SUFFOLK

by

MATT SALUSBURY

being a

GUIDE

to

yet-to-be-formally identified ANIMALS
from the region briefly known as
THE CURIOUS COUNTY

including an *account* of over 150
MYSTERY BIG CAT sightings

A Slack-jawed Amazement Production

c/o Matt Salusbury
PO Box 80185
London N1P 3SS

PRINTED IN SUFFOLK
by Leiston Press

MMXXIII

Designed and typeset by
Matt Salusbury
and Leiston Press
with thanks to Charley Allan
MMXXIII

Front cover: late 15th-century panther gargoyle on St Peter's Church, Theberton. Image enhanced to remove modern drain-pipe coming out of its mouth. Inset: still from video footage of a black leopard(?) at Wortham, by kind permission of Lee Acaster.

Start of Part One: (page 23) woodwose on top of St Mary's Haverhill, shot from below.

Start of Part Two: (page 90) dragon slain by St George in stained glass memorial to Colonel Doughty, killed at Gallipoli in 1915, at St Peter's Church, Theberton.

Start of Part Three: (page 203) Horringer village sign, with a spotted black panther from the arms of the Earls of Bristol.

Back cover: See page 348.

A Slack-jawed Amazement Production
PO Box 80185
London N1P 3SS
mysteryanimalsofsuffolk@gn.apc.org
bigcatsofsuffolk.com
Printed in Suffolk by Leiston Press

ISBN 978-1-915721-09-9

To Jane Salusbury,
to Kate Salusbury
and to
Smute and Thomas

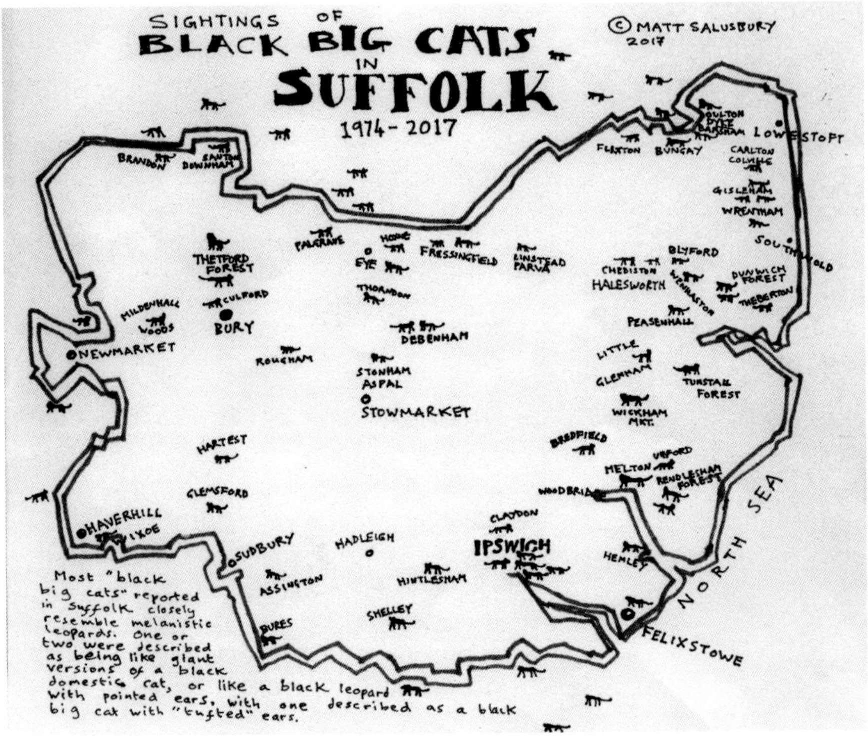

SIGHTINGS OF BLACK BIG CATS IN SUFFOLK 1974–2017

BRANDON
SANTON DOWNHAM
THETFORD FOREST
MILDENHALL WOODS
CULFORD
BURY
NEWMARKET
PALGRAVE
HOXNE
EYE
FRESSINGFIELD
LINSTEAD PARVA
THORNDON
DEBENHAM
ROUGHAM
STONHAM ASPAL
STOWMARKET
HARTEST
GLEMSFORD
HAVERHILL
WIXOE
SUDBURY
HADLEIGH
ASSINGTON
HINTLESHAM
BURES
SHELLEY
CLAYDON
IPSWICH
FLIXTON
BUNGAY
OULTON DYKE
BARSHAM
LOWESTOFT
CARLTON COLVILLE
GISLEHAM
WRENTHAM
SOUTHWOLD
CHEDISTON
HALESWORTH
BLYFORD
WENHASTON
DUNWICH FOREST
THEBERTON
PEASENHALL
LITTLE GLEMHAM
TUNSTALL FOREST
WICKHAM MKT.
BREDFIELD
UFFORD
MELTON
RENDLESHAM FOREST
WOODBRIDGE
HEMLEY
FELIXSTOWE
NORTH SEA

Most "black big cats" reported in Suffolk closely resemble melanistic leopards. One or two were described as being like giant versions of a black domestic cat, or like a black leopard with pointed ears, with one described as a black big cat with "tufted" ears.

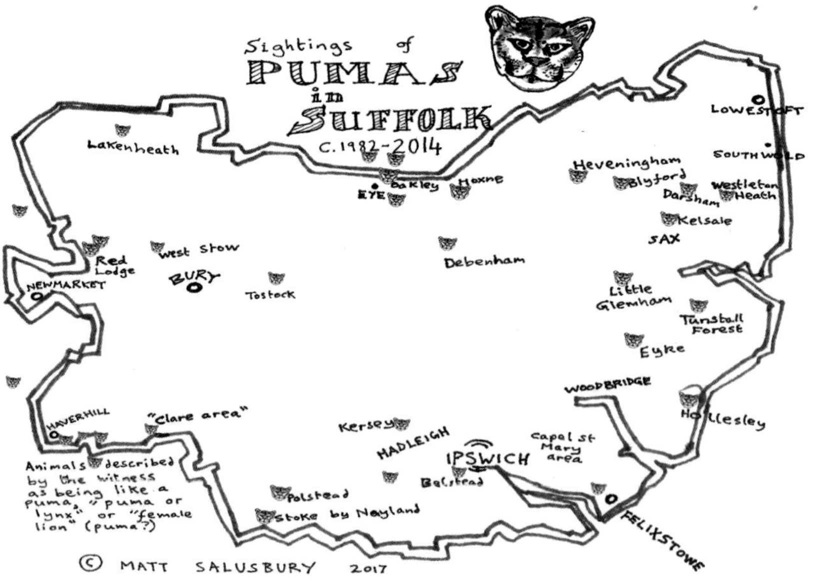

CONTENTS

Researched mostly by folding bike and public transport 2014-2021. If there is any public transport left in Suffolk by the time you read this, details will be on www.suffolkonboard.com. Shown here is the author crossing into Suffolk from Essex on the White Bridge over the Stour at Cattawade.

Preface

My childhood was spent under the wide skies of East Suffolk, on the edge of what was once called Snape Warren – several square miles of heathland and reed beds north of the Alde estuary. Across this, almost as far as Aldeburgh on the coast, was a varied route through heather, marsh and woodland designated "the Sailors' Path" on old Ordnance Survey maps. I imagined smugglers flitting furtively inland with rum and other contraband. The earliest part of our ramshackle house incorporated two eighteenth century cottages, where, by local lore (mentioned somewhere by folklorist George Ewart-Evans), a group of smugglers had been apprehended and later executed; their shades were said to haunt what had become our bathroom, though no one I knew had ever encountered them.

The most picturesque part of the Sailors' Path was a series of seven footbridges over irrigation dykes, close to a derelict Gothic gatehouse, a perfect setting for adventures with my childhood chums. Close by were the mud flats of the Alde, punctuated by a surreal sandy beach known as "Little Japan", created on the Wentworth estate some time in the twentieth century.

One day on the mudflats I encountered dozens of dead eels, with puncture marks as if they had been attacked by a vampire; it's true there was a heronry in the adjacent woods, but why would herons kill so many eels and leave them to decompose on the mud? I was about 12 years old and it was the first natural mystery that I remember; another, many years later on a different part of Snape Warren, was scores of dead toads, ideal for a witch's brew.

Just as dramatic, though hardly mysterious, were the corpses of myriad cooked adders and World War Two ammo and incendiary bombs among the blackened gorse and heather after a major heath fire in 1957; and an invasion of ladybirds on the coast that turned the sea wall at Slaughden red for as far as the eye could see. Had they flown across the North Sea?

I left Suffolk in the Sixties and didn't join Bob Rickard on *Fortean Times* for another decade, but it was childhood experiences such as these that had whetted my appetite for strange phenomena, along with the famous fortean Suffolk stories, including the merman of Orford and the Black Dog of Bungay, and I'm very pleased to see both put in detailed context by Matt Salusbury in his chapters on manimals and spectral hounds in this intriguing book.

Some fortean researchers have long suspected that Black Shuck and his ilk transmogrified into the Anomalous Big Cats (ABCs) – anomalous not least for their black coloration that have been witnessed across the UK for the last 50 years or so. Some will scoff at such poetic fancy, but it did seem that the decline in mystery canine reports accompanied the rise of mystery feline sightings. For many years I prepared annual surveys of nationwide ABC reports, mainly from local newspapers, which gave some indication of the phenomenon's spread right across the UK from John O'Groats to Land's End, although these reports – on average about 400 per annum – represented only a fraction of actual ABC encounters.

Matt Salusbury is to be congratulated on his extensive survey of these curious felids in Suffolk, which does seem to have a fair number of the enigmatic critters (whatever their phenomenal status might be).

Paul Sieveking, founding co-editor of *Fortean Times* magazine

England outline map: Wikimedia Commons Suffolk outline: Matt Salusbury

Introduction

I'd been living for about a year and a half in Suffolk when suddenly I found that random neighbours, local residents, fellow bus passengers, drinkers in the pub would casually mention that they – or a friend, husband, family member, customer – had seen a big cat a few years back. Some told me, in a matter-of-fact way, that they'd witnessed a big cat in Suffolk themselves, as if it wasn't even a particularly big deal. Eventually I didn't even feel surprised when a visitor from North Norfolk wandered in during my first shift as a volunteer in one of Suffolk's small museums, to tell me that – a couple of years before – he'd seen a puma nearby, or when a taxi driver told me about the black leopard he'd seen on a road some ten miles to the north back in around 1999.

Some were unsure whether what they'd seen was a big cat or not. Those who'd told me a partner or relative had seen a big cat didn't themselves necessarily believe them. One informant also threw in a couple of traditions about ghosts from the remote corner of Suffolk where they'd grown up in.

Some of the Suffolk people who'd told me about their own big cat encounters (or who passed on second-hand ones) had heard that I was on the Suffolk big cats' case. (I've been on BBC Radio Suffolk several times with presenter Jon Wright.) Others just told me about their big cat experiences out of the blue when I mentioned what I was doing in Suffolk, or after asking me what line of work I was in. A small handful of unsolicited accounts of modern Suffolk sightings of the impossible phantom East Anglian hellhound Black Shuck came my way as well. ("East Anglia" covers the counties of Suffolk, Essex and Norfolk. Or so I *thought* until this book was progressing, when it became clear that it sometimes takes in Cambridgeshire, or excludes Essex, depending on who you're talking to and about what[1].)

Many, but not all, big cat informants asked not to be identified, for reasons strange to outsiders, as we will discover. In Suffolk's villages and its small towns where everyone knows everyone, even to publish where a witness to a mystery animal comes from is to identify them. One redacted Freedom of Information Act disclosure by Suffolk Police described a caller contacting the police to report a sighting of something like a black leopard in the "Beccles-Bungay area". The two Suffolk towns of Beccles and Bungay are nearly seven miles apart (just over 11km), Bungay at the time had a population of 5,000 and Beccles double that, but the police were still concerned that tongues would wag to the point where everyone in that district would work out who the witness was.

The county of Suffolk is mostly rural and strongly agricultural – pigs or barley, sugar beet, turnips or broad beans are commonly raised on the acidic, sandy soil of coastal Suffolk, cows on the wet and more fertile watermeadow pasture and fens further inland. In April the fields are a bright yellow and the air thick with the honey-like smell of oilseep rape, grown for cooking oil. Within weeks of any given year's harvest, the next year's crop is already planted.

If you live in a city elsewhere in the UK the chances are you've probably seen the word "Suffolk" on some pub tap artwork. Adnams ales are brewed in Southwold, Greene King beer is brewed in Bury St Edmunds. A more recent introduction to the rest of the UK – Aspall's cyder (with a "y") from orchards near Debenham – is also made in the county. An early indicators of gentrification in London's neighbourhoods is the arrival in its suddenly posh butcher's shop of Blythburgh free range pork, all the way from Suffolk's Blyth Valley. The area around Blythburgh is said to have more pigs that people.

Suffolk has just over three quarters of a million humans. Bits of Suffolk are so empty that a car passing your house is a noteworthy event. To live off-road, off mains and off-grid, with your own water supply and septic tank, is common in Suffolk. Many Suffolk folk are so out of the way they expect to be out of mobile phone coverage most of the time. Before the Covid lockdown of 2020, one in six of them had never been on the internet. There are no motorways here either.

My apologies if you're impatient at all this talk about Suffolk's human inhabitants. When am I going to starting reading about its unknown animals? But to be honest, mystery animals are by nature very speculative. I have no photos to show you of the demon hellhound Black Shuck, nor of living woodwoses and wildmen, nor holiday snaps of the fairies of Stowmarket, nor old slides of Kessingland sea serpents, nor any "lantern men" caught on camera, nor images of the shug monkey. There's no blurry, controversial mobile phone footage of Suffolk's evil freshwater mermaids, or CCTV footage of spectral horses pulling phantom coaches driven by long-deceased, mad aristocrats. The Tuddenham dog-headed man has never tripped any trail cameras. I do have, though, one rather jaw-dropping video over a decade old, of a large black feline in a Suffolk field, which we'll come to later.

Seeing as Suffolk's mystery animals probably aren't going to show themselves, I'll have to rely mostly on stories by Suffolk-based humans who claimed to have encountered them. There are many such human stories.

Apart from that few seconds of footage of what looks like a black leopard in Suffolk, I have much by way of anecdotes, reports, sightings, witness testimony and folk legend. I have gathered dozens of interviews with big cat witnesses, plus dozens more testimonies emailed to me, plus scores of newspaper clippings of Suffolk big cat encounters. As well as testimony of an encounter with a shambling, hairy, eight-feet-tall, benevolent entity on the road to Peasenhall for good measure

I found I became preoccupied with the human drama of these encounters with Suffolk's mystery animals. Most of the human witnesses to big cats were affected deeply by their encounter, awestruck even. One described how they felt "privileged" to have seen three Suffolk big cats over quarter of a century. By contrast, a couple of other witnesses were quite blasé about their big cat sighting, as if it had been the most normal thing in the world.

There are also, as we shall see shortly, touching stories of human encounters with strange creatures in Suffolk from centuries past. For example, all the able-bodied men from around the border village of Bures mobilising to fight what may have been a crocodile escaped from King Richard the Lionheart's menagerie. Then there is the response of the crowds in Ipswich of 1784 who thronged to see "natural philosopher" and quack Dr Katterfelto and his "Moroccan Black Cat" and went away convinced both "are devils." And who cannot be charmed by the reaction of a Mr A.W. of Stowmarket, sometime around 1740, glimpse of a gathering of fairies? So parochial was A.W.'s world, that he could only describe the fairies' alien, otherworldly appearance "as if with spangles, like the girls at shows at Stow Fair."

I've heard or read many accounts by people engaged in some very Suffolk activities when they saw big cats – out combining (harvesting arable crops from a combine harvester) in a field of wheat, metal detecting, off-roading on motorbikes, "rough camping" in the woods as teenagers, or lamping (hunting rabbits with a gun and a torch at night). I'm told that gun ownership in East Anglia is significantly higher than in other parts of England. Most farmers will have both a firearms certificate for a rifle and a shotgun licence as well. Later we will hear stories from farmers who saw a big cat through their rifle sights but couldn't bring themselves to shoot it.

And why were so many of Suffolk's big cat witnesses driving to or from work at 5.30am when they had their encounters? Read on for an explanation. To truly understand the county I had made my home, to get under the skin of Suffolk, and also to really bring across how powerfully strange the experiences of contact with mystery animals can be, I had to document the only data we have to go on, which is mostly the stories of the humans who meet them.

What of Suffolk, then? (Skip this bit if you already live there!) It's the easternmost county of the mainland UK. The top right-hand corner of Suffolk is so far east it's known as "The Sunrise Coast", experiencing dawn about four to six minutes before London's sunrise. But in winter Suffolk gets darker up to eight minutes earlier than London too – it's actually further north of the capital than it feels.

Suffolk faces the North Sea with the Netherlands around 90 miles to the East. Battered food packaging bearing Dutch-language labelling can often be found on Suffolk's more rugged, mostly shingle beaches. There are some more traditional Suffolk seaside resorts with sand, too, such as Lowestoft (it has particularly fine, white sand) and Felixstowe. If you're a visitor to the area, though, you'd be advised to wear a wetsuit to swim in the unforgiving North Sea off Suffolk even in high summer.

Away from the coast, Suffolk is bounded mostly by rivers. The Waveney and the Upper Waveney form the county's northern boundary with Norfolk, this river becomes the Little Ouse in the west. The River Stour forms Suffolk's boundary with Essex to the south and Cambridgeshire to the east (it's the Stour Brook by the time you get to Cambridgeshire). Many Suffolk people describe their particular corner of the county in terms of its nearest river – the Blyth Valley, the Dove Valley, the Brett Valley, the Lark Valley, the Upper Waveney Valley, the Orwell Estuary, the Stour Valley, the Gipping Valley, Deben Vale, the Alde Valley. Much of Suffolk is so pancake-flat you wouldn't be aware you were entering one if its rather shallow valleys by car, you'd briefly notice a serious stretch of uphill or downhill arriving in or leaving one of its valleys by bicycle, though.

While some of Suffolk's rivers were once mighty navigable waterways, most of them have since silted up. A lot of the emptier land in the west of the county from Lakenheath all the way to the Cambridgeshire border is fenland reclaimed from the marshes. Babergh District, also known as South Suffolk, even has a green hill on its corporate logo, so different are its distinctive contours from the flat plains of mainstream Suffolk. South Suffolk includes the ridiculously beautiful former Wool Towns of Clare and Lavenham. The latter village is a surreal landscape of brightly-painted Tudor half-timbered houses as far as the eye can see. Lavenham, with over 130 listed buildings, was world famous even before one its houses featured as Harry Potter's ancestral home in the film of *The Deathly Hallows Part 1*. The first editions of the Harry Potter books were even printed in the county by Clay's of Bungay, part of a long tradition of industrial-scale printing in Suffolk. (Yes, this book was printed in the county too.)

Antiques and auction houses are big business in Suffolk, while fairytale retro weddings across Suffolk have become a huge industry. Some of Suffolk's villages really are the picture postcard vistas that time forgot. For a village to have an intact fifteenth century church – or an even older one – is not even a big deal in Suffolk.

While hills are a rarity in Suffolk, an exception is the range of flat-topped steep chalky slopes of the East Anglian Heights. These hills run all the way from Bury to Newmarket and Haverhill. There's also Stowupland (the clue's in the name) near Stowmarket, hilly enough to host a "Queen of the Mountains" section in the Women's Tour cycle race when it cames through Suffolk.

Suffolk is England's driest county. There's a coastal micro-climate along Suffolk's shore which is surprisingly benign. It can be pouring with rain inland but sunny on a little strip going from the sea to a few miles inland, to roughly near where the A12 main road passes. As we shall see, the low-lying water meadows and coasts of Suffolk are prone to sudden, weird mists and fog.

The good news if you're looking for mystery animals, is that there are an awful lot of places for them to hide in Suffolk. If it's animals you're looking for, whether mystery or mundane, you're in luck. Vast swathes of the county are given over to nature reserves and wildlife habitats. Birdwatching is absolutely huge in Suffolk. Minsmere is nationally famous as the jewel in the crown of the RSPB (Royal Society for the Protection of Birds) constellation of bird reserves, while the deer rut (red deer stags fighting) every October at nearby Westleton Heath is an annual event. Then there are the ancient woodlands like the Captain's Wood at Sudbourne near Woodbridge and at Staverton Thicks.

There are mighty forests in Suffolk, many of them planted relatively recently. The comparatively tiny Waveney Forest, the bigger Dunwich Forest, Mildenhall Wood, The King's Forest, the forests at Tunstall and Rendlesham and the greatest of them all – Thetford Forest, the UK's biggest lowland pine plantation, stretching all the way into Norfolk. Much of Suffolk is marsh – Minsmere, Snape, Trimley and the nature reserve at Orford Ness, one of the longest spits of shingle in Europe. Then there are the lakes, marshes and waterways of The Broads – the Suffolk and Norfolk Broads National Park to give it its full title.

There are also the heathlands of the Area of Outstanding Natural Beauty known as the Suffolk Coast and Heaths. There's another area of unique heathland, The Brecks – the area around Brandon and Mildenhall and continuing all the way over the Norfolk border.

This abundance of wildlife refuges means that there is some – known – English fauna that is found only in Suffolk, or that stays exclusively in Suffolk when visiting England on its annual migration. There are only a couple of places outside Suffolk where you can expect to see the Eurasian hobby *(Falco subbuteo)* on its yearly stay in the UK, having arrived from Algeria or Tunisia. This bird of prey has swept-back wings resembling those of the swifts and swallows it hunts. Hobbies plummet out of the sky, snatching dragonflies in mid-flight on the wing. The hobby takes over recently vacated crows' nests in Minsmere and North Warren reserves, and some other secret Suffolk locations.

Also unique to Suffolk within England are the butterwort, the marsh fragrant orchid and the rare wild cornflower *Centaurea cyanus*. The fen raft spider is Britain's biggest arachnid. It's large enough to eat tadpoles and it's found almost exclusively in Suffolk, at Lopham Fen, straddling the Suffolk-Norfolk border. The emerald damselfly is now restricted almost entirely to the Suffolk fens.

This out-of-the-way emptiness and relatively unspolt idyllic landscape mean that at any given time many of the people in Suffolk are tourists or weekenders, retired people or second-home owners, while the estuary from Ipswich down the Deben and all the way to Felixstowe is dotted with marinas for recreational sailing. Some fashionable retro-chic Suffolk seaside towns like Southwold double their population in the summer. In some Suffolk resorts, 40 per cent of all homes are holiday homes. It's quite possible that you yourself are reading this book having discovered it in one of Suffolk's many tourist attractions while holidaying there.

The people of Suffolk have a reputation for being laid back and not angered easily. The driving in Suffolk is supposed to be the most polite in the UK. (Although local newspaper *Coastal Scene* is filled with accounts of fatal collisions at high speed on the A12 main road around Saxmundham, often involving deer.) Framlingham (just "Fram" to those in the know) and the seaside resort of Aldeburgh frequently appear near the top of the table for the ten best places to live in the UK, according to right-of-centre Sunday newspapers read by older people.

But it's not all country idyll in Suffolk. Let us briefly celebrate urban and industrial Suffolk as well. Slow worms (Britian's only species of legless lizard) are recovering their numbers in Suffolk, their most impressive recovery is in the urban gardens of Ipswich. Urban otters are regularly seen passing through the town of Halesworth, swimming in its Town River in its urban Millennium Green and in back gardens in the town of Saxmundham. (The Otter Trust, an otter sanctuary that used to be near Bungay in North Suffolk, disbanded one of its refuges as otters ceased to be endangered.)

Also, a two-year Suffolk Wildlife survey into hedgehog sightings found that as of 2016, the county town of Ipswich was bucking a national trend in hedgehog decline, with "Ipswich in particular remarkable for its number of sightings".[2]

Two of the county's early waves of big cat sightings were also in Suffolk's county town of Ipswich – with a population of over 100,000. Even the fairies of Suffolk tended to be clustered around the undoubtedly urban location of Stowmarket, now the UK distribution centre for several multinationals, including Bosch electronics. The port of Lowestoft is Suffolk's second biggest town and also the most easterly town in the UK, with the UK's tallest onshore wind turbine. Lowestoft experienced an urban cluster of Black Shuck sightings in the 1970s. Another outbreak of big cat sightings involved the Haverhill Puma, a "puma or lynx-like" big cat seen several times at roundabouts at the entrance to an industrial estate on the edge of Haverhill, a pharmaceutial manufacturing centre and "London overflow" town tucked away on the borders in Suffolk's south-western corner.

While to the tourist Suffolk may seem like a chocolate box illustration, over 900,000 sea containers a year travel the Ipswich to Felixstowe railway line. Our biggest export out of Felixstowe is currently containers going back empty. You can't stand on a station platform at Ipswich for any length of time without a long freight train of containers taking several minutes to pass by on its way to or from Felixstowe, the UK's biggest container port. You can see the Port of Felixstowe's giant cranes all the way from the mighty Orwell Bridge at Ipswich, which has some massive docks of its own.

Then there's that giant white golf ball on the horizon that is Sizewell B Nuclear Power Station on the edge of Leiston, with its procession of pylons marching away from it. Électricité de France's planned successor reactor, Sizewell C, is currently "in consultation". Even comparatively small Suffolk towns like Framlingham, Saxmundham and Leiston are ringed by impressively-sized industrial estates and the South Suffolk town of Hadleigh is a centre for the food processing industry.

Oh, and did I mention Martlesham Heath, a former wartime airfield just outside Ipswich, now the headquarters of Suffolk Police, and the still functioning British Telecom research centre, where they perfected fibre optic communications?

It's not a very unified county. Bury St Edmunds and Ipswich's relationship is mostly one of rivalry over its shopping centres. West Suffolk and East Suffolk were separate counties until 1974, and there's a different feel in the West of the county. One thing you notice there, are more village playgrounds and mothers with prams or pushchairs, and not just at weekends – the rural population is younger, with more arrivals who still work in London, what with the better roads. The population is denser and less agricultural, with an infrastructure to match, although there are parts of West Suffolk that are also very isolated and empty.

Suffolk's infrastructure and communications don't exactly aid the county's unification. To get from Sudbury in the southeast corner to the county town of Ipswich will take you over an hour on the only bus service to cross the county – Beeston's double-decker route 91, or by train via Bury, or from Sudbury station back into Essex to change trains and back into Suffolk again, via Colchester. As for Haverhill, it's easier to get there from Cambridge or Stansted Airport by public transport than it is from the rest of Suffolk. My previous expedition in search of mystery animals – to the wilderness of Kerala, South India in search of alleged five-feet tall pygmy elephants – was a considerably easier undertaking than some of the journeys across Suffolk which involved me taking two trains, three buses and two five-mile rides on a folding bike that I undertook for *Mystery Animals*. In Suffolk, the car is king.

I confess the mystery animals in this book are distributed somewhat unevenly throughout Suffolk. Mystery animals are disproportionately well represented in the North, close to the border with Norfolk, fairies around Stowmarket and sea serpents off Kessingland. Big cat reports come disproportionately from Ipswich, North Suffolk and the Western edge of the county, with a historic range around the forests near the River Deben. Escaped rheas – large South American flightless birds – for some reason seem to congregate around Wickham Market. Freshwater mermaids tend to be found in the River Gipping or in pools and ditches in the area around Bury St Edmunds. I have found hardly any accounts of mystery animals from Suffolk's Shotley Peninsula, not that many from its Bawdsey Peninsula, surprisingly little mystery animal-related activity from the area around Felixstowe.

Do I believe any of this? Good question. The earlier chapters of this book are legends and folklore from a bygone – and more superstitious – age, and should be regarded as being for entertainment purposes only. Having said that, something is going on, because eminently sane, modern people report encounters with Black Shuck, with animal ghosts, with mystery lights that act if they're alive, even with the odd shambling hairy ape-like entity on the road from Peasanhall or seen from a lorry cab passing through Elveden. I will try to offer possible rational explanations for all of these.

There are many reports of mystery animals that I investigated but which I dropped from the final draft as I didn't think they were mystery animals after all. A mother and son reported an escaped exotic venemous watersnake seen in the river at Southwold near the Might Bridge. But then it became clear that they had in good faith misidentified a common grass snake – they're good swimmers and sometimes have the pale spot on the back of their neck that my witnesses had noticed. I have many more examples of such honest mistakes. I also dropped from this book an account of a satanic entity seen on the road near Saxmundham at night, as later conversations with the witness raised questions about their credibility. Since then I've begun to question my scepticism regarding the witness, as one of the seemingly fantastic stories they told me turned me about the forthcoming unveiling of a giant statue locally, which I'd not heard from any other source, turned out to be completely true.

I have organised this book with the mystery animals in ascending order of credibility, starting with the stuff of (mostly) legend, and moving with a disorientating jump nearer the end to flesh-and-blood exotic animals loose in Suffolk. Then much of the book will be taken up by Suffolk big cats. I do believe there are big cats in the wild in Britain. I keep changing my mind as to whether they're leopards, pumas, and lynxes that have got out from captivity and bred here in the East of England, or whether they are feral domestic cats who over the generations have somehow become gigantic, or even just misidentifications. I do stray out of the county in an effort to explain what animals the big cats sighted in Suffolk could be.

Suffolk is home to some former mystery animals once filed under "cryptids" (mystery animals unknown to science) but now accepted. In the 1890s, about the time gorillas and okapi were being discovered in Africa, a new species of mammal was coming to the light of science right here in England; yellow-necked mice were "discovered" in ancient woodland mostly in South Suffolk. Yellow-necked mice (*Apodemus flavicollis*) are one and a half times the size of a house mouse and are more common in deciduous woods in "ancient countryside." They're now thought to be the last survivors of a much bigger population that once had a much wider range. They like Suffolk's warm summers and live in woods for most of this season, venturing into the houses of the humans in autumn.[3]

Then there is the ant lion (*Eurolion nostras*), an insect long regarded as a fantastic beast of legend, turning up occasionally in English literature in the eighteenth century and nineteenth century. Its name didn't help its credibility, it is in fact the pincer-jawed larva of what turns into a comparatively boring, long-winged, lacewing insect resembling a dragonfly, only 3cm (1.2 inches) long in adult life.

In its smaller larval stage, the ant lion builds elaborate traps in the sand for passing insects that it ambushes. The first confirmed record of ant lions living in what was then Suffolk came from Gorleston near Lowestoft in 1931, after which it was apparently forgotten for the next 50 years. Interest was revived in 1990s and after fruitless searches for ant lions, two were eventually found in Minsmere in 1994. Now the ant lion is found in only three places in the UK – its Suffolk stronghold at Minsmere and nearby Dunwich Heath, and Holkham National Nature Reserve in Norfolk.[4]

A brand new species joined the fauna of Suffolk in 2019, with the discovery of the stem boring fly *Melangromyza moatesi* at Lackford Lakes nature reserve on the border with Norfolk. *M. moatesi* is named after Lackford Lakes volunteer Graham Moates, who discovered its larvae growing in the stem of the hemp agrimony plants found around ponds there.[5]

And there are several examples of a Suffolk mystery animal that never was. Take, for example, the mousehunt (or mousehunter) and the blacktail, animals both known to people of Suffolk in the early twentieth century. The blacktail was a kind of weasel, only bigger than a conventional weasel and smaller than a stoat. In *The Mammals of Suffolk*, the county's official Recorder of Mammals, Simone Bullion, describes an animal called a mousehunter (also called a mousehunt), a smaller type of weasel. Bullion said it was not a separate species at all, just a female weasel, they being quite a lot smaller than the males. She told me "at that time there was a lot of confusion re: stoats and weasels among the general populace and the belief was that there were more than two species… Re: the blacktail – I am sure this is referring to a stoat, because of the black tip to its tail. It could be a female stoat as again, there is a high degree of sexual dimorphism (males being bigger than females) in stoats, as there is for weasels… The principal prey of weasels is mice and voles, so that fits with the mousehunt definition." So mousehunts were just misidentified female weasels and blacktails were just misidentified female stoats.[6]

Why me, a recent immigrant to Suffolk? What are my credentials for the task ahead? Are you in good hands? In my day job I am a professional journalist, likely to be covering the rather dry world of education, or trade union affairs. I can do "serious" journalism as well as being an enthusiast for mystery animals. I am duty-bound by the National Union of Journalists' Code of Practice on journalistic ethics and on confidentiality to respect my sources' anonymity when they request it. In a couple of cases, I gave anonymity to big cat witnesses who hadn't asked for it, because I felt they really should have.

As a journalist, I talk to people, I check facts, I go back and look at sources – a glance at the footnotes will show I've traced many of my secondary sources back to the primary source where the assertion first appeared. My job is to ask, "Says who?" and find out whether "facts" are accurate, whether they actually stand up well enough to comply with the chilling libel laws of England and Wales. I am preoccupied as a journalist with the status of information – is it solid, verifiable evidence, reasonably likely to be true, or just conjecture, hearsay or rumour?

Well OK, much of the material in this book is just hearsay and rumour, but I have striven to label it as such throughout. I did throw out testimony from a couple of big cat witnesses because I felt they were too scatty and disorganised in their thoughts for me to rely on what they told me. Gentle requests for more detail produced a slightly different version of their story each time…

Since the dawn of this century I've also been a regular contributor to *Fortean Times* magazine, strapline "The World of Strange Phenomena" , for *Fortean Times* I have covered unusual topics from solar flares to Trotskyite UFO cults with (I hope) healthy scepticism and good humour, so strange phenomena are my specialisation. *Fortean Times's* founding co-editor Paul Sieveking, raised in the Suffolk village of Snape, was kind enough to provide the short preface to this book.

I've been hanging out with big cat experts for well over a decade. I have a track record for investigations into unknown animals too. My previous book *Pygmy Elephants* brought me into contact with a dozen or so proper zoologists and proper paleontologists, with whom I had to talk the talk and walk the walk of serious life sciences.

Like many recent Suffolk residents, I have been an immigrant from London, although my grandparents lived in Snape, so I spent my childhood summers in the county. I was pleasantly surprised when a farming contact told me of my work on Suffolk big cats and people's reluctance to talk about them, "You certainly summed up us Suffolk folk… I think that you've identified a subject that needs to be shared beyond our boundaries." After years of staring at an atlas of Suffolk, and then going out and seeing all the places, I can probably tell the difference between Wickham Market, Wickham Skeith and Wickham Street – and distinguish Tuddenham from Tuddenham St Martin and Saxham from Saxmundham – better than a lot of Suffolk folk.

There are footnotes at the end of each chapter, with sources, so as not to break up the flow of the narrative. If you're puzzled by repeated references in the footnotes of this book to "**FT**" in bold type, followed by two figures also in bold, that's the way *Fortean Times* magazine likes to do references to its back issues (issue number, colon, page number) and I've followed their convention. There's a glossary at the back, in case you're fuzzy about the difference between East Anglia and the East of England, or can't work out which Suffolk towns are known as Fram, Sax, Bury and Stow for short. (Unless you're a train announcer the Suffolk cathedral city internationally known as Bury St Edmunds is within Suffolk always just "Bury", always pronounced "berry.")

People ask me whether I have had any encounters with mystery animals in Suffolk myself. I gave myself the benefit of the doubt about whether I'd seen a strange-looking black leopard with its head leaning to one side from a train approaching Wickham Market – until I saw it in the exact same position on the return journey and realised it was a blackened tree-stump.

Harder to explain was the briefest glimpse of a strange, misshapen grey-white apparently hairless calf-like creature that shot past when I was in another train on a wet, misty day in the Spring of 2016, getting ready to get out at Darsham station.

Whatever it was trotted past the train right by the side of the tracks. It could just conceivably have been a lost calf or even a deer or faun, it was all a blur at around 50 miles per hour. I merely note that the phantom East Anglian hellhound Black Shuck, who we'll meet in Chapter 6, sometimes appears as a shape-shifting entity resembling a calf or was "calf-sized".

I wasn't supposed to take well over eight years to write *Mystery Animals of Suffolk* but I did, and I've enjoyed almost every minute of it. I just hope you'll enjoy the result! As a result of writing this book, I am no longer surprised to hear reports like the one I heard in 2018 from a man in Rumburgh who described to me something answering the description of a small puma he'd just seen near the track approaching Brampton Request Stop station earlier that same day.

I leave the last word to the correspondent known as "I.G.", writing from Ipswich in 1645 to describe the skeleton of a giant that had been dug up at Suffolk's Brockford Bridge: "It may be that you may say, I might have employed my time better then in troubling you with this matter, I assure you of the truth of this, and the wonder of the thing commanded me to impart this much unto you."

Matt Salusbury, Dunwich, Suffolk, 2023

An ant lion larva. Within the UK, ant lions are confined to a couple of locations in Suffolk and one other habitat in Norfolk.

1. I wrote this book in the reasonable belief that "East Anglia" is Suffolk, Essex and Norfolk. It is, in fact, rather a moveable feast. See "Jade Goody and the many faces of East Anglia," Lawrence Cawley, BBC News, 15 May 2016, www.bbc.co.uk/news/uk-england-36130219

2. "Hedgehog friendly town", *Suffolk Wildlife* magazine (Suffolk Wildlife Trust), May 2016.

3. *The Mammals of Suffolk,* Simone Bullion, Suffolk Wildlife Trust/Suffolk Naturalists' Society, Ipswich, 2009.

4. "Heath ready for stardom after supporting role in Springwatch", *East Anglian Daily Times (EADT)* 7 July 2014.

5. "New species of fly discovered at Lackford Lakes", Suffolk Wildlife Trust, 20 January 2020, www.suffolkwildlifetrust.org/news/new-species-fly-discovered-lackford-lakes.

6. Simone Bullion, County Recorder of Mammals, Pers. Comm. by email 10 August 2015; "blacktail" from *Westleton – Customs and Sayings recorded by the Women's Institute in 1922*, Westleton Women's Institute, Leiston Press, Leiston 2008.

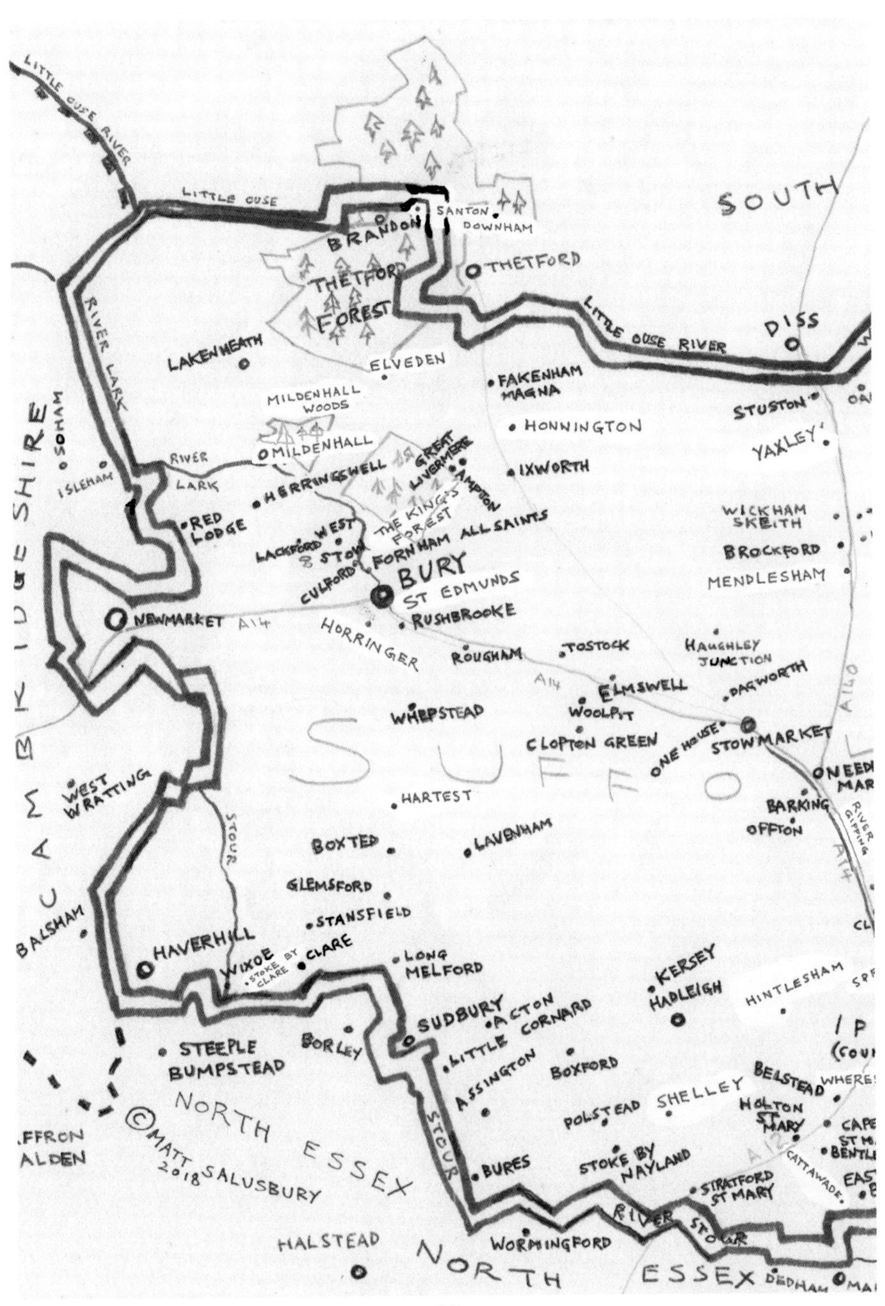
LITTLE OUSE RIVER
LITTLE OUSE
BRANDON
SANTON DOWNHAM
THETFORD
THETFORD FOREST
SOUTH
LITTLE OUSE RIVER
DISS
RIVER LARK
LAKENHEATH
ELVEDEN
FAKENHAM MAGNA
MILDENHALL WOODS
HONNINGTON
STUSTON
CAMBRIDGESHIRE
SOHAM
MILDENHALL
GREAT LIVERMERE
YAXLEY
ISLEHAM
RIVER LARK
HERRINGSWELL
AMPTON
IXWORTH
RED LODGE
THE KING'S FOREST
WICKHAM SKEITH
WEST STOW
LACKFORD
FORNHAM ALL SAINTS
BROCKFORD
CULFORD
BURY ST EDMUNDS
MENDLESHAM
NEWMARKET
A14
RUSHBROOKE
HORRINGER
ROUGHAM
TOSTOCK
HAUGHLEY JUNCTION
A14
ELMSWELL
DAGWORTH
WHEPSTEAD
WOOLPIT
CLOPTON GREEN
ONE HOUSE
STOWMARKET
A140
SUFFOLK
WEST WRATTING
HARTEST
BARKING
OFFTON
RIVER GIPPING
STOUR
BOXTED
LAVENHAM
A14
GLEMSFORD
STANSFIELD
BALSHAM
HAVERHILL
WIXOE
STOKE BY CLARE
CLARE
LONG MELFORD
KERSEY
HADLEIGH
HINTLESHAM
SUDBURY
ACTON
LITTLE CORNARD
BORLEY
STEEPLE BUMPSTEAD
ASSINGTON
BOXFORD
BELSTEAD
SHELLEY
HOLTON ST MARY
POLSTEAD
NORTH ESSEX
©MATT SALUSBURY 2018
STOUR
BURES
STOKE BY NAYLAND
A12
CATTAWADE
STRATFORD ST MARY
RIVER STOUR
HALSTEAD
WORMINGFORD
NORTH ESSEX
DEDHAM

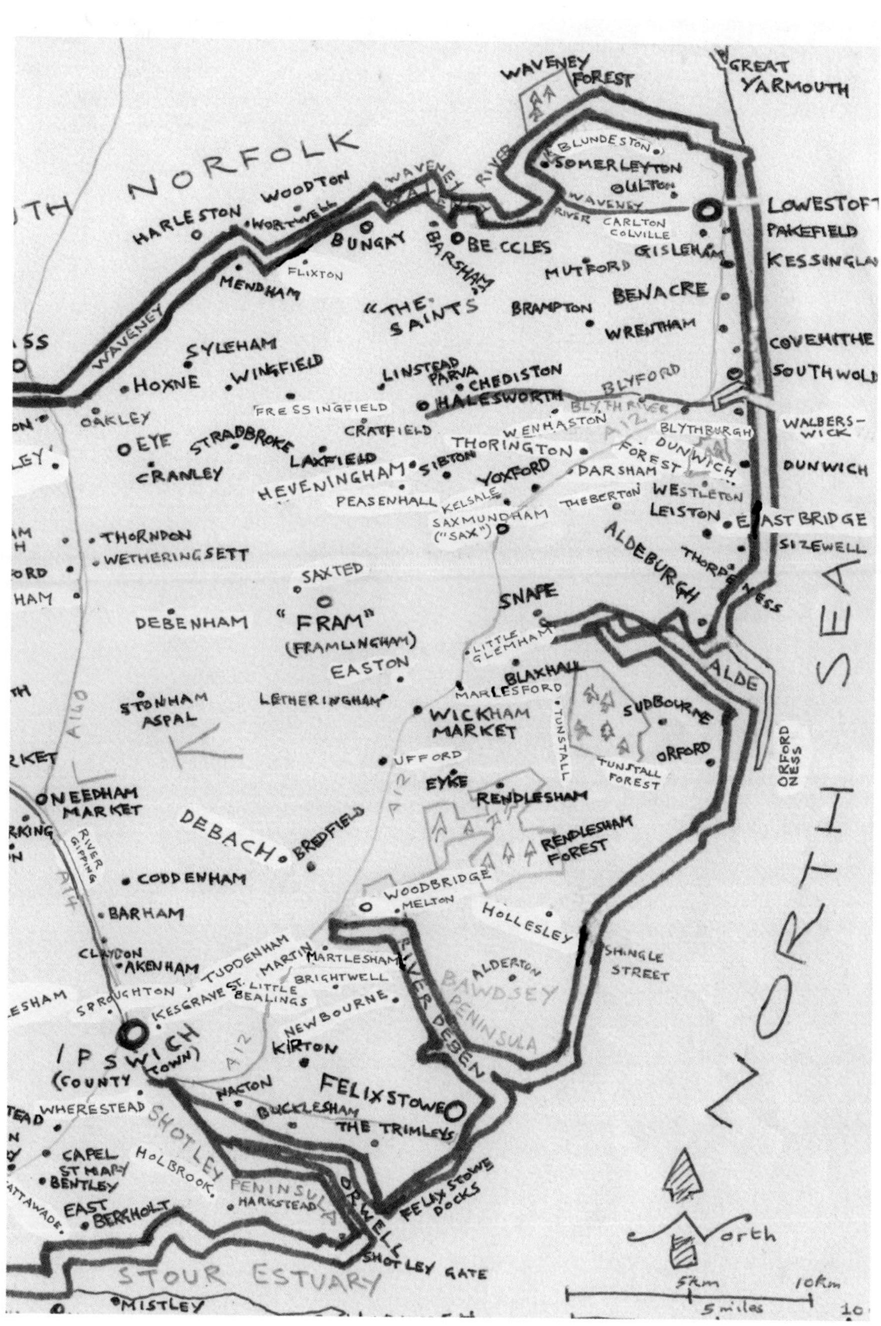
WAVENEY FOREST
GREAT YARMOUTH
NORFOLK
BLUNDESTON
SOMERLEYTON
OULTON
WAVENEY RIVER
LOWESTOFT
PAKEFIELD
HARLESTON
WOODTON
WORTWELL
BUNGAY
BARSHAM
BECCLES
CARLTON COLVILLE
GISLEHAM
MUTFORD
FLIXTON
MENDHAM
"THE SAINTS"
BRAMPTON
BENACRE
WRENTHAM
WAVENEY
COVEHITHE
SOUTHWOLD
SYLEHAM
HOXNE
WINGFIELD
LINSTEAD PARVA
CHEDISTON
BLYFORD
HALESWORTH
BLYTH RIVER
FRESSINGFIELD
OAKLEY
CRATFIELD
WENHASTON
BLYTHBURGH
WALBERS-WICK
EYE
STRADBROKE
THORINGTON
A12
DUNWICH FOREST
LAXFIELD
CRANLEY
HEVENINGHAM
SIBTON
YOXFORD
DARSHAM
DUNWICH
PEASENHALL
KELSALE
THEBERTON
WESTLETON
LEISTON
EASTBRIDGE
SAXMUNDHAM ("SAX")
SIZEWELL
THORNDON
ALDEBURGH
WETHERINGSETT
THORPENESS
SAXTED
SNAPE
DEBENHAM
"FRAM" (FRAMLINGHAM)
LITTLE GLEMHAM
EASTON
BLAXHALL
ALDE
MARLESFORD
STONHAM ASPAL
LETHERINGHAM
WICKHAM MARKET
TUNSTALL
SUDBOURNE
A140
ORFORD
ORFORD NESS
UFFORD
TUNSTALL FOREST
EYKE
NEEDHAM MARKET
RENDLESHAM
DEBACH
BREDFIELD
RENDLESHAM FOREST
NORTH SEA
RIVER GIPPING
CODDENHAM
A14
WOODBRIDGE
MELTON
BARHAM
HOLLESLEY
CLAYDON
AKENHAM
TUDDENHAM ST. MARTIN
MARTLESHAM
SHINGLE STREET
ALDERTON
BRIGHTWELL
SPROUGHTON
KESGRAVE
LITTLE BEALINGS
BAWDSEY PENINSULA
NEWBOURNE
RIVER DEBEN
IPSWICH (COUNTY TOWN)
KIRTON
NACTON
FELIXSTOWE
WHERESTEAD
BUCKLESHAM
SHOTLEY
THE TRIMLEYS
CAPEL ST MARY
HOLBROOK
BENTLEY
PENINSULA
ORWELL
FELIXSTOWE DOCKS
EAST BERGHOLT
HARKSTEAD
North
SHOTLEY GATE
STOUR ESTUARY
MISTLEY
5km
10km
5 miles

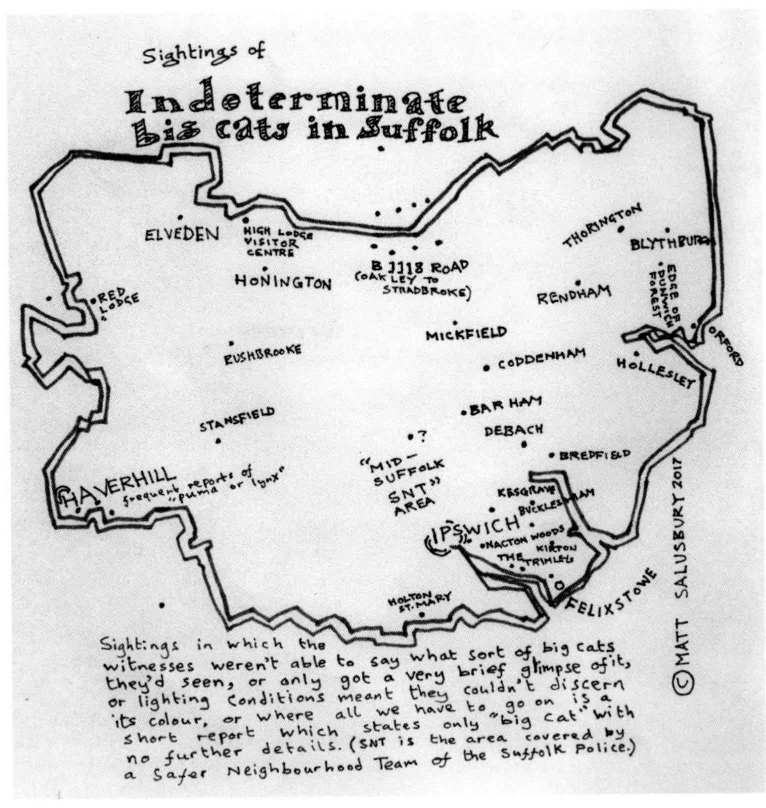
Sightings of
Indeterminate big cats in Suffolk
ELVEDEN
HIGH LODGE VISITOR CENTRE
B 1118 ROAD (OAKLEY TO STRADBROKE)
THORINGTON
BLYTHBURG
EDGE OF DUNWICH FOREST
RED LODGE
HONINGTON
RENDHAM
MICKFIELD
ORFORD
RUSHBROOKE
CODDENHAM
HOLLESLEY
BARHAM
STANSFIELD
?
DEBACH
BREDFIELD
"MID-SUFFOLK SNT" AREA
HAVERHILL
frequent reports of "puma or lynx"
KESGRAVE
BUCKLESHAM
IPSWICH
NACTON WOODS
KIRTON
THE TRIMLEYS
FELIXSTOWE
HOLTON ST. MARY
© MATT SALUSBURY 2017
Sightings in which the witnesses weren't able to say what sort of big cats they'd seen, or only got a very brief glimpse of it, or lighting conditions meant they couldn't discern its colour, or where all we have to go on is a short report which states only "big cat" with no further details. (SNT is the area covered by a Safer Neighbourhood Team of the Suffolk Police.)

Thanks are due

This book would not have been possible without Darren Mann of Paranormal Database, nor possible without John and Jane Salusbury who enabled me to be Suffolk-based for the best part of the 2010s.

Thanks also to Jon Wright of BBC Radio Suffolk, and to the Suffolk Records Office. And thanks to the museum people – Sophie Stevens, Mel Hollis and Theresa Carver of Colchester and Ipswich Museum Service; Alex McWhirter of Moyse's Hall Museum; Jane Hamilton and all at Dunwich Museum; Peggy Smith of Clare Ancient House Museum, Christopher Reeve of Bungay Museum; Mike Fordham of Halesworth Museum.

For permission to use their copyrighted material, for free: Lee Acaster, Russell Green, Mark Mower; Georgios Lyras; Nick Redfern; Matt Goodwin, Suffolk County Council Archaeological Service; Jack Hellhound of Hellhound Brewery; Benjamin Carr and Gabriella of Shuck Creative; Kevin Jolly of Mildenhall Fen Tigers and Andew Forsyth and Amy De Keyzer of the RSPCA.

The big cat experts: Rick Minter; Jonathan McGowan; Richard Freeman; wildlife filmmaker Mark Fletcher. And the conventionally-sized cat experts – Roger and Miranda Nodding of Framlingham and Saxmundham Cat Rescue.

Also John Daniel, Mark Frost, "Sam", Kevin Wood, Jonathan Mossman, Chris Field, also Charlie Haylock; "R2D2" at RAF Lakenheath; Hawk Honey and Matt Gooch (both SWT wardens); Brenda Sore; Paul Berry; Ian Day; Roger Mason; Janet Whitby; Russell Green, "Simon in Ipswich", Les Rayner, Sue Bradshaw, Mark Goodchild, James Perry, Kate Sutherland and many other big cat witnesses who asked not to be named.

The Suffolk churches people: Roy Tricker, Marion Welham of the Diocese of St Edmundsbury and Ipswich; James Hall of Ipswich Historic Churches Trust; Simon Knott's excellent Suffolk churches website; the Rev. Andy Wolton; the Rev. Simon Gill and Barry Wall.

And not forgetting Richard Muirhead for his librarianship talents; Ivan A. W. Bunn of *Lantern* and the Hidden East Anglia website; Jan Holloway; James Newton; "Phillip"; Kerry Stranix of Suffolk Wildlife Trust; Samantha Hutchinson of Norfolk and Suffolk Constabularies FOIA department; West Suffolk's unnamed FOI Coordinator, Recorder of Mammals for the County of Suffolk Simone Bullion; Katy Cody, Judi Hallett of Ufford Parish Council; Duncan Bradley of *Suffolk Free Press*; the late Kate Salusbury for expertise on peripheral vision; Ufford Park Golf Course; The Broads Authority; Phil Samponaro, historian 95th Bomber Group; Mike Ager of The Red Feather Club; Bev Bowry and John Clement; Maiya Pina-Dacier of Dig Ventures; the proofreading and editing team – Tom Salusbury, Tim Holt-Wilson, the late Jane Salusbury, Darren Mann, Claudia Civinini, Jon Downes, Gabrielle Bosley, Luke Eubule Reilly. Also to Tanzi, Alan in Thetford (carp expert), Alex Bass of Local Birding Tours, Samantha Hammond, David Wilshin, Bob Markham. And to Jane Inglesfield for putting up with me indexing in front of the telly.

I researched this book mostly by bike and public transport, so a big thanks to the transport crew for lifts to Suffolk's remotest corners – Kim Dyson, Paula and Julie and all drivers of the Connecting Communities bus service, John, Jane and Tom Salusbury, Keith Chambers of Darsham Taxis and to many others – space does not permit.

PART ONE –
NOT QUITE HUMAN

1. On the trail of Suffolk's woodwoses

In 2012, Suffolk briefly adopted the controversial slogan "the Curious County". So unpopular was the "Curious County" branding that Suffolk's MPs lined up to publicly denounce it. Among them was Bury St Edmunds MP David Ruffley, who at the time described the Curious County slogan as "idiotic and meaningless" and called for the then head of the region's tourism board, Visit East Anglia "to explain the concept" to local MPs.

Under pressure from the county's MPs and many others who hated the idea, the brand manager of Visit Suffolk, Amanda Bond, defended the Curious County concept. She noted Suffolk's pride in its "curious assets" which "made this county unique." She listed the gloriously bonkers slot machine arcade created by local artist Tim Hunkin that is the Under the Pier Show at Southwold, the strangely-shaped House in the Clouds holiday home in Thorpeness, "the mystery of Shingle Street"– an enduring legend involving rumours of burnt bodies recovered from the beach at Shingle Street during the Second World War.

Liz Cobbold of world famous Suffolk brewer Adnams was one of the few prominent voices in support of the Curious County idea, joining in with the hashtag #proudtobecurious, adopted by tens of thousands of Twitter accounts within its first weekend. But faced with an army of influential spoilsports, Suffolk remained officially the Curious County for less than a year.[1]

Bond promised she would henceforth stick to a more "traditional" portrayal of the county. As I was at the time planning to start work on a book on the mystery animals of Suffolk, I was devastated. No more Curious County! What an excellent tie-in opportunity that would have been. I was pleased to see that one of the cultural living treasures of Suffolk, the author and comic performer Charlie Haylock, chose to carry on regardless, titling one of his books *Don't Hurry Me – I'm Suffolk: A Celebration of the Curious County*.

Regardless of whether or not its weirdness has official blessing, there is indeed much that is curious about the county of Suffolk. It has more than its fair share of mystery lights. It has, allegedly, a huge number of ghosts, both human and animal, with phantom coach horses pulling phantom coaches a speciality – ideally with a headless coachman somewhere in attendance. Also outrageously common in Suffolk are encounters with the phantom black dog Black Shuck, as he was known, among many other names.

Curious assets

Suffolk is particularly rich in mystery creatures of tradition and folklore – some apparently not so mythical and a bit more real – that seem to cross the line between humans and other animals. The line between human and (other) animal is a surprisingly blurred one, and begs the question, what does it mean to be human anyway? Philosophers have pondered this question for centuries – what is it that makes us members of the species *Homo sapiens* unique? What sets us humans apart from other animals? Where does "human" end and where does "animal" begin?

Some of the alleged not-quite-human animals that are said to be found in Suffolk may – as we'll see – be misunderstood humans after all. Other alleged part-human or human-like denizens of this Curious County couldn't possibly exist according to what we now understand about the natural world. But in relatively recent times such "manimals" (man-animals) have been not only reported, but greatly feared.

A speciality on the mystery animal spectrum, a "curious asset" almost unique to Suffolk is its woodwoses, its wildmen-of-the-woods. There is at least one documented medieval account of a woodwose encounter in the county, also as a handful of alarming accounts from modern times of experiences involving such entities in Suffolk, as well as numerous fifteenth-century representations of woodwoses carved on the fonts and porches of Suffolk's churches. Most mysterious of all is that these woodwoses appear almost exclusively in Suffolk. They're very rare in other parts of Britain.

Many of the mystery animals in this book are a little on the insubstantial side – they're phantoms, creatures of myth, or – like Suffolk's big cats – just elusive and very, very good at hiding. But you can actually get to *see* Suffolk's woodwoses – its hairy wildmen – by the dozen, albeit as 500-year-old effigies of themselves in stone, just a foot or so high. The fact that they're not all in the same glass case in some museum in Ipswich but out in village churches often in the wilds of Suffolk, off the beaten track, makes woodwose-spotting in Suffolk all the more interesting. (Photos of Suffolk's woodwoses, arranged –mostly – alphabetically by location of the church they're in, start on page 28.)

Suffolk is said to have more medieval churches per square kilometre than any other county in the UK, so looking for woodwoses lends itself to pleasant trips to take in a cluster of them on a day out. The diocese of St Edmundsbury and Ipswich have even advertised occasional "woodwose bike routes" that cover two or three "woodwose churches" in a day at a more leisurely pace than my own Stakhanovite woodwose road trips of well over 20 miles each, taking in sometimes four "woodwose churches" a day.[2]

My somewhat obsessive quest for Suffolk's woodwoses began not in Suffolk itself but at the Community Centre in the village of Wolfardisworthy, Devon, at a conference of the Centre for Fortean Zoology (CFZ). Sharing space on the community centre noticeboard with posters advertising the Young Farmer's Tractor Pull was a little poster exhibition by the late Paul Vella, a government forensic scientist who spent a lot of his holidays going over to the Pacific North West of the USA looking for evidence of Bigfoot. Among the images he'd got off the internet was a photo of a curly-haired, bearded wildman with a club and shield, on the porch of a church in Peasenhall, Suffolk. The exhibition was all about presenting "evidence" for the survival of some kind of Bigfoot/yeti/apeman/Neanderthal creature in Europe within historical times.

I wish Suffolk's wildmen were as simple as that – actual surviving prehistoric hominids (humans or great apes) or real flesh and blood manimals somehow recorded for posterity – for some reason – on the fonts, porches, towers and roofs of Suffolk churches before they eventually became extinct. Unfortunately, it's not as straightforward as that; woodwoses are really a lot more mysterious.

We really aren't at all sure what those little hairy guys – they're all guys in Suffolk, with the possible exception of a once-female wildwoman we'll be introduced to shortly – are doing there, and why they're so prevalent in Suffolk in particular. As Roy Tricker, expert on Suffolk churches, told me of the Curious County's woodwoses, "I continue to be baffled as to their significance... They seem to be a total mystery." I've heard as many alternative explanations for woodwoses as there are examples of woodwoses to be found in Suffolk's churches.[3]

PART 1 – NOT QUITE HUMAN

What is a woodwose? Very good question. Woodwoses are also known as *wudewusa* in the Anglo-Saxon language, "the old man of the of woods" and – according to information on display at St John the Baptist Church, Saxmundham – the "old man of Suffolk." A "wose" is apparently another Saxon word for a "being" or troll. "Woodwose" is generally used interchangeably with "wildman". The Anglo-Saxon *wudewusa* is literally "wild being" and has nothing to do with living in the woods. Author P.G. Wodehouse's name has the same origin.

Generally woodwoses are medieval wildmen found carved on the fonts and porches of churches throughout the county. (The font is the structure, usually by the door and usually made of stone, for holding the water used in the baptism of babies into the Christian faith.) But what is this hairy man-beast, and do its numerous ecclesiastical appearances commemorate a real British Bigfoot that once stalked the English countryside?

Few churches in Suffolk Coastal District are without at least one woodwose, but there are also clusters around Mid-Suffolk in the Stowmarket-Needham Market-Elmswell area and around Eye in villages near the A140 road.

Most are believed to date from the 15th century ("the 1400s"). They are carved on the staves of stone baptismal fonts, or as reliefs hewn into the porch of a church, where they are usually to be found with a club and shield raised as they close in for combat with a dragon or wyvern (a two-legged dragon.) Some of the woodwoses are perched on the roofs of church porches.

There are even a few woodwoses on top of the towers of Suffolk churches. A huge gorilla-like stocky-bodied woodwose crouches on the top of the tower at the church of St Mary the Virgin in the town of Haverhill, down in the southeastern corner of Suffolk near the Cambridgeshire and Essex borders, resting on his straight club, thoughtfully stroking his beard as he stares into the distance. The church at Kelsale-cum-Carlton, immediately north of Saxmundham has two badly deteriorated seated woodwoses seated at the top of the church tower and flanked by two lions. A carved stone figure at the top of All Saints Church in Sudbury, while it's hard to make out when looking up at it from the ground, is a fifteenth century woodwose with big ears and a grinning face turned slightly to one side, as he holds a club in both hands. He's held in place by a metal bar after he fell off the tower in a hurricane in the 1980s.[4]

At the church of St Andrew's in Walberswick, the woodwoses are ruined – some of their heads are gone and you can just make out the wavy hair on the torsos that remain. When first I saw the ruined Walberswick woodwoses, I mistook them for a particularly hairy Adam and Eve. While the seaside village of Walberswick is a famously fashionable holiday resort, the haunt of Hampstead literati all the way from London and the Freud family in particular, Suffolk's woodwoses tend to be in out-of-the-way places that are unlikely to feature in glossy Sunday supplements any time soon.

The area of the county with the greatest density of "woodwose churches" is the Blyth Valley, inland from the "Suffolk Heritage Coast" and west of the A12 road, and some of the most spectacular examples of Suffolk woodwoses are to be found so far off the map there's actually a Lonely Wood round there, and several "Lonely Farm" addresses. Another sign that back in the olden days no one in the Blyth Valley expected help to come from anywhere any time soon in times of trouble is the proliferation of ancient farms with moats around them.

You could take in most of the woodwoses of the Blyth Valley and the western edge of Mid-Suffolk District in a day by car. A determined, fit cyclist in good weather could do them in a full day. I made a woodwose run from Halesworth station to the villages of Chediston, Cratfield, Badingham and onward to Darsham station in a day's cycle ride before sundown, including pub and tearoom stops for the rainy bits. Peasenhall and Sibton are do-able by bike in a long afternoon from Darsham or Saxmundham stations.

Holidaying "smart set" Radio 4 listeners (and – quite a few summers back – then Prime Minister Gordon Brown, up for his hols in the trendily retro holiday resort of Southwold, where beach huts change hands for over £100k and over a third of properties are second homes) mostly dash into the town of Halesworth just long enough to fill the 4x4 up with posh dinner party ingredients and then speed out again. Halesworth has its own miniscule museum, and is famed among trainspotters for its "moving platform" a combined railway platform and level crossing. But souvenir postcards of the less chic destination of Halesworth are hard to find in any of the town's shops. The parish church of St Mary's Halesworth does, however, have woodwoses on its font.

The standard woodwose-on-a-font configuration is four woodwoses facing outward, rarely more than a foot high, generally flanked by sitting lions, along with the angels and winged animals representing the Four Evangelists – Matthew, Mark, Luke and John. Most of Suffolk's woodwose-bearing fonts conform closely to this arrangement. Some of Halesworth's font woodwoses stand with their legs crossed, their clubs resting on the ground, flanked by the traditional smiling lions. There are well over a hundred of these octagonal fonts, usually with just the lions, across Suffolk. The fonts were mostly carved from stone all the way from Barnack in Cambridgeshire.

From Halesworth, the road to my next woodwose stop, the very small and mostly thatched village of Chediston, took me along a "roadside nature reserve" and then through miles of oilseed rape fields with the occasional field containing alpacas. Fields of yellow rapeseed are a common sight in the Spring in Suffolk's Blyth Valley

Please drive very slowly in the churchyard

The churchyard of St Mary's Chediston is a thoroughfare, with a battered "Please drive very slowly in the churchyard " sign. The woodwoses on the fifteenth century stone font in the otherwise bare church of St Mary's Chediston resemble Halesworth's, except that some of the woodwoses have surprisingly Christ-like beards and expressions, and the seated lions flanking them have broad grins. One Chediston woodwose has a shield covering his private parts, but all the woodwoses have such thick body hair you can't see anything anyway.

A nearby woodwose font halt is St Peter's Church, Sibton. The four Sibton woodwoses have more muscular limbs and thicker hair, and stare suspiciously at you as they guard the font. Most beasts in medieval art were in some way allegorical, and woodwoses were said to represent strength. They're also the right shape to fit neatly within the space of the upright staves of a font – tall and thin, holding up a club.

Also in the Blyth Valley, a comfortable cycle ride from Halesworth, is Wissett, whose church has four woodwoses on the font. Particularly interesting was the beard-stroking intellectual woodwose, deep in thought, and the less intelligent woodwose on the same font, whose toothy smile makes him look a bit of an idiot. The two other woodwoses on the font are both damaged, one carries a club and has his face vandalised, the other stands cross-legged.[5]

Wissett's woodwose font has evidence that it used to be painted in bright colours. Parish records for 1492 show a parishioner had paid for a lick of paint on its woodwoses, confirmed by flecks of turquoise still on the font. The woodwoses of Wissett and Middleton (see below) are the only Suffolk woodwoses to feature on postcards, on sale in their respective churches.

PART 1 – NOT QUITE HUMAN

The porch of St John the Baptist, Badingham, has a very worn outline of a woodwose with long hair on its head and a thick club raised at an equally worn wyvern (two-legged dragon) now so indistinct that some say it's a dog or a tiger – although it looked like a wyvern to me. Either the elements have eroded both protagonists away, or the religious reformers have defaced him. In any event, you can barely see their outlines.

The woodwose at St Mary's Church, Cratfield, is on the porch. He may be less than two feet tall, but he's impressive. With his legs tucked into the space available above the arch over the door, he has an angry expression, short curly hair on his head and a pointy beard. While most woodwoses on Suffolk church porches are fighting two-legged wyverns, this one's closing in for a fight with a fat dragon with two sets of legs.

Seven miles due south of Badingham lies the village of Sweffling, which also has a woodwose closing for combat with a wyvern on the porch of its church. If the Sweffling woodwose had body hair it's worn away, he's also lost some limbs.

Arriving at Peasenhall, you get a sense you are back in civilization. Not only are there signs for the mighty A12 road again (East Suffolk's link road to London, and the nearest it gets to a motorway, although single carriageway at this point), there are *two* tea rooms.

Woodwose spotters hold up as the finest example of the genre either Cratfield or Peasenhall porch, I have to say the latter magnificent example is my favourite. The woodwose above the porch at St Michael's Peasenhall is in slightly better condition than Cratfield's. He has the happier face of a serene although slightly comic yet slightly disturbing noble savage. Peasenhall Man's body hair falls in luxurious curls, and he has fine detail on his shield, while the wyvern approaching him across the porch is more serpentine than the obese one at Cratfield.[6]

Peasenhall means "the valley where peas grow", and the Peasenhall Pea Festival held every July celebrates the humble pea with various child-friendly activities such as pea-throwing and a costume competition which invites children to dress up as a pea (there's a lot of green make-up involved). The event made the "50 most fun things to do in Suffolk" listing a few of years back.

There's another Church of St John the Baptist in the ancient market town of Saxmundham, right next to its Tesco and Waitrose superstores. St John's has just two woodwoses on the font of its church, and I have to agree with the assessment of the church's own guide: "a splendid specimen in an excellent state of preservation."

Saxmundham's woodwoses are 18-inch Renaissance works of art – why they aren't as well known as the works of Michelangelo is beyond me. Their extraordinarily detailed little faces have all the dignity of Biblical patriarchs, their features could past muster as a slightly retro Neanderthal reconstruction. Flanked by the standard smiling lions (these ones have their tongues out), the burly, thick-limbed "Sax" wildmen sport late 15th century woollen hats and are otherwise naked under their thick, superbly detailed fur. One has his club raised, another has his club resting on the ground, his legs crossed.

It turns out my woodwose tours were just scratching the surface, taking in a mere eight examples of woodwoses in churches in the part of the county where they are most abundant.

There's also the top half of a statue of a fearsome woodwose propped on a windowsill at St Mary's Woolpit, not far from Stowmarket. (We'll meet Woolpit's green children and its doom-prophesying black dog later.) The Woolpit woodwose is "a symbol of strength and evil... said to come from India" according to a label in the church.

Woodwoses at Alderton (top left, charging with spear), Badingham (top left, facing left, with club), Barking (top row, centre), Blythburgh, (top row, right), Chediston (centre row, left), the Ancient House, Clare (kneeling, second row right), Cov-ehithe (bottom row, right, with faced hacked off) and Cratfield (bottom right, charging, with club).

PART 1 – NOT QUITE HUMAN

The Church of St Andrew at Alderton, half way down the Bawdsey Peninsula, was a ruin used as a barn before it was brought back into use in the nineteenth century. Its tower collapsed long ago, a warning sign advises you to stay away from its remains. On the church's porch is a tiny, worn away one-foot-high figure of a long-legged woodwose charging with a pointed stick (or the stem of a pine tree?) at what is assumed to be a dragon. The dragon's so eroded, though, that it's an identification based only on woodwoses charging at dragons on other Suffolk church porches. Only its long hair and beard lead us to believe the figure with the pointed stick is a woodwose, so unkind have time, neglect and the estuary's climate been to the porch of St Andrew's. The naked, bearded wildman with a club bending over to strike the dog-like dragon on the porch of St Mary's Church in the North Suffolk border town of Beccles is so eroded away you'd miss him if you weren't looking for him.

North of Stowmarket, on the porch of the church at Yaxley, there's a fine woodwose with a club fighting off attacking lions (or possibly a lion and a dog). The curls and twists of his hair and fur are rendered in fine detail. Sharing space with the Yaxley woodwose is a man in a fifteenth century costume with woollen hat, clutching a short sword and shield and battling something that could be either a curly-tailed, fat wyvern or an odd-looking chicken.

Not for from Yaxley is Mendlesham, where the two rather hard-to-photograph woodwoses are bigger than usual and are perched on the roof of the porch looking down at you, together with two lions. The woodwoses on the roof at Mendlesham are a frightening looking pair, brandishing their clubs in both hands with their legs bent as if about to attack. They have bushy eyebrows and hairstyles of matted hair that make them look like an evil Gaul from the Asterix books or a cursed Rastafarian escapee from *Pirates of the Caribbean*

The Church of the Holy Trinity at Middleton has some fine carved woodwoses on its font, with the wavy hair on their bodies rendered particularly skilfully. One has a damaged head. As on several woodwose fonts, this may have been to accommodate hinges to a font cover, added later.

There are some slimmer woodwoses with particularly fine detailing of their noble faces, clubs and hair on the font at the church at Barking near Needham Market (it used to differentiate itself from other Barkings as Barking-cum-Darmsdem.)

Nor are woodwoses just a rural phenomenon. They turn up in sophisticated urban Suffolk churches too. We've already encountered the woodwoses of the urban churches of Sudbury, Saxmundham, and Halesworth. We're about to meet the little woodwoses in the church of the port town of Orford. And the Church of St Michael the Archangel in the town of Framlingham contains the tombs of the Howard family, as well as that of Henry VIII's royal bastard Henry Fitzroy, Duke of Richmond and Somerset, but it also has little club-wielding woodwoses on its font, two of them are going bald. A short typewritten guide on display in the church, which itself looks a bit vintage now, says of its fourteenth-century, woodwose-bearing font, "it is carried on a stout pillar decorated with figures of pagan belief and superstition from which the baptized are liberated into the fullness of life by the Holy Spirit of God." This begs the question, how much superstition and pagan belief can a newborn baby accumulate? It's noteworthy that some of the churches' own guide booklets don't mention their woodwoses at all, almost as if they are in denial about them.

I've also had the opportunity to view the woodwoses in the disused St Clement's Church, Ipswich, smoke-damaged by a 1990s fire but now on its way to becoming an arts centre. The soot-encrusted woodwoses of St Clement's, the old ropemakers' church by the waterfront, have a more Classical look to them, suggesting a slightly later date. I only got a brief look at them, though. After being kindly let in to St. Clement's by the Ipswich Historic Churches Trust, I had to move aside panels or wire mesh and sheets of plasterboard to get to the font. Until recently, St. Clement's had been used as a scenery and prop store for Ipswich's New Wolsey Theatre.

I confess there are so many woodwoses in Suffolk that I haven't managed to see all of them yet. As I write, I've just finally been to see the ones around the font at Bildeston. The woodwose on the door of the font cover at Bramford and the head of a wildman sticking his tongue out at Nettlestead still await my examination.

I was impressed on my various woodwose tours how nearly all the local churches are left open to the public all day. (I'm told Wickham Skeith's church is usually locked, I confess to tiptoeing in during their service one Sunday and sneakily photographing what's left of the woodwoses there – fortunately, fonts are usually right by the door of a church, so such under-the-rader woodwose photography missions are possible.)

Iconoclasts

To add to the mystery surrounding Suffolk's woodwoses, a fair proportion of them have been damaged or deliberately vandalised in what looks likes some Islamic State or Taliban-style demolition of "graven images" and "idolatrous" antiquities. The Protestant faith took hold as a result of the English Reformation (starting in the 1530s, but reaching its most extreme form under Lord Protector Oliver Cromwell in the 1640s and 1650s). It was all about a return to the core values of the original teaching of Jesus, as revealed in the Bible, and especially the Ten Commandments. Commandment number three stated: "Thou shalt not make unto thee any graven image," making the woodwoses in Suffolk churches an obvious target.

We've already encountered the ruined, headless woodwoses at St Andrew's Walberswick, but the most extreme example is probably at Wickham Skeith, where there's only an outline left where one of the woodwoses was completely chiselled away. The spaces where something's been neatly removed from the font at Little Bealings, just outside Ipswich, looks like the gap you'd expect to be left were you to hack away woodwoses and lions. And something appears to have been chiselled out from between the lions on the font at St Mary Burgate.

The woodwoses at St Peter's church, Theberton, have their faces hacked away, and the woodwoses at Middleton, between Theberton and Westleton, are damaged, although some of the damage to their heads maybe as a result of adding hinges for a font cover later. The fine, hairy woodwoses at St Andrew's Covehithe have had their faces and hands chipped off. A leaflet for visitors to the church says they were defaced by William Dowsing's men in the Cromwellian period, but Dowsing's journal makes no reference to woodwoses or any images on the font, only to religious "pictures" including stained glass images and images of "cardinals". Other defaced Suffolk wildmen appear on church fonts at Redlingfield (near Eye) and at Old Newton, just north of Stowmarket and also at Bildeston.

It's possible they were defaced earlier, either by Henry VIII's commissioners, or (more likely) by King Edward VI's officials, enforcing an edict of 1540 ordering the smashing of religious statues. Or by parishioners or churchwardens on their own initiative – East Anglia was quite enthusiastically Puritan, and would have become embarrassed by the "old hat" woodwoses from the Catholic days of at least 160 years earlier.

PART 1 – NOT QUITE HUMAN

Woodwoses on the font at Framlingham (left), Halesworth (centre) and on top of the tower of St Mary the Virgin, Haverhill (right).

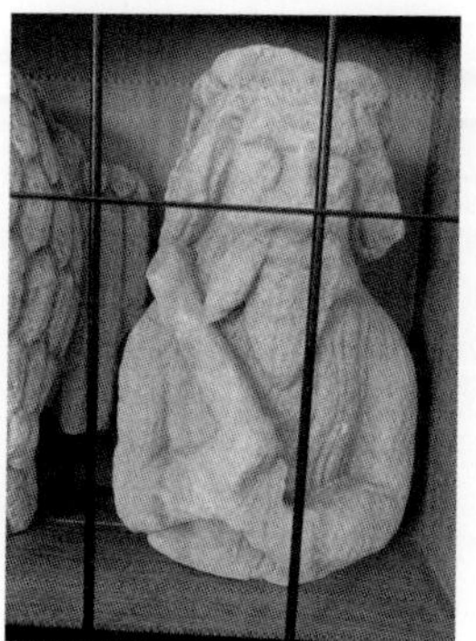

Ruined woodwose at Letheringham, found in a local garden (left), on the roof of the church at Mendlesham (centre) and at Middleton (right).

Restored by Victorians, these woodwose at Nacton (left and inset) and Waldringfield (centre) have hooves, a typical octagonal woodwose font at Orford (right).

The provenance of the surviving top half of the woodwose statue in St Mary's,Woolpit isn't known for certain, but it's thought it could have come from the well shrine of Our Lady at Woolpit, demolished by Henry VIII's reformers.[9] The officials of Edward VI showed particular intolerance to statues in churches, and are believed to have inflicted the most damage on East Anglia's devotional art.

Some local woodwose-bearing fonts only survive because the idolatrous bits were plastered over until the commissioners had gone away. The smooth sides of the font in the church at South Cove, between Wrentham and Covehithe, make it look as if it was plastered over a long time ago, could it still have woodwoses hidden underneath that plaster?

Some plastered-over woodwoses weren't uncovered until the plaster was chipped away in the nineteenth century, when the Oxford Movement gripped the Anglican church, and church decoration was "in" again, with new stained glass windows and so on.

The commissioners of Henry VIII began enacting an edict ordering the destruction of (some) religious statues in churches during the Reformation in the 1530s. But most of the ruined woodwoses on the fonts at St Andrew's Church, Walberswick and others were possibly defaced in the short reign of Edward VI, or later – by self-appointed Cromwellian iconoclast William Dowsing and his deputies.

Laxfield-born Dowsing, who was Provost Marshall of the Eastern Association, Cromwell's civil war army of the East of England, carried out an ordinance from the Earl of Manchester that charged him with destroying "superstitious imagery". He visited over 250 churches in Suffolk and Cambridgeshire (taking in a quarter of all of Suffolk's churches) for that purpose, and noted it all obsessively in his diary.

By the time Dowsing came round, many of the woodwoses had already gone in the great purge by Anglican reformers in the 1540s. Suffolk was a strongly Protestant region anyway, and some of the pictures of saints, crucifixes, altars, rood screens (partitions separating altars from the congregation), inscriptions and initials referring to the Virgin Mary would already have been removed by the congregation before the official iconoclasts came calling.

It's thought that many of the woodwose-chiselling incidents took place during the days of the Tudor reformers, and many plasterings-over of woodwose fonts occurred in this time, 110 years before Dowsing. A few months before the great storm and alleged appearance of the Devil in the form of a black dog at Bungay in 1577, (we'll meet him in Chapter 6) there was a report complaining that the churchwardens had taken down church furnishings against the wishes of the Bishop of Norwich. Elizabeth I (1533-1603) even passed edicts restraining her subjects from the destruction of ecclesiastical decorations, concerned that local congregations were taking the process too far.

Some of the damage to the woodwose fonts may even have happened in Victorian times, after a few mishaps in the delicate process of chipping carefully away at the three-hundred-year-old plaster from church fonts. There are a few woodwose fonts that are Victorian restorations – at Newbourne, Nacton and Waldringfield. In the last two examples, Victorian stonemasons have re-done the woodwoses with hooves instead of feet, while the now rather hipster-looking contemporary woolen hats of the early Tudor period have mutated into outlandishly exotic turbans. (Everyday Tudor headgear probably looked even more exotic than turbans to Victorians.) It's possible that the feet became hooves because some of the woodwoses' toes had been worn away and damaged, so the masons improvised with what remained.

Most of the paraphernalia Dowsing and his associates were so keen on stripping out of Suffolk churches wasn't Medieval Catholic at all, but recent innovations by the Anglican High Church Archbishop William Laud under Charles I in the 1630s. Laud had ordered the installation of altar rails and steps going up to the altar. Fonts showing the very Catholic concept of the seven sacraments or bearing any initials referring to the Virgin Mary seem to have incensed Dowsing and Co. – as did angels, stained glass windows and any representation of nuns, monks or cardinals. Dowsing's crew seems to have left woodwoses alone at least some of the time, though. While woodwoses may strike us as pagan, they were at times under Dowsing's radar, as at least they weren't Catholic! Unlike the contemporary East Anglian witchfinders (we'll meet them, and the "imps" that feature in their accusations, in Chapter 9), Dowsing wasn't seeking to enrich himself from his East Anglian mission, he was motivated entirely by what we'd now call religious extremism.[5]

One of the strangest back-stories of a Suffolk woodwose is that on display behind bars in the Priory Church of St Mary, Letheringham, just down the road from Easton. Only the top half survives of this worn and battered, pointy-bearded woodwose with huge, staring eyes and thick moustache. He holds a short, curved, broken club raised in what's left of both his hands. But his ruined state isn't down to official iconoclasts, but to neglect by local landowners and churchwardens.

Letheringham church – it's in the middle of a field today, surrounded by paddocks for horses – was a ruin by the eighteenth century: its roof was gone, and a property dispute over the land it stood on exacerbated this state of affairs. A visiting antiquarian in 1780 described the "roof entirely down" exposing ruined "antient and curious monuments", possibly including our woodwose, who may once have stood on top of the porch. A restoration ordered by church authorities went seriously awry, with churchwardens instead selling of the entire contents of the chancel to a contractor, presumably for building materials, stone being rare in these parts. We owe the Letheringham woodwose's survival to his chance discovery in a local garden, where he was being used as a garden ornament.

Secular wildmen

However, not all Suffolk's woodwoses are ecclesiastical. Although they're hard to spot in the shadows of the dark wood on one of exterior windowsills of the Clare Ancient House in the Suffolk town of Clare, there are indeed two skinny, shaggy secular woodwoses – carved in wood – kneeling and holding some sort of emblem or coat of arms.

There's also a distinctly non-ecclesiastical Green Man pub at Tunstall. The Helmingham Hall Herbal and Bestiary, an illustrated manuscript from around 1500 originally at Helmingham Hall, Suffolk but now in the Yale Library, also has a hairy "Wildman" in it, holding a club in one hand and a snake in the other. It was thought to be a pattern book for decorating the hall.[6]

New discoveries of medieval Suffolk woodwoses are still coming to light. The broken-off handle of a gold spoon found by metal detectorists near Woodbridge was the subject of a coroner's court hearing at Ipswich in December 2015, seeking to establish the value of the find, with the help of British Museum experts.

This court case was a treasure trove hearing. Treasure trove legislation covers exclusively gold and silver "portable antiquities", seeking to establish whether the goods were buried on purpose or hidden with the intention of being recovered or whether they were just lost, or whether the heirs of whoever the treasure belonged to can be found. These factors all affect whether the treasure trove became the property of the Crown or the finder.

The spoon handle shows yet another little Suffolk wildman with his arms resting on his hips, with a club raised in his right hand. His legs were broken off below his thighs, but there's enough of them to tell he was standing at ease, with his legs slightly apart. The curls of his thick body hair are just visible, and the long hair on his head has the look of dread-locks tied up in a huge bob.

The woodwose spoon handle was dated to around 1400, which would make it "certainly one of the earliest depictions of the Wild Man" in England, according to Professor Ronald Hutton of the Department of History of the University of Bristol. According to Professor Hutton, the gold spoon handle would have been in the possession of someone "well-off… upper middle class", who may have been given it as a gift to "remind them how not to behave", as the "barbaric, chaotic and unrestrained" nature of such wildmen were an "awful warning" against any breakdown of the social or religious order.

Ipswich and Colchester Museum service confirmed to me they as of January 2018 they had raised the money to purchase the gold woodwose spoon handle for the Ipswich Museum and that it was in their collection.[7]

≠

Pakefield Man

Some 700,000 years ago, "Pakefield Man", the early pre-humans that crossed the Alps to arrive in Suffolk, left a sign of their presence here – 30 flint tools that were eventually pulled out of the cliff at Pakefield, a southern suburb of Lowestoft. These were some of the earliest known evidence of human activity in Northern Europe. The unlikely scenario of primitive proto-humans surviving somewhere in the wilds of Europe has, however, been dealt a blow by recent improvements in radiocarbon dating. This put back the extinction of the Neanderthals to 10,000 years earlier than previously thought.[8]

Are the numerous woodwoses in Suffolk churches just for show, or do they commemorate some kind of local English wildman-of-the woods, a British Bigfoot, or what cryptozoologists call "relic hominids"? There are indeed accounts of two historical Suffolk wildmen. These include the capture of a wildman in the Suffolk port of Orford whose description was remarkably similar to the manimal depicted on so many of the county's churches.

Cistercian abbot and historian Ralph of Coggeshall, writing in approximately 1200, recorded in his *Chronicon Anglicanum* how around 1161, "In the time of King Henry II, when Bartholomew de Glanville was in charge of the castle at Orford, it happened that some fishermen fishing in the sea there caught in their nets a wild man. He was naked and was like a man in all his members, covered in hair and with a long shaggy beard. He eagerly ate whatever was brought to him, but if it was raw he pressed it between his hands until all the juices were expelled. He would not talk, even when tortured and hung up by his feet. Brought into church, he showed no signs of reverence or belief. He sought his bed at sunset and always remained there until sunrise. He was allowed to go into the sea, closely guarded with three lines of nets, but he dived under the nets and came up again and again. Eventually he came back of his own free will. But later on he escaped and was never seen again." There are still longhaired woodwoses on the font at the church St Bartholomew in what Visit Suffolk describe as the "diminutive gem" that is Orford today.

And there's The Wild Man pub in Sproughton, a village on the western edge of Ipswich.

This pub's said to owe its name to a creature that during its construction, roughly contemporary with most of the woodwoses in the county's churches, "terrified the builders in a nearby waste." Its current pub sign features a cartoon figure wearing a spotted animal skin and carrying a spear and a club, reminiscent of *The Flintstones* cartoon. A local tradition, though, says the wildman was just an eccentric hermit who lived in the nearby Devil's Wood.[9]

Outside Suffolk, woodwoses in churches are rare in the rest of England, although there's a cluster of them over the Norfolk border and around Norwich. Norfolk woodwoses include one at All Saints, Hilborough clutching a severed head in its hand. There's also one at Beverley, Cambridgeshire, on a stately home. Still in the East of England, there's an exceptionally fine hairy wildman on the carved tomb of Sir Robert Whittingham, who died in 1471, at the church of John the Baptist in Aldbury, Hertfordshire.[10]

Zuilen, now part of the Dutch city of Utrecht, displays woodwoses ("wild men" or "savages" in heraldic terminology) on its coat of arms, as do the arms of the Dutch city of Bergen op Zoom, the Earl of Atholl and the late Duke of Edinburgh.There's also a 1499 painting of wildmen carrying shields with German coats of arms by the artist Albrecht Dürer.

As late as 1755, zoologist Carl Linneaus catalogued a sub-species of *Homo sapiens* which he called *Homo sapiens ferus* (*ferus* meaning feral), describing it as "four-footed, dumb and hairy." It is tempting to think that Suffolk's woodwoses commemorate an actual briefly captive wildman, or even a species of relic hominid living among us in the flat plains of East Anglia. But folklorist Gregory Forth in *The Wildman Inside and Outside Europe* (Gregory Forth, *Folklore* volume 118, no 3 Dec 2007) points out that unlike the Asian and American traditions of Bigfoot, the almasty apeman of the Caucasus Mountains and so on, there are very few surviving accounts of actual sightings of wildmen in Europe. At the time most of Suffolk's woodwoses were carved on the county's church fonts and porches somewhere in the fifteenth century, they were "thought to be mythical" or to "live outside Europe," according to Forth.[11]

Archaeologist and cryptozoologist Dr Myra Shackley, author of *Wildmen: Bigfoot, Sasquatch and the Neanderthal Enigma* (Thames & Hudson, 1983) described an "apparent paucity of phenomenological evidence" for European woodwoses.

The discovery of New World "savages" came at about the same time as reports of monkeys and apes started arriving in Europe. Some late medieval manuscript illustrations show bands of woodwoses fighting with tailed monkeys. St Mary's Woolpit has medieval monkeys and bears on its pew ends – possibly inspired by travelling menageries – but the monkeys are clearly a very different animal than the woodwose.

Occasional reports do turn up, in addition to the Orford and Sproughton wildmen there is the claim in the 1569 English translation of Pierre Boaistuau's *Histories of Wonderfull Secrets In Nature* that there was a 1409 wildman sighting in Norway, and a 1531 wildman capture in Saxony, Germany. At the time the woodwoses were carved people were one famine, one missed tithe payment, one episode of misunderstood mental health difficulties and one collateral damage incident during an escalated local dynastic feud away from starvation. Occasionally people would lose absolutely everything and turn feral.

European wildmen are thought to have been inspired by the classics of literature, such as the numerous versions of the *Romance of Alexander* in which Alexander the Great encounters "the Wildman" in India during one of his many exploits – some from history, some entirely fictional. The medieval Classicists in Suffolk's then numerous monasteries could also turn for inspiration to the Marsyas – a race of wildmen skinned alive by Apollo.[9]

A magnificent woodwose at Peasenhall (above) with fine examples at Saxmundham (below, left) and catching the evening sun at Sibton (right).

PART 1 – NOT QUITE HUMAN

Unlike the Asian and North American big hairy men, who were viewed as a different animal to humans, the Christian doctrines of Man made in the image of God and of The Fall meant that woodwoses had become "feral men" originally human but who had grown apart due to "outrageous hardship" or turned wild through an "upbringing among wild beasts." The woodwose's coat of hair was regarded as a consequence of their "wildness not their natural state", according to Forth. One distinguishing feature that set Europe's woodwoses apart from the wildmen and big hairy men outside Europe was that they had long hair on their heads, and beards, making them more human-like.

Some of the attributes of European woodwoses related by Forth were that they didn't speak, they seemed to enjoy thunderstorms, they had some kind of Tarzan-style "sympathy" with animals, as well as knowledge of medicinal plants. Sometimes woodwoses snatched and ate human children. Male woodwoses were said to occasionally abduct human women, while "wildwomen" (female woodwoses, sometimes depicted in medieval manuscripts and on coats of arms as hairy women with rather neat long hair and hairless breasts) had the power to disguise themselves as more mainstream women to seduce male humans.

The particularly fine specimens of little woodwoses on the font at St Mary's Harkstead, in the Shotley Peninsula, include one with very feminine features, longer hair and no beard. It looks like it may once have been a female woodwose. The Harkstead woodwoses show evidence of having been "recut" in later life, and there are some marks showing damage to the possibly gender-reassigned woodwose's chest, so he/she may have been a victim of Victorian prudery or misogyny during a later restoration.[12] (There's a photo on page 342.)

The Renaissance saw a rebranding of the woodwose as an extinct creature, or a savage human, like the "savage" peoples that were then being discovered outside Europe. By the seventeenth century, "wildman" had pretty much vanished from English literature and written sources, as a fascination for the newly discovered "wild" races of the New World had instead taken hold.

There was even a St Onuphrius, a woodwose saint in both the Orthodox and Catholic Churches. He was a fourth-century "Desert Father" of Egyptian Christianity who lived as a hermit for many years and had thick body hair and a loincloth made of leaves. The Welsh prophet Lailoken was a former wildman who'd lived as a lunatic in the Caledonian forests. Merlin, court magician to King Arthur, had originally been a wildman according to some versions of Arthurian legend.

Woodwoses may also have been inspired by Biblical wild men such as Nebuchadnezzar II, King of Babylon, who in the Old Testament's Book of Daniel was "humbled by God" while boasting of his achievements, and cast out from society. Probably the most famous portrayal of Nebuchadnezzar "cast out" is by the artist William Blake, who depicted a naked man with long white hair and a white beard crawling on all fours, his face in a tortured stare, and with his toenails growing into claws. Nebuchadnezzar went insane and lived like a beast for a period of seven years before he was cured. To Medieval Christians, he represented those redeemed by baptism. Fonts were not objects of veneration, though, so they were left alone by the religious reformers, unless they contained "Catholic" religious scenes such as crucifixions.

Debrett's Illustrated Peerage in its older editions had 28 British heraldic coats of arms with hairy wildmen or "savages", with or without clubs and some much rarer wildwomen. Such coats of arms were prevalent among the nobility of medieval France and Germany. King Charles VI of France was the only survivor among five nobles accidentally set on fire while capering dressed as woodwoses in a ball in 1393. Woodwoses as a heraldic symbol seem to have arrived among the English nobility in the fifteenth century, around the time the Suffolk woodwose fonts were carved.

It's also possible that woodwoses could symbolise the itinerant artisans who built the churches and carved the fonts – unsettled, roaming men seeking patrons at a time of huge expansion of church-building. "The club or ragged staff carried by many woodwoses is a common symbol donating a traveller from St Christopher." Could the woodwose carvings have depicted real people – caricatures of the stonemasons themselves as itinerant wildmen? A lot of these woodwoses have the features of actual people, and several woodwoses in different churches are clearly the work of the same artists.[13]

Woodwoses may turn out to be a cultural import from North Germany, via North German merchants of the trading ports that became the powerful confederation that was the Hanseatic League. This was a self-help organisation of merchants and ship-owners, already being referred to by name as "the Hanse" in the Royal Charter granted to the Suffolk city of Dunwich in 1215. The League came to include the North German cities of Hamburg, Lübeck and Cologne and the Dutch port of Groningen, Bergen in Norway, Gdansk in Poland and with numerous outposts as far afield as Tallinn in Estonia and colonies on the shores of the Baltic.

The League controlled pretty much all trade with Denmark, Sweden, North Prussia and Poland, and by the fifteenth century had warehouses or "offices" in King's Lynn, Norwich, Great Yarmouth and Ipswich. Cargo arriving from the Hanseatic League ports included the tall timbers from the vast forests of Poland and North Prussia used for shipbuilding, which they shipped to the shipbuilding ports of Suffolk such as Ipswich and Aldeburgh. Southwold had the status of a Royal harbour for the building of the King's ships from 1489 onwards, after the status was transferred to it from the port of Dunwich.

In those days, North Prussia contained some of mainland Europe's last remaining original pagans, who fought guerilla campaigns in the forests against the Teutonic Knights. These Tuetonic Knights were ethnic German settlers fighting an official Crusade against the pagans with Papal blessing. Woodwoses and wildmen were common on coats-of-arms of North Germany at this time, so it's possible the Hanseatic traders brought them with them to Suffolk.[14]

There's also a Flemish woodwose connection. The coat of arms of the city of Antwerp in Belgium is supported by a wildman and wildwoman, neither of them very hairy and both naked except for crowns and loincloths made from leaves, and both holding clubs. The "genre paintings" and prints created by the Flemish painter Pieter Bruegel the Elder (1525-1569) depict contemporary peasant traditions and festivals in Flanders – now the Dutch-speaking part of Belgium. Several of Bruegel's scenes include a well-known Flemish carnival play *The Death of the Wildman* performed in the streets in the background. This was a recognisable skit done by travelling players during carnival (at the end of Lent), in which an actor plays a hairy wildman who's shot by a hunter with a crossbow. Flemish people – as weavers, craftsmen and mercenaries in particular – were numerous in fifteenth and sixteenth century Suffolk. Many Suffolk church fittings – particularly the stained glass panels – are from Flanders. Bromeswell church (between Melton and Ufford) even has a bell with an old Flemish language inscription on it. Could Suffolk's Flemish immigrants, many of them craftsmen commissioned to do work on its churches, have brought over their wildman from their carnival play with them?

Yet another explanation for Suffolk's woodwoses, and why they're so peculiar to Suffolk, presents itself in the shape of crests on carved tombs of the de La Pole family in the church at Wingfield, in a remote corner of North Suffolk. The remains of Wingfield Castle, the seat of the de La Pole family, the Earls of Suffolk until the Tudor times, is now a privately-owned stately home nearby, but it's the tombs of the de La Poles we're interested in.

John de La Pole, Earl of Suffolk, who died either in 1491 or the following year, lies buried there, immortalised in a stone effigy that depicts him in full armour, lying next to his wife. John's head rests on his full-face helmet, which bears a crest showing his family's "Saracen" enemy from the Crusades centuries earlier. "Saracens" were the Muslim soldiers of the armies of the caliphates that faced the Crusaders, drawn mostly from present-day Turkey, Egypt or Iraq. The Saracen's eyes are closed, as if he has just been beheaded by a victorious Crusader forebear of John. The extraordinarily detailed head of the Saracen is a racist caricature – he has long curly locks, an elaborate beard, a headband, big earrings and an exaggerated, wide nose.

The same church has a less detailed stone effigy of Michael de La Pole, who died on active service at the siege of Harfleur in 1415, on Henry V's raid into France that culminated in the Battle of Agincourt. Michael's head also rests on a helm with a Saracen crest. This Saracen also has his eyes closed, and wears a helmet or skullcap and has the same wrinkled brow, locks, beard and exaggerated nose as the stone Saracen's head on John de La Pole's helm.

Both the Saracen's heads look awfully similar to the features of the bearded, hairy woodwoses on those church fonts all over Suffolk. Could the woodwoses have originated as "Saracens" on the de La Pole coat of arms, with their strong association with Suffolk and local pride? As a history undergraduate I recall being told in a lecture that a group of Cluniac hermits who moved into a cave in deepest medieval rural France had to be rescued from a mob of villagers who were convinced that the bearded hermits were "Saracens" who had tunnelled all the way from "the Holy Land" to France. Saracens were deliberately dehumanised by the propagandists of the Crusades, and the good people of Suffolk in those days could easily have confused the caricatures of Muslim soldiers with something less than human.[15]

The Elveden entity and the Peasenhall presence

But to bring the Suffolk woodwose phenomenon up to date, the Paranormal Database website received a report from a lorry driver who in May 2011, en route to Suffolk's busy international port of Felixstowe, was passing through fields near the village of Elveden along a busy stretch of the A134 road in the north-east corner of the country. From his cab he saw a light brown-grey ape-like creature, at first walking on all fours, with an "almost hyena-like movement", before it got up on its hind legs. The "semi-human like" creature looked up at the witness, showing its "forward facing eyes, long snout but a shorter face than a deer" and "small upright dog-like ears," before bounding off on all fours again. Elveden, home to England's tallest war memorial, also has associations with big cats and fairies, as we will see later.

Shortly after my first woodwose bike rides I interviewed "Phillip" (not his real name) who told of a strange late afternoon encounter in the summer of 2011 while walking with his partner back from a festival in Peasenhall towards their tiny campsite in Sweffling. From his description, Phillip's sighting was along a stretch of Rendham Road, with woods to the east.

In an experience which he estimated lasted some three minutes, Phillip "became aware something was watching us, following us... almost parallel with us." He "didn't know what it was," it began as "just a feeling I got," Phillip's "periphery vision on the left side saw this figure… if I turned my head I didn't see it." The entity was a "vague impression, it didn't look directly at us." Phillip caught the occasional "fleeting glimpse, like a snapshot." It was "there one minute and not there." (The description of an entity walking "parallel" but not visible if you look at it directly is noteworthy. Some of the Black Shuck phantom dogs in the traditions of Suffolk – we'll meet these in Chapter 6 – appear alongside witnesses on lonely country roads at night and walk in step with them, and are benign and protective – but only if you avoid looking them in the eye.)

Phillip's partner didn't see anything. Phillip described what he saw: on two legs, "seven or eight feet tall... silver grey, dark." He had the sense that it was "friendly". He'd had a similar encounter earlier in woodland in Wales, with an "impression of a tall and hairy" entity, "not as distinct" as his Suffolk manimal encounter.

An artist by profession, Phillip sent me a pencil drawing of the apparition on the road from Peasenhall. It showed a bulky, furry, biped in profile with stooped shoulders and an indistinct head, with trees in the background, more Bigfoot than woodwose. He confirmed that neither he nor his partner knew at the time of the wildman on the porch of the nearby churches at Peasenhall and Sweffling. Might those little woodwose carvings actually commemorate local protective spirits? Could the "tall, hairy entity" that Phillip experienced also have given the people of that corner of fifteenth-century Suffolk the impression of something "friendly"?

Since talking to Phillip, I've come across other accounts featuring sightings of another "impossible" modern East Anglian manimal apparition, a bit less man and a bit more animal. Bigfoot Research UK, which collects reports of alleged British Bigfoot-like creatures, lists two such creatures seen around Thetford, just over the Norfolk border. One was in 1986, on the A1075 road through Thetford Forest between Thetford and East Wretham.

An anonymous witness reported seeing "a strange hominid... a shaggy haired creature" about seven feet tall, which the witness at first thought was "an escaped zoo animal" before it got up on two legs, at which point the witness drove away, "scared". The creature they had glimpsed had "greyish white hair, small ears, a face with a sort of snout, and big eyes." A "similar creature" was reported in the "same general area" some 21 years later, in December 2007. I would normally ignore such a report. I merely note the similarity between whatever it was and the "brown-grey ape-like creature" with a "long, narrow snout" that also got up on two legs, seen at Elveden – just southeast of Thetford.[16]

The Cryptozoology News website also claimed, without giving a source, that Bury resident Geoff Knights (*aka* Crabtree) was visiting Offton Woods, near Stowmarket, in August 2015. Knights had previously worked around the woods, and said they'd been "left alone" since the mid-1980s. There he heard "primate vocalisations and crashing' sounds" before a "monkey-like animal" emerged from the foliage.

The creature Knights encountered was about 5 feet 8 inches (1.72 metres) tall, and had the physical features of a gorilla mixed with "the general shape of a man." Knights described how "I heard as clear as day. A monkey goes 'woow woow'. Then I turned and saw it." According to Knights, the creature was similar in colour to a chimpanzee, but walked fast on two legs, more like a human. It knocked branches with its arms, which he thought were "a third longer" than a human's. Whatever it was, it disappeared back into the woods, having sent the usually "pretty fearless" Knights fleeing in panic. There were "no pictures or videos taken of the incident," Cryptozoology News noted.[17]

The Suffolk Sasquatch

Then there was the Suffolk Sasquatch – "sasquatch" is a name for Bigfoot in the indigenous language of Canada's Halkomelem nation. A photo of the Suffolk sasquatch was circulating in 2004, showing a stooped, green, shambling bipedal thing, somewhat resembling the Swamp Thing character from the 1980s Marvel comic book series.

In the photo, it was standing in a clearing in front of trees, and had one arm raised and seemed to hold some kind of stick or staff in the other, and it was impossible to tell whether what hung from its body was fur or some kind of foliage, as if it were an earth elemental made from vegetation. A paranormal researcher who shall remain nameless recalls a photo of the Suffolk Sasquatch – said to have been taken somewhere at a secret Suffolk location – coming into his possession, in the very early days of digital photography.

Our researcher was told, "the figure had ran in front of the witness's car along a country lane" just outside Ipswich. So keen was our researcher to follow up that they were on the point of dropping some critical bit of work at their place of employment and asking for some time off to go out into the field and take a look, when the person who'd given them the Suffolk sasquatch photo 'fessed up and admitted the whole thing was "a deliberate hoax". They admitted it was a scarecrow.[18]

I'm afraid I will have to omit from our survey of not-quite-human man-creatures the "Queer character at Woodbridge" popularised in *Lo!,* the book by the great collector of anomalies Charles Fort. Often described as a "wildman," the accused appearing in court at Woodbridge in 1905 on an assault charge was no such thing. He was just a very anti-social and eccentric itinerant human.

When he appeared "in rags" on the path on nearby Martlesham Heath, holding a knife and shouting that he wanted what appeared to be "Baccy!" (tobacco), a passer-by called the East Suffolk Constabulary. The "wildman" had on his person some cash and a book of drawings, many of them of ships, annotated in a language that detectives at Scotland Yard couldn't identify. Our "queer character" (it just meant odd in those days) was acquitted of any offence and sent on his way with his book. From the report in the *East Anglian Daily Times* of 12 January 1905, he seems to have been definitely human. He'd possibly invented his own private written language or just spoke an obscure, hard-to-identify European tongue.[19]

That concludes our round-up of woodwoses, wildmen and ape creatures of the Curious County. Some are pure myth and folklore, fantastic creatures that survive only as figures carved in stone around Suffolk's churches hundreds of years ago. These woodwose carvings come with a mysterious origin and a curious distribution – common within the county of Suffolk but rarer outside it in the rest of England. There were, though, a couple of historic accounts of encounters with wildmen in Suffolk. As we have seen, there have been some more modern local encounters with... well, something tall and hairy and vaguely ape-like or vaguely human.

Woodwose on the exterior of St Edmund's, Southwold (top row, left), at Sudbury (centre), defaced at Theberton (right), more ruined woodwoses at Old Newton (bottom row, left) and at Walberswick (centre), hacked off woodwose at Wickham Skeith (right).

PART 1 – NOT QUITE HUMAN

Saracen's head at Wingfield (top left), Wissett woodwose (right), gold spoon handle found near Woodbridge (courtesy Suffolk County Council Archaeological Service), woodwoses at Norton (centre right), Woolpit (bottom left) and Yaxley (right).

The entity encountered on the road from Peasenhall by "Phillip" (top left, sketch copyright "Phillip", used with permission); the Suffolk Sasquatch, (right, contributor wishes to remain anonymous); more carved woodwoses, a Victorian "recarving" from the font at Southolt (above) and a woodowse from the porch of St Mary's church at Beccles. It's wielding a club, it's so worn away as to be barely visible (above right).

Yet more Suffolk woodwoses: on the porch of Sweffling church (left) and seated on top of the tower of the church at Kelsale right).

A woodwose on the tower of St Peter's Yoxford, grasping his long, forked beard. (right); Suffolk wildman pub signs (below): The Wild Man, Sproughton and The Green Man, Tunstall.

FOOTNOTES TO CHAPTER 1: On the trail of Suffolk's woodwoses

1."Curious Suffolk tourism campaign leads to MP demanding action", *Beccles and Bungay Journal*, 18 October 2012, www.becclesandbungayjournal.co.uk/news/curious_suffolk_tourism_campaign_leads_to_mp_demanding_action_1_1660519; "Suffolk: Curious County slogan row may reach House of Commons", *East Anglian Daily Times (EADT),* 18 October 2012, www.eadt.co.uk/business/suffolk_curious_county_slogan_row_may_reach_house_of_commons_1_1660329.)

2. Diocesan woodwose bike ride at www.cofesuffolk.org/index.cfm?page=yourchurch.content&cmid=464.

3. Much of this chapter first appeared in "The woodwoses of Suffolk," Matt Salusbury, *Fortean Times* **FT 318**, September 2014, updated at http://mattsalusbury.blogspot.co.uk/2014/10/the-woodwoses-of-suffolk.html; Roy Tricker, Pers comm by email 21 January 2015. It's unclear why, but most dictionaries give Bigfoot a capital letter.

4. The spike protruding from the head of the woodwose on the tower of All Saints, Sudbury, holds him in the place after he took a tumble in the Great Hurricane of 1987. Thanks to Barry Wall of the Sudbury. All Saints, Sudbury is an urban church and is usually kept locked. There's a list of keyholders on the door.

5. www.williamdowsing.org/journalnoindex.htm

6. *The Priory Church of St Mary Letheringham*, WD Akester, 1979, updated 2007. Dowsing paid a visit to Letheringham, but records only removing some Catholic inscriptions and a pictures of saints; *The Helmingham Hall Bestiary* is on the Yale Collections website at http://collections.britishart.yale.edu/vufind/Record/2038220.

7. "Rare treasure found in Suffolk depicts medieval 'Wild Man'", Evelyn Simak, BBC News website (Suffolk section), 12 December 2015, www.bbc.co.uk/news/uk-england-suffolk-35050026. Email from Rachel Kidd, Ipswich and Colchester Museum Service, 22 January 2018 confirming the spoon handle's now in their collection.

8. See the Lowestoft Museum's Pakefield Man display; Earlier Neanderthal extinction in *New York Times* 21 August 2014, www.nytimes.com/2014/08/21/science/neanderthals-in-europe-died-out-thousands-of-years-sooner-than-some-thought-study-says.html. Traces of the same species as Pakefield Man, *Homo heidelbergensis,* had since been found from an even earlier date along the beaches of North Norfolk.

9. Orford Castle was also the location for Vincent Price's climactic final scene in Tigon British Films Productions' 1968 horror film *Witchfinder General*. Sproughton wild man attack from *Phenomena – a book of wonders*, p. 111, John Michell and Robert J. M. Rickard, Thames and Hudson, 1977. The 120 bus from Ipswich Old Cattle Market bus station stops at the "Wild Man, Sproughton" bus stop once a day. *De Wildeman* (The Wild Man) is a fairly common name for a pub in the Netherlands and Dutch-speaking Belgium.

10. Whittingham intelligence from Jerry Glover, Letter to *Fortean Times* FT 321 December 2014 "Woodwoses".

11. *Homo sapiens ferus* from *Phenomena,* John Michell and Robert J.M. Rickard, Thames & Hudson, London 1977; "The Wildman Inside and Outside Europe", Gregory Forth, *Folklore* volume 118, no 3 Dec 2007, Forth quotes extensively from a 1952 article by Bernheimer.

12. A medieval manuscript shows woodwoses both male and female – the female woodwoses have bare breasts – living in a glade, with some of the men running off to fight flying wyverns with clubs. It's from the 15th-century *The Book of Hours* in the University of Syracuse Library, http://libwww.syr.edu/digital/collections/m/MedievalManuscripts/ms07/104v.jpg.There's the head of a "Green Woman" at the top of the ceiling under the porch at St Peter and Paul's Church, Clare.

13. Jerry Glover, Letter to *Fortean Times* FT 321 December 2014 "Woodwoses".

14. "Prussian wildmen", Dana S Alder, letter to *Fortean Times* **FT323;71** January 2015.

15. There's still a Saracen's Head pub in Sudbury, another Sacarens Head pub (without an apostrophe) nearby in Newton Green, a Turk's Head pub in Hasketon near Woodbridge and a Saracen's House Business Centre in a former pub in Ipswich.

16. www.bigfootresearchuk.com/ – page "Not found" as of 21 June 2015.

17. "'Bigfoot' Sighting in England, Claims Local Man", Cryptozoology News, August 23 2015, http://cryptozoology-news.com/bigfoot-sighting-in-england-says-local/.

18. Sorry, no references, anonymity requested on this one!

19. "A queer character at Woodbridge", *EADT* 12 January 1905, quoted in *Lo!* Charles Fort 1931, online at www.resologist.net/loei.htm. Many contemporary newspapers have regular headlines beginning "A queer character at..." followed by a location. These usually describe an eccentric vagrant appearing before the local courts.

2. There were giants in the earth

A gigantic head stands in a field on the edge of the Suffolk town of Eye.

The Curious County's two most famous giants were most definitely human, known to have been born to normal human mothers. The same cannot be said, however, for "the Bones of a mighty Giant dig'd up at Brockford Bridge neer Ipswich in the county of Suffolk" in 1651. While the remains of this particular giant then described as "The Wonder of Our Times," don't survive, a contemporary description hints at an unexpected identity.

Tom Hickathrift was a fenland giant with at least one parent – his mother – said to be human. That's if Tom was originally an actual person at all. Despite his very ordinary-sounding name, if there ever really lived a very tall person by that name, he seems to have walked out of history in great strides and passed into legend.

Not only do Tom's exploits seem impossible, even to a very tall human, most of them happen outside Suffolk. His stomping grounds were the fens of Norfolk and around the Isle of Ely in Cambridgeshire, there's only one brief Hickathrift story set in Suffolk.

Nor do the Tom Hickathrift stories give many clues as to his size, or even the size of his gigantic opponents. In some versions, he's not a giant, just a giant-killer with superhuman strength. Nor is it clear when Tom Hickathrift lived. Some legends portray him as a labourer at the time of the Norman Conquest, but he's best known from a book from around 1600.The most celebrated legendary exploit involving our Tom has him being paid "over the odds" to take an ox cart full of grain through a fenland route all the way to the port of King's Lynn in North Norfolk. The reason for his higher than usual fee became apparent when on the way he encountered a local ogre terrorising the neighbourhood. The ogre seems to have escaped from our opening chapter on woodwoses. He was hairy and had huge arms, so hairy that his hair got caught in the spokes of the cartwheel that Tom tore off the cart to defend himself with. In most versions of the story, Tom flipped the ox cart over and ripped off the whole axle, complete with one cartwheel, and held the axle as a kind of handle while he wielded the cartwheel like a huge club. After the obligatory massive fight, Tom eventually smashed the ogre's head with the business end of his cartwheel club.

Another Tom story has him leading a rebellion or rent-strike against a local "Lord of the Manor." The residents of the fens, who survived mostly by shooting wildfowl, catching eels with eel-spears and cutting for sale the very fertile peaty turf of the marshlands, were fiercely independent – as we'll see when we meet the Fen Tigers later in the section on big cats.

There's an eight-foot grave in the churchyard at Terrington St Clement, near King's Lynn and not far from the Lincolnshire border, said to be Tom's resting place, and his fight with the ogre is said to be depicted in the decorative plasterwork on the side of The Sun Inn, Saffron Walden, Essex.

The only Suffolk-based Tom Hickathrift story is a mention of him throwing a really big object at one of his antagonists (the Devil or another giant in various versions) but hitting instead the tower of the church in Beccles, which accounted for the inexplicable hole that could be seen in tower at one time, now long-since repaired. There's a problem with this story: a "dent" in the ground at the church at Walpole St Peter, on the North Norfolk border with Cambridgeshire, is also said to be the result of Hickathrift hurling a cannonball at the Devil.[1]

A much better documented and definitely human Suffolk giant was George Page. His grave in the churchyard at Newbourne, just outside Ipswich in the direction of the River Deben, commemorates him in a faded inscription as "the Suffolk Giant... exhibited in most towns in England." George was an impressive 7 feet 7 inches in height (2m 33.5cm), and died in April 1870 aged 27 (26 in some accounts) while on tour with the Whiting's Exhibition travelling fair. The Page Brothers were exhibited together as "the Suffolk Giants". George was an inch (2.5cm) taller than his brother Meadows, who continued to travel with the fair for another five years, before returning to his old job as a farm labourer and dying at a ripe old age in 1917.[2]

There used to be a Hulk's Grave in Mendham in Mid-Suffolk, on the south bank of the River Waveney (on the parish boundary of both Weybread and Withersdale) said to be the grave of a giant. It was also believed to be a place of execution, where "vagrants of the parish" were hanged and then buried. As late as 1922, witnesses recalled having to lead their ponies past the spot as they refused to move through the area. The site has now completely eroded away, there's nothing much left of see of the alleged giant's grave anymore.[3]

The Wonder of Our Times

A pamphlet appeared in 1651 in the form of a letter from "I.G," a merchant in Ipswich to his brother in London to update him on "the town of his nativity". I.G. recounts the discovery of the "Wonder of Our Times... the Body of a Mighty giant dig'd up at Brockford Bridge neer Ipswich in the county of Suffolk." It narrates how workmen digging in the "gravelly way" came across the bones. There's still a Brockford Bridge today. It's just south of Brockford Street on the A140, which goes from Stowmarket north to Diss. The "gravelly way" could have been a source of gravel – and possibly fossils, see below – from the old river bed of the River Dove, which would have changed course and shrunk over the years. The river's just a trickle under today's blink-and-you'll miss it Brockford Bridge over the A140, to this day there is an ancient-looking gravel footpath along the riverbank nearby.

The modern Brockford Bridge seems to be at the same location as the one where the "mighty Giant" was "dig'd up". Brockford Bridge isn't all that "neer" Ipswich, it's generally regarded as a Stowmarket address. It's a good 15 miles from Ipswich via modern roads, hardly "neer" in days when 30 miles a day by horse was considered a good day's journey. It's unlikely that the author of the 1651 pamphlet on the Brockford Bridge giant actually went all that way – an afternoon's journey – to see for himself. I.G. does mention a John Vice as having found the bones, with no further explanation as to who he was, so Vice may have been a mutual acquaintance of I.G and his brother, and an "our cousin" living nearby is mentioned, so I.G. may have learnt of the find by letter from them.[4]

Giant "bones" were uncovered at Brockford Bridge, although not a complete skeleton. All the teeth from the lower jaw were missing, and the pamphlet hints that the "shin bones" were damaged or partly absent. The giant's head lay almost "a quarter of a yard (nine inches or 22.5cm) lower than his feet", found in a North-South orientation, "his head to Ipswich-ward, and his feet towards Norwich."

Sixteen "teeth of an extraordinary bigness," were in the lower jaw. The body had a "scull" that was "the bigness of half a bushel" in size – half a bushel is about four gallons (just over 18 litres) or two average-sized buckets full of water. A leg bone (presumably a femur or upper leg bone) was "about the width of a middling woman's waist" and when the skeleton was laid out it was ten foot (3.04 metres) asize". It was four feet (1.21 metres) around the giant's rib cage from one shoulder to another. Presumably this ten-foot length for the skeleton would be when laid out on the ground as if reconstructing an upright human-like giant that had stood on two legs.

I suspect our "mighty Giant" was a fossilised prehistoric elephant or mammoth. There are plenty of specimens of both mammoths and fossil elephants from round the county of Suffolk and there's even a short geological period known as the Ipswichian Interglacial, which takes its name from local deposits laid down during a relatively short interval between Ice Ages.

Southwold Museum has a chest of drawers full of elephant remains – mostly teeth and bits of skull – on display. Ipswich Museum has some impressive local mammoth and prehistoric elephant remains, including most of a mammoth skull, as well as a full-size woolly mammoth model that was recently named Wool I Am, reconstructed based on mammoth remains found in what's now the Stoke Tunnel, the rail tunnel immediately south of Ipswich Station around the Maidenhall neighbourhood. Ipswich being a big town, there's a lot of digging going on, and deeper than in the agricultural areas of Suffolk, so Ipswich Museum's particularly rich in mammoth remains. The Museum also has a fine piece of most of a mammoth's skull dredged from off the coast at Lowestoft.

West Stow Museum's tiny palaeontology display has a fragment of a mammoth tusk and a piece of a prehistoric elephant's shoulder. Felixstowe Museum has a section of mammoth's tusk and a mammoth tooth, and even tiny Halesworth Museum has a small fragment of a mammoth's tusk thought to be from a warmer "interglacial" period between Ice Ages. Fishing

The Wonder of our times:

BEING

A true and exact Relation of the Body of a mighty Giant dig'd up at Brockford Bridge neer Ipswich in Suffolk, this present November 1651. his height 10. foot, his Head as big as half a bushell; with a description of the severall parts of his body, and manner of his interring.

Certified in a Letter from a Gentleman in the Country, to his Brother (a merchant) in London.

London: Printed by R. Austin, for W. Ley, at PAUL's Chain. 1651.

The cover of a 1651 pamphlet describing the bones of a "giant" discovered at Brockford Bridge, Suffolk. Fair dealing under the Copyright Act 1988 – front cover image for the purposes of critique or review, also out of copyright anyway.

vessels routinely dredge numerous mammoth bits, including their lower jaws, from off the coast of Suffolk. At Homersfield (*aka* South Elmham St Mary) on the River Waveney, there's a gravel pit – a bit like the "gravelly way" at Brockford – out of which mammoth tusks and teeth have been pulled.

Elephants usually have 26 teeth, including six enornmous molars. Especially in juveniles, they'll have teeth at the back still under the gum waiting to grow through, visible in a skeleton. Compared to human teeth, these are proportionately much larger than the skull they're attached to, which may be why I.G. singled out the teeth in particular as "huge."

If you looked at an elephant's skull believing it to be that of a very large human, its teeth would still be disproportionately large. The fact that there were no teeth in the top jaw of the Brockford giant is significant. Although they emerge from their own sockets, the tusks in elephants and mammoths are modified teeth from the upper jaw. Take away the tusks and it would be harder to identify the skull as an elephant's, and easier to mistake it for a very large human's. You could mistake the skull's tusk sockets for something like human nostrils.

Elephant and mammoth shoulder blades look just a bit like a human's to the untrained eye. The rib cage less so, but if you imagined you were dealing with the skeleton of an upright human, you could easily convince yourself it was the rib-cage of a very large, burly and well-built man – like the clumsy, lumbering monsters that giants were supposed to be in fairy tales.

While living elephants' feet are pillars of flesh designed to support several tonnes, the actual bones in them end in long, thin, surprisingly graceful toe-bones. (The toenails are all you can see sticking through that pillar of flesh in a living elephant.) The forearms could have been mistaken for a human arm ending in fingers, while parts of the less human-like back legs ("shin bones") seem to have been missing anyway.

A grown man wouldn't be able to put his arms round the skull of a full-grown adult modern African elephant skull, let alone lift it, so two buckets of water could comfortably fit in an elephant's cranium – the domed bit of its skull. The local Ipswich or Eye weights and measures people would have had an official "bushel" measuring container – probably an iron or brass bucket, and these were usually flat-bottomed, round, containers with low sides and handles at the top. (A bushel was originally a measurement of grain – around eight gallons or 36 litres.)

An elephant's skull is domed, like a human's, the right shape to hold two bushels, and not so different in shape from the bushel measuring containers that would have been around at the time. I can't imagine other prehistoric animals like a short-faced bear or sabre-toothed tiger or hippo, all with their more elongated skulls, being so easily passed off as a giant human's. My money's on *Elephas antiquus*, also known as the "straight-tusked elephant", as the true identity of the Brockford Bridge Giant. This was an older, slightly taller relative of today's Asian elephant, with a more domed head and with very long tusks that were straight right to just before their tips, when they curved. The jumbled bones of fossil elephants, especially when their tusks have fallen out of their sockets, do look awfully like giant humans, and there are several references to "giants" in Ancient Greek and Roman sources that are strongly suggestive of Mediterranean prehistoric elephants such as *Elephas antiquus* as well as mammoths. While mammoths fit the description, their tops of their skulls are a bit pointier than elephants', making them look less human-like.[5]

I found a reference to a "stupendous Elephant" in a menagerie of "foreign animals" visiting Ipswich in 1800, advertised in the *Ipswich Journal* as part of Pidcock's Grand Assemblage of Curious Foreign Animals and Birds. The advertisement claims it was the first time a live elephant had ever been seen in the county town, adding that the elephant is "so wonderful that without an ocular demonstration… Naturalists themselves are inclined to doubt." That was 150 years after the Brockford giant, so it's unlikely anyone local would have actually seen an elephant, or even recognised its skeleton, in 1651.[6]

Sadly, our correspondent I.G. records that many people from "adjacent towns" came to gawp at the Wonder of Our Times that was the Brockford giant, and "diverse" of them, "out of more folly I think broke the skeleton to gain part, or small pieces of the bones, to brag they had part of him. Some thought he was a Dane (a Viking?) … others imagine he might belong to Prince Arthur." (King Arthur). I.G said, "for my part, I shall suspend my judgement and leave it to wiser men."

To the people of seventeenth century Suffolk, both the Viking raiders and settlers of the ninth century and the possibly mythical Romano-British leader King Arthur were larger than life figures, giants among men. The pamphlet was illustrated with woodcuts of burly, Classical man's head and shoulders portraits, including possibly Hercules in his lion skin. The portraits were chosen probably because those were the woodcuts the printer happened to have to hand. Colchester and Ipswich Museum Service confirmed to me that their "Victorian natural history museum" started a couple of hundred years after this 1651 discovery, which was in the days of Lord Protector Oliver Cromwell, so they don't have identifiable specimens from the Brockford giant, however fragmentary, answering the pamphlet's description.

The Yoxman, a 7.9-metre (26-foot) bronze giant by sculptor Laurence Edwards, visible from the A12 road as it passes through Yoxford.

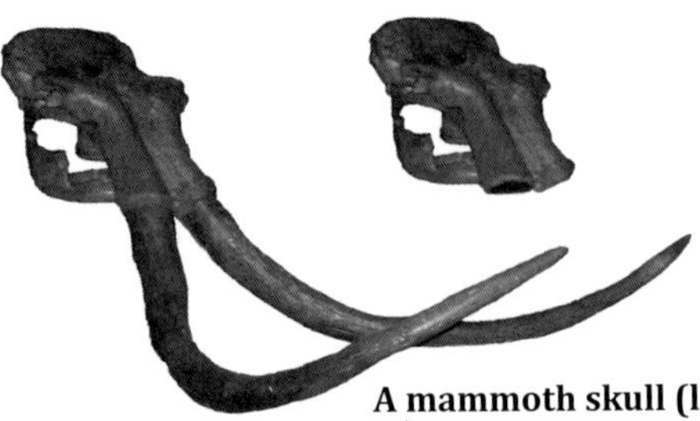

A mammoth skull (left) and the same skull missing its tusks (right), looking more like a human skull.

Reconstruction using a scale model of an incomplete mammoth skeleton laid out as described in the 1651 *Mighty Giant* pamphlet.

Mammoth tooth

Drawing of a small mammoth found in situ, with tusks missing

Selfie with Wool I Am, the mammoth model on display in Ipswich and (below) Halesworth Museum's mammoth tusk fragments.

Skeleton of *Elephas antiquus*, a prehistoric elephant and another possible identity for the "Mighty Giant dig'd up at Brockford Bridge." Photo: Georgios Lyras. Below: A life reconstruction of *Elephas antiquus*.

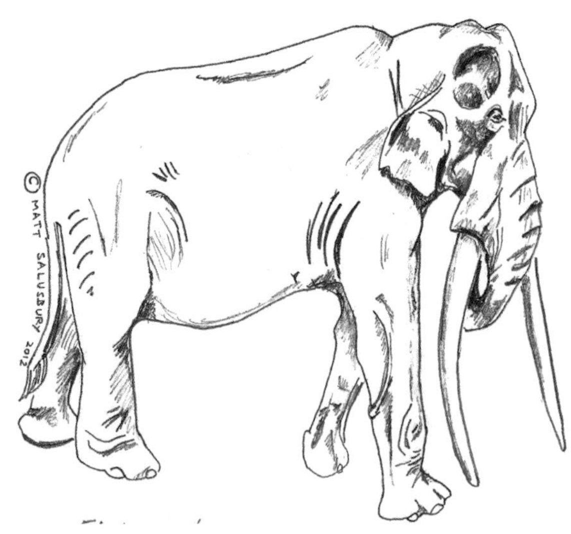

PART 1 – NOT QUITE HUMAN

FOOTNOTES TO CHAPTER 2: There were giants in the earth

1. The "There were giants" quote is from the Bible, *Genesis* 6, Verse 4; Hickathrift tales from *Haunted Suffolk*, Peter Jennings, Tempus Pubs, Stroud, 2006 . Tom has his own Wikipedia page at http://en.wikipedia.org/wiki/Tom_Hickathrift. Some sources have an alternative spelling – Hickerthrift.

2. *Diss Express*, 6 May 1870. *The Ipswich Journal* of 24 October 1863 records how Bury police prohibited on the grounds of taste the exhibition of the 24-year-old, three-stone weight – 19kg – "living skeleton" at the Bury Fair. See www.pipwright.com/Newspapers_in_Suffolk_1851_1875.htm

3. Hulk's Grave from Suffolk County's heritage website https://heritage.suffolk.gov.uk/hbsmr-web/record.aspx?UID=MSF686-Hulk's-Grave&pageid=16&mid=9.

4. *The Wonder of Our Times: Being a True and Exact Relation of the Body of a Mighty Giant dig'd up at Brockford Bridge near Ipswich in Suffolk...* pamphlet, I. G , printed by R. Austin, for W. Ley, at Paul's Chain, London, 1651, Thomason Collection list: E 646 (3), British Library digital resources, most of the text is at www.foxearth.org.uk/blog/2005/01/brockford-giant.html. East Anglian chronicler Ralph of Coggeshall also records that sometime between 1066 and 1263, "huge teeth" from a giant were found on a nearby seashore in Essex. The giant's teeth had been seen by the monks at Coggeshall, *Chronicon Anglicanum* www.bl.uk/collection-items/chronicon-anglicanum. The1640 Brockford Bridge land survey is from *The East Anglian; or, Notes and queries on subjects connected with the counties of Suffolk, Cambridge, Essex and Norfolk* https://archive.org/stream/eastanglianorno05whitgoog/eastanglianorno05whitgoog_djvu.txt; estimate of a day's journey by horse from www.westra.com/horses/history_travel.htm.

5. *Elephas antiquus* is also known as *Paleoloxodon antiquus*. Remains of a fossil *Elephas antiquus* (straight-tusked elephant) were excavated at Thorndon, three miles due northeast of Brockford Bridge. See *Proc Suffolk Inst Arch* no.18, p.253, 1924; "The Mammals of Suffolk", CB Ticehurst, *Proceedings of the Suffolk Naturalists' Society* no.2, 1932; "A Contribution to the Geological History of Suffolk", HEP Spencer, *Transactions of the Suffolk Naturalists' Society*, no.15(2), 1970; *Palaeolithic East Anglia*, JJ Wymer, Geobooks, 1984, with thanks to Tim Holt-Wilson.

The anecdote about not being able to lift or put your arms round an African elephant skull is from Lars Thomas, University of Copenhagen Museum, in *Pygmy Elephants*, Matt Salusbury, CFZ Publications, Wolfardisworthy, 2013, http://pygmyelephants.blogspot.co.uk; *The First Fossil Hunters – Dinosaurs, Mammoths and Myth in Greek and Roman Times*, Adrienne Mayor, Princeton University Press, 2011.

There's more on the geological context of the Brockford Bridge "mighty Giant" discovery at https://mattsalusbury.blogspot.com/2020/10/the-body-of-mighty-giant.html, in which co-author Tim Holt-Wilson gives reasons why he believes the"mighty Giant" is more likely to be *Mammuths primigenius*.

6. Historians debate whether the Roman Emperor Claudius's war elephants actually entered Colchester in around 44AD, having been deployed among the hostile British tribes of the Essex Marshes in a psychological warfare "shock and awe" operation, or whether they were taken further north into present-day Suffolk.

Tavern Street, Stowmarket, with no fairies in evidence. It was said of the Stowmarket fairies that "they never appeared as long as anyone was about", so the presence of at least one pedestrian on this often busy street may have scared them away.

3. Away with the Stowmarket frairies

Elves, it seems were originally not little people, they weren't invisible, they didn't fly. They weren't quite human, although even in Anglo-Saxon times there were tales of human-fairy hybrids and of "changelings" – fairy children secretly swapped for abducted human ones. If you met an Old English *ælf* (elf or fairy) he would look like an aristocratic male human. They were mighty fighters, and the name Alfred ("elf-wisdom") was a fitting name for a king. In Anglo-Saxon tales there was no mention of female fairies, they seem to have arrived on the scene later.[1]

The fairies of old were referred to as "the Good Folk", not because they were good, but out of hushed respect, as they were so capricious, mischievous, powerful and dangerous. And fairies in ancient tradition absolutely did not have little transparent wings like the cute fairies in the Victorian children's book illustrations, these were apparently inspired by those awful cherubs that had become popular by then. There was, however, a far from cute East Anglian "buttery spirit" – like a butterfly, said to haunt "dishonestly run inns" and exact vengeance.

JM Barrie's 1904 "fairy play" *Peter Pan*, with its Tinker Bell fairy, is said to have had its genesis in Suffolk. This was during a 1901 holiday spent by Barrie and his wife at Thorpeness in the company of the resort's founder, Arthur Llewelyn-Davies, his wife and five children. Barrie's photographs of three of the Llewelyn-Davies children play-acting at fantastic adventures in Thorpeness became a photo-book *The Boy Castaways of Black Lake Island*, which in turn evolved into *Peter Pan*.

Famous for its "Do you believe in fairies?" line, *Peter Pan* in turn inspired some of the more surreal architecture of the Suffolk resort of Thorpeness, and the islands in its artificial boating lake The Meare are still named after locations from *Peter Pan*.[2]

Tinker Bell was quite unlike the early fairies. These appeared in the epic Old English poem *Beowulf*, and were "Cain's kin", descendants of Cain, son of Adam, cast out by God for the first ever murder – of his brother Abel. Early exorcists of the Christian Church drove out fairies as if they were demons. And in Elizabethan England, Dr William Bullein, originally a Suffolk boy from Blaxhall but at the time practising as a doctor in London, in 1562 published *Bullein's Bulwarke of defēce againste all Sicknes*. This describes various Suffolk witches he had known. Among them was Mother Line – "a false witch" in Parham, who used ebony beads and charms to cause "the Fairy charmed and the Sprite conjured away." ("Sprite" being an alternative name for a fairy.)

Certain Little People

In 1499 an unnamed woman from "Bellings Parva" in Suffolk was tried before the ecclesiastical (Church) courts of the Bishop of Norwich, whose jurisdiction included East Suffolk. "Parva" is a Latin word for "small" used in several Suffolk place names today, so Bellings Parva is most likely the modern village of Little Bealings, just north of Ipswich. The accused was up in court on charges of "sorcery", specifically, she was alleged to have gained magical powers to heal, foretell the future, seek out the causes of bad luck and detect buried treasure. Testimony recorded that the magical powers of the Bellings Parva sorceress were granted to her by "God and Blessed Mary" and also by "certain little people" referred to as "lez Elvys" and "lez Gracyous ffayry" – the elves and the gracious fairies. She was convicted, but her sentence was a lenient one. She got away with just "purgation" – a humiliating barefoot walk at the head of the congregation to her parish church, carrying an expensive beeswax candle as a "donation" that she had to pay for.[3]

Anglo-Saxon elves were believed to cause illness by shooting little arrows at people, and little flint arrowheads found lying around were assumed to be evidence of these "fairy shot", which we now know to be the work of early humans from the Stone Age. The word "stroke" to describe the sudden and debilitating effects of reduced blood flow to the brain comes to us from the belief that such victims were "fairy-struck". Flint hag stones – pebbles with a natural hole all the way through them – when tied round the neck of a calf or horse would stop Suffolk fairies knotting their hair or tails or riding them at night to the point of exhaustion, a practice recorded in Woodbridge as late as 1832.[4]

Although they could be touchy and violent, and would kill to avenge any dishonour, neither the Anglo-Saxon elves nor the fairies that came after them were entirely evil. ("Elf" was an Anglo-Saxon word, the word "fairy" from the French "fey" came over with the Normans.) The Good Folk of Anglo-Saxon tradition would form alliances with mortal humans against the monsters that threatened the order of things. It was relatively common for people to claim to have enlisted the help of the fairies (or for the fairies to provide it unsolicited) in revealing witches.[5]

Characteristics peculiar to Suffolk fairies included being "sandy-haired", sometimes it was their skin as well that was "sandy". If you left out food for them, they would "watch your dough" in return. Carrying bread in your pockets or wearing daisy chains was supposed to keep the more malicious Suffolk fairies at bay. The scarier "hyter-sprites" of Norfolk were "sandy-coloured" and green eyed and could shape-shift into sand martins. While they would lead lost children home, they were dangerous if "crossed." While the fairies of Suffolk, and much of Southern England, wore bright, shiny clothes with decorative caps or hoods – greens and blues were popular colour in fairy fashion – the hyter-sprites to the North of Suffolk were distinctive for wearing mostly white.[6]

While the idea that we share the landscape with magical beings goes back at least to the Bronze Age and probably before, fairies became unfashionable in Europe with the spread of Christianity. It was not until the nineteenth century that folklorists began gathering accounts of fairy traditions and writing them down. (The Rev. Hollingsworth, who we'll meet shortly, was writing in Stowmarket in the 1840s, but documenting stories that were already up to 100 years old.)

The people of Suffolk had their own dialect names for fairies. They were commonly known as "frairies", and a correspondent to the *Ipswich Journal* in 1800 confirmed that "frairies" was pronounced "fray-ries". Fairies were also known as perries, and "perry dancers" were the Northern lights, which could on occasion be seen in East Anglia. Fairies were also known in Suffolk as "feriers" – which somewhat bizarrely seems to have mutated into "Pharisees."[7]

Pharisees were a significant Jewish social movement, school of philosophy and at times a political faction in the Roman province of Judea. Their strict interpretation of religious law based on the teaching of Moses led to a few run-ins between Pharisees and the followers of Jesus of Nazareth as described in the New Testament. Jesus's Sermon on the Mount has some short rants against them, singling out the "righteousness of the scribes and Pharisees" (*Matthew* 5:20) in particular.

"Pharisee" became associated over time with hostile, self-righteous conformism, although one Pharisee, Nicodemus, was sympathetic to Jesus's followers and at great risk assisted in the embalming and burial of Jesus. Before the days of the *New English Bible* (1961-1970), little effort was made to explain to congregations who the New Testament's historical figures actually were. So to most Suffolk parishioners Pharisees would have been seen as some sort of sinister villains, somehow out of favour with God, and otherwise so impossibly exotic, outlandish, otherworldy – they might as well have been Martians. Although the simple folk of rural Suffolk a couple of hundred years ago couldn't have known it, "Pharisee" was a strangely appropriate term for a fairy, as the word "Pharisee" is thought to derive from ancient Greek, Aramaic and Hebrew words meaning "separated" or "set apart," which Suffolk's sandy-haired fairies certainly were.[8]

There was a theory popular with folklorists that "Pharisee" to describe fairies in Suffolk had a Celtic origin. Folklorist George Ewart Evans, who settled in the East Suffolk village of Blaxhall in 1948, mentions the notion that "Pharisee loafs" or "ferisheen loaves" come from the Gaelic *fer-sidhe*, "Men of the Hill." (We'll come to fairy loaves in a minute.) Whether or not Ewart Evans himself believed that an Iron Age Celtic word from before the Romans (so at some point before 47AD) had survived for over two thousand years in Suffolk dialect, isn't clear. Another oft-repeated theory is that Suffolk dialect words for fairies do have a Gaelic origin, but that they were brought to the East of England (along with some fairy traditions) much more recently, by settlers from Ireland arriving in the West Norfolk fens in the eighteenth and nineteenth centuries, particularly after the Potato Famine of the 1840s and 1850s. There's not a lot of evidence, though, for these settlers dispersing all the way down to relatively remote corners of East Suffolk like Blaxhall.[9]

A far neater explanation for "ferisher," Pharisee" or "ferisheen" was offered in a reader's letter to the *Ipswich Journal* in 1752 (reprinted in the same newspaper in 1877). The reader, from East Kent, stated that the shepherds of *Kent,* as well as Suffolk, used to call fairies "Pharisees", and suggests it's a corruption of "forester", said to be the name by which fairies were known somewhere up in the North of England.

It is thanks to another *Ipswich Journal* reader that one of the most bizarre tales of Suffolk "frairies" survives. Most sources tell you that the tale of "Brother Mike" dates from 1877, but I found that the 1877 issue of the *Ipswich Journal* that includes it is in fact one of the paper's many reprints of much earlier Suffolk Notes & Queries, so this story dates from 1800. Another Suffolk Notes and Queries reprinted in the 1860s in the *Ipswich Journa*l, giving an original date of 1751, recalls "the father of the servant who used to tell us 'Brother Mike'," presumably this is the Brother Mike story of the little "frairies", so the story dates from before 1750, and is possibly even older than that.

"Little tiddy frairies"

Anonymous reporting of Suffolk mystery animals was a thing even then, the correspondent narrating the story gave his name only as "Brother Mike." Rendered in the West Suffolk dialect of St Edmundsbury, his story describes a farmer near Bury lying in wait for whatever was eating wheat stored in his barn. On a moonlit night at the stroke of midnight, "little tiddy frairies" appeared en masse running around the barn. They were "as big as mice," each making off with an ear of corn over their shoulder. Like a lot of Suffolk "frairies", they wore brightly-coloured clothes, they were dressed in "little blue capotes" (cloaks or coats with hoods), yellow breeches and blue capes, with red caps on their heads with long tassels.

There was one frairy, among the hundreds running around that barn, who was so small he was struggling to carry an ear of wheat. The farmer reached out and caught him, and the frairy cried out "Brother Mike! Brother Mike!" The farmer carried the frairy home "for his children" and kept him tied to a kitchen window, where he refused to eat and pined away and died.

The correspondent to the *Ipswich Journal* admits that there is a similar German story, *Der Schotendiebe*, "The Pea Robbers".

While you'd expect frairy traditions to be a deeply rural phenomenon, it's striking how Suffolk's "frairies" tended to cluster in the very urban setting of Stowmarket and the villages just outside it. (In conversation among people who live there the town seems to be just "Stow".) The Rev. A.G.H. Hollingsworth chronicled in his 1844 *The History of Stowmarket* several fairy stories told to him by the citizens of Stowmarket and the residents of villages in its environs, who requested the traditional anonymity when reporting the county's mystery animals. This was a sensible precaution in a town where everybody knew everybody else.

As if with spangles, like the girls at shows at Stow Fair

So the Rev. Hollingsworth's informant for our first Stowmarket frairy story is "Neighbour S–", at the time of writing "now near eighty", who described happenings her mother had told her about her own infancy (or her sister's, she wasn't sure anymore). She would, then, have been describing events around 1765. When her mother was "lying asleep" some weeks after giving birth, with her husband and the infant by her side, she "woke in the night" and the baby was missing. The mother jumped out of bed," and, sure enough, a number of the "little sandy things", the "frairies", had got the baby at the foot of the bed and were undressing it. They fled away through a hole in the floor, "laughing as if they shrieked," while the mother "snatched up her child." For months afterwards, Neighbour S's mother always slept with the child between herself and husband, with the baby wrapped in "bed clothes" that were carefully attached by safety pins to the pillow and sheets "that it might not be snatched hastily away."[10]

The same Neighbour S– told the Rev. Hollingsworth that another mother's child had been snatched by the "frairies", who had substituted in its place a changeling. The unfortunate mother "had had a child changed, and one, a poor thing, left in his place, but she was very kind to it, and every morning on getting up she found a small piece of money in her pocket. My informant firmly believes in their existence, and wonders how it is that of late years no such things have been seen." In recent years, commentators have noted the fairy child-snatching and substitution with a changeling in most stories happens at about the time that infants start to manifest the first symptoms of developmental disorders that we would now call autism or Cornelia de Lange Syndrome, suggesting tragic explanations for fairy changeling stories.

The Rev. Hollingsworth added that "The whole of the Hundred (district) is remarkable for fairy stories, ghost adventures, and other marvellous legends. Fairies frequented several houses in Tavern Street about 80 to 100 years since." This would have been around 1744-1764. "They never appeared as long as anyone was about. People used to lie hid to see them, and some have seen them. Once in particular by a wood-stack up near the brick-yard there was a large company of them dancing, singing, and playing music together. They were very small people, quite little creatures and very merry, But as soon as they saw anybody they all vanished away. In the houses after they had fled on going upstairs, sparks of fire as bright as stars used to appear under the feet of the persons who disturbed them."

Another fairy encounter from *The History of Stowmarket* also took place "about 100 years since" (so in the 1740s), at the house of a witness we'll have to call Mr A. W. This was the venue for "fairy visits and officiousness. A man lived there who was visited constantly by a fairy (or ferrier or ferisher). They used his cottage for their meetings. They cannot abide dirt or slovenliness, so it was kept tidy and clean. They cut and brought faggots for the good man, and filled his oven with nice dry wood every night. They also left a shilling for him under the leg of a chair. And a fairy often came to him and warned him not to tell any one of it, for if he did tell then the shilling, wood, and fairies would never come to him again. Unluckily for him, he *did* tell of his good luck, after which his little friends were never seen by him more. The fairy wore yellow satin shoes, was clothed with a green long coat, girt about by a golden belt, and had sandy hair and complexion."[11]

This would appear to be a variation on an almost identical story of a fairy in a long green coat and a golden belt who appeared to a man who lived in the village of Onehouse, a short distance to the northwest of Stowmarket, and now no longer as isolated as its name suggests. The fairy at Onehouse, however, didn't want the use of the house for meetings, he and his fairy kin brought gifts, and also left the occasional shilling under his chair, as a "reward for a clean house," but like the man in the "Mr. A. W." fairy encounter narrative, the man at Onehouse blew it by bragging about the arrangement, so no more shillings under chairs for him! The Onehouse story is a seventeenth-century narrative, so at the very least 40 years older than the one set somewhere around Stowmarket and documented by the Reverend.[12]

The most spectacular Stowmarket close encounter with the fairy kind was probably that witnessed in around 1822, by "S____", who insisted that he "was quite sober at the time." (He is, somewhat confusingly, a different person to "Neighbour S–".) His fairy experience took place along the Bury Road just outside the town, "in the meadow, now a hop ground (a field of hops) not far from three ashen trees." S____ "in very bright moonlight" on one of those clear Suffolk nights where the moonlight's so strong you can't look directly at the moon or you'll be blinded, "saw the fairies."

There "might be a dozen of them, the biggest about three feet high, and small ones like dolls. Their dresses sparkled as if with spangles, like the girls at shows at Stow Fair. They were moving round hand in hand in a ring, no noise came from them." Our witness "could see them as plain as I do you. I looked after them when I got over the style, and they were there, just the same moving round and round... I might be forty yards from, them and I did not like to stop and stare at them."

S____ ran home and called out to three women who were his neighbours to come and look for them, but they found nothing. Readers will be pleased to hear that while there might not be fairies in Stowmarket anymore, the Stow Fair is alive and well. Its entertainment has moved on somewhat from just girls in spangled dresses, which must have been met with slack-jawed amazement by residents of slightly rural Mid-Suffolk 170 years ago but which wouldn't cut much ice today. Held over a whole weekend in July, the Stow Fair has recently featured such rock legends as Dr Feelgood playing live at the Recreation Ground.

Another Stowmarket fairy story involved a local resident who mended a fairy's "bread peel", a flat steel or wooden paddle used to move loaves in and out of a hot oven. For this, our Stowmarket resident was rewarded with a magic cake that appeared out of nowhere. Yet another Stowmarket fairy story tells how a midwife was asked by a fairy to visit his wife to deliver a baby. When the midwife agreed, the fairy rubbed an ointment onto the midwife's eyes

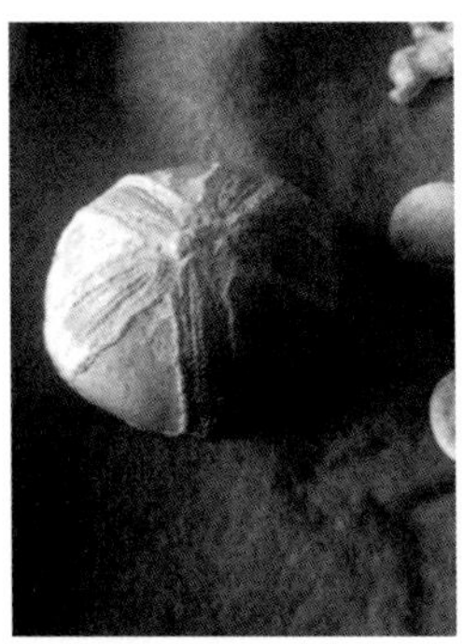

Fairy loaves from Suffolk, from (top) the private collection of Paul Berry, (middle row and bottom left) Halesworth Museum and (bottom right) Dunwich Museum archive.

PART 1 – NOT QUITE HUMAN

Sprites Lane and Sprites Primary Academy in Sprites Ward, Ipswich. Photo: Copyright Darren Mann. ("Sprite" is an alternative word for fairy.)

Hagstones – like these hanging up outside a house in Southwold – were hung around the necks of livestock to stop fairies riding them to exhaustion at night.

Carlton Green on the edge of Saxmundham, where a boy saw white-clad fairies silently dancing in a ring many years ago. Now it's a caravan park.

so that she was able to "enter fairyland" and see the fairies. (Whether there was some sort of parallel-universe version of Stowmarket within fairyland isn't made clear.) The job done, the midwife was brought back to our more mundane universe, the one that includes our version of Stowmarket. There a few days later, she was surprised to see in a butcher's shop the same fairy who'd given her the fairyland midwifery job. He was stealing meat, invisible to everyone else. Presumably, she could still see him through at least one eye, thanks to the fairy ointment still on it. She went to give the fairy a telling-off, and he asked her which eye she could see him with, whereupon he blew into that eye, depriving her of sight through it from then on.

There are very similar, but much older, stories from the west of England that go back at least to the sixteenth century, and the idea of having magical sight but losing one eye in the process goes all the way back to the one-eyed Viking god Odin. There are many stories around midwifery and fairies, which may have something to do with the hallucinogenic ergot fungus; a parasitic growth on rye that was also used by midwives to induce labour.[13]

Also part of Stowmarket fairies cluster, but a lot more recent, comes a report of a woman travelling with her husband by rail from Ipswich "some years ago" (this would be early in the twentieth century) who experienced a "curious apparition" as the train passed through Haughley. Her husband, a former engine driver, was later able to identify the place, but said he hadn't had any "unusual experiences" whilst working on that line. Haughley is roughly three miles northwest of Stowmarket, just after where the line splits having come north out of Stowmarket, heading east to Elmswell and then onward to Bury rather than taking the other line North to Diss, so an ex-engine driver would know it well. At the time of our story, there would have been a Haughley Junction station on the "Middy" (Mid-Suffolk Light Railway); the station's the office of a building firm today. Haughley's now best known for "Bluebell Sundays" in which carpets of bluebells at the Haughley Park stately home are open to the public each Spring.

Passing through Haughley, the lady saw a "dwarf-like man, dressed in peasant's clothes". His dress was "probably about two hundred or three hundred years old." The dwarf-like man seemed to come up through the floor of the carriage," then he was "crouching and looked up at the church as the train passed by it, then he disappeared into the floor again." The woman claimed to have second sight, as revealed to her by later incidents.[14]

Nimmey-nimmey not, my name is Tom Tit Tot!

As well as fairies, Suffolk apparently also have goblins, evil creatures distinguished by their pointy ears and pointy noses. There's a Suffolk variant of the Rumplestiltskin legend, in which a King (territory unnamed, so we don't know if it was supposed to be the Anglo-Saxon Kingdom of East Anglia) tells the best spinner in all the kingdom that she has to spin enough flax to fill the whole floor of the castle, if she fails, he'll have her head chopped off, if she succeeds, she gets to marry him.

A goblin appears and offers to do the impossible flax-spinning task by magical means, in exchange for her first-born. A friend of the champion spinner goes out to find out the name of the goblin. Just in time, he shouts through the window to the spinner what he's heard, he'd managed to eavesdrop on the goblin singing to himself, "Nimmie nimmie not, my name is Tom Tit Tot," a rather human-sounding name for a goblin. Tom Tit Tot the goblin (for it is he!) disappears when his name is proclaimed. This is where the story diverges a lot from the Rumplestiltskin story – in the Tom Tit Tot Suffolk version, the lady marries not the king, who had after all threatened to behead her, but that man who found out Tom Tit Tot's name. You can see why the Rumplestiltskin version became the more popular one, "Tom Tit Tot" doesn't quite have the same ring to it. There's a Tot Hill and a Tot Hill Farm north of Stowmarket, by the A14 roundabout, just south of the Travelodge hotel. There's also a Tommit's Lane in the village of Wetherden, also just west of Stowmarket, near Haughley. A "tom-tit" in Suffolk dialect is a wren or titmouse.[15]

Other Suffolk goblins were to be found in the woods around Oulton, just west of Lowestoft, where they held feasts, according to antiquarian A. D. Baynes. The churchyard of St Michael's Church, Oulton, is also said to be the haunt of fairies, alleged to emerge on moonlit nights and dance around the church, at least on nights when the howling of Black Shuck, or the wind, didn't scare them away from the churchyard. (See Chapter 6 on Suffolk's Black Shuck.)[16]

As well as goblins such as Tom Tit Tot, there was Tom Poker, a Suffolk bogeyman used by parents to terrify naughty children. Tom Poker would lie in wait in any dark, enclosed spaces such as household cupboards.[17]

Dancing around churchyards, or dancing silently in circles on meadows or greens, seemed to be a favourite pastime of Suffolk "frairies". We've already met the fairies of Stowmarket with their sparkling circle-dancing in a moonlit meadow, during which "no noise came from them." "Fairy rings" of discoloured grass were said to be the marks made by fairies dancing in circles (we now know these to be caused by fungus.) Mr C. Napthine of Westleton told the local Women's Institute in the 1920s that if you "go out at night you'd see the fairies dancing round the toadcaps (toadstools)".[18]

A surprisingly recent story of a "fairy-ring" of silent dancers comes from Carlton Green on the edge of Saxmundham – volunteers at the Saxmundham Museum told me they thought it sounded like the green space in front of where the caravan park is today. Mr B Waterman of Ipswich was a very old man when he recounted the story to Joan Forman in 1974.[19] Waterman recalled as a child aged nine, in the early years of the twentieth century, walking with his younger brother, on the road past Carlton Green and coming across a ring of "figures", looking like unremarkable adult humans except that they were clad in "white muslin" and doing some sort of "follow-the-leader" ballet, silently in a circle. Waterman noted that at that age he didn't know what a ghost was, and only later concluded what he'd seen were ghosts. But their description more closely fits Suffolk "frairies" than ghosts, albeit closer to dressed-in-white hyter-sprites on a visit from Norfolk than the traditionally colourful dress of thr fairies of Suffolk. Ghosts generally don't dance.

Ralph of Coggeshall, chronicler or East Anglian "wonders", left us two medieval tales about fairies and their strange interactions with the people of Suffolk. Ralph tells us of the now world-famous "green children of Woolpit" in his *Chroniculum Anglicorum,* although it is also to be found in an earlier source, twelfth-century Yorkshire chronicler William of Newburgh's *Historia Rerum Anglicanum.*

The Green Children of Woolpit were a brother and sister, found in a wooded hollow near Woolpit (it's a quarter of an hour's bike ride from Elmswell Station on the Ipswich to Bury line, Needham Market's not far, and there's an exit for Woolpit off the A14). The green children are shown in silhouette on the Woolpit village sign. They spoke a strange language, and they were dazzled by daylight, and their skin was green. The boy refused to eat the food he was offered, and pined away and died, but the girl learnt English, and ate mostly beans before adapting to a broader diet, and her green complexion changed to the more usual skin colour of most contemporary East Anglians. She was eventually baptised and – despite being initially "rather loose and wanton in her conduct" – married a Suffolk gentleman. She told her hosts she and her brother had been tending sheep in "St Martin's Land", a subterranean vegetarian paradise in perpetual twilight whose green-skinned people only sheared sheep of their wool and never slaughtered them for meat. Going after a lost sheep, they'd somehow stumbled into the weird alternative dimension (for them) that was medieval West Suffolk. Although it was not explicitly stated, many assumed the Green Children of Woolpit were fairies.

All manner of explanations have been put forward for the Green Children of Woolpit since the story was rediscovered in the nineteenth century. "St Martin's Land" was just Trimley St Martin near Felixistowe, or Fornham St Martin in West Suffolk on the River Lark, or one of The Saints, the villages between Beccles and the River Waveney that are still a little bit out of the way to this day. Or it was a garbled account of a historical event, and the Green Children with their strange language were just the children of Flemish merchants who'd escaped some sort of pogrom. (Such massacres were recorded in the reign of King Henry II.) They were malnourished child refugees from the civil war during the "anarchy of Stephen", the troubled reign of King Stephen of England (1135-1154), in whose time the Green Children story is supposed to have taken place. In this scenario, their green colour was just some kind of jaundice that later went away. They were aliens from Mars or Venus (a theory discredited when we learnt more about the environment on those planets), they were aliens from another dimension. And so on.

Dr Karl Shuker on his Shukernature blog mentions a description of the land of "Faerie" recounted by Giraldus Cambrensis in his *Itinerarium Cambriae* – Journey Through Wales – in 1188. It is similar to St Martin's Land – filled with woods and meadows but perpetually gloomy, with the sun and stars rarely poking through constant cloud. Shuker also points out that in the twelfth century Suffolk of isolated communities, stray children speaking even the dialect of the county's border with Cambridgeshire would be near unintelligible to the villagers of Woolpit, let alone Flemish foundlings. Shuker also suggests chlorosis – a condition caused by iron deficiency and common in adolescent girls up to the nineteenth century – as explaining the children's green skin colour.[20]

The other Ralph of Coggeshall Suffolk fairy story is 'concerning a fantastic spirit' and comes from the castle at Dagworth, which was abandoned in 1173 after an army of Flemish mercenaries under the Earl of Leicester sacked it. The story features a changeling and an invisible shape-shifter; a fairy named Malekin. In 1210, by which time the castle was in use as residence again, at least according to this story, Malekin frequented the castle home of Osbern of Bradwell, as an invisible entity speaking the Suffolk dialect of English, but talking in Latin to the priest, with both languages spoken in the voice of an infant. While many heard Malekin speak, she only appeared in physical form once – after much persuasion – to a serving girl who'd left out food for her, and then only on condition she didn't try and touch her.

To the servant girl, Malekin looked like a child dressed in a white. Malekin told members of the Bradwell household that she was a human child born in the then prosperous West Suffolk "Wool Town" of Lavenham. She'd been kidnapped from her mother by the fairies and returned seven years later. She eventually started to eat and drink, and claimed to have a magic fairy hat that made her invisible, and that she expected to be able to return to her human family in another seven years. Ralph noted briefly how "wondrous" the whole affair was. Dagworth is – you will by now not be surprised to hear – just north of Stowmarket, right near the Tot Hill junction of the A14.

PART 1 – NOT QUITE HUMAN

Fairy Hills, The Valley of the Elves, Pixey Green, Fiery Mount

There are other places in Suffolk – besides Stowmarket and environs – that have fairy associations. There's a Pixey Green in the Eye Valley, between Stradbroke and Fressingfield. Curiously, Pixey Green doesn't seem to appear on a lot of maps. Could a fairy enchantment be at work disguising it? In Thorington, in the Blyth Valley just West of the A12, just south of Wenhaston, there used at one point to be a field with the name of Fairies Hill, said to be the site of a lost prehistoric burial mound, but Fairies Hill doesn't appear on today's maps.[21]

There's also a Sprite End in the Trimleys, a dead-end off Spritehill Road, and there's a Sprites Lane in the Chantry neighbourhood of Ipswich, south of the River Gipping, not far from the Bredfield roundabout. There's even a Sprites Primary School nearby. ("Sprite", as we've seen, is another word for a fairy or elf.) There's a Spright's Covert near Reydon and a tiny Sprite's Wood on the eastern edge of Beccles. Another type of sprite was the woodsprite, the Suffolk dialect name for a woodpecker, presumably because of its mischievous, laughing call and its bright green and red fairy colours.[22]

There's also Elveden (usually pronounced with three syllables, as "El-vuh-d'n"). English language scholar Eilert Ekwall suggests that *Miracula sancta Withburge*, a biography of St Withburga, abbess of Dereham, includes a Latin description of what seems to be Elveden, "from the land of the king and martyr the blessed Edmund, which is called the valley of the nymphs (female fairies) in English." And there's a nineteenth century account by a young girl walking along a road in the village, who was passing a wood that bordered the road when she heard the sound of music "chiming, tinkling, beguiling, beneath that sound high-pitched laughter." As an old woman she would tell people about the music she heard and how it would snare passing horses and lure them down into the fairies' magic dell.

Elveden is an important junction, with a flyover, as the A14 from Thetford to Newmarket crosses the busy B1106 road, just after it emerges from Thetford Forest. At the time of the Elveden lady's fairy encounter, it was an important route for horses and carts taking freight to Thetford. The "magic dell" supposedly still exists today, as the Milestone Slip wood next to the lane going down to Redneck Farm. There is a problem with place name Elveden being "valley of the elves", however. Before Eilert Ekwall, most scholars agreed that "Elveden" came from the Anglo-Saxon *elfetednu*, meaning "valley of the swans."

Another Suffolk dialect expression was "elvish," meaning peevish or easily irritated, a reminder that elves and fairies were best treated with respect and left well alone.[23]

Fairies were said to frequent springs or wells in what became the fountain in Bell Vue Park in Lowestoft. This well was said to have fairy guardians, but it dried up 1903 following railway construction.[24]

Southwold had "The Fairy Hills" on a hill called Eye Cliff Hill, still visible in around 1879 when A. D. Bayne visited and described seeing "vestiges of ancient encampments, and in many parts of circular tents... most probably of Danish origin". An earlier source, of 1769 (paraphrasing Gardner's *Historical Account of Dunwich...* of 1754), noted that "On this hill, and several others that are near it, are the remains of a camp; and where the ground has not been broken up, there are tokens of circular tents, called by the people Fairy-hills, round which they suppose the fairies were wont to dance." Coastal erosion has long since carried away Eye Cliff Hill, which is now out to sea. Gun Hill – where a battery of guns left over from an ill-fated attepmt at war with France in the 1620s now stands – is all that remains of what was once Eye Cliff Hill. Several now-vanished burial mounds are known to have stood there.[25]

There was also an old house said to have been frequented by fairies on the edge of the woods near Capel Saint Mary, in East Suffolk near the Essex border, but the old house's exact location is unknown today. But if you absolutely need to see elves and fairies in Suffolk, the best place to go is the reconstructed Anglo-Saxon village at West Stow Museum, which has twice-yearly *Lord of the Rings*-themed events, with re-enactors in the roles of orcs as well as elves. The Greene King Brewery factory shop in the centre of Bury has costumed "beer elves" on duty in the run-up to Christmas.[26]

We have already heard the alleged "chiming, tinkling" music of the fairies at Elveden, and a more recent Suffolk frairy musical encounter story comes from the village of Ufford, just outside Rendlesham Forest and near Woodbridge. In 1933, a Miss Lucy Walpole and her sister lived in Fiery Mount, a house in the village. At the time, the Fairy Investigation Society was running a survey asking for any reports of fairy encounters. Miss Walpole put hers in a letter and sent it in.

According to the Society's archives, "Miss Walpole's sister heard on several occasions [at dawn] the sound, as if in the far distance, of a simple little tune (of about six notes) being played, as it was, she said, like the plucking of strings of a tiny harp or other stringed instrument… repeated many times."[27]

Chris Woodyard, in an article in *Fortean Times* examined the Fairy Investigation Society's archives, noting that reports of fairy harp music are less common than accounts of hearing tiny fairy handbells, flutes or other pipes. Woodyard offers misidentified birdsong or old water pipes re-purposed as fence posts resonating in the wind as explanations.

There's also Musical Ear Syndrome (auditory hallucinations from people losing hearing), tinnitus and high caffeine consumption. Given the location, near the Deben estuary, and time of day (dawn) the Ufford fairy harp music could well have been misidentified birdsong, possibly of an unfamiliar avian visitor to these parts. Plenty of exotic birds that are "rare migrants" to our shores show up in coastal Suffolk and its estuaries are often the first port of call for migratory birds arriving in England, with their distinctive and unusual birdsongs.

As with many of Suffolk's fairy places, the Fiery Mount (could "Fiery" be a corruption of "fairy" or "frairy"?) seems to have done a magical fairy disappearing act. The clerk of today's Ufford Parish Council, in answer to my enquiry, said they had no record of there ever having been a Fiery Mount in their parish. A new fairy survey has recently been completed, anyone who's had a close encounter with the fairy kind, whether it was within or outside Suffolk, is asked to contact www.fairyist.com.

Pharisee loaves

As well as making music for us, the fairies were also supposed to leave "fairy loaves" or Pharisee loaves. According to Suffolk lore, these were said to protect against horse infections and were worn on the tackle of horses, a belief that folklorist George Ewart Evans noted in Blaxhall in *The Horse in the Furrow*. Another Suffolk superstition about fairy loaves was that if you had one in your possession it always ensured a plentiful supply of (real) bread.

Fairy loaves were fossil sea urchins, and were found either in their original round shape – looking a bit like a fossilised roll or bun – or sometimes flattened, making them resemble a loaf of bread even more. There's a flattened *Echinocorys scutatus* sea urchin from Bramford, Suffolk, labelled as a bread supply-ensuring "fairy loaf" in the collection of the University of Oxford's Pitt Rivers Museum of anthropology, where it arrived via a Mr Balfour in 1919.

Halesworth Museum has plenty of fairy loaves on display, including some you can touch in their "handling tray" of fossils, Beccles Museum also has some, while Dunwich Museum has a fossil sea urchin in their archive (you'll have to ask to see it.) Collecting and keeping fossil sea urchins – whether or not they were felt to have anything to do with fairies, goes back a long way. One skeleton of an Anglo-Saxon woman dug up in a cemetery in Bury had a fossil sea urchin clasped in its skeletal hand.[28]

Sea urchins are echinoderms, a phylum (group of organisms) that includes starfish, and they all have a five pointed star on their fossils, like the five points of a starfish. Paul Berry of Framlingham, who showed me his collection of Suffolk fossils including some fossil sea urchins, showed me the five points of the star on one of them and said that he'd been told in his childhood over sixty years ago that the five points represented you, your future spouse, "the vicar," (at your future wedding) and your two first yet-to-be-born children.

The gravel pit on Westleton Common was once famous for its abundance of fairy loaves. But by 1922, Mr H Fisk was saying of the pit's fairy loaves that "children used to hunt for them" but in that modern age, were "quite finished with" collecting fairy loaves."[29]

But hang on, fairies are impossible and can't exist, can they? So what's going on? Why did people report seeing fairies and why do they still? (There are still modern reports of fairies in England from outside the county of Suffolk, albeit very few.)

Rational explanations for fairy encounters?

What are termed "ghosts" might be expected to manifest in old houses that have damp and mould problems. A study started in 2015 by Professor Shane of Rodgers of the civil and environmental engineering department at Potsdam University in New York looks at how airborne particles of the less well-researched "indoor moulds" might adversely affect the brain, possibly even triggering frightening hallucinations. As with "ghosts," so with fairies. It's interesting how, in such a rural county, so many fairy stories are clustered around an urban area like Stowmarket, with some stories taking place in and around houses, or at least indoors.[30]

The spectacular encounter with multiple fairies on Stowmarket's Bury Road in 1822 described above took place in a field of hops. I'm told sleeping with your head on a "hop pillow" – a pillow case stuffed with hops – is a traditional remedy for insomnia. Traditional herbal medicines usually have some sort of foundation in chemistry or biology. Could some psychoactive ingredient in a field of hops have triggered some sort of hallucination in S_____, the witness to this fairy encounter?

Then there's Charles Bonnet Syndrome, named after the eighteenth century Swiss naturalist and philosopher who observed Lullin, his 87-year-old grandfather, still of perfectly sound mind, experience all manner of bizarre hallucinations as his sight began to decline. Charles Bonnet Syndrome is now known to be much more common than once thought, one recent study put the proportion of people who suffer "impaired vision" and who also experience the syndrome at 40 per cent, although only a quarter of these will experience full-blown visual hallucinations. Most of the time they remain mentally lucid and realise that the outlandish visions they're having aren't real. The condition if often mistaken for dementia and schizophrenia, which is apparently why over a third of patients in one Charles Bonnet Syndrome study kept quiet about having it.

Lullin remained lucid until the end, but as his eyesight worsened, he described to his grandson increasingly weird visions that peaked in late 1759 – two young men in "magnificent" red and grey cloaks with hats trimmed in silver, while Lullin also saw a swarm of specks that turned into a flock of pigeons or butterflies, and a blue haze with yellow dots that turned into a patterned handkerchief – all reminiscent of the bright hues in the fashions of the Stowmarket fairies. He also saw carriages, birds and people appear in his room, of various sizes. Imaginary people or objects filling the room until they almost touch the ceiling are apparently a common hallucination. Lullin's birds and people would be seen to converse, but in silence, which makes the many reports of Suffolk fairies dancing "noiselessly" suddenly more interesting.

Those touched by the Syndrome in modern times see medieval landscapes, and modern buildings seem to them to suddenly have ancient architecture instead. One female sufferer reported hideous "witch-like figures" with hooked noses, and a boy riding on the bonnet of a car, who rose into the air when the car stopped.

Another woman, aged 73, under the influence of Charles Bonnet Syndrome saw a girl pass through a solid door in front of her, while a 69-year-old man who had the same condition would generally see visions in the evening – faces, old friends appearing in armchairs in front of him, strange shapes and animals. Yet another man with Charles Bonnet Syndrome, aged 87, would regularly, see a Highland cow in his living room, that stared at him as it fed on grass, as well as bears, darting blue fish and swarms of flies. Compared to this, the "little tiddy frairies" of Suffolk seem quite boring.

Nowadays we – and usually the people who experience these visions – understand them to be result of some sort of irregular brain activity. But back in the day, before opticians and psychology, they would have been seen as signs and portents and gifts from the gods, or the fairies. In some traditions only certain people could see fairies, those blessed (or cursed) with the "fairy sight," like the lady on the train travelling through Haughley.

Our current understanding of Charles Bonnet Syndrome is that it's a result of sensory deprivation. The brain is starved of its usual constant stream of visual data as its owner's vision starts to deteriorate, and starts to fill in the gaps to compensate for this loss. A more recent theory suggests there's some sort of censorship mechanism in the brain that weeds out irrelevant images from the subconscious, but that the mechanism fails when the visual data coming in falls below a certain threshold. In any event, the hallucinations usually stop not long after the sufferer becomes completely blind.[31]

Furthermore, between 10 and 20 per cent of people who gradually lose their hearing experience auditory hallucinations – they hear sounds that aren't there. This may help explain the fairy stringed instruments that the old lady at Fiery Mount, Ufford, heard at dawn in the 1930s. The girl who claimed to hear "chiming" fairy music in Elveden, though, was at the time much younger, and less likely to be going deaf.

While once there was a rich tradition of reporting fairy sightings, these seem to have tailed off dramatically since the 1930s, in Suffolk at least. Testimony of close encounters with the alien occupants of UFOs seem to have replaced stories of contact with fairies in modern times. It's interesting to note that in these modern narratives of close encounters with "aliens" from outer space, the aliens seem to share some of the characteristics of fairies – kidnapping, whisking people off to strange realms, disorientation and missing time experiences.

The Woolpit village sign (above) features the two Green Children of Woolpit. A mischievous pixie-like face (below) looks down from the wall of St Edmund's Church at Southwold

FOOTNOTES TO CHAPTER 3: Away with the Stowmarket frairies

1. "Elves in Anglo-Saxon England" [book review], Jeremy Harte, *Fortean Times*, July 2007.

2. Buttery spirit form *Lantern* 25, Spring 1979, www.hiddenea.com/Lantern25.pdf; JM Barrie Thorpeness connection from www.norfolkcoast.co.uk/location_suffolk/vp_thorpeness.htm, www.suffolktouristguide.com/Thorpeness-and-Peter-Pan.asp; "Timeline: Pan Through the Ages", *Daily Telegraph* 7 October 2015)

3. "Cardinal Morton's Register", Claude Jenkins, *Tudor Studies* pp. 72-4, London, 1924 – quoted in "The Making of the Early Modern British Fairy Tradition", Ronald Hutton *The Historical Journal,* 57(4), p1157-75, 2014 http://research-information.bristol.ac.uk/files/38162235/Fairies4_1_.pdf; *The Register of John Morton, Archbishop of Canterbury 1486-1500: III: Norwich Diocese sede vacante*, 1499/ Canterbury & York Society, 2000; Historic Witches and Witchcraft Trials for England, Marc Carlson, 2004 www.personal.utulsa.edu/%7Emarc-carlson/witchtrial/eis.html. Other Suffolk "Parva" place names today include Linstead Parva, Fakenham Parva and Thornham Parva. The Suffolk village of Little Stonham still has the official alternative name Stonham Parva. There's also a modern Great Bealings.

4.1832 calf riding from *Haunted Suffolk*, Peter Jennings, Tempus Publications 2006. Hag stones, plentiful on Suffolk's pebbly beaches, are so-called because it was believed that looking through the hole would allow you to identify who was a hag (a witch) and who wasn't, but as far as I'm aware it was never explained how. A man from rural Bedfordshire (East of England) told me his mother had told him hag stones were protection against Black Shuck (see Chapter 6), whose name is apparently pronounced differently in Buckinghamshire, as "shook".

5. In a witchcraft trial in 1550s, in Taunton, Devon, witchcraft suspect Joan Tyrony named one Simon Richards as a witch. How did she know? The fairies told her! This was a risky strategy, as claiming to be in cahoots with the fairies sounded awfully like witchcraft too. "Troublesome Things: A History of Fairies and Fairy Stories", (book reviews), Scott Wood, *Fortean Times*, May 2000; Origins of the words "elf" and "fairy" from "The Making of the Early Modern British Fairy Tradition", Ronald Hutton, *The Historical Journal*, 57(4), p1157-75, 2014 http://research-information.bristol.ac.uk/files/38162235/Fairies4_1_.pdf.

6. *The Folklore of East Anglia*, Enid Porter, BT Batsford, London; *Lantern* 17; *Lantern* 25; *Customs and Sayings recorded by the Women's Institute in 1922*, Westleton Women's Institute, Leiston Press, Leiston 2008.

7. Perries from *Suffolk Dialect*, Louise Maskill, Bradwell Books, Sheffield, 2014. The Northern Lights put on a brief show in the winter of 2014, when they could be seen in the skies above Suffolk and Essex.

8. https://en.wikipedia.org/wiki/Pharisees. Readers of a certain age who went to Church of England schools may recall "I danced for the scribe and the Pharisee/ But they wouldn't dance and they wouldn't follow me," from Sydney Carter's 1963 hymn *Lord of the Dance*.

9. *The Horse in the Furrow,* George Ewart Evans, Faber and Faber, 1960)

10. *The History of Stowmarket*, Rev. A.G.H. Hollingsworth, F. Pawsey 1844, 2003 edition by Mike Durrant.

11. "Ferisher" sounds awfully like "fresher", a Suffolk dialect name for a little frog. *Suffolk Dialect*, see above.

12. Onehouse story from *Albion – A Guide to Legendary Britain*, Jennifer Westwood, Paladin, 1985, with thanks to Paranormal Database http://paranormaldatabase.com; "Mr A.W." from *The History of Stowmarket:* Rev. A.G.H. Hollingsworth, F. Pawsey 1844, 2003 edition by Mike Durrant.

13. The Norse god Odin (Woden in Germanic mythology, from which we get the word "Wednesday",) is usually depicted as one-eyed and with a white beard. In his quest for knowledge, Odin lost an eye when he gouged it out and gave it in payment to Mimir, guardian of the Well of Urd, whose waters provided "all knowledge" to those who drank from them. Fairy midwifery story from *The East Anglian Miscellany*, 1907-8, Note 2344. Ergot-based hallucinations from "Mouldy Old Ghosts", Ghostwatch, Alan Murdie, *Fortean Times*, **FT 329;15** July 2015. Carbon monoxide poisoning in poorly-ventilated houses may also have caused mild hallucinations of fairies and ghosts, and may explain why to see some ghosts and fairies was an omen of your impending death!

14. *Railway Ghosts and Phantoms*, W B Herbert, David & Charles, London 1989 p16; some people were said to be born with "fairy sight", often inheriting the ability to see fairies invisible to others. In Scandinavian lore in particular, if you held the hand of someone who had fairy sight, you could see the fairies too. "The Fairy Touch", Fairies Folklore and Forteana", *Fortean Times* FT 320; 25 November 2014.

15. *Suffolk Dialect,* see above; "Tom Tit Tot" in *Folklore*, Volume 84, Spring 1973 identifies six variants of the story worldwide, in which Tim Tit Tot, under various names, can be a troll, a fairy woman dressed in green or a devil and the tasks they set differ from building a church to producing piglets.

16. *Haunted Lowestoft Revisited*, Ivan A.W. Bunn and Henry Baker, published by the authors, Lowestoft 2010, it quotes *Royal Illustrated History of Eastern England,* A. D. Baynes, Macdonald & Co, c.1873; *Haunted Suffolk,* Peter Jennings Tempus Pubs 2006.

17. *Suffolk Dialect,* see above.

18. *Customs and Sayings recorded by the Women's Institute in 1922*, Leiston Press, Leiston 2008.

19. *Haunted East Anglia*, Joan Forman 1974, 1985 reprint Jarrold & Co, Norwich.

20. Dr Karl PN Shuker's "Shukernature blog http://karlshuker.blogspot.co.uk and *Dr Shuker's Casebook*, CFZ Publications, Woolfardisworthy 2008.)

21. Thorington's missing Fairies Hill from www.hiddenea.com/suffolkt.htm#thorington, giving as its source *Blything Hundred*, P. M. Warner, University of Leicester PhD thesis, 1982, p.45.

22. *Suffolk Dialect*, see above; Sprites Primary School is now Sprites Primary Academy.

23. "Bewitched in the 'valley of the elves'", *EADT* 22 November 2014, p 13; elvish meaning peevish from *Suffolk Dialect*, see above.

24. *Haunted Lowestoft Revisited.*

25. Hidden East Anglia www.hiddenea.com/suffolks.htm, which quotes *Royal Illustrated History of Eastern England,* A. D. Bayne, Macdonald & Co, c.1873; *Southwold and its Vicinity,* Robert Wake, F. Skill, 1839, p.372; *A Description of England & Wales,* Newbery & Carnan, 1769, Vol.8, p.282. *Suffolk Ghosts and Legends,* Pamela Brooks, Halsgrave, Wellington, Somerset 2009 gives as a source for the Southwold fairy hills *Excursions Round Suffolk*, Thomas Kitson Cromwell, 1819.

26. Capel Saint Mary fairies from *The Ghosts of Borley plus Stories of Ghosts and Hauntings Along the Suffolk and Essex Border* Wesley H. Downes, via Paranormal Database.

27. "The Music of Fairyland", Chris Woodyard *Fortean Times* **FT 321;46-49,** quoting Marjorie T Johnson, *Seei ng Fairies: From the lost archive of the Fairy Investigation Society, authentic reports of fairies in modern times,* Anomalist Books, San Antonio NM 2014.

28. For more on the human history of fossil sea urchins, see my review of *The Star Crossed Stone*, *Fortean Times FT*278, August 2011, http://mattsalusbury.blogspot.co.uk/2011/07/star-crossed-stone.html.

29. Fairy loaves unfashionable by 1922 from *Westleton – Customs and Sayings*, see above.

30. Prof Rodgers's study from "Mouldy Old Ghosts", Ghostwatch, *Fortean Times,* FT 329;15 July 2015, see also "The Real Ghostbusters Investigate Mold, Not Moans, Within Haunted Houses", *Medical Daily* 2 April 2015, www.medicaldaily.com/real-ghostbusters-investigate-mold-not-moans-within-haunted-houses-327950#.

31. "Cattle in the living room", Mark Greener, *Fortean Times* **FT 321;54-55**, December 2014.

Gun Hill in Southwold. Its slopes are all that remain of the long eroded-away Eye Cliff, which in the eighteenth century still had the ruins of a "Fairy Camp".

This freshwater mermaid is by the bridge over the River Gipping on Ipswich's London Road.

4. Freshwater mermaids and miscellaneous manimals

"Pray resolve me in your next Week's Paper, whether there be any such Thing in Nature as Mermen and Mermaids, I being not yet satisfied in the verity thereof, notwithstanding the Reports of Seamen and others." That was the plea from a letter writer to the *Ipswich Journal*, 27 May 1721.[1] The vexed reader of the *Ipswich Journal* may well have believed in mermaids, possibly because his parents had told him from an early age to believe in mermaids (as they might convince their infants to believe in Father Christmas today). His parents would have a very practical reason for doing so, as we will see.

With the possible exception of the Orford "merman" we met earlier found by fishermen in their fishing nets off Orford Ness, which was probably an ordinary human gone feral, Suffolk's merfolk were all female – mermaids rather than mermen. And "Reports of Seamen" didn't feature in Suffolk mermaid traditions. The Orford merman was the only merperson found off the coast, as all the Suffolk mermaids were freshwater mermaids, found in the county's rivers, lakes, wells, pools and even its drainage ditches.

Rendlesham had a "Mermaid's Pond," also known as the S-pond, as it was shaped like a letter "S". A reader of the *Ipswich Journal* in the 1870s – a man who wrote to the newspaper describing his childhood there some 50 years earlier – recalled there were trees around the edge of the S-shaped pond at one end, and the grass around it "in early spring full of flowers." (It's near Cottage Wood and a tumulus, and now just north of the sewage works.) But if our *Ipswich Journal* reader who was a boy back in 1814 strayed too near the edge of the pond, "our nursemaid would call out to us not to go so near 'lest the mermaid should come'" and hook him and his playmates in with a crome fork, which was a sort of rake with curved teeth, used as a muckraker.[2]

The author of *The Book of Days* wrote in the 1860s how he was told by one Suffolk child that mermaids were "them nasty things what crome you into the water," while another child from the county told him he'd actually seen a mermaid once, "a grit hig thing loike a feesh." Kate Welham of Bacton, near Stowmarket, recalled being told as a child in around 1908 to stay away from mermaid-infested ponds.[3]

Just outside Bury in Babwell Fen Meadows, once the private fishing lake of the Abbot of St Edmundsbury, there were in the mid-nineteenth century "an abundance of beautiful water" fed by springs, and in "the low grounds" near the road. (This is probably what's now the Fornham Road.) A mermaid was to be found in the body of water then known as the Mermaid's Pits. They were named after a "love-sick maid" who had drowned herself there, and who then turned into a mermaid; whether or not she was an evil mermaid who pulled in children wasn't known, but there was supposed to be an "abundance" of mermaids in the drainage ditches and ponds locally. Local mothers warned their children to stay away from these. There's now a Mermaid Close here, just off the Fornham Road, with a small body of water nearby.[4]

A look at Google Earth shows some features round there that appear on older maps as pools but have now been drained. Some of the Mermaid's Pits may have fallen on hard times, ending up as the settling ponds at what's now the Silver Spoon factory. It was previously the British Sugar factory, manufacturing raw sugar from sugar beet in a process that involved washing the beets in a lot of water, which had to end up somewhere. For this reason sugar factories tended to be built near where there was a ready supply of water. The smell of sugar beet tended to attract coypus, (we'll meet these large rodents later,) and the East Anglian sugar factory settling ponds usually had a "terrible smell" attached to them, according to a source who worked in other East Anglian sugar plants back in the 1970s. You can still see the silos of the Bury Silver Spoon plant as a landmark near the station,, with big piles of sugar beet often stacked nearby. In any event, these settling ponds today would be no place fit for a freshwater mermaid to lurk, however evil.

Not far from Bury, on the River Lark at Fornham All Saints in West Suffolk, and just a little bit further up river at Hengrave, there was said to be a mermaid, either in the river or in the well. The mermaid (apparently without the use of a curved rake) would grab and drown children who ventured too close or even touched the water. There was also a phantom woman on a horse who was seen to ride across the surface of the nearby mere (lake) on certain days of the year. The ghost story writer MR James grew up nearby, at Great Livermere, and penned many a short story about "antiquarians" researching the more peculiar corners of forgotten Suffolk history and archaeology and ending up meeting a sticky end at the hands of some ancient malevolent East Anglian entity that they'd stirred up. The area around Fornham All Saints, with its massive Neolithic and Bronze Age monument (now threatened by housing development) inspired James's ominously-titled ghost story *A Warning to the Curious*.[5]

The people of the fens were thought (by others) to have some fairy or mermaid blood in them, or were believed to be born web-footed. The "half-mermaid" fen-dweller girls in particular were feared. It was whispered of them that they loved to play near pools and dykes and push their normal playmates in.[6]

There was yet another freshwater mermaid said to live somewhere in the River Gipping at some unknown point in history. The mermaid that frequented the Gipping would prey on children who played near the deeper waters of the river. Then there's The Mermaid pub on the banks of the River Gipping, the old Stowmarket Navigation canal at the point where the London Road crosses it in Ipswich, just before it comes out into the Orwell. We'll look at the River Gipping in more detail, and the Gipping Valley, in our section on big cats. As it wasn't clear exactly where the mermaid was to be found, it was wise for children to stay away from the Gipping altogether.[7]

The entity in Wimbell Pond near Acton (just east of Long Melford) may or may not have been a mermaid. A chest of money is said to lie at the bottom of the pond. Those who have thrown stones into the pond have heard it make a ringing noise as it strikes the chest, and seen a small white figure whimpering, "That's mine."[8]

You've probably already guessed the perfectly rational explanation for all of Suffolk's freshwater mermaids. Until recently, Suffolk children were expected to be out of the house and out and about all day, and not expected to show up again until teatime. The temptation to play – unsupervised – near ponds, lakes, drainage ditches, rivers and meres was great. Parents made up stories about absolutely lethal and terrifying mermaids living in these bodies of water in an attempt to keep their children away from them. In other parts of England, there were witches instead of mermaids living in wells.

PART 1 – NOT QUITE HUMAN

Ginger werewolf of the East of England coast

Via the Centre for Fortean Zoology's own Nick Redfern, comes a story "passed down from generation to generation from a family in Kent", about the Shirley family, who were picnicking in "an area of woodland" on the East Coast of England sometime at the end of the 1940s. Pat Shirley had been told the story by her grandfather, who was there, but she wouldn't tell Redfern where the incident had happened (or possibly by the time the story had been passed down to her, the location had been forgotten).

Pat Shirley's grandfather told her that during their woodland picnic somewhere on the East Coast, he'd caught the briefest of glimpses of a werewolf-like manbeast "covered in flaming red hair" and "possessing a pair of huge and powerful jaws." It then vanished into the trees.[9]

A look at an atlas shows that wooded stretches of the East of England coast – from the Thames Estuary in Essex and all the way up to Lincolnshire – are limited. There's nothing very much going on by way of noticeable woodland near the coast anywhere in Essex. Nor is there anything noteworthy by way of woodlands on the Lincolnshire coast either. So a wooded stretch of coast in the East of England would probably be in Norfolk or Suffolk.

Some stretches of the Suffolk coast with woodland nearby do spring to mind – around Sizewell, along the Dunwich coast as far as Dingle, and if you strayed inland from Walberswick beach you'd find yourself along some farm tracks and bridleways lined with dense avenues of trees on both sides. Benacre and Covehithe have woods close to the shore, and right behind Aldeburgh (away from the beach) there are woods.

I don't pretend to be an expert on North Norfolk, but the Norfolk seaside resort of Sheringham to this day advertises itself as "twixt sea and pine", with pine forests near the beach. Maps suggest that areas behind the North Norfolk beaches of Horsey, Stalham, Holkham Bay and Hunstanton also have some woodlands.

That's the state of our East of England wooded coastline today, but what about in the 1940s? There may well be some little wooded stretches of the shore that have simply fallen into the sea since then, through coastal erosion. I recall that when I was a child, in the 1970s, there were trees at the top of the cliffs at Dunwich and at Iken Cliff with ropes hanging from their branches for children to swing on, and roots to clamber over, and these are both long gone. The great fallen trees that lie on their sides on the beach at Covehithe are all that remains of what was once a wood at nearby Benacre, lost to coastal erosion and floods in recent times.

I invite readers to peruse large-scale 1940s maps of the East and England coast to pinpoint the location of an incident that I find it hard to believe could have happened in the first place.

The dog-headed man of Tuddenham

Tuddenham St Martin, just north of Ipswich, is home to the Magpies, Ipswich's rugby club. Local business Tuddenham Hall Foods is England's biggest asparagus grower. In Tuddenham St Martin, in the 1980s and 1990s, there was "a tradition of sorts" of a local "dog-headed man" that would "seem to be passed down from older brothers and fathers in that area," according to Chris Field, who as a child moved into the village.

Chris told me a friend's dad had "told us a few things" about the dog-headed man, possibly while "trying to put the scares on us." To this day he's unsure as to whether the dog-headed man of Tuddenham was supposed to be "a spirit creature" or what, exactly, it was supposed to be. He did tell me there were "tales of a man with a wolf's head in the area," and that these were "linked to certain locations, bridges and river ways." Chris admitted that in the area around Tuddenham, some of the woodlands "do have a certain energy… the feeling like you're being watched, copses that make you feel unwelcome." These were often the places locally where Tuddenham youths would play "manhunt" or "it", games no doubt made more exciting by the prospect of the dog-headed man lurking behind you in your hiding place![10]

Something like the dog-headed man of Tuddenham may have wandered 16 miles north-east to terrify two teenage boys. A Suffolk informant (we'll call him "Paul") described being stalked by *something* one summer night in 1995 while "wild camping". The noises it made while "stomping around", and the sounds of branches breaking on the forest floor, made Paul feel that it that walked on two legs, although he didn't get a look at it.

This incident took place in Dodds Wood, near Sweffling, on the Glemham Estate. "Paul" and a friend spent their teenage years "roughing it" in unofficial campsites. In the summer of '95, the two friends built one with a fire pit in Dodds Wood. Paul and friend stayed up most of the night after hearing *something* walking around the edge of their camp. The "stomping" and "branches breaking" came closer until an hour before dawn", when the noises finally receded. The boys returned the next night, with Paul's dad's dog. The noises resumed. When the dog "started going berserk and barking like mad... whatever it was... ran off very fast and we could hear the branches breaking as it ran." Days later, during a thunderstorm, Paul heard a "huge howl that went on for more than half a minute," which came from the friends' camp area.[11]

That concludes our round-up of Suffolk's demi-humans. Some were just stories made up to scare kids, others – while obviously impossible – have nonetheless been encountered by sane adults in disturbingly recent times. From waterborne mermaids we now turn to sea monsters.

A dog-headed humanoid figure on the roof of the church at Blythburgh (top). Or is it a ginger East of England werewolf? Above, a street sign in Ipswich.

FOOTNOTES TO CHAPTER 4:

Freshwater mermaids and miscellaneous manimals

1. See www.pipwright.com/Newspapers_in_Suffolk_1720_1800.htm..

2. Suffolk Notes & Queries, *Ipswich Journal* (1877) quoted by the Fairy Investigation Society website www.fairyist.com/fairy-places/east-anglian-fairies/mermaid-s-pond-rendlesham-suffolk, also in *Paranormal Suffolk: True Ghost Stories,* Christopher Reeve, Amberley Stroud 2009.

3. *The Book of Days*, R. Chambers, W & R Chambers, 1863-4); *Paranormal Suffolk: True Ghost Stories*, Christopher Reeve, Amberley Stroud 2009

4. *A Handbook of Bury St. Edmunds*, Samuel Tymms, F. Lankester, 1859. Alex McWhirter, Heritage Officer for West Suffolk at Moyse's Hall Museum, Bury said his enquiries on the Mermaid's Pits on my behalf had "drawn a blank."

5. Alan Murdie, Ghostwatch, *Fortean Times*, **FT 325;18,** March 2015, quoting "Folklore from S.E. Suffolk", Lady E. C. Gurdon, *Folklore*, December 1892. According to *Suffolk Ghosts and Legends*, Pamela Brooks, Halsgrove, Wellington, Somerset 2009, the antiquarian and topographer John Gage, writing in 1822, put the Mermaid's Pits further away from Bury and near Fornham. Brooks also quotes "Suffolk Notes & Queries" in an 1877 reprint in the *Ipswich Journal* as saying that the well in the village of Fornham also had a mermaid.

6. *The Folklore of East Anglia*, Enid Porter, BT Batsford, London 1974.

7. Paranormal Database.

8. *The Folklore of East Anglia,* see above.

9. "The Werewolves of Britain" Nick Redfern, *FATE* magazine, March 2006; http://cryptomundo.com/bigfoot-report/werewolves-uk/, also in *Mystery Animals of Britain and Ireland*, Graham McEwan, Hale, London 1986.

10. Chris Field, telephone interview, 9 September 2015. There is a Dog's Head Street right in the centre of Ipswich, but this apparently has its origin in the pub sign of a medieval Flemish inn that once stood there.

11. "Paul", by email, 30 September 2015.

Mermaids lure sailors away from drink and into the Sailor's Reading Room at Southwold, a mermaid figurehead on the Galleon Fish Shop at Aldeburgh.

PART TWO – HERE BE DRAGONS

5: Kessingland sea serpents ahoy!

The North Sea off Suffolk's coast, as well as the county's rivers and estuaries were at one point allegedly teeming with sea and river monsters.

Aside from the child-murdering freshwater mermaids who we've just met in the "not quite human" section, the denizens of Suffolk's coasts and rivers are said to include fish and crustaceans of monstrous size, sea serpents with multiple humps behind a long neck, a strange moose-like giant swimming mammal and even "sea dragons" and crested serpentine river dragons. Some of the sea and river dragons and "cockadrilles" that infest Suffolk's waters even clamber out onto land to terrorise the surrounding medieval villages. Just as Rendlesham has become Suffolk's Grand Central Station for UFO mysteries, so the large seaside village of Kessingland, in the suburbs of Lowestoft, has become over the years *the* place to see passing sea serpents. In many cases, though, boringly rational explanations present themselves for the apparent abundance of Suffolk's sea and river monsters.

Monstrous fishes

When Lowestoft's herring fisheries reached their zenith in around 1913, if you looked out to sea you could observe several hundred herring drifters (fishing boats) at once, with sometimes as many as a hundred nets in a line, stretching out for two miles. So huge were the regular catches of the Suffolk herring drifter fleet that it often took crews 12 to 15 hours to haul them in. There were once smokehouses all along the coast to process the catch. Girls migrated all the way from Glasgow to work in the filleting sheds of the Suffolk coast. By the 1950s, overfishing had driven the Suffolk fleet into sharp decline, with herring and cod fished to the point of "commericial extinction" locally. Now the great fishing fleets are gone. At the beginning of our current century, you could come out of Lowestoft Station and see a trawler, winching gear and all, tied up in the harbour right in front of you, but the last Lowestoft trawler operator ceased trading in 2002.[1]

Now there are only much smaller "longliner" fishing boats fishing along Suffolk's coast. The little fishing ports of Aldeburgh and Orford are still active, you can still see piles of lobster pots in the front gardens at Sizewell. Mussels from the Deben are particularly sought after.

Back in the glory days of Suffolk fisheries, the fleets would sometimes land such exceptionally huge catches as to surprise even themselves. The *East Anglian Daily Times* reported on 13 May 1907 that the fishermen of Lowestoft had landed "such a glut of mackerel that had never been seen in the town before", over "two million fish in one week." But they were victims of their own success. The sheer weight of mackerel had caused some of the drifters' nets to sink and be lost forever, and with such a surplus of fish, the mackerel price had been driven down. On other occasions, the county's fisherfolk found themselves facing some truly monstrous fish.[2]

Sometime not long before 1884, a fisherman by the name of Hannant, fishing out of Corton, just north of Lowestoft, was out fishing from Mr Gowing's herring fleet vessel when he landed an enormous cod, "a fine codfish." Hannant "cut it open, there rolled out a full-grown baby, slightly cut on the chin by the knife, both cod and baby immediately pitched overboard," with "no crowner's (coroner's) inquest." Presumably, a sudden wave striking the boat had tipped the baby-eating cod and its stomach contents into the sea.[3]

Mother Lumpkin's Hole, in Middleton, west of Westleton, is a deep hollow in the bed of the Minsmere River near Reckford Bridge, which, according to local rumour, was the habitat of "carp as big as pigs, and pike the size of baby sharks". According to local rumour, a wagon along with its team of horses once vanished into the hole. A local resident recalled in 1969 how in earlier life he'd been warned away from the Hole for fear that he be dragged in by the dreadful monster that lived there.

The hole's not visible today, but the Minsmere River still flows under the Reckford Bridge. The bridge is right by the "Middleton – Please drive carefully" sign on the road from Westleton. The Minsmere River sometimes floods over it.

Leaving aside the immense variation in size among the world's various species of shark, *Saxmundham News* back in 2014 did report that Graham and Matt Bedding pulled out a 36 lb 14 oz (16.71kg) mirror carp from the fishing lake at Carlton Meres Country Park near Lonely Farm, up the road from Saxmundham and a short distance from Middleton. This carp was a local record-breaker, while not the size of an adult pig, it was comparable to a very respectably-sized piglet.

My East Anglian carp fishing enthusiast source told me that the mirror carp and any carp in the Minsmere River would have had to have been introduced, like the one at Carlton Meres. They also said that what determines how big carp can grow in England is the length of the warm summers, they generally don't put on much by way of growth in the cold winters, when they're often in a sort of torpor. While pig-sized carp are just possible in stocked lakes in the south of France, even in England's driest county and with the benefit of the generous Suffolk coastal microclimate, hog-sized carp are unlikely.[4]

A Summerie of Englysh Chronicles by John Stow, believed to have been written at the end of the sixteenth century, records that on "IX Dec AD 1568" at Downham Bridge in Suffolk "17 monstrous fishes, some of them 27 feet in length" were taken. (It's Santon Downham today.) It's just possible that a solitary sturgeon or porpoise or even a pilot whale could find its way that far up river (the Waveney was a mightier body of water in those days, navigable and with ports), but *seventeen* of them at once?[5]

And then there is Southwold's monster crab. *The Halesworth Times* of September 1857 relates how on the twelfth of that month, "an enormous crab, with claws measuring five feet, was caught on the beach in this town. It was found with a long rope attached to it, and was conveyed in a cart (having previously had its claws detached) to the Town Hall, where it may be viewed by the curious of crustacean research."[6]

We are convinced we saw a sea serpent

And so to the seas immediately off Kessingland, from which several sea monsters have been seen over the years. The earliest written report of something odd in the sea off Kessingland seems to be the account from *The Gentleman's Magazine* of December 1750, which relates how "The creature was about five feet long from what could be viewed of it above the water, with a head like a dog and a beard like a lion. The skin was spotted like that of a leopard. It passed in a leisurely fashion, finally disappearing beneath the waves to the great amazement of all those watching from the shore..."

From its description, the 1750 *Gentleman's Magazine* mystery animal off the coast of Kessingland does seem awfully like an out-of-place seal or sea lion. Grey seals and common seals (the latter also known as harbour seals) are a fairly common sight off the Suffolk coast, and harbour seals have spots. That still doesn't explain the "beard like a lion", while lions don't have beards, they have manes. A particularly big, shaggy sea lion that had strayed all the way from the South Atlantic might fit the bill, although sea lions aren't spotted.

The *New York Gazette* of a few months later, of 13 May 1751, was written at a time when New York was a loyal colony of the British Empire, so naturally gossip from London was still just as interesting as news from the thirteen colonies of America. The *Gazette* reported that there was "Advertised for Shew in London: Two Ostriches; the Male weighing 300 1-4th, 10 Feet in Height. A Sea Monster, taken on the Coast of Suffolk, 5 Feet long, and 4 Feet round, with a Head like a Dog, a Beard like a Lion, and a Tail like a Fawn; the Skin is covered with Down as soft as Velvet, and is spotted like that of a Leopard. The fore Fins, which resemble the Hands of a Man, are used by this Creature, to wipe its Eyes and wash its Face. lt is kept in a Cistern of salted Water, is very gentle, and will roll and tumble at Command."

The animal caught off the coast of Suffolk does bear a striking resemblance to the animal seen off Kessingland, and to a seal or sea lion, now apparently in captivity.

In London in those days, you could charge people to see a novelty like a live seal and tell them it was the eighth wonder of the world. It's entirely possible that some enterprising scam artists, inspired by *The Gentleman's Magazine* story, just got hold of a seal and passed it off as "the sea monster taken on the coast of Suffolk." Most 1750s Londoners would have been none the wiser.

Fast forward some 160 years, and our next Kessingland sea monster is better documented and considerably bigger. In July 1912, the great novelist Sir Henry Rider Haggard (*She, King Solomon's Mines*) was working on a novel at home in Ditchingham, which is mere yards over the Norfolk border, in the suburbs of Bungay. He was contacted by his daughter Lilias, who was holidaying with his sister not far away at Kessingland Grange.

Lilias's letter to the great novelist read, "We had a great excitement here this evening, and we are convinced we saw a sea serpent! I happened to look up when I was sitting on the lawn, and saw what looked like a thin, dark line with a blob at one end, shooting through the water at such a terrific speed it hardly seemed likely that anything alive could go at such a pace. It was some way out over the sandbank, and travelling parallel with the shore." Running to fetch some binoculars, Lilias returned with these just in time to "make out it had a sort of head at one end and then a series of about 30 pointed blobs which dwindled in size as they neared the tail. As it went along it seemed to get more and more submerged and then vanished. You can't imagine the pace it was going. I suppose it was about 60 feet long."

Henry went to Kessingland Grange, where the cook and the gardener confirmed his daughter's story. He then forwarded Lilias's letter together with his own to the *Eastern Daily Press,* where it was published on 24 July 1912.

And then, on a clear August morning in 1923, Captain F E B Haselfoot of the survey ship *HMS Kellett,* was taking observations off the coast not far from Kessingland, when Haselfoot and the navigator Lt Commander R M Southern observed something unusual. Haselfoot wrote that he "observed rising out of the water about 200 yards from the ship, a long, serpentine neck, projecting from six or seven feet above the water. I observed this neck rising out of the water twice, and it remained up, in each case, for four or five seconds. Viewing with the naked eye only, I could not make out precisely what the head was like."[8]

Then in July 1978 a holidaymaker strolling on Kessingland beach, who admitted that "I would be inclined to think that I had imagined everything if I had not read the story of the

Kessingland Sea Serpent," wrote to the *East Anglian Magazine* to tell them how, amid calm seas, he'd observed something that "looked like the head of a seal on a long neck sticking up out of the water. There seemed to be some humps behind the head, but the creature only remained visible for a matter of a few seconds before diving beneath the surface." In the long-established tradition of Suffolk mystery animal witnesses, the holidaymaker ticked the "requests anonymity" box.[9]

Moving south along the coast from Kessingland, our next Suffolk sea serpent encounter is from July 1978. Looking out to sea from Britain's most famous "secret hidden beach" at Covehithe, a witness described seeing a creature that had a head like a seal, with a long neck and several humps. He added that the encounter was over very quickly.[10]

A more recent anomalous sighting off the coast at Covehithe was a young piglet that tumbled off the cliff at the end of 2014 and landed in the North Sea. At the time of writing, you could see pigsties and plenty of piglets in the fields between the cliffs and the coastal path through the woods down to the beach. The cliffs are eroding away fast, so even a careful piglet could easily fall off them. This particular piglet seemed to be the adventurous type, though, and was very soon swimming off towards the Netherlands at surprising speed, possibly aware of the fate the humans had in mind for it. The farmer called the RSPCA, who could just about make out a tiny, shrinking dot on the horizon, before he commandeered a boat and rowed out to rescue the piglet. He commented that the piglet seemed surprisingly "unfazed" by its adventure, especially given how freezing the North Sea can be, even in summer.[11]

Just below Covehithe, and visible from Covehithe beach on a clear day, lies Southwold, once home to now vanished "fairy" earthworks, as we have seen. On 21 October 1938 a "sea-serpent" was seen off the Suffolk coast at Southwold by two local fishermen casting their nets. It was reported to have been grey and some 60 feet (some 20 metres) long with a single hump, and moving fast. When approached by the two fishermen it made off at astonishing speed. The vicar of Southwold apparently saw it too from the shore.[12]

However, a letter to the *Lowestoft Journal* of 16 January 1976 by Southwold resident Mr A. Barrett Jenkins claimed to explain what the monster really was. Jenkins said he'd seen the monster himself, and that his father, a local photographer, had hired a fisherman to row him out to photograph it. But when they got to the spot, they discovered that the "monster" was nothing more than some big timber logs bolted together. The "humps" were an optical illusion, caused by the timbers bobbing in an out of sight together amid the waves. The "monster" was later towed ashore, where a few interested people gathered to see it.[13]

From Southwold, via Walberswick, Dunwich and Sizewell, our journey south along the Suffolk coast next takes us to the surreal village resort of Thorpeness. There, at around 8pm on a clear June evening in 1931, three women – Mrs Sybil M. Armstrong, her children's governess and her cook – spotted a many-humped sea serpent from the sitting room of a rented bungalow on a cliff at Thorpeness. They saw a dark object moving about 400 yards offshore. Mrs Armstrong went outside and could make out an object with an animal's head, a long back and several humps behind. (A sketch she made of the monster moving at sea had six roughly evenly-spaced humps of about the same size, except for the hump at the end, which was a little smaller.) *Lantern* added that the creature's humps were black and rounded, and that its head swung from side to side. Mrs Armstrong called the residents, who watched as the creature hauled itself over a sandbank, revealing fins in "the shoulder region" which it beat while in the water, throwing up a lot of spray, and appearing to be a lighter, tawny brown colour when out of the water. It slithered down the far side of a sandbank into the sea "with a great commotion" before disappearing from view. Mrs Armstrong the following evening observed fishing boats trailing lobster pots right near where the animal had disappeared, and estimated it to have been about 60 feet long, although *Lantern* put it at some 30 or 40 feet long.[14]

A monster of a very singular nature

South of Thorpeness is Aldbeburgh and after that the next port along the coast is Orford, in the estuary behind Orford Ness, which at 16 miles long is Europe's biggest shingle bank. Orford Ness is now a nature reserve, with some very weird abandoned buildings from the Cold War era. As well as the "merman" we encountered in Chapter 1, a wildman netted off the coast at Orford Ness, and some possible predation on the local foxes by big cats (as we'll see later), out of the seas between Orford and Southwold came a very nasty little sea dragon.

The story comes originally from an account in *The Gentleman's Magazine* of 1749. (As we have just read, the magazine had regular spots cataloguing the latest occurrences of high strangeness.) There story's set somewhere "between Orford and Southwold" – as these places are some distance apart, it suggests an encounter quite a long way out to sea, where it could have been hard to pinpoint exactly where you were.

There's a retelling of the story in the 1823 *Encyclopedia Britannica Dictionary of Arts, Sciences, and Miscellaneous Literature* Volume XIX. This draws heavily on the article in the *Gentleman's Magazine,* describing the sea dragon as a "monster of a very singular nature." In the words of a witness who had seen the creature's corpse, its "head and tail… resemble those of an alligator; it has two large fins, which serve it both to swim and to fly; and though they were so dried that I could not extend them, yet they appear, by the folds, to be shaped like those which painters have given to dragons and other winged monsters that serve as supporters to coats of arms. Its body is covered with impenetrable scales; its legs have two joints, and its feet are hoofed like those of an ass: it has five rows of very white and sharp teeth in jaw, and is in length about four feet, though it was longer when alive, it having shrunk as it became dry."[15]

The animal was captured by the two fishermen, who displayed its dead body. "It was caught in a net with mackerel; and being dragged on shore, was knocked down with a stretcher or boat-hook," the account continues. "The net being opened, it suddenly sprung up, and flew above 50 yards: the man who first seized it had several of his fingers bitten off; and the wound mortifying, he died. It afterwards fastened on the man's arm who shows it, and lacerated it so much, that the muscles are shrunk, and the hand and fingers distorted; the wound is not yet healed, and is thought to be incurable."

In the opinion of the *Britannica* writer, although "It is said by some to have been described by naturalists under the name of the Sea-dragon. We must add to the account now given of the monster called a sea-dragon, that we think it extremely probable that the animal was nothing more than a distorted or overgrown individual of some of the well known species of fish."

The definitions for "Sea-Dragon" in the 1823 *Britannica* refers to the creature taken between Orford and Southwold in 1749. It's entirely possible that the much less terrifying "Suffolk monster" from Kessingland in *The Gentleman's Magazine* of 1750, the one that looked like a seal, is somehow the same animal as the sea dragon taken between Orford and Southwold, and that somehow the story has become awfully confused and embellished in the telling. They are very different-sounding animals, although someone was exhibiting a creature at least

Stereo telescope for sea monster observation at Southwold (top left, there's one at Felixstowe too.) These long-eared, fire-breathing dragons (above and below left) on the porch at St Edmund's Church, Southwold have bodies that look remarkably like crocodiles. Could they have been based on contemporary drawings of crocodiles?

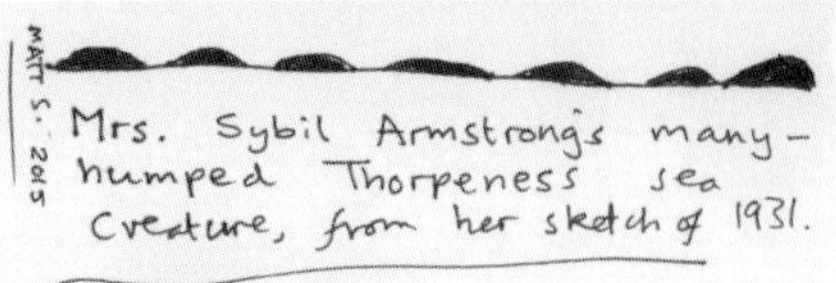

Artist's impressions of Sybil Armstrong's sea serpent (above) and a local record-breaking carp caught in 2014 (above right). This wyvern (two-legged dragon, right) does battle with a woodwose (see Chapter 1) at the Church at Peasenhall.

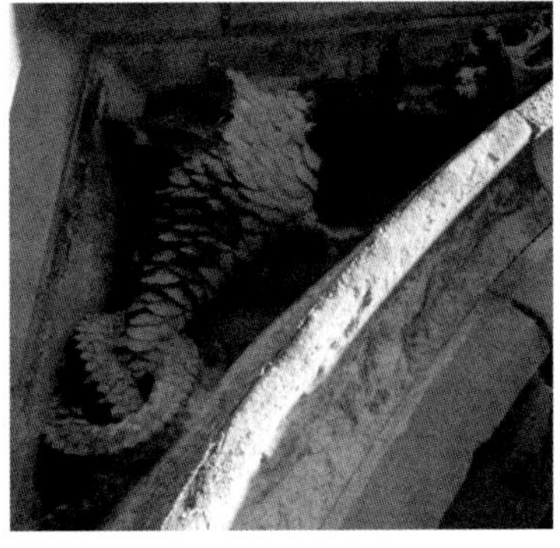

passed off as the "Suffolk sea monster" alive in London. Could the 1749 sea dragon have been followed by attempts to put a live seal on show in London, pretending it was the same murderous alligator-like sea dragon thing?

Dragons and serpents at sea, on land, and in the rivers

As well as our particularly vicious little sea dragon, there was once a "water dragon" attacking medieval Sudbury and Bures, both in South Suffolk, on the banks of the River Stour. In 1405 (or in some versions much earlier, recorded by a document dating to 1405), this crested monster clambered out of the local river and terrorised Sudbury and Bures and the neighbouring villages. There is said to be a document dating from 1405 that relates this South Suffolk dragon attack, but none of the sources I've found name it, nor say where the document is, nor even if it still existed at the time they were writing. I haven't been able to confirm its provenance beyond Dr A. Jessop's *Frivolia: Essays* of 1876.

Most retellings of the Bures dragon story in modern English, with their considerable variations, appear to be from a translation from Middle English. These usually give the location as "close to the town of Bures, near Sudbury" and don't mention a dragon attack on Sudbury at all. Sudbury's now a seven-minute train ride from the village of Bures.

The unnamed document relating the dragon's attack on Bures notes, "there has lately appeared, to the great hurt of the countryside, a dragon, vast in body, with a crested head, teeth like a saw, and a tail extending to an enormous length." The dragon killed a shepherd and ate many of his sheep, before "workmen" of the local estate, retainers of Sir Richard Waldegrave, arrived and fired arrows at it, but they found that when their arrows ("darts" in one version) struck the dragon's body, it "remained unhurt, for the arrows bounced off his back as if it were iron or hard rock." Arrows that hit the animal's spine gave out a ringing noise as if they'd struck a "brazen plate" and just bounced off, the animal's hide proving impenetrable. After this, "all the country people" (all the able-bodied men of the district) were mobilised for a dragon-destroying operation ("in earnest" according to another version,) and when the dragon saw "that he was again to be assailed by arrows", he fled in the long reeds of the marsh never to be seen again.[16]

Sudbury and Bures are both on the border with Essex (the River Stour forms the boundary) and half of the modern village of Bures is actually in Essex. Some of Sudbury's suburbs were in Essex, but were annexed to Suffolk in the 1970s. In this borderland, rivalry between the men of Suffolk and the men of Essex was fierce in days when attitudes were more parochial.

One form of Suffolk-Essex rivalry was the different versions of the dragon story. The residents of the village of Wormingford in Essex, just over the Stour from Bures, naturally begged to differ over what happened. In their version, it was their own village that came under attack, and it definitely wasn't by a crested water dragon. Oh no, said the Wormingforders, the Bures folk had it all wrong. In the Wormingford narrative, it was a "cockadrille", a crocodile that was one of the first acquisitions of the royal menagerie at the Tower of London, supposedly brought back by King Richard I as a gift from the exiled King of Jerusalem during his Crusade. This would put the acquisition at sometime not long after 1194, well over 200 years before the alleged 1405 document.

According to an unsourced explanation on display in Wormingford Church, King Richard's crocodile became fully grown and was easily able to smash its way out of its cage with a swish of its tail, after which it escaped into the nearby Thames and found its way into the Stour, where it wreaked havoc on the Suffolk-Essex border. It was eventually slain by Sir George de la Haye in a field called Bloody Meadows, who in some versions impaled it with a spear, after it had put up a rather feeble fight more indicative of an ordinary mortal crocodile than a huge, crested, armour-plated dragon. In yet another take on the story, the cockadrille appeared at a ford on the Stour. There it killed "many travellers" before it in turn was slain by Bertram de la Haye, who felled a tree on top of it.[17]

A short distance from Bures and Wormingford is a suspiciously similar tale of Suffolk-Essex rivalry, also involving dragons and an ancient document that it seems nobody can actually produce.

Little Cornard and Ballingdon are now both suburbs of Sudbury, while Little Cornard has a Kedington Hill, formerly "Kydyndon Hyl". Part of Ballingdon – a mile from Little Cornard – is still in Essex, including Ballingdon Hill, in olden days "Blacdon Hyl." The "Welcome to Suffolk" sign now stands on the top of Ballingdon Hill, roughly at the extent of the queue for the traffic lights at the bottom of the hill, when you wait to cross the bridge to get into Sudbury on a busy day. In case you're wondering what all these hilly bits are doing in flat-as-a-pancake Suffolk, the geography of South Suffolk is characterised by gently rolling hills. (See, for example, the hilly landscapes painted by local boys Thomas Gainsborough and John Constable.

A "small, leather-bound book" supposedly in the Canterbury Cathedral Library, although I've not been able to trace any mention of it back beyond W.A. Dutt's *Suffolk,* (Methuen, 1904) relates how on 26 September of the "year of our Lord 1449", two "terrible dragons", one black and one red and spotted, were seen fighting for about an hour "on two hills, one being "Blacdon Hyl" and the other being "Kydyndon Hyl." The red spotted dragon "obtained victory" over the black one and they both retired to their hills. The narrator diplomatically omits to say which of the two dragons was from Essex and which was from Suffolk.

Apart from its similarities to the Sudbury, Bures and Wormingford stories, there is another problem with this narrative. A very similar incident features in the story of the boy Merlin, later to become King Arthur's entirely fictional court wizard. In this tale, a red dragon (Wales) defeats a white dragon (the Anglo-Saxons.) It looks awfully like another tale of border rivalries transposed to the Suffolk-Essex border. And Kedington Hill is also supposed to have been 'Killingdown Hill,' the place – supposedly – of an earlier battle between either Boudicca, queen of the Iceni, and the Romans or between Saxons and invading Danes.[18]

A Serpent among us

To the people of Suffolk in the seventeenth century, the term "serpent" included anything snake-like or dragon-like with a long thin body, with or without wings or legs. Natural history treatises of the day had illustrations of serpents with little legs and wings, combs, crests and frills. The most famous serpent of all was The Serpent who tempted Eve in the book of Genesis in the Old Testament. He had a serpentine body and – initially – legs, until God cursed him and he lost them.

So when something deeply strange turned up in the countryside around Mendham, North Suffolk, a correspondent writing to his brother described is as best he could, as a "Serpent." Thomas Flatman of Mendham, on the River Waveney west of the villages known as "The Saints", wrote to his brother on 25 September 1662. At his brother's request, Thomas sent "newes of the Serpent among us – I have not seene it myself but can name you 20 yt (that) have, all agreeing punctually in th(eir) relac[i]on and descripe (description) of ye same; tis

PART 2 – HERE BE DRAGONS

Monstrous fish – on the promenade at Lowestoft (top left, inset), on a memorial at the church in Blythburgh (left), sticking out its tongue on the Ancient House, Halesworth (left, inset). The mouth of Hell represented as a gigantic fish on the Wenhaston Doom (top right).

Another dragon bites the dust at the hands of St George in stained glass at the church at Yoxford (below, left). This crocodile on an artificial island close to the boathouse and tearoom at Thorpeness is a realistic model, to lend an atmosphere of *Peter Pan* fantasy to a day out on the boating lake (below, right).

A cat-headed, winged serpent carved on The Old Bell Inn, reputedly the oldest pub in Ipswich (above) and an artist's impression of the Waveney Monster sighting (below).

above a yard and a half longe (4½ ft, 1.36 m), an head like a toade but very large. A yellowish ring around ye neck, 2 wings as broad as a man's hand (and) like a Batts (a bat's wing), 4 yellowe short legs like a ducke as bigg as a lusty mans Thigh . The Belly yellowe speckled with blacke spotts, head and backe all covered in scales wch (which) shine in the sunne (and) reflect all manner of coullers (colours). Hee was seen eating a water henne (moorhen?), is most often seen before sunrise in the morning and about noon when the sun shines bright and hott. Here (in Mendham) is one affirms he surprised the Serpent one morning and being in a place where he could not retreat he ris; & spring at ye man but mis't him."

The letter was signed, "Yo heartily affectionate Bro, T Flatman, Mendham." I can't begin to explain what it could possibly have been.[19]

The Waveney monster

Back in the early 1980s, a small motorised boat was cruising along the Waveney River, between Somerleyton on the Suffolk side and round a series of bends inland towards Burgh St Peter on the Norfolk bank. On board were local men Colin Denny and Noel Rochford. Both were "coypu men" working with Coypu Control, a vast, £2.5 million scheme (in 1980s money) that took the best part of a decade to eliminate the invasive alien species of coypu from the East of England. (We'll look in detail at these large aquatic rodents in Chapter 12.)

Rochford and Denny were out early one March morning on the Waveney where it bends northwards, on the lookout for swimming coypu to shoot with their Ministry of Agriculture-issue single-shot pistols. Rochford was steering the craft. They were heading towards Haddiscoe and the Burgh marshes, nearing the cut at Burgh St Peter where boats are moored. Suddenly they spotted "a large creature", which they estimated at "possibly 10ft in length (3.04 metres), with thick fur and big eyes, come out of the water," making a noise "almost like a loud snort."

Denny said of the creature, "It wasn't a seal. This thing weighed a tonne or maybe more. It was a huge thing and when the head came out of the water, it was a bit frightening. It had brackish fur like a coypu and a big shaped head. It was enormous," Rochford confirmed his own belief that "it certainly wasn't a coypu or a larger relative," Mark Mower, author of *Suffolk Tales of Murder & Mystery*, also interviewed Rochford and Denny, and his book adds that the two coypu men had seen the creature "from 15 yards (around 14 metres)," having "a dozen short glimpses above and below surface" for some 20 minutes in total. Mower described it as having a "large head like a moose", and said there have been other sightings of it.

Rochford told the *Lowestoft Observer* years later that "When I told the Ministry, officials just laughed and said: 'It's another of your jokes.'" When the Min of Ag failed to take them seriously, the two witnesses appealed to the public for help in identifying the animal.

The result was the "Waveney Monster Hunt", in which Denny and Rochford were persuaded by the *Eastern Daily Press* to pose in their little Coypu Control launch on the Waveney in March 1984. The hunt culminated in the Norfolk and Suffolk Broads holiday and boat hire company Hoseasons putting up a £10,000 reward for a close-up photo of the "Monster." It remains unclaimed to this day. *Suffolk Tales of Mystery and Murder* suggests the "Waveney Monster" could have been a bull Atlantic grey seal come in off the coast (there's a seal that's regularly seen in Suffolk's River Blyth). The Otter Trust at nearby Earsham said it was unlikely to have been a muntjac, the exotic species of dwarf Asian deer that have made their home in Suffolk. Denny later thought it could have been a swimming capybara – the world's largest living rodent, that swims with only its eyes and nose above the waterline. Capybaras, though, are nowhere near 10 feet long, while no capybara escapes were reported by local zoos.[20]

Gilbert Addison, who was employed by a Minister of Agriculture research laboratory from 1973 to 1978, commented that the Waveney Monster was "most likely a Chinese water deer, which swim very easily." Were it a Chinese water deer, it would have been on the northern edge of Suffolk a quarter of a century before they established themselves in that county (see Chapter 12), So it would have been a rarity in the region, harder for the 1980s Coypu Men to correctly identify.[21]

A possible explanation for "sea serpents" seen off the Suffolk coast could be whales. Whales are rare in East Anglian waters, so rare that were you to look in a recent natural history book, it would tell you there aren't any in Suffolk's waters, they're certainly rarer off Suffolk than in the East Anglian coastal waters off Essex and Norfolk. Their so rate locally that observers wouldn't be expecting whales, and could easily misidentify them for something more outlandish. Mrs Armstrong's sea serpent, for example, had fins around its shoulders, like a whale.

The Lowestoft Journal of 16 January 1976 recalls a reported collision involving a "somewhat decrepit little Welsh Brigantine" and an enormous "whale" off the Suffolk coast. The insurer paid up without any complaint.[22]

In recent years, however, whale sightings have become more common off the Suffolk coast, people are expecting to see them and are therefore becoming better at identifying them. Dunwich Heath nature reserve even has a hide on the cliffs for watching porpoises, whales and seals. (A suspicious number of enormous Suffolk sea serpents had a head "like a seal"!) Global warming means more species of whales and porpoise are moving into East Anglian waters.

"It was a sight I never expected to see off the Suffolk coast," said Mr Ballard, a witness to the first confirmed humpback whale seen off the coast from RSPB Minsmere nature reserve in 2013. A humpback whale turned up off the coast of Minsmere again the following year, spotted by Bird Guides from the reserve on 23 October. Suffolk Wildlife Trust recorded the sighting, but there was no photo for confirmation by the end of the season. It will be interesting to see if sightings of Suffolk sea serpents diminish as better documented sightings of Suffolk coastal whales increase.[23]

Extraordinary eel

Finally, Michael Fryer in a letter to *Fortean Times* described seeing an extraordinary eel in the River Stour somewhere on the Suffolk-Essex border in the mid-1970s. It was in a deep, peaty slow-flowing section of the Stour, dredged regularly in those days. At the bottom of a pool about six feet (1.2 metres) deep at the base of a weir, Michael spotted an eel 1.4 metres (4.5 feet) long, "far bigger than the maximum" – around three feet three inches in length, or about a metre. This extra-large eel nudged its way along the river bottom before disappearing into shadow. We'd be unlikely to see anything like that again in the Stour though. Fryer noted that its eel population has crashed by 90 per cent since that day in the early 1970s.[24]

That ends our short history of the sea serpents and dragons of Suffolk's seas, rivers and ponds. Some are puzzling indeed, some are dubious or were quite possibly misidentified whales, swimming deer or even a seal passed off as a sea monster. We now climb out of the North Sea and onto land to encounter one of Suffolk' best known monsters – Black Shuck.

PART 2 – HERE BE DRAGONS

Coiled serpents on the facade of the Army Careers Centre in Silent Street, Ipswich. Below: an oarfish, possible identity of the Kessingland sea serpents. It can reach up to 8 metres (26 feet) in length.

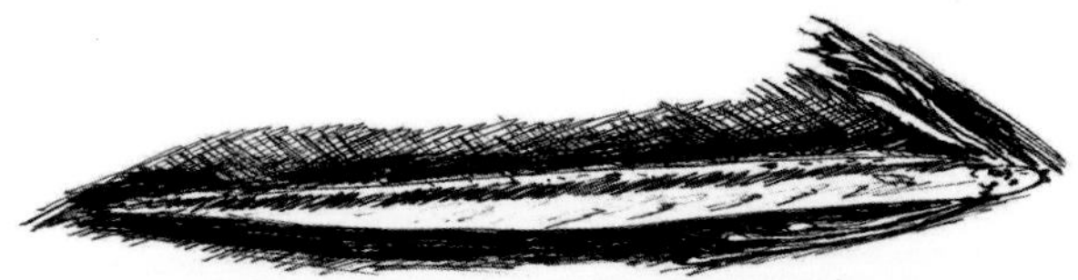

Christopher Saxton's 1575 map showing a fish or whale off the coast at Dunwich (below, out of copyright), and a dragon carved in wood on a sixteenth century house in Lavenham (bottom).

FOOTNOTES TO CHAPTER 5: Kessingland sea serpents ahoy!

1. Cod were taken off the Red List of "fish to avoid", having recovered from a population collapse – *Guardian*, 25 September 2015 www.theguardian.com/uk-news/2015/sep/25/north-sea-cod-taken-off-red-list-of-fish-to-avoid-as-numbers-improve.

2. www.pipwright.com/Newspapers_in_Suffolk_1901_1914.htm.)

3. *Unnatural History Notes,* 1884 p 20 -21, quoted in *Lantern* 25, Spring 1979, www.hiddenea.com/Lantern25.pdf.

4. Paranormal Database, which quotes *Suffolk Remembered*, Allan Jobson, Robert Hale, London, 1969. Of the 21 common shark species in UK water, the small spotted cat shark is an unimpressive 10cm on hatching, and the porbeagle shark is 57cm at birth, not enormous for a pike. See The Shark Trust website, www.sharktrust.org/en/british_sharks.

5. Stow quoted in *Lantern* 17, www.hiddenea.com/Lantern17.pdf.

6. Southwold monster crab from www.pipwright.com/Newspapers_in_Suffolk_1851_1875.htm.

7. *Haunted Suffolk*, Paranormal Database. Iceni Post blog http://icenipost.com/the-kessingland-sea-serpent-or-may-be-an-oarfish/ speculated it could have been a ribbon fish or an oarfish.

8. Iceni Post blog, http://icenipost.com/the-kessingland-sea-serpent-or-may-be-an-oarfish/.

9. Iceni Post, see above.

10. Paranormal Database, which quotes *Ghosts of Suffolk*, Betty Puttick, Countryside Books, Stroud, 1995. The very remote beach of Covehithe, a mile's walk down a narrow track across fields and woods from the nearest parking spaces, frequently features as Suffolk's best-kept secret in newspaper articles.

11. "Suffolk piglet rescued from sea by RSPCA" , BBC News, 4 December 2014, www.bbc.co.uk/news/uk-england-suffolk-30326967

12. *Modern Mysteries of Britain,* Janet & Colin Bord, Grafton, London 1988 and "Timberrr.... it's a sea serpent!", *Lantern* 13, 1976 which quotes *In the Wake of the Sea-Serpents*, Bernard Heuvelmans, Hill & Wang, New York, 1969.

13. "Timberrr.... it's a sea serpent!" see above

14. *Modern Mysteries of Britain,* Janet and Colin Bord, Grafton London 1987, also in *Mystery Animals of Britain and Ireland,* Graham J. McEwan, Richard Hale, London 1986; Sybil M Armstrong described the encounter in a letter to the *Times* shortly afterwards; "Timberrr.... it's a sea serpent!" see above.

15. *Suffolk Ghosts and Legends*, Pamela Brooks, Halsgrove, Wellington, Somerset 2009 has a retelling of the story which quotes *Britannica* in its edition of 1810, near identical to that of 1823.

16. *Here Be Dragons*, Ralph Whitlock, George Allen & Unwin, 1983. The story apparently comes from *Frivolia: Essays*, Dr A. Jessop, Unwin, 1876. The "darts" variant is from *Frivolia*.

17. George de la Haye spearing the dragon is on a window in the church in Wormingford, whose name commemorates a "worm" – a serprentine dragon. The Bures website claims villagers of both Bures and Wormingford always believed the "dragon" was an escaped crocodile. www.bures-online.co.uk/dragon/history_files/WormDragon.pdf

18. *Hidden East Anglia* www.hiddenea.com, which quotes W.A. Dutt among others.

19. *Flying Snake* vol 2 issue 1, which quotes "Letter from Thomas Flatman", 25 September 1662; MS Rawl. *Early Modern Letters* 107, fol. 204, Bodleian Library, www.flyingsnakepress.co.uk.

20. "Unsolved mystery of the Waveney monster", *Lowestoft Journal,* 10 April 2009, www.lowestoftjournal.co.uk/news/unsolved_mystery_of_the_waveney_monster_1_509964; *Suffolk Tales of Murder & Mystery,* Mark Mower, Countryside Books, Newbury 2006; Mower interview at www.youtube.com/watch?v=Lfs5lPr4cdE #theotherside.

21. Gilbert Addison's comments via Tim Holt-Wilson, 3 July 2021.

22. Quoted in "Timberrr.... it's a sea serpent!" see above.

23. "Pod of pilot whales spotted off Lowestoft" *Lowestoft Journal* www.lowestoftjournal.co.uk/news/were_whales_spotted_off_lowestoft_coast_same_group_as_those_seen_near_essex_1_3853976 19 November 2014; Emma Webb of MarineLife, talk on "From porpoises to fin whales – cetaceans of East Anglia", Suffolk Wildlife Trust Mammal Conference, September 2014; "Humpback whale off Minsmere?" *Bury Mercury* 23 Oct 2014, www.burymercury.co.uk/home/video_have_you_seen_the_humpback_whale_reported_off_rspb_minsmere_1_818072.

24. Extraordinary eel from "Letters", *Fortean Times,* **FT39:72-73**, April 2020..

PART 2 – HERE BE DRAGONS

6. Suffolk Shuck

The strange cultural phenomenon that is Suffolk's phantom black dog, Black Shuck, deserves a book of his own (most assume Shuck is a "he"), and indeed there are several books about him, whose authors have already done a better job than me. (There's a bibliography at the back). Folklorists seems to refer to phantom Black Dogs in capital letters, presumably to distinguish them from ordinary mortal dogs that happen to be black.

Shuck can't possibly exist, of course. Nonetheless, he is still being reported. When I came to do the modest Shuck research I did for this book, I'd assumed he was a creature from the deepest rural backwaters of Suffolk, confined to a bygone, vanished age where superstition and ignorance held sway, when few people were literate. It was eyebrow-raising to discover exactly at which points during Shuck's long history the two peaks in East Anglian Shuck sightings occurred.

The first Black Shuck sightings peak was in the 1920s, in the age of mass print media, movies and the beginning of radio. And the second spike in Shuck experiences was during that groovy, cool, fab, bell-bottom trousered, kipper-tied era that was the 1970s, at the end of which I was in my teens. Chopper bikes were fashionable, The Wombles were on the telly, colour TV was proliferating into people's homes and Britain was entering the Common Market (now the European Union) and getting used to decimal currency. Successful local campaigns saved the Ipswich to Lowestoft railway line from being axed and saved most of Suffolk's Waveney District from being annexed to Norfolk. At this time, the ancient horror that was East Anglia's Black Shuck was still at large, scaring the residents of Seventies Suffolk as never before.

Nor were these 1970s Shuck encounters – at a time when the UK's Queen Elizabeth II was celebrating her Silver Jubilee, when the punk phenomenon was first exploding into our cultural lives, and when there were queues for the first Star Wars film – set in some isolated corner of the county where the "white heat of technology" had not yet penetrated. Some contemporary close encounters with Shuck were remarkably urban, in Suffolk's second biggest town, no less.[1]

This wave of Seventies Suffolk Shuck sightings may have been Shuck's last hurrah, as after that reports of Shuck encounters tailed off. The Shucks that have occasionally manifested in the Curious County since then seem to have lost many of their supernatural powers. The reasons for Shuck's apparent decline is as interesting as Shuck himself. Some have noted the appearance at around the same time of another shiny black-coloured, very different mystery animal that seemed to take Shuck's place, as we shall see later...[2]

The classic Black Shuck is a large or very large black dog, sometimes with shaggy fur, sometimes with a shiny, glossy coat, and with shining red eyes, or eyes "the size of dinner plates". In some versions, to look directly into its red eyes "is death," although a remarkable number of witnesses lived to tell the tale. But Shuck doesn't always have anything unusual about his eyes – indeed, he sometimes forgets to bring along his head!

Shuck is a phantom – he appears suddenly and vanishes, sometimes disappearing through walls, and witnesses who try to fight him off report that their weapons pass right through him. Nothing is that simple about Shuck, though, he is often a bit of a trickster. Insubstantial phantom he may be, but some have reported feeling his hot, noxious breath on them, some reported being bitten by him (it?), and some of the frightening entities that go by the name of Shuck aren't always even dogs. Sometimes he changes size, or shape-shifts into another animal, or does both. And he seems to come in several variants that are either downright evil, or benevolent and protective, or sort of neutral. Even the black colour isn't standard – there's a fair number of white Shucks scattered around Suffolk too.

Black Shuck isn't just a "ghost dog" either, he's more than that – he's a trickster, a demon; sometimes he's the Devil appearing in dog form (although the most noteworthy Suffolk Satanic Black Dog incarnations behaved very differently from the classic Shuck). A small proportion of Black Shuck entities are connected to witchcraft and magic. For convenience, we'll come to Suffolk ghost dogs other than Shuck near the end of this chapter.

Places in the county where Shuck (Black or otherwise) has been encountered include Great Livermere and the lanes of Theberton sometime around the 1920s. A Mrs Carter of Westleton reported to the local Women's Institute in 1922 that at some time earlier, she'd seen "a huge figure like a black dog" on the Red Stile, on the Westleton to Darsham Road, and when it went past she heard a noise like a clanking chain. Many people had been "thrown about there terribly" at the Red Stile by some unseen force, she added.

The Barham Beast, from Barham near Ipswich, was encountered around 1910 by two men walking home along the village's Norwich Road by Barham Church Lane, close to Barham Hill. A large, rough-coated dog with big, yellow eyes chased them. One man tried to fend it off with a stick (or a whip in some versions of the story) but the stick passed right through the creature, which ran off and dived through a brick wall, at which point it disappeared. In some accounts the man who tried to strike the Barham Shuck is named as Kent, and the encounter is dated to just before World War Two.

At Reydon near Southwold, a couple out riding in their two-wheeled carriage at the dawn of the twentieth century encountered a Shuck which ran under their horses. The man struck at the beast with his horsewhip (a stick in some versions of the story), only for the whip to pass right through it. Similarities between the Barham and Reydon stories lead me to suspect that one is a garbled version of the other!

A "large phantom dog was seen around the ruins" of Dunwich in 1926. Pretty much all that was left of the City of Dunwich by then would have been Greyfriars Monastery or the Leper Chapel next to St James's Church. (Dunwich was among the top ten biggest medieval cities in England before a series of storms caused its decline, with much of it abandoned by the end of the thirteenth century; the ruins gradually succumbed to coastal erosion.) In South Suffolk, the area West of the village of Boxford, along Boxford Lane (the A1071) and all the way west past Little Cornard and over the county border into Essex is said to be patrolled by a Shuck.[3]

Since the sixteenth century, there have been reports of a phantom dog of a type known as a galleytrot around Walberswick, particularly on the nearby heath, on the road between The Bell pub and the vicarage, and on the beach leading south down to Dunwich. Local legend claims the galleytrot is the Devil himself, appearing in dog form. Some reports of the galleytrot seen near the Bell Inn, said to date back to "the 1500s," have him as a soul-stealing, calf-sized creature with big, round, red eyes, and a growl "so horrendous it could send you straight to hell."

There were several wartime encounters with this Shuck. A World War Two coastguard fired his pistol at the Walberswick galleytrot, and the bullet seems to have gone right through it. An American serviceman and his wife living in a remote, flat-topped hut on the edge of Walberswick marshes during the same war, were disturbed by a loud banging noise late one night, after which they saw through their window a galleytrot trying to get into the hut. The Shuck's assault on the hut followed, and it lasted several hours, during which it appeared to throw itself repeatedly against the side of the building. Come daylight, the couple want to investigate but couldn't find any sign of any damage to the property, nor could they find any dog tracks. Elaborate hazing by the locals springs to mind as a possible explanation.

Historical novelist Penelope Fitzgerald, back in the days when she worked in a bookshop in Southwold, was leading a pony across Walberswick Common when a "white dog like a pointer" ran off through the bracken, without making any sound at all. Locals told Fitzgerald the same entity had been seen "waiting for someone" on the Common on several occasions over the past hundred years. In the 1980s, two women reported seeing the Walberswick galleytrot – illuminated in car headlights, black in colour and a calf-sized entity with glowing eyes – and there have been more recent Shuck sightings on The Green, at nearby Southwold, just the other side of the River Blyth.[4]

Another wartime phantom hound, a "suspicious dog", was pursued by locals down Callow Hill Lane in Ampton (near Great Livermere, just off the A134) in the 1940s. The "suspicious dog" was at large at a time when vigilant villagers were on the look out for German agents and fifth columnists ahead of a feared invasion of the East of England. The dog was accompanied by a suspicious man. Both man and dog suddenly disappeared after a brief pursuit. This is likely to have been a more ordinary "ghost dog", though. Black Shuck has no human master, phantom German spy or otherwise. Shucks have been spotted in pairs, though – Wissett, north of Halesworth, has *two* phantom Black Dogs, both said to haunt the two little humpback bridges in Mill Road, near the village, although in an alternative version of the story, it's a single apparition known as the Shaggy Dog.[5]

Shuck was also said to roam the East Anglian coast from Felixstowe in the South and all the way north to Hunstanton in North Norfolk. *East Anglian Daily Times* columnist Martin Newell recalled in 2014 that a Suffolk man told him some time previously he'd seen Shuck one evening in the marshes of Felixstowe, and that Felixstowe's coastal Shuck was said to have a "thick, unkempt coat."[6]

The Felixstowe Shuck connection is interesting because the Felixstowe Kennels were apparently the home of the first Irish wolfhounds known to have been imported to England, arriving sometime around 1893. A wolfhound bitch named Felixstowe Mavourneen began a line of pedigree Felixstowe wolfhounds. (By 1919 the Felixstowe Kennels had moved to Witnesham, just north of Ipswich.) Some of the earlier pedigree Irish wolfhounds in England, bred at the Felixstowe Kennels, were "black and tans" (black with a lighter underside), and "black" is one of the American Kennel Club's "allowed" wolfhound colours for pedigree wolfhounds today. Black wolfhounds are popular (although not particularly common) in Scandinavia and there's even a shiny black "Russian wolfhound" breed. Could some turn-of-the-twentieth-century nocturnal encounters with a terrifying, huge shaggy hound have had their origins in a nearby breeding facility for Irish wolfhounds, a still unfamiliar breed at the time?[7]

In East Anglia, particularly Suffolk, Black Shuck has strong associations with churchyards and cemeteries, among the many names by which it is known locally is the Churchyard Beast. It is said that in the yard of St Michael's Church in the village of Oulton, on the edge of Lowestoft, the sound you can sometimes hear is the howling of Black Shuck, although others say it's the wind. There was a Black Shuck sighting at nearby Oulton Broad, reports of which were said to have inspired Sir Arthur Conan Doyle's 1901 story *The Hound of the Baskervilles*, but this Shuck Baskervilles origins story isn't supported by evidence.[8]

Sometimes Shuck is a portent of imminent death or disaster, although Ivan A.W. Bunn in his excellent analysis of East of England Shuck traditions noted that of 74 Black Shuck-related portents of death his research uncovered – the majority of them from Suffolk – only 17 actually came true within a year. Sometime in the nineteenth century at Woolpit, on a road approaching the village, a man was said to have been confronted by a talking Shuck, who informed him he'd be dead before the week was up. The story goes that he died the following night. A remarkably similar story set on the Woolpit Road in Clopton features a Shuck called the "Clopton Thing" with "two saucer eyes" that would not move out of the way, and which "grew larger" before it spoke, to tell a traveller, "I want you within a week." He too died the next day. The Clopton Thing may well be a different version of the Woolpit story. Clopton today appears on most maps as Clopton Green, just over half a mile south of Woolpit.

A more modern Shuck death portent came from Bungay in January 1970, in which a Mrs Whitehead of the town's Earsham Street saw Shuck in the middle of the road, running in the direction of Earsham so fast it hardly touched the ground. Mrs Whitehead had stepped out to go to a phone box to call a doctor as her mother had been taken ill, and the appearance of Shuck in the street was seconds after her mother died. There's a tradition in the Lowestoft area that you could avert your death as a result of seeing Black Shuck by refraining from mentioning it to anyone for at least a year afterwards.[9]

At other times, Shuck could be a benevolent protector, who would manifest himself on the road. The phantom dog would appear alongside people walking home at night – particularly women and girls alone – and start walking in step with them. The roads north of Dunwich were said by some to be the territory of a protective Shuck (also on occasion a portent of death), but only protective towards those who showed respect to it when it appeared. "Showing respect" in Shuck lore either meant not showing any fear, or never turning your back on it, or not looking it in the eye, so that Shuck would walk alongside you on the periphery of your vision.

Studies in the field of medicine and psychology (some of them controversial) suggest that some perfectly sane people have problems interpreting and processing data coming in on the periphery of their vision – "peripheral vision disturbance". Where most people would identify strange optical effects on the edge of their vision as just that – a blur caused by turning your head quickly, or something on the periphery of what you can see that's not quite in focus, some would interpret such data as images of things – or creatures – that they felt they could actually see. Such "disorders" are thought in some cases to be hereditary (that's one of the controversial bits).

It's possible that in some isolated communities with a not very wide gene pool, there were families who interpreted what they saw on the edge of their (uncorrected) vision as something that walked in step with them, but that "disappeared" if they looked directly at it. (We saw a similar phenomenon with the Peasenhall Bigfoot from Chapter 1.) It's not much of an explanation, but attempts to explain Shuck are of the clutching-at-straws variety.

At the north end of Aldeburgh there was said to be a "bogie beast", a Shuck who if you showed no fear would walk to heel with you. But if you weren't walking in his direction, he'd snarl and seize you by your clothes. Hugh Braun, who worked on the 1930s Bungay Castle restoration, writing to folklorist Theodora Brown more than 30 years later, told her "A child of ten whom I used to escort from school [in Bungay]... told me that she knew Old Shuck quite well and that he sometimes fell in beside her as she walked home from school. She had no fear of him and used to be quite sorry when, after a while, he disappeared."[10]

Another Shuck that "vanished" if you looked at it directly was one with which people had many encounters on the Lowestoft-Beccles road. This shuck was seen around the Water Bars and the bridge over the Hundred Stream around the village of Barnby in the 1930s. The creature was referred to as being "big and black" and "having no head." Sometimes it disappeared as soon as you looked at it. In around 1939, a woman tried to grab hold of the black dog near the Hundred Stream bridge (Shuck seems to have had its head on at the time), it instantly shrank to the size of a cat before doing its disappearing act.[11]

Other variations on Black Shuck, also known as Padfoot, Hateful Thing, Old Shug, Skeff, Bogie Beast and Old Shock, (from *scucca*, a Saxon word for a demon) include Shucks that manifest themselves as calves, sheep, donkeys, "things with saucer eyes" or even large black cats. A woman who'd been to school in Bungay in the last years of the nineteenth century recalled many years later a local nursery rhyme about Black Shuck, that went: "Scratch Cat of Bungay/Hanging on the door/Take a stick and knock it down/And it won't come anymore." She insisted Bungay's Shuck was a cat. "Shuck" is also a word for a tramp in the local dialect of Lowestoft, and Tramp's Alley – an old footpath that leads from Gunton Church immediately north of Lowestoft and goes down to the cliffs – is said to be the haunt of Black Shuck.[12]

Old Shock was said to be a calf-sized black dog encountered on footpaths. It threw witnesses around, inflicting bruises and trauma on them. In the eighteenth century, a Shuck was seen on one occasion around the village of Melton, on the River Deben, near the site of the Sutton Hoo Anglo-Saxon ship burial. It had a donkey's head and a smooth, velvety coat. Near the Horse and Groom pub, Goodman Kemp tried to capture it (or tried to shoot it in one version) and whatever-it-was bit his hand before vanishing.

Weirdest of all was the Shuck near Thetford that transformed itself into a white rabbit with flaming red eyes. It's interesting to note that Thetford was known for the Thetford Warrens, the centre of England's rabbit fur industry, until the trade collapsed in the 1920s.[13]

Shuck is often associated with bodies of water. Among the many names to describe Shuck in East Anglia was "Water Dog." Ivan A. W. Bunn's analysis of East of England Shuck traditions in the 1970s noted that the "overwhelming majority" of stories he'd collected took place within a mile of water, particularly streams, bridges and marshes. The village of Burgh, near Woodbridge had a bullock-sized white Shuck, known as "Bath Slough", said to emerge from a boggy pool. It was last seen in 1823.[14]

A select few of the Suffolk Shucks are, according to tradition, the result of witchcraft. Thomas Everard from Halesworth, a witchcraft suspect convicted and hanged thanks to East Anglian Witchfinder General Matthew Hopkins, in his confession stated that while serving as an apprentice he was "frightened by a dog, like a water dog." References to local Shuck traditions were probably inserted into the testimony of East Anglian witchcraft suspects – under torture – to give their confessions local colour and an air of authenticity, to help add credibility to all the nonsense about suckling imps. We'll meet these imps and animal familiars, including a "red dog," from Suffolk's witchcraft trials shortly.

A former Lady Walsingham told ghost story collector James Wentworth Day that she had seen Black Shuck leaping over the wall of Leiston churchyard one night in the last years of the nineteenth century. She and a companion, Lady Rendlesham, had decided to sit up all night in the churchyard of St Margaret's Leiston waiting for Black Shuck to appear. The church is a Victorian building that replaced the medieval church when it was clear that the population of the industrial town had got too big for the previous one. Auto-suggestion seems to have been at work, because eventually Lady Rendlesham – a very old lady by the time she related the event to Wentworth Day in the 1920s, saw a dog with glowing eyes bound up the road and clear the five-foot church wall. She then saw its "sleek shadow go slinking away among the tombstones." While it's nice to think that the power of Lady Rendlesham and Lady Walsingham's shared anticipation somehow conjured a Leiston Shuck into being, as we will see later, a more mundane explanation is more likely.[15]

There is a tale from Lowestoft of an elderly Italian sailor who befriended a local fisher-boy, and who tried to persuade the boy to join him in foreign climes. The Italian eventually left Lowestoft, and asked the boy to look after his large black dog. Boy and dog used to go for a swim every day off Lowestoft's Ness Point – the most easterly point of the mainland UK.

The story goes that one day, the boy and the dog swam out too far, at which point the dog wouldn't let the boy swim in, and attacked him. For a brief moment the dog seemed to transform into the old Italian. The boy was covered in bites, but a passing fishing smack pulled the boy out of the sea, and the dog swam away as if it were a porpoise born in the water.[16]

Bungay and Blythburgh's Strange and Terrible Wonders

Mention "Black Dog" in Suffolk and the name "Bungay" quickly comes up. This town, sticking out into Norfolk where the River Waveney bends, is the epicentre of Suffolk's Black Dog culture, with the town's identity and civic pride closely tied to one particular phantom black dog manifestation, back in Tudor times. Any discussion of the Black Dog of Bungay usually takes in the subject of the Black Dog of Blythburgh, and the scorch marks it allegedly left on the door of Blythburgh Church at the same time as its Bungay appearance on that terrible day in the summer of 1577.

World famous though Bungay's Black Dog is, it's a very atypical Suffolk phantom hellhound. It's doubtful whether it was supposed to be the same phantom animal as the county's shape-shifting death omen, sometimes malevolent, sometimes headless, sometimes protective trickster that is Shuck.

The Bungay and Blythburgh Black Dog stories have come down to us largely via a single pamphlet, *A Straunge and Terrible Wunder wrought very late in the parish Church of Bungay, a town of no great distance from the citie of Norwich*, written by Abraham Fleming and published within weeks of the alleged events it describes. Fleming was the vicar of St Pancras Church in London, so far away from Bungay that he had to explain to his audience where Bungay was, it was a place he probably never visited. He claimed his pamphlet was based on eyewitness accounts. Fleming, who complained about having to supplement his modest living from the Church with other work, was a prolific author.

A *Straunge and Terrible Wunder* relates how on 4 August 1577, a great thunderstorm broke over the market town of Bungay, and over Bungay's St Mary's Church in particular. There really was such a storm on that day, as confirmed by the St Mary's Bungay churchwarden's accounts book, which describes a "great and ferfull tempest" featuring rain, hail and lightning "as was never seen the lyke."

More controversially, Fleming's pamphlet describes how darkness fell during the storm and that "the divel in such a likeness" appeared, galloping through the Church in "incredible haste." Fleming is vague about whether it was a dog or not. He refers to something "like a dog… a dog as they might discerne it," having already related how everything had gone "dark, and yea with such a palpable darkness". Elsewhere in the account the entity that canters through the church is just a "Horrible shaped thing". There's a not very good illustration of a dog on the front of *A Straunge and Terrible…* but author Christopher Reeve [17] suggests this is because the London printer happened to have a woodblock of a dog handy.

In Fleming's account, there's a service in progress when the "Horrible thing" charges through St Mary's Church on its trail of destruction, and the church is filled with the congregation. Fleming has the Black Dog seize two parishioners kneeling in prayer, after which he "wrung the necks of them bothe" and they "strangely dyed". The beast also inflicted some unusual wounds (burns?) on the back of another man who survived. The clerk of the church, who'd gone outside to clear the guttering (in the middle of a church service!) was thrown to the ground by a violent clap of thunder, and the church clock was "broken in pieces."

Then the action moves to Blythburgh, 12 miles away according to the pamphlet, although the road routes are a little different now, the AA Mileage Calculator estimates it's almost 14 miles today (21 km). Back in 1577, Blythburgh was a prosperous port on the River Blyth, although the silting up of the river and a devastating fire have turned it into a not very big village today, still with one of the biggest churches in Suffolk. Fleming describes how on the same August morning "the like thing entred, in the same shape and similitude" and again ran amok through Holy Trinity Blythburgh's busy church service. He appeared swinging from a beam, before he "slew two men and a lad", burning another on the hand. Other Blythburgh parishioners were "blasted" before the Black Dog flew out of the church in a "hideous and hellish likeness." Scorch marks on the inside of St Mary's Blythburgh's door are still visible today, said to be the work of the pyromaniac Black Dog. More recently, Lowestoft rock band The Darkness immortalised the 1577 assault on Blythburgh's church door in their song *Black Shuck,* and can you guess which four-letter word they found to rhyme with "Shuck" in the chorus?[18]

The *Straunge and Terrible* narrative ends with the observation that it was no doubt "a spectacle of God's judgement which the fire of our iniquities has kindled," followed by a "necessary prayer" to "deliver us from evil, Amen!" In the midst of the trauma and confusion of the English Reformation, there were so many of Queen Elizabeth II's spies and informers monitoring print media, so Fleming refrained from saying exactly what recent local "iniquities" had displeased God. But Reeve notes[19] that the events in the pamphlet were recorded just after St Mary's Bungay's Puritan churchwardens had taken down a partition between the church and chancel, contrary to the "Queen Majesty's laws" and the wishes of the parishioners.

There are a number of problems with Fleming's story. Hollinshed's history book *The Chronicles of England, Scotland and Ireland*, whose first edition was in 1578, had a revised 1586 edition to which Fleming contributed. It mentions the incident, with a "tempest" of "lightning" in Blythburgh, with something like a "flash of lightning" and "cracks of thunder" that cause the damage and leaves scorch marks. This account is more detailed; it could be first-hand in places, and could be based partly on parish records. There's little mention of a dog, and there's less attention to Bungay, with only a mention of the death of "two men who sat in the belfry" with one man injured when "a clap of thunder" blew apart the "wheels of the clocks." Satanic black hounds are conspicuous by the absence from the account in *The Chronicles*. None of the contemporary French and Flemish pamphlets on the same incident, which include *Histoire Marvellouse,* (A Story of Marvels) refer to a dog at all. Continental sources that refer to the incidents all state that the deaths were caused by lightning.

The parish records of St Mary's Bungay include a payment of eight pence to four women who laid out the bodies of those killed by falling bells in the storm. The records refer to John

The Black Dog of Bungay on the Town Council offices (top left), at the Bungay Black Dogs FC training ground at Ditchingham (top right); said-to-be Black Shuck's claw marks, visible as dark horizontal streaks on the right-hand side of these double doors of Blythburgh Church (right), St Mary's Bungay churchyard, scene of a 1970s Shuck encounter (below).

Fuller and Adam Walker, slain "in the tempest in the bells. 4 Aug. 1577." The "bells" is the belfry or bell tower, and ringing church bells to frighten away evil spirits during a thunderstorm was still standard procedure in Elizabethan England.

It seems that Fuller and Walker had rushed to the church belfry to ring the bells when the storm started, probably in an otherwise empty church. The parish records suggest they were killed not by burns or strangulation by a Black Dog but by lighting hitting the bell tower, sending the church clock and bits of the tower collapsing on top of them. St Mary's Bungay's burial register records Adam Walker and John Fuller, "stryeken deade both within the steple of the Churche" while its churchwarden's register has an entry on repairs to the belfry, with brief detail on parishioners killed or injured "in dyv'se places of the legs & feet".

The citizens of Bungay were angered by Fleming's sensationalist account of their local tragedy. There were complaints to the Privy Council and the Bishop of London about unlicensed "pamphlettes" concerning an incident in "Bongay… neere unto Norwich," which is probably *A Straunge and Terrible Wunder*. A local guide to Blythburgh suggests that the burn marks on its church's door aren't even lightning damage, but made with a red hot poker by a farrier in the days when the church was commandeered by Cromwell's New Model Army in the late 1640s.The church briefly became a farrier's shop for shoeing the army's horses.[20]

Parishioners were visited upon/By a curious beast

A remarkably similar incident to that in the *Straunge and Terrible Wunder* occurred some sixty years later, and points to a natural phenomenon as its cause, though a phenomenon no less exotic than phantom Black Dogs. The Great Thunderstorm of Widecombe-in-the-Moor in Devon struck a busy parish church in 1638 during a service just like the one described by Fleming. A contemporary woodcut shows a dark sky, thunder, hail, bits of the tower falling off and a ball of flame escaping from a cloud and rushing towards a church.[21]

This ball of flame burst through a window of the church, tore off some of the roof and killed four of the 300-odd worshippers, injuring 60 and severely damaging the church. The vicar's wife in particular was "burnt in a very pitiful manner." Several of those killed at Widecombe – including a rather normal-sounding dog – died from being thrown against pillars and walls or out of the door of the church with great force. Sound familiar?

Widecombe legend subsequently grew up about the Devil, appearing as a man with cloven hooves riding a black horse, calling at the nearby Tavistock Inn, paying for his ale with coins that then turned to dried leaves on his way to capture and carry off to Hell local gambler Jan Reynolds. But the consensus today is that Widecombe was hit by ball lightning – an exotic and not yet completely understood form of lighting, but lightning nonetheless. The Widecombe parishioners seem to have been thrown about by a concussion wave generated when the ball lightning struck.

Could the events attributed to a Black Dog at Bungay and Blythburgh in fact have been ball lightning, leaving strange burns and victims "blasted" by waves of high-pressure air?

Other historical accounts of what could have been ball lightning striking churches include a "dreadful cloud with thunderstorms and lightning" from which emerged a "dog of immense size" that ran to and fro on the altar of Trier Cathedral in Germany in 1160, and at Danbury Church in Essex in 1402, in which the Devil appeared in the likeness of a grey hooded monk, burning someone as it passed between their legs amid thunder and chaos, and destroying some of the steeple. The clock mechanism at Godshill Church on the Isle of Wight was apparently wrecked by ball lightning entering the church sometime in the eighteenth century.[22]

A "diabolical dog" came into the church at Messina, Italy in 1341, destroying some of the altar furnishings, and within the living memory of some of Fleming's contemporaries, a "tempest of thunder and lightning" hit St Nicholas's Church in Cornhill in the City of London in 1538, accompanied by a "thing of ugly shape was seen to come in at the south window", leaving a scorch mark resembling a lion's claw. The bells of St Nicholas rang of their own accord, apparently a common occurrence in such mega-storms. Back in Suffolk, on 8 February 1906 a huge fireball badly damaged the eastern end of Barsham church, with an enormous yellow-white "circle of light" appearing in the sky, according to one witness.[23]

As our various church-bothering ball lightning incidents show, in the confusion parishioners often interpret what they see as a Satanic dog or other apparition. So at Bungay and Blythburgh?

Our church-bothering Black Dogs are nothing like the usually more benign Suffolk Shucks. They bring no portents of death, only death itself, they don't talk or walk in step in a protective way, or fade or vanish, or change size or shape, they just leave a trail of destruction. They are believed to be the Devil himself in canine form, nothing like the trickster spirit that Shuck usually is – leaving the odd bite and scaring the living daylights out of travellers but delivering nothing like the Black Dog's death toll at Blythburgh or Bungay.

Doggie entities – more like Shuck than the Terrible Wunder appearing on that fateful day in 1577 – continued to be reported in both Blythburgh and Bungay. In Bungay in particular, there were "many sightings in Bungay since – none of which resulted in any deaths," according to Bungay Museum curator Christopher Reeve.

There were said to be sightings sometime before 1978 around Blythburgh along the A12 road that runs through the Western edge of the village and a policeman by the name of Craig Jenkins was said to have seen Black Shuck somewhere around the A12 around Blythburgh at some point in relatively recent times.[24]

Shuck researcher Ivan A. W. Bunn received a letter in the autumn of 1973, from a man from Lincolnshire with no previous knowledge of East Anglian black dog traditions. He told how he was laying new drainage pipes across the Blythburgh Marshes behind the massive Holy Trinity Church at Blythburgh (so huge it's known as "the Cathedral of the Marshes") when he suddenly heard a dog loudly panting behind him. He turned round and there was… nothing. It was only when he told some locals in the pub that they produced a book full of local Shuck stories. As we will see, a couple visiting nearby Dunwich Forest a quarter of a century later who heard panting or growling no longer assumed it was Black Shuck but an Alien Big Cat.

Many of the twentieth century Shuck encounters around Bungay were a short stroll over the Waveney bridge and into Ditchingham, minutes over the Norfolk border. The Bungay Black Dogs FC football teams have their pitch there. Ernest Whiteland of Ditchingham saw a shape come towards him that fell into step with him then disappeared while he was walking home one night from very nearby Bungay in 1938. An old man was walking his bike uphill when a huge, shaggy dog with fiery red eyes came towards him, then passed right through him. This could possibly have been the same sighting as that experienced by a man from Aldeburgh near the Ditchingham railway station in that year. There were several other contemporary Ditchingham sightings, possibly confused versions of the ones above. Witnesses described the Ditchingham Shuck as around 28 inches tall, black and shaggy with large glowing red eyes.[25]

A Mrs Hall saw the Bungay Dog running through the streets of Bungay twice, but so fast she couldn't see much detail. She recalled that in 1917 she saw it pass through the solid door of Holy Trinity Church (a short distance down the road from St Mary's, scene of the sixteenth century carnage). She also witnessed the Bungay Dog near the town allotments some time in the 1950s, and saw it disappear there.[26]

Christopher Reeve, an expert on Bungay's Black Dog, notes that articles in the regional press in the 1930s and 1940s led to a "barrage" of accounts, and Ivan Bunn also noted in 2015 when I bumped into him at London's Liverpool Street station that press reports of Shuck sparked "waves" of sightings in the 1970s.

Back in 1977, Ivan Bunn, who'd already been studying Black Shuck for two years, insisted that "this phantom is not purely a legend but has been repeatedly right up to the present day." Suffolk Shuck reports were ridiculously frequent in the 1970s, possibly as a result of it being a golden age of paranormal book and magazine publishing, when people were on the case both locally and globally as never before. The 1970s seems to have been a renaissance for Shuck too, although also his swan song.

While Bunn's researches were turning up "hitherto unrecorded characteristics" in Seventies Shuck sightings (as far as he was aware, at least), he said that contemporary reports usually don't mention some of Shuck's more spectacular aspects. The Seventies Shuck tended not to be headless, not to have one eye in the centre of its head, not to have horns, not to wear chains, nor to resemble a calf or grow in size or shape-shift or foretell deaths either. He didn't even seem to walk in step with witnesses that much.

Nor was he bear-sized or calf-sized, even his red eyes weren't mentioned so much anymore. He was increasingly just a strange, rather big dog that tended to appear out of nowhere. He would still do his vanishing act, although increasingly this was just reported by witnesses as not being able to work out where he could have gone. Instances of latter-day Shucks vanishing into thin air, or "flickering" in and out of existence are rare. Modern Shuck witnesses were left wondering whether they'd in fact seen just a huge, black but otherwise ordinary dog.[27]

They came thick and fast, the Seventies Shuck sightings, particularly around Lowestoft, where Black Shuck chronicler Ivan Bunn is still based. Observant readers will already have noted that Mrs Whitehead's death-portent Shuck experience in the streets of Bungay, the panting of the invisible Shuck heard on Blythburgh marshes, and the string of Shuck sightings by PC Jenkins and others around the A12 at Blythburgh were all from that decade.

Peter Jennings's *Haunted Suffolk* records a sighting in the early 1970s of a large white dog seen by a woman who was walking in Beccles cemetery, near the Crown Inn. The dog faded away as she approached. Keith Flory contacted the Hidden East Anglia team to tell them about the night in "early 1973" when, going home to Woodbridge from a night shift not long after midnight, he was followed by a Great Dane-sized Black Shuck who bounded after his motorbike all the way down the town's Old Barrack Road – effortlessly keeping up with him all the way until Flory finally lost his pursuer in Seckford Hall Road by the A12.

A woman spotted Black Shuck in the bushes at Lowestoft's Belle Vue Park in 1975, although her husband saw nothing. Folklorist Theo Brown, also based in Lowestoft, went and inspected for himself the locations of Suffolk Black Shuck reports, and claims to have had an encounter of her own with the Black Dog in the churchyard of St Mary's Bungay in the 1970s. And I was contacted via Twitter by Jim Bradley, a Norfolk-based birdwatcher, who told me "my friend's father who I would say is now in his 60s" encountered the Black Dog himself "in Orford in the late 70s… He and a friend were out walking and a black dog, calf-sized, wandered onto the track and stared at them. It eventually lumbered off into the scrub. They followed its path but the beast had seemingly disappeared, no trace whatsoever."[28]

Not only did Shuck's supernatural powers begin to diminish around this time, people eventually started to become embarrassed to say they'd seen him at all. By the early twenty-first century, Reeve noted that many felt "awkward" about recounting their Shuck experiences. By then, with the exception of local five-year old kids, they increasingly feared "ridicule."

Around 2012 a film production company approached Reeve about a Black Shuck feature film – a taxi driver confirmed to me that he'd been ferrying people around scouting for locations, but it since seems to have been trapped in what the film industry jargon calls Development Hell – in development but not progressing to production.

By then, Reeve told me, he couldn't find anyone who would give him new accounts of Shuck experiences. Small children still seem to see Shuck locally, or at least have no inhibitions about relating other people's sightings. Reeve's own then five-year-old niece told him, "But he's alive – I saw him!" And after his talk at Bungay Primary School, one girl told Reeve, "My granny's seen him." There were similar comments from other pupils.[29]

There was excitement in June 2014 when it was announced that "Devil Dog Black Shuck Returns!" and Shuck was all over the *Daily Mail* ("Who let the Devil Dogs Out?") and the BBC One Show. A spokesperson for Dig Ventures, the company that organised a 2014 Suffolk archaeological dig that found the skeleton of a big dog, explained it was all the result of a "throwaway comment in a parish newspaper" that "matured into a fully-fledged monster tale eagerly lapped up by the world's media."[30]

Leiston gets a bad press, possibly because of the presence of the decommissioned Sizewell A and the active Sizewell B nuclear power stations just down the road, and because it's an industrial town with little of the rural charm of the posh holiday resorts such as Aldeburgh, a mere two miles away. Leiston has the Long Shop Museum with a working steam engines, while the imposing ruins of Leiston Abbey are a couple of minutes down the B1112. The dig at Leiston Abbey in the summer of 2014 did indeed turn up the bones of a seven-foot long dog, excavated in one of the Abbey's demolished monastic kitchen buildings, and there was speculation that the dog in question may have been contemporary with the Bungay and Blythburgh incidents in the 1570s and somehow inspired A *Straunge and Terrible Wunder*.

After the furore subsided, and radiocarbon dating was carried out on the remains, it turned out to have been a "huge farm" dog, most likely from the beginning of the nineteenth century. In the words of Dig Ventures, "an exceptionally large male canine skeleton" of a dog that was elderly, with worn teeth and arthritis in its joints.

Dig Ventures later estimated the dog skeleton's height as 72 cm from shoulder to floor, putting it in the range of Great Danes or mastiffs. Radiocarbon dating put it "either 1650-1690, 1730-1810 or post 1920". The rubble in the trench it was buried in suggested the dog "was alive at the end of the eighteenth century." It was at a time when dogs were beginning to be not just work animals but treasured pets – an attempt by Parliament to levy a "dog tax" had been seen off due to the outcry among dog-owners, and the sense that dogs were members of the family had taken hold. The Leiston Abbey dog lived long into retirement and was given a decent burial, suggesting it was much missed. No hellhounds, then.[30]

I have not been actively seeking Shuck sightings, but while gathering witness testimony on Suffolk's big cats (we'll meet them later), a couple of original Shuck stories from the past thirty-odd years did come to my attention. Alan Murdie, who writes the Ghostwatch column

PART 2 – HERE BE DRAGONS

Big Dog Ferry, Beccles (top), a diabolical hound on the Guildhall at Eye (above left); wolf on Bury's Sicklesmere Roundabout (above); Old Barrack Road, Woodbridge, was the scene of a Shuck motorbike chase; Shuck jumped over the wall of Leiston churchyard (below left) and a black greyhound on the coat of arms of Needham Market in the church at nearby Barking.

in *Fortean Times,* recalled travelling by car with a friend at night from Bury to Colchester in 1986. Somewhere around the "back roads" of the Suffolk-Essex border, they slowed down to approach a rural crossroads where his friend was startled to see an "enormous dog" sitting up, close to the four-way sign by the crossroads as if guarding something. Murdie himself didn't see anything. Murdie's own investigations into ghost lore revealed that Shuck had a more benign reputation south of the Suffolk-Essex border, where sightings of him were rarer.[31]

We've already heard Jim Bradley's account of a suspected Shuck of the Seventies seen by his father's friend in Orford. And one contributor to this book related how "a guy" out near Coddenham, 8 miles north of Ipswich on the A14, "told me a story about a friend of his who took his dog for a walk on a windy, rainy day and they were apparently chased by a big dog, as soon as it got nearer to them it would vanish and the process started again. I assumed this was all bullshit but he is adamant it happened."[32]

"My dad saw Shuck in the Seventies"

An interesting pattern in recent Suffolk Shuck testimony is emerging, best described as "my dad saw Shuck in the seventies". (I wasn't seeking Shuck testimony, but when word got out that I was after Suffolk big cat sightings, unsolicited Shuck sightings started to come my way.) All my informants are male, and all the testimony is secondhand – sons describing the Shuck sightings of their fathers in the 1970s. As noted earlier, that halcyon flared-trousered era of chopper bikes and kipper ties also saw the most recent peak in Shuck sightings.

A couple of Shuck informants said they'd never before communicated to anybody else what their father had related to them in the Shuck department, one informant felt they could only tell me because their father had since passed away. Some informants expressed regret at not having pressed their dear departed dads for more on their Shuck sightings, or mourned that fact that they couldn't get their dads to talk about the incident. It's as if there's a complicated Shuck-experience component to father-and-son relationships in the Curious County.

The other pattern emerging in these testimonies of seventies Shuck sightings is more the absence of a pattern – they are all very, very different. While the magical powers of Shuck seem to have been gradually shaved away over time, the variety of shuck encounters has if anything increased.

A man from Rattlesden told me his father, back in the 1970s, was driving on the A140 from Ipswich to Stowmarket one night when he collided with Black Shuck in the dark. He got out of the car to take a look and found... nothing. The next day there was a strange deposit on the bonnet of his car, "like eggshells."

Another bizarre encounter was from a man identifying himself as "Major Pickle" on the Twitter platform. He disclosed that his father had (eventually) told him that on Sunday 5th August 1973, he (Major Pickle's father) and a friend were driving from Henstead to Bawdsey to go canoeing. Henstead's a small, mostly agricultural village is immediately west of the A12, between Wrentham and Kessingland. It's now best known for the Henstead Exotic Garden and for its Arts and Crafts Centre.

Coming round a corner on the road near Henstead, the two canoeists saw a huge black dog with something like a mane standing in the road, just looking at them. It "seemed to be there and was just gone" according to Pickle's account many years later. When his dad got out of the car to look at it there was nothing to be seen except for the (then) open fields in the area. It was what happened next that made those two 1970s canoe enthusiasts think that he'd had a brush with a beast of ill omen. The friend with whom my informant's dad used to go canoeing had always mapped and researched their canoeing route. They'd regularly been canoeing off Bawdsey before, but "they never encountered anything like this". A freak tidal whirlpool came up and their canoe went right into it, they almost drowned. They capsized and were washed up on the then restricted Ministry of Defence-owned Bawdsey Island Radar Station, "an interesting experience during the Cold War". As a result of inadvertently trespassing on a Cold War-era defence installation, they kept quiet about all the events of that day.

Major Pickle said of his dad's encounter on the road near Henstead, "To the day he died he was convinced it was Shuck and the story never changed in any way." He asked his dad if it could have been a big cat, he insisted it was a really big dog.[33]

While "my dad saw Shuck in the seventies" accounts are still emerging over 40 years later is surprisingly common, more recent accounts are rare.

A post in 2009 on the Centre for Fortean Zoology's blog from "Woody" related his encounter in the summer of 1994. Along with his then new dog Max, he used to regularly go for a run by "Martlesham Creek, across a small boating club and into farm land that ran parallel to the Church lane at Martlesham" where horses "were grazed there by the river Deben, that runs to nearby Woodbridge." It was there that Woody "started to notice that Max began to run very close to my feet almost tripping me… I was instantly aware of being watched, checking behind me about 50 yards back stood a huge black dog, my own wouldn't take his eyes off it. It stood stock still, watching us ... (I) put my dog on a lead" and walked out of sight of it. "Max turned again and growled back the way we'd just came. There stood the big black dog again... I began to worry a bit. So grabbing a solid stick… I carried on walking." There followed three or four more sightings of the same black dog, always the same distance away, always with the same stance, and "with me very nervously looking over my shoulder until we got level with Martlesham Church, when Max turned, growled and practically broke the lead in his eagerness for a fight only, in true, good ghost story fashion, there was nothing there!"

Woody and Max then "ran like hell the remaining mile or so home and locked the doors." Woody admitted "the dog I saw may just have been someone's… be it a bloody big one, but I like to think that Max saw Shuck off."[34]

Shuck witnesses of the twenty-first century are more likely to concede that it's just possible it may have been an ordinary pet or gone-feral dog they saw. When a "shaken driver" reported how he "came face to face with what he fears was a white wolf stalking the back roads of Suffolk" in November 2009, he believed he'd seen a flesh-and-blood escaped exotic animal rather than a Suffolk Shuck phantom animal. Nigel Stebbing was reportedly able to photograph the "white wolf" from the window of his van at Kersey, near Hadleigh. The driver didn't think he'd seen a phantom dog or hellhound.[35]

From Rendlesham Forest comes a 1980s story of an encounter by Paul and Jane Jennings shortly before they got married. Their Shuck experience occurred "on a cold winter's afternoon in 1983", as related by Nick Redfern in his article "Weirdness in the woods". Paul and Jane "were terrified by the sudden manifestation… of 'a big black dog'. … walking along a pathway… they came face to face." Said Jane, "It was almost like it was waiting for us.'" The beast's head "was clearly canine in appearance… much larger than that of any normal dog. Yet... its body seemed to exhibit characteristics that were distinctly feline" although these characteristics weren't named. It had an "eerily mournful expression upon its face… Suddenly, the beast began to 'flicker on and off for four or five times', then finally vanished… an overwhelming smell that reminded the pair of 'burning metal'" lingered afterwards.[36]

Shuck is supposed to be even more common on the fens of Norfolk than he is in Suffolk, especially in Breckland, and some Norfolk Shucks sound scarier. The Peddar's Way footpath in Breckland has a Black Dog all of its own. Other Norfolk Shuck variations include one at Geldeston that has fiery eyes and hangs around the churchyard, and a Shuck by the River Waveney[37] that only growls and gets violent if you show fear. Coltishall, North Norfolk, has another headless Shuck, a bridge-dwelling dog. A Shuck encountered by a woman in Great Yarmouth in the nineteenth century was a solid animal that stood on its hind legs – she felt its paw on her shoulder and smelt its "noxious" breath on her. *East Anglian Daily Times* columnist Martin Newell was told by a Norfolk local to "be careful" when writing about Shuck, and claimed a woman had told him of a Shuck encounter she'd had returning from a dance in Cromer early one summer morning in the 1950s. The Shuck in Overstrand, on the North Norfolk coast, was in different variants either a cyclopean Shuck with one eye in the centre of its head, or headless, or it had two huge eyes and a rough coat.[38]

Essex Shucks – they occur as far south as far as Malden in London's suburbs – include an exploding Shuck that set fire to a horse-drawn wagon at Hatfield Peverell. Signs of similar Shuck pyrotechnics were reported in an undisclosed East Anglian location in *Notes and Queries* for 1850, where a witness showed his neighbours a spot where Black Shuck had been seen, with a patch of ground looked "as if gunpowder had been exploded there." Hockley in Essex is the location of a 1958 encounter in which an old lady was joined by a "gigantic black hound" walking in step with her before it suddenly disappeared. And there are 1930s accounts of a midwife cycling home through lanes near Tolleshunt Darcy, Essex, and experiencing a huge black dog that effortlessly kept up with her bicycle.[39]

The science and psychology of Black Dog apparitions

Simon Sherwood, Professor of Psychology at the University of Northampton, has studied Black Dog apparitions. (He doesn't use the local term Shuck, as his research covers the whole of the UK.) At a talk at the Centre for Fortean Zoology's Weird Weekend 2006 convention, Sherwood noted that the Black Dog is well known in folklore but has not been examined from a psychological perspective.

Prof Sherwood said that in other parts of England outside East Anglia, the Black Dog is also known as Barguest (a word used Up North to describe a shape-shifting goblin) and its saucer-sized eyes can be yellow instead of the usual red. Other characteristics of Black Dogs across England that Sherwood described include shape-shifting into a man rattling chains or dissipating into a black cloud. (The nearest chain-rattling Shuck to Suffok I've come across is the dog-shaped one at Gorleston, on the Norfolk bank of the River Waveney that wore rattling chains hung round its neck, and which threw a man over a hedge with great force.) Some beyond-Suffolk Shucks have large ears, or they could be horns. Some are transparent, some ignore the observer completely "as if on some kind of automatic patrol."[40]

Sherwood differentiates three types of Black Dog. Firstly, there are shape-shifting dogs associated with a particular place, Black Dogs whose appearance foretells a death in a particular family, and Black Dogs who appear on a particular day. In a classic case from Uplyme, Devon in 1858 a witness walking down Dog Lane was followed by a red-eyed dog that grew in size up to the tree line before turning into a cloud. Folklore researcher Theo Brown collected similar stories from the area up to the 1950s.

Prof Sherwood's own interest comes from a bedroom encounter as a child, in which a horned dog with yellow eyes bounded towards his bed before vanishing. This encounter appeared to be confirmed by a local story about a Black Dog in a poltergeist haunting. Sherwood gets postings to his website from people who still encounter Black Dogs but don't know about the legend, or who live in countries that don't even have a Black Dog tradition. A posting to his site in April 2006 from a witness to an encounter in St Peter's Church Yard, Brackley (Northamptonshire) described a "large black shaggy dog", possibly with horns, running at him before it was "enveloped in darkness and faded away."

The big question in apparition research is – according to Prof Sherwood – are apparitions objective or subjective? Are apparitions physical in some sense? Are they actually there? Sometimes apparitions such as Black Dogs are seen only by one person in a group, Prof. Sherwood feels "your electromagnetic field environment in certain states of mind can see an apparition." Then there's hypnogogic imagery (vivid images just as you go to sleep, often accompanied by sleep paralysis), a phenomenon that's well documented, and there is also a credible case for Black Dogs being a "projected archetype of our fears." Prof Sherwood also admits that while magnetic field experiments can reproduce some of the phenomena associated with, for example, ghosts, they have never been able to reproduce any Black Dog effects in a lab. "We need to look more closely at the types of people who experience Black Dogs, and the circumstances of the apparition occurring," he concludes.

How magic works – allegedly

We've looked at Shucks attributed to witchcraft, like the "Water Dog" whose appearance was used in evidence at a witch-trial, or the one Lady Walsingham conjured up in Leiston.

Simon Jones – Britain's only openly pagan magistrate – was in the audience for Sherwood's talk at Weird Weekend 2006. Jones confessed to being a modern white witch, and said he had conjured up thought forms – of skeletal monks, although no Black Dogs as yet – to scare people away from sites he was using to perform magic. According to Jones, such magically-produced thought forms could be brought into being from a distance and could "like a computer programme," act independently once created. Such thought-form apparitions would have to be remotely "recharged" with magic energy from time to time.

I have a problem accepting the existence of magic at all. But Jones's matter-of-fact-sounding model explaining Black Shuck and other ghostly apparitions as magically-created thought forms used by witches (white or otherwise) to guard sites used for their rituals is a better one, or at least a less bad one, than any others I've encountered. It would certainly explain the "automatic patrol" mode of Shucks that appear to walk in step with witnesses before vanishing, and why they're terrifying dogs or sinister, hooded monks – their appearance is, in the manner of a *Scooby-Doo* episode, to scare people away from a particular place. Such entities could linger in an area long after a wizard had use for them.

I caught up with Simon Jones, Justice of the Peace, at the 2014 Weird Weekend, and he elaborated on the pagan white magic model of created thought-forms. He said he wasn't sure whether magicians and wizards like himself actually created these pre-programmed magical spectral guards, or whether they just tapped into and controlled something that was already there, something which for convenience he called "nature spirits."

He added that different people might see "nature spirits" differently – when one of these entities is out and about, some might experience it as being a black dog, or a little man or an

Ness Point in Lowestoft (top left,) the mainland UK's most easterly point, where legend tells how a swimming Shuck tried to drown a local boy. Nearby Wilde Score (top right) was home to a "White Dawg" phenomenon. Logo of Shuck Creative packaging (above left), based near Ipswich. Walberswick's The Black Dog Deli (above right). The dragon slain by St George on this chest at St Edmund's Church, Southwold, looks remarkably like a huge dog.

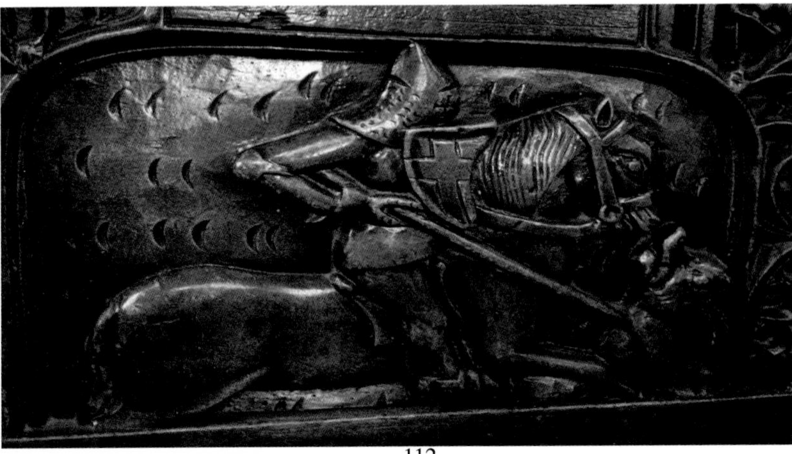

eight-foot shambling ape thing. Jones said cowled, ghostly monks and black dogs were among the typical apparitions that magic-users like himself either conjured into being or tapped into. He was interested when I told him the story of one of East Anglia's most bizarre Shucks.

This is the apparition from Clopton Hall, just south of Chedburgh in West Suffolk. A legend states that St Felix, the Burgundian bishop who brought Christianity to the Kingdom of East Anglia had a hoard of gold buried at Clopton Hall, and he instructed a monk and a dog to guard the buried treasure. Over the years these two entities merged into a single presence, a monk with a dog's head that guards St Felix's treasure for all eternity. In other versions of the story, the site of the former Clopton Hall was said to have been near Woodbridge, or elsewhere in Rattlesden parish, and the mysterious guardian of the treasure is the other way round – a gigantic hound with a monk's head, and it lives up Whitefoot Lane. There is said to be a White Shuck in the vicinity of nearby Woodbridge, which may have something do to with that Whitefoot Lane street name.

Listening to Jones's matter-of-fact description of magicking up phantoms to guard ritual sites, Clopton's dog-headed monk does sound like a couple of such magical guardians gone horribly wrong, like a corrupted computer file. This explanation involves suspension of disbelief, but when making sense of Shuck we are in straw-clutching territory.[41]

When did Black Dogs become black big cats?

Several commentators have noted that Alien Big Cats – often shiny black leopards (we'll meet them later) – seem to replace Black Shuck around the time his recent decline began. Mark Mower –whose *Suffolk Tales of Murder and Mystery* examined Shuck stories and some of the earlier Suffolk big cat reports – noticed this, as did Merrily Harpur in *Mystery Big Cats*. Here she puts forward the idea that Britain's alien big cats aren't flesh-and-blood either, but they're a very different kind of spirit animal, interacting with humans in a very different way to Black Dogs. We've heard the old Black Shuck nursery rhyme from Bungay that called Shuck a "Scratch Cat", and the couple in Rendlesham who saw a "flickering" Black Dog in 1980s Rendlesham noted its long face (like a leopard's) and its many "feline" characteristics.

This "Alien Big Cats replacing Black Dogs" phenomenon isn't just confined to Suffolk either. Glen Vaudrey, who's studied both Black Dog traditions and big cat sightings in the Western Isles of Scotland, notes that most recorded encounters with the islands' "faerie dogs" – usually in the dark – happened before 1949, and after that. "Mystery black dog hauntings on the lower part of the Hebridean island of Mull seem to have ceased, to be replaced – apparently – by sightings of a mysterious black cat."[42]

Shuck is much more than a ghost. In tradition, he doesn't seem to have ever been a mortal dog that came back from the dead as a phantom; he's more interesting than that. Shuck seems always to have been there, as a spirit, at least since the Vikings arrived, although claims that Shuck is a Norse introduction to our shores seem to have been exaggerated. Just as Shuck encounters have become less weird in recent years, so have more mundane ghost dogs proliferated in Suffolk, often accompanied by human masters, which Shuck (if you'll excuse the pun) would never have been seen dead with.

Suffolk ghost dogs include the disembodied head of a Jack Russell – no date given – reported by one old lady at Great Barton (it's just outside Bury.) The Jack Russell head floated about the correct distance from the ground you'd expect it to be.

The ghostly howl of a wolf was said to be heard whenever snow was on the ground in Woolpit, said to be the place where the last wolf was killed in England, or at least in East Anglia. There's a problem with that story. Woolpit is more likely to take its name from a local Anglo-Saxon leader called Wulfa. A mysterious wolf (a ghost?) was found guarding the severed head of the East Anglian King Edmund the Martyr, first patron saint of England, after the Danes captured him somewhere around Hoxne in 869, and the coat of arms of Bury St Edmunds used to have a wolf guarding the severed head on it. For reasons of taste, the former county town of West Suffolk now displays only a howling wolf, while the statue of a howling wolf on Bury's Sicklesmere Roundabout guards only a more tasteful empty crown. [43]

Residents of Wilde Score, an alley going downhill from the High Street to the coast in Lowestoft, have experienced a ghostly "White Dawg" phenomenon, and TS Farm Stores of Tonning Street, Lowestoft, was the setting for a haunting in 2010 by a young man with a black dog, accompanied by banging sounds. Lowestoft's Tramp's Alley, also a Shuck haunt, was the location of a man with a dog who suddenly appeared a short distance from a group of campers on a early morning walk in 1987 – the man was staring out to sea, and then man and dog both vanished. North Parade – the road behind the promenade at Southwold – is the alleged haunt of ghostly woman walking a dog. They are said to stroll together down the hill towards the beach, having been drowned in a sudden tide some years ago.[44]

Black Dog culture

Whether or not there is any substance in Shuck stories, Suffolk has a strong Black Dog culture; he's a great source of local pride and part of the county's identity. There's Shuck Creative, a company that design luxury packaging just north of Ipswich, and Woodbridge has a Shuck Food Festival every autumn. Ipswich has a Black Dog Motorcycle Club (it didn't have a black dog on its logo last time I looked), and Hellhound Brewery, which recently moved from Hadleigh to Brampton, brews a Black Shuck Porter, a dark "breakfast stout" beer with a suitably red-eyed hellhound's head on the label. The Black Dog Deli in Walberswick (now also with a branch in Halesworth) serves excellent salads, and picnics to go that include a "black doggy bag", although it seems to be slightly taking the micky out of the Black Shuck legend by having a harmless-looking Scottie dog as its logo. Among its products on sale is Howling Black Dog Chilli, all the way from an industrial estate in Martlesham near Woodbridge. A poster on the wall of a car park among empty warehouses on Ipswich Waterfront once assured those who park there that Black Dogs Security are patrolling, although at the time of writing their website seemed to be down. The Blackdog Antique Centre operates in Halesworth, having moved from Bungay. Also in Halesworth is Shuck Brewery, a mircrobrewery producing organic pale ale, its logo features a black dog with a frothing pint glass.

Bungay, epicentre of Black Dog culture, is today home to the Bungay Black Dog FC football teams (their ground is actually just over the Norfolk border in Ditchingham), and the Black Dog Running Club. The Black Dog was essential to the economic revival of Bungay in the depression of 1933, when the silted-up Strathe Navigation (the River Waveney) closed to trade. Bungay's Black Dog culture owes much to Dr Leonard Cane, who set up social housing in the town and invented the Black Dog tradition to bring in much-needed tourism, and possibly to overcome resistance to the installation of the first electric street lamp by putting a Black Dog weathervane on top of it. (It was moved later to the top of the market town's Buttercross in the market square.) The story about the Black Dog appearing at the ruins of Bungay Castle, and it being the "transmogrified" soul of the evil local medieval landowner the Earl of Bigod, seems to have been made up at around that time. There are Black Dog street signs with the characteristic lightning bolt in Bungay today, he appears – running with his tongue hanging out – in the town's coat of arms and on the ironwork of the gate in front of the tourist office and the tiny Bungay Museum. In the now decommissioned St Mary's Church, Bungay there's a modern tapestry of him running amok among a terrified sixteenth-century congregation.[45]

Who let the dog out?

There is a simpler explanation for many Shuck encounters – actual living dogs, whether domestic ones on the loose or feral dogs. Among early reports in the wave of black leopard sightings in Ipswich in 1996 was an animal seen by many witnesses in the Kelly Road neighbourhood. One local resident expressed the view that what they had seen was in fact a black Labrador named Whiskey that (according to the local resident, at least) "everyone knew" was allowed to roam the streets 24 hours a day by his owner. Christopher Reeve has an elegant explanation for the Black Dogs seen amid the chaos of lighting strikes at Bungay and Blythburgh churches back in 1577. Dogs were often brought to church in those days – the St Mary's Bungay warden's accounts record payment in the 1560s for "driving dogs" out of the church. It's conceivable a parishioner's dog panicked in the chaos and ran around biting people. [46]

I have seen working Suffolk farm dogs – sometimes with a collar, sometimes without – let out for a while by farmers, safe in the knowledge they won't wander far, and told to "go and earn your keep" by doing their bit for rabbit population management. Far from running amok, these working dogs have been tucking into rabbits when I've encountered them. When they're done, the dogs will let themselves back in. The practice still seems quite common.

One can imagine Ladies Rendlesham and Walsingham in an age before dog licences or dog food, seeing a Leiston local's perfectly well-trained dog who'd been let out for a self-catering feed one dark night, and erroneously concluded they'd encountered Black Shuck himself!

Testimony of our most recent Black Shuck encounter, though, comes from a man convinced that he met a flesh-and-blood creature – it urinated, left bite marks on his bottom and even wore a collar. As everybody knows, Black Shuck has no human master.

Nonetheless, this recent Shuck encounter – while mundane by the phantom hellhound's usual standards – does highlight the fact that strange, large, frightening black dogs do mysteriously appear seemingly out of nowhere. This may explain some historic Shuck sightings.

Our witness, Edward Wilson, best known as the author of the William Catesby series of spy novels, takes a daily "afternoon jog" through Chediston, west along the quiet, narrow lane from the church and through the village. It was midday in November 2020, about half a mile west of the church, that as Edward recalls, "I saw a dog… a very big dog." "It was "completely and utterly black… exactly like a big Alsatian… I'm sure it had a collar." The collar made him look around for its owner, but there was none in sight, "odd, because you don't see dogs on their own" round there.

The animal wore a "strange... black collar with a silver bauble, it didn't look as if it had a place you could attach a lead to." Edward was struck by the dog's resemblance to Black Shuck... pointy black ears, staring eyes, the teeth." As soon as Edward saw the dog, "it started... staring and barking at me." Edward, a decorated US Special Forces veteran, was at first unfazed and resumed running as usual. The dog went "one pace of front of me" and then turned and "bit me on the backside… quite a firm bite" which didn't draw blood.

Then "it got really frightening." The dog "started trotting – very friendly – alongside me, went into a field next to me" between it and Edward and "started running along beside me."

When Edward turned as usual and retraced his steps as he reached the end of the village, he saw the dog ahead – "I must have taken my eyes off him", then the animal "completely disappeared." A little later on his jog back through the village he caught sight of the dog once more – "in front of me, trotting along happily" and it at one point was "weeing ahead of me", then it disappeared yet again, "I don't know where it went."

Edward reported the incident to the police, believing a mortal, unattended and dangerous dog may be at large. Halesworth police told him they had "checked a local dog owner near there" but concluded "nothing definitive" and gave Edward an incident number.

Elements of this more recent encounter fit the Shuck pattern. Whatever-it-was displayed a physical resemblance to Shuck, it did a typical Shuck disappearing act after it seemed to walk in step with its observer – like those more benign Shucks from Dunwich and Bungay. But would our witness have even noticed Shuck similarities were he not in East Anglia, where a background Shuck traditions can influence our perceptions of what we experience?

When I got in touch Edward again in January 2023 for an update, he told me that Suffolk Constabulary had recently got back to him to tell him they'd traced the owner. The dog's onwner lived not that far away from Chediston. An officer had "had words with her" about keeping her dog under control. So Edward Wilson's encounter with a strange black dog became yet another example of a Suffolk Shuck encounter that had a prefectly mundane explanation.[8]

A Black Dog weathervane at Walberswick Ferry (left) and the green and white dog from the Gooch family coat of arms that watches over the Benacre Estate.

PART 2 – HERE BE DRAGONS

FOOTNOTES TO CHAPTER 6: Suffolk Shuck

1. Queen's Silver Jubilee 1977; The first Star Wars film, at the time just *Star Wars*, now *Episode 4: A New Hope*, had its original UK release in 1977; birth of punk rock music generally agreed to have been in 1976.

2. Loss of Shuck supernatural powers post-1970s from "Analysing the Hell Out of the Beast", Ivan Bunn and Mike Burgess, Hidden East Anglia website, also *Lantern 18*, www.hiddenea.com/Lantern18.pdf.

3. Great Livermere Shuck from "Ghostwatch", Alan Murdie, *Fortean Times* **FT220**, which cites two unnamed books by local author Beryl Bryson; Aldeburgh Shuck from *Forgotten Ports of England,* George Goldsmith Carter, Evans Bros, London 1951 – Carter was a teenager in Aldeburgh in the 1920s when he heard the story; Barham Beast, Westleton Red Stile Shuck from *Westleton – Customs and Sayings recorded by the Women's Institute in 1922*, Westleton Women's Institute, Leiston Press, Leiston 2008; Reydon Shuck and Dunwich Greyfriars phantom dog from *Haunted Suffolk,* Peter Jennings, Tempus Publishing, Stroud, 2006; Boxford to Middleton Shuck from Paranormal Database. There's a list of Shuck locations in East Anglia at www.hiddenea.com/shuckland/locationlist.htm.

4. *Cave Canem*, ASSAP, which quotes *The World's Greatest Ghosts*, Nigel Blundell and Roger Boar, Octopus 1983; Paranormal Database, *Ghosts of Suffolk*, Betty Puttick, Countryside Books, 1998; WW2 coastguard's Shuck shooting and The Green, Southwold encounter from *Paranormal Suffolk: True Ghost Stories*, Christopher Reeve, Amberley, Stroud 2009. The Shuck of the Dunwich ruins, see above, is also described as a galleytrot. The Penelope Fitzgerald encounter – undated – is in *Suffolk Ghosts and Legends*, Pamela Brooks, Halsgrove, Wellington, Somerset, 2009. It's likely to have been before 1975.

5. Paranormal Database and Hidden East Anglia, www.hiddenea.com/shuckland/wissett.htm which quotes Patricia Willis: "The Wraiths of Wissett", *East Anglian Magazine* Vol. 41, No. 9, July 1982, p. 392; Ampton "suspicious dog" from *Haunted Suffolk,* see above.

6. Felixstowe to Hunstanton coastal Shuck range from *The Folklore of East Anglia*, see above; Felixstowe marsh sighting from "Black Shuck the Hell-hound legend that won't lie down", Martin Newell, *EADT,* 07 June 2014.

7. www.irishwolfhounds.org/felixstowe.htm, which quotes *The Magnificent Irish Wolfhound* by Mary McBryde.

8. The Yeth Hound of Dartmoor tradition is generally considered the most likely inspiration for Baskervilles; Oulton churchyard Shuck from *Haunted Lowestoft Revisited*, Ivan A.W. Bunn and Henry Baker, published by the authors, Lowestoft 2010, includes reprint of *Haunted Lowestoft*, Borderline Science Investigation Group, Lowestoft 1975.

9. "Analysing the Hell Out of the Beast", www.hiddenea.com/shuckland/analysing1.htm, Ivan A. W. Bunn and Mike Burgess, Hidden East Anglia website, also *Lantern* 18 www.hiddenea.com/Lantern18.pdf; Woolpit talking Shuck from Paranormal Database; Bungay 1970 death portent from *Paranormal Suffolk:* see above; Clopton Thing from *Cave Canem*, Chris Huff, ASSAP www.assap.ac.uk/newsite/Docs/Black%20dogs.pdf; How to avert death by Shuck sighting from "The Hellhounds of East Anglia", Ghostwatch, Alan Murdie, *Fortean Times*, **FT340;18-19**, May 2016.

10. Thedora Brown, known as Theo, did most of her work on the folklore of Devon and Dartmoor, but she also wrote articles on Shuck, including "The Black Dog", *Folklore*, Vol. 69, no. 3, September 1959.

11. Dunwich protective Shuck from Paranormal Database, *Shock!* – see below – and Dunwich Museum exhibit; Aldeburgh bogie beast from *Paranormal Suffolk:* see above; Bungay protective Shuck from a letter from Hugh Braun to Theodora Brown, 28 June 1969, in the Theo Brown Collection, University of Exeter 1969, quoted by Dr David Waldron in *Shock! The Black Dog of Bungay*, Dr David Waldron and Christopher Reeve, Hidden Publishing 2010; Barsham headless Shuck from Hidden East Anglia's "Analysing the Hell Out of the Beast," Ivan A. W. Bunn and Mike Burgess, www.hiddenea.com/shuckland/analysing1.htm.

12. Bogie beast variants and Thetford rabbit Shuck from *The Lore of the Land*, Jennifer Westwood and Dr Jacqueline Simpson, 2006; *The Folklore of East Anglia*, see above, also on the Thetford Shuck; Scratch Cat – another version ends with "no more" – from Christopher Reeve's *The Black Dog of Bungay*, pamphlet on sale in St Mary's Church, Bungay, 1988.

13. Melton donkey-dog from *Paranormal Suffolk:* see above; Dr Simon Sherwood experienced a bedside encounter as a small child in 1974 in Spalding, Lincolnshire, in which he saw a Black Dog with horns, www.blackshuck.info/. Could a Mr Kemp taking on Old Shuck at Melton and a Mr Kent battling the Barsham beast some 200 years later indicate a garbled version of the same story?

14. Burgh Bath Slough from Paranormal Database and from Hidden East Anglia www.hiddenea.com/shuckland/woodbridge.htm.

15. Water Dog in Everard's testimony from *Paranormal Suffolk:* see above, Christopher Reeve, Amberley Stroud 2009; Leiston Church wall-leaping Shuck from *A Ghost Hunter's Game Book*, James Wentworth Day, 1958; The incident's also in *Alien Animals,* Janet & Colin Bord, Granada 1980 and *Mystery Animals of Britain and Ireland*, Graham

J. McEwan, Richard Hale, London 1986.

16. Ness Point Black Dog from *Haunted Lowestoft Revisited* and numerous other retellings. *Suffolk Ghosts and Legends,* Pamela Brooks, Halsgrove, Wellington 2009 quotes *In the Footsteps of Borrow and Fitzgerald,* Morley Adams 1914 as placing the Italian Shuck story not in Lowestoft but "in a small seaside hamlet", which Brooks thought might be Walberswick.

17. *Shock!* see above..

18. The Darkness's Black Shuck lyrics at www.azlyrics.com/lyrics/darkness/blackshuck.html and the track at www.youtube.com/watch?v=jeRY-jxKuqA.

19. *Shock!* see above.

20. *The Black Dog of Bungay* Christopher Reeve, pamphlet on sale in St Mary's Church Bungay, undated; *Shock!* see above; Poker explanation for scorch marks from *Holy Trinity Blythburgh: Cathedral of the Marshes*, Hugh Roberts, Mary Montague, Barry Naylor, Jarrold, Norwich 1999.

21. For the Great Thunderstorm of Widecombe (sic) see https://en.wikipedia.org/wiki/The_Great_Thunderstorm.

22. Trier ball lighting incident in *Annales Francorum Regum* 1160, and in *Shock!* see above, which quotes folklorist Theo Brown; Danbury Grey Friar phenomenon from *Historia Anglicana Walsingham* of 1653, quoted in *Lantern* 17, p 7, www.hiddenea.com/Lantern17.pdf; Godshill, Isle of Wight ball lightning strike from *A History of the Isle of Wight*, 1871, quoted in "The Enchanted Isle," Roger Clarke, *Fortean Times* **FT 343;33**, August 2016.

23. *Shock!* see above. *Paranormal Suffolk,* see above. Historian John Stowe, who was a child at the time of the Cornhill incident, wrote an account sometime before 1605 in which the bells were already been rung when the thunder started, and the bells continued to ring because bell-ringers "for fear... fell down and lay as dead," leaving to bells to come to a halt on their own. In Stowe's version the bell ringers then go down from the belfry to find the lion's claw scorch mark. Stowe is quoted in *Mystery Animals of Britain and Ireland*, Graham J. McEwan, Richard Hale, London 1986); Barsham church-wrecking fireball from *Quarterly Journal,* Royal Meteorological Society, 32, p.170, quoted in *Modern Mysteries of Britain,* Janet and Colin Bord, Grafton/Collins, London 1987; Fans of the Tintin books will also recall the fictional exotic ball lightning that came down the chimney of a stately home full of archaeologists and annihilated the Inca mummy of Raspa Capac, "he who unleashes the fire of Heaven," levitating Professor Calculus in his chair, as depicted on the cover of *The Seven Crystal Balls*, Herge, Casterman, 1948.

24. Reeve's comments from *The Black Dog of Bungay* Christopher Reeve, pamphlet on sale in St Mary's Church Bungay, undated; twentieth century Blythburgh A12 Shuck sightings from *Haunted Suffolk* Peter Jennings, Tempus Pubs, Stroud, 2006, no date given for PC Jenkin's encounter.

25. *Paranormal Suffolk:* see above; "Invented Traditions and Regional Identity – the case of the Bungay Black Dog", Dr David Waldron, *CFZ 2011 Yearbook*, The Centre for Fortean Zoology, Woolsery N. Devon, CFZ Publications, ed. Jonathan and Corinna Downes; Aldeburgh man's Ditchingham sighing from *Haunted Suffolk*, Whitehead's 1938 encounter in *Alien Animals*, Janet & Colin Bord, Granada 1980 which quotes Alisdair MacGregor's *The Ghost Book*.

26. Mrs Hill from *Paranormal Suffolk,* see above; Bungay press reports from *Shock!* see above.

27. Bunn's comments in *Lantern* 18, www.hiddenea.com/Lantern18.pdf.

28. Belle Vue Park sighting form *Haunted Lowestoft Revisited*, see above; 1973 Woodbridge sighting from www.hiddenea.com/shuckland/woodbridge.html; 1970s Orford encounter from Jim Bradley, Pers Comm. by email 29 April 15.

29. *A Strange & Terrible Wonder: the Story of the Black Dog of Bungay,* Christopher Reeve, Peter Morrow & Co, 1988 quoted in *Shock!* see above.

30. Leiston Abbey dig's find of dog remains, see http://digventures.com/2014/10/28/digventures-and-the-bbc-one-show-devil-dog-black-shuck-returns/ and http://www.dailymail.co.uk/news/article-2629353/Is-skeleton-legendary-devil-dog-Black-Shuck-terrorised-16th-century-East-Anglia.html, with thanks to Maiya Pina-Dacier, Community Manager of Dig Ventures.

31. "The Hellhounds of East Anglia", Ghostwatch, Alan Murdie, *Fortean Times,* **FT340;18-19**, May 2016. The most likely location for such an encounter at a crossroads on a drive from Bury to Colchester approaching the Essex border would be around Bures on the B1508 or Nayland on the A134. Could this manifestation of Black Shuck have been guarding Suffolk from all the Essex boys and Essex girls?

32. Pers. Comm by email 19 12 14, sorry, anonymity requested.

33. Testimony from "Major Pickle, Minister of the Countryside", via Twitter Direct Messaging, 19-29 April 2018.

34. "The Gurt Dog Returns", Max Blake, comment by "Woody", 6 July 2009, Fortean Zoology blog, CFZ, http://forteanzoology.blogspot.co.uk/2009/07/max-blake-gurt-dog-returns.html)

PART 2 – HERE BE DRAGONS

35. "Is a white wolf prowling Suffolk?", *EADT,* 19 November 2009.

36. "Weirdness in the Woods: Strange Creatures of Rendlesham Forest," Nick Redfern, undated; http://monsterusa.blogspot.co.uk/2009/03/weirdness–in–woods.html used with his kind permission, the article quotes *Explore Phantom Black Dogs*, Bob Trubshaw, Heart of Albion Press, 2005.

37. *Haunted Suffolk*, Peter Jennings, Tempus Publications 2006.

38. Coltishall bridge dog in *Mystery Animals of Britain and Ireland*, Graham J. McEwan, Richard Hale, London 1986; Peddar's Way Black Dog in *Alien Animals,* Janet & Colin Bord, Granada 1980; Great Yarmouth bad breath Shuck from *Lantern* 18 www.hiddenea.com/Lantern18.pdf; Cromer sighting from "Black Shuck the Hell-hound legend that won't lie down," Martin Newell, *EADT* 07 June 2014; Over the Cambridgeshire border in Wicken Fen, not far from Newmarket, there's yet another Shuck, according to *Cave Canem*, Chris Huff, ASSAP www.assap.ac.uk/newsite/Docs/Black%20dogs.pdf.

39. Hockley Shuck in *Mystery Animals of Britain and Ireland*. In some versions of the story, the wagoner tries to hit the Shuck with a stick, the stick catches fire and the wagoner is burnt to ashes along with his horse and his wagon. This and the "gunpowder Shuck" from *Phenomena*, John Michell and Robert J.M. Rickard, Thames & Hudson, London 1977 and *Mystery Animals of Britain and Ireland*, see above, which quotes Eric Maples' *The Realm of Ghosts*; Tollhurst Darcy Shuck from "Black Shuck the Hell-hound legend that won't lie down", Martin Newell claimed in *EADT* 07 June 2014 to have read of the Tolleshunt Darcy Shuck.

40. Gorleston Shuck with chains from *Lantern* 18, www.hiddenea.com/Lantern18.pdf.

41. "Black Dog Apparitions", talk by Prof Simon Sherwood, Weird Weekend 2006, Exeter, author's own notes; Conversation with Steve Jones JP, Weird Weekend 2014, Hartland, 16 August 2014; *Alien Animals*, see above The dog-bodied Clopton Hall entity with a monk's head is from Paranormal Database which quotes *The Ghost Book*, A. A. MacGregor, Robert Hale, 1955, p 71; Similar to the dog-bodied, human-headed monk at Clopton Hall is the "beast in priest's garments", an anti-clerical carved pew end in St Mary's Church, Hadleigh in South Suffolk. This depicts a monk or priest with huge teeth that's seized a severed human head in its jaws, it's on all fours and under its ridiculously tight-fitting cassock or habit it has an animal's body with hooves.

42. *Suffolk Tales of Murder & Mystery,* Mark Mower, Countryside Books Newbury Berks 2006; Mystery Big Cats, Merrily Harpur, Heart of Albion 2006; *Mystery Animals of the British Isles: The Western Isles*, Glen Vaudrey, CFZ Publications, Wolfardisworthy 2011.

43. Great Barton ghost Jack Russell from *Haunted Suffolk*, see above; Woolpit ghostly wolf howls from *Haunted England*, Christina Hole, 1940, quoted in *Suffolk Tales of Mystery and Murder*. The last wolf in England is generally thought to have died somewhere in one of the isolated forests or wildernesses of the Derbyshire or Yorkshire sometime between 1485 and 1509.

44. Wilde Score White Dawg from *Haunted Lowestoft Revisited*, TS Farm Stores haunting and 1987 Tramps Alley haunting from Paranormal Database. Southwold ghost dog and dog walker from *Haunted East Anglia*, Joan Forman 1974, 1985 reprint Jarrold & Co, Norwich.

45. Bungay Black Dog traditions from *Shock!* see above; "Invented Traditions and Regional Identity", see above.

46. Reeve's explanation from *Paranormal Suffolk:* see above. Dogs in church seem to have once been a nationwide problem. I saw in a church in Llanynys, Denbighshire, a set of "dog tongs" from the sixteenth or seventeenth century used to separate dogs fighting during services.

47. Phone interview with Edward Wilson, 25 January 2021.

Numerous equestrian ghosts are said to travel the roads of Suffolk, this sign (top left) is at Walberswick. A phantom fish carried by a spectral fisherman haunts Southwold Beach (top right). A phantom coach pulled by phantom horses is said to emerge from the driveway of Roos Hall (above left) near Beccles. Toby's Walks near Blythburgh is named after a lynched Jamaican cavalry soldier whose ghost in some accounts drives a hearse pulled by headless horses (above right).

Trainers and stable hands exercise race-horses in Newmarket, where the ghost of famous jockey Fred Archer has been seen riding his favourite horse on a local exercise track.

PART 2 – HERE BE DRAGONS

7. Land of the headless coach horse

Scientists wonder where all that "missing" mass in the universe could have got to. The universe, it seems, weighs much less than it should do, according to current theoretical physics. Where *has* all that mass gone? Various exotic states of matter have been dreamt up to account for the missing mass – dark matter, string theory, dark string, WIMPs (weakly interacting massive particles) and so on. I beg to suggest another possible explanation as to where all the universe's unaccounted for matter can be found. It's in the form of ectoplasm, the alleged supernatural substance that holds together all those ghosts in Suffolk, ghosts who – if every ghost tradition is to be believed – would probably outnumber Suffolk's population of a mere 700,000 or so living mortal humans.

Even Suffolk's vibrant UFO scene is drowned out by the volume of noise about ghosts. Suffolk can even boast one of Britain's most famous writers of ghost stories – MR James, who was a Great Livermere boy. His best-known ghost stories are set in Suffolk – "'Oh, Whistle, and I'll Come to You, My Lad'" (1904) and "A Warning to the Curious" (1925). Rival pubs in Bungay vie for pole position as "the most haunted pub in Britain" – Bungay's The Three Tuns pub currently holds the crown, with an absurdly high number of (human) ghosts – 24. Bury St Edmund's is doing well in the "most haunted" stakes, its Cupola House, which burnt down in 2012, was a claimant to "most haunted house in Britain", being (allegedly) haunted by one of the cathedral city's many phantom monks and a Grey Lady.

The Suffolk village of Wissett, near Halesworth and with a population of around 200 living souls, is said to have at least *four* ghosts, more than many towns. Lowestoft has at least six ghosts, excluding animal ghosts, with ghostly airmen a Lowestoft speciality. Overnight ghost-hunting vigils at Felixstowe's Landguard Fort, up there with The Three Tuns, Bungay in terms of the number of its alleged phantom residents, could cost you £60 a night.[1]

Most of Suffolk's ghost population, unfortunately for mystery animal enthusiasts, seems to be the ghosts of humans, although Suffolk shares with Somerset and the North of England galley beggars, which while they are among the undead don't seem to have ever been a living person. Galley beggars are skeletal entities that exist purely to scare people, and delight in carrying their head under their arm, or lifting their head off from their neck with their hands.

In among the huge alleged population of Suffolk ghosts are a striking number of *animal* ghosts. Some of Suffolk's ghost dogs are regarded as just that – phantom dogs seen with their ghostly human walkers; they are a separate phenomenon to the "Black Shuck" we met in the previous chapter. And there are phantom horses in abundance. Suffolk was the centre of heavy horse breeding up until 1914, and for the breeding of war horses up until the fall of full armour from fashion in Elizabethan times. The county is home to the oldest known breed of draught horses for heavy pulling work, the chestnut-coloured Suffolk Punch. The ancestry of every Suffolk Punch horse alive today can be traced back to "Crisp's horse of Ufford", born 1768.

Suffolk was a county of working horses, so it was logical that Suffolk would leave behind some working horse ghosts too. (There were an estimated seven million horses in the UK in 1914.) Gypsies were once numerous in Suffolk – they tended to know their working horses, so there was work for them there.

Some of Suffolk's ghost horses – whether visible or invisible – were on their own, without riders.On the road out of Blythburgh, at a spot called the Heronry, there once used to be burial mounds. One remaining unexcavated mound is said to house a phantom horse, a "heath horse" that emerges on moonlit nights and gallops silently towards the village on an ancient track before disappearing into the nearby sea. We know there were horse burials in Suffolk – Mound 17 at the Sutton Hoo Anglo-Saxon burial site on the bank of the Deben near Melton had a young warrior and his horse buried under it. And on Walberswick Common it is said that you can hear phantom horses gallop across the common, but only in daylight.[2]

Blythburgh has other invisible horses. On Blythburgh Common, people report hearing horses galloping up towards them, then they hear them gallop away. The invisible galloping horses here are associated with Sir Robert Brooke, who enclosed the Common in seventeenth century clearances during which four people were killed. These very similar invisible horses, on the Common, in adjacent villages, could be garbled retellings of the same tradition.[3]

Out on the Shotley Peninsula at Stutton Hill near Holbrook, as late as the 1960s there was a spot where people reported being overcome by an "uneasy feeling", sometimes they would hear the sound of horse's hooves as well.

More fairies than ghosts, but still phantasmal and scary, were the water horses. You had to be on the lookout for them in November in particular, in the area from Dunwich all the way up the coast to Corton. Water horses would gallop out of the sea and along the beach and frolic in the fields inland, then tempt you to ride them and then drown you.[4]

Then there was the somewhat less terrifying and more endearing Tommy the Horse – a horse ghost seen grazing alongside his still living stablemate, and frolicking in the meadow, on misty evenings at Grange Farm, Henstead, outside Lowestoft.[5]

Sometime before 1922, Mr J. Spall of Westleton encountered a "white horse", a mysterious "loose horse" out on the road in the middle of the night while driving in his own cart through what's now Waveney District and back to Westleton with three horses pulling a "load of whins" (gorse) he'd collected. Spall would have gathered locally abundant gorse either to crush up for winter feed for his livestock, especially horses, or for fuel – for bread ovens in particular. At "Wangfer" (Wangford) at the Southwold turn, he came across this strange animal, and shooed it away with a stick, before noticing that his own horses were all "a muck and sweat" with fear, but he observed that his horses were "cold to the touch" by the time he got to The Plough pub at Wangford. He didn't say whether he thought the "white horse" he'd seen off – and which had so affected his own horses – was a ghost.[6]

The sound of an invisible horse was heard around Piper's Vale in Ipswich, near the north side of Ipswich's Orwell Bridge, at the turn of the twenty-first century. And in the winter of 1991, a witness giving her name only as Laura said she was searching a barn for her missing cat in one of Newmarket's many stables near Park Lane when she heard the sound of a horse arriving, in metal shoes, and went outside to look, only to find… nothing. Two colleagues had reported hearing an invisible horse moving around there too, and one had been told that the stable's previous owner that the place had been haunted by the ghost of racehorse that had been heard but never seen.[7]

One Suffolk phantom horse was not heard but felt. Jack Goddard went looking for moths in Jay's Hill in Sotterley – south-east of Beccles – and felt the hot breath of a horse on him, but saw or heard nothing there.[8] Then there was the invisible donkey heard frequently by Mr J. Spall of Westleton, who lived with his wife in a cottage near the Westleton churchyard, and would hear at midnight a noise coming from the yard outside his house, a sound "as if a donkey with a clanking chain" was moving about.[9] While invisible horses were the most commonly unseen animal ghost, Dunwich was said to have herds of invisible grazing cows, once heard by locals moving along the roads in this area, and on the cliffs, which were once of course green pastures. Nobody in Dunwich today that I talked to has ever heard this story, it does sound awfully like the "some say you can hear the sound of ghost bells tolling in the sunken Dunwich churches" nonsense.[10]

Ghost riders

As well as "loose" phantom horses, donkeys and cattle at large on their own, Suffolk has an abundance of equestrian ghosts ridden by phantom riders.

In Blythburgh there is a spot just south of the A12 bridge over the Blyth River where an older man leading a black horse has been seen, along with a woman in her twenties wearing a long dress frilled at the hem, and a large hat. Sometimes the man leading the black horse is a younger highwayman in "breeches, boots and a skirted coat", while the twentysomething woman is clutching a hat against her frilled skirt.

In 1974, Kessingland landlady Elaine Burke reported that her guest, a Grimsby-based lorry driver going up north via Blythburgh on the A12, jammed on his brakes when the man leading the black horse and the girl in the frilled skirt and hat appeared in the road right in front of him. In a state of some distress, he climbed out of his cab to find… nothing.

While witness accounts tend to dwell in some detail on the eighteenth century style of the girl's dress, Joan Forman did some digging around in the early 1970s and found the same trio – man, girl, horse – had been seen in various forms on Blythburgh Common for some 200 years. In some versions, the man was a farm labourer whose niece used to bring him lunch every day when he was working with his horse in the fields, and found him dead near his horse one day, and died of a broken heart. In other variants, the girl is holding the man's arm (her uncle's?) and in yet more variations on the story, the woman is riding the horse.[11]

Another Suffolk ghostly horse and rider, from the other side of the county, involves someone who in life was something of a national celebrity.

The town of Newmarket styles itself as "the Home of English Horse Racing." King Charles II set up his horse racing stables here in the 1660s, as the gentle hills and well-drained, chalky soil of the area around the town made it ideal for exercising racehorses. If you leave town by train headed for Bury, you find yourself immediately in a long railway tunnel that goes under the exercise tracks known as the Gallops.

Fred Archer, "The Tin Man", was one of the most famous jockeys from the late nineteenth century, and was based at Newmarket. Fred was unusually tall for a jockey. He shot himself aged 29, a suicide which could have had something to do with his jockey's extreme weight-loss diet, exacerbated by the death of his wife and by drink. The Newmarket town councillor I met on a visit to Newmarket commented that most jockeys are around seven to ten kilos below their optimal body weight, "so it's no wonder they go off the rails sometimes!"

Since 1927, horses have shied away or swerved at a particular spot in the exercise track at Hamilton Stud Lane where jockeys and members of the public report seeing Fred Archer riding at a gallop on his "favourite horse", probably a horse named Scotch Pearl. Fred has also been seen riding Scotch Pearl on the heath, and several accidents on the Newmarket Course had been blamed on this equestrian apparition.

As with all ghosts, there are a couple of problems with this story. One, racehorses are said to be notoriously jittery anyway. As anyone who's watched them on Newmarket's exercise tracks will know, they don't need a ghost to spook them, a falling leaf will do nicely. Two, the ghost of Fred Archer on horseback has been seen in Cheltenham too, on the edge of the Cotswolds, often enough to make it "Cheltenham's famous ghost." The spirits of Fred Archer and Scotch Pearl must be powerful indeed if they can appear in two places at once.[12]

Among a ridiculous number of ghosts said to reside at Felixstowe's Landguard Fort are horsemen seen crossing a "drawbridge that no longer exists." There's said to be the ghost of a horseman in the yard by the Old Bell Inn, Stoke Bridge, near Ipswich Station, home to various unexplained things that go bump in the night.[13]

On heathland near Dunwich around the Red Stile on the way to Heveningham, a ghostly landowner on a phantom racehorse wages class war from beyond the grave, charging around the heathland and worrying the locals.[14]

In Icklingham, on the A1101 near Mildenhall, near the Temple Bridge that crosses the River Lark, a "headless shape on horseback" has been seen galloping over the meadows, startling passing (living) horses and cattle. Sometimes the apparition's invisible, and manifests as only the sound of horse's hooves. The "headless shape" may be Simon Theobald of Sudbury, a former Bishop of London decapitated by rebels in the Peasant's Revolt of 1381. While the murder took place in London and most of his body was buried there, his head was brought back to his native Sudbury for burial. In other variants of the story, he's not a headless bishop but a former highwayman, buried with his horse in a nearby mound, who startles local cattle out of revenge on the local community that brought his highwaymanry to an end. Sadly, as in most Suffolk headless horseman traditions, there's quite a lot of detail on the phantom rider, but little to none on what we're more interested in, which is the ghost he rides on.[15]

Oddest of all the Curious County's phantom horse and rider double-acts is the Kirkley Runner, the headless horseman that gallops down Carlton Road to the Kirkley Bridge in Lowestoft and vanishes. He once terrified a woman who was pushing a pram. Curiously, there was no known local tradition of a headless horseperson in Lowestoft before encounters involving the Kirkley Runner started, out of the blue, in the 1970s.[16]

Our Suffolk ghost riders on horseback are comfortably outnumbered by spectral coaches pulled by phantom horses. There are indeed enough phantom coaches in Suffolk to form a reasonably-sized traffic jam, were they arranged end-to-end, which would almost reach the size of the traffic queue of the sort seen each July on the roads around the Latitude Festival at Henham Park near Blythburgh.

Ideally, the classic Suffolk phantom coach and horses should have headless coach horses pulling them, with extra bonus points for a much rarer headless phantom coachman driving the coach. Preferably, Suffolk phantom coaches should bear the crest of a decaying aristocratic family, and be driven in a manic and reckless fashion by a particularly unpleasant and dead member of that family, where possible pulling up or leaving from a the site of a ruined and abandoned stately home, or the site of a stately home that's not there anymore.

Most Suffolk phantom coach horses reportedly wear the tackle and equipment of the eighteenth century, pulling vehicles from that era, with ghostly human drivers and passengers in clothes contemporary with that era – three-cornered hats and frock coats for men, bodice dresses and bonnets for women.

Some phantom coach horses and the coaches they pulled have been encountered since those times, there are even ghost stories in which witnesses mistake the ghost coaches they've seen for those owned by their neighbours. Many witnesses saw eighteenth century coach horses in the nineteenth century – while the style of the vehicle, horses and the dress of the occupants was already old fashioned, they could still name the type of coach the horses were pulling. More recent sightings, in our age where cars have long replaced horse-drawn vehicles, are rarer. Some witnesses describe suddenly seeing a "Victorian" coach and assuming that they must have seen either ghosts or costumed re-enactors.

The most problematic element of the already hard-to-believe phantom coach and horses genre, is of course, the bit about the coach horses being headless. While human phantoms with no heads, including headless horsemen, can reasonably be explained as the ghosts of people who died by beheading, as far as I am aware there is no historical evidence for any horse beheadings, let alone beheadings of teams of four coach horses at once.

The impossibility of the whole phantom coach and horses thing notwithstanding, younger members of the aristocratic Bigod family can be seen travelling on certain nights of the year in a coach drawn by horses with flames and smoke pouring from their nostrils, moving on narrow lanes round Bungay and on to Geldeston Church over the border in Norfolk and back, either seen or heard but never both. And yes, the Bigod family's coach has headless coachmen too.

Also in the lanes around Bungay, on the road which crosses the bridge over the Waveney at the edge of Bungay and takes you into Norfolk and the nearby village of Ditchingham, there's another phantom coach pulled by a team of four horses, once seen at Lion's Grave on the Ditchingham Road. At least one driver has reported that this particular phantom coach seems to charge at oncoming traffic, turning away at the last possible moment. It could of course be the same coach as the Bigod's coach that cruises the lanes around Bungay.

A disproportionate percentage of Suffolk's phantom coach and horses phenomena are reported on the roads around Bungay, Beccles and Oulton, at the northern end of the county near the south bank of the Waveney River, which does raise the possibility that some of the many local phantom coach-and-horses are in fact one and the same.

One of at least three different nocturnal phantom coaches pulled by a team of coach horse ghosts up and down the Beccles to Bungay road is the one pulled by four very fast coach horses towards Acton Park and the point known as Nursery Corner, on some nights. The gates of the local Acton Park are said to burst open at midnight, with the phantom coach and its team of horses racing out to Nursery Corner, or from nearby Barsham all the way to Hassett's Tower in Norwich, or leaving the village of Barsham in the direction of the now busy B1062 Beccles to Bungay road.

This phantom coach and horses is associated with the Blennerhassetts of Barsham. In one account the coach is driven by "old Hassett," with sparks flying as the phantom horses' hooves strike the ground, and with the coach sometimes even taking to the air. In another version, a ghostly member of the Blennerhassett family leaves the village on Christmas Eve in a coach bearing the Blennerhassett family crest, and pulled by headless horses, to Hassett's Tower in Norwich and back by sunrise. Barsham Hall is a ruin on farmland on a track off the Bungay-Beccles, you can spot it on an Ordnance Survey map as "Barsham Hall, Remains of".[17]

At the western edge of Beccles, also on the Bungay Road, is Roos Hall (it's still there). The Roos Hall phantom coach, featuring headless horses and in some versions a headless coachman, allegedly pulls up at the Hall and departs each Christmas Eve.[18]

There's also a story of a phantom coach pulling up at night up at nearby Beccles Hall, an Elizabethan hall that was dismantled and made into a farmhouse. The apparition appears to have killed local poacher and ne'er do well Jarge Mace, sometime in the late eighteenth century. Mace's body was found unmarked the morning after the apparition, but with its face in a fixed stare, as if in terror.[19]

Northeast of Beccles, in Oulton, there's Oulton Street, which has a phantom carriage travelling from house to house, or a solitary black horse galloping over the stones at midnight, depending on who you ask. The Oulton phantom coach story seems to have its origins in a garbled account of a local incident involving a man in a black carriage who abducted an eighteenth-century bride on her wedding day. The story was thought at the time of its telling to be a diversionary smokescreen for smugglers.[20]

Another phantom carriage with horses conveys a veiled woman at Oulton, and its backstory is associated with an adulterous woman who'd run off with her husband's murderer, and who came back in a carriage to murder her daughter by her husband, in an attempt to hide her past. It does sound awfully like the mortal intrigues in the story around the Oulton Street coach, doesn't it?[21]

And not far from Oulton, near the A12 at the Pleasurewood Hills theme park near Foxburrow Hotel, just north of Lowestoft, a couple walking out at night "many years ago" had a silent but terrifying encounter with a huge black horse rearing up at them, which turned out to be pulling a dog-cart driven by a cloaked, masked, bearded figure.[22]

Leaving the Waveney Valley and going south to the Blyth Valley, we go to Wissett, whose phantom black dogs we've already encountered. There's a spectral horse and cart associated with the village's Hallelujah Pond, a large pool ringed by trees in a field nearby Hallelujah Cottage. The Wissett phantom horse and cart is said to retrace the final journey of a horse and cart that fell into the pond, with its driver (and possibly the horse too) drowning.[23]

There was also a single, late twentieth century, encounter with a phantom horse and cart at Thornham near Eye, on Lord Henniker's gravel driveway. The present Lord Henniker's father told of hearing horses and wheels on the gravel driveway; investigating, he found nothing.

At Hintlesham Hall, just of the A1071 between Hadleigh and Ipswich, I was told by a woman who'd lived locally in the 1960s that there had once been a sighting of a "headless coachman coming down the drive." My source couldn't recall whether he was accompanied by coach and horses – headless or otherwise.

In Pettistree (near Wickham Market) there's a headless horseman who has been seen trotting down the high street in the early hours, spotted by at least two people since the 1990s. And further south at Polstead, not far from the Essex border, Mrs Hackford was driving her car near the village green on a summer late afternoon in 1991 when a horse and carriage conveying an elderly lady and two men, all on horseback and in Victorian costume, rode past her coming the other way. Mrs Hackford looked behind her immediately after the carriage passed, but it had vanished.[24]

In the area around the site of Boulge Hall (just north of Woodbridge), which was already derelict when it was demolished in 1950, the ghost of Mrs Short was said to emerge from the hall's gates in a coach pulled by headless horses. Mrs Short was known as the Queen of Hell during her lifetime on account of her sharp temper. Another version of the tale has the phantom in the coach driven by a Mr Fitzgerald, who built Boulge Hall in 1801.[25]

The Big Wood at Mutford (between Lowestoft and Beccles) was the scene of an encounter in which three men on horseback pulled up near the witness, they were escorting a coach in which sat a woman wearing a cloak, with feathers in her hair, but no face – no eyes nose or mouth were visible, her face was just "smooth flesh." When the witness screamed, the coach and horses rode off.

A single, headless horse pulls a carriage along Quay Lane on the road from Reydon to Wangford on dark nights. This is the Wangford north of Southwold, after which country and western singer Hank Wangford named himself, and near where Mr J Spall of Westleton saw his nocturnal "white horse". The Quay Lane ghostly horse and carriage is believed to be driven by a former – long deceased – owner of Reydon Hall, which is still very much standing.[26] There's also said to be a spectral coach and horses at the South Suffolk village of Long Melford.

In a category never known for its restraint, the most over-the-top Suffolk phantom coach and horses combination has to be the phantom hearse driven by Toby Gill, "Black Toby", to Hell each night (via the A12 and Blythburgh). Naturally, Black Toby's phantom hearse is drawn by four headless horses, with "muscular Jamaican" Toby Gill at the reins, wearing the uniform of a drummer in Sir Robert Rich's 4th Dragoons regiment, circa 1750.

Tobias Gill was found in a drunken stupor, camped out on the heath between Blythburgh and what's now the A12, in an area now known as Toby's Walks. (It used to be a picnic site, but in more recent years it's said to have become a "dogging" site, so Suffolk Coastal have put a barrier up where the picnic site car park used to be.) Near Toby's camp, servant girl Anne Blackmore was found dead, and Gill was convicted of her murder and hanged nearby. According to tradition, the deed was done using a mail coach which drove away with a rope tied to it, looped round a tree and with the end tied in a noose round Gill's neck. In an alternative version of the story, the ghost of Gill is driving the mail coach rather than the headless four-in-hand pulling a hearse towards Hell.

It later emerged that Blackmore's body was unmarked, and that she may have died of natural causes. Gill's lynching, while clearly an act of racism, could also have involved local smugglers settling scores. The dragoons (light cavalry issued with rifles) often supported the Excisemen in their local anti-smuggling operations and gunfights with smuggling gangs.

The main problem with the "Toby Gill driving a hearse to Hell pulled by four headless horses" scenario is that Toby's ghost is generally said to wander the heath on foot and alone. (The name for the local beauty spot – Toby's Walks – has nothing to do with whether the ghost travels on foot or driving a coach and horses; "Walks" in Suffolk is a name for a place where you can graze sheep.) Joan Forman, who briefly lived at nearby Blyford in the early 1970s, notes in *Haunted East Anglia* that "the story of a single spectre – that of Toby himself – seems credible... In the headless horses I frankly do not believe." Forman asked around extensively in the neighbourhood and there had been no Toby Gill sightings – with or without the Hell-bound headless coach horses – that anyone still alive in 1974 could remember.

According to the local guidebook *Blythburgh – a Suffolk Village*, the legend of a funeral hearse drawn by four headless horses and Toby driving to Hell each night started sometime in the nineteenth century, well over 50 years after Gill's lynching. His story could by then have become mixed up with another nearby phantom coach and horses (headlessness optional) – or the several other equestrian ghosts that crowd the heathland around Blythburgh – there are plenty of them to choose from![27]

And the allegedly very haunted indeed Borley Rectory, less than a mile over the Essex border near Sudbury, was also said to have a phantom horse and carriage, seen by various people, some of whom said it was driven by two headless coachmen. Borley Rectory is no longer standing, demolished after being damaged by fire in 1939.

The philosophically most demanding Suffolk ghost is a silent fisherman seen walking along Southwold beach with a rod and a large fish in his hand, or slung over his shoulder, and carrying a Tilley lamp. I've heard of other versions in which the fish is at the end of a fishing line, and the fisherman is carrying a rod. The ghost fish is "dead" and inanimate, which is most bizarre. Surely if it were a ghost it would be animated as if alive? This would make our ghost fish the only ghost ever recorded that manifested as dead, rather than animated. The whole point of being a ghost is that you are somehow animated and "alive" beyond the grave, there's not much point in being a ghost if all you do is get to manifest as an inanimate, lifeless corpse.[28]

Ghost cats

We've already looked at ghost dogs in our section on Black Shuck, but what about Suffolk's ghost cats?

In St Peter's Street, Ipswich, near the waterfront and a short walk from the station, is what's now the Thomas Wolsey pub. Previously known as the Blackadder, there were reported sightings in the pub of a ghostly cat, as well as a phantom monk and a ghostly girl. The current landlord told me that as of late 2014, there has been no reported ghost cat activity, although people occasionally report feeling "uncomfortable" in the upstairs meeting rooms. He added that the last people who ran it "reckoned there was a baby floating round," a ghost baby presumably. In the same street there is a magnificent cat in bronze on the statue of Cardinal Thomas Wolsey, Henry VIII's chief minister and one of the most powerful men in England at the start of the Reformation. Wolsey grew up nearby, and was said to be a cat-lover who brought one of his cats with him to formal meetings.

A spectral cat suffocates guests (although not fatally) in Room 3 of the Horse and Groom pub, Melton, by lying on their throats in the middle of the night.[29] There's also a house near the Crown Street Hotel in Lowestoft, said to have a ghostly black cat that runs up the stairs and disappears. In Leathes Ham, on the north shore of Lake Lothing in Lowestoft, an old lady saw a cat with "gret yellow eyes" that disappeared when she bent down to stroke it. The entity known as Old Yellow Eyes in Fakenham Magna was also said to be a ghost cat.[30]

One moonlit night in 1939, James Wentworth Day, East Anglian broadcaster and author, investigated the burnt-out and empty Borley Rectory. Something shot between his legs and into the remains of the house. He described it as a "gigantic black cat", local enquiries revealed that many other people had seen a huge, phantom feline dashing into the house.[31]

While the Borley Rectory phantom cat was supposed to be a giant, all the other Suffolk ghost cats are supposed to be conventionally-proportioned domestic cats. A minority of British big cat investigators, particularly Merrily Harpur, believe that Britain's mystery big cats are phantoms too, of a special kind of spirit entity, "daimons" that behave differently to Black Shuck and to other ghosts. That would at least explain the obvious lack of any big cat roadkill. Nearly all of the big cat investigators in these isles, though, work on the basis that big cats are real flesh-and-blood animals, from known species with Latin names, as we are about to see.

What is going on with all these ghosts, animal ghosts especially? Why would animals survive bodily death and come back as ghosts? If this were true, why isn't the world filled with dinosaur ghosts? And why is it that so many of the relatively few animal ghosts seem to be in the company of ghostly humans, either as pet dogs or as working horses serving as mounts or pulling phantom coaches for human ghosts?

In Chapter 3, as we saw with the urban fairies of Stowmarket, mouldy old houses with their poor quality air and mould may be able to "trigger psychosis", and this could possibly explain the ghost cats in pubs and hotels too. Moulds in ancient houses affecting the brain, though, doesn't explain the large number of outdoor animal ghosts.[32]

Nor should we assume that animal ghosts are dead animals returned to the grave. Until the beginning of the nineteenth century, rural people saw ghosts – human and animal – as purposeless "wandering spirits" that vanished at dawn, they weren't associated in rural tradition with any animals that have ever been alive, they were just spirits in the form of an animal that were somehow *there*. It was only with the rise of the literate classes fed on a diet of romantic novels that ghosts came to be seen as entities who walked the Earth with some sort of mission – to bring messages from beyond the grave, correct injustices or reveal their buried bodies or buried treasure and so on. Recent research, though, while not telling us anything about whether or not animals can come back as ghosts, does suggest that animals can have near death experiences like those that some humans go through.[33]

Another forgotten nationwide nineteenth-century phenomenon was an outbreak of ghost impersonators. Some of these were taking advantage of an existing local legend, while others were just putting on a white sheet to scare people where there were no particular ghost legends already doing the rounds. Female domestic servants walking at night were particularly vulnerable to being targeted by misogynist ghost impersonators and their pranks. There were frequent reports of Victorian mobs attacking ghost impersonators who'd been discovered.

This was at a time when most people at some point in the year walked to or from work in complete darkness. The introduction of street lighting and police patrols, at least in towns, meant that by the 1870s ghost impersonators, and the fear of ghosts on the road, became "fancies of a bygone age." But much of rural Suffolk didn't get electricity till the 1930s at the earliest. I know of some homes there that still don't have it. Many living in Suffolk have never had street lighting. Animal ghost impersonation would be harder to pull off than impersonating a human ghost, but you do start to wonder about Victorian ghost hoaxers up to their usual mischief when you hear stories of people hearing the sounds of a phantom coach and horses (or donkey) outside their house on a dark Suffolk night and find there's nothing there.

A perfectly rational explanation offered for the sound of a phantom coach and horses passing in the night comes from the Isle of Wight. The Reverend Sinclair and his wife arrived at the island's Chale Rectory in 1940 and heard stories of "the driving into the yard at midnight of a carriage and pair (of horses), which was said to have been heard, but not seen, on many occasions." They were astonished when they too heard the jingling of horse tackle, creaks and the sound of horses' hooves. After they put down rat poison, the phenomenon ceased.[34]

Fret assessment

There is another natural, though alarming and peculiarly East Anglian phenomenon, that could explain ghostly encounters on the road a dark nights. This also account for why there are more phantom horses around coasts, estuaries and rivers than further inland. Peculiar coastal mists, known locally as frets, form with astonishing suddenness in coastal Suffolk.

I once travelled on a clear, warm August night by car on the Walberswick to Dunwich road. Suddenly, wispy sheets of stray mist started billowing up and floating in front of the car headlights, looking very much like winding sheet phantoms. I've been on Walberswick Beach on a hot summer's day, when suddenly within under a minute I was surrounded by thick mist through which you couldn't see fifty feet ahead of you. Beyond was a solid wall of fog. After about an hour it lifted, with equally sudden speed. I've crossed the Orwell Bridge in a bus on an early September morning in a thick mist through which you could barely see the other end of the bridge.

George Orwell, writing in *The Lion and The Unicorn*, in an attempt to inspire socialists to fight in World War Two, described some of the "essentials" of the British landscape. This included "old maids hiking to Holy Communion through the mists of the autumn morning." The passage is today best known for some bizarre misquoting by former Prime Minister John Major, in a speech to the Conservative Group for Europe in April 1993, in which it was garbled to "old maids bicycling to Holy Communion through the morning mist."

In any event, hiking and especially bicycling to Holy Communion in Orwell's part of the world – he was from Ipswich – wasn't through a feeble, barely discernible, wispy Mist Lite, a Home Counties mist that just lent a bit of atmosphere. Suffolk's "mists of the autumn morning" were scary, thick, impenetrable dangerous East Anglian things, with visibility suddenly down to 100 or even 50 feet (30m or as little as 15m). Is it any wonder a lot of ghosts are reported round here?

Smugglers' tales

As briefly alluded to earlier, smugglers' tales play a role in the Suffolk phantom coach and horses phenomena, especially the scarier headless ghosts. It's noticeable how many of the terrifying encounters with ghosts (and with Black Shuck too) are at night on isolated roads near the coast, or near a (then) navigable river not too far from the sea.

Smuggling in Suffolk was an absolutely huge industry, particularly at its zenith in the eighteenth century. The Hadleigh Gang of smugglers could easily outnumber the Excisemen (Customs officers) and the dragoons mobilised to support them in any gunfight. In the mid-eighteenth century, an estimated 200 men with 100 horses at their disposal were involved in the smuggling enterprise at Pakefield, Covehithe, Sizewell Gap, Slaughden and other locations nearby. Perhaps this explains why so many ghosts on the roads of coastal Suffolk were of apparitions of horsemen, coaches or horses and carts?[35]

An *Ipswich Journal* report of September 18 1794 (reprinted in that newspaper in 1864) covers in just a few lines, as if it's not really all that newsworthy, how a father-and-son team of Excise Men assisted by a detachment of the 1st Regiment of Dragoon Guards, seized at least 250 gallons of "foreign brandy and geneve" (Dutch gin) in the village of Alderton on the Bawdsey Peninsula and impounded it in the Woodbridge Customs & Excise office. There were huge import duties levied on goods from outside Britain and its colonies – especially spirits, tobacco and Belgian lace, and a considerable slice of government income came from these duties. Imported spirits were always in big demand, so smuggling was a very profitably enterprise for a lot of people in a part of the country where cash was scarce. And the Netherlands was a mere 90 nautical miles away from the Suffolk coast.[36]

George Ewart-Evans's conversations with his neighbours around Blaxhall in the 1950s, recorded in *Ask The Fellows That Cut The Hay,* recalls smuggling being a big thing in their living memory, and that shepherds were particularly prized by smugglers, who paid them to obscure their tracks by driving sheep over these tracks once they had gone.[37] As Suffolk author Mark Mower points out in a Visit Suffolk video, "It was in the smugglers' interests to create ghostly figures and apparitions". With all the tales told to you down the pub (possibly by someone "in" with one of the huge smuggling gangs) about headless phantom coach horses pulling their bad-tempered dead aristocrat drivers to Hell, if you heard the clatter of horses' hooves at night on the road you'd probably run away in terror. You'd be unlikely to investigate whether the coach was laden with contraband Dutch gin. Especially if death from pure terror seemed a possibility, as we saw earlier in the case of the unfortunate poacher Jarge Mace in the ruins of Beccles Hall. And as for the sinister ghost fisherman wandering Southwold Beach with his fish and his lit Tilley lamp (which would date it from some time after 1818), what better cover could there be for a smuggler signalling to a boat from the shore?[38]

The overwhelming majority of phantom coach-and-horses stories in this survey come from East Suffolk near the coast, rather than from Mid-Suffolk or West Suffolk further inland. I hope it's not due any inadequacy in my research into West Suffolk traditions. I suspect it's something to do smuggling being an activity that was concentrated near the coast.

Some of the ghost stories told around Lowestoft and Oulton in particular seem to have been given a hand in their dissemination by self-styled "King of the Gypsies" and author George Barrow, who died in 1881. The local gypsy community – big in North Suffolk, with its healthy trade in horses until well into the first half of the twentieth century – could have had their own reasons for putting around rumours of ghostly horses putting phantom carriages.

The gypsies of the day would have particular spots where they wanted to put some distance between themselves and the settled locals, including spots used for some harmless and innocent purposes. They'd have had favoured out-of-the-way pitches where they could stop and set up camp in the reasonable expectation of being left alone. A quick word over a pint down the pub – one of the few occasions where gypsies and non-gypsies met informally – about phantom coach horses in that locality could see to that. Lowestoft historian ML Powell describes an Oulton Broad resident seeing spectral horses pulling a phantom gypsy caravan coming up their drive towards them one night, then turning round and "disappearing" down the drive. It could of course been an *actual* gypsy caravan up to something they didn't want the locals to know about. Local legends of ghostly horses pulling ghostly vehicles at night – legends possibly helped along by the gypsies themselves, could have provided a perfect smokescreen.[39]

Among the communities of gypsies that regularly passed through Suffolk, there were stories of strange encounters with animals that had something not quite right about them. One such account comes from sometime around 1870. It concerns the Smith family, who found themselves in "a field in Suffolk". At night their usually very affectionate donkey would "recede" from them whenever they approached. One of the family went to fetch it, but however hard they tried to approach it, the donkey always seemed to be the same distance away. Eventually, their donkey "vanished". Early next morning, they found their donkey had wandered off their campsite and been found and taken to the local animal pound. This begged the obvious question, what had they encountered the previous night?[40]

Recent archaeological evidence from outside the county points to a rational – although in itself bizarre – explanation for the phantom coaches pulled by headless horses. We have already looked at a Suffolk Saxon horse burial, and how these could have led to legends of ghostly horses bursting forth from now long vanished mounds. In 2018 came the discovery of England's first Iron Age chariot burials – up until then, all of Britain's Iron Age chariot burials had been in Wales This latest discovery, which predated the Romans, was in Pocklington, Yorkshire. One chariot was buried together with two horses in full harness – they had presumably been slaughtered just before burial, after over two thousand years only their skeletons remained. The chariot had been positioned and then buried as if the horses were leaping up a slope and out of the ground. Over the millennia, repeated ploughing of the field where the horses and chariot were buried had destroyed the remains of the part of the burial that was closest to the ground – the heads of the upright horses that pulled the chariot. So when twenty-first century archaeologists uncovered the remains of the chariot and the skeletons of its horses, the horses were headless. The skeleton of a "high status" man in his forties was found crouched in the chariot.[41]

Imagine other such Iron Age chariot burials somewhere in England, with horses in full harness buried upright, as if pulling the chariot. Iron Age Suffolk was home to the powerful Iceni and Trinovantes tribes during the Iron Age, which left plenty of archaeological evidence, so such an unrecorded discovery in the Curious County could have been a possibility.

Now imagine what might happen if simple country folk of, say, the eighteenth century, stumbled across one of these, perhaps while ploughing a field. They would find the skeletons of headless horses, together with the remains of a chariot. The closest thing in their experience to a chariot would have been a coach or a buggy or trap. (The last two vehicles were two-wheeled coaches, ubiquitous at the time. Could the discovery of an Iron Age chariot burial, with the horses, minus their heads due to erosion or ploughing, have given rise to legends of phantom coaches pulled by headless horses?

PART 2 – HERE BE DRAGONS

FOOTNOTES TO CHAPTER 7: Land of the headless coach horse

1. I have to say that I visited Landguard Fort by day, and I would struggle to find a less spooky place. Atmospheric, yes, spooky? No.

2. Blythburgh Heronry heath horse from *Ghosts of Blythburgh, Southwold & Walberswick,* Allan Scott-Davies, Artspace, Suffolk, 2010; Walberswick invisible horses from Paranormal Database, which quotes *The Haunted Pub Guide*, Guy Lyon Playfair, Harrap, London 1985. This also mentions a phantom man appearing in Walberswick Commons and in the ruined part of St Andrew's Church; The mound-dwelling Walberswick heath horse may be the same local entity as The Monster of the Green mentioned by *East Anglian Magazine* p 38-41, vol. 23, quoted in *Lantern* 25.

3. *Ghosts of Blythburgh,* see above.

4. My Shotley Peninsula sound-of-horses-hooves informant, who grew up there in the 1960s, requested anonymity and also described a twentieth-century account of a "crisis apparition" of a local man at the moment of his death nearby. Water horses from *Lantern* 25, also *Haunted Suffolk*; Peter Jennings, Tempus Pubs, Stroud, 2006.

5. *Haunted Suffolk,* see above.

6. *Westleton – Customs and Sayings recorded by the Women's Institute in 1922*, Westleton Women's Institute, Leiston Press, Leiston 2008.

7. Both from Paranormal Database, which cites *Encyclopedia of Haunted Places*, Jeff Belanger, Career Press Inc, 2009 for the Pipers Vale horse, a witness contacted the website to tell them about sounds of a horse in Newmarket.

8. *Paranormal Suffolk: True Ghost Stories,* Christopher Reeve, Amberley Stroud 2009. No date is given for this incident, but there was a Jack Goddard contributing articles about moths to *Suffolk Naturalist* up to 1963.

9. Invisible ghost donkey from *Westleton – Customs and Sayings,* see above.

10. *The Ghost Book* Alasdair Alpin MacGregor, Robert Hale 1956. There is a tradition from the nineteenth century of the "sound of bells from Dunwich churches sunken beneath the waves." After a series of floods or storms in 1286, 1287, 1328, 1347 and 1362, many of the wooden houses in Dunwich were blown down or washed away. Skilled workers in Dunwich moved to nearby ports. Suddenly, Dunwich lost much of its workforce, and no longer had the manpower to do the regular task of clearing the harbour of shingle. Dunwich harbour became untenable, the town was gradually abandoned, with coastal erosion continuing to eat away bits of the town. The churches gradually fell into ruin, with their disused bells salvaged for re-use elsewhere. Given the scarcity of stone locally, much of these churches would have been taken apart for building materials before the sea covered them. There could never have been the "sound of bells tolling in churches sunk beneath the waves." See "The Bells! The Bells", *Discover Dunwich*, 1, 2019, www.dunwichmuseum.orguk/assets/Discover-Dunwich/discover-dunwich-colour-FINAL-half-term-dates-02-19.pdf

11. *Haunted East Anglia*, Joan Forman 1974, 1985 reprint Jarrold & Co, Norwich, the story's also in *Ghosts of Blythburgh, Southwold & Walberswick*, Allan Scott-Davies, Artspace, Suffolk, 2011.The spot where the black horse and two people are seen is near the same mounds on Blythburgh Common from which the "mound horse" is said to burst out.

12. Paranormal Database, which quotes *The A-Z of British Ghosts*, Peter Underwood, Chancellor Press 1993; Ghost of Fred Archer on horseback in Cheltenham from PJ Cadavori blog http://pjcadavori.blogspot.co.uk/2014/03/cheltenhams-most-famous-ghost.html.

13. Paranormal Database. The former Old Bell Inn building has become a funeral director's premises.

14. Paranormal Database, which quotes *This Haunted Isle*, Peter Underwood, St Michael's Abbey Press, 1983. "Are these the scariest places in Suffolk?" *EADT,* 31 October 2015 puts the phantom squire on horseback at what's now Dunwich Heath NT nature reserve, which is nearer Westleton, and describes the squire as "Victorian". Local ghost stories say the squire is a member of the Barne family, once local lords of the manor, of Edwardian vintage.

15. Paranormal Database, which quotes *East Anglia – Walking the Lay Lines and Ancient Tracks*, Shirley Toulson, Fontana 1976; *The Folklore of East Anglia* Enid Potter, BT Batsford, London 1974 has the detail about the revenge-exacting highwayman and his horse buried in the mound.

16. *Haunted Lowestoft Revisited*, Ivan A.W. Bunn and Henry Baker, published by the authors, Lowestoft 2010.

17. Numerous sources, Paranormal Database cites *The Ghost World,* T F Thiselton Dyer, Ward & Downey, London 1893, online at Project Gutenberg at www.gutenberg.org/files/45362/45362-h/45362-h.htm and *The Lore of the Land – A Guide to England's Legends from Spring-Heeled Jack to the Witches of Warboys,* Jennifer Westwood and Jacqueline Simpson, Penguin, 2005. I wimped out of actually going to the now very isolated "Barsham Hall,

Remains of", it looked like it was going to be an awfully long way down a track and it was getting dark. I did cycle along the track through the village of Barsham along which the phantom coach is supposed to ride.

18. Numerous sources, Paranormal Database cites *Supernatural England,* Eric Maple, Guild Publishing 1988; see also www.bbc.co.uk/suffolk/content/articles/2008/10/30/roos_hall_gc_feature.shtml

19. *The Folklore of East Anglia*, see above. *Paranormal Norfolk* (Frank Meeres, Amberley, Stroud 2010) places this story at Breckles Hall, Attleborough, Norfolk, with the poacher named George Mace. (It's also spelt "Breccles".)

20. *Haunted Lowestoft Revisited,* Ivan A.W. Bunn and Henry Baker, published by the authors, Lowestoft 2010.

21. *The Ghost World*, T F Thiselton-Dyer, Ward & Downey, London 1893, online at Project Gutenberg at www.gutenberg.org/files/45362/45362-h/45362-h.htm has the Oulton House ghosts as being "a wild huntsman with his hounds" rather than a veiled woman in a coach.

22. Oulton, Oulton House and Pleasurewood Hills equestrian apparitions all from *Haunted Lowestoft Revisited*, Ivan A.W. Bunn and Henry Baker, published by the authors, Lowestoft 2010.

23. *Lantern* 38 and Paranormal Database, which quotes "The Wraiths of Wissett", *The East Anglian Magazine*, Vol.41, No.9, July 1982.

24. Hintlesham source requested anonymity. A ghost hunt by "paranormal investigators" for BBC Points East in 2010 mentioned plenty of human ghosts, mostly of infants or children, but no phantom coachmen, www.youtube.com/watch?v=yoF4f0QDWJg; Pettistree headless horseman and Polstead carriage from Paranormal Database.

25. Paranormal Database, which quotes *The Lore of the Land - A Guide to England's Legends from Spring-Heeled Jack to the Witches of Warboys*, Jennifer Westwood and Jacqueline Simpson, Penguin, 2005.

26. Paranormal Database, which cites *Ghosts of East Anglia,* Mills H. West, Countryside Books, Newbury, 2003. This Wangford is not to be confused with Suffolk's other Wangford, near Lakenheath.

27. *Haunted East Anglia,* see above; *Folktales and Legends of East Anglia,* Geoffrey M. Dixon; *Blythburgh - a Suffolk Village*, Holy Trinity Church Blythburgh/Jarrold, Norwich 2003.

28. *Haunted East Anglia,* see above, also *Ghosts of Blythburgh,* see above.

29. *Haunted Suffolk*, see above. The same pub also has a "white lady." Gail Nina Anderson in *Fortean Times* – **FT 323;75** – describes in the dark in her bedroom as a teenager hearing and feeling the weight of a cat – a large one, jumping on to the bed, walking towards her, putting her hand around its front leg, which felt real, feeling its paw, and then turning on the light and it has vanished, with no sign of it. We interpret such experiences as a dream, or some kind of hypnogogic state, the state immediately before falling asleep. People tell Nina, a university lecturer specialising in "the Gothic", that they quite often experience this phenomenon, with either a cat or a person sitting on the end of the bed. Such a phantom cat features in Sheridan La Fanu's 1872 vampire novel *Carmilla*.

30. *Haunted Lowestoft Revisited*, see above.

31. *Mystery Big Cats* Merrily Harpur, Heart of Albion 2006 which quotes *Mystery Animals of Britain and Ireland,* Graham J. McEwan, Richard Hale, London 1986.

32. "The Real Ghostbusters Investigate Mold, Not Moans, Within Haunted Houses", *Medical Daily* 2 April 2015, www.medicaldaily.com/real-ghostbusters-investigate-mold-not-moans-within-haunted-houses-327950#.

33. "Spurious Spirits", Jacob Middleton, *Fortean Times*, **FT 297;33-37** February 2013; animal near death experiences in http://whofortedblog.com/2014/04/28/animals-near-death-experiences/

34. Foxearth Historical Society www.foxearth.org.uk/blog/2005/01/rat-run.html.

35. *Haunted Suffolk*, see above; for more on the sheer scale of Suffolk smuggling see The Vulcan Arms website, http://vulcanarms.freehostia.com/history.php smuggling in Suffolk.

36. The 1st Dragoons would 19 years later distinguish themselves at the Battle of Waterloo.

37. At the time of writing, Ewart-Evans's recordings of *Ask The Fellows*... for the BBC were at www.bbc.co.uk/programmes/b00rv8yk.

38. Visit Suffolk's #TheOtherSide, www.youtube.com/watch?v=Lfs5lPr4cdE#theotherside.

39. *Haunted Lowestoft Revisited,* see above, which quotes *Lowestoft Through the Ages,* ML Powell, Flood & Son, 1952.

40. Gypsy Ghost Stories, *Fortean Times*, **FT 407:34,** July 2021. It quotes *English-Gipsy Songs*, C G Leland, Prof. E. H. Palmer, J. Tucker, Trubner & Co, London, 1876.

41. "Further chariot burial discovered at Pocklington", Current Archaeology, January 2019, https://archaeology.co.uk/articles/news/further-chariot-burial-discovered-at-pock.

PART 2 – HERE BE DRAGONS

8. Return of the shug monkey

I hesitated on whether to include Suffolk's shug monkeys among the Black Shucks and phantom dogs, or whether to put them in with the fantastic land animals like the crested dragon that predated on the good people of Bures. Some put the shug monkey among the werewolves and manimals. While the shug monkey occasionally walked upright, it seems it was never supposed to be even partly human. Shug monkeys are a cross between an ape, a lion and a huge dog. They spend most of the time on all fours (moving much faster than in their clumsy and occasional bipedal walks) and only got mixed up with werewolves later, and possibly even conflated with some of Suffolk's mystery big cats in more recent times. So enigmatic and hard to pin down is the shug monkey, even by the standards of mystery animals, that I've given it a little section all of its own.

The hellhound Black Shuck's many alternative names included Old Shug and Old Shock, the latter said to come from the Anglo-Saxon word *scucca*, meaning demon, and it was sometimes described as a demon or malicious spirit. But the shug monkey is described in most accounts as a strange animal that seemed to leave tracks and behave like a flesh-and-blood entity, unlike Black Shuck, which was a phantom and always male. While Shuck seems to be a personal name for one individual in particular, it's not even clear if shug monkey is a one-off or some kind of rare species of living thing. And here's another eyebrow-rasing observation – despite the shug monkey's medieval or possibly even earlier origins, the heyday of Suffolk shug monkey sightings seems to have been as lately as the 1950s, and there was a shug monkey alert among East Anglia's paranormal researchers in 2009.

About the only thing we can say with certainly about Suffolk's shug monkey is that it has ape or monkey-like features, but with "shining eyes". It's not a monkey, and it's an import from just over the Cambridgeshire border, from whence it seems to have wandered eastward into the Curious County.

According to *The Sutton Companion to British Folklore, Myths & Legends*, the shug monkey is found especially on the B1052 road between the Cambridgeshire border villages of Balsham and West Wratting and around the nearby Honey Hill and Slough Hill – all less than three miles away from Suffolk. "Shug Monkey" beer is brewed by Elgood's brewery of Wisbech, also in Cambridgeshire. To confuse matters, there's also the Beast of Balsham, a mystery big cat from that area, reportedly most active in the years leading up to 2006.

The *Sutton Companion* briefly describes shug monkey as a "myth thought to have been introduced by Norse settlers," a "black, shaggy entity with monkey-like features," and this makes me wonder if "shug" isn't just a corruption of "shaggy". Bury St Edmunds-based ghost investigator Alan Murdie described shug monkey as being like a huge dog, having only "the face of an ape," and speculates that both shug monkey and Shuck come from Viking legends about phantom wolves. Some include shug monkey in among the weirder types of Black Shuck manifestations, which is certainly a field already crowded with weirdness, what with Black Shuck in all his calf-headed, exploding, shape-shifting and size-changing variants.[1]

Murdie was of the view that the shug monkey tradition can't be traced back beyond 1954, and a letter from a former Cambridgeshire Police officer using the name "A. Taylor", who wrote to East Anglian writer, broadcaster and reactionary James Wentworth Day. *Here are Ghosts and Witches,* Wentworth Day's book from 1954, describes shug monkey in a single long paragraph. This has shug monkey roaming right up to the border with Suffolk.[2]

Another sighting of old monkey-face, also from the 1950s, was told to ufologist and paranormal investigator Nick Redfern many years after the event, and was said to have occurred in Rendlesham Forest. The area does get an awful lot of attention from enthusiasts of the strange, and due to what's become known as RFI, the Rendlesham Forest Incident, the appearance of some mystery lights in the sky on Boxing Day night 1980.

Depending on who you ask, the mystery lights were a hoax, or the misidentified light from Orford lighthouse (demolished in 2020), or time-travelling extraterrestrials from another dimension who landed after firing laser beams into a secret nuclear arms dump from a flying craft marked with heiroglyphics. (The story keeps changing.) What this does mean is that there's always someone asking around about the Rendlesham Forest UFO incident, which does turn up testimony on other weird stuff in the vicinity. These include numerous Rendlesham big cat sightings, bears (stand by for the rational explanation), wild boar and of course the shug monkey.

In the early 2000s, local resident Sam Holland told Redfern that soon after New Year's Day 1956, he was walking through the woods with Harry, his spaniel, when a "bizarre-looking creature" emerged from among the trees some 12 metres (40 feet) ahead of him, walking on four "huge, muscular legs... like a lion's."

At first Holland thought he'd spotted an exotic big cat escapee from a zoo (British big cats in the wild weren't yet a phenomenon in those days). But it soon became apparent that whatever-it-was had a thick, glossy black coat and was "easily ten foot" long, which would rule out any known prehistoric mammal carnivore as well as anything alive in the 1950s. It was when it turned its head towards Holland so he could see its "terrible face" that Holland realised he was up against some high strangeness, and that's when Harry the spaniel started whimpering in fear. Holland described a head like that of a silverback gorilla, a "huge neck", flared nostrils and powerful jaws. It looked intently at Holland and Harry and then sauntered off into the undergrowth. Holland would later describe what he'd seen as "a combination of ape, dog, lion and rhinoceros."[3]

Redfern added that Rendlesham researcher Maxine Pearson found a shug monkey footprint. I haven't been able trace Pearson.

CFZ Director Jonathan Downes admits "an ex-girlfriend of mine – an East Anglian paranormal researcher –was in possession of some video tape which showed the paw print of some huge animal – like that of a cat or a dog, but far bigger and with strange flattened finger nails rather than claws. She thought that it was a print from an alien big cat of some description, but my immediate thought was of the semi-mystical 'shug monkey'. When I later found that my friend and colleague Jan Scarff who was brought up in the vicinity of the air bases also knew about the so-called 'shug-monkey' I became even more interested, and I have been collecting reports for some years."

Downes added that he and Redfern "between us... have built up a convincing image of a large, dark coloured shambling beast which is presumably zooform in nature." By "zooform" (a term Downes invented) he means an entity that manifests as some sort of animal or part-human part-animal that couldn't possibly exist but is nonetheless reported, often associated with a particular area. Shambling "British Bigfoot" creatures, phantom black dogs with glowing eyes that flicker out of existence, ginger East of England werewolves and the impossible shug monkey fit into this category. Our understanding of biology and zoology tell us that such animals could never possibly have existed, yet still they come. The explanation, if there will ever be one, will probably be found in a still exotic corner of mass psychology or particle physics, or something.

Mr Hill, the undertaker at Southwold, is known to have had baboons in his little private zoo in the 1930s, but no escapes were reported, and there's no way the descendants of escaped 1930s baboons could have reached such gigantic size. Nor is there any contemporary mention of any escapes from Mr Wombwell's menagerie on its Suffolk tour of winter 1907, during which a "great blue and red-faced mandril baboon" was exhibited at Halesworth.[4] Even the largest known prehistoric baboon, *Dinopithecus*, five feet (1.5m) tall and weighing the same as a modern adult human, was a tiddler compared to the Rendlesham shug monkey.

The latest shug monkey alert was in 2009, when Jenny Pearce claimed to have seen a bear in Rendlesham Forest. Downes commented at the time that it was less likely to be a bear and more likely to be "something far less tangible, and far less easy to catch. It is, I strongly suspect, the return of the shug monkey, some ten years after its last spate of appearances." Hold tight for the rational explanation of the Rendlesham Forest bear, coming up in Chapter 12.[5]

An ape-like creature, signifying sin in medieval theology, looking down from the tower of the Priory Church of St Mary's at Letheringham

FOOTNOTES:TO CHAPTER 8: Return of the shug monkey

1. *The Sutton Companion to British Folklore, Myths & Legends*, Marc Alexander Marc, Sutton Publishing, London, 2005 paperback edition, p272; "Shug Monkeys and Werewolves – The Search for the Dog-Headed Men", Jon Downes and Richard Freeman, *Fortean Studies* vol 5; "Ghostwatch – Are Black Dogs wolves?" Alan Murdie, *Fortean Times*, **FT 278;16**, August 2011.

2. "Ghostwatch – Are Black Dogs wolves?" see above**;**. The report in question is in *Here are Ghosts and Witches*, James Wentworth Day, Batsford, London 1954. The shug monkey's also in *Mystery Animals of Britain and Ireland*, Graham J. McEwan, Robert Hale, London 1986, page 127.

3. Thanks to Nick Redfern for his assistance on shug monkey sources, and for permission to reproduce extracts from his works. "Seeking the sinister shug monkey," Nick Redfern, Mysterious Universe blog, http://mysteriousuniverse.org/2012/09/seeking-the-sinister-shug-monkey/; Redfern's shug monkey researches are also detailed in *Three Men Seeking Monsters,* Nick Redfern, New York: Paraview Pocket Books, 2004 (pages 36, 52, 165, 176-182; An unnamed Hollywood studio bought an "option" to make a film of *Three Men Seeking Monsters* a few years back, so shug monkey may yet make it to the big screen one day.

4. *Halesworth Times and Southwold General Advertiser*, 3 December 1907.

5. Still on The Track, Fortean Zoology blog, CFZ, http://forteanzoology.blogspot.co.uk/2009/03/return-of-shug-monkey.html. Downes told me he investigated the Rendlesham shug monkey in 1997. *Tales of Old Cambridgeshire,* Polly Howat, Countryside Books, 1990 asserts that the shug monkey had not been reported since World War Two.

Is it a dog? Is it a lion? Is it an ape? No, it's shug monkey! Attempts at reconstructing this elusive creature.

PART 2 – HERE BE DRAGONS

9. Upon evidence of the use of imps

Suffolk has always had its fair share of devils and demons. The Devil, Satan himself, made several forays into Suffolk in various folk stories, but he's usually driven away by determined bell-ringing or by the sheer holiness of the place – "silly Suffolk" as it was once known, came for *selig*, an Anglo-Saxon word for blessed, there being so many monasteries and holy men around in those days.

The church of Saint Botolph at Iken stands on a little hill rising out of the surrounding marshes, and it's believed to be the site of where Saint Botolph, a Dutch bishop who helped bring Christianity to East Anglia in the sixth century, had his first mission. It was said of him that he quickly earned a reputation for holiness – and power – by casting out the marsh devils and monsters infesting the area. It has been suggested that the "devils" of the marshes were just plumes of ignited marsh gas (methane), and that Saint Botolph just had the marshes drained to build his monastery, thereby driving out the devils.[1]

In a garden in Ballingdon, tracks were discovered in snow in a garden matching those of the "Devil's Hoofprints" whose appearance had caused such a furore in Devon days before in March 1855. The Ballingdon correspondent writing to the *Illustrated London News* felt they were the work of rats, whose tracks became less distinct as they climbed over drifts of deeper snow. There's also a legend that there once was a cupboard in Roos Hall, near Beccles, that contained an imprint of the Devil's hoof print made in a solid brick.[2]

There was also said to be a "howling demon" that was bound under the Homersfield Bridge over the River Waveney when it was built. The current bridge is the oldest surviving concrete bridge in Britain, dating from 1870. The magic binding of the demon under the bridge was said to work as long as water continued to flow under it. On one occasion at the end of the nineteenth century, when the flow almost dried up when it was dammed during repairs, "a user of the Bungay-road" reported hearing the demon, who "shruck and growled awful."[3]

Imps – little devils, small familiars – appear in the magnificent Wenhaston Doom, painted on wooden panels along a wall of St Peter's Church, Wenhaston, which dates to around 1490. The "Doom" is the Last Judgment at the end of the world. Person-sized devils blowing horns and tormenting the souls of the damned in Hell appear on the right of the painting, but in the centre is Satan himself conferring with a winged archangel, who is holding a set of weighing scales. In the scale on the left is a tiny naked human – a human soul, whose soul-weight is equal to that of the two tiny imps in the other scales to the right. These two rather cute imps – one a reddish colour and the other a natural brown – look vaguely like some kind of animal – mice or other rodents, or weasels or something. Lettering nearby suggests they are the souls of the wicked, already turned into imps at the last judgment. There are other Dooms painted on churches in Suffolk – at Bacton, Chelsworth, Stoke by Clare, Yaxley and Stanningfield. But none are as spectacular as Wenhaston's, nor do they feature imps. Strangely, the peak in reports of imps in Suffolk came not in the superstitious days of the Medieval Catholic Church, but in the times of the Protestant puritans during the English Civil War of the 1640s.

At the time, Suffolk was in the hands of Parliament's recently-established New Model Army, and the ever-present threat of a local rebellion by Royalist sympathisers remained. Into this tense environment came Matthew Hopkins, "Witchfinder General" (the title was never official, it was one he'd made up himself). Matthew Hopkins and Company included four "searchers" – two male and two female – whose job was to examine suspects for "private marks" on their body that might indicate pacts with the Devil, or hidden teats on which they could suckle imps. Hopkins was working under the remit of a Special Commission which charged him with, among other tasks, seeking out and acting upon any "compact with the Devil" he encountered, and taking decisive action "upon evidence of the use of imps."[4]

It may well have been in the interests of the regional Parliamentary powers-that-be to have Hopkins stir up paranoia and fear in the East of England, to keep the population in a distracted state of hysteria and terror. Some of the harmless old women he sent to the gallows (and in one case to burn at the stake) are known to have had a reputation as suspected Royalist sympathisers, or to have been neighbours of Royalist suspects.

An open campaign of persecution against Royalists would have been too dangerous – it may have led to open rebellion. At one point, some 120 witchcraft suspects were awaiting trial or sentence in prisons across East Anglia due to the actions of Hopkins and Company, they only got a brief reprieve "by reason of the near-approaching Cavaliers" (Royalists), making trials impossible.

When Royalist sympathisers were instead accused of witchcraft, those who expressed scepticism risked themselves being labelled as part of the satanic imp-suckling conspiracy. As in the twenty-first century with George W Bush post-9/11, suddenly "you're either with us or against us." Witchcraft was the War on Terror of the 1640s, used to justify all manner of human rights abuses. And just as the deluge of "evidence" obtained through torture in George W. Bush's "Detainee Programme" turned out to be fundamentally flawed, so the testimony of witches obtained in 1640s East Anglia turned out to be a pile of dangerous nonsense.

The Witchfinder General met at least three times with Parliamentary commanders, so it is possible that he was allowed by them to operate because he could try Royalist sympathisers without proper evidence. He amassed a reputed five-figure sum in charges to town councils for his witchfinding in 1645 money – ten shillings for each "examination" of a suspected witch, the same fee for each conviction, £6 in witchfinding fees to Aldeburgh, a staggering £23 to Stowmarket. Ipswich levied a special tax to pay off extra fees to the town jailer, as there were so many witchcraft suspects held in its prison.

The total death toll from the East Anglian witchcraft trials, which peaked in 1645, could have been as high as 472. By his own reckoning, Hopkins's assistant John Stearne put the total at 124 arrests, 68 hanged, with many others – mostly elderly at the time of their arrest – dying in prison. And the records of the trials contain references to more imps than you could shake a stick at.

Essex boy Hopkins (he lived just over the border from Suffolk in Manningtree, but he was born in Suffolk) claimed to have a copy of the "Devil's own list of all the witches in England" with him while he travelled around the East of England with his assistants John Stearne and Mary Phillips, both also of Manningtree. Those suspected of witchcraft by Hopkins and Company were locked in rooms with a small hole made in the door or wall through which imps could pass, with "watchers" keeping the suspect under surveillance, with instructions "if they see any spiders or flies to kill them. And if they cannot kill them, then they may be sure they are her imps."

Some imps weren't clearly described in Suffolk witchcraft trial testimony. Rose Parker, wife of Christopher, was found not guilty of feeding imps. Alice Denham was hanged when found guilty of charges including feeding imps, but we have little idea from trial transcripts what these imps were supposed to look like.

The Reverend John Lowes of Brandeston near Framlingham, after being kept awake for several days and nights and "swum" in Framlingham Mere, confessed in a delirious state to having "two imps" and that one of them was always putting him to doing mischief, including causing a ship off the coast of Harwich to be sunk. This testimony was accepted without anyone at the trial bothering to check whether any ships had recently been sunk off the Essex port of Harwich, or whether any such ships existed in the first place. Nor is there a description of the Rev. Lowes's "two imps." He withdrew his confession on the scaffold but they hanged him anyway.

From other trials we learn only the colour of imps. Anne Pearce, wife of Robert Pearce of "Steak"[7] in Suffolk had a "grey and a black imp", and sent them both out to "vex... destroy and torment" her enemies. Anne Leach and Elizabeth Clarke of Mistley in Essex (just over the Suffolk border on the other side of the Stour Estuary, and Hopkins's headquarters) seem to have shared one of their imps, and dispatched this "black and grey imp" to go out and kill cows. An unnamed Suffolk "old woman", a witch for the past 50 years, had been bewitching "cattle, corn, etc." as well as bewitching five of her family members "to death". All this was carried out by "Imps which came to her in several shapes", their form unspecified.[8]

Where Suffolk imps are described, they are usually suspiciously similar in form to small animals. A pamphlet published in London in 1645, *A True Relation of the Arraignment of 18 Witches* describes the witch trials at Bury, resulting in a mass execution there on 27 August of that year, and has probably the most detail on imps of any contemporary writings on the witch trials.

The *Arraignment* recounts trial testimony and witness statement on imps "sometimes in the shape of mice, sometimes in the shape of kittens, sometimes in the shape of snails, and otherwise in the shape of hornets wasps and divers other shapes". One of the (unnamed) witches charged at Bury "who had a grudge against a gentlemen and his wife in Suffolk... sent one of (her) Imps in the likeness of a little black dog" to play with their child, and the little black dog imp eventually "brought the child to the waterside and drowned it."[9]

Another witch, who "they say is to be burned" apparently regretted her actions, and had allegedly asked "divers godly ministers to pray in their several congregations that her imps may have no further power to do any such hurt."

Faith Mills of Fressingfield confessed to having two pet bird imps who forced a cow to jump over a stile. Mother Lakeland of Ipswich, one of very few witches in England to actually be burnt at the stake, stated in her trial that she had formed her own congregation to hold what we would regard today as a harmless Bible-reading circle. When questioned in the trial on whose authority she'd set up this group, she answered that it was "on the authority of the Holy Spirit." This didn't go down well. With everyone in such a panic over witches and Royalist plotters, people didn't want to hear about spirits, Holy or otherwise. Witnesses testified in her trial that Lakeland had three imps – two little dogs and a mole that she used in her witchcraft. Another of her imps of unspecified shape was sent to kill a Mr Beale, who was taken very ill but didn't die.[10]

There's also a curious link between witchcraft and phantom dogs like Black Shuck. Thomas Everard from Halesworth, a witchcraft suspect "found" by Hopkins, confessed that while serving as an apprentice he was "frightened by a dog, like a water dog."

A water dog was one of the variants on Black Shuck. The unfortunate Rev Lowes of Brandeston confessed to having been thrown from his horse when it was panicked by the sudden appearance of a mysterious "red dog" shortly before making his "compact with the devil." There were other such cases reported in witchcraft trials from Essex too. It seems that a phantom dog encounter heralded an imminent opportunity to make a pact with Satan and set up as a witch. Naturally, these accounts of phantom dog encounters were extracted under torture. Possibly, Hopkins and Company felt that adding some local colour and East Anglian Black Dog traditions (and playing on then very real fears of local phantom dogs) would add credibility to their victims' outlandish testimony.[11]

And the Suffolk imps were tame compared to some of those to be "found" in Essex, Norfolk, Cambridgeshire, Buckinghamshire and Hertfordshire. Witchfinder General Matthew Hopkins claimed to have come across familiars with such curious names as Griezel Greedigutt, Pecke in the Crowne, and Sacke and Sugar. Most of these resembled ordinary animals, but one-legged widow and alleged witch Elizabeth Clarke of Manningtree, Essex confessed to having a far stranger familiar she called Vinegar Tom, which she fed with her own blood. According to Hopkins, Clarke's imp Vinegar Tom initially appeared in the form of a greyhound with the head of an ox, but then shape-shifted into a headless four-year-old child that ran around in circles before fleeing the house.

How was the "use of imps" by witches arrangement actually supposed to work? According to *The Arraignment of 18 Witches*, it would begin with someone making "a covenant with the Devil". (This usually involved jumping into bed with him, in the case of female witches, however elderly). The Satanic covenant was usually followed by the Devil giving the witch a personal "mark" somewhere on their body, often in the form of tiny "teats or dugs" from which the witches suckled with their own blood the imps the Devil sent to them. The Rev. Lowes confessed to having a "teat on the crown of his head, and under his tongue".

Thus nourished, the imps would be sent out to do their bidding, usually "bewitching" people against whom they had a grudge. This "bewitching" would take the form of inducing crop failure, causing their cows to turn sick and die, wrecking crops through thunderstorms or floods, inducing horrible wasting diseases in their victims (of the order of making their tongues rot in their mouths, that sort of thing) or sending them mad.

These "teats" to feed imps were "but little," so small that they could be detected "between toes." The searchers would strip suspects naked, and as well as looking for "dugs and teats" they would hold suspects in confinement for 24 hours and watch them closely for signs of them being "perplexed" that their imps hadn't come to them for bloody nourishment and to receive orders on which crops and livestock to go out and trash or destroy. Naturally, you wouldn't have to be an imp-feeding witch to be "perplexed" at the prospect of being held in confinement naked and with the prospect of torture and then a death sentence over you.

Hopkins – a former quartermaster in the Eastern Association, the Parliamentary force that preceded the New Model Army – was extraordinarily well connected. He is known to have used the Rosicrucian Cipher, a code for Parliamentary spies. One of Hopkins's useful contacts was William Lilley, celebrity astronomer and occult adviser to the nobility, known as Merlinus Anglicus Junior (England's Little Merlin). Lilly's almanacs had a readership in the millions. Hopkins got most of his knowledge of useful things to say about the occult – pacts with the Devil, imps and all – through Lilley. Some of the occult stuff and nonsense that made its way into the witchcraft trials originated in the fifteenth century Latin language Catholic witch-

Imps weighed at the Last Judgement on the Wenhaston Doom (detail, top, and in Satan's scales, above left). Witchfinder General Matthew Hopkins (standing, in woodcut bottom right) "discovers" a menagerie of imps as "witches" (seated) confess to him , although this scene is from over the Essex border in Manningtree. From *A Discovery Witches,* possibly commissioned by Hopkins himself, out of copyright.

finder's manual *Malleus Maleficarum* (Hammer of the Witches), extracts of which would have come Hopkins's way via Lilley. Presumably, just as George W. Bush's "detainee" interrogators appear not have taken on board the *Maleficarum's* warnings, Hopkins hadn't studied in detail the bit in *Maleficarum* that warned about the dangers of relying on confessions extracted under torture.

Hopkins was devious and seems (unlike his East Anglian contemporary, the church vandalising iconoclast William Dowsing from Chapter 1) to have been in it entirely for the money. While Stearne, his assistant, appears to have believed in witches and the Devil, it seems that Hopkins probably didn't actually himself believe any of the testimony his Company extracted under torture. Hopkins knew his Bible, and drew on it for quotes, such as "Thou shalt not suffer a witch to live" from *Leviticus*, and a narrative on the persecution of witches by the Kings of Israel in *Kings*, but you could count the Biblical citations that supported his mission on the fingers of one hand.

Hopkins's fall eventually came. *The Moderate Intelligence*, a Parliamentary publication in September of 1645, called for "closer enquiries" before witches were convicted, noting that the Devil probably had better things to do than recruit "none but poor women" to settle scores using imps. John Gaule's 1646 book *Select Cases of Conscience Touching Witches and Witchcraft* denounced how "every old woman with a dog or cat by her side… pronounced for a witch". Hopkins and Stearne were questioned before the assizes in Norfolk.

But more important in ending Matthew Hopkins's reign of terror than any doubt of those convicted of witchcraft were the lingering suspicions that Hopkins with all his talk of imps and witchcraft had conned town councils out of a lot of money for his services. He died penniless, his late twenties in 1647, shortly after retiring from witch-hunting.

Just because the Witchfinder General was discredited, it didn't mean imps had gone away from Suffolk – definitely not! While Hopkins and Co. may have planted testimony on imps into the mouths of their broken torture victims, they were exploiting fertile territory. Belief in imps would persist in Suffolk for well over 150 years.

Zooform imps aplenty featured in the trial of the "Lowestoft witches", widows Rose Cullender and Amy Duny (or Denny), tried at Bury in 1664. Duny was indicted for causing the death of a child, and testimony centred on "a great Toad" which hopped out of the child's blanket when it was hung up. When this toad was seized with tongs and put on a fire, it burst into flames "like gunpowder." Children were said (by others) to have cried out that Duny had sent flies to put pins into their mouths, which they then vomited up (the pins, not the flies).[12] Testimony from other children stated that Duny and Cullender had sent imps to torment them, one child said they'd seized an imp in the form of a mouse, which they'd thrown on the fire where it flared up like gunpowder, other witnesses saw the gunpowder-like phenomenon but not the mouse. Another child said an imp was in the shape of a duck. Robert Sherringham alleged that Rose Cullender sent "Lice of an extraordinary bigness" after him.

Sir John Keeling, Sergeant at Law, was "most unsatisfied" with the imp evidence, which he correctly identified as based "upon the Imagination only of the Parties Afflicted." However, counter-arguments from the "most knowledgeable" Dr Brown of Norwich won the day, Dr Brown sensed "the subtlety of the Devil" was here at work. Both widows were hanged.[13]

Suspected witch "Mother Munnings" was up in court at Bury in 1694 in front of Lord Chief Justice Sir John Holt, on charges including keeping a "familiar imp" in the form of a polecat and a black imp and a white imp as well. She was acquitted, cross-examination established that the black imp and white imp were probably just balls of wool. [14]

A resident of Stonham Aspal was "swum for a witch" in 1752 – thrown into a pond to see if they would sink or swim. Swimming, rather than sinking, was not a good sign, as we will see. An old woman was thrown into a pit at Monk Soham because she "had a cat and must be a witch" and because she turned up to church in a black silk dress, "unnatural" apparel for someone of her humble circumstances. This was in the early nineteenth century.[15]

And witchcraft, apparently with imps, was back on the agenda in 1825 at Wickham Skeith, whose little church with its chiselled-away woodwoses we encountered earlier, not far from Mendlesham and Yaxley. An article in *The Times* of 19 July 1825 titled simply "Witchcraft", and giving as its source the *Suffolk Herald*, related events that had taken place more than two weeks previously. "Isaac Stebbings, a little spare man of 67" was "swum for a wizard in the presence of some hundreds of people!"

Stebbings's fellow parishioners included "a thatcher whose wife… is afflicted in mind" and also a farmer who is "occasionally disturbed." You can see where this is going already! "As in former days of gross credulity" somebody put forth "the surmise that they were 'bewitched'" with "Stebbings spoken of as the 'worker of the mischief'". The "afflicted" woman reckoned she had a means of detecting witches using a frying pan.

While she was carrying out this procedure, Stebbings came "dancing up to the door." Other irrefutable evidence Stebbings was a witch were accusations that he'd come round trying sell mackerel at 4 am, and that he allegedly had passed in front of one man's house several times when he was making candles, and that this man as a result couldn't "make his wax", the ingredients wouldn't melt or mix.

Stebbings was thrown into the village pond, and survived a 45-minute ordeal. He sank, which apparently meant he wasn't a witch, although some weren't satisfied and called for a retrial. Stebbings agreed, desperate to clear his name, and the following Saturday, with the local constable to keep the peace, Stebbings's second "swimming" was scheduled. With him was his companion Tom Wilden all the way from Bacton, nominated to be "swum" with him, as a sort of experimental control, being of the same weight and height approximately, to see if he'd pop out of the water like a cork too, a sure sign of being a witch.

The *Times* also mentions a "cunning man," an East of England euphemism for a wizard, who for a fee of £3 revealed that Stebbings was "with certainty" a witch. At the time Stebbings was swum, according to *The Times* (presumably the second attempt), the "afflicted farmer" who was "unusually perturbed", called out. *The Times* had him, "in an unusual voice," shout, "I can see the imps about me… I must frighten them away with my voice." At this point, the vicar and the churchwarden intervened to prevent Stebbings's second dunking, much to the disappointment of the "deluded multitude."[16]

And great were the deluded multitudes in those days, in Suffolk at least. One famous witchcraft sceptic, Richard Grey of Aldeburgh, practiced as a lawyer in London but then inherited some money and returned to Suffolk at the end of the eighteenth century, making it his mission to travel around (often sleeping rough) for the next 20 years trying to convince whoever would listen that neither witches nor their imps existed. This was not a popular idea.

When Grey came to Orford in the early years of the nineteenth century, they so didn't like his ideas about the non-existence of imps and witches that they tied him to a stake and piled up wood around him, ready to set fire to him. He only escaped when he promised never to show his face in Orford again. He retired to Aldeburgh.

More than 200 years after the Witchfinder General, *The Bury Post* reported that in Norton (west of Stowmarket) "there lives a famous old woman, of the name of Osborn … by trade a pedlar. This however is said to be merely a mask, to disguise her real profession – that of a fortune-teller; and she is also said to have the powers of a witch. Indeed, many persons are so terrified at the sight of her that they flee from her presence, and believe that to offend her in any way, or to refuse to buy of her goods, would bring upon them some dreadful visitation." Ms Osborn was said to have gained her powers from her late mother, "old Mrs Talbot of Cotton" who had bequeathed to Ms Obsorn her imps. These she had used to cause "poor Mrs W" to become "suddenly covered with white lice."[17]

A refreshing change from imps made up under torture was imps made up by parents. A type of mischievous imp unique to this part of England was a clim, which lived in the chimneys of nurseries and children's bedrooms. The clim could be summoned down the chimney by parents to scare naughty children into behaving themselves. Little is known about the clim or its alleged habits of appearance beyond the fact that it was scary enough to get children to shut up, and that it lived up a chimney.[18]

Wonders! Wonders!

While the alleged imps or familiars attached to most Suffolk people featured only in tales made up under torture, or in the delusions of others, one visitor to Suffolk seemed to cultivate the idea that his "Morocco black cat" was a familiar with diabolic powers.

Christian Katterfelto (also known as Dr Gustavus Katterfelto) was a Prussian lecturer on science and "natural philosophy" and a quack. He arrived in Britain in 1776 and travelled around the country for the next 23 years. He performed in London from 1780 for the next four years, using a solar microscope to show projected images of microbes, which he described as "insects" that he believed were behind the flu epidemic that broke out in 1782. He claimed to have a cure for this, and to have discovered perpetual motion. His catchphrase for introducing his projected microscope display was "Wonders! Wonders! Wonders!" Electricity, magnetism and the latest scientific discoveries that lent themselves to spectacular demonstrations also featured in his shows.

Back in his glory days in London he could charge a considerable two shillings and sixpence a head, and his audiences there had included the Prince Regent and Royal Family, the Archbishop of Canterbury and Dr Samuel Johnson, but eventually everybody who was everybody had seen his act, so he had to hit the travelling paid-lecture circuit. He was a skilled conjurer, and part of his showmanship was to hint that his powers had a demonic origin and even that he might have sold his soul to the Devil.

To complete this "demonic powers" act, in his shows he was always attended by at least one "Moroccan black cat." When Dr Katterfelto and his Moroccan black cat pulled into Glasgow, one spectator described it as "an animal of much merit, which gained him at one time in London, £3000… an 'occult' medical doctor with his Morocco black cat – a familiar."

Dr Katterfelto's Moroccan black cat appeared to have a long tail, at a subsequent performance no tail at all, while the conjurer would make its "kittens" appear in the pockets of audience members. Marie Antoinette, Queen of France, ensured she got one of these kittens. Other accounts of Dr Katterfelto's events say he appeared attended by "blackamoors" and sundry black cats, more than one. Trying to pass off your black cat as an imp may have been big and clever in London society, but to do so in Suffolk, was foolishly dangerous. Over a quarter of a century after Katterfelto had passed through Ipswich, they were still "swimming" witches.

There was a sense of anticipation in the air when Dr Katterfelto stopped at Colchester in August 1784 on his way to his next stop, Ipswich. The *Ipswich Journal* reported "Divine and natural Philosopher and the various Arts made use of by Sharpers to obtain illegal fortunes… at the Town Hall at Colchester, with very great applause and a crowded house"[19]

When the Doctor and his Moroccan black cat finally arrived in Ipswich in September, 500 came to see his week-long run at the Council Chamber. The *Journal* reported, "his various philosophical experiments are so astonishing and wonderful that they are beyond all description. Many persons will have it that he, or his famous Morocco Black Cat, are devils."[20] In the event, the county town proved more sophisticated than rural Suffolk, Dr Katterfelto's visit didn't end with a trip to the local pond. Dr Katterfelto passed on from Ipswich to his next sell-out destination. After another fifteen years on tour and 15,000 shows under his belt, he died on tour in modest circumstances in an obscure Yorkshire market town. The fate of his reputedly demonic Moroccan black cat familiar (or possibly familiars) is unrecorded.[21]

Impish face at the church at Barking, near Needham Market (left) and a devil sticking out his tongue at sinners at St Mary's Church, Halesworth (right)

FOOTNOTES TO CHAPTER 9: Upon evidence of the use of imps

1. *Suffolk Coastal Ebb & Flow,* Suffolk Coastal District Council booklet, via Paranormal Database. Marsh gas explanation from the Parish of St Botolph Without Bishopsgate, London, which points out that Botolph's monastery could just have easily been near Boston, Lincolnshire. www.botolph.org.uk/who-was-st-botolph/)

2. "The Devil's Hoof Prints", Mike Dash www.mikedash.com/assets/files/Devil's%20Hoofmarks.pdf.

3. *Norfolk Folklore Collections*, W. B. Gerish, Vol.3, p.193, 1916-18 via Paranormal Database.

4. *Witchfinder General – the Biography of Matthew Hopkins*, Craig Cabell, Sutton, London 2006.

5. *Witchfinder General:* J Gaule, *Select Cases of Conscience Touching Witches and Witchcraft* 1646.

7. If there is still such a place name in Suffolk today, I can't find it. The way the internet works makes it hard to find, too. Any search for "Steak" together with "Suffolk" brings up pub food or a certain kind of restaurant. It could be Stoke by Clare or Stoke by Nayland, both villages in the south of Suffolk, close to the River Stour and to the border with Essex, or Stoke Park, now a neighbourhood of Ipswich near Ipswich railway station.

8. Imps in several forms from *Arraignment of 18 Witches*, see below.

9. Note the similarity between this imp and Black Shuck legends involving a phantom Black Dog, usually found near water.

10. *The Folklore of East Anglia*, Enid Porter, BT Batsford, London 1974.

11. Everard's water dog from *Paranormal Suffolk: True Ghost Stories*, Christopher Reeve, Amberley Stroud 2009. Norfolk assizes interrogation from https://en.wikipedia.org/wiki/Matthew_Hopkins.

12. In *Revelation*, 16:13 in the New Testament, John of Patmos describes his vision of the Apocalypse, in which "I saw three impure spirits that looked like frogs; they came out of the mouth of the dragon, out of the mouth of the beast and out of the mouth of the false prophet." So being associated with the sudden, strange appearance of a frog or toad would presumably count against you when the Witchfinder was in town.

13. There's an account of the trial at www.lowestoftwitches.com/the_trial_report.htm.

14. "Mother Munnings" and her alleged imps from *The Encyclopaedia of Witchcraft and Demonology,* R. Hope Robbins, Paul Hamyln, London, 1959.

15. Swimming in Stonham Aspal from Foxearth Historical Society www.foxearth.org.uk/blog/2005/04/weighed-down-by-bible.html)

16. The *Annual Register* for 1825-1826 repeats pretty much the same story, but minus the bit about the farmer shouting about imps, and there's a variation in that he sold some candles that didn't melt properly, rather than causing other people's homemade candles not to work. https://books.google.co.uk/books?id=FnNIAAAAYAAJ&q=wickham#v=twopage&q=wickham&f=true.

17. *Bury Post*, 8 August 1855 www.pipwright.com/Newspapers_in_Suffolk_1851_1875.htm. Outside Suffolk, but still in East Anglia, imps were hard to get rid of, and had to be in some cases elaborately destroyed by relatives when a witch died. When witch Susan Cooper of Whittlesford, South Cambridgeshire, died in 1878, the children ran home from school to stomp on the soil of her grave so the "imps wouldn't get out". A nineteenth-century witch at Lodden, Norfolk was said to have rat-sized, miniature human-like imps with bat wings that she kept in a box. In Horseheath, Cambridgeshire, the local witch was supposed to own five imps resembling white mice that she carried in her red underskirt. Jabez Few of Willingham, Cambridgeshire, who died in 1928, had white rats that village children called his imps and which came when he whistled. These examples are from *The Folklore of East Anglia*, Enid Porter, BT Batsford, London 1974 which quotes *Cambridge Antiquarian Society Proceedings* 1915.

18. *Suffolk Dialect,* Louise Maskill, Bradwell Books, Sheffield, 2014.

19. Suffolk Notes from 1784 reprinted in the *Ipswich Journal*, 9 September 1884. Sharpers are con artists, hence "card sharp." Dutch scientist Antonie Philips van Leeuwenhoek used microscopes of his own design to see "microbes" a century earlier.

20. *Ipswich Journal*, 18 September 1784, Pip Wright's Suffolk newspapers website, www.pipwright.com/Newspapers_in_Suffolk_1720_1800.htm.

21. *Darlington and Stockton Times*, 17 October 2008, www.darlingtonandstocktontimes.co.uk/news/3767854.Hooked_on_the_tale_of_a_flamboyant_travelling_showman/; www.historyextra.com/book-review/katterfelto-prince-puff; www.amostcuriousmurder.com/BellGeordie.htm; "Katterfelto" was sometimes spelled with one "t".

PART 2 – HERE BE DRAGONS

10: Hobby lanterns, will-o-the-wisps and the Felixstowe Fire Demon

Witnesses insist "it wasn't the lighthouse" (at Orford Ness, above, now demolished) causing mystery lights in the Rendlesham UFO Incident.

Some encounters that have taken place within Suffolk involved something so bizarre it's unclear whether it was supposed to be a living entity or not.

A case in point is the experience of a Mr Turner sometime at the close of the nineteenth century, returning via Bulcamp (opposite Blythburgh, the other side of the River Blyth) and "coming down to Westleton seeing something on the road." Mr Turner tried to "smack his stick into it," but whatever it was it "fared on as if it went into a fleece of wool, then flung him onto that fence and made him walk to the end of the fence." Mr Turner feared that whatever-it-was would "fling him into the holl (ditch), but that it didn't."[1]

Ridiculous as such encounters with living balls of wool may sound, they were in the folklore of many parts of the British Isles, and multiple reports of run-ins with malicious balls of fleece came from England and Ireland in the nineteenth century. They were generally lumped in together with the fairies, probably because they were regarded as "magical." "Fairy" was originally an adjective meaning "magical"; there were even "fairy giants" in Ireland.

Then there is the Growing Stone of Blaxhall. From the footpath that goes through that village of Blaxhall, you can see the Growing Stone through a hole kindly cut in the fence by the owner of Stone Farm, where the Growing Stone resides. (The Growing Stone also features on the village sign, along with racing motorbikes from the local motocross circuit and some of George Ewart Evans's "fellows who cut the hay".)

While the Growing Stone may not actually be an animal, it's growing, so it has to at least be alive, right? The Growing Stone was, in that already much-used phrase, "said to be" the size of a small loaf of bread a century ago (or a century before whenever the story is being told) and is now a boulder weighing over five Imperial tons (5.08 metric tonnes).

Geological scrutiny, however, has not been kind to the Growing Stone of Blaxhall's backstory. It turns out to be a 10,000 year-old "itinerant" boulder, brought to Blaxhall by the action of glaciers during an Ice Age. A growing stone is already pushing the bounds of credibility, but an inert stone that after a period of around 10,000 years suddenly puts on a growth spurt is even harder to believe. Five-ton boulders, and indeed the supply of stone bigger than shingle, are rare in Suffolk, so even a five-ton Ice Age itinerant boulder could come to be regarded locally as something rather special.

Most of "so weird we're not even sure if it's alive" Suffolk phenomena, though, involve nocturnal mystery lights, moving as if under the control of something intelligent, and interacting with the observer in a way that suggests something living. These mystery lights, for centuries assumed to be alive or the work of something alive, were known in Suffolk as hob-o-lanterns, hobby lanterns, lantern-men, will-o-the-wisps, Jack-o-lanterns or even Jenny Burnt Arses.[2] (The carved-out pumpkin Jack-o-lantern decorations of today are caricatures commemorating a feared creature associated with a glowing light that was much more terrifying.) Elsewhere in the Curious County these creatures with the dancing lights were called Joan the Wad – said to bring good luck – Pinket or Spunkie, or corpse candles. In some hob-o-lantern traditions, the entities were the souls of unbaptised children, or the drowned. Some could disguise themselves as beautiful girls. On the Slaughden peninsula, the remains of a once-proud port and royal shipyard that's now a narrow spit on the end of Aldeburgh, there were said to be lights associated with nameless "things" or "little beings" that pelted you with shingle.

While in past centuries unexplained lights were assumed to be the work of fairies or the Devil, the modern explanation for will-o-the-wisps is that it was misidentified jets of ignited marsh gas – methane – or perhaps some sort of St Elmo's fire phenomena. St Elmo's fire – an electrical discharge seen during thunderstorms, a little bit like lighting – is more often associated with tall, pointy and often metal structures like ship's masts, aeroplane wings, chimneys and church steeples. But the blue glow of St Elmo's fire, sometimes accompanied by a buzzing noise, has also been recorded during thunderstorms around grass, leaves and cow's horns.

John Wentworth Day reported that these mystery lights were once so common in Syleham, on the Suffolk bank of the River Waveney, that the phenomenon was known as Syleham Lights. Day added these were most probably self-igniting plumes of marsh gas, and after the Syleham Marshes were drained, these were much diminished.[3]

However, ignited marsh gas and St Elmo's fire don't account for the tendency of Suffolk's will-o-the-wisps and hobby lanterns to lure travellers to their doom, to move in zigzagging figures of eight, or for the characteristic of the invisible lantern men (or whatever they were) to not only lead you astray with their phantom lights, but also to dash a traveller's own lantern out of their hand and "burst it all to pieces." The Slaughden "things," whatever they were, had snatched the lantern from the hands of a shepherd on at least one occasion. Lamp-snatching hobby lanterns – who led you off the path after extinguishing your own lamp – were said to be at large around Dunwich too up until around 1924.[4]

Travellers should avoid whistling, as lantern men would always come to kill you if you did. And whatever you do, don't show them your lantern, or they'll dash it out of your hand and "burst it all to pieces". Although in other stories, you could distract the hobby lanterns by whistling or make them go away by lying flat and holding your breath.[5]

The *East Anglian Miscellany*, published between 1933 and 1943, includes a letter from a Mr G Fell on hobby lanterns, which describes an incident from his boyhood in Sudbourne, just north of Orford.

Fell describes in around 1882 encountering hobby lanterns: "I expect very few people have seen one." He recalled two fields in Sudbourne where "on certain nights one of these objects could be seen on these fields. They look like a dull red light, like a lantern with the glass smoky. It moved to and fro across the field, about walking pace, always in the same track above the ground: it never went near the hedge." Whatever it was, it seemed to disappear whenever Fell and his boyhood chums approached within 100 yards (30 metres), and then light up again when they withdrew.

At Orford Ness, a few miles east of Sudbourne as the crow flies but over on the other side of the River Alde, at the end of the narrow spit of land, is Lantern Marshes. This features in a map of 1600 as "Lanterne Marsh", which seems to predate any beacon or lighthouse. Could the mystery lantern-lights of Sudbourne have been around for some centuries before Mr Fell experienced them?[6]

There's also a Lampland Marshes on large-scale maps immediately south of the village at Walberswick. There were said to be jack-o-lanterns in Eastbridge and at Rendlesham, and up until the 1920s at Mumbery Hills (near Westleton) and in the "low" (low ground) of Dunwich Walks, appearing between Michaelmas (29 September) and Christmas Day. Miss Tish Spall of Westleton advised of hobby lanterns, "don't go among them or they'll jump about and put your lantern out." She described how she herself had been "well-led" (beguiled and led astray) over a distance of a mile and half away from her route by hobby lanterns at Westleton Walks. "Woody" a witness to a possible Black Shuck, said that Martlesham Creek is "full of stories of fairy lights and ghosts… a lot of weird stuff round the church at Martlesham".[7]

The 1980 Rendlesham Forest UFO Incident still continues to attract a lot of attention. There's even a *The Rendlesham UFO Incident* "found footage" sci-fi horror film, also known as *Hanger 10*, in which by far the best performances were by the wintery Suffolk skies and the long-abandoned bunkers of the airbase. Given the attention still lavished on "Rendlesham," it's curious how another Suffolk "unusual lights" incident has been all but forgotten except by obscure UFO buffs on the other side of the Atlantic. The incident that made the front page of the Ipswich *Evening Star* on 21 September 1965, with the headline "Felixstowe Glowing Object Mystery" somehow seems to have become almost as obscure as the East Anglian airship wave of 1909. Although just like Rendlesham, the Felixstowe Glowing Object Mystery seems to have acquired some extra embellishment in the telling.[8]

By the time of the 1965 Felixstowe Glowing Object Mystery, *Flying Saucer Review* was already complaining, "our newspapers no longer print anything about flying saucers." But as mainstream *Evening News* science writer Robert Chapman explained at the time, "mysterious lights" just didn't make the grade anymore. The term "UFO" had just entered circulation, and the nuts-and-bolts ufologists (who believed UFOs were physical craft) were beginning to come into conflict with "contactees" who looked to the Space Brothers to save mankind. "Occult theories" about UFOs were also on the rise, and the aliens that people described meeting were becoming more "hostile" and more scary.[9]

Mumbling about a man in the flames

The "Glowing Object Mystery" involved three Felixstowe residents in their early twenties – lorry driver Geoffrey Maskey, his girlfriend Mavis Forsyth and Michael Johnson, who lived a few doors down from Maskey. It was Maskey who was driving them all one night down Walton Avenue, back then in 1965 a fairly quiet road on the edge of town, but half a century later the road along the very busy waterfront of the Port of Felixstowe, Britain's biggest container port. The "last street-lamp" on Walton Avenue, where they stopped for Johnson to get out, presumably for a quick wee in the nearby woods, is now right by the huge roundabout where container lorries leave the port for their onward journeys.

The *Star* report opens by describing a "high-pitched humming noise…. a great orange tinted object moved across the sky… a man staggered from a hedge and collapsed." The humming noise was heard as Maskey and Forsyth waited in the car for Johnson. The sound was quickly followed by a "long oval object in the sky… a dull orange colour". The glow from it lit up most of Walton Avenue for about half a minute. It was then that Forsyth and Maskey realised their friend was still in the woods, and in a panic, they reversed the car back to look for him. At this point, Johnson emerged staggering from the bushes and collapsed. His friends noticed "a lump and marks on his neck," and he was "mumbling about a man in the flames getting him," before he lost consciousness, so his friends dragged him into the car and drove him to Felixstowe Hospital. There, Johnson was diagnosed as suffering from "a severe shock" and transferred to the better resourced Ipswich and East Suffolk Hospital. As the paper went to press, the hospital still wasn't letting visitors in to see Johnson.

By the time the American Monsters website wrote it up in 2011, the "Glowing Object" had morphed into "The Felixstowe Fire Demon." Details had attached themselves to the story that weren't in the original *Evening Star* report. The three youths had been on their way by car to Essex (off their route, and they were heading the wrong way for the ferry to Harwich). A normally dark night became "Stygian blackness", Johnson was given amnesia and couldn't recognise his friends when he regained consciousness in hospital in the morning. Additionally, Johnson had acquired "unusual burns" on the back of his neck and a bruise above his ear.

The account in American Monsters goes way beyond a "man in the flames trying to get him," this has become an "unseen force" that compelled Johnson to walk out of the car at Walton Avenue and head into the woods, where he encountered "a humanoid being" with "large sloping eyes that were glowing in the darkness." The creature was "engulfed by orange flames" and caused Johnson to black out.[10]

Was there really a "man in the flames" that early autumn night on Felixstowe's Walton Avenue? While the "Glowing Object Mystery" seems to have strayed into UFO territory, it sounds like something more in the local tradition of hobby lanterns than actual scary occupants of craft from outer space. The humming sound that accompanied the event suggests some sort of electromagnetic phenomenon. And Johnson's confused, "mumbling" state could well have been the result of some hitherto unexplained electromagnetic effect on his brain, triggering "shock" and possibly even delirium and hallucinations.

In any event, the strange orange glow was back in the skies over Felixstowe on the hot summer night on 1 July 2006, when witnesses reported two "orange orbs" over Old Felixstowe and the skies to the north. A witness described these orbs as "moving extremely fast, they appeared to chase each other. The objects were watched for around ten seconds before dropping behind the horizon, disappearing from view."[11]

My dog saw a UFO

Nor was Michael Johnson the only Suffolk man known to have been injured by some sort of mystery glowing light entity that falls squarely into the "so bizarre we don't even know if it's alive" category.

Thomas Meyer, a postman, was walking with his dog on Sizewell Beach just before seven in the evening in late February of 1975. Suddenly, he noticed a bizarre greenish yellow thing like a pumpkin – glowing "like a TV screen" as it headed in from the North Sea and hovered a few feet above the beach. The dog saw it too, and ran off – it was found cowering over a mile away. The mystery glowing thing gave off a strong odour like acid drops, and Tom felt heat radiating off it. This "heat" made him so ill that he was off work for a long time. (He was partially paralysed according to some accounts.)

A lighthouse keeper and local fisherman told ufologist Jenny Randles, who investigated the incident, that they'd seen something similar, and there was TV interference in the town of Leiston, just down the road, during these events. Randles speculated that whatever it was might have been an earthlight – a hypothetical build-up of an electrical charge caused by underground geological activity when tectonic plates rub together, or an exotic plasma thrown up by some kind of not-yet understood "meteorological tsunami"[12]

Luminous balls of light were seen passing through walls of the Queen's Head pub at Blyford (between Blythburgh and Halesworth) pursued by a group of people in 1969, with some accounts describing these lights disappearing into a wardrobe, observed by the landlady but not the landlord, in "the early seventies." In 1970, a workman in the kitchen of the Bird's Eye factory at Rant Score, Lowestoft, felt a touch on his shoulder when working there and saw that it was caused by a floating, glowing blue ball that then passed through a wall.[13]

The Rendlesham Forest Incident has gone down in history (it's on the National Archives website) as a "UFO incident". As we've already noted, however, that particular stretch of Suffolk Coastal District has been prone to strange lights, often moving as if under "intelligent control", going back to at least the nineteenth century. Two men saw in the 1970s "a pair of lights" hovering over the coast near Orford Castle, near Rendlesham. The lights were hovering quite close to the water, and these darted away at "an incredible speed" as they approached.[14]

Unusual lights

What became the Rendlesham Forest UFO incident began as a police call out about "unusual lights" on Boxing Day night in 1980. Two Suffolk Police officers also investigated the reports at 4.11am the next day, but reported no trace of anything.

Retired US Airbase commander Colonel Charles Halt claimed at a later UFO conference in Woodbridge that some US personnel based at Rendlesham had "lost 40 minutes" during their search of the nearby woods in response to a report of unusual lights, and that their communications equipment went "off air" at the time. John Burroughs, Bud Steffens and James Penniston, who were part of the search team, later told of feeling "static" as they observed the flying object's flashing lights and hieroglyphic-like markings.

Halt, who was base deputy commander at the time, was not present during the first encounter, but was told next morning. Then on the evening of December 27, Halt heard officers shouting, "It's back, the UFO's back." He went to investigate with a team who found three "impact holes" in the ground and damage to the treetops.

Soon afterwards, the search team spotted a "mysterious object" with a moving red light in a field between the woods and a nearby farmhouse. Whatever it was "came towards us into the forest, moving, bobbing up and down in the trees. It was oval, about 100 to 150 yards away, with a dark centre and red around it," with "sparks" coming from it before it "exploded and disappeared" a minute later.

They then saw objects high in the sky – one was "elliptical" before it shape-shifted into a "full circle", then two "very bright lights" in the sky approached from the south, one came overhead at very high speed and sent down a laser beam of about 10 to 12 inches (up to 30 cm) in diameter. Halt revealed he'd received statements from RAF Bentwaters and the nearby RAF Wattisham base, stating "at Wattisham, they picked up what they called a bogie – an enemy craft – and lost it near the Forest."

Alternative theories claim the light came from either the Orford Ness lighthouse or some kind of military tests, while ex-USAF security policeman Kevin Conde later claimed in 2003 that he and colleagues had hoaxed the whole thing using a loudspeaker and car headlights.

Sceptics have pointed to inconsistencies in various witnesses' accounts and more detail being added over time. A 2015 poll by travel magazine *Wanderlust* downgraded Rendlesham to only the *third* best place in the UK to see UFOs, after Bonnybridge in Scotland and Broad Haven in Wales.[15]

"Rendlesham" is now firmly entrenched in the canon of UFO "close encounters," with extraterrestrials, time travellers from the future or beings from another dimension said to be involved, depending on who you ask. Or in another version, it's a complex psychological warfare cover story for some Cold War shenanigans around an airbase that may or may not have had a secret store of nuclear weapons, or a fake store of non-existent nuclear weapons dreamt up to confuse Soviet agents.

Sceptics say it was just the misidentified light from the now demolished Orford Ness lighthouse nearby, which is a bit of an insult to the witnesses' intelligence. A more reasonable suggestion is that it was some sort of military activity at Orford Ness, then a restricted military zone, although the above-top-secret Cobra Mist programme to build "the world's most powerful radar" that Orford Ness had housed was suddenly cancelled in 1972. The Atomic Weapons Research Establishment had also ended its bizarre experiments at Orford Ness involving exploding miniature models of nuclear bombs there long before 1980.[16]

Alleged visitors from outer space and top secret Cold War black ops notwithstanding, it strikes me that Rendlesham's tale of people running around the woods on a dark midwinter night in a confused state, chasing mystery lights "bobbing" around the forest floor is beginning to sound familiar. These were mystery lights that produced sparks, exploded, disappeared, fired "laser beams" and induced missing time experiences. To me, this sounds more like an encounter with a traditional mischievous Suffolk coast hobby lantern or Jenny Burnt Arse than with anything from other worlds or from the devious minds of military intelligence.

The hobby lanterns and strange lights in the coastal Suffolk sky persisted long after the Rendlesham Incident. A "green meteor" was seen heading towards Orford Ness in the autumn of 1999. Brenda Butler, the local ufologist who did much to popularise the "Incident", still guides groups through the forest and runs Rendlesham "skywatches" on the last Saturday of each month. Brenda has spent a lot of nights at Rendlesham and Tunstall Forest. She claims to regularly spot UFOs and the "mysterious beings piloting these ET craft." She also claims to have seen "orbs" floating in the forest, and a strange light there described as being close to the ground. Other believers have reported "aports" in the Forest – small stones apparently falling out of the sky after appearing to teleport themselves from nowhere to a point a short distance above the ground. This phenomenon sounds remarkably similar to the nameless "things" of Slaughden, that pelted passers-by with shingle, who we met a few pages back.[17]

Something vaguely intelligent

A contributor to Paranormal Database described how in January 2010, on the footpath from Hollesley leading to Shingle Street, she watched with her partner as a single greenish glowing ball of light danced around the path and the marsh behind the beach. Shingle Street is so-called because a lot of the shingle or pebbles washed away from the beaches to the north ends up piled up here, formed into bizarrely-shaped mounds and lagoons.

The following month, also at Hollesley, a local woman using the alias Babylonian Angel reported seeing two hobby lanterns while sitting on top of an old World War Two pillbox, at around half past eleven on a still and cold night, with a misty sea and some low cloud in the skies. She described how "the light began moving in spurts of quick arches" and "slow figures of eight", how it "bobbed back and forth" before quickly heading towards her and then away from her. When it was less than 50 meters away, she could see it as a "green-tinged white light... my partner... remembered it being a white light." Close up, it just looked like a point of light, but further away it looked like a light shining from the centre of a transparent sphere, with "fine wiggling lines... like those lightning/plasma balls you get in novelty shops." The light moved towards them and backed away for about 15 minutes, before Angel became frightened on seeing there was another light, "exhibiting the same strange movement... about 20 degrees to the left of Orford lighthouse."

Angel was sure "something vaguely intelligent was behind the motion of the lights... the first one had come to check us out." She and her partner left soon afterwards. Four days later, she "had other experiences with an orange light over Rendlesham Forest while camping".[18]

So what's going on with the hobby lanterns, then? Are these mystery lights really alive? One of the more bizarre theories on the origin of these mystery lights is that held by Andrew Collins, author of *LightQuest*, who suggests that they are "the product of sentient light forms and light intelligences... sentient energy forms and complex plasma constructs... manifestations of a higher dimensional reality," mixed with a bit of "quantum entanglement" and some "multidimensional experiences" thrown in for good measure. Collins claims that "some mysterious balls of light are sentient, and will interact with humans."[19]

I suspect that the answer to Suffolk's mystery lights will lie not in the animal kingdom or in "multidimensional reality" but in currently exotic particle physics or meteorology, just as currently exotic physics will one day explain the strange burns inflicted on the parishioners of Blythburgh and Bungay by "ball lighting" attributed to Black Shuck. (Although I await with interest theoretical physics's explanation for how an electromagnetic or meteorological effect can knock a lantern out of your hand.)[20]

Is there, then, something peculiar to the geology or in the weather system of the Suffolk coast that gives rise to these entities? I recall a friend telling me they'd talked to a car breakdown repairman who told him he was on call one night and experienced a "missing time" experience in Rendlesham Forest, which he didn't regard it as having anything to do with UFOs. Is there just something intrinsically odd about that particular part of the Curious County that causes mystery lights that look like they know what they're doing? It's interesting to note that hobby lights seem restricted to the coast and the marshes and forests immediately behind the coast – it doesn't seem to be a county-wide phenomenon encountered inland too, in contrast to much of its mystery fauna.

Some of the scarier hobby lights and jack-o-lanterns may have been yet another crude tactic to scare people away from local smuggling operations, in the manner of a *Scooby-Doo* episode. Smugglers needed their own signalling system, and needed to stop others signalling when they didn't want any attention, which may explain who the nameless "things" were that suddenly reached out of the dark at you on remote stretches of coast to snatch away your lantern. A notice in The Fox Inn pub in Darsham, for example, referred to a jar of toenail clippings intended to scare away witches, and a local static jack-o-lantern mystery light source used as cover for a smuggling operation.

Bob Markham, a retired geologist with the Ipswich Museum, told me that the geological strata of coastal East Anglia being "of recent age" also helps explain the region's abundance of mystery lights. Suffolk's strata is among the youngest in the UK. It's so young, says Bob, that there's still animal and vegetable matter decomposing down there. The phosphorous in this decaying matter rises to the ground – often aided by small underground earth tremors – in the form of phosphine gas, which ignites spontaneously on contact with other gases.

The owls are not what they seem

Hobby lanterns may turn out to be animals after all. Just when you thought East Anglia's mystery lights couldn't get any weirder, enter "the luminous owls of Norfolk."

These were bright, nocturnal white lights seen flitting around the fields and woods of Suffolk's northerly neighbour, their behaviour said to closely resemble that of a barn owl. This phenomena started in 1908, when gamekeeper Fred Rolfe came forward to say a glowing barn owl had startled him by passing close to his face one night near King's Lynn.

Sightings of luminous owls became common around Twyford and Fakenham (North Norfolk), although one luminous owl sighting was as far south as the village of Rushall, just five miles from the border with Suffolk. Local naturalists such as RJW Purdey got involved – his reported nocturnal observations included a luminous barn owl seen through binoculars, appearing as a "lamp surrounded by mist". *The Zoologist* reported "exceeding bright" owls at Haddiscoe Marshes.

Purdy believed that owls acquired their glow from roosting in trees with phosphorescent fungal spores on them. He boldly declared all East Anglia's will-o-the-wisps to be just luminous owls. The matter seemed settled after Norfolk engineer Edward Cannell managed to grab a dying luminous owl as it landed in his garden at Lower Hellesdon. Cannell described it as "phosphorescent in nature," with a "faint glow."

While the men of science regarded the matter as solved, Mr Roberts – the Norwich taxidermist who received the owl cadaver from Cannell – was unimpressed. Mr Roberts said it was an ordinary female barn owl, adding, "I have seen nothing luminous about it." Many – including Charles Fort in his book *Lo!* – observed the "faint glow" of phosphorescent fungus came nowhere near the "exceedingly bright" white light observed in luminous owl phenomena. Fort suggested it wasn't so much a case of will-o-the-wisps being just misidentified phosphorescent owls, more phosphorescent owls being misidentified will-o-the wisps.

Fred Silcock on The Owl Pages website suggests barn owls may be naturally luminescent, able through some not yet understood biological mechanism to turn their luminosity on and off, possibly to dazzle their prey. Silcock notes that for a predator that hunts at night, they do have a lot of white plumage. He also observes that in Australia, which also has barn owls, there's an equivalent to hobby lanterns, Min Min lights, that flit around like birds. He cites an account from Australia of a barn owl flying into someone and knocking their lantern out of their hand. Further study is needed, admits Silcock.[21]

So we remain unsure whether Suffolk's mystery lights are even alive, whether they even fall into the "animal" category, let alone what they are.

Evening Star

Ipswich, Tuesday, September 21, 1965 No. 24,437

Felixstowe Glowing Object Mystery

The "Felixstowe Glowing Object Mystery" makes the front page of the Ipswich *Evening Star* in September 1965 (above), with photos of two eyewitnesses. The Cobra Mist radar facility in Orford Ness (right) is surrounded by the Lantern Marshes, home to lantern-snatching, pebble-throwing mystery lights.

UFO LANDS IN SUFFOLK

And that's OFFICIAL

The Rendlesham Forest UFO Incident breaks in the *News of the World*, two years after the alleged events of Boxing Day Night 1980 (left).

Rant Score in Lowestoft (right) with Gulliver, the UK's tallest wind turbine, in the distance. Just in front of it is the Bird's Eye factory, where glowing balls of light passing through walls troubled workers in the 1970s.

FOOTNOTES TO CHAPTER 10: Hobby lanterns, will-o-the-wisps and the Felixstowe Fire Demon

1. Mr Turner's encounter retold by Mr J. Spall of Westleton, an old man by the time of his 1922 interview, which is in *Westleton – Customs and Sayings recorded by the Women's Institute in 1922*, Westleton Women's Institute, Leiston Press, Leiston 2008. These rolling balls of wool are known elsewhere in England and Ireland as rolling wool bogies. For nine examples of this phenomenon, see "The Mysterious Rolling Wool Bogey," Simon Young, www.academia.edu/24973729/Young_The_Mysterious_Rolling_Wool_Bogey

2. The name "hob-o-lantern", which seems to have corrupted to "hobby lantern", may have had something to do with hobgoblins, or just hobs. These were small hairy spirits said to inhabit people's houses, particularly in the North of England and the English-Scottish border. "Hob" is thought to have come from a local dialect word for "Robert." In Lancashire, "hobs" were said to sometimes bring bad luck to households, and there are stories of them moving house with families, despite the families' efforts to lose them. There's a Hobland Plantation in what was once the northern edge of Suffolk but now just over the Norfolk border, on the edge of Great Yarmouth.

3. *Here are Ghosts and Witches*, James Wentworth Day, Batsford, London 1954.

4. Slaughden "things" from *Forgotten Ports of England*, George Goldsmith Carter, Evans Bros, London 1951; St Elmo's fire on leaves and grass in Weather Phenomenon and Elements – The Fire of St Elmo" in The Weather Doctor website, www.islandnet.com/~see/weather/elements/stelmo.htm; "Burst it all to pieces" from *The Folklore of East Anglia*, Enid Porter, BT Batsford, London 1974, which is also the source for the alternative name Jenny Burnt Arses. Readers may recall from Chapter 9 on imps that the "marsh devils" cast out by St Botolph at Iken are now thought to have been ignited plumes of marsh gas.

Fans of the *Men In Black* films may recall that Men In Black Agents Jay and Kay erased the memories of UFO witnesses. Then while these witnesses were still in a suggestive state, they then gave them a "weak-ass story" about how what they'd seen was "swamp gas from a weather balloon… trapped in a thermal pocket and reflected the light from Venus."

Lamp-snatching Dunwich hobby lanterns are from Paranormal Database; Joan the Wad, Spunkie, Pinket and their origins as drowned girls and shape-shifting ability from *Lantern* 8, 1974-75, www.hiddenea.com/Lantern8.pdf. In other parts of the British Isles, hobby lanterns could sometimes lead you to buried treasure, but no such luck in Suffolk.

5. *Don't* whistle at hobby lanterns from *The Folklore of East Anglia*, see above *Do* whistle at hobby lanterns from *Lantern* 9, spring 1975, www.hiddenea.com/Lantern9.pdf.

6. "Magic Lanterns," Alan Murdie and Robert Halliday, *Fortean Times*, December 2005, which quotes *East Anglian Miscellany* 1933-43.

7. Tish Spall testimony from *Westleton – Customs and Sayings* see above; Martlesham fairy lights from a post by "Woody" to CFZ blog, 6 July 2009 http://forteanzoology.blogspot.co.uk/2009/07/max-blake-gurt-dog-returns.html.

8. *Rendlesham UFO Incident*, Altitude Films 2014, distributed as *Hanger 10* in the US, where Rendlesham is not well-known. Official trailer at www.youtube.com/watch?v=G4GijLIkmHM; East Anglian airship wave of 1909 from http://ufo.se/english/articles/wave.html.

9. *Flying Saucerers – a social history of UFOlogy*, David Clarke and Andy Roberts, Alternative Albion, Loughborough 2007.

10. "Felixstowe Glowing Object Mystery", *Evening Star,* Ipswich, 21 September 1965; "Felixstowe Fire Demon: (England)", American Monsters, Rob Morphy, 16 October 2011, http://www.americanmonsters.com/site/2011/10/felixstowe-fire-demon-england/. The incident occurred two years before Felixstowe's first container facility, the North Crane, was built, beginning Felixstowe's transformation into the huge container port it is today. The London Gateway container terminal in Essex is set to overtake Felixstowe as England's biggest.

11. Paranormal Database, http://paranormaldatabase.com.

12. "UFO Casebook – my dog saw a UFO", Jenny Randles, *Fortean Times,* **FT 280;31**, October 2011. Someone who lived nearby back in those days of terrestrial TV recalled to me that the local TV reception was never all that great at the best of times during the early 1970s.

13. *Haunted East Anglia*, Joan Forman 1974, 1985 reprint Jarrold & Co, Norwich; Bird's Eye Factory glowing ball from Paranormal Database, http://paranormaldatabase.com which also discusses the Blyford Queen's Head phenomenon.

14. Paranormal Database, http://paranormaldatabase.com.

15. "Listen: To US commander investigate 'UFO attack' at Rendlesham in 35-year-old recording," *Daily Express*, July 14 2015, www.express.co.uk/news/weird/590814/RENDLESHAM-US-commander-alien-attack-UFO-laser-explosion-woods-Lt-Col-Charles-Halt; Conde hoax claim from *Most Secret – the hidden history of Orford Ness*, Paddy Heazell, History Press/National Trust, Stroud 2010; *Wunderlust* poll at www.wanderlust.co.uk/magazine/blogs/weird@wanderlust/where-to-spot-ufos-in-britain. See also https://mattsalusbury.blogspot.com/2020/01/colonel-halt-returns-to.html.

16. *Most Secret,* see above. The remains of the Cobra Mist radar array occupy Lantern Marshes, and together with the "pagodas" used by the Atomic Weapons Research Establishment, these are now part of a National Trust nature reserve open to the public, accessible by ferry from Orford Quay, see www.nationaltrust.org.uk/orford-ness-national-nature-reserve. Orford Ness Lighthouse was finally demolished in 2020 as the sea encroached.

17. "X-files shed light on UFOs", *Coastal Advertiser* 6 August 2010; "Magic lanterns", see above; alleged stone falls in Rendlesham Forest from The Why Files, www.thewhyfiles.net/rendlesham2.htm.

18. Paranormal Database, www.paranormaldatabase.com, who told me it would not be possible to contact the witness directly; "Babylonian Angel," comment of March 2010 in response to the article "Magic lanterns", see above.

19. *LightQuest – Your Guide to Seeing and Interacting with UFOs, Mystery Lights and Plasma Intelligences*, Andrew Collins, Alibris, andrewcollins.com. It should be pointed out that its conclusions are probably not peer-reviewed for the resilience of their empirical evidential basis." The "ET" in "ET craft" is short for "extraterrestrial."

20. The Defence Intelligence Staff's *Unidentified Aerial Phenomena in the UK Air Defence Region: Executive Summary* (2000, also known as Project Condign) concluded that the small proportion of UFOs were Unexplained Aerial Phenomena (UAP). The report stated these were most likely unusual meteorological phenomena not yet fully understood by science. It called these "Buoyant Plasma Formation," similar to ball lightning, capable of producing unexplained energy fields or plasma. Possible causes for UAPs could include super-heated meteorites hitting the atmosphere and creating exotic plasmas from the gases there. http://www.disclosureproject.org/docs/pdf/uap_exec_summary_dec00.pdf. One of my proofreaders, with a life sciences background, reminds me "there is no exotic physics."

21. "The luminous owls of Norfolk," Dr David W Clarke, *Fortean Studies* vol. 1, John Brown Publishing, London 1994, which wrongly places the Norfolk village of Rushall in Suffolk and quotes *Lo!,* Charles Fort 1931, www.resologist.net/loei.htm. Fort's huge reading list regularly included the Norwich-based *Eastern Daily Press* but very rarely the Ipswich-based *East Anglia Daily Times*, which may explain why his works have much data from Norfolk but less from Suffolk. The British Library's Newspaper Library at the time of writing still has an incomplete collection of *East Anglian Daily Times*. So there may be historical accounts of Suffolk luminous owls awaiting discovery!

"A Review of accounts of luminosity in Barn Owls Tyto alba", Fred Silcock, The Owl Pages website, www.owlpages.com/articles.php?section=Studies+and+Papers&title=Min+Min&page=1.

"The owls are not what they seem" heading comes from the 1990s TV drama series *Twin Peaks*, video clip at https://www.youtube.com/watch?v=mbi7rq-TSk8.

A glow-worm – a female *Lampyris noctiluca* beetle – signalling to a mate in Dunwich Forest.

11: Mysteries made mundane

We are about to leave behind folklore and tales told to children to stop them playing near ponds. We are just pausing to catch our breath before we take a deep dive into stuff which is undoubtedly real.

Why do we tend to scoff at people who claim they saw fairies or wildmen, or imps, while we take at face value reports of, say East of England wallabies? Our out of place gyrfalcons, or a "white wolf" loose in Kersey, as seen in Chapter 6.

Why do people who see wallabies loose in Suffolk or who see large flightless birds – escaped emus and rheas on the run, careering dangerously across the A12 – regard them as "just" escaped exotics and out of place migrants, rather than imagining some supernatural origin to these wonders? Where does the fantastic end and the mundane begin?

Even if there are – as I will propose in the remainder of this narrative – black leopards, pumas, lynxes and bobcats living among us in Suffolk, isn't the truth of this as astonishing and as wondrous as any real or imagined encounters involving living balls of wool that attacked people? Isn't a Suffolk that we share with pumas, black leopards and lynxes equally as astonishing as any flying "serpent among us" in 17th-century Mendham or any scorch marks and trauma left in the wake of Black Shuck or the Felixstowe Fire Demon?

Many witnesses report being awe-struck by their fleeting glimpse of a big cat in Suffolk, as we shall see. Many of them describe their brief encounter with a big cat as life-changing. Even if Suffolk's big cats eventually turn out be "just" the fourth-generation descendents of exotic pets, it won't take anything away from the profound sense of wonder experienced by the big cat witnesses.

It was less than a few decades ago that we dismissed reports of otters seen in the wild in England. No, conventional wisdom said, otters have died out here. You must have misidentified something else. Until otters, with a little help from captive breeding programmes, re-established themselves. Yes, you are seeing otters again.

Then it was polecats. No, you couldn't possibly be seeing polecats in Suffolk, because polecats were hunted to extinction locally at the turn of the 20th century. You couldn't conceivably have seen polecats. You must have misidentified something else. Then polecats began their inexorable march eastward, gradually re-establishing themselves in the county, to the point where they regularly turn up as roadkill on the Suffolk coast. (See the next chapter for the story of polecats returning to Suffolk.)

Now it's pine martens. They were extinct in Suffolk by the 1950s. You couldn't possibly be seeing English pine martens, you must have mistaken something else that you saw for a pine marten. Until very recently, people who claimed to have seen a pine marten in the East of England were scoffed at as if they said they'd seen fairies in the streets of Stowmarket or as if they'd reported aliens flying in UFOs over Rendlesham.

Guess what? Pine martens are now re-established in the West of England and are also marching west. I received a report of a live pine marten seen on the edge of Tunstall Forest not long before this book went to press. (See the next chapter.)

And for almost the past half century, people have been reporting big cats in Suffolk, with increasing frequency.

PART 2 – HERE BE DRAGONS

You can't possibly be seeing big cats in Suffolk, there are no big cats in the wild in Suffolk – or indeed Britain. You must have been mistaken. But... otters and polecats and pine martens.

How will people of the distant future look back on this controversy around sightings of big cats in Suffolk? Will they titter at our primitive early 21st century folly in ever believing that there were big cats out there in the East Anglian countryside? Will they guffaw at us from across the centuries, labelling my Suffolk big cat investigations as part of a curious early second millennia fad, like the preoccupation that Stowmarket folk in the 1840s had with fairies? Will they compare belief in the big cats of Suffolk to the hysteria around "the use of imps" in the Civil War Suffolk of the 1640s?

This is why I have included here the escapees, exotics, introduced species and the many, many, sightings of big cats of Suffolk, together in the same book as the Suffolk wildmen, the Stowmarket fairies, the many manifestations of Black Shuck and the several Kessingland sea serpents.

I believe the big cats of Suffolk to be flesh-and-blood animals. But it would be foolish of me to deny that these stories come out of the same context, the same continuum, as the tales of Black Shuck and the Jenny Burnt Arses. As with the large number of credible accounts of big cat sightings from the Curious County, there are many detailed stories of Suffolk Shuck too, and many identifiable patterns in those accounts.

The people who still to this day tell their Shuck narratives are reasonable people still very much alive. While Black Shuck is impossible, *something* happened to the people who had their Shuck experiences, something that affected them. And as we saw briefly in Chapter 6, there are similarities between Black Shuck – the shiny black East Anglian beast with glowing eyes – and the shiny black leopards reported from across Suffolk whose eyes glow in headlights.

The last peak of Suffolk Shuck sightings in the 1970s came at around the time that sightings of – mostly black, nocturnal – big cats began to be reported in Suffolk. As Dorset big cat investigator Jonathan McGowan points out in his recent work *The British Big Cat Phenomenon,* East Anglian phantom hellhound Black Shuck shares with black leopards several distinctive characteristics. As we have seen, McGowan is not the first commentator to note uncanny similarities between some quite feasible British big cats and the impossible Shuck.

Shuck has glowing eyes, like a leopard. Shuck sometimes walks in step with those who witness it – behaviour that some people who've had real-life encounters with leopards observe. And Black Shuck is reported as sometimes leaping through the trees – not dog-like behaviour at all, but perfectly normal for a black leopard – leopards are comfortable climbing trees. Based on these observations, McGowan suggests that these leopard-like traits of Black Shuck point to Shuck not having been a phantom hellhound after all, but it was black leopards seen in poor light at night all along, fooling fearful folk into thinking it was Black Shuck they'd encountered.

To me, this theory is an even bigger stretch than taking Black Shuck at face value and accepting that phantom shape-shifting, vanishing and (in Essex) exploding hellhounds actually exist. The "Shuck was a black leopard" hypothesis would require a population of black leopards that had established itself in the East of England by the late eighteenth century or earlier and somehow evaded detection. Given the huge body of surviving written accounts of fox hunts (and stag hunts and hare hunts) from that time, you'd expect to regularly find narratives of the fox hounds flushing out black leopards and chasing these leopards up trees. But this is not the case.

No, for me the similarity between Black Shuck sightings morphing into sightings of glossy black big cats hints not at a neat "Black Shuck was black leopards all along" explanation. To me it sets alarm bells ringing, it's suggestive of something big cat investigators like me don't want to hear – that there is something going on in the "pyscho-social" realm, with changes over time in how people process and interpret strange experiences that they've had. People saw fairies in the 1840s, now they report "aliens" arriving in UFOs. Is the transformation of Shuck into the mystery black leopards seen today any different?

This "Black Shuck morphing into black leopards" phenomenon presents a problem that East Anglian big cat investigators would be foolish to try to ignore. It is for this reason that I have to accept, with some reluctance, that my narrative of a half century of Suffolk big cat sightings belongs in the same bestiary as Shuck and the wildmen and the freshwater mermaids and the Dog-headed Man of Tuddenham St Martin, if only to recognise the need to approach the subject with some caution and a little scepticism and humility.

Returning to the people of the future looking back at our early 21st century big cat investigations, though, I suspect that derision at my credulity for believing in Suffolk big cats would not be their reaction to this work. More likely, there will be futuristic head-scratching at what all the fuss was about. I imagine that the folk of the not-so-distant future will regard the big cats of Suffolk not as mystery animals at all but as mundane animals – accepted as being as much as part of the county's established fauna as grey squirrels and muntjac deer and other introduced species we now take for granted.

For the record, I do believe that big cats live among us in the county of Suffolk, although I find I keep changing my mind about what exactly they are. There are a fair number of misidentifications, when the animals seen (including some seen by me) turn out not to be big cats at all, or turn out not even to be animals. We'll come to that comic interlude when we get to Chapter 20.

I also confess that I frequently find myself looking at some of the very few photos and scarce footage or alleged Suffolk big cats that exists and changing my mind about whether or not they really are images of big cats in the wild in the Curious County and environs. Sometimes I will look anew at such images and conclude that they can't possibly be big cats after all. How could I possibly have been fooled? What was I thinking?

Then I'll look at the images once more and change my mind yet again – wow, whatever-it-was is on second thoughts absolutely *huge*, the muscles and the way it move mean it must definitely be a leopard or a puma or a lynx or an absolutely enormous domestic cat gone wild after all. Then I question how I could ever have had any doubts in the first place. Then I'll change my mind yet again, and decide this Suffolk big cat stuff is all nonsense – it really belongs in Part One – along with the evil freshwater mermaids and with the neat little wildmen that seem peculiar to Suffolk churches and other fantasies.

Then a report will come in from another sighting of a big cat with exactly the same description as the one I had just started to have serious doubts about, with the new sighting reported from the next village to the sighting I'd just written off. Or I'll read of a sighting from elsewhere in the country that follows the same patterns as the big cat sighting I was about to bin. From the other end of England we hear reports of "pale pumas", off-white coloured big cats like that puzzling footage I got earlier. Or confirmation comes from another source that some leopards can have pointed ears like a domestic cats rather than the rounded ears they usually have, so that anomalous Suffolk sighting of an animal like a leopard but with pointed ears starts to make sense. And so on. It's maddening! For now though, I tend to agree with the big cat investigator with whom I spent a few hours at a secret location on England's South Coast ten years ago while he casually checked the memory cards on trail cams he'd set up in his search for evidence of local big cats. "This isn't a joke," he said, "this is real!"[2]

A rhea wanders around its paddock in the Suffolk village of Chediston. These giant flightless South American birds have become popular pets and "super weeders" in the county. Can you also spot the other introduced exotics, llamas and alpacas, in the background?

FOOTNOTES TO CHAPTER 11: Mysteries made mundane

1. *The British Big Cat Phenomenon – Differing theories, eye witness reports, and the predator's diet*, Jonathan McGowan, Hangar 1 Publishing, North Haven CT, 2022

2. "Big cats in Dorset - London Cryptozoology Club expedition, with Jonathan McGowan", 14 June 2013, Matt Salusbury blogspot, mattsalusbury.blogspot.com/2013/06/big-cats-in-dorset-london.html

A medieval dog-ape creature on a church pew in the Suffolk village of Barking.

Deer populations have reached critically high levels in the county of Suffolk, to the point where there are regular deer culls and the ecosystems of some heaths are threatened by overgrazing by deer. Most Suffolk deer are the result of deliberate introductions by stag hunts or escapes from deer parks.
Deer are believed to play a crucial role in the diet of Suffolk's big cat population, with many discoveries of deer carcasses within the county showing signs of predation by big cats.
Shown here are red deer hinds (females) on Dingle Marshes.

12: Exotics, escapees, out-of-place animals

Up to now, most of the mystery animals in this book have been the stuff of legend, belonging more to folklore than to natural history. Some are insubstantial, behaving more like phantoms than real, flesh-and-blood actual physical animals. Some – despite being reported – couldn't possibly exist according to scientific laws as we currently understand them, barring a sudden discovery of some really weird effects of quantum physics that could accommodate both Black Shuck and the Stowmarket fairies. (The more we learn about quantum physics the odder it becomes, so we live in hope.)

But from now on, we are almost certainly dealing with living animals with real biology, demonstrable behaviour and legitimate, scientific-sounding Latin names. Meet the "exotics", the out-of-place introductions and animal escapees of Suffolk.

Driven to extinction, risen from the dead

Some two and a half million years ago, the Red Crag formation was laid down along Suffolk's coasts. It was a time before modern humans arrived, there were two-toed sloths and porcupines in Suffolk. We've already met one of Suffolk's prehistoric elephants back in Chapter 2, their remains mistaken for a "Mighty Giant." The Red Crags have yielded the remnants of red pandas and teeth possibly from *Cacharadon megalodon*, a huge prehistoric shark. A fossil northern hemisphere albatross has been hauled up from the Red Crag at Boyton near Hollesley. And we'll eventually encounter "Owen's cat", a European puma whose mortal remains were dug up in the county.

More recently, animals have been driven to extinction in Suffolk by humans. Evidence from Woolpit suggests they were hunting wolves there until Saxon times. The skulls of at least 19 wolves or large dogs were unearthed near the medieval city walls at Bury St Edmunds. King Edward I's 1281 proclamation calling on Englishmen to annihilate wolves included a bounty for wolves' heads, so these skulls were probably presented in lieu of taxes.[1]

Suffolk has seen not just animal species disappear, but entire Suffolk habitats that have vanished or will vanish soon. Many of Suffolk's current nature reserves are expected to be lost to the sea within the next 70 years or so, and bits of land are being bought up as "Plan B" nature reserves for the future when the current ones have gone.[2]

The cuckoo, the tree pipit and the sedge warbler are all birds that have almost gone from Suffolk. The last report of a pine marten in Suffolk was in 1956, they too have long since vanished from the Curious County. Pine martens are now reappearing in counties in the West of England and Wales, though. Recent evidence suggests they may be reviving in Suffolk too. In June 2020, Suffolk Wildlife Trust recorded that a reliable source had reported a dead pine marten on Felixstowe Beach, which they were unable to recover for analysis. It's possible that the pine marten's body could have been washed down one of Suffolk's rivers – the Orwell, the Deben or the Ore, to have ended up there. Matt Goodwin saw a pine marten from his car early in March 2023 while driving through the edge of Tunstall Forest on the Snape Road, near the entrance to one of the mountain bike trails. He works in pest control and traps polecats for a living, he keeps polecats and ferrets so he can tell pine martens apart from polecats. He told me he saw the pine marten climb a tree as he drove past.[3]

Red squirrels were common up to the 1970s, especially in Thetford Forest, but by the time I had my only sighting of an English red squirrel, in Staverton Thicks as a child in around 1975, they were already rare. Disease and competition for resources with the alien "greys" – grey squirrels introduced from North America – did for them. Following a failed attempt at reviving their numbers, the Thetford Forest Red Squirrel Project was finally abandoned 1992, after a parapoxvirus outbreak decimated the red squirrel population and due to the difficulty of "removing greys." The last sighting of a "red"in Suffolk was in Thetford Forest in the early 21st century. Within mainland Britain, "reds" are now mostly confined to Scotland.

Egrets were hunted to extinction across the UK, for their white tail feathers to decorate Victorian ladies' hats, to the point where birdwatching books of the 1970s had them down as non-native, "rare vagrants" to East Anglian shores. Now little egrets (*Egretta garzetta*) are fairly common around some of Suffolk's estuaries and even in the drainage ditches around Eastbridge and the edges of Lowestoft.[4]

Hazel dormice (*Muscardinus avellanarius*) are also back from the brink, after disappearing from much of Suffolk. Sleeping dormice have been fond in nest tubes (in fact long, thin boxes) left in hedgerows in 16 sites including Polstead, Hadleigh, Bentley, Assington, Belstead and South Ipswich. This indicates that dormouse reintroduction programmes in South Suffolk have been a success.

The Suffolk Wildlife Trust nature reserve at Bradfield Woods, just under seven miles due south-east of Bury, has been the most successful dormouse reintroduction site to date – most of these sites were picked because there were part of the animals' "historic range", there were Victorian records of dormice having been there. During the Bradfield Woods reintroduction, a "nut search" for nutshells with the top neatly chewed off in a particular way revealed that there were pockets of surviving native dormice. The same phenomenon occurred at the dormouse reintroduction site at Tiger Hill – the only known habitat for dormice in Suffolk by the 1990s. Now there is "gene mixing" between introduced dormice and native survivor dormice from a population that had been there since Victorian times. Recent DNA studies show the Suffolk's dormice are a genetically distinct population that have been isolated from other dormouse populations in England for a very long time.

Now there's a "multi-agency" effort at reintroducing dormice underway at Bull's Wood, and at Priestly Wood near Needham Market. We can no longer tell if the dormice turning up in the nesting tubes are from introduced stock or from a rediscovered population that had always been there. In addition to its surviving native (and re-introduced) hazel dormice, Suffolk gained a new mammal species with the discovery of a single edible dormouse (*Glis glis*), trapped in a house near Saxmundham in 2015. Edible dormice are believed to have been released into the wild around 1902 by Baron Walter Rothschild at his home and private zoo near Tring. They were regarded as a delicacy by the Romans, hence their name. The English enclaves of surviving edible dormice, though, are a long way from Suffolk. It's thought the Saxmundham-area edible dormouse may have made its way to Suffolk from one of these populations with a shipment of timber.[5]

Avocets (*Recurvirostra avosetta*) arrived in 1940 at Havergate Island, just off Orford, after farmers had abandoned it, with its fields turning into lagoons. Avocets have since established themselves at RSPB Minsmere as well. Other Suffolk Lazarus species are the fen raft spiders in Lopham Fen nature reserve, which straddles the South Norfolk-North Suffolk border. When the fen raft spiders were discovered at Lopham Fen, they were on the brink of extinction, and were revived in part thanks to deliberate re-introductions.

Also back from the dead are polecats (*Mustela putorius*), hunted to extinction by gamekeepers in the county by the early twentieth century. There's now a more enlightened attitude to pest control, and a modern abundance of roadkill for them to eat. Polecats started showing up at Red Lodge on the border with Cambridgeshire in the early 2000s, and moved gradually eastward into Suffolk to re-establish themselves. Surveys of polecat sightings and polecat roadkill in Suffolk up to 2015 by the Vincent Wildlife Trust indicate that Suffolk's polecat revival includes more and more polecat-ferrets – hybrids between the brown-coloured wild polecats and the white or cream-coloured gone-feral once-domesticated ferrets (*Mustela furo*), particularly in South Suffolk. Polecats and polecat-ferrets are turning up that are "polecat-like, silver, sandy" or "albino" in colour, according to the survey.[6]

I've found polecats as roadkill at Wissett and near Blyford. A source in Suffolk pest control told me that as part of his work he had recently caught a polecat in a trap intended for squirrels, near Stowupland. He already kept ferrets and tried to keep this polecat in captivity too, but its behaviour was so completely different from any of the ferrets – even those occasional throwback ferrets that have the brown colouring of polecats – that before long he felt he had to release it. One of my Twitter followers in North Suffolk tells me she's occasionally visited by a polecat who seems irresistibly attracted to the roof of her husband's workshop. Clearly, increasingly bold polecats are firmly re-establishing themselves in Suffolk.

Goshawks were secretly re-introduced into the wild in the 1970s by falconry enthusiasts, having gone extinct in Britain a century earlier. The species was popularised by Suffolk-based writer Helen Macdonald, whose *H is For Hawk* describes her relationship with Mabel the goshawk, who flew in the West Suffolk skies above the heaths and forests around Mildenhall, Lakenheath and Thetford. Thetford Forest is now the place to see goshawks, and even has a "Goshawk Trail", but I've been told that in recent years wild goshawks have turned up further east, with occasional sightings in Rendlesham and Dunwich Forests.

Ospreys, too, are starting to call in on their way through Suffolk at a secret location somewhere in the Blyth Estuary. Three nesting sites have been made for them from donated telegraph poles with steel structures on the top, into which fits an osprey nest. They were first spotted roosting there on their migratory route in 2009 and "single ospreys" have since regularly been spotted in the Blyth Estuary roosting as they pass through.

Climate change is reversing the decline of other species that have up to now been very rare in Suffolk – the stone curlew (*Burhinus grallarius*) and Roesel's bush-cricket (*Roeseliana roeselli*) among them. The restoration of dykes in Oulton Marshes means the Norfolk hawker – one of England's rarest dragonflies – is re-establishing itself in the county of Suffolk.

A surprising proportion of our so-called indigenous British fauna – including our own *Homo sapiens* species and an estimated one quarter of all mammal species in the UK – are introductions anyway. Some were brought deliberately to the East of England by humans, others were let loose into the wild accidentally, while some species seem to have introduced themselves into Suffolk without any help from humans.

House mice arrived from the Middle East, brought accidentally by humans in the Neolithic period, around the fourth millennium BC. Brown hares were apparently introduced to southern England in the Iron Age immediately preceding the Romans.

It was the Romans who seem to have brought plague-carrying black rats with them, also from the Middle East. The species has now been annihilated from Britain and displaced in this country by the brown rat, whose ancestors arrived on ships from Central Asia as late as 1720.

Occasionally, black rats are discovered in ports. They were briefly common in wartime Ipswich, with so many comings and goings of naval vessels. There was a 1984 "infestation" at the port of Lowestoft, but Suffolk's ports today have a very good record of containing invasive species arrivals, any black rats coming in by ship are quickly detected and isolated. [7]

More recent notable rodent introductions include gerbil escapes into Woolverstone Hall School grounds in 1992, a mid-1960s hamster infestation at a florist's shop in Bury and a mid-1970s guinea pig colony at Freston Hill layby, at the Ipswich end of the Shotley Peninsula. Fortunately, none of these populations established themselves permanently.[8]

The Normans in the eleventh century introduced the fallow deer still found in Thetford Forest and around the Stour Valley (at Tattingstone among other locations). Another Norman introduction (or possibly re-introduction) into East Anglia was the rabbit, much prized for fur and meat right up until the early twentieth century. Some of England's earliest man-made rabbit warrens of the twelfth century were established in Suffolk because of its mild winters. In eighteenth and nineteenth century East Anglia, warrens were a lucrative enterprise, with tens of thousands of rabbits bred for their pelts or meat in local warrens. Thetford Station was an important transit point for the rabbit fur trade. In the 1920s, the rabbit fur trade collapsed suddenly, many rabbits were let loose. Black rabbits are still found around Thetford, and over the nearby Suffolk border, a result of exotic rabbits from the fur trade.

Red deer and roe deer were rare in Suffolk by Tudor times, fallow deer were confined mostly to enclosed deer parks. Suffolk's roe deer were locally extinct by the eighteenth century, the roe deer found in the county today are the result of a reintroduction at Santon Downham in 1884. All of Suffolk's red deer are apparently the result of nineteenth century releases into the wild by the Norfolk Hunt.[9]

Invaders must die!

While there are concerted efforts to re-introduce some vanishing species in Suffolk, there are similarly determined enterprises aimed at wiping other introduced species off the face of the earth (or from Suffolk at least). Suffolk Wildlife Trust is currently engaged, with the help of local landowners, in a mink-trapping campaign using rafts at "National Key Sites" in the River Deben, Minsmere, North Warren and Sizewell, among other Suffolk locations. Mink (*Neogale vison*) prey on water voles, and have brought about their decline to the point of near extinction locally. But the native water voles (*Arvicola amphibius*) are now returning to the River Stour following a successful mink trapping campaign by "committed landowners".

Mink were brought to the UK from North America in the 1920s and farmed extensively for their fur, with a peak of around 700 mink farms by the 1960s. But as the industry declined many were released into the wild. They're very agile and cunning, so they often got out of their enclosures, and some believe that it was only continuing escapes that sustained the UK's wild mink population. There were also a few tactically ill-considered releases of mink by animal rights activists, included one big mink farm break-in that featured an undercover police officer infiltrating the animal rights movement. The first reports of the American mink in the wild in the UK were in the 1950s. A former work colleague recalls in his childhood the early 1960s the panic around mink, with the tabloids warning that they would break into houses and attack children. (So far as we know, they never did.) The species had been had become established in Suffolk by the 1970s, pushing out the water voles from their wetland habitats.There's now an Eastern Counties Mink Hound Pack, hunting each summer using hounds to flush out mink for them to shoot on land where landowners invite the hunt in as pest control. One of the hunt members said on the occasion of some particular vicious stripping-out of ornamental garden fishponds in Felixstowe by (probably) mink, "They quite often kill a lot at a time... They are horrible creatures. It's not just fish they attack – they will eat anything, including ducks and moorhens." As we'll see later, some of the messier animal kills found and attributed to Suffolk big cats could have in fact been down to mink.[10] A ban on mink farming in the early 2000s means no more escapes, so the mink in Suffolk may finally be in decline. The revival of polecats, who compete with mink for food, may hasten mink local extinction.

We've already met some of the "coypu men" who spotted the Waveney Monster while out on a 1980s anti-coypu patrol. Those engaged in the campaign to exterminate mink from Suffolk can draw comfort from the huge and ultimately successful series of seek and destroy missions on an equally invasive alien species that has now – officially at least – been eliminated from the county's wetlands. Or has it?

Coypu, also known as nutria, are large South American rodents with webbed hind feet. They're *big* – adults can have bodies up to 60 cm (nearly two feet), with another 45 cm (18 inch) of tail behind that. They arrived in the UK in 1929, and were bred for their fur. At its peak the industry had 49 fur firms nationally, but the coypu fur trade had ended by 1945. Some coypu escaped from a fur farm in Norfolk in1937 and quickly spread across Norfolk, into Suffolk and beyond, establishing themselves in the wild by the 1940s. The Ministry of Agriculture's Coypu Control Programme was set up in 1962, originally to run only for the next four years. *Myocastor coypus*, to give the animal its Latin name, had reached the peak of their wild population by 1966 – 320 of them were destroyed that year in Minsmere alone. In the words of the Min of Ag of the day, "It became clear that this animal was capable of causing serious damage to agricultural crops, especially sugar beet and other roots."[11] Coypu also burrowed through dykes, becoming a threat to river and flood defences. Finally, in 1977 the Ministry of Agriculture was given £2.5 million for a 15-year eradication programme that saw 35,000 coypu killed.

Britain's last wild coypu trapping was on the Ouse, near St Noets, Cambridgeshire in 1988. The last confirmed coypu sighting was at the end of 1989, and the coypu was pronounced officially eradicated in England in that year, two years ahead of schedule. Two possible coypu sightings in Suffolk in 1991, at Ipswich Golf Course and at Great Bealings, could well have been misidentifications.[12]

However, people continue to report coypu in Suffolk. Natural England in response to a Freedom of Information Act request admitted there had been sightings in 2005 of Suffolk coypu in Brantham, in 2008 at Newmarket, and in Depden (southwest of Bury) the previous year – "inconclusive" was their comment on all of these. Of a Saxmundham coypu sighting in 2008, Natural England commented "Inconclusive, no other evidence." A photo said to be of a coypu snapped somewhere in Suffolk in 2010 came their way too, unsurprisingly "Inconclusive" in their view. Nor did the 2009 "Coypu... Other signs, droppings" sighting from somewhere in Suffolk impress Natural England. Their total for the number of cases of alleged coypu reported in the period 2001-2010 was eleven, the number "Confirmed" was a big round zero.

Perhaps Natural England's most revealing comment on post-1989 coypu sightings was on an alleged 2005 sighting from Feltwell Common, Norfolk: "Captured and killed, Otter confirmed." When such sightings are followed up and investigated, it turns out people aren't too skilled at identifying coypu and distinguishing them from other animals.[13]

The Suffolk Naturalists Society were reporting back in 2010 "accidental arrivals" in the county including alien mossy liverworts on the trunks of Australian ferns at garden centres and "strange" fungi from overseas turning up on woodchips on flowerbeds. "Invasive species" of plants identified just within South Suffolk's Dedham Vale as of 2016 included giant hogweed, Japanese knotweed, Himalayan balsam, Australian swamp stonecrop, floating pennywort, parrot's feather and creeping water primrose.

A poster on the Suffolk Biological Records stall at the 2015 Suffolk Mammals Conference proclaimed "Invasive species alert! Warning of Quagga mussels." These prolific mussels from Ukraine suck up a lot of the plankton that other organisms in the local food chain depend on, and have recently turned up in the Thames, brought here on the undersides of ships. The latest devastating alien invader is ash die-back fungus, recently arrived in Suffolk from the Netherlands on saplings brought over for plant nurseries.

As well as mystery animals, Suffolk has it own mystery animal *diseases*. The most puzzling of these is Seasonal Canine Illness (SCI), which suddenly afflicts dogs who've been exercising even for just 90 minutes in Rendlesham Forest. (There was a 2013 case in Thetford Forest too, while in recent years local noticeboards have warned of apparent cases in Dunwich Forest too.) Sickness, diarrhea and lethargy affect dogs within 24 hours of walking in woodland. These attacks afflicting dogs always seem to come in the autumn months, and were first noticed in 2009. Toadstools have been ruled out. What exactly causes SCI remains an enigma. While harvest mite infestation has been identified in dogs affected by SCI, the actual cause of SCI has yet to be confirmed.

Victims of SCI have included Sparkie and Ruby, owned by Caroline Peters from Felsted, Essex. Her dogs "collapsed" and were "fighting for life" in a specialist vet's in Newmarket as of October 2015 after the briefest of runs around Rendlesham Forest.[15] There have also been occasional outbreaks of "mystery bird flu" among Suffolk-based poultry in recent years, with suspicion falling on migratory birds as the carrier.

East of England escapees

The wild land mammal you're most likely to actually *see* in Suffolk – the muntjac deer – is another recent accidental introduction, the result of escapes from a deer park in Woburn, in Buckinghamshire, in the early 20th century. The little horned, fanged muntjac deer are now so numerous they've acquired the status of vermin and there are occasional official muntjac culls – muntjac venison has appeared on the menu in some Suffolk eateries.

There are also Chinese water deer in the Curious County, believed to have found their way to Suffolk following an escape from a safari park just over the Norfolk border. Common in the Broads and the Waveney Valley, they can be found around Benacre and Covehithe, the Twitter account of RSPB Minsmere confirmed to me "there are a few Chinese water deer at Minsmere but rarely seen" and they've been spotted around Dunwich. A North Suffolk informant tells me CWDs, as they are known in wildlife management circles, have started to show up on the edge of Eye. Further south, a warden told me a small group of CWDs regularly cross the Alde River at low tide and enter the Orford Ness NT reserve. In their native China, CWDs are threatened by hunting, so they'll soon be more common in the East of England than in China.

There is a commonly-held belief that the East of England's muntjac deer are a hybrid, a cross between Reeve's muntjac from China and Indian muntjac. Speculation on muntjac hybridisation goes back all the way to the writings of Charles Darwin, and there are well-documented cases of – sterile – muntjac hybrids in Thailand and apparently fertile Reeve's muntjac/Indian muntjac hybrids in the wild in parts of India. Regrettably for mystery animal buffs, though, it seems the East of England's muntjac are all pure-bred Reeve's muntjac, escaped from a single safari park. While there was a postwar mass-breakout of Indian muntjac from an enclosed deer park in Buckinghamshire, it seems they all died out before they had the opportunity to hybridise with the Reeve's.

The presence of these smaller, introduced deer is relevant when we start to look at Suffolk's mystery big cats shortly. As Jonathan McGowan, a big cat investigator from another part of the country told me of big cats, "they follow the deer." While a leopard or a puma could take down one of Suffolk's red deer or fallow deer with a little difficulty, escaped exotic Chinese water deer and abundant muntjac are the ideal-sized prey for a British big cat. Indigenous muntjac of a slightly different kind are the preferred diet of leopards in parts of Indonesia.

Forester Paul Berry recalls how he saw "something like a monkey running up the lane" in Deedman's Lane "a few years ago". (It's south of Saxmundham, not far from Dodds Wood where something on two legs frightened teenage campers back in Chapter 4.) Paul assumed it was an escaped pet, as a neighbour had a private zoo when he lived in Badingham in the Blyth Valley in the 1970s. Back in Badingham, the neighbour's captive monkeys were always escaping, "he lost about 25… one ended up my father's tree… my mother fed it for a few months." The *Lowestoft Journal* recorded the brief escape from the then Suffolk Wildlife Park in Kessingland of Rambo, a Barbary ape, who got out twice in 1966, and a Himalayan monkey called Lucy who made it as far as the roof of a house in Kessingland's Church Road. Manning's Amusement Park in Felixstowe – it's still there – once had an "island of monkeys" among its attractions, back in the 1930s when it opened, but I've not come across any escapes from it.[16]

Insect immigrants

The purple emperor butterfly *(Apatura iris)* steadily declined throughout the twentieth century, until it disappeared from Suffolk and was confined to a few woodlands in southern England. The only confirmed colony in the county is in Theberton Wood, said to be the result of a "freelance" (unlicensed) introduction in the early 2000s. The Theberton colony is doing well, with confirmed sightings coming from nearby Minsmere and one even showing up in more distant North Warren in Aldeburgh.

The Butterfly Conservation Suffolk group has been tracking purple emperors in Suffolk since the early days of the internet, and there been have reports of recent sightings including around Bonny Wood near Needham Market, Mellfield Wood near Bury, at Holton, near Halesworth and at Bradfield Woods. This would suggest that the purple emperor is gradually recolonising its former range in the East of England, spreading out from Hertfordshire since the 1990s.[17]

The long-tailed blue butterfly *Lampides boeticus*, with its distinctive trailing tail, is a pest on the Continent but is a rare migrant to our shores that was thought not to survive British winters. It's being sighted increasingly in southern England on the coast, and breeding pairs have been seen. It may have settled in Suffolk and other coastal counties. And it's thought there's a "faint possibility" that "small colonies" of the Clifden Nonpareil or blue underwing butterfly "are establishing themselves in Suffolk," according to zoologist Karl P. N. Shuker.

Willow emerald damselflies (close relatives of dragonflies) were exclusively continental European and North African animals, until a plume of warm air blew some of them from the

Continent to Suffolk in August 2007, with specimens first recorded in Trimley St Martin on the edge of Felixstowe. Since then, willow emeralds have been logged at over 30 locations in Suffolk, they are now "thriving" and spreading into neighbouring counties.[18]

There are some Suffolk alien crustacean interlopers as well. In the South Suffolk village of Great Wratting, about four miles from Haverhill and along the Suffolk bank of the Stour (and at other locations) the river is populated by non-native alien American signal crayfish, which are pushing out the native white-clawed crayfish. The American invaders escaped from a local fish farm some time ago. The large, aggressive Chinese mitten crab, which probably entered the Stour Estuary via the ballast tanks of ships entering Harwich or Felixstowe, are now out-competing native crabs and endangering marine engineering projects with their burrowing.[19]

Deliberate introductions

While South Suffolk was once known for the high quality wool from its sheep, the most expensive wool made in Suffolk today is likely to come from the county's alpacas. The animals, originally from Peru and related to llamas and camels, are bred for their high quality, super-waterproof fleece. Alpacas are increasingly common in the pastures of Suffolk. There's even a gone-native "Long Melford strain" of alpacas from Suffolk. Some people who keep free-range hens in the county have alpacas as "fox guards" protecting chickens and lambs from predators. Alpacas gather together in tight packs when threatened, and alert their owners to danger with their screams. One alpaca handler I met at a village fete in Westleton told me her hand had never quite been the same after she was floored by a particularly savage kick from the clawed back foot of a "full male" alpaca. And she told me that on no account should you put "full male" alpacas in a field with your ewes – they will try to rape them.[20]

One exotic grazer seen in Suffolk, after absconding from the Suffolk Wildlife Park, was Stormin Norman, a Bactrian camel who briefly went on the run at the end of 1991, according to the *Lowestoft Journal*.[21] But most of Suffolk's recently introduced grazers are put there by wildlife management people as part of a plan. The exotic grazers are usually there to keep the foliage on the rare "grazing marsh" ecosystem pruned to the correct short height, with a bit of help from the rabbits and deer.

As of late Spring 2012 there were a total of 300 sheep and 80 ponies on Suffolk nature reserves grazing – often for the benefit of rare ground-nesting birds. The Forestry Commission estate at Dunwich Forest and the nearby RSPB Minsmere reserve took delivery of a total of 28 wild Dartmoor ponies in 2009. The males were all supposed to be geldings, but clearly some of the females were pregnant when they moved to Suffolk, as three foals have already been born to the Dunwich Forest Dartmoor pony herd. At the Sandlings around Minsmere and East Sheep Walk between Minsmere and Walberswick, there are bizarre-looking, multiple-horned Hebridean sheep to keep the grass grazed. Exmoor ponies are also to be found grazing Hollesley Common. Konik ponies, also known as Konik Polska ponies, are on active service keeping the ground cover cropped on Dingle Marshes, at Minsmere and at Redgrave and Lopham Fen. Konik ponies ("Konik" just means "pony" in Polish) are sandy coloured with dark manes, well camouflaged in reeds. They're adapted to marshes, are low maintenance and don't mind getting their feet wet.

These exotic introduced grazers have been joined by Highland cattle on Minsmere, with a surprise calf born to a cow considered too old to have any in 2015. Some of the sheep grazing the nearby National Trust reserve at Dunwich Heath had a surprising addition at the beginning of 2013. Shepherd Andrew Capell, who tended Dunwich Heath's herd of 100 sheep (including some Hebridean sheep) found a bewildered male red deer faun living among his flock. Believed to have been accidentally left behind by his herd, it was hoped he'd rejoin it when it next came by.[22]

Donkey DNA discovery and reptiles on the run

Some of North Suffolk's donkeys may even have North African ancestry. A shuttle mission by the wartime US Army Air Force unit the 95th Bomber Group, based at RAF Horham in the Dove Valley, brought back an African donkey on a B17 Flying Fortress bomber, and the 390th Bomb Group based at RAF Parham near Framlingham are also known to have brought back at least one donkey on a return flight from Algeria. As Professor Phil Samponaro, Lead Researcher, 95th Bomb Group Memorial Foundation told me, "I suspect others made the trip from North Africa to other bases," others being other donkeys adopted as mascots.[23]

We have already covered the alleged escapee medieval "cockadrille" (crocodile) of Bures and Wormingford, in Chapter 5. (Or was it a crested dragon?) Margaret and Stephen Finch had an encounter with a common snapping turtle *(Chelydra serpentina)* described as "ferocious", "ill-tempered" and "very aggressive" in July 2012. It was in the Finch's garden in Grundisburgh, near Woodbridge. The RSPCA inspector who took delivery of the snapping turtle thought that it had "been owned once" and had been living in the nearby water meadows until heavy rains forced it out.[24]

A venomous mangrove snake in a consignment of Malaysian timber was discovered by warehouse workers unloading at the end of April 2015 at Ransomes Europark in Ipswich. The snake was very thin and dehydrated, and "he must have been in that crate for more than six weeks" according to RSPCA inspector Jason Finch (no relation), who removed him to "specialist RSPCA care." Jon Biscoe, supervising the delivery, noticed the black snake with yellow stripes and immediately concluded of "it was very obvious he was too exotic to come from anywhere nearby."[25]

Within sight of Suffolk, just over the other side of the River Waveney and just inside Norfolk at the lakes around Wortwell, there was an alligator alert back in 2011.[26]

If there was anything to this alligator panic, whatever it was probably drifted into Suffolk at some point. A source in local media tells me that small reptiles (thought to be baby alligators and snapping turtles) are seen occasionally swimming in the pools in Ipswich's Hollywells Park. The belief of those who work round the park is that people dump cute little baby alligators there when they get too big. My informant says the witnesses to these released juvenile reptiles swimming around Hollywells don't expect them to survive the winters, even in England's driest county.

Exit, pursued by a bear

Ramblers and dog walkers were advised to take care after reports of two sightings of a brown bear around Rendlesham Forest in the Spring of 2009. Two emails of witness testimony emerged, along with two YouTube videos. One of these videos had still photos of a bear in what was clearly Rendlesham Forest, together with audio commentaries by two people who'd seen the bear in the woods. One of these was Jenny Pearce, who told in the video clip how she "saw it moving through the trees ahead. It was much bigger than a dog. I picked up my son and left for the car straight away." The other video, apparently made by someone filming at a run, showed blurry footage of a bear moving through an identifiable Rendlesham Forest.

As we saw earlier, some people who'd been investigating the shug monkey phenomenon around Rendlesham came to the conclusion that it wasn't a bear, but the more mysterious shug monkey that had been encountered in the area before. Alas, the Red Rose Chain Theatre Company, who were about to put on an outdoor production of Shakespeare's *A Winter's Tale* in the forest, admitted they had made the whole thing up. Red Rose Chain actor and designer Jimmy Grimes came forward to tell how he'd created two email accounts for the fake witness testimony, and how he'd run through the woods filming footage on his mobile phone, into which he'd later Photoshopped footage of an actual bear. The still images of the bear were also Photoshopped into genuine photos of Rendlesham Forest. Jenny Pearce and the other witness were made-up characters played by actors.

Red Rose Chain, who have an enviable reputation for making Shakespeare accessible to "the kids," pulled off the whole stunt to popularize their *Winter's Tale* production in keeping with their philosophy. Shakespeare's *A Winter's Tale* features the famous stage direction "Exit, pursued by a bear," hence the elaborate bear hoax.[27] Nick Deptford claimed to have photographed a bear in Rendlesham Forest in March 2009 and also earlier, according to his You Tube video on the subject (www.youtube.com/watch?v=B3W673xd-Rg). But looking at the blurry photo, it's more likely to have been a muntjac or wild boar.

Confirms report of exotic species

A wild boar? Yes, a wild boar! There were an estimated 800 in the Forest of Dean in South West England as of 2014. A man was even killed in a fatal collision with a wild boar on the M4 motorway near Swindon at the beginning of 2015. Conservationist Scott Passmore notes that wild boar are "classed as feral", as non-native escapees – if wild boar officially became a native species in Britain, the government would need to have a strategy for it, which would cost actual money. So for the moment there is the pretence that all of the wild boar loose in the UK have recently escaped from captivity, rather than being born here. While still "classed as feral," wild boar are the responsibility of landowners.[28]

Whatever the policy, Freedom of Information Act disclosures by Natural England tell a different story. That organisation has investigated six kills in Suffolk of wild boar by "a local gamekeeper" – three in 2006 and three in 2009. There was a comment at the end of all six reports: "Confirms report of exotic species." Natural England's reports on wild boar also include the repeated phrase, "continual recording of sightings in the area." While some wild boar kill locations are just recorded as "Suffolk" by English Nature, a 2006 report includes the Suffolk location "Ixworth", near Bury.

All three 2009 kills of wild boar were of males; one was thought to be a juvenile. English Nature at the time believed "All three animals appear to be part of group of 15/16 animals released from a local farm. No license held, case with Trading Standards." (No location was given for the three wild boar kills in 2009, other than "Suffolk.") Simone Bullion, Recorder of Mammals for the County of Suffolk, told me in the tea break at the 2014 Suffolk Wildlife Conference that the county was by then "wild boar-free." A source in North Suffolk, who didn't want to be identified, told me a wild boar was shot in the Suffolk village of Stuston (near Diss) in 2013. My informant said the animal was seen on the Common, then moved onto private land, where the landowner charged a man £50 for the privilege of shooting it.

Philippa Godfrey, from Tunstall, told me that she'd heard reports of wild boar in Tunstall Forest and all the way down towards the coast at Orford, about four miles to the southwest.

There's even a possibility that if there are wild boar in Tunstall or Rendlesham Forest, they may end up being food for other escaped exotics gone native – big cats, possibly black leopards, as we will see quite soon.[29]

We apologise for the delay, this is due to rheas on the line

A mystery bird of prey, unidentified, attacked a domestic cat in Puddle Brook, Haverhill in November 2009. The cat managed to retreat into bushes and hide.[30] The unknown cat-attacking raptor seen at Haverhill could have been one of a variety of much-travelled foreign "accidentals" – or possibly domesticated escapees – that are showing up in Suffolk.

Alex Bass of Local Birding Tours spotted a young gyrfalcon at the far end of Westwood Marsh, near Dingle, during one of his morning tours on in February 2015. Gyrfalcons *(Faclo rusticolus)* are the world's largest falcons, they're buzzard-sized. Those who observed through binoculars the one at Westwood Marsh got a good enough look at it to see that it probably wasn't ringed, suggesting it was an "accidental" that had flown all the way from Iceland rather than an escapee from captivity. Harris hawks *(Parabuteo unicintus)* are native to North America and Iceland, although they're spotted "fairly regularly" in Suffolk, according to Bass, who saw one at North Warren RSPB reserve near Aldeburgh, by the site of the old railway line in 2015. There also have been sightings "on and off" of a red-tailed hawk in the Brecks, a long way from its usual range in North and Central America and the West Indies. It's impossible to tell whether these are "accidentals" or formerly captive escapees, says Bass – Harris hawks have also been known to hitch rides on transatlantic container ships. There is a controversy in birder forums about whether there are any breeding pairs of Harris hawks in England yet, Bass says he hasn't found any evidence of them breeding here so far.[31]

One out-of-place Suffolk bird of prey that was definitely an escapee was the golden eagle that in May 2015 escaped from its perch on "private premises" in Stratford St Mary in the south of the county. It was soon found just over a mile away, wearing a ring and tethers.[32] Within the UK, wild golden eagles are now confined to the moorlands of Scotland. Other extraordinarily rare bird visitors to Suffolk include the flamingo that dropped into the River Ouse and Minsmere in 2011, believed to have escaped from Hampshire's Marwell Zoo. [34]

Introduced birds on the run, of an altogether bigger kind, have been found in Suffolk, for some reason clustered around Wickham Market and the railway that passes through it. There's an East Suffolk Lines station at Wickham Market, also known as Campsey Ash.

Rheas are a brown or white-coloured South American flightless running bird, related to emus and more distantly related to ostriches. Unhelpful newspaper reports describing an "ostrich-like" rhea on the loose in Suffolk have led to garbled stories of "ostriches" at large in the Curious County, but these are actually rheas. (There is an Ostrich Inn at Wherstead on the shore of the Orwell River and not far from the Orwell Bridge, but it's nothing to do with ostriches. It was originally Oyster Ridge, the spot where you'd expect to find oysters, and the place name corrupted to "ostrich" over the years.) Although they're smaller than ostriches, the tallest of the rheas can still reach an impressive five feet (1.5 m) tall. They can run at 40 mph (64 kph). The males make loud booming mating calls. They like to eat lizards, beetles, grasshoppers, roots, fruit and small roadkill in particular in their native South America, but will eat practically anything. They're partial to all sorts of weeds, which is why some people keep them as an alternative super-weeder for use in especially overgrown land.

One rhea briefly delayed the East Suffolk Lines train service travelling from Ipswich to-

Alpacas at Darsham (above), a found coypu skull from the private collection of Paul Berry (right), a Reeve's muntjac (below) and a captive emu in its field by the A1071 near Hintlesham (below right), photo: © Google Street View.

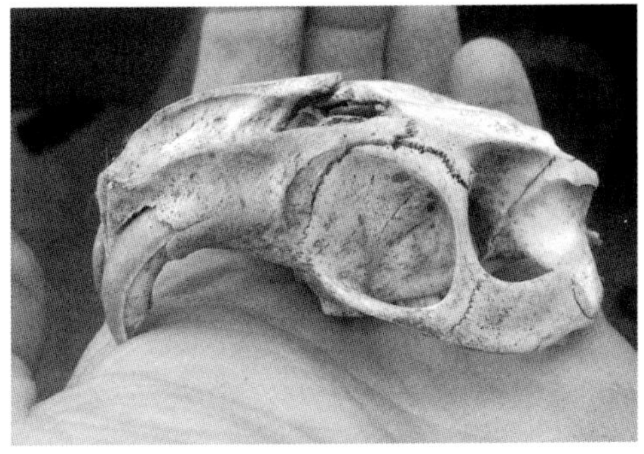

wards Saxmundham near Wickham Market in May 2012, as it wandered on the railway tracks. (Short delays due to horses, dogs or deer on this line aren't all that unusual, but rhea delays are.) A "stunned train driver was forced to slam on the breaks" as it "strolled" into the path of the train, according to one newspaper report, with the caveat that it was the *Daily Mail*.[34]

The rhea eventually walked off the tracks of its own accord and Pat Andrews, who was climbing a stile on a path right by the railway at the time, was able to take a close-up photo of the rhea standing around just after the train passed. The 2012 Wickham Market rhea on the line was never found, its whereabouts are still unknown and it hasn't been seen since (although see below for a suspiciously similar "emu"). Curiously, given its value, this rhea-on-the-line was never claimed by its owner. Could one of Suffolk's big cats have caught it?

Another rhea on the run two years earlier, though, (yes, also around Wickham Market) had reportedly escaped from a known estate near Campsey Ash and its adventure ended tragically. This 2010 runaway rhea was photographed near Woodbridge and seen near Eyke, Campsey Ash and Marlesford, where it was observed dashing across the busy A12 in front of cars. Steve Friend of saw it twice, once in April and again at the end of June, telling the *Daily Mail* "It seems to be doing well for itself. It has survived the winter."

After this particular Suffolk rhea had been at liberty since the previous Christmas, the RSPCA, concerned at the bird's habit of running across the A12, finally caught up with it in early June 2010. After a two-hour chase, RSPCA chief inspector Mark Thompson hit it in the thigh with a hypodermic dart from his rifle, dazing it into semi-consciousness. The rhea was loaded onto a trailer to go to its new owner, a rhea enthusiast who already kept some of the birds as pets on their land near Eye. But on arrival at its new home, the rhea "lay down for a while" and suffered "some sort of panic attack and died." Its death was probably the result of the stress of its capture.[35]

And another flightless bird, reportedly an emu, was spotted on the same Lowestoft to Ipswich train line again in July 2012. According to the *Lowestoft Journal*, a train driver logged the "baffling sight" at 11.20 on Monday 9 July as an emu was spotted running across the line "near Saxmundham," the next station north of Wickham Market. It caused "little disruption".

Emus are taller than rheas and have different colouration – blue necks with brown plumage on their bodies, although I suspect the average Abellio Greater Anglia rail company employee isn't trained to identify different giant, flightless birds. Given that this was only a month after the rhea sighting not far down the same railway line, I suspect the "emu" had been garbled in press reports in an attempt to explain to the uninitiated what a rhea is, rather like the aforementioned unhelpful "ostrich" report.

However, a bird "confirmed as an emu", escaped from its owner in Whepstead, West Suffolk, and went on a two-hour run early one August morning in 2016, covering at least 12 miles before turning up in a garden in the village of Glemsford to the south, where it was "secured." That's not all that impressive a distance when you consider that the emu's cruising speed when running is around 30 mph (51 kph). Startled motorists encountering the emu escapee on its wanderings south from Whepstead variously reported it to police as an ostrich or rhea.[36]

Strigiform seagoing stowaways

Other alien birds turning up in Suffolk include vagrant snowy owls *(Bubo scandiacus)* from the Arctic hitching a ride on ships coming into Felixstowe. They're powerful fliers, normally found in Iceland and Scandinavia, Siberia, Alaska, Canada and Greenland. "Ship assisted" snowy owls have been appearing up on the rooftops of houses in Felixstowe, having stowed away on container ships on the other side of the Atlantic that have brought them to that port. As many as 60 snowy owls were believed to have boarded a ship near Deception Bay, Quebec (North Canada) bound for a port in the Netherlands.

Back in 2001, snowy owls were "entertaining bird watchers" in southeast Suffolk, with one RSPCA inspector unsuccessfully trying to catch one among the rooftops of Felixstowe. It was expected these North American immigrants would eventually hitch a ride back over the North Atlantic on another ship the following Spring. Suffolk birdwatching tours operator Alex Bass told me that in recent times there was a snowy owl seen in Trimley, just inland from Felixstowe, over a period of a couple of years.[37]

What is believed to be the first successful breeding pair of black winged stilts *(Himantopus himantopus)* in the UK for 27 years bred in Cavenham (on Suffolk's western edge, between Herringswell and Lackford) in 2015 and then stayed at a secret location near Great Livermere (just north of Bury, near RAF Honington) that summer with their fledged chicks. The Suffolk stilts left the UK, presumably for Spain, with their four chicks in mid-August.

Self-introductions

Moyse's Hall Museum in Bury has in its collection a late nineteenth century stuffed sea eagle (*aka* white-tailed eagle, *Haliaeetus albicilla*) that turned up in 1891, some time after sea eagles had already disappeared from the East of England. According to the label attached to the specimen, it came the Museum's way via a Mr Cecil Nunn and was shot on the Rushbrooke Estate after being "chased" on New Year's Eve 1891 all the way from land near Bury via Moreton Hall, Rushbrooke, Rougham Hall and the local rectory and back to Rushbrooke. It had been "in the neighbourhood for some weeks" and had killed "fowls" and hares.

A story attached itself to the specimen, that it had been blown down from much further north (where there were still a few native English sea eagles at the time) by a great storm. The story goes that, in a state of some confusion, it flew into the face of a horse in a team of horses pulling a coach, and turned over the whole coach and horses before it was shot. Alex McWhirter of the Moyse's Hall Museum in Bury told me he'd spoken to someone who confirmed the story, and said the source for the story was a relative of one of the passengers in the coach way back in the 1890s. But there's nothing of this story on the label on the stuffed sea eagle that ended up in the museum and no other "substantiating evidence", so McWhirter thinks the story may be apocryphal.

Sea eagles disappeared from the rest of the UK, and an attempt to re-introduce them to Suffolk has been seen off. A half-million pound programme by Natural England and the RSPB for sea eagle releases on Suffolk's coast appears to have been cancelled after a group of landowners met at Benacre estate in 2009, concerned that the plan had been made without consultation. As farmer Robert Middleditch put it at the time, "the impact on lowland agricultural systems is not known as no eagles have ever been released into an area like this with farming such as ours, where there are outdoor pigs and poultry." The sea eagle re-introduction plan was off the table as of late 2015, although a few village shops still hadn't yet taken down their "No white-tailed eagles!" posters, just in case. Meanwhile, sea eagles are spreading westward across Continental Europe without any human intervention, so their eventual return to the East of England may be inevitable anyway. Sea eagles were officially re-introduced to Scotland's Isle of Mull in 2015 and some eaglets were released in the Isle of Wight in 2020. A visiting white-tailed eagle was spotted near Southwold in March 2015 and at least two were reported across the skies of locked-down East Anglia in the summer of 2020.[38]

And let's not forget the little owl, (*Athene noctua*) the species of owl you're most likely to actually see in Suffolk. In the late nineteenth century, these were known as "the Frenchman", as they suddenly introduced themselves to England from France.

Testosterone-fuelled mutant

Back on land, a "voracious, testosterone-fuelled mutant" could have found its way to Sudbury after one was "allegedly spotted" in the town's Friars Meadow. Biodiversity Around Town Scheme chair and local councillor Peter Clifford said a local woman had told back in the summer of 2008 that she'd seen a black squirrel "jumping through nearby trees."

At the moment black squirrels are confined to Bedfordshire and Cambridgeshire, the latter adjoining West Suffolk. At the 2014 Suffolk Mammals Conference, squirrel expert Professor John Gurnell of Queen Mary University, London played down the talk of black squirrels being "more successful" or "with higher levels of the male sex hormone testosterone, making them more aggressive and more attractive to females" (as *Suffolk Free Press* put it), and said it was an otherwise unexceptional melanistic variant of the originally North American – but now gone native – grey squirrel.[39]

Climate change in what's already England's driest county means we can have a good stab at predicting which birds are going to start re-introducing themselves as Suffolk continues to warm up. The next predicted avian alien invaders are the Eurasian hoopoe (there was one in Kessingland in 2014), the little bustard, the bluethroat and the black tern.

The common crane and the goosander duck are already on the county breeding list maintained by Suffolk's Biological Records Office, which documents arrivals and extinctions. The 400-year absence of cranes from the region ended with the arrival of a pair at Lakenheath in 2011, where they are now breeding. Bass also saw a flock of eight common cranes (*Grus grus*) flying over Sizewell Belts in March of the same year – he said they were either from a population establishing itself in Norfolk or more likely from the Netherlands. I am sworn to secrecy about yet another pair of breeding cranes whose Suffolk location I can't disclose.[40]

Wickham Market wallaby

Wallabies have been causing a stir in Suffolk since Mr Wombwell's travelling menagerie passed through Halesworth in 1907, with the *Halesworth Times and Southwold General Advertiser* of 3 December 1907 giving attention to one animal that "could not even be seen in the London Zoological Gardens. One of these was the albino Wallaby Kangaroo from Western Australia." But the albino "Wallaby Kangeroo" remained firmly in captivity throughout its tour. The *Lowestoft Journal* did record the escape of Benny the Bennett's wallaby from what was then the Suffolk Wildlife Park in Kessingland in January 1988.[41]

Whatever strange attractor has been causing rheas to cluster around Wickham Market seems to have been exerting a more mild influence on wallabies too – there's been one wallaby sighting in the area. Local man Nick Beagley, cycling from his home in nearby Pettistree towards Ipswich in 2004, had an "absolutely extraordinary" experience when a wallaby appeared, "hopping along the side of my bike before disappearing into the hedgerow." A dead wallaby was reportedly found in a ditch at Bucklesham, just east of Ipswich, also in 2004. An *Ipswich Star* reporter also admitted having spotted a wallaby "sitting by the roadside at Warren Heath on the edge of Ipswich" sometime prior to 2004. Kessingland's captive parma wallabies – a smaller species – were at the time all present and correct, although their spokesman said red-necked wallabies were known to live wild elsewhere in the UK, and "so they could live quite happily in Suffolk." A Suffolk Wildlife Trust spokeswoman told the *Star* they'd received no wallaby reports.

Paranormal Database received a report from a driver and passenger who saw a "young kangaroo" travelling along Ipswich's busy London Road at around 4 pm on the evening of 12 September 2011. Given the unfamiliarity of most Suffolk folk around the various species of kangaroo and wallabies, it could well have been a misidentified wallaby. Julian Eley filmed from his dashcam what is clearly a white wallaby hopping away from his car as he drove down a country lane between Glemsford and the Essex border one night in September 2017.[42]

From the prairie to the fen

Suffolk Wildlife Trust staff at the Redgrave and Lopham Fen, which straddles the North Suffolk-South Norfolk border, spotted a black-tailed prairie dog over several weeks in May 2012. It was assumed this North American animal had escaped from Banham Zoo in Norfolk sometime in the three months leading up to May, making it the third prairie dog seen in the fen over the previous two decades. The Castle Museum in Norwich has a stuffed prairie dog, originally found on the Redgrave to Lopham road in 1990, after an escape from the same zoo.[43]

Some introductions into Suffolk's terrestrial fauna appear to have mysteriously arrived out of the clear blue Suffolk sky. A rain of frogs was recorded in 1900 in the Mid-Suffolk village of Wetheringsett. A shower of small, yellow or dull green frogs one and a half inches long (around 3.75cm) came down on Wetheringsett Farm. In July of 1843 a "shower of frogs in enormous numbers" fell at "Lyston Hall, Suffolk" just west of Long Melford. The fallen frogs were "carried away in wheelbarrows". (The Hall was long ago demolished, but there's still a village of Liston just over the nearby Essex border.)

A local theory explaining the fall was that frogspawn was drawn up into the atmosphere by the heat of the sun. When it hatched out it was heavy and fell to the earth. As one commentator later noted, this theory didn't stand up because "the tadpole period has not been accounted for." Not a very sound theory, then. There was also a frog fall on Isleham and nearby West Row on the Cambridgeshire-Suffolk border back in 1954, landing on workmen on the road near Isleham, following a waterspout in the nearby River Lark.[44]

Stoke by Clare – on the Stour, and two miles east of the town called Clare, as the name-suggests – was visited by "numerous swarms of animals of unknown origin" making a sudden appearance after a rain shower and lingering on the village green for three days in mid-April 1800. Whatever the animals were, they resembled "grub grasshoppers" with long black legs,black heads and "goggle eyes." The villagers of Stoke by Clare were "too terrified to destroy them," the greenery the creatures had fed on had died.[45]

There were many travelling menageries in days gone by, so "escaped from the circus" (or zoo) was the lazy explanation whenever a big cat was seen on the loose. Ipswich and Bury were both on the circuits of the travelling menageries, with Bury's old greyhound stadium playing host to events usually billed as a "circus and menagerie." A researcher told me he came across a reference in the nineteenth century *Ipswich Journal* to "Indian prairie fiends" (possibly brown hyenas) in one menagerie that pulled in at Ipswich, but the Suffolk Record Office only has in its catalogue a couple of posters and handbills of an "American menagerie" on show in the county town from late 1940s, when the glory days of menageries were already over. Turn-of-the-twentieth-century Suffolk folk looked forward to the next visit of Wombwell's touring circus and menagerie, which transported its elephants on the Lowestoft line

PART 2 – HERE BE DRAGONS

Hebridean sheep at East Sheep Walk (above).

A polecat captured near Stowmarket. Driven to local extinction over a century ago, polecats are re-establishing themselves in Suffolk. Photo: Matt Goodwin (right).
Konick pony grazing Dingle Marshes (below).

using open flatbed railway trucks, while the Wombwell's elephants crossed the Blyth River on the Walberswick ferry, a much bigger craft in those days than the rowing boat it is today.

Mr F Hill, the undertaker in Southwold in the 1930s, had a small private zoo that included baboons and a black cockerel that pulled a tiny cart, diligently recorded by the town photographer, but no big cat escapes. Performing bears – mostly from Russia – were a common sight in the seaside towns of Suffolk in the early years of the twentieth century, and show up frequently in contemporary photographs. Travelling bears were a regular fixture in Framlingham; they used to sleep at night in an alley outside the Blue Boar pub in town, while their handlers slept in the local dosshouse.

The nearest I could find to a historical big cat escape in the Curious County was an incident in mid-nineteenth century Norwich in which an elephant briefly absconded from Mr Hylton's particularly slack travelling circus. (It got as far as an orchard on the edge of the city, but it's hard to hide in the suburbs if you're elephant-sized!) The same report recounts a complaint that a lion had "already nearly escaped earlier" from the same establishment.[47]

Captive big cats in Suffolk – that stayed captive – go back at least as far as 1789, when a *Bury Post* advertisement assured the citizens of that city that "the proprietor of the Royal Lion, from the Tower of London" would be back soon in Bury with his lion from the Tower's Royal Menagerie, in response to popular demand.[45] Well over a century later, Captain Daniels, the lion tamer of Wombwell's menagerie, astounded the citizens of early twentieth century Halesworth by going "into a den of five leopards, and putting them through various movements" and "performing" in a cage with various species of bears, along with some wolves.[48]

And there was Briton, the Suffolk-based lioness. In the 1930s she was bought as a cub from a circus by Suffolk eccentric Tornado Smith, who took her on the road along with Sparky the "lamb", actually a sheep for most of his performing life. Briton and Sparky featured in Smith's "Wall of Death" motorcycle stunt act, one of the first such acts in England and a big draw for holidaymakers at Southend. Briton the lion cub balanced on the motorcycle's handlebars for Smith's act. When she was fully grown she rode in his motorcycle sidecar. They settled in the Suffolk village of Boxford, where Tornado set up a rickety wooden Wall of Death for the amusement of the locals. Briton is accounted for, she couldn't have got out to start a Suffolk big cat population. Sadly, the coming of World War Two rationing spelled the end for her; she was almost certainly shot by Smith, now unable to feed her. Briton is said to be buried under the courtyard of Boxford's White Lion pub. She's immortalised on the village sign.[49]

Wherever they may have come from, there most definitely are big cats in the wild in Suffolk today. When I embarked on this project, my first impression was that there hadn't been many sightings of big cats in Suffolk, certainly not compared to other parts of the UK – I'm thinking of Devon, Dorset, Fife, and Gloucestershire in particular, where you're practically tripping over British big cats. Big cats in Suffolk at first appeared to have been a not very widespread phenomenon that had peaked in the 1990s and early 2000s.

How wrong I was. After my investigations over nine years, revealing over 150 Suffolk big cat sighting reports, taking in well over three dozen witness interviews, Suffolk's big cats now have enough data on them for a considerable section of this book all to themselves.

• Please report any invasive species you find in Suffolk – plant, animal, mysterious, mundane – to the Suffolk Biological Records Centre via www.suffolkbrc.org.uk.

Sign in Rendlesham Forest warning of the mysterious Seasonal Canine Illness (left)

Above: a young coypu stuffed and mounted and on display in the Dunwich Museum. Its outdated label says "coypu traps can be seen on the local marshes." Both the coypus and the traps are now gone, with only a few dubious coypu sightings since their official eradication in the late 1980s. Below: a rhea crossing the East Suffolk Line near Wickham Market.

FOOTNOTES TO CHAPTER 12: Exotics, escapees, out-of-place animals

1. *The Mammals of Suffolk*, Simone Bullion, Suffolk Wildlife Trust/Suffolk Naturalists' Society, Ipswich, 2009. As has already been noted, North Sea cod off the Suffolk coast had been overfished to the point of commercial extinction, and only recently came off the European Commission's Red List of endangered "fish to avoid".

2. "Heath ready for stardom after supporting role in Springwatch," *EADT,* 7 July 2014.

3. "Recording Suffolk", *Suffolk and Norfolk Life* magazine, August 2010; 1950s pine marten from *Oryx* vol. 3, August 1956, with thanks to Richard Muirhead; "Have you seen a pine marten in Suffolk?", Suffolk Wildlife Trusts, 10 June 2020 www.suffolkwildlifetrust.org/news/have-you-seen-pine-marten-suffolk. Tunstall Forest pine marten sighting – Matt Goodwin, pers.com. by email, 5 March 2023.

4. Lazy birdwatchers who can't be bothered to get out of the train can see egrets through the window of the Manningtree to Ipswich train at Cattawade as it crosses the Stour, or just before Ipswich at ponds on the edge of Jimmy's Farm. If it's egret-watching without getting out of your car you're after, try the road out of Ipswich, past Ipswich docks– the B1456 – passes under the mighty Orwell bridge and towards the Shotley Peninsula. There are egrets aplenty in the Orwell Estuary here. The Ipswich Buses 98 bus service will take you along the same route.

5. "Tracking down Suffolk's dormice – 15 years of detective work," talk by Dr Simone Bullion, Suffolk Mammal Conference, September 15 2014, author's own notes.Hazel dormouse DNA study from "The secret of Suffolk's dormice" and edible dormouse discovery near Sax from "A new mammal for Suffolk", both from *Suffolk Wildlife* magazine (SWT), May 2016.

6. "Polecats return", talk by Johnny Birks, Chair of the Mammals Society Suffolk Mammals Conference, Bury 15 September 2014, author's own notes. **7.** *The Mammals of Suffolk*, Simone Bullion, Suffolk Wildlife Trust/Suffolk Naturalists' Society, Ipswich, 2009; "The Distribution and Status of the Polecat *Mustela putorius* in Britain", 2014-2015, Vincent Wildlife Trust 2016, www.vwt.org.uk

8. *The Mammals of Suffolk*, see above. It quotes "Golden Hamster", Baker, S. J. & Hills D. in *Mammals of the British Isles*, S. Harris & D. Yalden, The Mammal Society, Southampton 2008.

9. *The Mammals of Suffolk,* see above. Red deer introduction from a display at Ipswich Museum.

10. "More mink attacks in Felixstowe", *EDP,* 29 February 2008 www.edp24.co.uk/news/more_mink_attacks_in_felixstowe_1_162022. "Police admit officer's role in mass release of mink by protesters, *Guardian*, 20 February 2018, https://www.theguardian.com/uk-news/2018/feb/20/police-admit-officers-role-in-mass-release-of-mink-by-protesters

11. Statement by the Minister of Agriculture to the House of Commons, *Hansard*, 21 December 1966.

12. *The Mammals of Suffolk,* see above..

13. *Reported Sightings or Signs of Exotic Species Compiled by Natural England's Wildlife Management & Licensing,* Natural England FOIA disclosure, September 2011. Nick Redfern investigated a single sighting of a wild coypu in the UK that post-dates 1989 –"two fat guinea-pigs running up the road" in Alrewas, Staffordshire. See "Out of Place Animals", Nick Redfern May 26, 2012, mania.com. A former Defra official, speaking off the record, dated coypu extinction in England to 1990. A 2016 Suffolk Police FOIA disclosure by Suffolk Police revealed "dozens" of reports to the police in which witnesses said they had seen "ghosts, aliens, witches and zombies" or "monsters", www.eadt.co.uk/news/suffolk-police-receive-dozens-of-calls-concerning-supernatural-sightings-1-5741007.

14. "Recording Suffolk", *Suffolk and Norfolk Life* magazine, August 2010. Dedham Vale AONB invasives via the Suffolk Biological Records Centre via www.suffolkbrc.org.uk.

15. "Dogs struck down by mystery illness", *EADT*, 20 October 2015.

16. See "The taxonomic status of feral muntjac deer (*Muntiacus sp.*) in Britain," D.I. Chapmana & Norma G. Chapmana, *Journal of Natural History,* Volume 16, Issue 3, 1982, www.tandfonline.com/doi/abs/10.1080/00222938200770311 with thanks to James Emerson @norwichbirder; Badingham monkey escapes from interview with Paul Berry, 25 April 2015. Kessingland escapes from Suffolk Records Office collection (Lowestoft) reference 1176/2/2/11/81 Kessingland Suffolk Wildlife Park, *Lowestoft Journal* press cutting file. Some data on escapes from other zoos comes from Freedom of Information Act disclosures by local councils, these escapes and recoveries have to be reported of under the Zoos Act. Island of monkeys from "Suffolk's got animal talent", *Suffolk* magazine August 2015.

17. Butterfly Conservation Suffolk website, www.suffolkbutterflies.org.uk/recording.html#Purple_Emperor; "The Secretive Emperor", Liz Goodyear, *Suffolk Wildlife*, SWT, May 2015.

18. UK Butterflies website, www.ukbutterflies.co.uk/species.php?species=boeticus; Shukernature blog, 19 July 2014, http://karlshuker.blogspot.co.uk/2014/07/the-clifden-nonpareil-bewitched-by.html; willow emerald damselfly arrival from *Suffolk Dragonflies*, ed. Nick Mason and Adrian Parr, Suffolk Naturalists Society, Ipswich 2016.

PART 2 – HERE BE DRAGONS

19. American signal crayfish from Wikipedia, Great Wratting http://en.wikipedia.org/wiki/Great_Wratting; Chinese mitten crabs from "River Stour: Dragons, aliens and a princess," Stephen Russell, *EADT*, 11 November 2010, www.eadt.co.uk/ea-life/river_stour_dragons_aliens_and_a_princess_1_721167, which adds that they're now in every English estuary from the Thames to the Humber.

20. www.melfordgreenalpacas.co.uk, although this alpaca stud farm has moved from Long Melford to Darsham. There are llamas and camels aplenty on display at the Oasis Camel Park at Linstead near Halesworth, www.oasis-camelpark.co.uk.

21. Kessingland Suffolk Wildlife Park, *Lowestoft Journa*l press cuttings file, Suffolk Record Office, (Lowestoft) reference 1176/2/2/11/81.

22. Faun among sheep from *EADT* 16 January 2013. Sudbury water meadow along the Suffolk bank of the Stour also has highland cattle. A Sudbury Town Council-commissioned postcard featuring one of the water meadow's highland cattle is available from Tourist Information in Sudbury Library. I've given up trying to keep track of herds of Hebridean sheep, Exmoor ponies, Highland cattle and Konik ponies used to graze Suffolk's various nature reserves. Exmoors and Koniks are in residence at SWT's Knettishall Heath in the Brecks on Suffolk's border with Norfolk.

23. Pers. Comm. by email from Phil Samponaro, 15 May 2015.

24. "Grundisburgh couple's unwelcome visit from ferocious turtle", *EADT* 19 July 2012, www.eadt.co.uk/news/video_grundisburgh_couple_s_unwelcome_visit_from_ferocious_turtle_1_1452012.

25. "Exotic venomous snake found in delivery at Ransomes Europark," *EADT* 29 April 2015, www.eadt.co.uk/news/exotic_venomous_snake_found_in_delivery_at_ransomes_europark_1_4051935.

26. "Visitors reassured following Norfolk alligator sighting," Annabelle Dickson, *Beccles and Bungay Journal*, 3 June 2011.

27. "Bear sighting in Suffolk woods was 'promotional' hoax staged by theatre group", *Daily Mail*, 31 March 2009, www.dailymail.co.uk/news/article-1165868/Bear-sighting-Suffolk-woods-promotional-hoax-staged-theatre-group.html; see also "Mystery bear in Suffolk forest Shakespeare hoax," *Daily Telegraph,* 30 March 2009, www.telegraph.co.uk/culture/theatre/5080987/Mystery-bear-in-Suffolk-forest-Shakespeare-hoax.html. The Red Rose Chain Theatre Company is at www.redrosechain.com/theatre-in-the-forest--about

28. "Call for wild boar cull after animals wreak havoc", The ***i*** Paper, 10 January 2015.

29. Conversation with Philippa Godfrey, volunteer at the Dunwich Dig, 3 August 2015.

30. "Cat's lucky escape from mystery bird," *Haverhill Echo* 11 November 2009, www.haverhillecho.co.uk/news/opinion/cat-s-lucky-escape-from-mystery-bird-1-461202.

31. Phone conversation on 6 December 2015 with Alex Bass of Local Birding Tours, based in Saxmundham, local-birding@aol.com, suffolkbirdtours@gmail.com.

32 BBC News, 6 May 2015, www.bbc.co.uk/news/uk-england-essex-32609103.

33. "Rare feathered visitor drops into Suffolk nature reserve," *Beccles and Bungay Journal*, 14 April 2011, www.becclesandbungayjournal.co.uk/news/rare_feathered_visitor_drops_in_to_suffolk_nature_reserve_1_865003.

34. "Train driver's shock as giant South American bird appears on railway tracks," Suzannah Hills, *Daily Mail,* 25 May 2012, www.dailymail.co.uk/news/article-2149881/Train-drivers-shock-giant-South-American-bird-appears-railway-tracks.html#ixzz1xrNQbfxY.

35. "On the run: The 4ft 9ins rhea tearing through rural Suffolk," *Daily Mail*, 23 June 2010; "Giant runaway bird dies of panic attack after RSPCA tries to 'rescue' it," *Daily Mail*, 1 July 2010, www.dailymail.co.uk/news/article-1291139/Giant-runaway-bird-dies-panic-attack-RSPCA-tries-rescue-it.html#ixzz3tXOpbQIp.

36. "Emu spotted on Lowestoft to Ipswich train line", *Lowestoft Journal*, 9 July 2012, www.lowestoftjournal.co.uk/news/emu_spotted_on_lowestoft_to_ipswich_train_line_1_1439268. As of Spring 2014, there was said to be a rhea on the loose on the Essex-Hertfordshire border, www.bbc.co.uk/news/uk-27060879. I did spot a captive emu, watching the traffic go past through a hedge on the A1071 just west of Washbrook, as I was travelling at speed on the Beeston's 91 bus service from Sudbury to Ipswich in February 2016. Retracing my route on Google Street View, there was a blurry image of the just-west-of Washbrook captive emu looking over a hedge for all to see; "Suffolk emu which gave owner and police the runaround found in Glemsford garden", *EADT,* 3 August 2016, http://www.eadt.co.uk/news/suffolk_emu_which_gave_owner_and_police_the_runaround_found_in_glemsford_garden_1_4642410 – Bernard King's emu secured at Glemsford seems to have been a different emu to the one visible on Google Street View near Hintlesham, see above.

37. www.birdcare.com/bin/shownews/219. Some North American snowy owls do occasionally fly – unassisted – as far as the Orkney Islands of Scotland. Many migratory birds from Continental Europe make their first landfall in

Felixstowe. We know migratory birds drop in on oil rigs. Trimley snowy owl from conversation on 6 December 2015 with Alex Bass of Local Birding Tours, suffolkbirdtours@gmail.com.

38. "Farmers concerned about return of rare bird", *Coastal Advertiser* – local *EADT* freesheet – 18 December 2009; "Rare white stork spotted in Southwold day after white-tailed eagle sighting", *EADT,* 20 March 2015, www.eadt.co.uk/news/rare_white_stork_spotted_in_southwold_day_after_white_tailed_eagle_sighting_1_4003448.

39. "Sudbury sighting of alien black squirrel", *Suffolk Free Press,* 12 June 2008; www.suffolkfreepress.co.uk/news/latest-news/sudbury-sighting-of-alien-black-squirrel-1-559165. North American grey squirrels were still rare in Suffolk in the 1930s and only became "endemic" in the 1970s; around the time I had my red squirrel sighting in Staverton Thicks.

40. Lakenheath cranes in *The Today Programme,* BBC Radio 4, 9 March 2011; Phone conversation on 6 December 2015 with Alex Bass of Local Birding Tours, based in Saxmundham, suffolkbirdtours@gmail.com; "Cranes fledge three young at Lakenheath", Birdwatch News Archive, 19 July 2015, www.birdwatch.co.uk/channel/newsitem.asp?cate=__16010.

41. *Lowestoft Journal* Suffolk Wildlife Park press cuttings file, Suffolk Record Office Reference 1176/2/2/11/81. According to the same file, a pangolin also escaped from Kessingland on 21 January 1972.

42. *Ipswich Star,* 23 October 2004; www.ipswichstar.co.uk/news/wallabies_on_the_loose_in_suffolk_1_101642; http://paranormaldatabase.com; "'White wallaby' spotted on the Suffolk/Essex border," BBC News Suffolk, 25 September 2017, www.bbc.co.uk/news/av/uk-england-suffolk-41392819/white-wallaby-spotted-on-the-suffolk-essex-border. I also received a secondhand report of a wallaby said to have been seen "around Sudbury" in October 2017.

43. Norwich Castle Museum prairie dog from *The Mammals of Suffolk*, see above.

44. Letter to *East Anglian* magazine April 1958 p310, quoted in *Lantern* 28 p8, 1979, www.hiddenea.com/Lantern28.pdf. See also *Fortean Times* **FT24;4** and http://office23-thefalls.blogspot.co.uk/2011/04/frogs-wetheringsett-suffolk-england.html. Lyston Hall fall from Charles Hoy Fort's Notes, 1841-45, which quotes *Meteorological Magazine*, 21 September 1886, http://www.resologist.net/notes/1841-to-1845.html:

45. *Suffolk & Essex Free Press* 25 March 1885, in Pip Wright's Newspapers in Suffolk 1876-1900, www.pipwright.com/Newspapers_in_Suffolk_1876_1900.htm.

46. Framlingham bears from "Suffolk's got animal talent", *Suffolk* magazine; August 2015; bears in East Anglian seaside towns in *A Visit to Southwold,* A. Barrett Jenkins, Southwold, 1985; near-escape of a lion from *Suffolk Chronicle,* 25 January 1845, reproduced in *I Read It In the Local Rag: Selections from Suffolk and Norfolk Papers 1701-1900*, Pip Wright, Poppyland, Cromer 2006

47. *Bury Post,* October 1789, http://www.pipwright.com/Newspapers_in_Suffolk_1720_1800.htm.

48. *Halesworth Times and Southwold General Advertise*r of 3 December 1907, www.pipwright.com/Newspapers_in_Suffolk_1901_1914.htm.

49. "Curious tale of the Wall of Death rider who buried his lion..." *Daily Express,* 21 July 2013, www.express.co.uk/nes/uk/416360/curious-tale-of-the-wall-of-death-rider-who-buried-his-lion-outside-a-rustic-villa. Why Boxford? Because it's a short ride to Southend, and because Tornado Smith's father was the landlord of the village's White Lion pub; Pathé newsreel showing Briton, Sparky, Tornado and his wife "Marjorie Death" at Southend in 1936, www.youtube.com/watch?v=fFfGKljkkBo.

Britain's most easterly newspaper

LOWESTOFT Journal

FRIDAY, APRIL 25, 1997

FRIENDS SHARE BINGO JACKPOT — PAGE 3

NEW LAW ON DOG MESS — PAGE 6

FIREMEN'S FIRST DAY RESCUE SURPRISE — PAGE 7

Big cat spotted

JOURNAL EXCLUSIVE by TERRY REEVE

A LARGE cat-like animal is roaming farmland in the Wrentham area, causing concern to farmers, it was claimed this week.

4 EVENING STAR, Monday, July 1, 1996

Huge cat seen near cemetery

HAS the black panther of Ipswich been stalking the town's pet cemetery?

One person who reports a sighting there is 26-year-old Pamela Cook, of Spenser Road, Whitton.

She recalls how a few weeks ago she was driving her friends to the pet cemetery in Tuddenham Road.

One of her friends has a pet buried there and they were paying a night-time visit.

Pamela recalled: "All of a sudden this black thing darted out. I caught it in my headlights. It was huge, nearly as big as a tiger, with a black shiny coat. It looked like a large cat.

"We were going to call the police, but we didn't because we thought they would think we were stupid."

Stressing that they were not drinking, Pamela said: "We went back there on four nights ago but we couldn't find it."

If you've seen the mysterious animal then call us on 01473 282256.

We are also offering a £250 reward to anyone who is able to capture a picture of the beast. Send them to Evening Star Claws Hunt, 30 Lower Brook Street, Ipswich, IP4 1AN

Controversy over wild cat-alogue

MYSTERY MOGGIE: A lynx which was reportedly found at Beccles.

"hoaxes", including a photo of a supposed black panther in Wales printed by two national tabloids last April that turned out to be a full-size black stuffed toy.

Mr Bamping said: "This is a good example of how easy it is to produce a hoax.

"This year we have been able to study evidence in greater detail and ...

Suffolk big cats make headlines – a *Lowestoft Journal* exclusive, 25/04/97 (top), one of the first reports from the Ipswich big cat wave in the *Evening Star*, 01/07/96 (above left), the Beccles Lynx in the *EDP* 08/04/96 (above right).

Big cat sightings may be linked to ferocious attack

A MAN who claimed he released a male puma into the wild has come under fire from a woman who believes she could have lost 16 pullets to the beast.

Frances Cutler of Wormingford, near the Essex/Suffolk border, was horrified when she discovered the devastation in her chicken run.

"Whatever got them buried some of them in the run and either took 11 carcasses away or ate them on the spot. There were so many feathers inside the run, all the perches were upside down and all the nesting boxes had been upset.

"We've had chickens for a long time and I'm a country person and I'm sure it ...

Meanwhile reports of further sightings were still coming in to the EADT yesterday, after a man claimed he had released his pet puma into the countryside when it had outgrown its cage.

A man who was taking his son to the disabled riding centre at Shelly saw a large black cat about 400 yards away in a field.

A couple driving through Assington only hours before a sighting was reported to Suffolk police saw what they initially thought were foxes playing in the road.

"As we got nearer we realised they ...

More patrols on streets to catch vandals

That big black cat is prowling again

Two more 1996 *Evening Star* reports, with sightings in Assington and Ipswich.

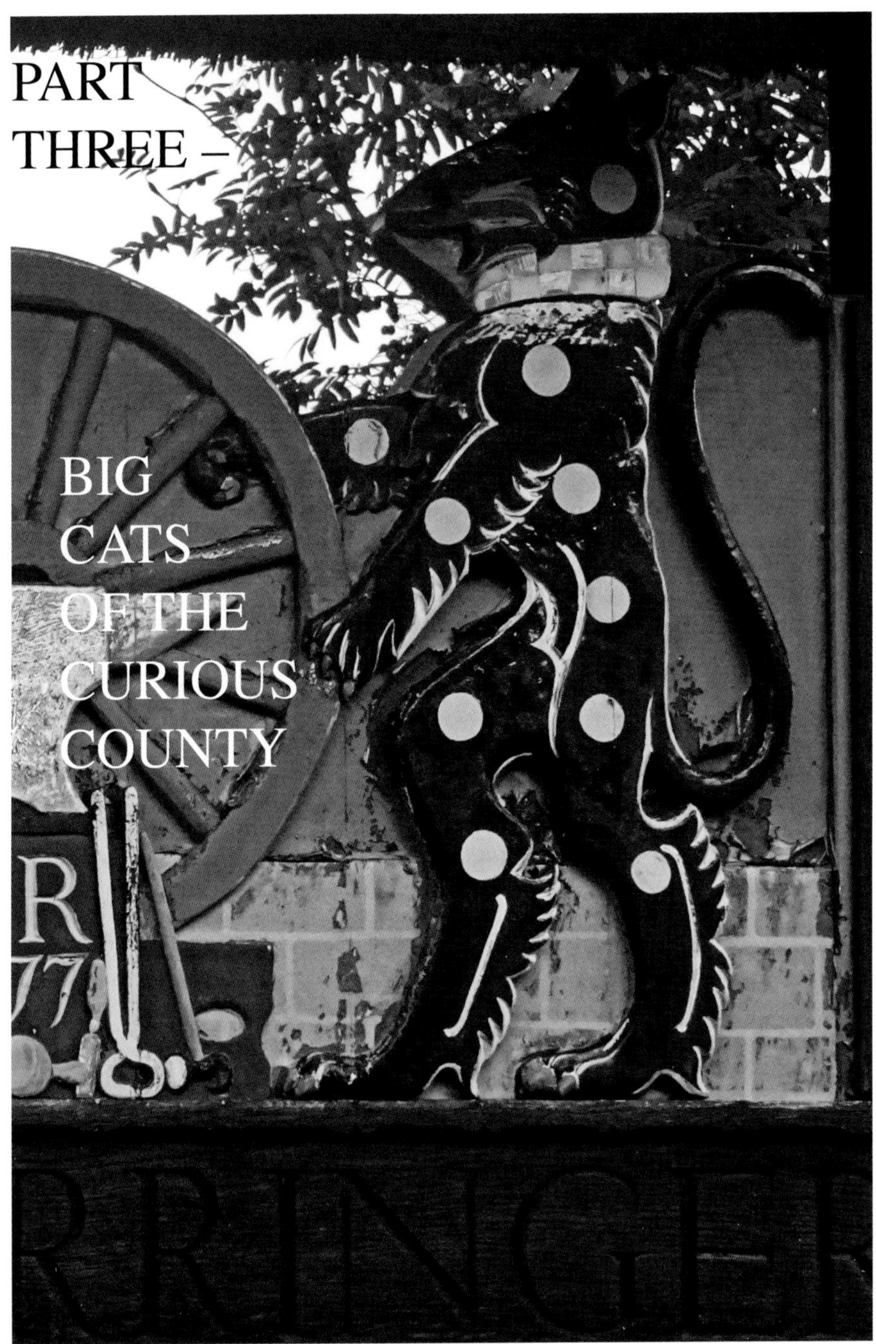

PART THREE – BIG CATS OF THE CURIOUS COUNTY

PART 3 – BIG CATS OF THE CURIOUS COUNTY

13: From the Theberton panther to alleged airmens' acquisitions

At some time in the 15th century (the century beginning in 1400) a heraldic spotted panther was carved in stone and added to the side of St Peter's Church in the village of Theberton, near Leiston, serving as a drainpipe. This panther gargoyle had spots – perfectly circular spots carved in relief. Some years after that, a more modern drainpipe was rammed into the panther's mouth, making it look as if he was smoking some kind of vast spliff. (I restored the panther to its original 14th century state for the cover of this book, photoshopping out the drainpipe. The "panther spliff" was just confusing to most people I showed it to.)

The Theberton panther was a mythical, heraldic animal, like a unicorn or dragon. Confusingly, "panther" came to be used to describe both leopards in Africa and India and pumas in the Americas. Melanistic leopards became known as "black panthers", and zoology acquired a genus with the Latin name *Panthera,* which includes lions, tigers, leopards, jaguars and snow leopards but not pumas or lynxes. Strictly speaking, there is no such animal as a "panther".

The heraldic panther is usually shown with coloured, circular spots ("roundels"), with the spots frequently a combination of some blue and some red. There's a fierce white heraldic panther with red and blue circular spots and wire whiskers at Hampton Court Palace.

The panther is often depicted with something like flames coming out of its ears and mouth, although what's emanating from it is actually supposed to be a lethal, super-strength scent that it lets out with a roar. This intoxicating musk was used to stupefy creatures – particularly dragons – and lure them to the monster panther's cave lair in a hypnotic daze, where the panther would eat them up. The water pouring out of the mouth of the panther on a wet winter's day in the village of Theberton may have been meant to simulate the deadly scent exuded by the mythical panther. Sometimes, particularly on medieval German coats of arms, the panther looked more like a donkey or a calf, or a composite animal with four horns.

The Romans tended to depict the mythical panther creature as being like a realistic spotted leopard – probably choosing this likeness because leopards really had spots and were fierce and frightening. Roman mosaics often depicted the god Dionysus riding on a "panther" that looks like a spotted leopard. (Back in the days of the Roman Empire, leopards were still native to what's now eastern Turkey.)

A white panther with yellow or gold spots was the badge of Henry VI of England (reigned 1422 to 1461 and again from 1470 to 1471), and an emblem of his Lancastrian dynasty. But King Henry's white panther bore only a passing resemblance to a big cat. It looked more like some kind of devil-unicorn, with an angry face sprouting gold serrated horns, and with nasty-looking sharp pointed hooves. The more realistic panther at Theberton – looking remarkably like a big cat with its mouth open and its snout screwed up as if in a snarl – may have been contemporary with Henry VI. It could have been a take on the royal panther emblem of the day.

Neither Marion Welham, the Diocese of St Edmundsbury and Ipswich's Church Heritage and Tourism Officer nor Roy Tricker, Suffolk church architecture expert, were able to tell me anything about the Theberton panther. Nor did they know of any other examples of heraldic panthers in the diocese's 478 churches. As Roy admitted, "Church guides often don't draw attention to water spouts and guttering." St Peter's Church, Theberton's own guidebook only notes that its panther is one of three "splendid gargoyles." [1]

The 15th century heraldic panther on the side of St Peter's Theberton forms a link between the intangible spirit world of folklore and myth and the very real world of zoology. We have a ridiculously fantastic beast in impossible colours, luring dragons to their doom with a roar and a wafted cloud of scent. Yet the artist has moved away from the spiky, fantastic depiction of a panther. The Theberton panther is a quite realistic depiction of something between a domestic cat and a big cat, albeit with circular heraldic spots ("roundels") in raised relief.

Enough of the charming folklore already! Like our Theberton panther, we are now leaving the phantasmal realm of mythical perfume-exuding panthers, woodwoses, will-o-the-wisps, spectral black dogs, galleytrots and hobby lanterns and leaping into the real world of those proper flesh-and-blood physical animals, the big cats.

And as luck would have it, in 2008, just on the edge of the same village of Theberton, on the road to Westleton, Tony and Sara Bloor who ran the shoe shop in nearby Leiston encountered something like a melanistic leopard (a black leopard). Also, one of their parents saw the same animal on the same stretch of road two years earlier.[2]

A quick zoology lesson – the big cats loose in the UK are thought to be either melanistic – black – leopards, (*Panthera pardus*) or pumas (*Felis concolor*) which are usually a sandy brown colour, or lynxes – (*Lynx lynx*) the spotty ones with the tufted ears. Other possible species that could be some of Britain's big cats include bobcats and servals and caracals – the last two look a bit like lynxes – or golden cats. Later on, in Chapter 20, there will be more detail on exactly what animals Suffolk's big cats could be.

Owen's cat from Newbourne

In the stores of the Ipswich Museum, there are the blackened carnassial teeth of a puma, adapted for shearing flesh. The teeth of this big cat were dug up from Newbourne, a spring between Ipswich and the River Deben. The great Victorian naturalist Richard Owen (he went on to coin the name "dinosaur") took an early interest in this discovery, and described it formally to science in 1846, naming it *Panthera pardoides* and interpreting the find as coming from something resembling a leopard. It became known more informally as Owen's cat. More recently, Owen's cat was renamed *Puma pardoides* – on re-examination it was found to be more like a puma than a leopard. (We'll go into the important difference between the leopards of Asia and Africa and the pumas of the Americas presently.)

Regrettably, this does not mean we can say, "case closed", and that we have conclusive evidence that big cats were on the prowl in 1840s Suffolk. Oh no! Owen's cat was dug up from the local Red Crag formation, along with the bones of prehistoric red pandas, porcupines and the teeth of giant sharks. *P. pardoides* walked the earth around two and a half million years ago. It was a now-extinct European puma, closely resembling pumas exclusively native to North and South America today.

Sadly, the evidence for modern big cats in Suffolk doesn't get as solid as actual teeth or other body parts. The best evidence for big cats in Suffolk is burst of mobile phone video shot in Wortham, a few seconds long, showing what seems to be a black leopard moving across a field some distance away. There's also a single, faint photo of a pawprint said to be from a big cat, taken in Dunwich Forest in 1998, by a couple from Beccles who earlier that day reported hearing growling and panting sounds. Natural England has revealed that it had in its possession photos showing "alleged predation on fox carcasses" allegedly by a big cat at Orford Ness and a "Photograph: Inconclusive" of another big cat "seen/reported" somewhere in Suffolk in 2010. But whatever these photos are, it seems they can no longer be found. There's also a photo of the front half of muntjac deer found up a tree in Knettishall Heath nature reserve[3]

Other witnesses to Suffolk big cats have reported seeing paw prints in earth or mud, including one set of "horse-sized prints, seven inches in diameter but with claws" in the earth on a property adjoining Foxhall Road, Ipswich in 2007. A resident of Bredfield found what she thought were the tracks of a big cat in the snow in her garden in 2003, and a gamekeeper found tracks he thought were from a "dark and cat-like", Alsatian-sized cat he'd seen earlier in countryside near Great Livermere. A resident of Brandon in West Suffolk I spoke to recalled there being many big cat footprints outside the town in one of the snowy winters early in the 2010s, but he couldn't remember which year. Another witness described to me how a farmer showed him the footprints of a big cat in mud by the side of the river in Wilby. I've come across half a dozen more cases of witnesses reporting finding what they believe to be the paw prints of a big cat, often after seeing a big cat in the area.

It's easy to misidentify dog tracks as being big cat tracks. But there are recognisable differences. The tracks of a dog are more symmetrical, with pads at the same level as each other. The tracks of all known types of cat are asymmetrical, a bit like the fingers on the human hand, their pads will not normally line up with each other. While dog tracks usually show claw marks, cats can retract their claws. They'll be walking with their claws in, except for rare occasions when they're walking on slippery mud and may need their claws for extra grip.[4]

Two Suffolk residents who had encounters with big cats reported finding scratch marks, one of these also found "its business" (scat, as big cat poo is known) in the field where he'd seen a "shiny black" big cat earlier that day. Another witness – Kevin Wood from Woodbridge – claimed to have seen the dead body of a big cat by the side of the road while driving somewhere in Suffolk. When he came back to the same spot later that day, the body had been "removed." I heard a similar story from the Eye area, with a witness spotting the corpse of a sandy-coloured big cat by the side of the road as he rode to work on his motorbike in 2013. There wasn't room for a big cat cadaver on his bike, he was in a hurry, and it had gone when he returned later that day, he said.[5]

As well as field signs, occasional "kill signs" are reported – evidence of prey killed apparently by a Suffolk big cat. Some time around 2000, Mark Frost, who saw a "shiny" black cat in a field of crops while working a combine harvester in Hemley, said that a neighbouring landowner found a newborn calf "killed" in the adjoining field. A member of staff at Dunwich Heath National Trust nature reserve, who's seen a big cat on the reserve himself, told me he'd also found a deer carcass "opened up", and more conclusive evidence of predation on deer carcasses suggestive of a big cat, and that a visitor to Dunwich Heath NT reported to him finding "half a seal" on the Suffolk Coastal Path, inland from the beach.[6]

Suffolk Police in February 2012 confirmed to the Ipswich-based *Evening Star* newspaper that a man had reported to them finding on a farm track in Akenham, just outside Ipswich, signs that "a big cat had attacked a deer. The man had found the deer (carcass) with marks around its throat," according to a police spokesman.[7]

One big cat witness claimed to have seen a big cat in Hollesley, after which they saw "tree scratches as evidence" of a big cat in the area. The same witness in 2005 found near Earsham an animal so mauled by whatever had killed and nibbled on it that he couldn't even tell what it was – his guess was a young otter or a squirrel (the Otter Trust sanctuary was nearby). Whatever it was had its rib cage taken out, and all its internal organs "gone". There was "not a drop of blood… or any scraps" left around it, and whatever it was that had mauled it must have cleared three locked gates or three sets of fences to get to it. A witness who'll have to remain anonymous said he'd also found a fox skull about 20 feet up a tree somewhere in Suffolk. Foxes aren't good climbers, and they go to their holes, definitely not up trees, to die. The witness's son was with him for one of these finds and took a photo, but it seems to have since been lost. Leopards in particular frequently drag their prey up into trees to finish them off in peace, or store their prey in trees to eat later.[8]

North Suffolk resident Chris Field told me that in around 2005, between Tunstall and Snape, near the crossroads by the church, on land where "they grow onions and carrots," he found a muntjac carcass that showed signs of "a killer bite on the back of a neck… a spaniel-sized bite," and signs of quite deep "incisions" that look like they were made by some pointed teeth, as well as what Chris described as a "cat spoor" nearby. He felt whatever it was had been "disturbed" before being able to eat its kill, which had been at some point during the previous day, as the muntjac corpse had "not gone hard" yet.

In early 2021 I received a report of a deer carcass found just outside Risby (west of Bury), with my source describing how "skin is moved away (from) bones as cats do. There were also... holes in the skin that appeared to be substantial puncture wounds."

We have only one convincing short video of a live Suffolk big cat of which I am aware. We do have a photo of a footprint. The evidence from big cats in Suffolk is not great.

In other British counties, along England's South Coast, I've been out photographing evidence for big cats with one of the experts on the subject, Jonathan McGowan, who's been tracking big cats near his native Bournemouth and elsewhere for many years. Within five minutes of getting out of the car in some reedbeds near Bournemouth, Jonathan was picking up and pulling apart big cat scat to show me the deer hairs it contained. Very soon we were pulling "leopard wool" – the black hairs of a melanistic leopard – off barbed wire, and coming across the odd paw print and big cat claw scratch marks in the wet earth. We stumbled across several big cat "larders" – piles of sika deer bones, including ribs neatly cut by the shearing carnassial teeth of a big cat, in contrast to dog's carnassial teeth, that would have just messily crunched up the bone. Even out in the reed beds of Dorset, the few big cat tracks we found were very hard to make out in the photographs I took – my photos of them are rubbish.

I'm afraid to say, in contrast to the abundance of evidence you can find in other parts of the UK – the Forest of Dean, Dorset, bits of the Welsh border and the Scottish county of Fife in particular – evidence for big cats in Suffolk is poor to non-existent. Simone Bullion, Recorder of Mammals for the county of Suffolk, told me in 2015 that Suffolk's biological records centre, who work closely with Suffolk Wildlife Trust, never got reports of big cats. She added that if anyone ever called them with a big cat sighting for which there were fresh field signs, they'd send someone out to take a look.[9]

Apart from that single short video, all we have is anecdotes about field signs rather than actual field signs, people saying they found a mauled dead deer or relating how – some years ago – they found a dead animal with teeth marks suggestive of a big cat. And there are also reports of sightings of big cats themselves – lots of them.

I thought at first there would be few accounts of sightings of Suffolk big cats, but it turns out over the years there's been a deluge of these. As of the end of 2021, I'd gathered testimony and reports – some secondhand via newspaper reports and big cat investigator groups, some through interviews with people who've contacted me – of around 170 big cat sightings across

Suffolk. That's a conservative estimate – it's hard to work out where one sighting ends and another begins in some cases, whether two reports from different sources are talking about the same sighting of the same animal. I've included a few credible reports of big cat kill signs and field signs in this figure.

And that figure of around 170 excludes many other sightings that are from places three miles or less over the county boundary and just inside the neighbouring counties of Norfolk, Essex and Cambridgeshire. These "other East of England" big cat sightings are all so near to Suffolk that if there's a real animal involved, you can bet they're in and out of Suffolk on a regular basis. This is a book on mystery animals of the county of *Suffolk* that you are reading. But as we shall see, big cats couldn't care less about county borders.

My 170-odd sightings and reports of kill signs and their chains of circumstances that caused them to be written down and emailed to me or to someone else – or described to me over the phone – are of course random quirks of fate. My stumbling over that record of a big cat sighting all those years later is equally coincidental. Big cat experts tell me you're more likely to see British big cats between February and March – there's less greenery for them to hide in, they're expecting they've got the woods pretty much to themselves on winter weekdays and aren't expecting to encounter many people. And it's thought that big cats need to put more effort into getting enough to eat in the winter, which is why you'll see more of them.

However, I couldn't help noticing how many newspaper reports of Suffolk big cat sightings are in the height of summer. I suspect local newspaper editors regard the summer months as a series of "slow news days", simply because the football season's over, Ipswich Town aren't playing, so there's no opportunity to fill pages and pages of speculation about how Ipswich Town are going to do next Saturday. Big cats will have to do.

I suspect also that many people in Suffolk who've seen big cats have kept quiet about it and never told anyone. A farmer who had a sighting of a glossy black leopard on his farm, after mysterious deaths or losses of quite lot of livestock, asked me to be vague about where and what sort of farm it was. He told me his "standing" in the "farming community" would be seriously affected if it got out that he had any unresolved problem with livestock loss. I got the feeling it was not a good idea to ask him to elaborate on why this should be. I also suspect what is not said, that some farmers who see big cats know their neighbours, know they are heavily armed and fear they're going to shoot the local big cat if word gets around

One wildlife warden who was happy to talk to me about his big cat sighting didn't want to be named; my witness was much more reluctant to talk about what we agreed to describe as "more conclusive evidence of predation on deer carcasses suggestive of a big cat". All sorts of agencies get involved once dead livestock come into the equation and it's understandable that some of the witnesses feel they don't need the hassle that making such a report will bring down on them. Often there's "the authorities" in some form to whom the witness should have reported such kills and hadn't. In a county of 700,000 souls, where in most places everybody knows everybody, witnesses anticipate all sorts of grief if they then tell somebody else and it gets out.

Understandably, some in the farming community who've seen big cats are reluctant to come forward after what happened south of the county border, in the village of St Osyth in Essex in August 2012. A large ginger domestic cat named Teddy Bear was mistaken for an escaped lion. Very soon there were two police helicopters overhead, reportedly 19 marksmen on the ground, and at least one local farmer on lockdown, confined to his farm under curfew by Essex Police

The Theberton panther as it is today, with its modern drainpipe still in place. I airbrushed it out of the front cover image as it confused people, they thought it was a spliff.

(years before the Covid pandemic). With that sort of overkill, you could forgive East Anglia's farmers for refraining from reporting any big cats they might see. [10]

And let us not forget that keeping things to yourself is a time-honoured Suffolk tradition. You don't tell anyone at which secluded spot on the coast the samphire is. In the more urban bits of St Edmundsbury, you don't tell anyone which roundabout the sloes are growing on, for that sloe gin and sloe vodka that you make every autumn by adding the berries to it.

You only tell the *East Anglian Daily Times* journalist – the one you know personally – where the breeding pair of blackwing stilts are roosting, and even then you don't tell them 'till after the chicks have fledged. Wardens are coy about whether there are hobbys or goshawks on certain reserves. (I've heard that in some cases, wardens know they are there but they're keeping schtum about it.) You don't tell anyone but your close friends and neighbours that badgers are helping themselves to the food you put out for the chickens, and I'm still absolutely not allowed to say anything at all about that pair of courting cranes and where they were, and even in what year. As Joan Forman noted of the eighteenth-century Suffolk smuggling industry, "East Anglians are good at keeping their mouths shut."[11]

Reluctance to report sightings notwithstanding, for sightings you need people. So however many big cats our unspoilt Suffolk countryside and wilderness may hide, there are only just under three quarters of a million residents (plus a lot more visitors in the summer, of course) to see the big cats, and then actually go to the trouble of telling someone who takes any notice. While some clusters of Suffolk big cat sightings may be in the more remote parts of the county, these are often along some surprisingly busy roads.

There have been several big cat sightings in Rendlesham Forest over the years, but I had no idea until I actually went there how busy the road through Rendlesham Forest is. The road through the forest is an important commute from Woodbridge to Orford and down to the Bawdsey Peninsula. And a lot of anecdotes about "black panthers" in Rendlesham Forest only survive because so many people happened to be asking around in Rendlesham and environs due to their interest in another, more famous Suffolk mystery – the Rendlesham Forest UFO Incident of Boxing Day 1980.

Around 2005 there were waves of big cat sightings along the remoter stretches of the A143 from Bury St Edmunds to Diss, and the B1118 that runs parallel to it near the Suffolk bank of the River Waveney and down to Hoxne. There have been multiple sightings of something described as a "puma or lynx" between two roundabouts on the A1092 bypass east of Haverhill on the border with Essex. One wouldn't expect Suffolk's big cats to be an urban phenomenon, but one of the earlier waves of big cat sightings was along the Foxhall Road in Ipswich, an important route out of the county town and east in the direction of Martlesham. In Ipswich there are more people around to see any big cats. There was a "stooped... large feline" seen crossing the major A12 road at Holton St Mary in 1998, just as the road enters Suffolk from the south, and I also interviewed a witness who saw a brown big cat jumping a hedge after crossing the A12 further north at Kelsale near Saxmundham. Recently, I've started to hear reports of big cat activity along the busy A14 around the Rougham turn-off. The story of big cats in Suffolk is often the story of where people happened to be travelling the county's busier roads at a particular time.

It's also striking just how many of those reports that give a time for a sighting list the encounter as "at 5.30am" or describe a big cat caught in the beam of car headlights on a lonely country lane late at night, often around 11 to 11.30pm. The labour market in this predominantly rural county can be precarious. I've spoken to a number of Suffolk men who have at various points of their working lives changed jobs to become ambulance drivers, night shift security guards, bus drivers, taxi drivers or delivery drivers for a time. Such a work history would frequently put you on the road very early in the morning or late at night, at the time when big cats are out and about. Leopards, pumas, lynxes and such, are what's called crepuscular – most active at dawn and at dusk. The fact that so many Suffolk big cat encounters happen at these times of day lends weight to their authenticity.

Let loose mountain lion mascots from World War Two?

When did the big cats arrive in the Suffolk countryside? There is a tradition in British big cat lore that some of them could have been introduced by American airmen in World War Two, who were said to have airlifted pumas (also known as cougars or mountain lions, and native to the western United States) in their bombers as mascots for their units. In such stories, the airmen reluctantly had to turn them loose at the end of World War Two as they were unable to take them back. (Australia has a similar tradition, with better evidence for it, about US airmen bringing over pumas as mascots for their Pacific theatre of operations.) I've talked to one big cat investigator who tells me that former US airmen have admitted to releasing puma mascots at the end of World War Two, but he wouldn't elaborate.

Certainly, Suffolk was Airstrip One in World War Two. (Local boy George Orwell coined the term Airstrip One to describe Cold War Britain in *Nineteen Eighty-Four.)* There was a military airfield of some sort about every five miles in Suffolk in World War Two.

I even heard a rumour that RAF Horham – the North Suffolk headquarters of the USAAF 95th Bomber Group's Flying Fortress squadrons in World War Two – had a puma mascot. A contact who lives locally said he went to an event at the Red Feather Club – the wartime pilots' bar that's now a museum. At the event he recalled seeing a video with black and white film footage of a serviceman of the USAAF (the contemporary US Army Air Force) with a puma on a lead. A Red Feather Club volunteer suggested to me that this might have been footage of the 95th Bomber Group taken while it was still stationed in the United States.

Military photographs of the time show that individual soldiers (ground troops) also had their own pets. A few servicemen smuggled them from the United States, but more often soldiers' pets were local animals – puppies, kittens, dogs, cats or birds – found in the field, left homeless by the war. These animals often tended to be small enough to fit into a large pocket of a uniform.[12] Some of these foundling mascots, mostly dogs (but even some adopted children) found their way back to the US after the war, brought back home by American servicemen openly, rather than being smuggled out.

The Royal Air Force had airborne mascots –"cockpit companions" that tended to be animals you could fit in the cockpit of a single-seater fighter with you. Jack Russells were for this reason a popular breed for airborne mascots. There are US Air Force fighter squadrons thata still have official bulldog mascots, but these stay on the ground. Other known RAF mascots and Royal Australian Air Force mascots included goats, puppies, kangaroos, monkeys found in Borneo and Alsatian dogs – all staying firmly grounded throughout the war.

Among ground troops, the London Irish Rifles had – predictably – Irish wolfhound mascots. Wotjek, a bear picked up in Iran, became Corporal Wotjek, mascot of the 22nd Transport Company Polish II Division. The Royal Navy had a reindeer mascot at its base at Scapa Flow which ended up at the official Royal Navy Zoo. The Navy, of course, had big ships that could accommodate big animals. The only big cat mascot from World War Two I've come across was Dolly the lioness, with the South African Pioneer Corps, on service in the Western Desert. She had her photograph taken looking cool wearing a Pioneer Corps forage cap. Dolly, sourced from southern Africa, presumably travelled to combat in a spacious troop transport ship. I've found no records of big cat mascots crossing oceans on aircraft.[13]

"Mascots" on bombers were mostly cartoon characters or pin-ups painted on the nose, "nose art" as it was known. While such painted-on "mascots" had official approval, live pumas were unwelcome.

Tempting though it is to believe that the brave men of the USAAF not only played a role in liberating Europe but also introduced East Anglia's big cats, there is a problem with this scenario. The recollection years later by Gale D. Moore, a US airman stationed with 493rd bomber group in Debach, near Woodbridge, hints at these. His unit flew Liberator bombers on missions "Somewhere in Europe". The manner of the arrival of airman Moore and his crew at Debach was not one that lent itself to bringing a puma with them.

Moore described "California To Combat... in Eighty-One Days"[14], which began with him boarding his Liberator with his crew at a California airfield, flying it to "their destination". Only when they turned east instead of west was it clear their destination was somewhere in Europe rather than somewhere in the Pacific. Via stopovers in Texas, New Mexico, Tennessee and Florida, Trinidad, Belem (Mexico), Belize and Brazil, the Liberator went on to recently-liberated Dakar, Senegal. There Moore and his crew slept in tents. Then on to Morocco for ten days, after which their plane was ordered to be stripped down for parts.

In Morocco, a crew whose plane had gone ahead left behind a "white American Eskimo pup". Rumours were already circulating among airmen that "the English were real sticklers for keeping animals out of England" so one of Moore's crew "decided to take the little dog with us and try to smuggle him under his coat while the rest of us were cleared" through UK customs and quarantine. So US airmen would expect to be shaken down for any pumas on arrival. Casually shipping a puma in a cage stowed in the bomb bay starts to look less likely. Moore and Co. were put on transport planes and via Casablanca were flown to England, then for training in Northern Ireland before finally arriving at Debach. They somehow managed to smuggle "the little puppy into Debach", through a complicated subterfuge involving stuffing it into a jacket during a customs search, with a crew member putting on a distraction. While US airmen could get away with a puppy hidden under a jacket, getting pumas past quarantine was harder. Not even Able Seacat Simon, domestic cat hero of the Cold War who survived *HMS Amethyst's* dash down the Yangtze to escape Chinese Communists, could evade British quarantine, where he died after arriving from China in 1949.

Moore was eventually stationed with 493 Bomber Group in Debach, where he found many of the bombers crews that had left the US had taken the seasonal "northern route" across the Atlantic. This allowed some to arrive in Wales within a mere five days rather than Moore's 36. Another US bomber crewman at Debach, Staff Sergeant Ed Bowery, recalled crossing the Atlantic aboard the passenger ship *Queen Elizabeth*. Given the long, convoluted trips many bomber crews made to East Anglia, puma smuggling opportunities seem remote.

Left: Fossil teeth of "Owen's cat" the European puma, from 700,000 years ago. The remains, from Newbourne Spring, are now in the stores of the Ipswich Museum. Photo: © Colchester and Ipswich Museum Service. Below: a paw print believed to be a big cat's, photographed by a couple in Dunwich Forest in 1998. Photo: © Mark Mower. Inset: drawing attempting to show what the full print in the faint photo might look like.

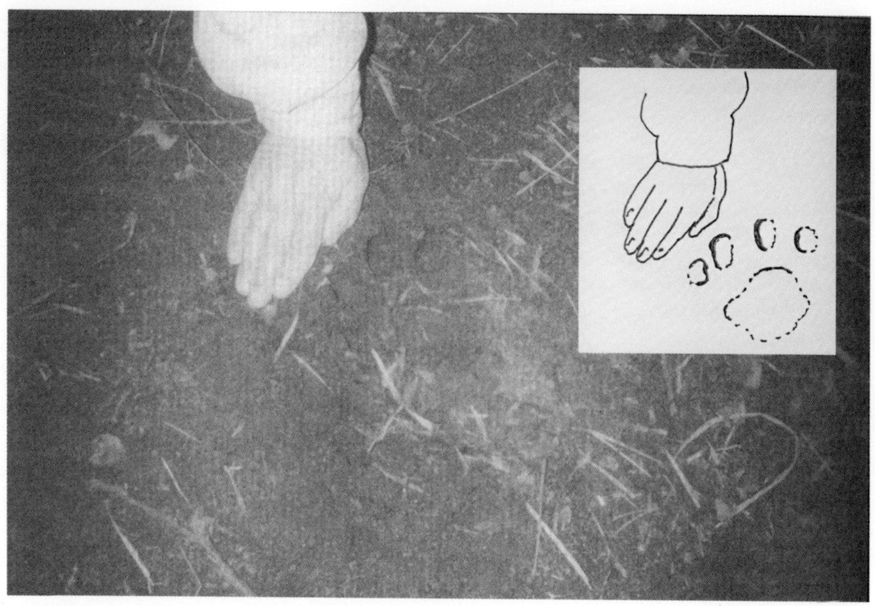

FOOTNOTES TO CHAPTER 13:
From the Theberton panther to alleged airmen's acquisitions

1. Elsewhere in the county, the Borough of St Edmundsbury's much more recent coat of arms features a black panther with gold spots, inspired by the emblem of the now defunct Rural District of Thingoe which was merged into the Borough. Thingoe's black and gold spotted panther originates in the coat of arms of the first Earls of Bristol, whose seat was in Ickworth. An impressive modern black panther with yellow spots can be seen on the village sign of Horringer cum Ickworth nearby. (See the photo on page 188.) The Palace of Westminster's visitors' entrance to Westminster Hall has a white medieval heraldic panther with black spots high up in the huge Victorian stain glass window at the top of the steps. This panther is based on the "Royal Beasts" in medieveal coats of arms.

2. "What lurks within the Suffolk countryside?" *EADT* 3 April 2008, www.eadt.co.uk/news/more_sightings_of_big_cats_come_to_light_1_188020

3. Wortham black leopard video from 2010 filmed by Lee Acaster; Wilby big cat footprints from 2020, witness requested anonymity; Dunwich Forest footprint photo from *Suffolk Tales of Murder and Mystery,* Mark Mower, Countryside Books, Newbury, Berks 2006, used with his kind permission. No more details are available, the "Beccles couple" wish to remain anonymous. As we went to press Natural England's FOI officer told me that neither the "inconclusive" photos of the Orford Ness fox corpse nibbled by a big cat from *Reported Sightings or Signs of Exotic Species Compiled by Natural England's Wildlife Management & Licensing Compiled by Defra Rural Development Service Prior to September 2006*, nor the Suffolk big cat photo referred to in the same document, could be traced. Some archive material stored on paper was then inaccessible due to Covid or may have been destroyed.

4. "Big cat spotted again" *Diss Express* 16 May 2008, www.cfzresources.com/database/cats2007/20070527_big_cat_spotted_again.htm and *Diss Express* 12 May 14 May 24 May, 25 May, 7 June; *Evening Star* (Ipswich), date not given, quoted in *BCIB Yearbook 2007*; "Black cat spotted in North Suffolk", *EADT* 16 July 2003, http://www.eadt.co.uk/news/black_cat_spotted_in_north_suffolk_1_60729

5. Mark Frost emailed Jon Wright's BBC Radio Suffolk show (01 01 15); Kevin Wood emailed Jon Wright's BBC Radio Suffolk show (01/01/2015). He had a sighting of a live black big cat just west of Easton on the Hacheston road around 1990, it wasn't clear from his email whether his sighting of the roadside big cat corpse some time before 2015 was in the same area. Regrettably, I'm not at liberty to divulge my source for the biker who spotted a big cat cadaver on the way to work.

6 Member of staff at Dunwich Heath NT who wishes to remain anonymous, interviewed 5 September 2014.

7. "Akenham: Police receive reports deer attacked by big cat", *Ipswich Star,* 18 February 2012 www.ipswichstar.co.uk/news/akenham_police_receive_reports_deer_attacked_by_big_cat_1_1213378. A witnesses told me that big cats that they had seen on other occasions appear to have killed their hens. A black leopard near Eye was said by the witnesses to be behind these kills.

8. Hollesley tree scratches from BBCR sightings map 2013, http://britishbigcatresearch.weebly.com/sightings-map.html; I can't give a source for either of the kill sign anecdotes, other than to say that they were based on two interviews in the Spring of 2015. Sorry. Clients don't like contractors talking about what they found on their land. It has been suggested to me that the fox in the tree could have been the work not of big cats but of "escaped eagles" – see Chapter 12. Snape muntjac with big cat kill signs from phone interview with Chris Field, 9 November 2015. I have not been able to verify a rumour of the still existing bones of a deer that were found up a tree in the Long Melford area.

9. Risby deer carcass report via Rick Minter by email, 7 March 2021. I am not at liberty to name his source, nor to publish photos or video footage of the corpse.

10. Big cat expert Rick Minter, explaining on a BBC Radio Gloucestershire show on 14 November 2015 why farmers don't talk about big cats, said it's because they are "a blight on their business." Teddy Bear, believed to be the St Osyth Lion, was said to be a ginger Maine Coon cat in some reports, *EADT* 1 September 2012, www.eadt.co.uk/home/the_st_osyth_big_cat_sighting_getting_your_lions_crossed_1_1500406Essex

11. *Haunted East Anglia*, Joan Forman 1974, 1985 reprint Jarrold & Co, Norwich.

12 See a selection of these mascots from the US National Archives, Washington DC Prologue, Animal Buddies 1996 www.archives.gov/publications/prologue/1996/fall/buddies.html; One of my interviewees described relatives' accounts of the USAAF's sudden departure from some of its Suffolk bases in 1945, and it sounds like something out of *The X-Files*. At RAF Eye and RAF Parham, everything from machine guns to jeeps were – according to these accounts – covered in tar paper to preserve it, then a huge hole was dug, mountains of equipment were placed in the hole and – under armed guard – locals were employed to fill the hole in. Grass and trees were planted on the top. The Americans put their equipment beyond use, but in anticipation of a possible imminent Soviet invasion, not that far beyond use.

13 There's a photo of Dolly at https://commons.wikimedia.org/wiki/File:%22Dolly%22_a_proud_%22British_ Lioness%22_is_fighting_with_allied_front-line_forces._She_is_mascot_of_a_South_African_Pioneer..._-_NARA_-_196357.jpg; Boy and Girl were lion cubs, found abandoned a day old and taken in as mascots by the Scots Guards, who were stationed in Kenya in the run-up to Kenyan independence in 1966. They and their four cubs never left Kenya, though. When the British pulled out of Kenya and the Scots Guards returned home, Boy and Girl were given to Kenya-based naturalist George Adamson. At eighteen months old they both played the part of Elsa the lioness in the film *Born Free*. Adamson was planning to release Boy and Girl back into the wild but Boy attacked and killed the young son of Adamson's assistant, and was eventually shot by Adamson.

14. 493rd BG Museum, Debech website http://493bgdebach.co.uk/vetmems.php.

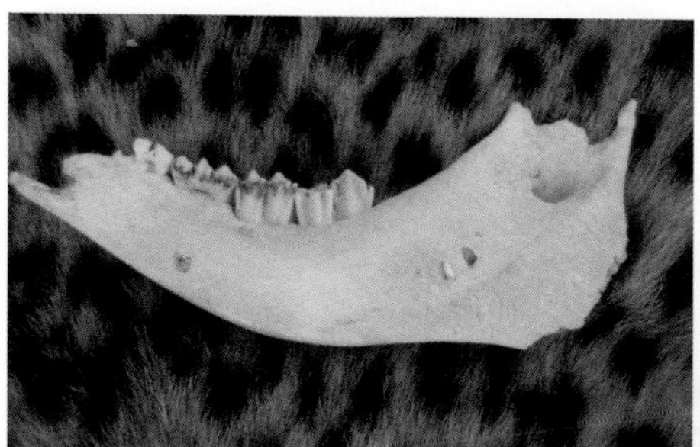

Sika deer jaw with puncture marks made by the teeth of a big cat – from Dorset, not Suffolk, from the collection of Jonathan McGowan (top). Big cat on the coat of arms of Joseph Harringer on his tomb at Lavenham.

More Suffolk big cats – the Garrett Lioness emblem on a steam engine built by Garretts of Leiston (top) and the three silver leopards on the arms of the Barne family at Dunwich.

If Suffolk's big cats really are escaped exotics and their descendants, they are most likely to be melanistic leopards ("black panthers" , top) from Asia and Africa or pumas (centre) from the Americas, or Eurasian lynxes (bottom.)
Leopard: Colin M L Burnett Creative Commons share alike; Puma: Jean Beaufort, "public domain licence"; Lynx: Magnus.johansson10 Creative Commons Attribution-Share Alike 2.0

14: The Debenham Lion and the big cat known as "Claws"

The earliest credible case of a big cat in Suffolk was the close encounter with a big cat reported by Jimmy Freeman while driving past the edge of Rendlesham Forest late one night in the mid-1970s. Interviewed by ufologist Nick Redfern in 2005, he felt that it had happened in either January of 1976 or 1977, but the details of the event were as fresh in Freeman's mind as if they'd just happened.

"Rendlesham Forest has big cats"

Freeman recalled that it was a dark, cloudy and slightly misty night, so it was a slow drive along the road through the 1,500-acre Forestry Commission conifer plantation some time between 11.15 and 11.30pm. Rendlesham Forest at the time surrounded the "twin bases", RAF Woodbridge airbase and RAF Bentwaters, from which the United States Air Force's Phantom jet fighter-bombers in those Cold War days made regular flights over the surrounding countryside. Suddenly "something large and shadowy" charged across the road in front of Freeman. It was "long, sleek and utterly black in colour." He had no doubt that he'd had a brief sighting of a huge cat, and that "Rendlesham Forest has big cats."[1]

Suffolk's big cats seemed to lie low in the years immediately following Jimmy Freeman's Rendlesham Forest sighting, which from its description would have been a melanistic leopard. British big cats hadn't really taken off as a cultural phenomenon yet. There was, however, a peak in sightings of phantom black dogs in the county in the 1970s, as we have seen.

Jimmy Freeman's Rendlesham Forest sighting probably slightly predated a significant piece of legislation that many believe led to the British big cat fauna that's established itself today. By the late 1960s it had become fashionable to keep big cats as pets. You could buy lion cubs in the pets department at Harrods in those days, and there were no regulations at all about keeping them.

An acquaintance in London had a relative who was a London Fire Brigade captain in the 1960s, who described how he had a callout to a fire in a tenement block in Whitechapel, and how he and his crew put up a short ladder and started scrambling over a wall to get to the back of the building. When the first firefighter jumped over the wall and landed in a cobbled yard at the back, suddenly a lion lunged at him. Fortunately the lion was chained up in the yard and couldn't reach the fireman. The fire crew hastily scrambled back over the wall, found another way in to put the fire out and forgot about the incident. Apparently, encounters of this sort weren't all that unusual in those days.

Out-of-the-way parts of the country with a lot of open space and not many people about, like a lot of Suffolk, were in those unregulated days the sort of place you might expect people to keep big cats – possibly people who weren't suitable owners. Such secluded places might also be the parts of the country where you'd expect less conscientious owners to still keep big cats even after subsequent laws were passed requiring owners to apply for a licence from the local authority to keep such animals.

A retired RSPCA inspector who worked in Croydon before moving to Ipswich, who gave his name as Stanley, recalled how he'd come across five families in the late 1960s who had lion cubs as pets. Inevitably, some owners discovered they were too much to handle and gave them to wildlife parks when they got too big, but Stanley claimed there was a Sixties "glut" of lion cubs, the wildlife parks ("safari parks" as they called themselves then) were beginning to run out of room for these giveaway lion cubs already.[2]

The Dangerous Wild Animals Act came into force in 1976. This required owners to apply for a licence from the local authority to keep any of the "dangerous wild animals" from a long list, which included all the big cats from jungle cats and up (more on jungle cats later), exotic domestic cat-wildcat crossbreeds like Bengal cats (leopard cat-domestic cat crossbreeds) and wolfdogs (wolf-dog hybrids, although the ban on these was lifted in 2006) as well as numerous primates, reptiles, venomous spiders and scorpions. The Act made it an offence to keep any of these animals without a licence. Nor was getting a permit from the council a formality – the local authority would only grant a licence if it was not a nuisance, not "contrary to the public interest", if it was happy with the security of the animal's accommodation, and if the owner had taken out liability insurance. And licences are costly – £250 as of 2021.

Many of the less competent big cat owners – those who in the words of one falconry enthusiast "shouldn't even have a goldfish" – were just smart enough to realise their homemade cages and pens wouldn't be up to scratch. They probably couldn't be bothered with the form-filling and expense anyway. These people are believed to have let their animals loose.

The British Big Cats Society (BBCS) back in 2006 declared on its website[3] that it had "gathered evidence of at least 23 releases of big cats into the wild since the Dangerous Animals Act was passed in 1976." The "original owners are now owning up" to having let loose lynxes, pumas, a panther, jungle cats, ocelots, caracals and "a host of exotics" into the British countryside, claimed the BBCS. Paul Sieveking of *Fortean Times*, who's been keeping an eye on British big cat reports since the early 1970s, documented several confessions of big cat releases reported in the press. These included a panther and a cougar let loose in Derbyshire in 1974, a pair of "panthers" given their freedom in Nottinghamshire in the same year and various big cats introduced into the wild in the Malvern Hills, Worcestershire, in 1976, the deed done on behalf of some Dangerous Wild Animals Licence dodgers.

In 2016, a third-hand claim emerged in *The Telegraph* newspaper that circus impresario Mary Chipperfield had in the 1970s released three pumas, including a "breeding" pair somewhere on Dartmoor, en route to their new home after the Chipperfields' zoo in Plymouth was forced to shut down. The story goes that Chipperfield couldn't face the prospect of losing these pumas to a life of captivity somewhere else. When the new owners at Dartmoor Zoo opened the truck, it is now alleged, there were only two pumas inside instead of the anticipated five. The legal obligation to report and record escapes of dangerous zoo animals in the UK didn't come into force until the Zoo Licensing Act of 1981.

This legislation brought in compulsory licensing of zoos, with a long list of reasons that the authorities could cite for not granting a licence – "if they are not satisfied that the standards of accommodation, staffing or management are adequate," if any member of staff had a conviction under any animal welfare legislation, and so on. There was a now long list of people who could veto a zoo's licence, including the county's Chief Constable and the local fire chief.

Some less reputable "zoos" were hardly worthy of the name. As a small child I remember going on holiday in Devon in around 1968, and at least two of the local country pubs each had a sad little zoo round the back as an attraction for the kids, with monkeys, parrots and owls. When licensing of zoos came in, a lot of these less viable establishments and hobby zoos disappeared. Fly-by-night zoo owners who should never have been in the business, facing the daunting and expensive task of attempting to become street-legal, would have been tempted to open their rickety cages and let their animals try their luck in the British countryside. Given how poorly many of them had been looked after, escape was a no-brainer from the big cat's point of view. It's possible that the "huge cat" seen by Jimmy Freeman in Rendlesham was one of the earliest post-Dangerous Wild Animals Act leopards already released. Another less fortunate post-Dangerous Wild Animals Act escapee (not deliberately released, he escaped) was the lion shot on 6 January 1984 somewhere in Norfolk, a day after it escaped, according to Defra, the government department then responsible for licensing dangerous animals.[4]

And it wasn't just leopards (black or spotted) that were supposed to have been turned loose in great numbers. There were pumas kept in sheds and barns and homemade pens in those days, and possibly lynxes. And there were other, more exotic cats not quite as impressive in size but nonetheless very exotic – servals with both spots and stripes and huge, bat-like ears, and caracals ("African lynxes") with their pointed black ears ending in the most extravagant tufts. Other big cats out there in the UK today may be lesser-known exotics like the African golden cat, the Asian golden cat, the jungle cat, or bizarre hybrids of any of these. We'll get acquainted with these candidates for the county of Suffolk's big cats a little later.

The first newsworthy British big cat famous enough to get its name in the papers was the Surrey Puma in the 1960s in the south of England. Its first sighting could have been as early as 1959, but it first came to widespread attention with a flurry of sightings in 1964, which was when the phenomenon became "the Surrey Puma", Britain's first named Alien Big Cat. There was a "Shooter's Hill Cheetah" in south London in 1963, but it never captured the popular imagination in quite the same way as the Surrey Puma, which is still reported today.

As we will see, the Surrey Puma was still famous enough to be the likely inspiration for the name given to Suffolk's own Haverhill Puma, the animal seen along the A1017 that bypasses the southern edge of Haverhill. This was despite several witnesses saying it wasn't particularly puma-like, describing it as a "puma or lynx." We'll return to this Surrey Puma, big daddy of all British big cat sightings, later.

Meanwhile, at around the same time as the Surrey Puma was hitting headlines, similar reports were coming from a location much closer to Suffolk. Janet and Colin Bord in their book *Alien Animals* (Paul Elek, 1980) mention that something very like the Surrey Puma was being reported from the East Anglian county of Norfolk in 1964, although such sightings never showed up on the news radar in the way the Surrey Puma did.

Surrey Puma fever had died down by the time Jimmy Freeman saw his "long, sleek, utterly black" 1970s large feline at Rendlesham, and it was a while later before the next British big cat flap hit the news, with the wonderfully scary-sounding "Beast of Bodmin", a black leopard loose on Bodmin Moor, Cornwall. The Beast of Bodmin, first seen around 1982, set the fashion for alliterative British big cat names. (The equally terrifying-sounding Norfolk Gnasher, who we'll eventually meet in this book, follows this tradition.) Well known though the Beast of Bodmin became, it didn't really take off as a cultural brand until 1995, some sixty Beast of Bodmin sightings later and after a Royal Marines mission to go and look for it on the Moor. A 1995 Defra report concluded there was "no basis" for the belief in a black panther roaming the Cornwall countryside. Cornwall's Newquay Zoo to this day has a "Beast of Bodmin Moor" puppet show, and since 2009 it's been home to the "Little Beast of Bodmin," a common palm civet (a mongoose-like distant relative of the cat family) that ended up there after being found in a garden near Bodmin.

Back in Suffolk, the area around Honington was the scene for one of only a handful of other 1980s Suffolk big cat reports I could find. Janet and Colin Bord's *Modern Mysteries of Britain* records several sightings of what had by then become known as Alien Big Cats (ABCs), as in "alien" to the UK, although whether they can today still be regarded as alien exotics is debatable. It was unclear whether the Honington big cats seen in April 1985 were a single creature or a possible family.

At around the same time, some 14km or eight miles to the west, and also recorded in *Modern Mysteries of Britain*, residents of the Suffolk village of Elveden reported several sightings of a large cat or cats. Recorded sightings of big cats from the eighties are rare, though – investigating big cats had not yet really become a thing. The odd big cat sighting showed up in anthologies of mysteries or forteana because they were strange and mysterious, there were as yet no people or groups dedicating a lot of time to looking for evidence of big cats.[5]

The Debenham Lion

Paul Berry from Framlingham was driving through the large Mid-Suffolk village of Debenham with his wife, it was in 1982 as far as they can recall. Suddenly they saw what Paul called "the Debenham Lion" walking nonchalantly across the road in front of them from left to right, quite unbothered about having been spotted. "That was big!" said Paul of the creature. It was about four and a half feet long and two feet high (1.37m long, 60cm high) and sandy coloured. After seeing it they saw a lion in a zoo and felt that it resembled one. Its head was "almost like a lion's head." While Paul didn't recall seeing them himself, he said his wife noticed and commented on the "tufts" on its short ears. (I showed Paul a photo of a tufted-eared caracal cat, and he said it looked nothing like that.)

Drinking in a nearby pub shortly after seeing the big cat, Paul met a group of off-duty Suffolk Police officers, and was introduced to "a Debenham policeman", over 30 years later he recalled his name was something like "PC Minx." Minx told Paul that his was the Debenham Lion's "third sighting in a couple of weeks." The Debenham Lion seems to have since become a locally-known phenomenon – in recent years, a match report of a game between Debenham FC and Wickham Market FC compared the tenacity of the former team to that of the Debenham Lion (and its cubs), so it still seems to be cultural reference understood locally. It's since been suggested to me that the Debenham Lion could have been one of the UK's earliest pet "red" (ginger) Maine Coon cats. But the Debenham Lion reportedly had short, *rounded,* tufted ears, and no mention was made of a long, thick coat.

Other recollections by Paul of his forestry work around Suffolk include going to do a job around Hollesley circa 1975 and around Nacton Woods sometime around 1980, and on both occasions being warned to be on the lookout for big cats.[6]

Some time "around 1990"– the witness couldn't be sure of the year when he recalled the event a quarter of a century later – Kevin Wood from Woodbridge was driving along the Hacheston Road (just west of Easton), at 5am, when he saw a "large black cat that looked at him. It bounded away." And an anonymous source told me that in around 1991, in the Wherstead area (it's just south of Ipswich where the Shotley peninsula starts), he came across a patch of ground in a very remote area where metal stakes six to eight inches long had been driven into the ground as part of a snare for foxes. Something very strong seems to have blundered onto one the stakes and managed to pull it right out of the ground and leave it there. He believes it would have to be something the size, strength and agility of a big cat.

From the last decade of the twentieth century there followed numerous big cat sightings across the county of Suffolk. These continue to this day. This phenomenon strongly suggests there is a rich variety of big cat species (and hybrids of various species) lurking in the Suffolk countryside, and in its towns and suburbs as well.

Lynxes or bobcats, two of them running

Camping in Staverton Thicks with a mate, sleeping on a platform on a tree, is definitely cool when you're eighteen years old. It was in the Summer of 1995, or it may have been 1996, (our witness wasn't too sure when he recalled the events in early 2015). The huge RAF Bentwaters US Air Force airbase whose perimeter fence is only 500 metres away from Staverton Thicks, had only recently closed with the end of the Cold War. The strange domes and watchtowers of Bentwaters are still visible from the end of Rendlesham Forest, the Bentwaters Cold War Museum is housed in one of its command bunkers, while the base is still used for spooky film locations. Its tarmac has also borne the skid marks of many a stunt filmed for *Top Gear*. The tree platforms where two eighteen-year-olds found themselves camping all those years ago seem to have been for spectators of some sort of Motocross stadium near the edge of the base, by then abandoned.

Staverton Thicks (or just "The Thicks" to those that know it) is an eerie landscape, with something of *The Lord of the Rings* about it. It's an overgrown medieval deer park and primeval woodland, and while the nearby Forestry Commission conifer plantation has most of its trees in neatly-planted ranks, The Thicks is a woodland of gnarled old ancient holly trees, many of them hollow. It's an enigma how the habitat survives at all, out here in England's driest county, as holly trees like it wet.

As a child in the 1970s my parents took me to The Thicks. On one trip we saw a red squirrel (a great rarity even then). On the same visit we spotted a man out walking with a hawk perched on his gloved hand. On a return visit in 2015 we gave up, we couldn't find the elusive public right of way through private land that gets you to the Thicks, a right of way that's barely marked on a map.

It was early one summer morning some 25 years ago that John Daniel had just got up at their unofficial Staverton Thicks campsite when he suddenly saw "lynxes or bobcats… two of them running." They were "muntjac-sized… one slightly smaller than the other." As for their colour, they were "not spotted, tabby," and John believed they were lynxes or bobcats because they had "tufted ears, no tails." They disappeared into the cover of the bracken.

John's friend "didn't believe" John when he told him he'd just seen two big cats. So John "beat them out of the bracken" so his friend could get a brief bird's eye view of them from the tree platform. John's friend, interviewed two decades later, was more certain that they were lynxes that he'd seen. He described how they "bounded away, shoulder blades moving as cats do" and how they were "quite long-legged."[7]

The following year, a veritable wave of Suffolk big cat sightings took hold, although it should be pointed out that this may just be a statistical phenomenon, in that *Fortean Times* magazine was at the time particularly diligent in collecting local newspaper reports of big cats. (The magazine's brief is "the world of strange phenomena".)

A "brown alien big cat" was seen in Felixstowe that year. Also in early March 1996, a big cat was spotted in Assington, near Sudbury. Suffolk Police had taken a call at 11 am on 3 March from a member of the public who'd seen a "large-black Panther-like cat with a tail as long as its body" in a field near the village. The caller said it looked "non-domestic." Police said the sighting was "not confirmed by anyone else."[8]

A couple of days later came *another* big cat sighting in Assington, A couple driving through the village on 5 March saw what they at first thought were foxes playing in the road. But as they got nearer, they "realised they weren't foxes – they were darker, possibly slightly stripey and more like enormous cats." The couple told Suffolk Police as well as the *EADT*. There's a curiously coincidental place name near Assington – Tiger Hill! [9]

A "large black cat" was seen from quite close in Hartest, and yet another big cat seen not far away in Stansfield. Also in South Suffolk, down near the Essex border, came reports of a big cat seen around the village of Shelley, hours after the sighting in Assington. On 5 March 1996 a man driving his son "to the disabled riding centre at Shelley saw a large black cat about 400 yards away in a field." [10]

There were eventually enough Suffolk big cat sightings, particularly in and around Ipswich, to give the county's black-coloured big cat a name, "Claws" (with a capital "C"). This was a not very strong pun on the great white shark "Jaws" in the book and films of the same name. "Claws" and other names for Suffolk's big cats never really caught on, with the exception of the Haverhill Puma.[11]

An urban big cat phenomenon begins

The *EADT* in March 1996 revealed that it had been contacted by an anonymous man claiming he had released a young male puma into the wild after it got too big for his cage. He didn't give a location for the release, or a date. He did tell the *EADT* that the puma was 17 months old when he let him out into the wild, and that he answered to the name Khyber. The anonymous former owner of Khyber said he'd been out looking for Khyber since letting him go, but added that "they move so quickly, it is no use."

Either the man claiming to have released a puma – he didn't say where, but in the days just before the internet it would have to be somewhere in East Anglia for him to be an *EADT* reader – was telling the truth, or he was making the whole thing up.

He didn't say when he'd let Khyber free, but the bit about having "been out looking" suggests it had been recent. Clearly, in this scenario, a law already in force for over two decades didn't stop complete idiots somewhere in the East of England getting hold of pumas. Pumas in captivity live between 15 and 18 years, so if Khyber did exist, the Suffolk pumas we're seeing today could be his children or even his grandchildren. [12]

"Big cat sightings may be linked to ferocious attack", said the *EADT,* which reported that Frances Cutler of Wormingford, a mile the other side of the Essex-Suffolk border, "believes she has lost 11 pullets to the beast." (Pullets, as every *EADT* reader knew at the time, are young hens under a year old.) "Whatever it was" either took away 11 carcasses or ate them on the spot, and buried some other bodies of young hens in the chicken run, presumably to come back for them later.

Ms Cutler, who'd kept chickens for a long time, was "sure it wasn't foxes," although she didn't say why. No date was given for this Wormingford chicken atrocity. It was the *EADT* "story about the big cat sighting" and their publication of a claim by an anonymous man to have released a puma into the wild that "got me thinking" according to Ms Cutler. She hadn't considered mink as a possible culprit for the pullet massacre, for example. [13]

Big cats began to pop up on the edges of the county town of Ipswich too, with a report of one seen on the A12 bypass near Ipswich – from the description, this was likely at the Copdock Interchange. In early June of that year a car full of people saw a cat "nearly as big as a tiger" with a "black, shiny coat" cross Ipswich's Tuddenham Road, near the pet cemetery. Pamela Cook from Whitton was driving with friends to the pet cemetery on Tuddenham Road, for a night-time visit to the grave of a friend's pet, when a "black thing darted out. I caught it in my headlights… It looked like a large cat." Fear of ridicule stopped her calling the police. Ms Cook and friends went back a few nights later to take a look but didn't find anything.

The black big cat seen in Ipswich and environs had apparently been spotted earlier along Hadleigh Road in nearby Sproughton, on the edge of Ipswich's Chantry Park, near the River Gipping. A woman told me a quarter of a century later how her mother had stopped dead while driving her along the Hadleigh Road sometime back in the summer of 1995 when she saw a black big cat, like a "black panther", cross the road ahead of her.

By this point, an *Evening Star* Claws Hunt was on, with the Ipswich-based newspaper offering a £250 reward for "a picture of the beast". So far as I know it's still gone unclaimed, like the still uncollected £10,000 prize for a close-up shot of the Waveney Monster. [14]

There was at least one other big cat sighted in that year in the town of Kesgrave – the suburb immediately to the east of Ipswich, as well as a "big black cat" seen on Ipswich's Kelly Road. A Kelly Road resident, however, later contacted the Paranormal Database website to cast doubt on whether it really was a big cat, insisting the big black cat was "actually a dog called Whiskey, he was a large black Labrador who used to roam the area 24 hours a day, and that witness was mentally disturbed… he was away with the fairies." Also just east of Ipswich, at Martlesham, between the Foxhall and Seven Hills roundabouts, yet another sighting of a big cat emerged. The Foxhall Road, which runs out of central Ipswich and heads east towards Martlesham, was already becoming a big cat corridor.

Up at the other end of the county, straddling the Norfolk border, lies Thetford Forest, England's largest lowland pine forest, with some of the tallest fir trees in the country. And it was in the summer of either 1996 or 1997 (by 2015 the witness couldn't give a year with certainty) that Ian Day of Kesgrave was mountain-biking along a gravel fire track when he caught a glimpse – down another track – of a big cat. It had a long, low but stout body shape and an "undoubtedly cat-like, long drooping tail." Ian said it was "dark in colour" and "about springer spaniel-sized but half as long again", and stood "50 cm high at the shoulder."

While Ian "did a U-turn to look for it," he didn't investigate further as "I was a bit twitchy and on my own, there was nobody else around." He has "lived my whole life in the countryside and I know for certain that it wasn't a fox or other large native mammal, the way it walked with a slow stride was also very much that of a cat."[15]

Lynx patrols around Wrentham

Big cats began to make an appearance in the northeastern corner of Suffolk too, less than two miles (around 2.6 km) inland from the North Sea coast, with a "large cat-like animal," seen by multiple witnesses roaming farmland in the Wrentham area. A "beast like a lynx or cougar" (a cougar being a puma) was sighted several times in the days leading up to 23 April 1997, "causing concern among farmers" who had already started "night patrols," after the big cat's appearance had been "linked to the death of a number of lambs," according to the *Lowestoft Journal*.

A driver on the A12 north of Wrentham had seen whatever-it-was "leap a roadside fence" and Sergeant Colin Read, based at the nearby Southwold Police Station, appealed for witnesses. The Sergeant advised local people "not the panic" as it was "only the size of a large fox", although he wanted to "alert farmers" as it would be likely to take lambs or piglets. Sergeant Read mentioned "a number of unconfirmed reports by farmers" of an animal described as three feet long and "brown or fawn in colour" and said he'd prefer to take it alive, to be handed over to a wildlife park. (The Suffolk Wildlife Park at nearby Kessingland confirmed they had no big cats at the time that answered the animal's description. The lynx-like servals only arrived at Kessingland some years later, when it rebranded as Africa Alive!) The Department of the Environment had been consulted, and they'd confirmed that the animal was "not protected" and could legally be shot.

It was on one of the Wrentham area "night patrols" during a mid-April weekend that a farmer spotted the mystery cat, "fawny brown" and "larger than a fox... low to the ground" with "pointed ears." He thought it was a lynx because of its "short tail". It approached his farm's security lights confidently, as if it were used to them, at which point the farmer could see its "bright eyes" reflecting the light. Another Wrentham resident was driving on the B1127 from Henstead to Beccles a turn off the A12 just north of Wrentham heading east – when he saw a large tawny animal "leap across the road."

Also, a taxi driver told me in 2016 – without me bringing up the subject of big cats – that he'd seen something like a black leopard on a road near Wrentham in around 1999. [16]

A "stooped, large feline" was reported in May 1998 in the area of Holton St Mary, near the Essex border. It's not known whether this was the same big cat seen by "two wildlife spotters" that was "running across the A12 at Holton St Mary." [17]

Then there was the frightening sound, described as "a cross between a large growl interspersed with panting", heard in Dunwich Forest by a couple from Beccles out walking one day in September 1998. The growling-panting noise caused the Beccles couple to flee to their car in terror, their anxiety possibly heightened by the sight of the large paw print they found and photographed in the vicinity earlier that day. It's a faint image in the photo, in which you can just make out three deep pads as wide as the fingers of a human hand held up against the print for comparison. The print's asymmetrical in the way that cat prints generally are and dog prints generally aren't, and there are no claw marks visible on it (cats can retract their claws, dogs can't.) It's not a very clear photo, but footprints and notoriously hard to photograph well, and it's as good as evidence for Suffolk big cats gets! [18]

Those unfamiliar with the distinctive call of the red deer that can be heard in Dunwich Forest – it's like a growl, a bark, a cough and the mooing of a cow all rolled into one – could easily mistake a red deer call for the growl of a big cat. So when I first read this story, I was tempted to dismiss it as an example of the phenomenon of "woodland panic" that sometimes seizes quite rational people in deep forests, until I heard about the sighting of a "lynx-like cat" in Dunwich Forest eight years later and the multiple encounters with a "black panther" in Dunwich Heath two years after that, which we'll return to shortly. [19]

There was even a contemporary celebrity big cat sighting, or a sighting by someone who's a celebrity if you live in Suffolk. Charlie Haylock has a regular spot on BBC Radio Suffolk and was Suffolk dialect coach to Ralph Fiennes for the film *The Dig*.

One day in 1999, Charlie was driving through Stonham Aspal, not far from the Suffolk Owl Sanctuary. He recalled years later being "on the curve" on the edge of Stonham Aspal in his car when he saw "a big black panther, a big 'un as high as my wing mirror." Charlie and the black panther "were a couple of feet from each other," he recalls the black panther "looked him in the eye," then "stopped, then walked on."

Charlie heard of another such sighting locally soon afterwards. Immediately after his own encounter, he drove straight to Debenham police station, where the initially dismissive Suffolk Constabulary were eventually persuaded to send out two officers in a car to investigate. Suffolk Constabulary, the UK's smallest county police force, is so tiny that sending out two whole officers represents a considerable manpower commitment for them.

It turns out that a black big cat "bigger than a big Labrador" had been seen along the same stretch of road a couple of years before Charlie Haylock's encounter. Andrew Storer, who now runs the Black Dog Deli in Walberswick, was riding his moped from Debenham along "the S-bend at Aspall" on the B1071 just before the village one summer night back in 1997. It's a tricky bend to take in the dark on a low-powered moped, so a scooterist who regularly took that route would likely have been alert and vigilant at the time. Storer told me nearly 20 years later how, coming round the Aspall S-bend, he saw a bigger-than-labrador-sized big cat in the headlights of his moped ahead of him, and not just a glimpse of reflected eyes either. What his headlights illuminated was "definitely a cat's face" and "it was black."[19]

A "shiny black" big cat put in an appearance at around this time in a field in Hemley, near Waldringfield. In 2000, Mark Frost, working a combine harvester in a field of crops, saw a particular big cat, which "got out of the crop into woodlands." Mark "got on to the radio" to a colleague nearby, who said he'd seen it 45 minutes earlier. They investigated and found "its business" (scat or big cat poo) and some scratch marks near a hole in the field. As mentioned earlier, a neighbouring landowner reported a calf found killed in the adjoining field.[20]

That big cat stomping ground from the 1970s, Rendlesham Forest, was the scene of another big cat encounter in April 2002, with a "black animal in the distance... almost in a pouncing position" seen by Anne Downing and her daughter. Anne said of the big cat she saw in the forest, "when we got too near it simply fled into the bush."

Centre for Fortean Zoology director Jonathan Downes told me in 2015 that he'd been in conversation in "a bar in Sheffield nearly 20 years ago" with Pete Robbins, co-author of *Left at East Gate*, one of many books on the Rendlesham Forest UFO Incident. Jonathan related how Pete Robbins had told him "there had been a string of black panther reports from Rendlesham Forest," presumably in the years leading up to 1995.

Mystery cats at the turn of the century

By the early years of our twenty-first century, there were already organisations dedicated to investigating big cats springing up in the UK, although these were generally more active where the evidence for big cats was more promising than in Suffolk, so generally based in Scotland, the southwest or the south coast of England. Nonetheless, people were reporting big cat sightings to these groups daily, via the relatively newfangled internet. In 2003, Big Cats in Britain recorded 28 big cat sightings reported to them from Suffolk, compared to 113 in Norfolk and 129 in Essex. Big Cats in Britain also received an email from someone who had a farm near Wrentham who claimed that in the area around Wrentham and Kessingland, a "black panther larger than a Labrador," with a "thick tail, no tapering" moved in sometime around 2002 and "was seen regularly round there... up to 2006." As has just been noted, Wrentham already had previous "form" for lynxes, with multiple sightings and even farmers' patrols and local police out looking for one back in 1997.[21]

The Department for the Environment, Food and Rural Affairs (Defra) and English Nature were getting reports too. English Nature became Natural England, which later released a lot of old Defra "legacy data" under the title of *Reported Sightings of Signs of Exotic Species Compiled by Natural England*. This included a reference to a big cat in Ipswich in October 2002, with the comment, "Sighting, carcass (Not available) Not conclusive." Presumably, it was one of those maddening occasions when somebody reported seeing a cadaver of a big cat, but they weren't actually able to produce the body. There have been a remarkable number of these up and down the country.

There was also big cat activity on farmland "behind Eyke". In 2003. John Daniel, the same man who'd seen the lynxes or bobcats at Staverton, was out lamping (shooting rabbits by the light of a torch or lamp at night) with another man, when their torch beams caught a big cat, that they were also able to see through their rifle telescopic sights. This was a "large, sandy coloured cat" which John later identified as a puma. John told me the presence of a "sandy-coloured cat in Eyke at the time was common knowledge" locally. John also heard of a sighting by a local woman named Debbie who "was walking her dog along a forest track and saw a black panther cross her path."[23]

These comings and goings of "utterly black cats," sandy pumas and lynxes or bobcats around Rendlesham throw up an interesting phenomenon that we'll see more of anon: different types of big cat seen in the same area, often at around the same time. Two things could be happening here. Either people aren't very good at identifying them, with a remarkable number of Suffolk big witnesses describing a "puma or lynx" – two quite different-looking cats. Or we're witnessing something that happens in Africa and Asia – different species of big cat occupying the same habitat, living under each other's noses but going after different prey, and only occasionally coming into conflict. Pumas and bobcats usually manage to stay out of each other's way in Canada, but pumas do prey on lynxes when they get the chance, while leopards are skilled at avoiding lions. Servals take smaller prey in the same habitat as leopards, only occasionally ending up as leopard's dinner.

Sometime before July 2003, there was talk of a "panther-like animal" roaming through villages and "isolated rural areas" including Blythburgh and Peasenhall in the Blyth Valley. [24]

Contemporary with these Blyth Valley encounters was the sighting by Janet Whitby, who was driving one of her children's friends back home to nearby Middleton. Over a decade later she recalled that it was sometime between 2003 and 2005.

It was a summer's day, and Janet was driving south along the B1225 Blythburgh to Westleton Road (she lived locally). Coming to the area around Potton Hall, she drove past Brick Kiln Farm where the Dunwich River at this point crosses the road, close to the Lymballs Lane turn-off to Darsham. (This stretch of the Dunwich River at the time was obscured by dense thickets, it's since been cleared.) Suddenly, a "huge cat crossed the road… walking, not running." It was the "size of a large dog". It had the sun right behind it, so Janet couldn't tell its colour. She could "tell it was a cat, not a dog," because it had "distinctive paws" and a distinctive walk, it walked in a different way to a dog. Its face was "rounded… not pointed like a dog's."[25]

"Was that... a lion?" That's what David Ellis asked his wife as they were driving south from Lowestoft along the A12 through Darsham very early one clear Saturday morning in 2003. Roughly opposite the Little Chef (now the Two Magpies bakery). Lying on the verge, sunning itself and apparently asleep, was "a female lion (or possibly a puma)... clearly visible... pretty recognisable." The couple were on their way to an event with an early start in Sussex, at least three more hours away, so they didn't stop.[26]

At around the same time as the encounter on the Blythburgh to Westleton Road and the

"Darsham Lion", Jack and Irene Wilcox reported seeing "definitely a large black cat-like animal with a long tail" which "seemed to take no notice" of them and was "not in hurry," as it loped across the road near isolated farm buildings on the Framlingham to Fressingfield road. Something "believed to be looking for food" left paw prints in the snow in a garden in Bredfield, near Woodbridge, in February of that year, while Bredfield resident Dominique Thomas told *EADT* she was aware of previous sightings in the village. Another Bredfield resident, Jane Richards, saw a "panther-like animal... mooching across the grass in the distance" near the village when she was out walking her dog the following February. [27]

Something feline was at large around Eyke again in October of that year, not the sandy puma this time but a "black feline" again, bigger than the witness's pet Labrador, prowling in the garden of Jane Fooks, who chanced upon it when she went to get something from her car. Others had seen it too, according to Jane. This Eyke encounter was almost simultaneous with a "dark and cat-like animal" with a shiny coat and a long tail, and maybe even a bit bigger than an Alsatian, seen by Mike Jennings of Kelsale while out shooting in countryside near Great Livermere. Whatever it was moved 100 yards across the field and looked back at the shooting party before going through a hedge. Mike reported that a local gamekeeper had found big cat footprints.

Somewhere in a stately home near Beccles (allegedly)

Then there was the Beccles Lynx. This first came to light in April of 2003, when some photos were passed to the British Big Cats Society. These showed the dead body of a Eurasian lynx lying on its side on the ground. The story accompanying the photos was that the lynx had killed 15 sheep before a farmer shot it near Beccles back in 1991. Then the farmer is supposed to have stored the corpse of the Beccles lynx in the freezer and eventually to have sold it to an unknown "wealthy landowner" who had it exhibited in their stately home somewhere near Beccles. The informant claimed both the police and the "Government had asked him to destroy the body." Before long, Danny Bampling of the British Big Cats Society was expressing doubt, noting that some highly realistic life-size soft toy big cats were turning up, and that it was easier than they had at first thought to use one of these to hoax a big cat.

A 2006 Freedom of Information (FOIA) request eventually untangled what really happened, and sorted out the origin of the Beccles lynx. A gamekeeper had shot it in Great Witchingham, Norfolk, in 1991, thirty miles away from the Suffolk border. It was stored by the gamekeeper in a freezer near Beccles. This is nowhere near where it had been shot, but apparently Beccles is close to the undisclosed wealthy landowner for whom the gamekeeper was supposed to be arranging for it to be stuffed. Norfolk Police paid a visit to the gamekeeper, to ask him to assist in the their enquiries regarding the poaching of some rare birds. They didn't find any rare birds in his freezer but they *did* find the Beccles lynx.

Defra (then responsible for the licensing of wild animals) seem to have determined that the dead lynx in the freezer had escaped from a zoo or "private ownership," so it was not a protected species and the gamekeeper who had it in his freezer could apparently do what he wanted with it. A subsequent (limited) FOIA disclosure by Natural England, *Reports received by Defra of escapes of non-native cats in the UK* suggests the animal that became known as the Beccles lynx escaped early in 1991, and was "reported" (reported escaped?) in early 1992, so it could have been out and about in the wild for a year, long enough for it to reproduce and become a parent of the Staverton Thicks lynxes seen by a teenage John and his friend a few years later. As we will discover later, the fatal shooting of one feral lynx in East Anglia in 1991 doesn't seem to have stopped reports of lynxes in Suffolk.

Natural England's brief disclosure of the chain of events suggests Defra may have known where it had escaped from, although they aren't letting the public know for reasons of data protection. Most of this came to light in response to a FOIA request in 2006.[28]

If its back story is to be believed, somewhere among one of the halls and stately homes near Beccles – there are many of them just off the busy B1062 road between Beccles and Homersfield, and along the Suffolk bank of the Waveney River – there's presumably still the Beccles Lynx in a glass taxidermy display case.

By now Suffolk Constabulary were taking the county's big cats seriously, and the Ipswich *Evening Star* of 23 July 2006 reported that "according to police statistics," 2004 was "the busiest year for big cat sightings", with 18 reported across the county in that year. This was contradicted by a Freedom of Information Act disclosure, which logged only four "cases of big cats reported to Suffolk Constabulary" in that year.[29]

In the spring of 2004, an animal variously described as "a large unidentified cat" between four and a half and five and a half feet long, including the tail, or a "large black cat" or a "big black panther-like cat at least four feet high and five feet long" (1.21 metres high, 1.5 metres long) put in several Suffolk appearances. It crossed the road ahead of a female witness driving through Tunstall Forest on 20 April. I also heard an account of a local man named Rick who "spent a lot of time in Tunstall Forest" and who once "followed a black panther on his mountain bike along a forest trail" there before the black panther "noticed him and went off into the forest."

Whatever black big cat or big cats were out and about locally back in 2004 so unnerved a Dairy Crest milkman on the road into the village of Melton in May that he refused to finish his rounds. Contemporary with this sighting was one by lorry driver Martin Emery. He contacted the police after getting a good look at something black and panther-like alongside his vehicle while driving near Linstead Parva, in the Blyth Valley not far from Halesworth. Martin said he also saw a footprint near the scene of his encounter which he thought was from a big cat.

Not long after this, not far from Tunstall Forest, just west of the A12 at Little Glemham, Paul Berry (he of the 1980s Debenham Lion sighting) saw on a farm track a "big cat… bloody great thing" that "jumped a four-foot fence". It had a "lightish colour" and he saw it for a couple of seconds illuminated by an outside light. Paul recalled that it was just after dusk, around 4.30pm, "the sheep were in their barns" on the Little Glemham Estate where he was working, so it would have been January or February 2004 or 2005.[30] That summer of 2004 also featured the appearance of a big cat around the little fishing port of Orford.

That same summer, at the northern end of the county, two young anglers packing up at the end of the day saw a melanistic big cat in Falcon Meadow, Bungay. Falcon Meadow is technically speaking in Norfolk but it feels very much part of the town of Bungay in Suffolk. The Waveney is a narrow trickle at this point, just wide enough for canoeing. Falcon Meadow is a park connected by a footbridge over a weir on the river to the centre of Bungay.[31]

James Bloomfield, then aged 22, and his teenage brother were preparing to leave as the sun was setting, it was 9.30 that evening in late July 2004. Suddenly they caught sight of a "black puma-like creature" standing a foot above the two-foot grass nearby. They described it as having a tail "about three feet long", it had a head "like a house cat's but five times bigger."

As we will see later, there aren't any black pumas, so a melanistic leopard is a more likely candidate for the Falcon Meadow big cat. its head was "like a house cat's but about five times bigger" notwithstanding. Reports of big cats had already been emerging from the area around Bungay for some years before the Bloomfield brothers' encounter. A Suffolk Police Freedom of Information Act disclosure noted that on 17 May 2011 an "informant" in the "Beccles/ Bungay Safer Neighbourhood Team area" reported "seeing a black Pantha" (panther), and that "This appears to be a re-occurrence of previous sightings over the last ten years" locally.

Just a month after the July 2004 Falcon Meadow sighting, Sue Bidwell and her husband, were on the road near Loddon, near Bungay and just over the Norfolk border. Sue was getting a driving lesson from her husband. He told her to stop the car so they could both get a better look at a "big black cat – like a puma" by the road with a "long body, big head, long tail." Whatever it was, it was tall enough that it cleared the grass that was between two and three feet high.

And in 2005 there were multiple sightings of a "black panther" around the Norfolk town of Diss, and on both banks of the River Waveney, on both sides of the Norfolk and Suffolk border. Other reported big cat sightings in Suffolk in that year of 2005 included the ones in Wenhaston and Chediston, quite near each other in the Blyth Valley, also at Carlton Colville on the edge of Lowestoft, one in Ipswich and one in Mickfield, along the A140. Mickfield has a nature reserve, offering small prey and cover to passing big cats. It's not known which one of these sightings was the one recorded by Defra in that year as occurring in a place described as just "Suffolk", followed by the comment "inconclusive."[32]

Sixty sightings a year

By then the big cats of Suffolk were outdoing other East Anglia big cats with the frequency of their appearances. The British Big Cats Society's Danny Bampling told the *Eastern Daily Press* that there had been a total of 60 big cat sightings in Suffolk in the period from April 2004 to July 2005, compared to only 54 in the normally more big cat-active Norfolk and a mere 50 in Essex. Danny estimated that about a third of the reported sightings were genuine, the others were "mistaken" or "too vague." Coastal big cats began to be reported more frequently at around this time, in a corridor going from the seaside town of Kessingland, southward all the way to the nature reserve at Dunwich Heath. Once again, witnesses were reporting different types of cat in the same habitat.

One informant reported seeing a lynx on his farm near Wrentham four or five times between 2004 and 2006. The same witness said a black panther "bigger than a Labrador" with a "thick tail, no tapering" had "regularly" been seen nearby since about 2002 and for the next four years. He lived two and half miles away from Kessingland, home of the Africa Alive! wildlife park, from where he said he would regularly hear the early morning calls of the park's captive big cats. On 3 April 2006, at about eight o'clock in the morning, our Wrentham-based witness was listening to Kessingland's captive big cat calls as usual, when he heard in response "exactly the same noise coming from the opposite direction." Africa Alive's big cats at the time would have included recently arrived lions – who have more of a roar than a call – as well as cheetahs and servals, the latter also known as African lynxes.

A short drive from Wrentham along Blower's Lane is the village of Gisleham, near Kessingland. An East of England Ambulance Service paramedic told me he'd been out on this country lane late at night on an emergency call in 2006 and he "thought he saw" from the window of his ambulance a big cat "dark" in colour crossing the road.[33]

If there was a lynx around Wrentham, it was occasionally venturing south. A dogwalker in Dunwich Forest at one of the many crossroads of the Forestry Commission tracks caught a glimpse of a light brown "lynx-like" cat, standing three foot six at the shoulder line, (1.06

metres) with "its tail hung low to the floor, turned up." (While there's a considerable variation in tail length, lynxes generally have short, stubby tails. It could have been a serval or a caracal. Their tails are longer, but probably not long enough to hang "low to the floor.") While the dogwalker said his wife didn't see the "lynx-like" cat, his dog definitely did, and chased it into the foliage.

It's possible the Wrentham lynx was the same animal as the lynx-like cat seen in Dunwich Forest. Wrentham, eight miles (12.8 km) by road from Dunwich, is a hop, skip and a jump away for a lynx, even allowing for the need to move inland to go round the Blyth Estuary – or swim across it. Lynxes are quite strong swimmers.

An awful lot of Suffolk people have dogs. There's plenty of open space for them, and a significant number of big cat sightings in Suffolk feature witnesses who are "dogwalkers." They usually report that their dogs react to the big cats, often giving chase, in one case fighting with a puma, as we'll see later. The fact that dogs react makes it less likely that big cats are just a mass hallucination. While lone humans may sometimes see things that aren't there, it's harder to induce hallucinations in a human and their dog as well.

And not far from Dunwich, two generations of the same family saw a "giant black cat" on the same Westleton to Theberton road over a two year period, on what seems from their description to be just after the B1125 turns left from Westleton into the busier B1122. Leiston residents Tony and Sara Bloor reported that their father had seen the animal while driving on that stretch of the same road at night in 2008, two years before their own sighting of the "giant black cat" that crossed the road in front of them and scrambled up a six-foot verge (1.82 m) and then escaped through a hole in a wooden fence. *The East Anglian Daily Times* noted that when Tony and Sara came forward in 2008, "residents in nearby villages have reported similar experiences." [34]

At the same time that lynx-like cats were seen up on the Suffolk coast, big cats were showing themselves in South Suffolk as well.

Let's call our South Suffolk witness "Sam". She saw a "large black panther-type animal" in 2006 (or possibly earlier), hunting in a cornfield near her home village of Glemsford.

The big cat Sam saw in Glemsford "jumped out of the corn with arched back and dived back in, me and a friend saw footprints in the same field a week later about the size of dinner plates," which would have to be a slight exaggeration. "Sam" added that there was another sighting of the same animal in the same year, in the field behind Glemsford Primary School, and that "three local people had seen this big cat in that year" around the nearby village of Hartest.

Glemsford is near Thomas Gainsborough's Sudbury. Also nearby is the village of Hartest, known for the steepest hill in Suffolk and for the vineyards nearby. It was a few miles south of Hartest that a driver travelling home to Sudbury one evening (sometime before 2012) caught "a glimpse" about 20 yards ahead of the car of something large and feline. The driver described it as "a large beige cat... bigger than your average muntjac deer" that leapt from the cover of the trees on the right hand verge of the road, touched down momentarily in the middle of the road and continued with another bound into the field on the left, and off into the darkness. He was driving with another witness, a passenger, who also saw it. "As we have both talked to other locals who claim to have seen big cats we came to the conclusion that, although we were elated to have seen it, maybe it wasn't that unusual," added the driver.

And from nearby Sudbury on 28 September 2010, came a report from a user of the Paranormal Database website. At 5:30 am, "while driving home this witness watched a large black cat… as large as a Boxer dog", run from out of a hedge into the car headlights. The creature continued to run along the road for a short distance before vanishing into another hedge."[35]

The relatively empty countryside around Glemsford has seen several big cat encounters.

The River Stour at Wixoe. The Stour marks the border between South Suffolk and Essex. As well as inspiring artists, the river valley on the Suffolk bank of the Stour has been the location for several big cat sightings.

FOOTNOTES TO CHAPTER 14:
The Debenham Lion and the big cat known as "Claws"

1. "Weirdness in the Woods: Strange Creatures of Rendlesham Forest," Nick Redfern, undated; http://monsterusa.blogspot.co.uk/2009/03/weirdness–in–woods.html

2. Stanley was a caller to BBC Radio Suffolk's Jon Wright show on 1 January 2015.

3.www.britishbigcats.org/news.php#oldnews6)

4. Confessions of various 1970s big cat releases in Derbyshire, Notts. and Worcs. From "Big cats still stalk Britain," Paul Sieveking, *Fortean Times*, **FT344;20**, September 2016. "Beast of Dartmoor mystery solved after famous circus owner Mary Chipperfield 'set three Pumas free in 1970s'", *Daily Telegraph,* 21 July 2016, www.telegraph.co.uk/news/2016/07/21/beast-of-bodmin-mystery-solved-as-dartmoor-zoo-released-pumas-in/.The problem with the "Beast of Dartmoor mystery solved" explanation is that all but a few of the many Beast of Dartmoor sightings are of a black leopard-like animal, and pumas are never all black, as we will see in Chapter 20. Norfolk lion escape from *Reports received by Defra of escapes of non-native cats in the UK 1975 to present day*. (Defra stands for the Department for Environment, Food and Rural Affairs.) The 1984 Norfolk lion escape would seem to be have been from the old Cromer Zoo, now no longer in operation. http://scotcats.online.fr/abc/realcats/index.html

5. *Modern Mysteries of Britain,* Janet and Colin Bord, Grafton, London 1988, records in its "County Gazetter of Strange Events" reports of sightings of a big cat in the "Elveden/Honington area" in April 1985, with "pheasants killed; no cats missing from zoos or wildlife parks," no source is given.

6. Interviews with Paul Berry 23-25 April 2015. A 2014 Debenham FC match report with Debenham Lion reference is at www.debenhamlc.co.uk/nmr.html. The Parish Clark of Debenham in 2016, in response to my enquiry, told me he was unaware of anyone who'd heard of any Debenham Lion.

7 Kevin from Woodbridge emailed Jon Wright's 1 January 2015 BBC Radio Suffolk show about his Hacheston Road 1990s sighting. No details on the witness to the possible Wherstead field signs at their request. Phone interview with John Daniel on 3 February 2015 and subsequent emails and face-to-face conversations. John's friend Chris Field who saw the two lynxes from the platform told me he thought the platforms were part of a motocross circuit near the caravan park, not the disused Rendlesham airbase. I interviewed him in late 2015.

8 "That big cat is prowling again", *EADT*, 4 March 1996.

9. "Big cat sightings may be linked to ferocious attack", *EADT* 6 March 1996.

10. "Big cat sightings may be linked.., see above.

11. "New sighting of big cat 'Claws', *Evening Star,* 25 November 2010, "Claws back on the prowl". *Coastal Advertiser* 12 March 2010 www.ipswichstar.co.uk/news/suffolk_new_sightings_of_big_cat_claws_1_737147; "Black cat sightings on the up", *Evening Star* March 16 2006, www.ipswichstar.co.uk/news/big_cat_sightings_on_the_up_1_107380.

12. "That big cat is prowling again", *EADT*, 4 March 1996.

13. "Big cat sightings may be linked.." see above.

14. The witness to the 1995 Sproughton sighting will have to remain anonymous. "Huge cat seen near cemetery", *Evening Star,* 1 July 1996. Ms Cook reported the sighting as being "a few weeks before" 1 July. I'm told the pet cemetery is no more, there's now a swimming pool on the site.

15. *Fortean Times* 101, 1996, which quotes, all from 1996 – *EADT* 4 and 6 March, 23 April, *Sudbury Mercury* 8 March, 12 and 19 July, *Bury Free Press* 14 March, 12 July, Ipswich *Evening Star* 25 April, 6, 12, 21, 24 and 28 June, 2, 4, 18 and 26 July, 29 November, *Eastern Daily Press* 20 June, *Diss Express* 23 and 30 August; Ian Day, email of 1 March 2015.

16. "Big Cat Spotted", Terry Reeve, *Lowestoft Journal,* 27 April 1997. The "beast like a lynx or cougar" quote is from an online cut and paste from "Puma's paws for Thought," unsourced newspaper article of April 1997 – http://classics.6te.net/cat/index.htm. This article is a listing – unsourced – of Norfolk black big cat sightings. The local taxi driver (requesting anonymity) told me about his 1999 Wrentham sighting in December 2016.

17. Teletext 25 May 1998 – possibly this is the big cat "running across the A12" mentioned in "Claws back on the prowl", *Coastal Advertiser*, 12 May 2010. "Jogger reports 'big cat sighting' in Suffolk field," Tom Potter, *EADT* 15 January 2015, www.eadt.co.uk/news/jogger_reports_big_cat_sighting_in_suffolk_field_1_4380274

18. Photo (at the end of Chapter 13) reproduced here by kind permission of Mark Mower, author of *Suffolk Tales of Murder & Mystery,* copyright 1998 Mark Mower. Mark could provide no more information, as the Beccles couple had asked to remain anonymous. Compare this to the witness in Blythburgh in 1973 in Chapter 6 on Suffolk Shucks, who wrote to Ivan W. Bunn, after hearing disembodied panting which locals he talked to assumed was Black Shuck.

19. *Suffolk Tales of Mystery and Murder,* Mark Mower, Countryside Books, Newbury 2006.

20 Conversations with Andrew Storer, August 2016; Charlie Haylock phoned in to Jon Wright's BBC Radio Suffolk show on 1 January 2015. The "S" bend at Aspall is in fact at Debenham on the Aspall Road.

PART 3 – BIG CATS OF THE CURIOUS COUNTY

21. Mark Frost emailed Jon Wright's BBC Radio Suffolk show, 1 January 2015.

22. "Big cat seen in Suffolk," *Evening Star*, 16 October 2003, in which Anne Downing recalled seeing with her daughter a big cat 18 months earlier; Email to Chris Moiser of BCIB, Big Cats in Britain Yearbook 2006, CFZ Press, Woolsery 2006.

23. John Daniel, phone interview 3 February 2015 and subsequent emails.

24. Blythburgh and Peasenhall sightings briefly covered in "Black cat spotted in North Suffolk," *EADT* 16 July 2003, www.eadt.co.uk/news/black_cat_spotted_in_north_suffolk_1_60729

25. Janet Whitby, phone interview 5 January 2016.

26. Darsham "lion" sighting (probably a puma) in an unpublished letter to *Fortean Times* from David Ellis, May 2003, forwarded to me by *FT* co-editor Paul Sieveking on 1 November 2016. Extracts from it are published here in the reasonable belief that it was intended for publication. David Ellis cannot now be traced.

26. All reports in this paragraph are from "Black cat spotted in North Suffolk," *EADT* 16 July 2003, www.eadt.co.uk/news/black_cat_spotted_in_north_suffolk_1_60729 except for Jane Richards's Bredfield sighting, which is from *Suffolk Tales of Mystery and Murder*, Mark Mower, Countryside Books, Newbury 2006.

27. *Reports received by Defra*... see above; http://news.bbc.co.uk/1/hi/england/norfolk/4830320.stm. The BBC News website report on the Defra investigation has Defra concluding that the lynx was shot near Great Witchingham, Norfolk. There was in Great Witchingham in 1991 a Norfolk Wildlife Centre and Country Park – its website has a distinctly 1990s look and showcases its European lynxes at www.norfolkwildlife.co.uk but says "We are no longer open." It was briefly saved by new investors following a winding down order from Her Majesty's Revenue and Customs in 2006, and eventually re-opened as The Animal Ark, a petting zoo with farm and domestic animals. This too appears to have closed.

28. *Evening Star* 23 July 2006; Suffolk Constabulary Freedom of Information Request No: F–2014–02424 September 2014, request by Bethany Whymark of the *Bury Free Press*.

29. Phone interview with Paul Berry; 23 April 2015 and face-to-face interview 25 4 15.

30. Tunstall Forest sighting via Paranormal Database; Linstead Parva, Orford and Bungay sightings from "Anglers report Big Cat sighting" BBC News England, 2 August 2004, http://news.bbc.co.uk/1/hi/england/suffolk/352954.stm; Tunstall Forest mountain bike chase report via John Daniel, pers. comm. 10 March 2021.

31. Suffolk Police FOIA disclosure Request no: F-2014-0072, 14 March 2014. A "Neighbourhood" in Suffolk Police terminology can be a vast area. Loddon sighting from *Suffolk Tales of Mystery,* see above. The Wenhaston and Chediston, Mickfield, Carlton Colville and Ipswich sightings were in a round up in the *Evening Star,* sometime around 23 July 2006, cut and pasted and unreferenced on an online forum. The Defra "Suffolk" sighting was from Natural England's *Reported Sightings of Signs of Exotic Species Compiled by Natural England.*

32. "Controversy over wild cat-alogue", Lorna Marsh, *Eastern Daily Press,* 18 March 2006; "More sightings of big cats come to light," *EADT* 20 March 2008, www.eadt.co.uk/news/more-sightings-of-big-cats-come-to-light-1-188020 ; Wrentham lynx and black panther from *Big Cats in Britain Yearbook 2006*; Conversation with an East of England Ambulance Service paramedic, 29 September 2014.

34. Dunwich Forest lynx reported to BCIB, *Big Cats in Britain Yearbook 2006;* Westleton to Theberton road sighting from "What lurks within the Suffolk countryside?" *EADT* 3 April 2008 www.eadt.co.uk/news/more_sightings_of_big_cats_come_to_light_1_188020.

35. "Sam" by email 5 July 2014 – she estimates the lynx incident was some time before 2006. Sudbury sighting from Paranormal Database. There's a Cats Lane in Sudbury.

Tongue-in-cheek reconstruction of a big cat investigator (left) encountering the Beccles Lynx, said to be on display in a stately home in the Beccles area.
Can you also identify in this entirely fictional scenario the coastal Suffolk landed gentry family coat of arms featuring leopards (see Chapter 13) or the famous horse and jockey whose ghosts are said to appear in West Suffolk (Chapter 7)?

PART 3 – BIG CATS OF THE CURIOUS COUNTY

15. Serving South Norfolk and North Suffolk – and crepuscular coastal cats

A surprising number of local institutions have the corporate motto "serving South Norfolk and North Suffolk". Personally I find it hard to get my head round the concept that Suffolk (originally the "South folk" of the East Angles) would have a bit of itself that's actually "North", and vice versa, but I'll leave this consideration aside and note that much of the Suffolk big cat action has occurred in that strange twilight world between counties that is South Norfolk and North Suffolk, once the territory of Queen Boudicca's Iceni tribe.

In any event, South Norfolk and North Suffolk has been the backdrop for plenty of comings and goings by… you guessed it … big cats. Specifically, there's been a lot going on in the big cat department in an east-to-west corridor on either side of the River Waveney, which forms the boundary between Norfolk and Suffolk, and along the A143 road. This road starts in Norfolk, and runs southwest and crosses the Waveney River to enter Suffolk just east of the Norfolk border village of Scole, before progressing onward towards Bury St Edmunds. Roughly parallel and to the south of the A143 is the B1118 road that runs near the other bank of the Waveney over in Mid-Suffolk District.

Further to the West is Thetford Forest, one of the biggest conifer plantations in England. The forest straddles both sides of the Norfolk-Suffolk border, occupying Suffolk's northwestern corner and the area known as the Brecks. In the mid-noughties, motorists cruising the roads along both sides of the Suffolk-Norfolk border along the Waveney Valley were experiencing big cat encounters. The area was then becoming a big cat hotspot, which it apparently remains to this day.

The earlier encounters in the Thetford Forest big cat cluster started mostly on the Norfolk side. On 8 May 2005 a couple of miles over the Norfolk border in Thetford, a "caller spotted large black animal walking in the woods, looked like a big cat", according to a subsequent Norfolk Constabulary Freedom of Information Act disclosure. The following February, the same police force recorded that a "caller has seen large black cat", somewhere along the "A134 Suffolk" – probably in the Barnham, Honington or Ingham area, around the Thetford Forest or the smaller Kings' Forest nearby. The better-resourced Norfolk Police force are often the first responders to such callouts. The A134 at this point is a major commuting route into Bury.[1]

Also in North Suffolk, but further east, East Anglia's big cats were on the move. In the weeks leading up to mid-June 2006, in fields between Oakley and Billingford near the A143, Stuart Gifford saw a "dark beige coloured creature" which he thought was a puma. "The way in which it moved left me in no doubt it was a big cat, the musculature and the way it held its head," he said. Days later, a female *Diss Express* reader who didn't want to be named had an encounter with a big cat in open countryside near Hoxne. This one was "dark coloured with a long thin tail and about two and a half feet tall (76cm). There was no doubt in my mind that it was a big cat," she said. There were two similar sightings on the same road in the same week.

A black, glossy-coated "German shepherd-sized animal with a loping gait, low to the ground" was seen by Janet Walters walking her dog on 1 April 2006 in fields at Fersfield. Sometime before October 2006, around Diss, other big cats had been reported in Thornham Parva, Wortham, Oakley, Billingford, Eye and Bressingham – the latter "a dark coloured animal… German shepherd sized with a longer body" seen by Martin Ayre in his garden.[2]

The County Town's second wave

In an apparent re-run of the wave of big cat sightings that Ipswich had experienced in the 1990s, the action seemed to move to Suffolk's county town once again in 2006, and particularly to the Foxhall Road.

Early one morning at the end of August 2006, along the Foxhall Road as it runs just south of the Foxhall Speedway Stadium, Derek Kendall of the One Stop newsagent was out delivering newspapers when he saw something that was "the shape of a cat… but quite big. I don't think it was as large as a panther but bigger than any domestic cat I've seen."

The area by the speedway stadium – and around the Nuffield Hospital – another Foxhall Road big cat sighting location – is densely wooded in some places and not frequently used by the public. Jane Cody, editor of the local *Kesgrave News* magazine, told me the stadium's surroundings would be "a good place for shy wild animals to hide out," noting that she'd seen around the stadium "a small deer hide away in a very wooded area when it saw me and the dog". Big cat witness Jonathan Mossman told me that seeing deer in quite urban parts of Ipswich had been "not uncommon" since the beginning of this century. So if you're still scratching your head about why big cats would hang out in that part of a county town with a population of currently over 130,000, the above deer anecdotes may offer a clue.

Very soon after the 2006 speedway stadium sighting, a big cat was seen on the Holywells High School playing fields, in Ipswich's Racecourse neighbourhood. Local resident Vera Westlake woke up one August night at 3.30am and looked out of her window, to see on the playing fields what she described as a "big cat… large animal, incredibly black" illuminated by streetlights. There was yet another big cat sighting soon after in the Rushmere neighbourhood.[3]

On 5 August 2007 on Foxhall Heath, west of the speedway stadium, Cindy Lucas was left "shaken" by her encounter with a black cat, a "huge animal… really long, low slung like a cat but very, very big." Cindy had also heard of an earlier big cat sighting by a friend in Martlesham who had been out shooting rabbits at night. During the morning rush hour a couple of weeks later, at Rushmere Heath, there were two sightings of a "black cat-like creature larger than a Labrador" that crossed the A1214 to open land by Woodbridge Road East. And someone who left a comment on the *EADT*'s website who gave their name as "Martlesham Resident" recalled in 2015 having seen a "big black cat… when out walking my dog early one morning… did not tell the police" nor did they give a year or date for their sighting.

In November 2007, back in the Foxhall Road, this time on property opposite the St Elizabeth Hospice, Jacqueline and Richard May – who owned the land – spotted eleven clear "giant paw marks", prints the size of a horse's hoofprint, wide apart, believed to be a big cat's. They were seven inches in diameter with "claws or toes". The Ipswich *Evening Star* commented, "witnesses are sure it's not foxes or muntjac, both species come into their garden." [4]

Seven years later, just when we thought "Claws" had moved out of Ipswich for good, it showed up again. On 6 June 2014. Suffolk Police reported that a big cat was reported to them as having been sighted in – where else? – Foxhall Road – and that "officers checked for missing animals from zoos and questioned people in the area, but nothing was found."[5]

East of Ipswich

While reports of bit cats in Suffolk's county town tailed off, evidence of big cats seemed to into the villages surrounding Ipswich, particularly in the area to the east of the A14 road on the west bank of the River Deben.

PART 3 – BIG CATS OF THE CURIOUS COUNTY

In the village of Kirton, Paul Newman was out walking his dog in June 2008, when he saw the head and shoulders of a big cat emerging from bushes. And two years later, also in Kirton, at the junction of Park Lane and Bucklesham Road, taxi driver Paul Smy saw a "large cat about the size of a leopard ... moving slowly without a care in the world," which he said was also seen by a woman in her car who'd stopped at the junction on the way back from the school run. Paul had lived and worked in Africa previously, where he'd seen leopards. The report of the incident in the *Evening Star* said the animal was "Claws", an animal of heath and woodland that had first been sighted on the Foxhall Road way back in 1998, although the *Star* claimed to have been tracking "Claws" since 1995. The *Star* claimed that "Claws" had become inactive that year, but was now "on the prowl once more." The article neglected to say what colour "Claws" was, by then it assumed that a sighting of a leopard in Suffolk meant a black leopard.[6]

And in the last days of May 2009, at Wilford Bridge near Woodbridge, there was a "black panther-type big animal… very long and quite stocky" with a very long tail, "much longer and thinner than that of a dog" and with ears that were "tufted," seen by golfers on the second tee of Ufford Park Golf Course. The Ufford tufted big cat was seen walking along the fairway of the first tee by a witness who "continued playing but kept looking back to see if it was following me, but it wasn't."

One of the more convincing Ipswich big cat sighting I've heard of was from sometime in 2010 ("about two years ago" its witness recalled in 2012). Big cat investigator Jonathan McGowan, who's more at home looking for big cats in Dorset, was a passenger in a car driving through Ipswich when he saw a puma by the side of a "motorway" junction. There are no motorways in Suffolk, but some Ipswich dual carriageway bypasses on the A12 and A14 are busy enough to be mistaken for a motorway if briefly glimpsed whilst passing through. Possible candidates for the junction where Jonathan saw his puma (he knows his big cats!) would be the A14 Junction 53 at Belstead, or Claydon (scene of a black leopard sighting), Wherstead, Ransomes Europark and the A12's Junction 58. All have fields or woodland nearby.

A short distance north of Ipswich, on a farm track in the village of Akenham, a Suffolk Police spokesman revealed that on the morning of 18 February 2012, a dead muntjac had been found with signs of predation suggesting to the finder that it had been the work of a big cat. According to Suffolk Police, a "man called to report that a big cat had attacked a deer. The man had found the deer with marks around its throat."[7]

Sometime before March 2010 "cat-like beasts, creatures" had been seen in Debach, (just north of Woodbridge) according to the *Coastal Advertiser* of 12 March 2010. Something like a puma or African golden cat appeared there in September 2014. Roughly contemporary with that, something like a puma was seen crossing the A12 at Kelsale, just north of Saxmundham. This big cat was "a brown one", and the witness just saw the "back end of it and its legs… jumping into the hedge" after it crossed the road. He only got a "glance…four or five seconds" of an animal he estimated was forty to sixty feet away (12-18m).[8]

Crepuscular coastal cats cluster

Back in 2013, I went looking for evidence of big cats in Dorset, where the field signs are much more plentiful than in Suffolk, with local big cat investigator Jonathan McGowan. We took the chain ferry from Bournemouth over to the little harbour at the famous Shell Bay Beach. As we waited in the car for the traffic by the ferry terminal to clear, Jonathan mentioned casually that few beach-goers are aware that there are "leopards on the beach at night."

Leopards, or some kind of big cat, would appear to have been in recent years "on the beach at night" along Suffolk's coast as well. The first hints of big cats moving up and down our coast was a sighting at the end of July 2006 reported by BBC News, described in their online news report two years later.[9]

This may have been something to do with some contemporary possible big cat kill signs from the National Trust nature reserve at Orford Ness, England's longest shingle spit and a former top secret weapons research establishment. Natural England had photos (which can apparently no longer be traced) of the fox carcasses found around Orford Ness that were said to have been predated on by a big cat, but regarded these as "inconclusive"."[10]

In possibly the same year (our witness had trouble recalling in 2014 exactly which year it was), a visitor to the Dunwich Heath National Trust nature reserve reported to one of the wardens that he'd found "half a seal" on the coastal path, which is far enough inland from the beach that it couldn't have been dragged there by the seagulls that predate on exhausted or dead juvenile seals that are often blown ashore in windy weather. The warden thought the visitor's report was "ridiculous" and dismissed it as nonsense.

Then the same warden (he didn't want to be named), as well as one of his colleagues, found the carcass of one of the red deer that passes through Dunwich Heath. It had been "opened up." The warden didn't want to go into detail about the several deer carcasses he's found at Dunwich Heath, except to say that he's seen "more conclusive evidence of predation on deer carcasses" suggestive of a big cat.[11]

Then in 2008, our witness was clearing up after a "do" at Dunwich Heath NT, and was driving around the reserve in its National Trust electric "mobility cart". It was raining heavily, so there was no one about. By Dowcra's Ditch, named after the reserve's founder, our witness spotted what he thought was a dog sitting in the ditch. Oh dear, he thought to himself, the boss isn't going to like that – dogs off leads not being allowed on the reserve. But then he noticed how the animal was sitting, "on his haunches". It was then that he realised it wasn't a dog at all, but a "big black big cat – bigger than a Labrador, with a very long tail." The tail was "thin but not particularly exceptional," and he didn't get a look at whether the tail's end was thick or tapered. They watched each other for a while before the big cat moved off, "in bounds."

Not long after that, a visitor reported to our warden another "black panther" sighting on the reserve, at Nightjar Corner, not far from Dowcra's Ditch. And then, at the start of the next season, when all the tourists started arriving (usually around April), yet another visitor sought out our warden. The visitor told him they'd come looking for him at the end of the last season (early September 2008) and couldn't find anyone, so they'd made the effort to come all the way over to Suffolk again to tell them what they'd seen earlier.

This is the story told by the visitor who had been so eager to find a warden to share it with. The visitor had taken the footpath away from RSPB Minsmere – it starts just south of Dunwich Heath – inland towards Eastbridge. Not far from Eastbridge along the footpath is a narrow gate that walkers have to go through. When he'd gone through the gate and was closing it after him, our visitor saw a black big cat behind him. He described how they sat there watching each other for a short while before the big cat bounded off.

I went to take a look at the location. It seemed like the perfect ambush site for a big cat out hunting. The path from Minsmere goes through the British Energy estate, with its marshes, where there are otters. Otters are on the big cat's menu, as are pheasant in particular, and any waterfowl they can catch (I saw plenty of duck). I saw tracks of otter and deer when I was there

– deer being the favourite food of British big cats, as we have seen. When I came through the gate in the opposite direction – from Eastbridge – I emerged from an open field into a shaded area with trees and a bramble thicket on either side, creating a sort of tunnel either side of the footpath. When I came out of this cover, pheasants on the path ahead took flight. It's the perfect spot for a big cat to sit around all day out of sight and jump out at any passing wildlife.

After his own sighting and the similar reports from visitors, suddenly the comment earlier about "half a seal" on the coastal path which our witness had dismissed as "ridiculous" began to make sense, as the work of a scavenging coastal cat that had found a dead or dying seal stranded on the beach and hauled it away to the shelter of the more secluded coastal path to eat as much of it as it could.

Seals and porpoises occasionally end up beached on East Anglia's coastline. There are other edible strandings for big cats to enjoy – tides will occasionally deposit drifts of starfish on the beach, and quite big dogfish, or bits of them, are to be found from time to time washed up on the Heritage Coast.

Take the road south past the edge of Rendlesham Forest, keep going through the village of Butley and you eventually come to the Bawdsey Peninsula. The peninsula is so out of the way that it was chosen for the site of Hollesley Bay open prison. On the winding road down to the nearby beach at Shingle Street, on Easter Sunday 2008, Heidi Hawley, a prison officer on her way to work, saw a "giant" dark and fawn-coloured cat, initially mistaken for an Alsatian, the size of a large dog, "beautiful" with "great big eyes".

It ran across the road in front of her, clambered up a steep bank, turned round and looked her in the eye before finally disappearing into undergrowth. Colleagues were aware of "similar sightings in the area in the past." *The East Anglian Daily Times* caused confusion by running the story with a photo of a lynx – with the caption "A lynx – similar to the big cat seen in Suffolk", although the word "lynx" didn't appear in the text. Shingle Street would be of interest to a big cat – there are sheep (unusual for this part of Suffolk) and lots of reed beds to hide in.[12]

Sometime in 2013, a "tan cat with black markings" was spotted in Hollesley, scene of that earlier Easter Sunday encounter between a prison officer and the "Shingle Street lynx". An unnamed witness reported the sighting to the British Big Cat Research group, adding that they had then found a "stool – faeces, hair samples, prints, impressions in the grass etc. Tree scratches as evidence".[13]

It was a very long time before I heard of any other big cat sightings from the Bawdsey Peninsula. While I was on a press visit to the National Trust's newly redeveloped Sutton Hoo estate in the summer of 2019, its Property Operations Manager Alison Girling told me that one of her regular volunteers had recently seen a black leopard cross the road at Ramsholt. This is village just six miles to the south of Sutton Hoo on the same bank of the River Deben, so the other side of the peninsula from Shingle Street. Ramsholt's best known for its Ramsholt Arms pub, in whose beer garden Jack Malik first plays the Beatles' "Yesterday" to his amazed friends in the film *Yesterday*. I contacted Alison later to ask if the Sutton Hoo volunteer wanted to tell me more, but I've heard nothing yet.[14]

Returning to our catalogue of early twentieth-century big cat sightings on the Suffolk coast, further down the Suffolk coast at Felixstowe, a Felixstowe feline was spotted in March 2008. Unlike the "brown" big cat spotted in Felixstowe back in 1998, this one was a "black panther-type animal", reported by a resident who saw the animal in the allotments near Garrison Road[15]

The coastal cats since then seem to have been more active further north up the coast, just over the other side of the Suffolk border and around Gorleston, Norfolk. Sometime before August 2013 there was a "black puma" observed in the area.[15]

There was another sighting of a big cat on the Suffolk coast, just north of Aldeburgh much more recently, in November 2021. Frazier Seagar and his wife Ru got a good look at a black leopard stalking geese in wetlands there, as we will see in detail the end of Chapter 18. Migratory geese arriving in wetlands on the coast around November would be an obvious addition to the diet of any big cats locally.

Evidence from elsewhere in the UK suggests big cats frequent our beaches in search of prey. A dogwalker on a footpath through a rural beauty spot at Cullen in Morayshire, Scotland in the Spring of 2012 discovered the rotting corpse of a "huge beast", a "giant cat" with "razor-sharp" teeth and an 18-inch tail, which had possibly died after tumbling down a cliff. It was too small to be a jaguar or a leopard but could have been an older leopard cub. And next to the body were the remains of what was probably its last meal – six mauled seagulls.[16]

Big cat sightings in the lower Waveney Valley

Big cats were showing themselves in the lower Waveney Valley at around this time. In the summer of 2007, a big cat that was a three-foot high animal, "four to five foot plus tail" in length, and with a "huge", very long, five-inch-thick tail which "hung down… curled at the end" was spotted by a motorist on the B1062 Flixton Road west of Bungay, on a road that runs close to the Suffolk border. The animal was near the entrance to the Flixton cement works, and it walked "gracefully and slowly" crossing the road from the cement work pits and into nearby woods. The witness reporting it said the "other driver" coming in the opposite direction also saw it.

This came a few days after a sighting on the night of 5 August 2007 near the village of Woodton, a couple of miles over the Suffolk border in Norfolk from Bungay – a "large, black, Labrador-sized cat" was seen by a family in the beam of their car headlights as they drove round a corner. It bounded across the road and up a verge, according to a report in the *Big Cats in Britain Yearbook 2007*.

Sometime in the years before August 2013, a big cat believed by the witness to be a lynx was seen more than once within a 10 mile radius of Blundeston, just north of Lowestoft and a mile in from the coast, in the extreme northeastern tip of Suffolk. Ian Miller told *EADT* "his wife had seen big cats" in the area that "could jump six to eight feet".[17]

In October 2014 there was an email from a Suffolk Wildlife Trust warden in my inbox, which began, "I was asked to contact you about big cat sightings in the lower Waveney valley." Moving inland from the coast at the top right-hand corner of Suffolk, starting from Lowestoft Harbour and going West through a short ship canal and inland along Oulton Broad, you come to the man-made Oulton Dyke near Lowestoft.

It was early in 2011 on the shore of Oulton Dyke, with the snow on the ground, that wildlife warden Matt Gooch and his colleagues were struggling to restart a stalled tractor. When finally it roared into life, the noise of its engine seems to have flushed out a "black thing" that had been hiding in the long grass. The animal was "too big and loping to be Labrador" and had a "long tail".

At first Matt wondered whether it was a Labrador on the loose, but its movement was "very cat-like." The big cat "loped across marshes, disappeared." Then it started snowing, so Matt and colleagues couldn't find any tracks. Matt said he'd heard of "a couple of sightings" of a very similar animal earlier. There was a local farmer who later decided they didn't want to be named, who'd reported to Matt having "regular" close encounters with the same creature. [18]

As we have seen, much of Suffolk's big cat action occurs on the very edges of the county. Moving west and inland along the Waveney. Veritable clusters of big cats continued to be reported in that region.

In April of 2007, a "big cat... larger than a big dog with brown grey fur" and "movements too fluid for a dog" was seen standing close to a hedge in a field near the North Suffolk border village of Oakley, by Halesworth resident Russell Carlton.

The grey fur suggests a puma, while they're usually sandy brown or beige in colour, they can be grey, dark chocolate brown or even reddish brown. A "dark coloured cat... two and a half feet tall" with a "long, thick tail" was spotted in fields on the way through Hoxne the following month, by an anonymous female witness driving along the B1118 to Stradbroke. And two months later, in August 2007, on the road between Mellis and Wortham, a driver observed for 30 seconds a "large black cat... long and wiry", seen in a field. It crouched down and slunk off into the undergrowth[19]

A big cat was allegedly illuminated in the beam of some car headlights yards north of the South Norfolk-North Suffolk border at East Harling near Garboldisham on the B111, in the first few weeks of 2008. This time it was a "light sandy, tan colour big cat" with a "three-foot long tail" – a description very much like that of a puma.

In the small North Suffolk market town of Eye in August 2008, in a meadow just before the road bridge at the end of Lowgate Street, a driver going to work in the nearby village of Occold saw a big black cat. This one was the size of a Labrador dog, but longer, with a long tail and small head. The witness thought it might have been the same big cat seen earlier in Cratfield. And this was around the same time that a witness testing their home's outdoor security light one night somewhere in Suffolk (perhaps in their excitement they forgot to give a location when they reported it to the Big Cats in Britain group,) found not only that their light was working, but that it illuminated something resembling a "puma or lynx" that "loped" through foliage at the end of their driveway, leaving very large, clawed footprints three inches across. This resident from somewhere in Suffolk insisted there were no dogs in their area.

Blyth Valley big felines

Back in the Blyth Valley, another big cat was seen by Brenda Sore of Peasenhall, near the transformer station at the southern edge of the village, just before dusk one evening in June 2008. She recalled being "scared" by a large feline that crossed the road some distance ahead of her, then "turned round and looked at me," and stood watching her over its shoulder for a long time. It was "black", and so far away it was difficult to gauge its size, but Brenda estimated it was "two feet six inches in height, three feet long." Its tail "came down at an angle and turned a bit", she later described its tail as "curled down, went up again". What she described was something very like a melanistic leopard or possibly a melanistic African golden cat, but for one curious detail. Unlike a leopard, it had "pointed ears."[20]

Blyth Valley big cat encounters continued, with a big cat-like animal, "dark" coloured and "like a puma or lynx, with a long tail" seen in a field by an Anglia Buses route 88A bus driver on the Blythburgh to Wenhaston road, sometime in either 2011 or 2012. The bus driver saw an a van from a well-known animal rescue organisation "riding around" at the time, although it's not known if its presence in the area was just a coincidence.

Mike Fordham is best known locally for his work with the Halesworth Museum, which is right next to the station and well worth a visit.

In 2012 or 2013 ("two years ago, or three" recalled in May 2015), Mike saw a big cat in the water meadow between the back of his back garden in Blyford and the Blyth River. The cat was "certainly bigger than a muntjac – dark, I would say black, with long thick tail", with the tail the same thickness throughout. The Blyford big cat was "walking across pasture with high grass, 80-90 yards away" and there were pheasants in front of it, which allowed Mike to estimate its size. He thought that as the meadow grass was quite long, it's possible that the pheasants couldn't see the big cat.

Mike added that a long time ago he used to go shooting (he doesn't anymore), so he was quite good at judging distances. He'd seen his neighbour's domestic cats in the same area, and this big cat was of a different size altogether. Unlike his neighbour's gardens, Mike's garden had a wildlife corner down at the back, where he used to go and watch barn owls and other animals. He said the meadow at the back had muntjac in abundance. There's a bus stop near Mike's house which is on the 88A bus route, it's not far from the spot where the Anglia Buses driver saw the "dark" coloured cat probably in the same year. [21]

Roger Mason, who lives in Norwich but often visits the Suffolk Heritage Coast, was driving with his wife away from the Minsmere bird reserve, travelling along the road through Westleton Heath, less than three miles from the beach, one summer evening in 2012 when he drove past what he described as one of the quarries. Sandmartins fly in and out of one of the little inland cliffs around the disused quarry here.

Mason spotted in the quarry what he described as a puma. He got a look at it for about ten seconds. Its body was facing away from him, but he could see clearly its back legs, its back and it tail, which drooped down and then curled up again, thick at the end. The animal was sandy in colour, and moved slowly, close to the ground, like a stalking cat, but "huge". Mrs Mason couldn't see it from the passenger seat.

There's plenty for a puma to eat on the Westleton Heath RSPB reserve. Herds of a hundred or even 200 red deer are not unusual, one of the RSPB wardens told me. The "deer rut" in October is an annual tourist attraction. So great are deer numbers locally that they threaten the purple heather foliage covering the heath with their grazing, and are culled each winter. There are also plenty of hares and rabbits, as well as birds roosting among the heather. While it's busy at weekends, parts of Westleton away from the paths and in the thick heathland cover where a big cat would be left alone during the week.[22]

Southeast of Halesworth is the Heveningham, famous for one of Suffolk's biggest firework displays at Heveningham Hall each November. A "big cat was believed to have been spotted" and reported to Suffolk Police in the area in late June 2014. The local "Safer Neighbourhood Team was informed and farmers in the area made aware."[25]

By December 2009, whatever it was had crossed into the Norfolk, with a Norfolk Police log from that time recording "caller saw a puma in the fields" at Scole. I've heard a third hand account of a Mrs Green encountering a big cat in Thorndon, a village near Eye, in 2012.[24]

Sometime before August 2013, at least one "black puma" was allegedly at large around the Somerleyton area, with Ian Miller – a witness to another big cat sighting in Gorleston – telling the *Eastern Daily Press* that a black big cat had been seen (recently?) around Somerleyton.[25] The relatively small Waveney Forest is nearby, known for its wildlife-rich habitat, so a big cat would feel at home here.

PART 3 – BIG CATS OF THE CURIOUS COUNTY

Eye saw a big cat

One of the more impressive-sounding sightings of big cat activity in the northerly part of the count y of Suffolk was in the Eye Valley, along one of the Waveney's tributaries, the Dove. The experience left its witness "in awe." At around 8am on a sunny July morning in 2013, John Daniel saw on his farm near Eye a "very, very cat-like" large black cat, with a "muscular build", Alsatian-sized with a long, thin tail that was "not bushy," and the tail was "agitated, moving about". The big cat's colouration was "a proper black… like a black dog in very good condition."

John at first thought what he had seen was a dog. He was alerted to the animal when he saw a cock pheasant strutting up and down twelve feet away from it, in the same way he'd previously seen cock pheasants defensively strutting up and down when there were foxes nearby.

It was then that John realised what he was seeing was something like a black leopard lying down, sunning itself in the early morning sun. John got a close look at it through the telescopic sight of his rifle, although he never for a moment considered shooting it. He had a rifle with him because he'd recently had a problem with a lot of predation of free range chickens. Something had been effortlessly scaling a four-foot electric fence and taking chickens or leaving them partly skeletonised or beheaded. John had taken to patrolling the ditch around his farm with a rifle, but whatever it was invariably came and went, leaving a considerable commotion among the hens, whenever John had just gone on a short break from his vigil.[26]

What was that? Did an East of England Ambulance Service paramedic catch a glimpse of a black leopard from the window of his ambulance whilst on call late one night on Blower's Lane, Gisleham (above)?

Claws back on the prowl

HE has stalked Suffolk for years, creeping through the county's heaths and woodland on the hunt for prey.

Sightings of the county's very own big cat – nicknamed Claws – have been numerous and date back as far as 1996 when startled residents in Ipswich's Foxhall Road watched as a panther-like beast weaved through the undergrowth.

The Evening Star has been charting the sightings of the big beast for the past 15 years and now it seems as though the secretive creature is on the prowl once again.

Taxi driver Paul Smy was so amazed when he saw a big cat crossing a field, that he stoppped and brought traffic to a standstill.

Mr Smy believes he saw a large cat-like animal crossing a field at Kirton as he pulled up at the junction of Park Lane and Bucklesham Road.

"I looked across the field ahead and couldn't believe what I was seeing," said Mr Smy, of Langer Road, Felixstowe.

"It was about a quarter of a mile away yet it looked really

CAT SIGHTING: Taxi driver Paul Smy in Kirton where he claims to have seen a panther

"It was just moving slowly without a care in the world."

"My worry is if it is a pan-

The *Coastal Advertiser* of 12 March 2010 reports yet another sighting of the Suffolk black leopard known as "Claws", this time in the village of Kirton on the road to Felixstowe.

A particularly lonely stretch of the B1118 near Hoxne, location for many a big cat sighting.

PART 3 – BIG CATS OF THE CURIOUS COUNTY

FOOTNOTES TO CHAPTER 15:

Serving South Norfolk and North Suffolk – and crepuscular coastal cats

1. The 2005 Thetford sighting and 2006 Suffolk A 134 sighting are both from Norfolk Police Freedom of Information Request Reference No: FOI 424/11/12, December 2011, which had extracts from call logs. Locations may be vague for reasons of data protection. The South Norfolk towns of Thetford and Scole were both once in Suffolk before their annexation in 1832.

2. All from *Diss Express* 16 June 2006; Fersfield sighting "Dog walker sees 'Big Cat' prowling", *Diss Express* 27 October 2006; Martin Ayer's Bressingham sighting from *Diss Express*, 1 September 2006, quoted in *Big Cats in Britain Yearbook 2006*, CFZ Publications, Woolsery 2007.

3. Both *Evening Star* 25 August 2006, www.eaweb.co.uk/archive/index.phpt–1322.html, but the webpage is down at the time or writing.

4. Undated Martlesham Heath sighting www.eadt.co.uk/news/is_there_a_panther_or_big_cat_loose_in_suffolk_1_4181532, scroll down to the "comments" section, comment by Martlesham Resident; Cindy Lucas's sighting *Evening Star*, 10 August 2007; Rushmere Heath mid–August 2007 sighting *Evening Star*, 14 August 2007, citing "Steve Fulcher, driving to work" as the witness; 9 November 2007 prints discovery *Evening Star* (Ipswich), date not given, quoted in *Big Cats in Britain Yearbook 2007,* CFZ Publications, Woolsery 2008.

5. "Is there a panther or big cat loose in Suffolk?" *EADT* 5 August 2015, www.eadt.co.uk/news/is_there_a_panther_or_big_cat_loose_in_suffolk_1_4181532.

6. Kirton head and shoulders sighting from *Evening Star* (Ipswich) 17 June 2008, quoted in *Big Cats in Britain Yearbook 2008,* CFZ Publications, Woolsery 2009. This may or may not be the sighting mentioned by *Coastal Advertiser* of 12 March 2010, which said there had been a sighting in Kirton two years earlier; Paul Smy's 2010 Kirton sighting from "Claws on the prowl once more", *Coastal Advertiser* March 12 2010.

7. Ufford tufted cat from a Big Cats in Britain report of 29 May 2009, none of the tufted cats are normally black, although melanistic servals are quite common, ghostly grey melanistic caracals have been known, and black bobcats occur in the wild. All are tufted; the junction at Sproughton is unlikely to have been where Jonathan saw the puma, it's too small to look like a "motorway junction", Conversation with Jonathan McGowan, 17 August 2012; Akenham muntjac kill from "Akenham: Police receive reports deer attacked by big cat", *Evening Star*, 18 February 2012 www.ipswichstar.co.uk/news/akenham_police_receive_reports_deer_attacked_by_big_cat_1_1213378.)

8. Phone interview with Mark Eagle, window cleaner, from Kelsale, 19 April 2015.

9. "Big cats in Dorset – London Cryptozoology Club expedition, with Jonathan McGowan", author's website, http://mattsalusbury.blogspot.co.uk/2013/06/big–cats–in–dorset–london.html; "Anglers report big cat sighting", BBC News website 02 August 2004, 2004 Falcon Meadow sighting from "Anglers report big cat sighting", BBC News (Suffolk), 2 August 2004, http://news.bbc.co.uk/1/hi/england/suffolk/3529254.stm.

10. *Reported Sightings or Signs of Exotic Species Compiled by Natural England*. Natural England told me as of early 2021 that any of their still extant photos of the fox allegedly predated on by a big cat could not be traced. Would a big cat kill and eat another predator, one of my proofreaders asked. Yes – badgers, domestic cats, foxes, small dogs if they can take them without drawing too much attention to themselves, whatever they can lay their paws on.

11. Interview with Dunwich Heath NT member of staff 5 September 2014, his colleague earlier told me he'd also seen for himself a deer carcass "opened up" but felt he wasn't expert enough to comment further on this.

12. "Big cat sighting revealed in Suffolk", *EADT* 29 March 2008 www.eadt.co.uk/news/big_cat_sighting_revealed_in_suffolk_1_187892.

13. British Big Cat Research group sightings map 2013, http://britishbigcatresearch.weebly.com/sightings-map.html. The British Big Cat Research people are still active.

14. Conversation with Alison Girling, Property Operations Manager, Sutton Hoo NT, 10 August 2019.

15. "More sightings of big cats come to light", *EADT* 3 April 2008 www.eadt.co.uk/news/more_sightings_of_big_cats_come_to_light_1_188020. I had a look for the Garrison Road allotments in 2015 and I couldn't find them. If they are still there, they're out of the way and well hidden.

16. "Is this new evidence of a big cat in Britain? Dog walker finds remains of terrifying creature near Scottish beauty spot", *Daily Mirror* 18 May 2012, http://www.mirror.co.uk/news/uk-news/big-cat-remains-found-by-dog-839016. It used to be filed under "Weird News" on the *Mirror's* website, but it's recently moved to the "Cats" section.

17. Flixton and Woodton sightings from *Big Cats in Britain Yearbook 2007,* see above. Blundeston jumping cat from "Norfolk puma spotted in Gorleston" *EDP* 28 August 2013, http://www.edp24.co.uk/news/norfolk_puma_spotted_in_gorleston_when_you_see_a_lion_going_for_a_kill_it_was_like_that_1_2356562).

18. Matt Gooch, SWT Warden, phone interview 4 December 2014 and BBC Radio Suffolk Jon Wright show 1 January 2015, Matt responded to an SWT email appeal asking witnesses to contact me. He told me he'd seen a letter from The Broads Authority that had been circulated in December 2010, referring to a visitor reporting having seen a big cat. The Broads Authority press office said they'd had a look and found no record of such a letter, and suggested it could have been a misremembered letter from the nearby Broadland District Council in Norfolk, or from English Nature.

19. Large, wiry black cat on the Mellis road from *BCIB Yearbook 2007,* CFZ Publications, Woolsery 2008; Hoxne grey puma from *Diss Express*, 3 April 2007; Hoxne dark coloured cat *Diss Express*, 10 June 2007.

20. Sandy-coloured East Harling puma, Eye sighting and Garboldisham big cat all from *BCIB Yearbook 2007,* see above. I couldn't find a record of a Cratfield big cat sighting, but I spoke to some Cratfield residents in 2015, who did remember talk of a big cat locally at that time. There were contemporary sightings at nearby Linstead Parva and Peasenhall. *Big Cats in Britain Yearbook 2008*, telephone interview with Brenda Sore 31 March 2015.

21. Blythburgh to Wenhaston road big cat from a conversation with the partner of the witness, September 2014; Mike Fordham, phone interview 2 September 2015

22. Conversation with Roger Mason, 21 February 2016.

23. "Is there a panther or big cat loose in Suffolk?", *EADT* 5 August 2015, www.eadt.co.uk/news/is_there_a_panther_or_big_cat_loose_in_suffolk_1_4181532)

24. Scole puma from Norfolk Constabulary Freedom of Information Act Request; Mrs Green's Thorndon big cat Pers. Comm. by email from John Daniel, February 2015.

25. "Norfolk puma spotted in Gorleston" *EDP,* 28 August 2013, see above.

26. Phone interviews and emails from 3 February 2015 onwards. At the witness's request, some details altered.

Artists's impression of a puma tucking into a washed-up seal carcass very early in the morning on one of Suffolk's beaches.

***The Hay Wain with Melanistic Leopard*, with apologies to John Constable above) and *Mr and Mrs Andrews With Puma,* with apologies to Thomas Gainsborough (below). These are modern parodies – while South Suffolk landscapes featured prominently in their work, neither artist featured big cats in these paintings!**

PART 3 – BIG CATS OF THE CURIOUS COUNTY

16. The Haverhill Puma and others

We will catch up with the big cats of South Norfolk and North Suffolk border again shortly, as the busiest area for big cat encounters along the northern frontier of the Curious County seem in the last few years to have moved west, to the area around Thetford Forest. But Suffolk's large felines also seem to be showing up again along the eastern edge of the county, on the border with Cambridgeshire, and once again on its southern border, along the River Stour that demarcates Suffolk's frontier with Essex.

Our quest for large members of the family *Felidae* brings us once again to the gentle rolling hills and ancient "Wool Towns" of South Suffolk, where Thomas Gainsborough painted his Suffolk portraits in the early eighteenth century, and where John Constable painted his landscapes – Constable said that it was gazing on the banks of the River Stour that inspired him to become a painter.

In early February 2009, "in broad daylight", a witness who contacted the Paranormal Database website told how they had spotted what he referred to as two "deers" in a field outside Bures, right on the Suffolk-Essex border, and a station stop on the Gainsborough Line to Sudbury. What was unusual about these "deers… running across a field" outside the village was that they were being "followed by large black cat… running at speed". The big cat was seen by two witnesses who were taking a break from "off-roading" – it was running so fast it was flicking mud into the air, a sign that it was a real physical animal and not a hallucination or phantom apparition. Another sign that it was a real physical animal was the "large print" they found in the area, twice the size of "our retriever", but unlike a golden retriever's, the print had no claw marks. Sadly, no actual photos of the beast of Bures or its paw prints were passed on to Paranormal Database.

Sometime before March 2010, "cat-like beasts, creatures" had been seen near the South Suffolk town of Hadleigh, according to the *Coastal Advertiser* of 12 March 2010, while on 1 March 2012, at a location given with deliberate vagueness by Suffolk Police as within the "Babergh East Safer Neighbourhood Teams area," a "big cat, possibly a puma, light grey all over" was reported, according to a Freedom of Information Act request. (The colour is notable. You may remember another Suffolk grey puma, reported near Hoxne in 2007. Given the distance pumas cover in their regular nocturnal ramblings, the Babergh East SNT report and grey puma and the reports from around Hoxne could refer to one and same animal.) The police report noted that "Informant reported their dog has been chased" somewhere in the patch of the police division that includes Hadleigh and the small town of Capel St Mary.

In 2012, someone "out metal detecting" along the A1092 road running along the Suffolk Essex border, somewhere between Long Melford and Wixoe, saw a big cat, according to a secondhand report. Given the wealth of Saxon and Medieval artefacts lying just underground in Suffolk's fields, metal detecting is a fairly common pastime in Suffolk. It's not unusual to pass fields with several detectorists at work in recently harvested arable fields, with the landowner's permission of course.[1]

Haverhill's "puma-like" cat and the Beast of Balsham

Tucked away in the bottom left-hand corner of Suffolk, near where the counties of Suffolk, Essex and Cambridgeshire meet, is the town of Haverhill. It was a postwar "London Overspill" town where many Londoners resettled from the 1950s, Cockney accents are still common in Haverhill.

The town has its own – named – big cat, the Haverhill Puma, possibly named after the Surrey Puma from way back in the early 1960s. Even though it's got a cool "puma" name, we shouldn't therefore assume that the Haverhill Puma is actually a puma. Its witnesses describe a "puma or lynx" or just a "big cat" without any distinguishing detail. The Haverhill Puma's colouration varies in different reports, while it would seem to have a curious affinity for traffic roundabouts.

The first known Haverhill big cat sighting I've come across – from the days long before the "Puma" name attached itself to it – was in the words of one of the witnesses and "unforgettable experience" back in late September 1999. Ronald Bartlett was driving with his wife along the A1071 Haverhill bypass, heading east towards Sudbury at dusk, around 7pm. There are several roundabouts in quick succession on the bypass on the southern edge of town, right on the Suffolk-Essex border. From Ronald's description, the Bartletts was approaching the Sturmer roundabout, the last of these as you head east.

Suddenly they saw what at first they thought was a black fox, before they realised it was a big cat approaching the road from the left side, "50 metres away, right in front of us." Ronald had to brake quite sharply to avoid it. In leaps and bounds the big cat crossed the road and the island in the middle of the roundabout and onto the bank on the other side of the road where it "stopped and faced me!" Ronald noticed the big cat was black in colour, with a tail thinner than an Alsatian's, it had "blue or green eyes glowing in the car's headlights," he couldn't be sure of the colour of its eyes.[2]

The next episode in our chronology of Haverhill big cat reports wasn't until August 2007, in the car park of the Haverhill Sainsbury's supermarket. When a night shift worker was driving out of it, they saw an animal that was "Tall and wiry with a white tipped tail, couldn't say how big it was. Thought it was a fox at first… too big for a domestic cat." It is of course possible that what the departing night shift worker saw was in fact a fox. The occasional fox that's much bigger than usual, as well as the occasional black or grey fox, have been reported across the UK in recent years.[3]

Then the *Haverhill Echo* was on the case, documenting what quickly became known as the Haverhill Puma. The *Echo* published an account of a "puma or lynx" sighting along the A1017 Haverhill bypass in the summer of 2010. Once again, the sightings were along that series of roundabouts close together along the A1017, near the entrances to the various edge-of-town industrial estates and business parks.

After that "another man, who did not wish to be named" told the *Echo* they'd seen the Haverhill Puma in the same place, in the form of a "puma or lynx" picking its way along a hedge, as if stalking, in 2012. And there was a follow-up of sorts in early July of that year, when the testimony of another Haverhill Puma witness appeared in the *Echo* under the headline "I saw the Haverhill Puma too".[4] The Haverhill Puma was back again near the bypass once again, on land near the Puddle Brook playing fields, seen in headlights well after lighting-up time one summer night in July 2012. It was described by witnesses as "definitely too big to be a domestic cat, dark, either dark brown or black… It had a very long tail that curved down and curled up at the end."[5]

The Haverhill Puma may well have been the same animal as another named British Big Cat, the Beast of Balsham, named after a village of that name just over the Cambridgeshire border. There were multiple sightings of the big cat attributed to the Balsham area, including some in which the Beast of Balsham strayed into Suffolk. It was an animal said to be a "long, lithe black panther" with a slim tail that's "not bushy." There were multiple encounters with the Beast in the year leading up to May 2006 around Balsham, usually in fields, and sometimes in Balsham's residential Woodhall Lane, with one sighting around dusk. One man claimed to have seen the Beast of Balsham ten times over the years. Zoologist Margaret Johnson was reported as being one of those among a group "hunting for signs of the Beast of Balsham". [6]

Great cats of the Gipping Valley

The River Gipping rises in North Suffolk, between the villages of Yaxley and Wetheringsett and meanders south through Stowmarket and all the way to Ipswich, where it briefly becomes the Stowmarket Navigation canal and then transforms into the mighty Orwell Estuary. A long time ago, Ipswich used to be called Gippeswyk in honour of the river that ran through it.

Big cats would favour Suffolk's river valleys like the Gipping. There is cover among the reeds and the drainage ditches. Wetlands are, as we have seen elsewhere and will see again in other examples, "big cat country." There are waterfowl, pheasants, and more exotic items on the menu like otters. Big cats follow the deer, and deer come down to the river where there are often few people around. It will come as no surprise that there have come big cat reports from the Gipping Valley. We've already come across one encounter of a black big cat, back in 1995, by the Gipping at Sproughton on the edge of Chantry Park, back in Chapter 14.

Reports are less numerous than elsewhere, possibly because outside the towns of Stowmarket and nearby Needham Market, there are fewer people about in that part of Mid-Suffolk.

Most people who've seen big cats in the Gipping Valley – as in the rest of Suffolk – were on their way somewhere. I talked to Jonathan Mossman, who with his friends Carl Scarfe and one other, on a moonlit night in the summer of 2006 was walking from Ipswich to his home in Claydon, in the southern end of the Gipping Valley, just outside Ipswich. Moonlit Suffolk nights once you're away from the light pollution of its towns have to be experienced to be believed – the moon is often strong enough for you to have a shadow and distinguish colours close up, and easily read by it. On occasion I've had to avoid looking directly at a Suffolk full moon, it's been so bright it's blinding.

Jonathan, Carl and his friend were about half way between Ipswich and Claydon that moonlit night, they were passing a park that bordered the then traffic–free road. Suddenly they became aware of a big cat watching them from the other side of the road, next to some fencing, and its shoulder height was, in Jonathan's words, "just shy of the fence post."

It was "all black, with the body shape of a feline," its shape was "pretty much (that of) a domestic cat." It had a long black tail whose form "matched that of a feline… long, slender" and the tail didn't move that much. It looked at the three walkers with "big eyes" as it stood there "near enough motionless."

As Jonathan and his friends were "trying to get home, didn't want to stop", they realised they would have to approach the big cat to get past it. He recalled being "very scared" at the prospect, and that he and his friends wrapped their stout chain rings round their knuckles, expecting the worst. (Chunky chain key-holders with a clip connecting them to the belt loop of your jeans were fashionable at the time, Jonathan recalled.) As the three walkers hurried past the big cat, it "got lower" to the ground, took "a couple of paces forward," then "turned off" and "ran backwards" through an open gateway into the park, into a field, before it "trotted away not particularly fast."

A big cat with "a tail as thick as a man's arm and sweeping" was seen at Barham Hall, near Claydon and the River Gipping, at five minutes to seven in the morning of 10 May 2008. The witness neglected to mention what colour the big cat was – they said that at first they thought it was a bin liner blowing in the wind, so it's safe to assume that it was black, or at least dark, in colour. They checked with the people at the local stately home, Barham Hall, who told them that Barham Hall "had no cats."[7]

"David in Bury", who contacted BBC Radio Suffolk immediately after my New Year's Day show on big cats in the county, has seen four big cats over a 20 year period. One of these was a "big cat, black," with "quite a long body… as long as a greyhound" and with a "thick tail." David, who worked as a UPS courier at the time, saw his big cat in headlights at around 12.30 one night in 2010. This was also in Barham, "where the traffic lights are now" (there weren't any lights there at the time of his sighting.)[8]

Other big cats locally included one recorded as being "one metre in length and dark in colour, not black, with a mottled effect on its fur," seen near Coddenham on 23 March 2010, according to Suffolk Police data. Something believed to be the black panther known locally as "Claws" was also reported as leaving "huge" footprints on the nearby landfill site at Great Blakenham, according to an anonymous tip-off to the *Evening Star*.

A "very large cat" was at large somewhere in the same general area on 4 August 2012, when a caller reported to Suffolk Constabulary a big cat seen "walking across a bridge" somewhere in the Mid-Suffolk South Safer Neighbourhood Team area. There being many bridges around the southern edge of Mid-Suffolk District, the sighting could have taken place almost anywhere in the Gipping Valley.[9]

In the southwestern corner of Suffolk, near the banks of the River Stour, was another appearance by a South Suffolk big cat, in the "Clare area," somewhere near the town called Clare (or village, depending on who you ask.) According to Suffolk Police, on 13 July 2011 the "Informant reported seeing a Puma" thereabouts.[10]

A memoir by deerstalking lawyer David Barrington Barnes, titled *On the Deer Path* and self-published in 2012, also describes signs of a puma on the loose somewhere in southwest Suffolk, on land Barnes names as "the Eve Estate", although he told me that confidentiality precludes him from revealing its real name or location. It is out of respect for this principle that I refrain from speculating here where the Eve Estate could have been. I believe I can safely say, however, that the little we have to go on would put the Eve Estate and its puma comfortably within Haverhill Puma territory or within the Suffolk part of the Beast of Balsham's range.

According to Barnes, "the then gamekeeper on the Eve Estate was adamant that the estate is visited by a big cat or big cats in the form of a puma." That gamekeeper had found several deer carcasses in the middle of fields, "reduced to little more than desiccated skin and bones" with their skin "rolled up rather like a roll of paper or foil," a clear sign of the fastidious eating habits of big cats, who peel back the skin of their prey with their rough tongues. The local deer were either "jittery" or completely absent in the days around such finds. This is consistent with the studies of lynxes introduced into Switzerland after 1970, which found that lynxes eventually had to move on every few days, as deer got used to them and became extra vigilant.

Barnes also heard of puma sightings from a tractor driver on the estate, once in grassland

and once in woodland, with the puma seen attentively watching a woman out walking. A man who ran local pheasant shoots reported to Barnes two puma encounters while out lamping at night, after which the man's wife's dogs were growling "in a scared manner" for days afterwards. The puma may even have been glimpsed by Barnes himself at night in the headlights of his truck, but he admitted he couldn't say with certainty whether the "big catlike animal" jumping over a newly-planted hedge was the puma or not, "so fleeting was my view." If it was just a domestic cat Barnes had seen that night, he added that it was "a giant of the species."[11]

I have reconstructed the Haverhill Puma, depicted above on the A1017 Bumpstead Road roundabout, as if it were a puma. However, witnesses to the Haverhill Puma described it as something like a "puma or lynx."

Haverhill Puma country, where the three counties of Cambridgeshire, Suffolk and Essex meet.

FOOTNOTES TO CHAPTER 16: The Haverhill Puma and others

1. Babergh South SNT grey puma from Freedom of Information Act Request no: F–2014–00782, Suffolk Constabulary, 14 March 2014; A1092 Suffolk-Essex border sighting report from multiple big cat witness "Sam" in Glemsford, who in 2015 recalled her friend's sighting was "a year ago… maybe two", Pers. Comm. by email 9 January 2015. The recent BBC comedy series *Detectorists* was shot in and around the Suffolk town of Framlingham.

2. Email from Ronald Bartlett, 6 March 2021, with thanks to Rick Minter.

3. Haverhill Sainsbury's encounter from *Big Cats in Britain Yearbook 2007*; CFZ Publications, Woolsery, 2008. "I saw the Haverhill puma," *Haverhill Echo*, 5 July 2012, www.haverhillecho.co.uk/news/latest–news/i–saw–haverhill–puma–too–1–3990317.

4. "Another sighting of Haverhill puma", *Haverhill Echo*, 10 July 2012, www.haverhillecho.co.uk/news/latest–news/another–sighting–of–haverhill–puma–1–4015576.

5. "Hunting for signs of the Beast of Balsham", *Haverhill Echo*, 11 May 2006, www.haverhillecho.co.uk/news/latest–news/hunting–for–signs–of–the–beast–of–balsham–1–452812. As we will see anon, there have been plenty of other big cat sightings in the county of Cambridgeshire along its Suffolk border and beyond. Readers with good memories will recall that Balsham was the stomping ground of the shug monkey encountered in Chapter 8.

6. *Big Cats in Britain Yearbook 2008*, CFZ Publications, Woolsery, 2009, wrongly described as "Bartham".

7. Jon Wright's BBC Radio Suffolk show, 1 January 2015."Bury" is Bury St Edmunds.

8. Coddenham sighting from Suffolk Police FOIA disclosure, Request Number: F–2013–03389, 23 November 2013; Great Blakenham "Claws" prints from "Suffolk: New sightings of big cat 'Claws'", *Evening Star* 25 November 2010, www.ipswichstar.co.uk/suffolk_new_sightings_of_big_cat_claws_1_737147; Mid–Suffolk South SNT sighting on a bridge from Suffolk Police FOIA disclosure Request no: F–2014–00782, 14 March 2014.

9. Suffolk Police Freedom of Information Act Request no: F–2014–00782 14 March 2014. Clare, Suffolk takes its name from the same medieval aristocratic family after which County Clare in Ireland is named.

10. *On The Deer Path*, David Barrington Barnes, 2012, self-published, http://onthedeerpath.co.uk/books.html; David Barrington Barnes, Pers. Comm. by email 23 August 2016 and 4 January 2017. For more on the Swiss reintroduction of lynxes, see Chapter 20 and also *Great Cats – Majestic Creatures of the Wild,* ed. Dr John Seidensticker and Dr Susan Lipman, Merehurst, London 1991

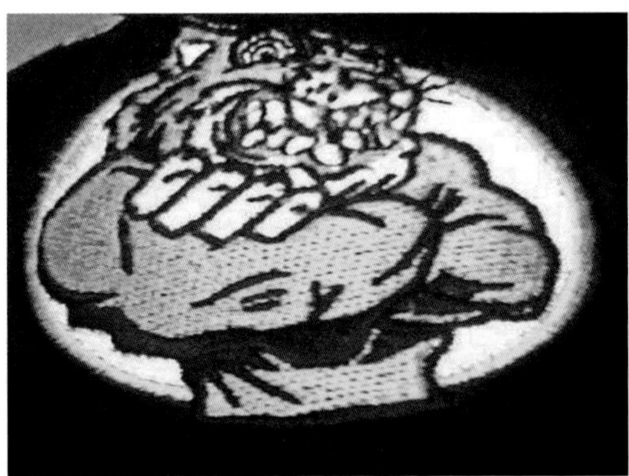

Detail from the author's own Mildenhall Fen Tigers baseball cap, in the speedway team's colours of orange and black. Logo reproduced by kind permission of Mildenhall Fen Tigers.

17. Mildenhall Fen Tigers!

The West Suffolk town of Mildenhall ("Mildenhall High Town" to give its rather grand-sounding full name) is perhaps best known for RAF Mildenhall, the base for the US Air Force's 100th Air Refuelling Wing, whose Boeing Stratotanker planes provide mid-air refuelling for NATO aircraft in Europe, or will do for the next few years at least. The base is eventualy scheduled to shut up shop and move out to Germany. Mention "Mildenhall", though, and many people will tell you about the speedway stadium on the edge of town, the venue on Saturdays for "home" races featuring the Mildenhall Fen Tigers speedway team, complete with their magnificent logo featuring a tiger. Speedway's huge in Suffolk.

Confusingly, the Mildenhall Fen Tigers aren't named after a big cat. There is a local big cat with that name said to be native to the region since the 1980s, which is known as the "fen tiger" or "fenland tiger." But this isn't supposed to be a tiger either, it's most frequently described as – and has even appeared in photographs showing it as – a skinny black leopard-like thing with thin legs. No, the "fen tiger" big cat of mostly Cambridgeshire and the northwestern corner of Suffolk are both called tigers because they're named after a regional type of person. I said it was confusing!

The term "fen tigers" appears to have been coined to describe the human inhabitants of the fens –the extensive marshland in the region that was eventually reclaimed for farmland. Dutch engineers worked to reclaim the fens, but the fen dwellers fiercely and tenaciously resisted them all the way. Before the fens were drained, the people of the fens somehow eked a living cutting peat, shooting game – mostly waterfowl – and catching eels by spearing them with eel spears. For three hundred years, the people of the fens resisted with extraordinary hostility any attempts by the engineers to drain the land and replace the hand-to-mouth existence that was their ancient way of life with agriculture. The fen people feared – rightly – they would lose their ancient rights to shoot gamebirds and other privileges, and the agriculturalists had their eye on the fenland because, once drained, it was some of the most fertile land in the country.

It was this fierce hostility that earned the fen folk the name "the fen tigers". Naturally, when the time came to name Mildenhall's speedway team, based on the edge of the fens near the Suffolk-Cambridgeshire border, "Mildenhall Fen Tigers" was the obvious choice.[1]

So when in 1982 a skinny black big cat started showing up in Cottenham, Cambridgeshire, looking nothing like a tiger, it nonetheless quickly became the Fen Tiger. The Fen Tiger, though, seems to describe several types of big cat. Cambridgeshire Police's Wildlife Officer PC Paul Carter, who started taking an interest in the Fen Tiger in around 2004, noted that "the animals vary from a large black panther to a smaller brown-spotted lynx."[2]

Over seventy sightings of "large cats" were recorded across Cambridgeshire between 1998 and 2014. We have already covered the 2006 wave of sightings in Balsham, Cambridgeshire, of a "long, lithe black panther… slim, tall" and with a tail that was "not bushy." While the epicentre of Fen Tiger and Beast of Balsham encounters was in Cambridgeshire, animals with similar descriptions also strayed into West Suffolk. At least one wave of Cambridgeshire sightings seemed to precede an outbreak of big cats in West Suffolk.[3]

A good example of the "Cambridgeshire first, West Suffolk next" big cat phenomenon was the 2008 cluster around Isleham, which started when "a couple reported seeing a knee-high, black feline creature with a long tail, which had a bulbous tip, in Isleham, Cambridgeshire on

August 26 at around 10pm," according to the *Newmarket Journal*. Isleham is only a mile from the Suffolk border. Less than a month later, a big cat was reported in nearby Red Lodge, Suffolk, where villager Jackie Ellerton saw a "feline creature" twice the size of an ordinary cat early one morning. It was standing on derelict land opposite her house in Russet Drive. But this was unlike the "knee-high, black feline" from Isleham, and Jackie said it was "huge and spotty and not like an ordinary cat."

The neighbourhood around Russet Drive, Red Lodge is an estate of closes meandering north from the River Kennett, which forms the border with Cambridgeshire, towards two roundabouts and a main road. The "derelict land" – a potentially big cat-friendly virgin meadow with long grass, some gullies and woodlands in the background – was still there when I visited in 2015. Along the river is Red Lodge Heath, an enclosed nature reserve with a gate unlocked during the day that a big cat could push open with ease, where muntjac and the occasional roe deer, as well as occasional wandering horses, are reported.[4]

None of the local residents I spoke to – including the conservation volunteers who were out tending the Heath and who know neighbours who walk their dogs there very early in the morning and "couples" who are there after dark – had seen or heard anything about a big cat.[5]

The Cambridgeshire-Suffolk border seems to have gone relatively quiet after that, or maybe the forces of serendipity that ensure the recording of earlier accounts of big cat encounters from that region just didn't come together. As we will see shortly, 2008 in particular was a busy year for the Fen Tiger in Cambridgeshire, but not up at the eastern end of the county nearer Suffolk. We next hear of the Fen Tiger on its travels into Suffolk in 2012.

Large – as in the size of my Labrador

Reach, Cambridgeshire, is about four miles from Newmarket. A poster to a gun dog training forum who gave his name as Keirk described in early 2012 how he'd been out in Reach one Saturday morning with "the dog" at around 7am, on a path on the local nature reserve near some farm buildings. He noticed a rabbit dart across the bridleway just ahead of him, then he saw a large black cat – "large as in the size of my Labrador" walking down the lane away from him, 20 metres away. It had "a long tail, held low." It didn't see Keirk or his dog, it went off into a hedge. His account ends with the words, "I sound like a nut job don't I? The wife thinks so."

Another account (undated as the witness could no longer remember the year of his sighting) was in Suffolk, at the Fornham All Saints golf club. The witness was working as a security guard, patrolling in the dark with an Alsatian dog, when he saw a big cat "shoot across in front of me… dog very nervous."[6]

The same David in Bury who'd fleetingly seen a big cat that night in Fornham All Saints saw another one in 2012, when he was working as a taxi driver out of Bury, on a pick up in West Stow. On this occasion, David was at Culford, a ten-minute drive west of Bury and near West Stow, when he saw a big cat cross the road, leap over the gates to the grounds of Culford School and vanish. The woodland pasture of the enclosed 480-acre Culford estate would in particular appeal to a big cat looking for something to eat.

West Stow is popular picnic site, also the home of Suffolk Museum Service's West Stow Anglo-Saxon Village, a reconstructed village from the Dark Ages which hosts Saxon re-enactments. At Moyse's Hall Museum in nearby Bury St Edmunds I was told that a visitor to West Stow had twice reported seeing a "golden puma" in its extensive grounds. My informant politely told me he thought the visitor might have been "on drugs" at the time. But other people had reported contemporary sightings of "sandy" pumas from that part of the county.

When I visited West Stow in 2015, a member of staff said he'd heard of a report from a visitor of a "puma" seen down by the River Lark (300 metres from the museum) in 2013, but he thought it was a muntjac misidentified by one of the visitors who'd come from outside the East of England and didn't know their exotic deer. I took a look at the trickle at the bottom of a ditch that is the Lark at this point. Big cats would have the place to themselves after the museum closes in September all the way through to its re-opening around Easter, and Lackford Lakes nature reserve is a short walk away.

Readers with good memories will remember the dead muntjac with its tongue and "in-nards removed" we read about earlier, found in the Lackford area, near West Stow, in 2014. And David in Bury – he contacted BBC Radio Suffolk after my appearance talking about big cats – also reported that "my guvnor Bill Boast", working with the Suffolk County Council "educational coaches" service, had seen a big cat "chasing a small deer" at Rushbrooke, just south of Bury, at the end of 2014.

Sometime before Bill Boast saw a big cat pursuing deer at Rushbrooke, a black leopard also passed through woods near Rougham, less than two miles away from Rushbrooke by winding roads, with lots of little woods on the way. David Willis, a resident of the town of Thurston to the north of Rougham, described in 2015 how he saw "some years ago" a big cat at a distance of 30-50 metres (98-164 ft) while travelling south through the woods near Rougham on his motorbike early one morning. It fitted the description of the black big cats seen around Suffolk, its body was "over two feet long"(60 cm), and ended in a tail the same length. It "cleared the road in one leap."[7]

Still in West Suffolk, but back up against the Cambridge border, in Fen Tiger and Beast of Balsham country, John Berrett of Barton Mills and Mrs Berrett were in Mildenhall Woods, near their home, in September 2014 when they spotted through a gap in the trees a "large cat-like" creature whose tail was "very long and looping." Newspapers at the time made no mention of the cat's coloration but noted the discovery of a "deer carcass stripped to the bone" not far from the same spot in Mildenhall Woods a few days later. Lorry driver Gerry Brown contacted me in 2021 to say that "many years ago" he was driving his lorry through the southern end of Mildenhall Woods along the A11 very early one summer morning – delivering newspapers to Norwich – when a "large black cat ran across the road in front of me and disappeared into the woodland that flanks the area".[8]

The area around Mildenhall and up to the Cambridgeshire border to the west seemed to be in the grip of a veritable cluster of puma sightings only a few years ago. Samantha Hammond contacted me shortly before she told the *Bury Free Press* and Suffolk Police about what she saw on 11 November 2014, while out in woods near Red Lodge looking for a friend's lost dog. That's the same Red Lodge where Jackie Ellerton saw a "huge and spotty" cat back in 2008.

Sam saw "two sandy-coloured pumas", one slightly smaller than the other and with spots on its legs." They were "pacing" together in a field on the edge of woodland. They were "definitely pumas" in Sam's opinion, although one of them was "spotty" on its front legs. She was disturbed to hear "a noise like a dog yelp 15 minutes later", although it could just as easily been one of the many and varied vocalisations that big cats make rather than – as she feared – her friend's missing dog being attacked by big cats. Gloucestershire-based big cat expert Rick Minter told me juvenile puma cubs still with their mothers can have spots on their legs – a detail that's quite obscure, not something you can look up online so easily.

People often ask me, where are Suffolk's big cats, then? Where should we look for them? Were I to go out looking for big cats in Suffolk today, my money would be on West Suffolk, from the banks of the River Stour where Suffolk meets Essex, along the Suffolk-Cambridgeshire border, around Mildenhall and Red Lodge. That is where big cats have often been reported – "sandy pumas" as often as the melanistic leopards. Suffolk Police logs, as we have seen, report something like a puma, even a "grey" puma. That Mildenhall to Red Lodge corner of West Suffolk is the area I'd expect to find field signs – scat, prints, scratch marks, possibly even discarded hairs on a barbed wire fence, or even dropped big cat whiskers. The West Suffolk border with Cambridgeshire is where one might – if they looked very hard – expect to find big cat kill signs.[9]

2015 opened with a big cat sighting from the Suffolk-Cambridgeshire border region that better fits the description of the melanistic Fen Tiger. Newmarket, famous for the horse races and the National Horseracing Museum, is a little enclave of Suffolk surrounded on three sides by Cambridgeshire. If you go to the edge of Newmarket early in the morning, you'll see the jockeys and stable hands exercising the racehorses in the paths and tracks and bridleways around the stud farms on the edge of town. On any given day, there are 3,000 rather jittery thoroughbred racehorses in Newmarket, and many of these will cross Newmarket's roads as they're given their daily exercise. (Some riders report seeing the ghost of tall jockey Fred Archer riding his favourite horse, as we saw in Chapter 7.)

The White Lion pub in Newmarket has one bar in Suffolk and one bar in Cambridgeshire, and I was told by a man I met in the street claiming to be a Newmarket town councillor that until recently, when the landlord called "Time!"then the drinkers all just moved into the bar in the other county, which had different licensing laws and a later closing time. On one of the bridleways parallel to the A11 immediately east of Newmarket, you're in a strange narrow little corridor of Suffolk. At its narrowest point, around the Bury Hill Exercise Tracks, Suffolk is well under a quarter of a mile wide, with Cambridgeshire immediately to your north, starting at Well Bottom Road, and with Cambridgeshire also to the south. When you travel by train out of Newmarket station heading west towards Ely and Cambridge, you've left the county of Suffolk within seconds.

The witness to our West Suffolk big cat sighting in the first days of 2015 didn't know whether they were still in Suffolk when they saw a black big cat from the window of the Newmarket to Ely train, in open countryside moments after it left Newmarket station in the direction of Dullingham. According to the witness, the black big cat was running alongside the train.[10]

"Are you yanking my chain, or am I yanking yours?" asked the conductor on the Newmarket to Ipswich train when I asked him if there had been any big cat reports on the line. He shared the robust big cat scepticism of most West Suffolk people I encountered, and suggested the "black big cat" seen running alongside the train was a misidentified black racehorse, "there are plenty of them about" and they're panicky enough to be stampeded by a passing train. There weren't any horses in the fields immediately before Newmarket when my train pulled in, though.

Hideous screams in Thetford Forest

We have already come across reports of big cats in Thetford Forest, from both sides of the Norfolk-Suffolk border that cuts through it. You may remember Ian Day of Kesgrave's springer spaniel-sized big cat near the forest's High Lodge Visitor Centre almost 20 years ago. Mike Hume of the Friends of Thetford Forest told me that as of September 2014 he'd not heard any intelligence on big cats in the Forest, and that "all I have heard of is Hebridean sheep, which are used to graze parts of the Stanford Battle Area, getting out and being mistaken for something other than what they are." (The Battle Area, Europe's biggest, is marked on most maps as a prohibited Danger Area where NATO's troops practice with live rounds. The scenes of Walmington-on-Sea's Home Guard on manoeuvres from *Dad's Army,* as well as its closing credits sequence, were filmed there.) But yes, there is more to relate on the subject of big cats from around Thetford Forest and from that northwestern corner of Suffolk where it meets Norfolk.

A gloomy dark winter Saturday, at dusk "many years ago" on the A1065, the Mundford Road north of Brandon, so far North that it was already a couple of miles into Norfolk, was the setting of the "quite unnerving" encounter recalled by "Beaver Bob" from Brandon, a "Top Brandonian" posting on Brandon Forums. By 2014 he could no longer recall in what year it had happened. His sighting was just north of Grimes Graves, the old flint mines that were in operation for thousands of years, right up to the nineteenth century. It's noticeable that nearly all the facades of the older houses in the Suffolk border town of Brandon are made of blocks of flint, and there's a pub in Brandon called The Flintknapper's Arms. Many of Suffolk's 400-odd parish churches, in a county where stone is hard to come by, have exterior flourishes and decorations made from blocks of Brandonian flint.

Running across that A1065 road "very fast" near the Grimes Graves was "a very large black panther." Beaver Bob saw it "clearly in my headlights."[11]

At the end of January 2007, a witness contacted Big Cats in Britain to say he'd caught a "glimpse … a pure black big cat… larger and sleeker than a Labrador" and it was "running after deer in Brandon Forest at high speed, through trees and bushes." A couple of months later, in Thetford, the Norfolk town whose suburbs are up against the Suffolk border, another sighting, this time a "large jet black cat" with a "long tail" came to BCIB's attention. Brandon Road in Thetford (less than a mile into Norfolk) was also the location given in a Norfolk Police log from September of that year that recorded "caller reports sighting a female lion by the wooded area". When Europeans first arrived in America, they mistook the pumas they encountered for lionesses, hence the alternative name "mountain lion" for pumas or cougars. A puma is a likely identity for this "female lion."[12]

In 2007, sightings of a black big cat in the Thetford Forest area were becoming frequent. On 23 November 2007, a BBC employee whose sister lived nearby in Santon Downham was cycling on the Black Trackway cycling track when a "huge black cat" with a long tail crossed his path. It was reported to Big Cats in Britain, with the comment that a Forestry Commission official (he presumably worked nearby, as they have an East of England headquarters at Santon Downham) had said there had been "a number of reports of sightings in the area."[13] Sounds of "hideous screams like a cat and dog fighting" were heard by three women walking their dogs, also in Santon Downham, in April 2008. Given the range of known big cat vocalisations, the sounds could just have easily been made by a big cat on its own – particularly a lynx.[14]

Then there was the testimony of "R2D2", who is "from Texas" and "knows his pumas." He routinely takes his Staffordshire Bull Terrier for walks right by the landing lights by the viewing area of RAF Lakenheath, the home of a US Air Force fighter jet squadron, one of the last left in Europe. He chose the name "R2D2" as his internet moniker on Brandon Forums. Let us not forget that the robot R2D2's original function in the earliest *Star Wars* film was in-flight repairs to an X-wing fighter. All these observations lead me to speculate that "R2D2" may have been part of the ground crew at RAF Lakenheath.

In any event, in June 2011, R2D2 was exercising his "Staffie" (Staffordshire bull terrier) by the landing lights near the viewing area, when suddenly his dog flushed out of the undergrowth a "tan puma… definitely a puma." They fought, and the puma eventually slunk away.

Fighting with dogs is atypical behaviour for the pumas of the western USA, who could usually be relied on to flee up trees away from dogs. So predictable was this behaviour that hunters used dogs to flush out pumas and chase them up trees where they could get a clear shot at them. This behaviour enabled hunters to bring pumas to the brink of extinction until hunting was regulated in the 1960s. You might expect a British puma, descended from pumas raised in captivity, to show different behavioural traits to the more mainstream puma populations of the Americas.

"R2D2" had previously found dead sheep on the heath halfway between Lakenheath and Brandon "clearly attacked" by a predator, as had a friend who was a local policeman.[15]

Suffolk Police received three big cat reports in the first half of 2015. In late April, there were "concerns" of a "panther on the loose" at Herringswell, just south of Red Lodge. The "matter was referred to rural crime officers but no big cats were found." Then another "panther" was allegedly sighted on 28 April in Wrentham, where readers will recall both a lynx and a black leopard were reported in earlier years, as well as the sound of something answering the captive big cat calls coming from the neighbouring wildlife park at Kessingland. The Wrentham "panther" seen in 2015 was "reported to officers" a few days after the Herringswell sighting, plenty of time for a big cat to cross the county of Suffolk from west to east, if it was the same animal.

A month later, at the end of June 2015, there were "concerns" of a "panther on the loose again," this time in Tunstall, the big forest where at – as already noted – a driver saw a black leopard eleven years earlier and where there may be wild boar for any big cats present to eat.[16]

The late 2010s saw the prospect of a new twist to the story of big cats in Suffolk, a much-reported proposal doing the rounds. There is still a vanishingly small chance that big cats in Suffolk may suddenly go from being a mystery to becoming mundane, making this book redundant. The Lynx UK charity in April 2016 opened consultations on a plan to reintroduce between four and six Eurasian lynxes into several locations in the UK, including Thetford Forest. The lynxes would be fitted with radio-collars, with their location always monitored.

Starting in 1970, Switzerland successfully re-introduced lynxes and Slovakia and Germany are re-introducing them now. Lynx UK were reported by BBC News Scotland as saying there was a "moral and ecological" case for the return of the Eurasian lynx, supposedly not seen in the wild in these parts for the past 1300 years. Since 2009, Professor David Macdonald of Oxford University's Wildlife Conservation Research Unit has been advocating lynx re-introduction to keep down deer, now at critically high numbers especially in East Anglia. The Scottish Wildlife Trust are keen on the idea, following the success of the recent re-introduction of beavers to Scotland. Initially, farmers and landowners around Thetford Forest were keen on the Lynx UK plan, presumably they'd seen damage done to farmland and woodland by deer.

But "stakeholders" gradually became less keen on the plan, as many realised that yes, while lynxes do eat deer, they're also likely to get through a lot of rabbits – very common around Thetford Forest after the local rabbit fur industry collapsed around 1912, resulting in them being let loose in large numbers – and hares, not so common. And sheep, and lambs. The Beccles Lynx is alleged to have killed 15 of these before being shot. The Sheep Association for sheep farmers came out against the Lynx UK plan nationally. Natural England came away from an "initial" meeting with Lynx UK lawyers saying the plan would "need very serious consideration in terms of its impact".

In June 2016 the Lynx UK Trust announced that while Thetford Forest "ticked all the boxes," they had for the moment ruled it out as a site for lynx re-introduction. The concerns of the Sheep Association had been noted, but more importantly, forest sites the Trust had looked at in Northumberland and Aberdeenshire just looked more suitable. The Trust's chief scientific advisor Dr Paul O'Donoghue told the *EDP* that "while Thetford would not be one of the first release sites, it could be considered again in the future."[17] The lynx introduction plan for Aberdeenshire is scheduled to go ahead at the time of writing.

But lynxes, it seems, are in Suffolk already. Although I've not heard of any in Thetford Forest itself, there were those lynx-like "hideous screams." Cambridgeshire Police's PC Carter believed that a "smaller, brown spotted lynx" was among the big cats roaming around the Cambridgeshire border and wandering into Suffolk around 2008. Lynxes and "tufted cats" have been seen around Glemsford, and Dunwich Forest, and Wrentham, and Ufford Park Golf Course, and all the way back to those two "lynxes or bobcats" seen in Staverton Thicks all those years ago. As we will see anon, a captive bobcat (a close relative of a lynx) went on the run in West Suffolk in 2020, causing havoc among the poultry before his recapture.

Flaviu the Carpathian lynx, who went on the run in Dartmoor for three weeks in July 2016 after gnawing his way out of his new home in Dartmoor Zoo, was eventually recaptured. How did Devon and Cornwall Police find him? With a state-of-the art thermal imaging camera-equipped drone. As these drones proliferate, if big cats do exist in the Suffolk countryside it becomes more and more likely that evidence of them will come to light.

There has been relatively little by way of recent big cat activity in the county, although I am occasionally contacted with brief reports from around Suffolk (and beyond). Most of reports that have recently come my way have been historic accounts, many very detailed and credible and some backed up by video evidence – but mostly involving big cat encounters some 10 years ago. Among these have been – in the months leading up to December 2017 – are brief, secondhand reports of big cats seen around the A140 road between Yaxley and Thornham.

One mystery cat sighting to which I have been alerted is among Suffolk's oddest. "Simon from Ipswich" and his daughter saw what they think was "two lynx cubs" along the narrow road leading to Eastbridge, near Leiston, early on the evening of 29 October 2015. "There was a dead rabbit or something in the road and it was either eating or investigating whilst the other one went into the hedgerow. It was like a small stumpy very fluffy grey and black kitten like looking creature from the back, (I) didn't see its face but I've never seen anything like it before." [18]

The "classic" Suffolk black leopard known as "Claws", whom we met in previous chapters doing the rounds in the 1990s, seems to have put in some more recent Suffolk appearances. Or – given that 18 years is considered a good innings for a leopard in captivity – its descendants have. The more recent reports that have reached me – both of encounters that have just happened and historical recollections from some years before – tend to feature the classic melanistic leopards.

Tony Wheal of Starston, Norfolk, described in a letter to the *EADT* how he and his wife had seen not one but *two* "very large jet black cats… one behind the other" coming down the road towards their car as they drove past the entrance to Chippenham Hall, near Fressingfield, while returning home from a supper party at around midnight on 24 April 2015. Chippenham Hall's not far from Cratfield, where as we saw in Chapter 14 there were reports of black big cats around 2008. For what it's worth, there's a Catkin Farm at nearby North Green.

Wheal, who had "many years of wildlife experience" described the two big cats as "noticeably larger than ordinary domestic cats, being well over two feet in the body plus the head, with the tail held horizontal, curving up at the tip." A mother black leopard and her older cub is a possible explanation for why anyone would see two normally solitary leopards at once.[19]

Suffolk Coastal's "large village" of Wickham Market, near the source of the Deben, saw some distinctly scary big cat activity in the early days of 2016. Local teenage A-level student Elliot Evans was finishing the regular run he does every other evening, which takes him through the then empty Simon's Cross playing fields near the school on the northwestern edge of the village. As dusk started to fall, he did some sprints which took him towards the tennis court. It was then that Evans became aware of what he at first thought was a large dog. Very soon he realised he "was being stalked" by something, according to the *Daily Mirror* newspaper.[22] Growing nervous, Evans shone the torch of his mobile phone and "met the eyes" of whatever it was. The eyes were "too far apart for it to be any dog." It was a "black panther… it must have been between four and five feet long". Evans glanced behind him to see that it "began coming towards me." He sprinted away across the rest of the sports field.

I visited this sports field, at the northeastern edge of Wickham Market behind the primary school, by the road out towards Easton. I noticed there's a high hedge around the edge of this sports field, and it's right next to allotments – as we've noted earlier, big cats would like allotments, as there are usually plenty of rabbits to be found on them. There's even an abandoned but still accessible World War Two pillbox almost hidden among trees in the corner of the sports ground for any local black leopards to shelter in.

Evans did his own research and came into contact with David Galvan, a former local representative of the British Big Cat Society. Galvan described "a long history of encounters by people with big cats in the area." He'd even seen one himself.

There are a lot of little woods where a big cat could hide out to the northeast of Wickham Market, around Easton, and also to the south and southwest of the big village. There's even a small area of woodland known as Catt's Wood just north of Wickham Market, where one might expect a big cat to feel particularly at home. It's possible that the black leopard seen at Wickham Market in early 2016 was the same – now very elderly – black big cat seen in nearby Easton back in 1990, or possibly even one of its cubs. (See Chapter 14.) As we've already seen, there was a lot of activity involving a black leopard reported from the village of Bredfield, near Wickham Market, just over a decade ago.

Black big cats are back

In October 2016, I was contacted by a witness who saw a "slender" shiny black big cat with a "small head", like a domestic cat but three feet long plus its tail, on the Boxted to Hartest B1066 road – as we've seen, a busy big cat corridor over the years. A year later, the same witness told me their daughter had just seen "a large black cat" in the same spot, "4-5 feet long jet black long tail which curled up at the end." A friend of theirs had seen something similar two weeks earlier on the Sudbury to Long Melford road, seven miles away.

PART 3 – BIG CATS OF THE CURIOUS COUNTY

Big cat investigator Rick Minter told me that in the early days of 2017 a journalist from a certain national newspaper – I'm only allowed to say it was one of the "red tops" – got in touch about a video said to be from Hintlesham, Suffolk – it's east of Hadleigh, on the A1071. This seemed to show a black leopard. For whatever reason, the paper has so far not run the story and the journalist ignored my attempts to get in touch with her. Odd indeed! From what I can understand, there could be an issue with the copyright of the video.

In any event, a licensed deerstalker based in the Blyth Valley told me he'd seen "definitely a black leopard" while deerstalking on a nature reserve with a colleague (who also saw the black leopard) somewhere near Hintlesham in around 2012.

I've also received two brief reports from witnesses with whom, for reasons too complicated to go into, I haven't been able to arrange detailed follow-up interviews before this book goes to press. A man who works in Halesworth told me he'd seen a black leopard more than once on land around Peasenhall. He also told me he'd overheard "shooting farmers" in the pub in Laxfield describe the fatal shooting of a black leopard.

Big cats have been reported in Mildenhall Woods (below).

FOOTNOTES:TO CHAPTER 17: Mildenhall Fen Tigers!

1. Other speedway teams in the same league include Glasgow Tigers, Sheffield Tigers, Leicester Lions and the Ipswich Witches based at Foxhall Road, Ipswich. There's also a Sicklesmere Panthers football club, representing a Suffolk village just south of Bury, the Lowestoft-based Waveney FC's numerous youth teams are named after cougars, panthers, jaguars and other big cats, while the Lowestoft Leopards basketball team has a melanistic leopard as its logo. Halesworth's recently revived cricket team is the Halesworth Pumas. The late Dave "Boy" Green, a Norfolk boxer from the 1970s, was also billed as "The Fen Tiger."

2. "I tawt I taw a puddy cat, I did," *Newmarket Journal* 8 September 2008 www.newmarketjournal.co.uk/news/latest-news/i-tawt-i-taw-a-puddy-cat-i-did-1-546538. Paul Sieveking, indefatigable cataloguer of British big cat newspaper reports since the early 1970s, gives a much earlier 1974 date for the emergence of the animal known as the Fen Tiger, "Big cats still stalk Britain," Paul Sieveking, *Fortean Times*, **FT344;20**, September 2016.

3. *Bury Free Press* 15 Sept 2014; "Hunting for signs of the Beast of Balsham", *Haverhill Echo,* 11 May 2006 www.haverhillecho.co.uk/news/latest-news/hunting-for-signs-of-the-beast-of-balsham-1-452812.

4. Fly grazing, the practice by irresponsible owners of letting their horses go and find their own pasture on public land or somebody's else private land, became such a problem nationally that legislation came into force in 2015 allowing council officials and the RSPCA to seize fly grazing horses and put them up for adoption.

5 Isleham sighting from "I tawt I taw a puddy cat, I did", *Newmarket Journal* 8 September 2008. www.newmarketjournal.co.uk/news/latest-news/i-tawt-i-taw-a-puddy-cat-i-did-1-546538; 2008 Red Lodge sighting from "Second wild cat sighting in space of month", *Newmarket Journal* 24 September 2008, www.newmarketjournal.co.uk/news/latest-news/second-wild-cat-sighting-in-space-of-month-1-546620.

6. Reach sighting from Gun Dog Training Forum, 6 May 2012, www.gundogtrainingforum.co.uk/phpbb/viewtopic.php?t=11942#p142533, Fornham All Saints sighting by David in Bury, who phoned in to Jon Wright's BBC Radio Suffolk show, 1 January 2015.

7. David in Bury phoned in to Jon Wright's BBC Radio Suffolk show 1 January 2015; SWT nature report on Culford estate www.culford.co.uk/Libraries/Foundation_Documents/Suffolk_Wildlife_Trust_Report_August_2012_as_word_for_web.sflb.ashx; "Golden pumas" anecdote from a conversation with Alex McWhirter, Moyse's Hall, September 2014. Staff at Moyse's Hall also do shifts at West Stow.Conversation with a member of staff at West Stow Anglo Saxon Village, 23 May 2015. Like most people I talked to in West Suffolk, he was sceptical. Where's the road kill in the form of the occasional big cats inevitably getting run over then, he reasonably asked. Rougham woods sighting from "My own big cat sightings", letter to the *EADT* by David Willis, 19 August 2015, with thanks to Paul Sieveking.

8. The Berretts' Mildenhall Woods sighting from "Suffolk woodland or foreign jungle?" *Bury Free Press* 15 September 2014, www.buryfreepress.co.uk/news/local/latest-news/suffolk-woodland-or-foreign-jungle-barton-mills-resident-spots-big-cat-in-mildenhall-woods-1-6296519; Deer carcass stripped to the bone from *Cambridge News* 25 November 2014..

9. Multiple big cat witness Samantha Hammond, by email 11 November 2014, "Puma cubs' spotted in Red Lodge during search for lost dog", *Cambridge News* November 25, 2014. I've met two other multiple Suffolk big cat witnesses and heard testimony from another, and I've found out that in Gloucestershire and Monmouthshire, the same witnesses routinely seeing big cats is not that unusual. A later *EADT* report on Suffolk Police disclosures of big cat sightings put the sighting one day later, on 12 November, and gave the location as Warren Road, a quiet main road that passes through the new-build area of Red Lodge, with strips of woodland nearby. See "Is there a panther or big cat loose in Suffolk?" *EADT,* 5 August 15.

10. Email from Sam Hammond, 9 January 2015, reporting a sighting by a friend.

11. Post by "Beaver Bob –Top Brandonian" Brandon Forums, 5 June 2014, http://forum.brandonsuffolk.com/default.asp.

12. Brandon deer-chasing sighting and Thetford jet black cat both from *Big Cats in Britain Yearbook 2007*, CFZ Press, Wolfardisworthy 2007; Thetford female lion sighting from Norfolk Police Freedom of Information Request Reference No: FOI 424/11/12, December 2011. The story goes that the European arrivals thought the pumas were lionesses and asked where the male lions were. The Native American guides, for whatever reason, told them that the male lions weren't to be seen as they lived only on mountain tops, hence "mountain lions," also known as "catamounts" – cat of the mountains. There's no way a lion could live in modern England for any length of time. They are open savannah animals, hunting in packs, not that good at hiding, and they would bring themselves to everybody's attention by eating really big prey like horses and cows. Lions on the loose in the East of England have usually been shot within a day of their escape, like the one in Cromer, Norfolk in 1984 http://scotcats.online.fr/abc/realcats/index.html

13. *Big Cats in Britain Yearbook 2007*, CFZ Press, Wolfardisworthy, 2007, reported to BCIB via Terry Dye of BCIB Cambridgeshire.

14. *Big Cats in Britain Yearbook 2008,* see immediately above.

15. "R2D2," posts to Brandon Forums 8 September 2014 and subsequently. Note his use of the authentic American English "tan" to describe the puma's colour, a made-up "sock puppet" pretending to be an American airman would have called it "brown." He also described his dog as a "Staffordshire Bull Terrier", while a British English speaker would probably describe him as a "Staffie." The encounter isn't far from where I believe the "Eden Estate" is, where deerstalking lawyer David Barrington Barnes documented multiple puma sightings, as we saw in Chapter 16.

16. Herringswell, Wrentham and Tunstall "panthers" from "Is there a panther or big cat loose in Suffolk?", *EADT* 5 August 2015, www.eadt.co.uk/news/is_there_a_panther_or_big_cat_loose_in_suffolk_1_4181532. The article quotes Suffolk Police as saying there were no big cat sightings reported in 2013 or 2014,which contradicts their own disclosure of a big cat seen in the "Clare area" in 2013, see above.

17. "The lynx effect – wild cats could be released into Thetford Forest" *EADT,* March 9, 2015; Natural England statement on their website www.gov.uk/government/news/natural-england-statement-on-the-possible-reintroduction-of-lynx; "Scheme to reintroduce lynx to Thetford Forest is dropped", Bethany Whymark, *EDP* Environment, 20 June 2016, www.edp24.co.uk/news/environment/scheme_to_reintroduce_lynx_to_thetford_forest_is_dropped_1_4583805.

18. "Escaped lynx recaptured in Devon", *Guardian,* 31 July 2016, https://www.theguardian.com/world/2016/jul/31/escaped-lynx-recaptured-devon-flaviu-dartmoor-zoo. Flaviu was captured in the twenty-fifth trap set for him by zookeepers, aided by intelligence from the Devon and Cornwall Police drone. "Simon from Ipswich" comment posted on author's blog, 29 October 2015; for more on 2021 bobcat escape in West Suffolk, see "West Suffolk bobcat escaped while being transferred to zoo, FOIA disclosure reveals", 28 July 2021, http://mattsalusbury.blogspot.com/2021/07/west-suffolk-bobcat-escaped-while-being.html.

19. "Puzzled by big cat sighting", letter to *EADT* from Tony Wheal of Starston, *EADT* 12 August 2015, with thanks to Alan Murdie and Paul Sieveking.

20. "Schoolboy comes face-to-face with huge black PANTHER when out running", *Daily Mirror*, "Weird News" section, 15 January 2016, www.mirror.co.uk/news/weird-news/schoolboy-comes-face-face-huge-7185521; "Jogger reports 'big cat sighting' in Suffolk field," Tom Potter, *EADT* 15 January 2015, www.eadt.co.uk/news/jogger_reports_big_cat_sighting_in_suffolk_field_1_4380274

A taxi driver claimed to have seen a big cat leap over the (then closed) gate at Culford School

Cropped still images from video footage of a black leopard(?) in Wortham, Suffolk, from August 2012.
They are from a colour video which is linked from https://bigcatsofsuffolk.com.
© Lee Acaster, 2012, 2021, reproduced with his kind permission.

18: Pandemic predators

I have come to the conclusion there is a parallel universe out there, superimposed on "normal" Suffolk, like all those secret places for wizards in *Harry Potter* that are there right under our noses but which we can't see.

I continue to have fleeting glimpses into this parallel-universe Suffolk, in which big cats – including one looking like a giant weasel – nonchalantly flit in and out of the county, farmers shoot leopards and bury the evidence, and in which an escaped bobcat turning up at the vet's after absconding en route to a zoo apparently isn't even a big deal.

It's early 2023 as I write this update. In the meantime, there have been a few significant big cat developments.

As I write, Suffolk and indeed most of the world is coming out of the grip of coronavirus, with England having experienced lockdowns – there have been fewer people out and about in recent times. My informant in North Suffolk told me back in the Spring of 2020, when the first Covid lockdown was young, that there had been much more big cat activity locally. This is consistent with a lot more sightings of known species of normally shy wildlife across the UK as there were then fewer people travelling and much less traffic.

There have been the usual misidentifications, some possibly fuelled by Covid cabin fever. One big cat sighting that made the news early in the lockdown, turned out to have a rather mundane explanation. A "large wildcat with big claws" spotted on the roof of a house in Cambridge in April 2020, within the first month of coronavirus lockdown, turned out be a neighbour's large ginger Maine Coon cat.[1]

One reliable-sounding report from the recent age of coronavirus lockdown that did come my way by email was from the summer of 2020, in a brief "lockdown easing" between Covid curfews. In those times more people were travelling again. One of these travellers was Sue Bradshaw. She reported how she was driving east along the A14 at around 60 mph near Bury St Edmunds, with no one about. She thinks it would have been somewhere around Rougham, which as we have seen earlier was the location of a big cat encounter sometime before 2015.

A "very large black cat" suddenly "dashed across the road in front of me. Its movement can only be described as catlike." Sue admitted that she had "failed to register exactly where it was" in relation to her car, as she was "so stunned."

Sue described the animal, which she saw for only a few seconds as it crossed the road from right to left, as muscular with a "square jaw". It had a face that from the side (she only saw it side on) was flatter than that of a domestic cat. On returning home, she searched for images for what she had seen, found images of a puma and was "convinced that is what I saw." As noted in Chapter 20, there's no apparently no such thing as black pumas, but the briefly-glimpsed silhouette of a black leopard and that of a puma are very similar.[2]

A source referred me to a volunteer in wildlife conservation (as we went to press I hadn't yet got permission to name them,) who testifies to multiple sightings of a lynx in Bradfield Woods nature reserve, near Bury, in the early 2010s.

Another source, this one in Suffolk pest control, reported seeing the footprints of a big cat, clearly "larger than a domestic cat", in mud by a riverbank near Wilby, which would be the River Dove or one of its tributaries, in the late Spring of 2020. (Wilby's a small village not far south of Stradbroke.) He was shown the footprints by a local farmer, who'd called him in because he had "a rat problem."

The farmer also showed him a video he'd filmed, which he said was footage of a black big cat in a field, filmed in daylight using a mobile phone held up against binoculars. Like much mobile phone big cat footage, though, it was a just an indistinguishable distant dark blur, although greater in size than a domestic feline. The farmer also said the same big cat had been "very active last year" (2019).

Call the bobcat fosterer

Just before the first coronavirus lockdown took hold, in March 2020, I got a tip-off from a colleague in the big cat investigator community, about a story which broke in *The Sun* "newspaper" a week later.[3]

A vet near Bury (it's safe to say "a vet near Bury" without identifying them, as in an agricultural county there are so many vets locally) took in a male bobcat. It had been shot by a "terrified" farmer, who had first sought the advice of police about whether he could shoot whatever it was that was suddenly "savaging" his chickens.

The farmer had fired a shotgun at whatever-it-was (I would guess in the dark, at night,) to scare it away. It turned out to be a bobcat and the farmer had injured it – one pellet became lodged in his right eye. The RSPCA then managed to capture the bobcat and bring it to the vet. I was shown an X-ray of the bobcat (they initially thought it was a lynx,) with the lead pellets embedded in him, a photo which I don't have permission to reproduce here. I do, however, have permission to reproduce here one of the RSPCA's photos of the bobcat with a clearly damaged pupil in its right eye, in its cage at the vet's, looking a bit like an absolutely enormous, muscular tabby cat. (See page 280.)

I was also told that the vet's assistant had by chance done their internship on a conservation project with Iberian lynxes in Spain, so treating a closely-related bobcat for its injuries was relatively straightforward for the team there.

There was initially some confusion about whether the bobcat had an owner or even a microchip (microchipping your bobcat is mandatory under the Dangerous Wild Animals Act). But it soon emerged that yes, the bobcat did have a licensed "owner in the area", who had reported him as missing.

While waiting to find out if the bobcat would be claimed, the RSPCA seems to have called up their contact who they would ring whenever there was a lynx or bobcat that needed fostering. Ownership of lynxes and bobcats in West Suffolk – whether licensed or not – may be much more common than anybody thought.

Other evidence suggests there are more lynxes than anyone realised in West Suffolk. Back in Chapter 17 we heard accounts of strange screams coming from Thetford Forest and lynx sightings locally, including one in Red Lodge. A former local resident told me that around 2005, people regularly heard such screams around Santon Downham, and there was said to be a "lynx man" locally who "everybody knew" kept captive lynxes. The Press Association's investigation from 2016 showed that at the time there were Dangerous Wild Animals Act licences for seven lynxes and two bobcats in West Suffolk.[4]

The Sun reported that West Suffolk Council had as of late March 2020 begun an investigation into how the bobcat could have got out, as part of their duty under the Dangerous Wild Animals Act. I made a Freedom of Information Act request to West Suffolk, whose FOIA

Coordinator kindly responded with some eyebrow-raising revelations.[5]

West Suffolk's disclosure came with all references to "third parties" redacted, I could only work out from the context and from a job title which correspondence was from the bobcat's owner and which was from the RSPCA. It was from this disclosure that I learnt the RSPCA had taken the bobcat to the vet and arranged for it to be rehomed. West Suffolk's Service Manager (Environmental Health) wrote to the bobcat's owner (they could trace him through his DWAL (Dangerous Wild Animals Licence). They advised the owner that the Council "have today seized... an injured bobcat belonging to you and kept under licence by you."

The bobcat's owner soon replied with an apology regarding this "unfortunate escape". (The disclosure confirmed it was the only DWA escape West Suffolk had on record.) The owner explained, in a scene reminiscent of the opening of the original 1993 *Jurassic Park* film, that "the bobcat was being homed to a zoo when the escape happened, on loading the cat, he lurched forward with force and the carrier fell, hit the floor releasing the door, in which he then escaped."

The owner went on the say that "we have been rehoming all DWAL animals and will not be renewing our licence this year." There's also correspondence between West Suffolk and another entity – possibly the bobcat's owner – asking for data on all their DWAs. From this it seems that whoever it was whose bobcat escaped near Bury was winding down their big cat keeping operation. They confirmed to West Suffolk that in the year up to May 2020 they'd offloaded two caracals, two bobcats, (plus the one that West Suffolk seized and the RSPCA rehomed), one serval and two jungle cats to at least one third party. By June 2020 the owner had confirmed that "all bobcats have been rehomed" (the Council had a list of four bobcats licensed to that individual.)

The final email in the FOIA disclosure has the owner anticipating a visit from "licensing" to check that there were no longer being kept on the premises any DWAs for which a licence would be needed.

I've also been put in touch with a new source in East Anglian wildlife conservation who told me of reports coming into a wildlife management agency I'm not yet allowed to name of two fatal shootings of big cats in 2020 in a managed forest environment. One of these described a lynx shot "out King's Lynn way" in North Norfolk and a bobcat shot in Brandon in North Suffolk, that same historic flint-knapping town near where a Brandonian reported big cat footprints in the snow back in Chapter 13. The same source tells of a father-and-soon sighting of a lynx in Thetford, convincing enough to call out a Norfolk Police wildlife crimes officer.

Clammed up

Most maddening of all is a story I have heard which I have no means of verifying. It's a very Suffolk story, taking in the *omertà*, the code of silence that shrouds the killing of wildlife in East Anglia's shooting and farming communities. And it's consistent with Chapter 18's often-repeated rumours – heard in Suffolk shooting circles and elsewhere – about something similar that is said to have happened in 1990s North Norfolk.

I was contacted by a farmer in the Dove Valley who told me that a neighbour, also a farmer, had confessed to shooting and killing a black leopard the previous winter. This neighbour was prepared to lead me to the spot where he had secretly buried the corpse of the black leopard, on the understanding he would stay anonymous and get "no comeback."

Through my go-between and informant this was all set up, assurances were given that I could travel to a spot somewhere in North Suffolk and be shown where the grave was. The only thing preventing me from driving to the location to do the deed was the ban on all but strictly necessary travel in the first (Spring 2020) Covid lockdown. I didn't greatly fancy explaining to the police at a roadside "stop and account" under coronavirus regulations why I had the rotting body of a leopard in the back.

A friendly university was on hand to receive the big cat cadaver after a long journey, ready to do a DNA test. As it had been in the ground for only a few months, there was a chance there would be enough of the soft tissue left to determine whether or not the dead big cat was microchipped. They could also tell a lot about whether it was likely born in the wild or an escapee from captivity by its teeth – there would be a lot less wear on the teeth of an animal raised in captivity. They'd ruled out being able to work out where it came from based on the isotopes in its teeth – too expensive a procedure. And then…

And then the whole thing was off. The farmer had "clammed up", my go-between told me. He "regretted" ever agreeing to show an outsider like me where he'd buried the corpse of a black leopard. Even the inducement of a grand in cash from a documentary film-maker (I can't talk about that yet) wouldn't change his mind. My contact had gone all East Anglian on me. I am left with a story of the bones of a black leopard, buried somewhere in Suffolk soil, the evidence degrading away undisturbed and undocumented. I have nothing of the body of this North Suffolk black leopard to show you, just hearsay and secondhand testimony as infuriatingly insubstantial as old wives' tales and campfire ghost stories of woodwoses and dog-headed men from the opening chapters of this book. I continue to hear rumours of other fatal shootings of big cats in East Anglia.

I also heard from James Perry, who reported to me a brief sighting of a black big cat while travelling on the A13 Thetford bypass on the edge of Thetford Forest Park (just inside Suffolk) in July 2021. The animal was black, "a little grey around the edges," the witness felt it was less like a black leopard and had features – "thick legs" and a "pronounced ruff" round its throat meant that it more closely resembled a rare melanistic lynx.[6]

Among the most recent sightings to come my way is one involving a melanistic leopard stalking and leaping at geese on a nature reserve just north of Aldeburgh, behind the beach and within sight of Maggie Hambling's iconic *Scallop* sculpture on the beach there. It was November 2021, just before dusk, so at a time when you'd expect big cats to be at their most active. Frazier Seager and his wife Ru were admiring the landscape as they walked back towards Aldeburgh, when Frazier became aware of a black shape moving close to the ground near a hedgerow about 300 yards inland.

They watched for five minutes as it pulled itself along with its belly almost touching the ground. It moved further inland, zigzagging as it went, which is typical leopard stalking behaviour. It was Alstatian-sized, jet black and definitely a cat. Then it sprang and landed with its feet together. At this point it became clear what it had been doing – it had leapt at a flock of geese, which took to the air with an enormous racket – Frazier took out his phone and tried to film it in the gloom, but all that can be seen is a pixilated black dot, with the sound of honking geese and Frazier exclaiming "Geese are going *mental*!" The black leopard then disappeared into a ditch.

In May 2022, the *Eastern Daily Press* reported a black leopard seen by the bridge over the River Alde at Bruisyard, near Woodbridge.[7]

I end this chronicle of nearly 50 years of big cat sightings with two reports that – like many that have come my way recently – detail historic sightings of big cat encounters around a decade ago. They are at the time of writing among the most recent reports to reach me. They are from two different corners of the county of Suffolk, but both featuring black leopards. With the exception of the escaped West Suffolk bobcat and another lynx (see below,) all reports reaching me in the last few years concern black leopards – I haven't heard news of Suffolk pumas since 2018. Both these sightings below are from the then-unnoticed Suffolk big cat waves of 2010 and 2012, that only now are coming to light through reports made many years later.

After a seven year search, I am pleased to include in my big cat round one a sighting that seems to be the Holy Grail of big cat sightings in Suffolk – a sighting that has produced some clear video footage of what does appear to be a black leopard.

Long body, like a house cat casually walking

But first, cab driver Mark Goodchild told me how 11 years earlier he had been out driving around 10pm, it was a on a midsummer night in July 2010 so it still wasn't completely dark. He had "upgraded headlights" fitted to his S-Class Mercedes, so he got a good view of what followed.

He was on the A1088 Walsham Road heading west towards Ixworth. He'd just come out of the S-bend at the Kiln Lane turn, into the straight stretch of road that is the approach to the A143 Ixworth roundabout.

Mark saw about 400m ahead "eyes glinting in the headlights, I thought it was a deer in the road", so he started to slow down. When he was about 50 metres from those eyes, he started to realise, "That's not a deer – it's the wrong shape, it's too long." And it had "green eyes… I saw the eyes are green." For a deer that's "the wrong colour… deers have reddy brown… or amber eyes" reflected in headlights. It wasn't moving from the road, so Mark dropped his speed to around 15 to 20 miles an hour. "It wasn't afraid of the car at all."

The animal with the green eyes was "just standing... on the other side of the road." By now Mark realised it couldn't have been a deer. Thanks to his upgraded headlights he could "see the body shape" – it was the "size of a Labrador, maybe a bit bigger, but a lot longer." Mark was "quite stunned when he realised what it was."

As Mark drove past the animal, it was level with his side window, "side on when you approached it." He glanced out to see it "within six feet… I could see the tail – close to three feet long". He described how the tail "curls up at the end – the same thickness all the way down." It had a "long body – like a house cat casually walking," its colour was "either black or very dark brown… very shiny." Mark watched the big cat for "30 seconds at least", he got "a long glimpse" of it, before it "went into some small bushes and long grass."

He then went home and looked up big cats on the internet. He looked up pictures of "panthers" (black leopards) – that was what he'd seen. He's since spoken to quite a few customers who've seen a black leopard locally. Two weeks after his August 2010 encounter, a customer from nearby Langham told him he'd found "what they could only describe as claw marks" on a post in their garden, the marks started five feet from the ground.

A friend of Mark's has since reported to him seeing his King Charles spaniel chased across a field by a "significantly larger" black big cat until the dog ran through the gate of their garden in the village of Barrow, the opposite side of Bury from where Mark had his encounter. This was in the locked-down summer of 2020. Another friend was said to have some phone footage of the same animal, while Mark has heard reports from a farmer "round Whepstead way" (south of Bury) who regularly sees a black big cat on his land very early on summer mornings.

Mark has been regularly driving up and down that stretch of the Walsham Road – where he had his big cat encounter – for 17 years. Shortly after his 2010 big cat experience, Mark noticed that while he regularly runs over rabbits in his car while driving on that stretch, he never sees any roadkill there. Often he will inadvertently run over a rabbit on the way to Walsham for a pick-up or drop-off, then drive back along the same route twenty minutes later and the dead rabbits have "gone."[8]

My God, that's a big cat!

Lee Acaster is a nature photographer, landscapes are his thing, primary woodland and coast. His stunning nature photos are on sale at www.leeacaster.com. While he doesn't describe himself as a wildlife photographer, "he's very into wildlife", he won Wildlife Photographer of the Year a decade ago. He's based in the Suffolk village of Wortham, near the southern bank of the Waveney. But he didn't have his camera with him when he had his big cat encounter back in early August 2012, which took place within sight of his back garden.

Recalling the events in 2021, Lee told how he "wandered down the end of the garden and saw a cat in the field" of wheat behind the row of houses that included his. "They'd just started harvesting… they've done (harvested) a strip of wheat… a strip round the outside of the field at some point. Beyond that is just wheat."

It was in that narrow "strip without wheat" that Lee saw a black cat. "I knew it was something unusual. I thought it was a cat at first" but "I knew it wasn't a cat or a deer or a dog… by the way it moved." He then realised "that's big – that's bigger than a cat." Lee described how "when I first saw it…. I could see it moving through the wheat… made me think there was something odd there, a normal cat wouldn't… come above the wheat." He realised "That's bigger than a cat… it was moving like a cat." It also had "big hind legs and a long, thick tail", which set it apart from a domestic cat.

At this point Lee "ran inside and grabbed my phone… trying to film it." His mobile phone footage starts with a view of the foliage at the bottom of Lee's garden as he finds a gap in it through which to film the black big cat at the far end of the neighbouring field.

Adrenalin was kicking in at that point, and Lee "didn't even remember to turn my phone the other way up" as he filmed, thinking "My God, that's a big cat!" He recalled how it "carried on slowly going through the field, it disappeared into the hedgerow… that's the last I saw of it."

Although he describes himself as "not normally one to believe in the paranormal," Lee finds big cats in that corner of Suffolk "very feasible." Of the field where he had his sighting, he says "all along there, there's rabbits and hares… any time of day there's 30, 40 rabbits along that field edge." From the way it moved, Lee thought the cat was "stalking, so basically that field is absolutely jam packed with rabbits all times of year… there's muntjac" too.

The field is close to two nature reserves, The Ling heathland and Redgrave and Lopham Fen, with small patches of woodland between these and the Waveney River – so Lee believes that if there was a big cat in the neighbourhood it would have an abundant food supply.

More recent reports of a black big cat in the neighbourhood have come to the attention of both Lee and Mark. The latter has family locally, he's heard "there's a lot going on in Botesdale and Rickinghall" by way of reported big cat activity and also around Redgrave.

In 2020 someone posted another video of a black big cat said to be at Redgrave on hyper-local online networking platform Nextdoor. It shows something black and blurry going behind some trees, it's much less clear than the Acaster video and I've not been able to trace the person who posted it. Mark notes that "you often get reports of big cats on Nextdoor" locally, "on the comments there's lots and lots of people who've seen big cats." Amid the chaos that is the posts and comments on nextdoor.co.uk, big cat investigators who can learn to filter out its parochial biases may be able to turn the platform into a useful tool for big cat reporting.

Lee also reports the discovery of evidence for a big cat kill signs, and – yes – he has photos too. He was on a nature photography field trip to Knettishall Heath nature reserve on the south bank of the River Ouse on Suffolk's border with Norfolk, near Thetford. The reserve is "quite heavily walked, not remote by any stretch," it's "part heath and part woodland". Lee's photography often takes him out before sunrise and "off the path". It was "around five or six in the morning" one day in 2020, when he glanced up into one of the trees on the reserve and saw the front half of a large male muntjac deer wedged into the space where a branch sprouted from the trunk, He estimates it was eight to ten foot up a tree.

"It was quite a big muntjac… This had been stripped… of flesh… it was stripped around the ribs… the head was kind of intact, but the throat, rib cage had all been stripped… it hadn't rotted off… it looked very much like a kill to me… fairly fresh, it wasn't rotting." Lee's heard of people in Suffolk illegally leaving out poisoned carcasses to kill birds of prey that are killing pheasants, but they probably wouldn't try it in a relatively busy nature reserve watched over by wardens. A photo of the muntjac carcass up a tree is included at the end of this chapter. It's in colour at http://bigcatsofsuffolk.com.

There is a still from Lee Acaster's 2012 footage of the black big cat at the end of the field on the front cover of this book and there are some more black and white versions of stills at the front of this chapter. Lee's 35-second footage shows the bushes and trees at the end of his garden as he seeks a vantage point to film, followed by some jerky footage – about six seconds – of a black dot moving from left to right across the "strip of wheat" in the distance. Cropped footage of just that section in the centre of the screen shows clearly a large, long-bodied, muscular black big cat walking from left to right. It climbs onto some raised grown then begins to disappear into a hedgerow. Lee admits "I thought it was a big cat, I was pretty convinced… but you can't really tell the scale."[9]

This is by far the best – the clearest – evidence for a big cat in Suffolk. What's most convincing about the Acaster video footage is the way the animal moves – it shows something too muscular and too big, too long bodied for a domestic cat. The way it jumps out over a rise in the ground is very big cat-like and convincing. So I have included with Lee's kind permission a link to the video online at http://bigcatsofsuffolk.com. It is as clear as evidence for big cats in Suffolk gets.

Last-minute lynx has the last laugh

As I put the finishing touches to this book in 2023, there is talk of re-introducing lynxes again. This time it is the island of Ireland (the Republic of Ireland and Northern Ireland) is where lynx re-introductions are under consideration, in an effort to control the population of introduced sika as they damage trees. Such proposed re-introductions are becoming part of a growing international re-wilding movement. There is also talk of re-introducing pumas to Florida, where they long ago died out (officially at least), to keep down to population of "wild hogs" (feral pigs) and mitigate the damage these cause.[10]

Our understanding of big cats in the British Isles, and in Suffolk in particular, has also been much added to by the recent publication of the four-volume *The British Big Cat Phenomenon*[11] by Jonathan McGowan, who has been spotting big cats and finding their tracks, scats (droppings), kill-signs, hairs and field signs for over 40 years. While McGowan's study area is mostly in Dorset, the circumstances of his sightings also have noticeable similarities with the many reports I'm hearing of big cats from the East of England, although he does say "I have reports from the middle of Ipswich." He notes that areas of Britain with the highest biodiversity are likely to be big cat territories. The nature reserves of Suffolk would fit the bill nicely.

There are insights in McGowan's books into the timeline of British big cat sightings. The surge in Britain's muntjac population began in the 1960s, contemporary with the first British big cat sightings. The 1980s saw a surge in big cat sightings and also saw a peak in releases of game birds – they were intended for paid-for pheasant shoots but they're also part of the big cats' diet.

Also in the 1980s, McGowan points out, work patterns changed and people were out and about in their cars late at night or very early in the morning a lot more. Deregulation, privatisation and the weakening power of trade unions in the 1980s meant people started driving across open countryside a lot a night to and from work. In earlier times there was much less nocturnal travel, usually with feebler headlights. Long commutes by car and anti-social working hours started to become common across Britain in the 1980s, which was a time when rural public transport also started to go into decline. No wonder there was a surge in sightings of big cats in that decade, given that big cats are most active at dusk and dawn.

McGowan admits that he saw a Maine Coon cat in the 1980s playing with a domestic cat that was a third of its own size and mistook it for a dog. This was before Maine Coons became well-known as pets, and it was contemporary with the "Debenham Lion"– a Suffolk big cat described by one witness as like a small lion but with tufted ears.

There are also big cats out there in the wild in Britain that don't fit the description of the know big cats, according to McGowan. There are, he says, black "running cats" that run after deer for long distances, quite unlike the short spurts that is all ambush predators like leopards and pumas are capable of. Remember the black big cat seen running after deer in Bures back in 2009, or more recently the black big cat in the Suffolk village of Barrow that chased a witnesses's King Charles spaniel across a field and all the way to the garden gate?

McGowan also attempts to answer the question, where is the big cat roadkill? Given Britain's road traffic density, big cats killed by cars would be repeatedly run over and squashed "pancake flat" in a couple of hours so as to become unrecognisable. McGowan and other witnesses have seen big cat roadkill on busy stretches of dual carriageway slip road where it's too dangerous to stop, when they return a couple of hours later there's nothing left – the corpse has been completely obliterated by being repeatedly run over. Among the possible big cat roadkill McGowan himself has encountered, there was the Blackwater Junction Black Cat – "totally pancaked out". It had been there for a long time, the skin had melted to the tarmac and its bones were all crushed.

The report of two pumas, one smaller with spotted legs in woods near Red Lodge in 2014 and another report of "two very large black big cats, one behind the other," seen together at Chippenham Hall near Fressingfield in 2015 start to make more sense in the light of the "hundreds" of reports of big cat cubs seen with their mothers that have come McGowan's way. These go back to the early 1990s and include many sightings of lynxes with their cubs in the ten years up to 2016. McGowan has seen dashcam video of a lynx cub and has seen police helicopter camera footage of a lynx and its cub from Wrangton, Devon – released through a Freedom of Information Act disclosure. McGowan's also found the footprints of big cat cubs together with those of their mothers', while he experienced his own sighting of two puma cubs playing in Dorset's Shillingstone quarry.

We will meet shortly a strange-looking, pale, almost off-white long-bodied cat filmed just over the Norfolk border in 2018. This begins to seem less strange in the context of the "pale puma" that McGowan reports as having been seen around Wimborne, Dorset. It was so pale it looked like a lion. McGowan adds that such "pale cats" have been photographed and his books include a blurry photo of a "blonde puma" similar in colour to the unusual animal filmed among the stubble of that field near Thetford Forest whose photograph appears shortly in the book you're reading.

There's also much detail in McGowan's work on variation in big cat ear shape – the big cats can have triangular, pointed ears. Malaysian leopards have the biggest ears, apparently. I am reminded of the black big cat seen by Brenda Sore near the transformer station on the edge of Peasenhall, like a black leopard but with pointed ears. I am also reminded of the black big cat like a "giant house cat" but five times the size, seen by two young anglers at Bungay's Falcon Meadow.

I leave you with one last account of a big cat seen in Suffolk, a lynx that seemed particularly unbothered at being observed by human witnesses. It's a last-minute lynx, our most recent sighting from late October 2022 – so regrettably too last-minute even to make it onto the maps at the end of this book.

Kate Sutherland emailed me to tell me she'd been travelling with others by car towards Bawdsey. They were "quite near there" (Bawdsey) "when we spotted a lynx on the drive of an isolated house. It looked exactly like the photo of the Eurasian Lynx on Wikipedia, about the size of a spaniel dog but more chunky. It had wide set eyes and ears with tufts on each ear."

The lynx "just stood on the drive and stared at us and even stayed there watching us as we reversed the car to check we had seen what we thought we had."[12]

So that's the state of play regarding big cats in the Curious County as of June 2023. I've no doubt we'll hear many more reports of them. Should you see a Suffolk big cat yourself, or its field signs, please report it to me via mysteryanimalsofsuffolk@gn.apc.org or via the link on bigcatsofsuffolk.com. Suffolk Wildlife Trust told me their wardens can come out and investigate if you contact them via www.suffolkwildlifetrust.org/contact immediately after seeing a big cat.

FOOTNOTES TO CHAPTER 18: Pandemic predators

1."'Large wildcat with big claws' spotted in central Cambridge", Ella Pengally, *Cambridge News*, 11 April 2020, www.cambridge-news.co.uk/news/cambridge-news/wildcat-spotted-cambridge-fen-tiger-18078609.

2. Email and phone interview with Sue Bradshaw, 20 January 2020.

3. "Big Cat Rampage: Bobcat goes berserk and savages farmer's chickens after escaping owner before being shot and captured", *The Sun*, 24 March 2020, www.thesun.co.uk/news/11248424/bobcat-captured-savaging-farmers-chickens/.

4. "Boar, lynxes and wild African cats among dangerous animals on private properties in region", Matt Stott, *EADT*, 23 May 2016, www.eadt.co.uk/news/wild-boar-lynxes-and-wild-african-cats-among-dangerous-animals-2269530.

5. FOIA disclosure by West Suffolk Council's FOIA Coordinator, FOI 385, 18 February 2021, https://bigcatsofsuffolk.com – "FOIA disclosures" page, also at https://mattsalusbury.blogspot.com/2021/07/west-suffolk-bobcat-escaped-while-being.html

6. Emails from James Perry, 21st and 30th October 2021.

7. "'Beast of Bruisyard' spotted minutes from Ed Sheeran's estate", *Eastern Daily Press,* 6 May 2022, https://www.edp24.co.uk.lifestyle/big-cat-sightings-in-norfolk-suffolk-894066.

8. Phone interview with Mark Goodchild, 15 June 2021.

9. Phone interview with Lee Acaster, 21 June 2021.

10. "Could reintroducing the lynx solve Ireland's sika deer problem?" Kevin O'Sullivan, *Irish Times,* 16 June 2022, www.irishtimes.com/environment/2022/06/16/could-reintroducing-the-lynx-solve-irelands-sika-deer-problem/

11. *The British Big Cat Phenomenon – Differing Theories, Eye Witness Reports, and the Predators Diet, The British Big Cat Phenomenon – Searching for Evidence and Territorial Marks, The British Big Cat phenomenon – sightings, field signs and bones, The British Big Cat Phenomenon – Environmental impact, politics, cover ups, and revelations*, all by Jonathan McGowan, Hangar 1 Publishing, North Haven, 2022.

12. Kate Sutherland, Pers. Comm. by email 27 October 2022..

The carcass of a large male muntjac found "eight to 10 feet" up a tree in Knettishall Heath nature reserve in 2020, evidence of a big cat kill? © Lee Acaster 2020

PART 3 – BIG CATS OF THE CURIOUS COUNTY

19. Big cats of the borderland

Suffolk's big cats show no consideration for county boundaries. Big cats answering the same description as those seen in North Suffolk are reported with even more frequency over the border in South Norfolk. There's the Haverhill Puma in the corner of Suffolk where it meets both Essex and Cambridgeshire, and there's a similar Beast of Balsham phenomenon in Cambridgeshire just to the west, while the predominantly Cambridgeshire-based Fen Tiger goes on the occasional jaunt into Suffolk too. The big cats of Suffolk's Stour Valley turn up south of the River Stour in Essex as well. All this would suggest the big cat phenomenon is not some peculiar madness that afflicts only Suffolk folk, but something real.

This being a book on the mystery animals of *Suffolk*, the following is a whistle-stop tour. The reports of big cat activity immediately over Suffolk's borders that come my way are even more random and anecdotal than my Suffolk data.

Cambridgeshire's got a lot of ocelot

The big cats of Cambridgeshire seem more abundant, more varied – there's a Cambridgeshire "ocelot-like" cat not reported in Suffolk – and more aggressive. Audience responses to a BBC Cambridgeshire feature on the Fen Tiger claimed a big cat had killed a greyhound in a back garden in Chatteris, while Cambridgeshire Police logged a "large wild cat" reportedly attacking domesticated cats in Great Shelford in 2010, as well as a sheep attacked by an "unknown animal, possibly a cat." Cambridgeshire Police Wildlife Officer PC Paul Carter believed that as of 2008, in his county "the majority of reports to the police come from farmers who claim they have had cattle and sheep attacked by a lynx-type feline."

As for the origins of Cambridge's big cat, they seem to go back earlier than Suffolk's. Back in 2001, one Cambridge academic described how he knew a man, a "country type" who'd talked to witnesses who'd described to him a small panther slightly larger than a Labrador, that ate rabbits, pigeons, pheasants and sometimes domestic cats. Apparently, this animal had been roaming the countryside around Cambridge since the early 1960s.

The first recorded sighting of what came to be known as the Fen Tiger was in Cottenham, Cambridgeshire (20 miles west of Brandon) in 1982. There was even a video of it shot by William Rooker of the British Big Cats Society, which shows a skinny black puma-like animal with long, thin legs. Cambridgeshire's big cats seem to be caught on camera more often than Suffolk's. There's also footage of a black big cat on a wall at Girton, Cambridgeshire. A couple of blurry photos of a black cat with pointed ears – it's hard to tell if it's a domestic cat or not – came the way of Big Cats in Britain in 2008 from Gamlingay, near the Bedfordshire end of the county.

Sightings of the Fen Tiger seemed to die down after the Cottenham encounter, but were being reported in the same area again from 1994, and there have been "numerous" sightings of the Fen Tiger since then. Big Cats in Britain recorded a Cottenham encounter in 2008 with something "dark coloured, with a tail hanging down and curling up" which "moved like a domestic cat" and had "cat-like features."

Other notable Cambridgeshire big cats include the sandy-coloured puma seen running at near the A14 at Fen Ditton and the big cat "the size of a Labrador" seen in Haslingfield, West of Cambridge in 2008. In the same year, there was also the "large mystery feline" reported to the *Cambridgeshire Evening News* after an encounter on the A14 at Elsworth, also West of Cambridge, as well as a "ginger" big cat, two feet high, five feet long including a two foot tail" observed for a few minutes at Coln.[1]

Whatever it was seemed to move south and deeper into Cambridgeshire, away from the Suffolk border in the early years of the twenty-first century, and then back up to the Fens towards Suffolk around 2008.

Various readers of a BBC Cambridgeshire Fen Tiger round-up in 2008 reported seeing a "dark tabby" 80cm-high (just over two feet high) big cat "like an ocelot... with a very long thick tail and small feline head," and something that left prints near Manea station, while the *Cambridge Times* printed photos of "large, cat-like prints found in Chatteris" on 31 March 2008. Another "ocelot-like animal" was the one seen between Histon and Waterbeach and reported to the *Cambridge Evening News* by Cambridge University cleaner Vernon Whiterod.

Cambridgeshire Police disclosed some big cat data at the beginning of 2014, revealing eight calls about "large cat" from the public in the previous year, including an unconfirmed report of a "panther seen in a back garden" in Friday Bridge near Wisbech. Police had also logged a "very large wild cat... possibly a lynx" at Little Eversden in 2010, and in the same year a "big black cat who walked across the road" at Comberton near Cambridge and a "heavily mauled deer carcass" found in Melbourn.

Cambridgeshire, like Suffolk, had its double big cat sightings, with the police disclosure logging a call by a cyclist who claimed in 2012 to have seen two large black "panther-like creatures in the snow." There was also a black panther sighting on a country road near Shepreth, down the road from Shepreth Wildlife Park, which keeps captive big cats. The park sent out its own investigators after a string of local sightings, and set up cameras locally, but these recorded nothing.

On New Year's Eve 2021 a report came to me via email of a sighting of a "sandy-tan" big cat with a tail "about the same length of its body," seen by David Wilsham and colleague who were the crew of a supermarket delivery truck driving through scrub just outside Isleham, Cambridgeshire. David was the co-pilot and his colleague, who also saw the animal, was driving. As we have seen already in Chapter 17, Isleham is just a seven-minute drive from Suffolk. David was "fairly confident it was a puma." This would make it the first East Anglian puma report I've received since 2017.

The county also has more zoos with big cats than Suffolk's only wildlife park at Kessingland, and there has been the odd Cambridgeshire big cat escape or false alarm, although none of these would account for the big cats seen in East Anglia. In 2014, a visitor set off the "code red" big cat alarm indicating one of the pumas or tigers had escaped at Cambridgeshire's Shepreth Wildlife Park during a kids' Easter egg hunt. Staff ushered visitors indoors while they went to check on the tigers and pumas, all of which were quickly accounted for.

And at Hamerton Zoo, over on the opposite side of Cambridgeshire, Akea the cheetah escaped in October 2008, due to a faulty electric fence. He wandered into a garden in the nearby village, ate the tyre of a children's bike there and sank its teeth into its saddle before zoo staff arrived. Akea was "completely tame", the keepers put a harness on him with ease and kept him in the villager's stable until a crate arrived in which they could take him back to the zoo.[2]

PART 3 – BIG CATS OF THE CURIOUS COUNTY

The Norfolk Gnasher

Norfolk can outdo the double big cat sightings of Suffolk and Cambridgeshire, with a sighting of *three* "jaguar-like" big black glossy cats the height of Alsatians observed near Norwich Airport, quite a long way from the Suffolk border, by an informant of Big Cats in Britain.[3]

Like Norfolk's hyter-sprite fairies and its cow-sized cyclopean or headless versions of Black Shuck, some of which make their appearance disgorged from an enormous fish, Norfolk big cats are scarier and more numerous than Suffolk's, with an older pedigree. Janet and Colin Bord in *Alien Animals* traced reports of big cats coming from Norfolk as early as 1964. Hevingham near Aylsham is supposed to have become a Norfolk big cat hotspot since 2006.

The "Norfolk Gnasher" as it has become known, is supposed to have eaten at least one swan. And in August 2006 in Burston, just a few miles over the Suffolk border and beyond Diss, an anonymous witness reported a "large cat, tawny brown colour" which he thought was trying to kill his own domestic cat in his garden. The much bigger tawny brown cat was "fast" but not as agile as his own moggy, who presumably got away.

The Norfolk Gnasher has a higher profile than the lesser-known Suffolk big cats, thanks to the efforts of among others Keith Simpson, from 2010 to 2019 MP for Broadland, the Norfolk constituency immediately north of Suffolk. Simpson has raised titters in the "Westminster Village" for his repeated Parliamentary Questions about the Norfolk Gnasher, with some less imaginative MPs jokingly asking Simpson if his big cat was in fact in Westminster.

Simpson was alarmed by Norfolk Police figures from 1997, which showed they'd received over 50 reports of big cat activity in the county. According to the *Independent,* Simpson told the House of Commons that one Norfolk farmer found a half-eaten lamb half way up one of his trees, and that others have suffered attacks on chickens and even a horse. Carrying prey up trees to eat in peace is a trait of big cats, leopards in particular, although goshawks and some of the eagles that occasionally visit East Anglia (See Chapter 12) could also carry off most of a lamb into in their talons.

Norfolk Police received a report from Diss in 2006 from an informant who "believes the sheep may have been bitten/clawed by the 'Norfolk puma'", while two years later, in the Saxlingham Nethergate area (way up north in North Norfolk) a caller to the police described some kind of puma hybrid that was attacking a duck. A decade later, an animal described as "the infamous Norfolk panther" was back in Saxlingham Nethergate, photographed roaming a freshly harvested local field. My first impression of the photos, said to be of a "Labrador-sized" cat with short legs and low to the ground, is it more resembles a huge domestic cat than a black leopard, and that it's hard from the photos to gauge the scale.

The Norfolk Gnasher seems to have a brazen disregard for police efforts to track it, showing up in Martineau Lane, Norwich, close to the Norfolk Police headquarters in February 2013. As we have seen, the Beccles Lynx was in fact from Norfolk. And there are lions and even a tiger reported in Norfolk, which suggests either that the big cat fauna of Suffolk's northern neighbour really is more exotic or that Norfolk folk aren't good at big cat identification. One caller to Norfolk Police described "what looked like a lion or tiger walking in the road" in Attleborough in 2008, while a lion was seen in Toftwood in 2006 by someone who called the police. As we saw earlier, a "female lion" (probably a misidentified puma) was reported to police in Thetford, Norfolk in 2007. To complicate matters still further, Defra records that a lion *was* shot around Cromer in Norfolk in January 1984, a day after its escape from captivity.

Norfolk, like Suffolk, has had at least one of those maddening cases of a dead big cat seen but not recovered. A caller to Norfolk Police in 2006 said he'd seen in Acle, by the A47 road, "a dead puma at the side of the road on the grass verge."[4]

Late one night in the early days of 2007, on the edge of Geldeston, (Norfolk) a "very dark, jet black" animal woke up a resident when it triggered a motion-sensitive security light in his garden. The witness (he didn't give his name) saw through his window, illuminated by his security light, something "a similar shape to a domestic cat, much larger and significantly longer in proportion." It had a "muscular, long bushy tail" but he "didn't notice the shape of its ears." It was seen sniffing at something fifty feet away from the window, before it finally walked away down the drive.[5]

Having been on BBC Radio Suffolk three times talking about big cats, by 2019 I had become one of the default go-to people for big cat reports in East Anglia as well as just Suffolk, I was contacted by an informant in North Norfolk, who told me that she and her family had between them three "actual sightings" of big cats locally, in Felthorpe, Whitwell, Frettenham and the Blickling Estate. In one of these encounters, "my son had a fright in some woods near to where he was working" and heard noises. After listening to audio files of big cats sounds, he is "convinced he heard a leopard." And "he saw something big running through the trees and a lot of crashing and banging, he thought it was deer at first but then he saw something black and velvety." His photo of it was the usual "dark mass" that lower-resolution mobile phones capture. My source said she'd heard talk of a black leopard "in Frettenham back in the mid-90s" and "rumours went around that it had been shot by someone". I've since heard the same rumour – a black leopard shot dead in North Norfolk – from other sources in the Suffolk pheasant shooting fraternity.

My Frettenham informant's husband also saw a big cat on a country lane near Whitwell Hall from his Land Rover, "a cat in the road licking itself like a domestic cat… it casually got up and slunk off into the hedge… its size took up the width of the road." The same North Norfolk source mentioned getting a call from a friend in a state of excitement in September 2015 who'd just had "a black leopard cross his path."

Norfolk resident Mr S. Braden told me in October 2017 that his wife had just seen a "black or brown" big cat on Track 61, one of the forest paths at the northern edge of the bit of Thetford Forest that's in Norfolk. He added that he'd seen it himself in the area "at dawn a year ago."[6]

I have more concrete evidence of something odd, even by the standards of mystery animals, from just over the Norfolk border. Whatever-it-is likely roams into the county of Suffolk too.

"Are you the one that's into big cats?" That was the call I got in October 2018. Our caller identified himself as Russell Green. He'd just been out with his partner inspecting land he owned late on the previous sunny October afternoon, he'd driven across his field and got out of the car to walk around. The field had just been harvested, there was stubble. We agreed to be coy about exactly where it was, this being East Anglia – let's just say it was somewhere a very short distance over the border with Norfolk, so just inside Nelson's County (as Norfolk likes to call itself), near the eastern boundary of Thetford Forest and close to the forest's edge.

At the far edge of a field, Russell spotted something odd. He sent me a 46-second video that he shot. It shows something cat-like in the distance, walking slowly across the field past a fence behind it with a lot of foliage around. The animal appears to have a thick fur, a small head, a very long body, and a bushy tail. What's unusual is its colour – it has a cream, off-white colouration. It keeps to the field's edge and walks with its body low to the ground. Its legs appear relatively short, although it's hard to be certain of this as it was in stubble about 30cm (a foot) high.

The animal is filmed on the zoom function of a mobile phone, so it's blurry and pixilated. Russell can be heard crunching around in the stubble, his partner says something inaudible and he calls for her repeatedly to "Get the car! Get the car! Quick!" Why? "I want to drive over to it!" Russell then walks across the stubble towards the animal, which pauses a couple of times and seems to turn its body towards the camera before proceeding in its strange, low-to-the-ground, flowing walk. With the author's permission I've parked the footage at https://youtu.be/BHeELKLbezc and it's linked from my own website bigcatsofsuffolk.com.

I thought, based on the fence posts, it wasn't all that big, but I defer to big cat investigator Rick Minter, who has much experience than me in these matters. He believes, based on the scale of the fence, it's getting on for puma-sized.

Russell kindly returned to the location two days later, shooting for me footage of the fence and the hedge with one of the trees that was part of it, which you can clearly see in his earlier video in the background behind the animal as moves across the field. He filmed a "massive" tree and took in the distinctive "cross fence post", a row of which is clearly visible in the footage of a big cat, or whatever-it-is. He comments that the top of the fence post comes up to just below "my neck, and I'm 5ft 11 (1.8m)." It's this careful comparison of the features in the background that lead myself and others to conclude we're dealing with a big animal.

Russell's follow-up video from the field's edge also shows a large patch of long grass at the edge of the field by the posts that has been flattened, as if something big had recently laid down in it. The video's at https://youtu.be/98Yj2BJP6l4 and also linked from bigcatsofsuffolk.com.

Possible identifications for the big cat Russell filmed include a puma. Although it's an unusual colour for a puma, it's possible that it's not cream coloured at all, the colouration is a trick of that spectacular early evening autumnal East of England sky, with that wonderful East of England light turning golden pink before sunset. So what we're looking at could actually be an albino animal, or even a pale grey one.

So odd is the animal in the field that it's not even clear whether the video shows a feline – it looks more like an enormous weasel or otter in shape. Its odd dimensions reminded me of a jaguarundi, *(Herpailurus yagouaroundi)* a South American species of wildcat with a very elongated body, short, rounded ears and a narrow, flat head ending in a pointed face. So unlike other cats is the jaguarundi that at the time of writing its Wikipedia page states, "jaguarundi shows several features seen in mustelids such as otters and weasels", while one of the nicknames given to the jaguarundi is "the otter cat".

Two jaguarundis whose owners lived in West Suffolk and had Dangerous Wild Animals Act licences showed up response to the Press Association's 2016 FOIA request to councils. So we know that as of a few years ago, jaguarundis were being kept in captivity in the area.

There are, however, two factors working against our strange-looking feline in a field of stubble being a jaguarundi. Firstly, it's probably way too big. Jaguarundis vary in size from not much bigger than a domestic cat to twice that size. Whatever is in the footage in the field is apparently much bigger.

Secondly, there's its colour. Jaguarundis are usually either red or grey. The two colour "morphs" of jaguarundis were once thought to be a separate species. Cream coloured off-white jaguarundis are unknown. They are, though, very shy and elusive jungle animals and we know little about their lives in the wild, so there may be rarer colours of jaguarundi out there, or bigger jaguarundis that those already documented. How bigger, different coloured jaguarundis would end up on the Norfolk-Suffolk border, though, is another matter.

Also, the luxurious, thick fur of our mystery elongated weasel-like cat doesn't match the short, wiry hair of a jaguarundi. The fur and colouration are closer to Norwegian forest cat, This is a particularly large breed of domestic cat that comes in a variety of colours including a "bi-coloured" black and white version. Black and white Norwegian forest cats that are mostly white are common amongst the breed. Norwegian forest cats do have thick fur and bushy tails, but they're also known for their long legs and pointed, often tufted ears. They don't have the long body of that odd feline from just over the Norfolk border. Could whatever-it-is from just over the Norfolk border be some kind of hybrid that's bigger and weirder? Unlikely. It's thought that jaguarundis may be too distantly related to domestic cats to produce offspring with them. Claims to have bred jaguarundi/domestic cat hybrids have never been confirmed.

The weaselly, otter-like look of the animal in the footage recalls another, much more bizarre phenomenon. Christopher Josiffe, author of *Gef! The Strange Tale of an Extra-special Mongoose*, was among those who noted the resemblance of a still from the footage of whatever-it-was in that field somewhere near Thetford to the poltergeist-like entity that terrorised the Irving family at their farm in the Isle of Man in the early 1930s. It became known as Gef the Talking Mongoose.

Gef was the subject of study by psychic investigator Harry Price (who suspected a hoax) and psychologist Nandor Fodor (who didn't believe Gef was a deliberate deception) and others. Gef left dog-like footprints and shed some hairs, fleeting glimpses of him were seen, with Gef described as a small animal with a bushy tail and long eyelashes. He was said to hunt and kill rabbits and there are a couple of photos of an indistinct bundle of fur perched on top of a gate that were said to be of Gef. The disembodied voice of Gef described himself variously as The Eighth Wonder of the World and as "a ghost in the form of a weasel".[7]

Having seen the footage, Adrian Read contacted me to say he thought the animal was an albino fox, although the head is probably too small for a fox. Russell said he'd seen an albino fox locally, but it looked completely different.

I tried to interest the media in the footage of the strange otter cat walking in that field, but to no avail. It became clear why – I tried to get their attention the day after several national newspapers had fallen for a story about a big cat seen on a housing estate in Hertfordshire. This quickly turned out to be a prank on a local community Facebook group that got out of hand. The poster of the joke about a big cat seen on their estate was horrified at the ease with which the "dailies" and other well-known news outlets had fallen for it. Having been burned, the media were staying well away from big cat reports for the rest of the week.

I have been sent convincing photos of possible big cat predation on the carcass of a roe deer that had been shot in the Norfolk end of Thetford Forest during deer cull of 2020. By the time the deerstalkers got to it there were fresh bite marks on its legs and puncture marks that had broken its skull. It had been dragged by something, leaving clear marks in the grass. A local landowner my source talked to said he'd seen a "puma-like cat" in the area several times, "about ten or fifteen years ago", which would have been somewhere between 2005 and 2010.

My informant also told me that a sighting by a father and son in Thetford in 2020 led to a Norfolk Police Wildlife Crimes Officer callout. The Diss Community Noticeboard Facebook page had a discussion on a "lynx" seen in the Norfolk town of Diss in July of the same year.

PART 3 – BIG CATS OF THE CURIOUS COUNTY

Essex exotics

We've already met the St Osyth Lion, a flap involving 20 police officers, marksmen and helicopters around St Osyth, north east Essex, after a local caller misidentified ginger Maine Coon cat "Teddy Bear" as a lion. For a brief period in 2012, the St Osyth Lion was bigger on social media in Britain than the then recent death of first man on the moon, Neil Armstrong.

An Essex big cat was seen in 2009 "slinking around" right next to the Essex Police station in Wivenhoe, by a police officer. The big cat got very close to him, triggering a police hunt for an animal described by Essex Police's Wildlife Crimes Officer Sergeant Lou Middleton as the "Black Beast of Essex". The hunt lasted several hours and found nothing.

There has been much by way of North Essex big cat activity nearer the Suffolk border. In the town of Halstead – not far from Sudbury – there were two sightings in 2008, one in a spinny at the end of a garden, next to a graveyard which muntjac pass through. The cat was "considerably bigger than a domestic cat" and black with a patch on its left side, with a "long, thick tail." And in Halstead's North End, a big cat crossing the road jumped and brushed against the exhaust of a passing motorcycle, according to the motorcyclist. A Ryanair pilot spotted a "black panther-like" animal on the B1383 travelling north from Stansted Airport towards Saffron Walden, one night in the same year. In November of 2008, another witness saw a "jet black cat with rounded ears" in woodland near the airport.

Neil Meads of UK Big Cats claimed to have found evidence for Essex big cats in field trips in the area around his home in Bishop's Stortford (it's on the Essex-Hertfordshire border, not far from Haverhill in Suffolk,) between 2000 and 2002. Closer to Suffolk, train conductor Ian Edge, working on the Sunshine Coast Line linking Colchester to Walton-on-the-Naze, spotted a "huge, jet-black" cat by Kirby Cross train station, near Frinton-on-Sea, early one September morning in 2009. From a train window he saw it in a field, "swishing" its tail. In the summer of 2005 there were sightings of a puma-like creature near the Essex ferry port of Harwich – at the mouth of the Stour Estuary opposite Felixstowe – and at nearby Jaywick, a dilapidated holiday village with the distinction of being officially one of the most deprived areas in England.

An email from Essex Police FOIA Officer Steve Grayton of September 2012 in response a Freedom of Information Act request admitted that "Essex Police does not record the information requested centrally and as Essex Police do not hold all of this as recorded information in the form of a single detailed breakdown, to provide a detailed breakdown such as you describe would qualify as the creation of new information which the Act does not require." Grayton also cited the costs involved in complying with such a request. So it seems that unlike Suffolk's tiny constabulary, Essex Police doesn't even have any figures for the number of calls it gets from the public about big cats.

A black Essex "alien big cat" was filmed in Hallingbury (near Bishop's Stortford) in March 2015, while a "black panther" was spotted in Finchingfield, Essex near the local Equestrian Centre on 1 August in the same year. Essex Police told the *Haverhill Echo* at the time they hadn't received any big cat reports. Linton Zoo in nearby Cambridgeshire said all their melanistic leopards were accounted for, while they would expect "more obvious signs like carcasses" if there were a black leopard on the loose."[8]

Leaving aside regional curiosities like the Cambridgeshire ocelot-like cat, the distances big cats routinely travel in the wild mean it's likely that some of the big cats being reported in the counties neighbouring Suffolk are the very same individuals that Suffolk people encounter in the Curious County itself.[9]

A cropped still from mobile phone footage (above) showing a strange cat-like animal walking on the edge of a field, just over the Norfolk border near Thetford Forest, with a blown-up screenshot showing a close-up of the animal (below). © Russell Green. See bigcatsofsuffolk.com for the video.

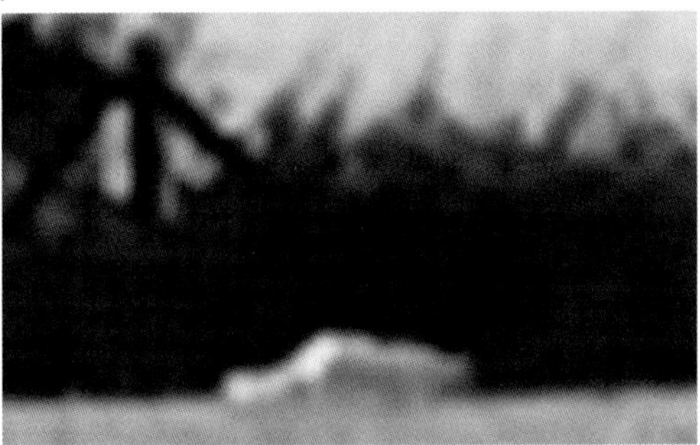

A jaguarundi, also known as the "otter-cat" (below). This one's at Prague Zoo. Photo: Bodlina~commonswiki, Creative Commons Licence.

PART 3 – BIG CATS OF THE CURIOUS COUNTY

FOOTNOTES TO CHAPTER 19: Big cats of the borderland

1. 1960s Cambridge Tiger from "The Wolf of Gubbio and the Cambridge Tiger", *Proceedings of the 15th International Congress for Analytical Psychology*, British Association of Psychotherapy (Jungian), Cambridge 2001; Cottenham sightings www.bbc.co.uk/cambridgeshire/content/articles/2008/04/02/big_cat_history_feature.shtml (BBC Cambridgeshire) Gamlingay, Coln, Elsworth, Haslingfield sightings from *Big Cats in Britain Yearbook 2008,* CFZ Publications, Wolfardisworthy 2009*;* for the Beast of Balsham see www.haverhillecho.co.uk/news/latest-news/hunting-for-signs-of-the-beast-of-balsham-1-452812)

2. Cambridgeshire Police FOIA disclosures "Lost cocker spaniels, ET, ghosts, zombies and misuse of police sirens...", *EDP*, 5 January 2014, www.edp24.co.uk/news/lost_cocker_spaniels_et_ghosts_zombies_and_misuse_of_police_sirens_are_all_part_of_a_cambs_policeman_s_lot_1_3177257 and "Has mysterious 'Fen Tiger' been seen in your area?", *Cambridge News*, 2 January 2014, www.cambridge-news.co.uk/mysteriousFen-Tiger-seen-area-Official-data-sightings-Cambridgeshire-released-police/story-22365969-detail/story.html#ixzz3Md3fAC2v; Fen Ditton sandy cat from *Big Cats in Britain Yearbook 2007;* "Shepreth Wildlife Park visitors fear they're on the menu rather than Easter eggs as tiger escape alarm set off", *Cambridge News* 20 April 2014, www.cambridge-news.co.uk/slideshow-Shepreth-Wildlife-Park-visitors-fear-theyre-menu-Easter-eggs-tiger-escape-alarm-set/story-22367546-detail/story.html#ixzz3Md1PJEJ7;"Mummy, there's a cheetah in the garden and it's eating my bike", *Independent,* 30 October 2008. Cheetahs are particularly easy to tame.

3. Norwich Airport triple sighting from *Big Cats in Britain Yearbook 2006,* CFZ Publications, Wolfardisworthy 2007.

4. *Alien Animals,* Janet and Colin Bord, Paul Elek, 1980. p. 50; Norfolk Gnasher eats swan from *Mysterious Creatures: A Guide to Cryptozoology – Volume 1*, George Eberhart, CFZ Publications, Wolfardisworthy 2014; Burston sighting from "Dogwalker sees 'Big Cat' prowling", *Diss Express* 27 October 2006; Keith Simpson MP from "Politics: Questions about the Norfolk Gnasher bring out the beasts in Westminster," *The Independent,* 3 December 1997; www.independent.co.uk/news/politics-questions-about-the-norfolk-gnasher-bring-out-the-beasts-in-westminster-1286556.html – Simpson's efforts to publicise the Norfolk Gnasher problem were assisted by Tony Bone, a former policeman who runs the Farmwatch organisation; Norfolk Constabulary Freedom of Information Request FOI 424/11/12, December 2011. "Is this the infamous Norfolk panther prowling near Saxlingham Nethergate?" *EDP,* 27 August 2016, http://www.edp24.co.uk/news/is_this_the_infamous_norfolk_panther_prowling_near_saxlingham_nethergate_1_4673316 Norfolk Gnasher near Norfolk Police HQ in "Police appeal after 'panther' sighting in Norwich, *Eastern Daily Press*, February 28 2013 www.edp24.co.uk/news/crime/police_appeal_after_panther_sighting_in_norwich_1_1960447; 1984 Norfolk lion shooting from *Reports received by Defra of escapes of non-native cats in the UK 1975 to present day.* There was a Cromer Zoo with at least one at the time of the 1984 lion shooting. It later closed. The current wildlife park in the Cromer area is no relation.

5. North Norfolk big cat reports by email to my website on 22 November 2015, anonymity requested. Mr S Braden's report of Thetford Forest sightings by email, 12 October 2015.

6. Geldeston big cat from BCIB Yearbook 2007, CF Publications, Woolsery 2008.

7. Emails and videos of the unusual long-bodied Norfolk border cat from Russell Green, 21 September 2018 and subsequently, used with his kind permission. "Know your cats – Jaguarundi, the otter cat". https://www.knowyourcat.info/lib/jaguarundi.htm; Dangerous Wild Animals Act licences for jauguarundi in West Suffolk from "Boar, lynxes and wild African cats among dangerous animals on private properties in region", Matt Stott, *EADT*, 23 May 2016, www.eadt.co.uk/news/wild-boar-lynxes-and-wild-african-cats-among-dangerous-animals-2269530; jaguarundi hybridisation from "Domestic x geoffroy's cat, jaguarundi, fishing cat hybrids", Sarah Hartwell, Messy Beast website, http://messybeast.com/small-hybrids/geoffroy-jaguarundi-hybrids.htm; website of *Gef! The Strange Tale of an Extra-special Mongoose*, https://gefmongoose.co.uk/.

8. "Big cats still stalk Britain," Paul Sieveking, *Fortean Times,* **FT344;20,** September 2016; "Public reassured after big cat sighting", Josh Thomas, *Haverhill Echo*, 7 August 2015, www.haverhillecho.co.uk/news/latest-news/public-reassured-after-big-cat-sighting-1-6891799#ixzz3z7AUDBMW.

9. Bishops Stortford field trips www.ukbigcats.co.uk/ourdiaryentry.asp?fieldtripvalue=13; Wivenhoe "black beast of Essex" hunt *Daily Star* 29 January 2009 www.dailystar.co.uk/news/latest-news/67620/Copper-is-attacked-by-big-cat; St Osyth lion *EADT* 20 September 2012 www.eadt.co.uk/home/the_st_osyth_big_cat_sighting_getting_your_lions_crossed_1_1500406; all 2008 sightings from *Big Cats in Britain Yearbook 2008;* Kirby Cross sighting from *Harwich and Manningtree Standard* 21 September 2009, http://www.harwichandmanningtreestandard.co.uk/news/4640513.Essex_Beast_spotted_again/; Harwich and Jaywick 2005 puma-like animal sightings *Harwich and Manningtree Standard* 21 June 2005, www.harwichandmanningtreestandard.co.uk/archive/2005/06/21/5422962.North_Essex__Increase_in_number_of_Beast_sightings

Tools of the trade: the author's cut-outs of a conjectural serval-type big cat (top) and a "domestic" (above), with a one-metre red and white painted "ranging pole" for scale. These cut-outs were used to investigate footage of a cat caught on CCTV footage in North Suffolk and to determine the animal's size.

20. Mutant mystery moggy misidentifications

I am of course aware of the possibility that I'm the victim of a massive leg-pulling operation. It is theoretically possible that all the many witnesses I talked to by email, phone or in person are engaged in some elaborate Suffolk prank on a city boy from London, based on some kind of impenetrable East Anglian humour that I'm too stupid to get.

I doubt it, though. I did leave out of this book a couple of accounts of a Suffolk big cat whose credibility I questioned, simply because the witness's story about who had seen it had changed – in one version they'd seen it themselves, in another a neighbour had, and the decade in which it had happened always seemed to vary each time I checked with them.

All my witnesses were frank about which details they didn't get much of a look at in an encounter that was over so quickly. Some readily admitted, without prompting, that they didn't get to see the cat's ears from that distance, they couldn't really gauge its size, or that it was all too much of a blur to note whether the big cat's tail looped down and then up again like a leopard's, whether it was thick at the end or tapered, and so on.

There is also the theoretical likelihood that all the many witnesses who contacted the East Anglian media or big cat investigator groups were having a laugh as well, that their descriptions of being "shaken" or "scared" by the encounters are all made up.

I have carefully checked the dates of all newspaper reports on big cats in Suffolk to see if there are any April Fools. There are none dated to around 1 April.

Other supporting evidence is the degree of consistency in accounts – people with no knowledge of other sightings in the same area report the same kind of big cats, from the North Suffolk black leopard cluster to the sandy or golden pumas of West Suffolk to the hard-to-identify "puma or lynx-like" Haverhill Puma and the lynx-like cats in a coastal corridor from Wrentham down to Dunwich Forest and the persistent historical reports – which I received years later – of a black leopard passing through East Suffolk in 2010 and again in 2012.

We have already heard of incidents of the Hebridean sheep that graze the Battle Area in Thetford Forest "getting out and being mistaken for something other than what they are." PC Paul Carter, Cambridgeshire Police Wildlife Officer, had been on the Fen Tiger's case for four years already in 2008 when he told the *Newmarket Journal* that "As most sightings occur after dark, it is possible that peoples' minds can play tricks on them," which was charitable and diplomatic of him. There are of course plenty of opportunities for honest misidentification, and for some rather crude and possibly inadvertent hoaxes.[1]

Panic on the streets of Sudbury

In the centre of the South Suffolk town of Sudbury, in the corner of the car park round the back of the bus station, easy to miss, is a tiny park called Siam Gardens. It's smaller than some Sudbury resident's own gardens. Sudbury Town Council's wardens in their hi-viz vests mostly deal with abandoned vehicles, littering, fly tipping, graffiti, dogs fouling pavements and vandalism. But community warden Bradley Smith got a call in February 2012 to tell him there was "a tiger on the loose" in Siam Gardens. He told the *Suffolk Free Press* that "We normally get calls about dogs on the loose, but never tigers." Suspecting "this must be a wind up", Bradley and his colleague Nathan Mitchell investigated. There in Siam Gardens was a tiger hiding behind a tree.

It quickly turned out that it was a tiger of "the large cuddly toy species." With the obligatory posed photograph of the two wardens crouching next to the large, realistic soft toy tiger in Siam Gardens (every day is a slow news day in Suffolk), the soft toy tiger was taken to the *Suffolk Free Press* offices for safe-keeping. A reader rang up and offered to take it off their hands in exchange for a £20 donation to the newspaper's favoured charity, so the Sudbury Tiger has gone to a good home.[2]

The Trimley Tiger

A year later, there was another Suffolk tiger sighting, this time it was a "Big cat spotted in Trimley St Martin!" according to the *Evening Star*. The tiger was spotted lounging on the roof of a property on the corner of Howlett Way and High Road where it could be seen "for miles around," watching over the "great grasslands of the Trimleys." (These are the villages of Trimley St Martin and Trimley St Mary, suburbs on the edge of Felixstowe. Their churches are at opposite ends of the same car park, so close to each other they share a graveyard.)

The effect of the tiger lounging on the roof was to make some motorists and passers-by "rub their eyes and look twice" before realising it was another soft toy tiger, albeit a rather realistic one, "of the type won accidentally at fairground stalls" as the *Star* succinctly put it. One of the workers renovating the house readily confessed to having found the soft toy inside the property and to have placed it on the roof "for a laugh," occasionally going up on the roof to change the tiger's position to add to the realism.[3]

There is a serious side to all this. In 2006, The British Big Cats Society's Danny Bampling, said that he thought maybe a third of East Anglia big cat sightings were "too vague" or "mistaken", citing several examples of high-profile recent big cat photos in the press which he was convinced were actually large, realistic soft toy black panthers. Such was the sudden proliferation of very convincing cuddly soft toy big cats that he expressed doubts at the time about the Beccles Lynx, and whether the photo of its corpse could have been a hoax – wrongly, as it turned out.[4]

A much stranger big cat misidentification story comes to us secondhand from Laxfield, via a source I agreed not to name. "My friend was out lamping at night with his gamekeeper and saw a dark shape hunkered down in one field. Looking at it through the rifle scope the gamekeeper swore that it was a big black cat and wanted to shoot it. My friend wouldn't let him shoot and they drove closer and closer, with the gamekeeper swearing more and more it was a big black cat, the closer they got! Well, when they were only a few feet away, this 'black cat' jumped up and turned into a nighthawker" – a clandestine detectorist out metal-detecting without the landowner's permission – "who promptly threw his detector... at the farmer, shouted 'Keep it' and ran off without a backward glance."

Evidence of big cat predation is also notoriously difficult to pin down. In parts of Suffolk, goshawks or red kites could have killed and mauled prey the size of a fox and downwards.

There was a wave of attacks on fishponds in gardens in Felixstowe in 2008 by a "mystery killer". In February of that year, Felixstowe resident Graham Cook lost all his fish in a single night, while Martin Downes of Ferry Road in Old Felixstowe had over 350 fish stripped from his pond in the space of fortnight, including 40 koi and golden carp found dead and "littered around the edge of the pond... all dead and mutilated, with chunks bitten out of them" in just one night. This closely followed a series of attacks over five nights on the pond of Mr Cook of Marcus Road, who reported that "50 fish went in all, some over 20 years old and weighing six pounds-plus." An estimated £2,500 of damage was inflicted in the Felixstowe fishpond carnage that winter, with the perpetrators evading capture. It turned out the "mystery killers" were... mink.[5]

Yes, it is a quite a funny story

Steven Johnson, director of the Cliff House campsite and holiday park in Dunwich, a short walk up the beach from Dunwich Heath NT where the black leopard was spotted in 2008, dated the campsite's own big cat furore to late 2004. "Yes, it is quite a funny story," Steven told me.

At the time, some contractors were building some new chalets by the campsite's pond, and were laying concrete pads as bases. There was, said Steven, "great excitement, the contractors said they saw a cat – a big cat – black. They said it was black." Then there was a big paw print that had appeared overnight, set in the drying concrete, "a nice clear one."

Steven has a flair for public relations. He made the national press with the true story of Daisy the dachshund finding a bone on the nearby beach, under the cliffs of Cliff House. It turned out to be a fossilised mammoth bone. "Daisy the dog finds a mammoth bone on the beach", ran the headline above the *Daily Telegraph's* picture story. His first thought on being shown the big cat footprint in Cliff House concrete was, "Great advertising!"

One of the big cat investigation groups – over a decade later, Steven couldn't remember which one – was sent a photo of the "nice clear" print. "They were so excited, they sent someone along. He was very convinced it was the print of a big cat. He made a plaster cast... sent it to the Natural History Museum for verification." After not hearing anything back for a while, Steven rang the big cat guy to see how it went. The big cat guy was very despondent. "DOG" was the Natural History Museum's conclusion.[6]

It shows how easy it is to misidentify a big cat footprint, even for the experts. It is of course possible that the contractors *did* see a big cat, and that the footprint was still from a dog. Perhaps Black Shuck is still around, shorn of his paranormal powers and now physical enough to leave footprints, and everyone just assumes these days when they see him that he's a big cat.

Mutant mystery moggy

I admit to feeling sympathy for all these intrepid but disappointed people who believe they've found a genuine Suffolk big cat, only for it to turn out to be a large soft toy, or the footprint of a large dog, or an illegal metal detectorist. Because I too was in a state of excitement for months over some CCTV footage of an animal briefly known as the "North Suffolk mutant mystery moggy".

In September 2015, I got a call from a free range poultry farmer in a secret location in North Suffolk who told me their CCTV security camera had captured what looked like a big cat. (I can reveal that his farm has free range hens. It's safe to do so as a drive round the area quickly reveals that most of the buildings between the location and Norwich – and there aren't that many – are vast sheds where free range chickens roost at night.)

My source and I both convinced ourselves we had seen some sort of young puma, or possibly a long-legged, pointy-eared lynx or serval. The 18 seconds of footage begins with a cat-like animal, shot in infrared on a dark night at around 1am, walking towards the farm gate. Its eyes are two huge blobs reflecting the light from the farm's infrared lamp. It walks towards a building just out of shot, at which point it trips a motion-sensor light and more details became visible. The mystery cat then turns and casually walks out of view at the bottom of the shot.

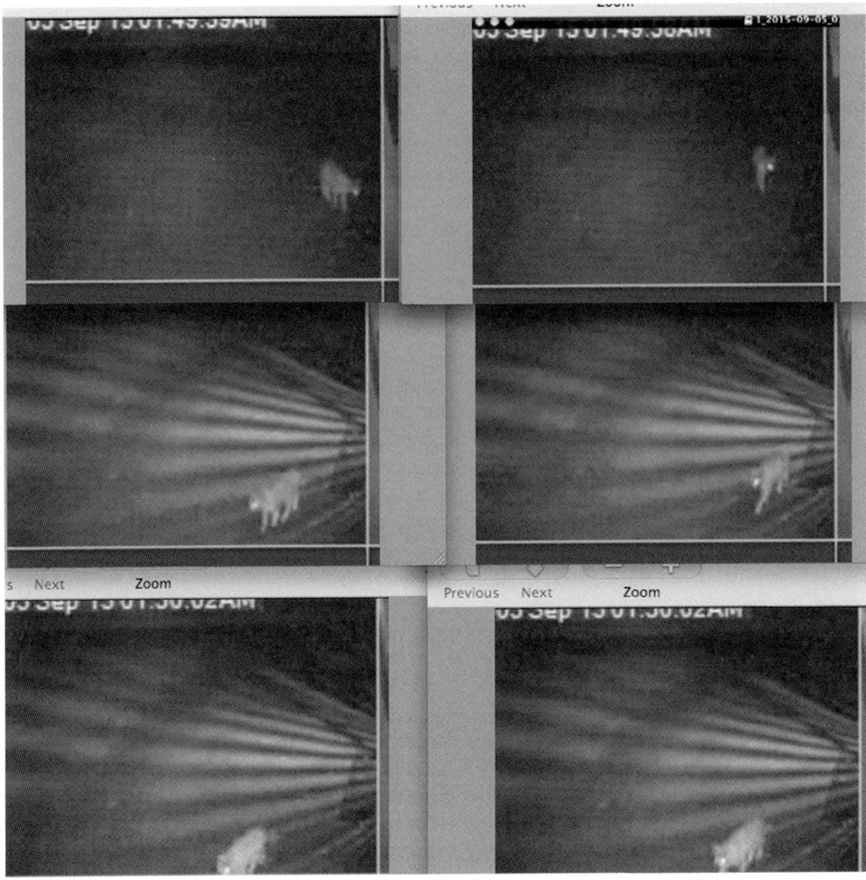

The North Suffolk mutant mystery moggy caught on CCTV – but see page 276 for an explanation! Copyright-holder requested anonymity.

(It's a CCTV camera bolted to a wall, so its field of view doesn't move.)

It's an odd-looking cat – long limbed, long-bodied with a small head and a relatively short tail. I wasn't immediately convinced it was a big cat, but my first reaction was that it couldn't be an ordinary domestic cat – its proportions were completely "wrong."

The video was recorded on a desktop PC, in low resolution and filmed mostly in infrared. It was hard to make sense of the footage. Sometimes the mystery cat appeared like a stripped-down, slim puma, like the pumas you see in South America. In a couple of frames, just after the light came on, it appeared mottled or spotted. In one frame we thought we saw long pointed lynx-like ears. It was as if the animal was shape-shifting, morphing from a puma to a spotted lynx, as if British big cats where ghost animals after all. But I realised most "data" was in fact artefacts produced by a low-resolution camera in poor light.

The cat walked past the mat

More problematic was the background in the footage – it was filmed in a featureless tarmac yard. There was absolutely nothing to give any kind of scale, except for the outline of a black rubber doormat in front of the door of a just-out-of-shot building. (We measured the doormat – it was just over 1.83 metres long.) When the light comes on, it throws the angular shadows of the bars of the gate over the mystery cat. Various people suggested some complicated maths involving the length of these shadows and the dimensions of the shadow thrown by the cat, the distance of the light source from the camera. We had to discount this – the light source is on a pole that shifts position slightly in the wind.

Soon I was on the scene with the farmer, doing some measuring, based on our estimate of how close to the 1.83m doormat our mystery cat had passed on its walk. In the footage it appeared to walk alongside the mat for a second. Based on instructions shouted to each other through the open door while watching the yard live on the CCTV camera monitors in the nearby farm office, we were able to set up some crude markers for the approximate (emphasis on approximate!) distance from the edge of the rubber doormat that the cat had passed by.

Measuring on-screen images and some crude maths led us to a very tentative estimate that we were dealing with a mystery cat just under a metre long excluding its tail. This would make it the size of a not very big puma. The way it hung its tail – pointing downwards then upwards at the end – seemed uniquely big cat-like at first, but I noticed some domestic cats held their tails like this too. We realised our calculations were not scientific. Further study was needed.

We resolved to await expert opinion and definitive measurements before releasing footage. Jon Downes, director of the Centre for Fortean Zoology, advised caution, recalling red faces over previous footage of a "big cat" that turned out to be an ordinary "domestic". A room full big cat experts at a gathering of the British Big Cat Research Group concluded that our footage was more likely to be a "mutant moggy" than our hypothetical "North Suffolk young puma." Even the prospect of a feral domestic cat close to a metre long, though,was an exciting one!

Mark Fletcher, an award-winning wildlife filmmaker whose work has included filming American pumas in the wild, kindly offered to do some "scaling" work for us, overlaying video images from the footage on something that could give an idea of scale. (He'd done this work before). First we needed to go back to the location in the CCTV footage with measuring poles and ideally some big cat cut-outs that could be positioned at various points in the yard for comparison.

I was finally able to turn up – during a gale, as it turned out – at the secret North Suffolk location with my improvised surveyor's-style measuring pole – ranging pole, in the jargon – one metre long, with a 50cm stripe in red and a 50cm stripe in white, as recommended to me by an archaeologist.

I'd sent three cardboard cut-outs ahead by post. One was a one-metre long, long-legged slim big cat. Trying to make sense of the blurry footage, I had given it a triangular chin and a short tail. Our first trial run with the cut-out in front of the CCTV camera showed that I'd over-estimated the legs – so I shortened these by tucking them in and taping them back. Our second cut-out, the "biggest possible domestic cat", was a cat outline with a more domestic cat-type body, and was 75cm long, this being the length at which big cats become "of interest," according to big cat investigator Rick Minter. Finally, there was a domestic cat cut-out, intended as a control. This was 50cm long, slightly smaller than Thomas, my then partner's adult tomcat.

So we obtained our CCTV footage of myself marching around a rainy, featureless yard in daylight with a one-metre ranging pole, following as best I could the path taken by our mutant mystery moggy. This was followed by "runs" with our various cut-outs. I sent these little films to Mark Fletcher, who got back to me with "overlays" that revealed that our mutant mystery moggy was, beyond doubt… an ordinary domestic cat! And a small one at that!

The video showing me in the yard, together with the ghostly image from the night-time footage of our mystery cat in the same spot superimposed on it, resembling a "ghost cat" from Chapter 7 on Suffolk animal ghosts. This video overlay clearly showed a small domestic cat next to my ranging pole laid on the ground. Its length didn't reach the end of the pole's 50cm red stripe. In the frames of me walking around the yard with the "domestic cat" cut-out, the cut-out was slightly bigger than the mystery cat. The superimposed image of our mystery cat barely cleared the top of my boots. As the farmer commented, "Disappointing, but you can't argue with that."

The affair shows how easy it is to misidentify animals as big cats, particularly in the dark. After this experience, I am wary of a report I recently received of a night-time encounter in which a driver saw "the eyes of a big cat" in his headlights at Yaxley. I am also cautious about the sighting by a motorist of a pair of eyes in his headlights that he thought to be those of a big cat, near the Tesco roundabout just outside Thetford late at night on 30 January 2015.[7]

But I feel my own big cat setback has been a useful exercise, the outcome shows the value of getting your mystery animal footage and photos properly checked out to avoid embarrassment. We had applied scientific methods and eliminated from our enquiries one mystery cat. Yes, a cautionary tale!

And finally, what about the weird proportions of our skinny, long-bodied, long-legged mutant mystery moggy? I showed the footage to a contact in East Anglian animal rescue. On condition of the usual East Anglian anonymity, he told me he thought it could be a Savannah cat – a cross between a serval and a domestic Abyssinian cat. They're "legal" from F3 – the third generation of being crossed with "domestics", but anything with more serval genes in it you'd need a licence to keep. Only a small number of people in the UK are licensed to breed F1 and F2 Savannah cats. My East Anglian animal rescue source tells me he's heard from one of these legal breeders that there are also unlicensed breeders out there in the East of England too, who are still breeding hybrid domestic cats with an awful lot of serval in them. He added that some of these have ended up being released. So our small North Suffolk mutant mystery moggy could in fact be carrying some exotic big cat genes.

An example of how easy it is to see animals that aren't really there. I saw this large, mysterious long-haired cat watching me from a driftwood log on Suffolk's Dingle Beach in 2014 (top). From a slightly different angle, however, it was revealed to be a burnt and blackened tree trunk that had washed up against another one (above).

CHAPTER 20. Mutant mystery moggy misidentifications

1. Thetford Forest intelligence from Mike Hume, Friends of Thetford Forest, by email 17 September 2014; PC Carter's comments at www.newmarketjournal.co.uk/news/latest-news/i-tawt-i-taw-a-puddy-cat-i-did-1-546538.

2 "Look what we found lion in town gardens," *Suffolk Free Press,* 28 February 2012 www.suffolkfreepress.co.uk/news/latest-news/look-what-we-found-lion-in-town-gardens-1-3567285; Duncan Bradley, *Suffolk Free Press* editor, Pers. Comm. by email 12 January 2015.

3. "Trimley: Big cat spotted in Trimley St Martin!", *Evening Star*, 27 April 2013, www.ipswichstar.co.uk/news/don-t-miss/trimley_big_cat_spotted_in_trimley_st_martin_1_2169527.

4. "Controversy over wild cat-alogue" *Eastern Daily Press*, 18 March 2006, http://www.eadt.co.uk/content/eadt/news/story.aspx?brand=EADOnline&category=News&tBrand=EADOnline&tCategory=news&itemid=IPED02%20Apr%202008%2010%3A16%3A58%3A417.

5. "More mink attacks in Felixstowe", *Eastern Daily Press,* 29 February 2008, www.edp24.co.uk/news/more_mink_attacks_in_felixstowe_1_162022.

6. Interview with Steven Johnson at Cliff House caravan park, Dunwich, 6 March 2015. The mammoth leg bone is now in the Dunwich Museum collection. "Daisy the dog finds the meal of her dreams, a mammoth bone", *Mail Online*, 3 October 2007, www.dailymail.co.uk/news/article-485477/Daisy-dog-finds-meal-dreams--mammoth-bone.html

7. "Driver spots 'big cat' on late night A11 journey", *Thetford and Brandon Times* 4 February 2015 with thanks to its editor Andrew Filchett. The sighting was technically just over the Norfolk border. Tim Holt-Wilson described to me getting into his car in Oakley, North Suffolk, one winter's evening, turning on the headlights and catching a glimpse of something long and black with a long tail moving away. It had disappeared when he got out of the car to look and listen. He feels what he experienced was a "trick of the light". Such scepticism of one's own nocturnal big cat sighting is healthy! Conversations with Tim Holt-Wilson, 26 September and 3 October 2016.

The ghostly "North Suffolk mutant mystery moggy" overlaid on daytime footage, revealing it to be a small domestic cat. Overlays by Mark Fletcher.

Less well-known and stranger-looking big cats: Asian golden cat (top), photo: Bryan flickr upload bot, Creative Commons Licence. Serval (above), photo: Thierry Martel, Creative Commons Licence.

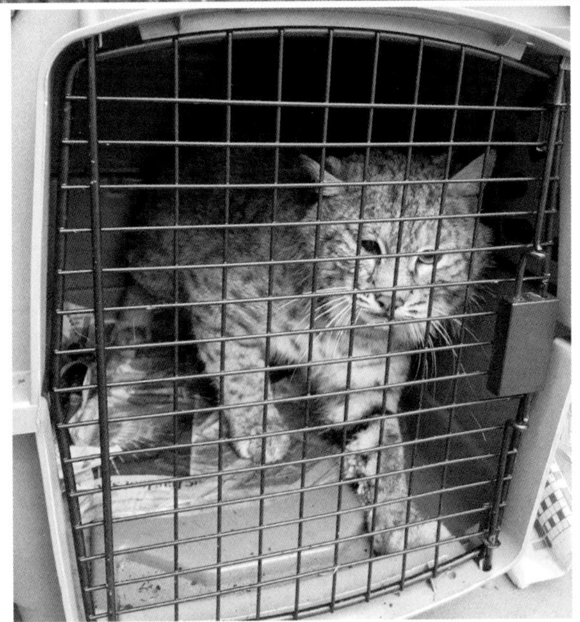

Caracal (top), photo: Leo za1, Creative Commons Licence. An injured male bobcat after its recapture in West Suffolk in 2020 (above). Photo © RSPCA, with their kind permission.

PART 3 – BIG CATS OF THE CURIOUS COUNTY

21: What are the Alien Big Cats?

It is probably safe to assume that the big cats that people report seeing in Suffolk are (misidentifications aside) real flesh-and-blood animals. Merrily Harpur, who has done much excellent research on British big cat sightings, has concluded that British big cats are "daimons" – "intermediate beings," spirits, some kind of manifestation of the collective unconsciousness or even some kind of "race memory" of actual prehistoric big cat when humankind was young and we were their food.

And what are we to make of the story told to ufologist Nick Redfern while he was on a tour of Rendlesham Forest with enthusiasts of the Rendlesham Forest UFO Incident on its twentieth anniversary – on a freezing day in February 2000? Redfern told me that among the 70 to 80 on the tour was a woman named Barbara Ash who related an account she'd heard of a "story concerning the sighting of a large black cat seen in Suffolk, England, in 1941 that allegedly transformed into a hare!" Local UFO investigator Brenda Butler told BBC News's Richard Haugh in 2010 how she and her fellow Rendlesham skywatchers have "seen the black cat, we've seen the little brown monks which float around, we've seen the disks, we've seen the craft in the sky, we've seen ghosts."

While this "British big cats are shape-shifting phantoms" theory neatly answers the question, "Where are the bodies, then?" I have to disagree with Harpur's conclusion. I am also deeply sceptical about secondhand stories of wartime Suffolk big cats transforming into hares. As we have seen, there are reports of ghost cats out there in Suffolk. But those that experience them are convinced that what they've seen is a ghost, and they are supposed to be the ghosts of domestic cats, usually haunting houses rather than the great outdoors.[1]

What kind of animal, then, are Suffolk's living big cats? Over the years, the phrase "Alien Big Cats" (ABCs) has been used to describe the introduced exotic big cats out there in the British Isles, although they've been in Suffolk for over 45 years, so any ABC around the county today would be third or even fourth generation immigrants, hardly "alien" anymore.

Leopards – for some unknown reason, black

The "black panther-like animals" most frequently described by witnesses in Suffolk (and across all of the East of England) would appear to be melanistic leopards – confusingly also called "black panthers." The character Bagheera from *The Jungle Book* is perhaps the most famous of these. Why all of them are black, with no reports of yellow leopards with black spots, remains a mystery. Perhaps there is something in the environment of Britain that makes being black a better adaptation than it is in Africa and Asia. It's thought the melanism (being a black version of an animal) might confer better immunity to diseases, for example. There are regions where native melanistic leopards are said to be quite common in the wild – the Aberdare Range in Kenya, is one example, as are some of Indonesia's islands.

Leopards are long-bodied. The "big black cat, the size of a Labrador dog, but longer" seen on the edge of the town of Eye in 2008 is a good example, as is the "big cat, black, quite long… body as long as a greyhound" seen by David from Bury in Barham at night in 2010. At a conservative estimate, at least 78 of the big cat sightings in Suffolk that I've collected more or less fit the description of a black leopard, going back to around 1975 That figure excludes many more reported less than a couple of miles over the border in neighbouring counties. Nearly all the sightings from North Suffolk near the Waveney, from around Ipswich, from the Theberton-Eastbridge-Dunwich Heath cluster and nearly all of the earlier reports from the forests west of the Deben and their surroundings seem to be black leopards. Add the bit of Norfolk that's walking distance from the Suffolk border and that's easily another dozen black leopard sightings, plus another Cambridgeshire border black leopard and two more from the Essex border.

While the leopards that are most popular with punters at zoos – often African leopards – tend to be the bigger varieties of leopard, there are some fifteen known leopard sub-species. Asian leopards are smaller – particularly forest-dwelling leopards, and the Somali leopard – the "nanopanther" is the smallest of all. Any British black leopard is likely to be a mix of several of these fifteen-odd leopard sub-species from various regions of Africa and Asia – and possibly of something other than a leopard as well.

There was a rumour going around that some of the early 1970s "black panthers" in captivity in UK were bred with black jaguars to fix the melanistic gene, to ensure that more of their offspring were black. (The Dangerous Wild Animals Act predated the film *Scarface* by four years, but "black panthers" were already cool among less responsible big cat fanciers.) While leopards are lithe and wiry, jaguars are much more muscular animals, with thicker legs and bigger heads than leopards. The "large black cat" seen sunning itself one summer morning in 2013 in that farm near Eye was described by its witness as having a "muscular build," while the feline seen in Lodden, Norfolk by the Bidwells on a driving lesson some nine years earlier was "muscular, with a big head". These are suggestive of a black leopard with perhaps a bit of black jaguar ancestry. We know leopards and jaguars occasionally breed in the wild, they are known to interbreed in captivity.[2]

Fewer pumas

"It had a very long tail that curved down and curled up at the end." That was how one witness described the "Haverhill Puma" he saw near the A1017 Steeple Bumpstead roundabout on the bypass at the edge of town, and right on the Essex edge of Suffolk, back in 2012. As we have already seen, numerous witnesses to Suffolk's big cats describe a very long tail that hung down and then curved up at the end. Some observers lucky enough to catch more than the briefest glimpse of the big cat's tail noted its end was thick and a little bushy, not tapered or pointed like a domestic cat's. This – along with the loping walk – convinces them they haven't misjudged the size of an ordinary moggy or misidentified a Labrador.

The long, curving thick-ended tail, together with the long body shape, the comparatively small head, the low-to-the-ground "loping" walk, with the animal moving in "bounds," accurately describe either a melanistic leopard or a puma (cougar or mountain lion). Pumas and leopards are generalists, both species are adaptable and you'd expect to find pumas hunting in the same Suffolk habitats as you'd find leopards. While leopards are generally the bigger of the two, their silhouettes are similar, they are about the same shape, and seeing as you're extraordinarily privileged to see even the briefest glimpse of one at all in Suffolk, you'd be unlikely to conclusively identify which one you'd seen, puma or leopard.

Witnesses I spoke to went online after their sightings and looked up big cats, or went to their local library in the days before the internet, and were convinced they'd seen either definitely a black leopard or definitely a puma. One witness sent me a variety of cut-and-paste internet images of pumas, commenting that it looked more like a particular photo, but the sandy colour was closer to another individual in a different photo. And Paul Smy, who'd lived in Africa where he'd seen leopards, identified the big cat he saw in Kirton as one of these. There was also "R2D2", from Texas, who "knew his pumas" and saw one scrapping with his Staffie near RAF Lakenheath.[3] Then there was the "big cat… bloody great thing" that we met earlier, and that "jumped a four-foot fence" on land on the Little Glemham estate in the winter of 2004 to 2005 that was a "lightish colour." This "lightish colour" suggests a puma.

And let's not forget, as we learnt in Chapter 14, the anonymous man who contacted the *East Anglian Daily Times* back in 1996, claiming to have released a young male puma named Khyber into the wild after he got too big for his cage.[4]

Rick Minter, who investigates big cats in Gloucestershire, where the evidence for them is much better than in Suffolk, told me, "in most areas when the pattern of reports is available over a year or over a day of reports at an event (I've done nine events this summer and got 132 reports amongst them) the trend is consistently three quarters black panther-type (melanistic leopard), a quarter puma-type and the odd lynx." Several other big cat investigators have estimated the proportion of British black leopards to British pumas in any given sample of reports, and it always comes in with a figure somewhere around the mid-twenties as a percentage of the sample that are pumas, with a few percentage points going to lynxes, the rest – around three quarters or slightly less – are melanistic leopards.

Using the same less than scientific method for counting Suffolk black leopard sightings up to 2021, I come up with 37 puma sightings in Suffolk itself, of which three were "multiple", a puma-like animal seen several times in the same area, or in one case two pumas seen together. I've also collected accounts of five possible Norfolk border puma encounters and one Cambridgeshire border puma, these animals presumably going in and out of Suffolk regularly. Pumas seem to have made their debut in Suffolk around 1996, or around 1982 if the "Debenham Lion" was a puma. Curiously, I've heard no more reports of pumas in Suffolk since 2017.

Pumas are technically speaking, not big cats, as they don't belong to the *Panthera* genus – tigers, leopards, snow leopards, jaguars and lions. Various features in their skulls and the inability to roar sets the pumas apart from *Panthera,* but for the purposes of large felines roaming around Suffolk we'll include pumas (family *Onca*) in the same big cat category. While pumas don't roar, their range of sounds includes chirps and even blood-curdling screams, the mating call of the female puma on heat. (See the glossary for the difference between a genus and a species.)

There were native European pumas 900,000 years ago at Newbourne, but pumas are now only native to the Americas, North and South, including all the way up to Canada. Opinion is divided on whether or not pumas are still native to the eastern United States – where they are confusingly referred to as "Eastern panthers" or "Florida panthers." There are numerous sightings of Eastern panthers, although pumas are supposed to have been driven to extinction by hunters in the East, and any pumas seen there are supposed to have wandered in from Canada or Mexico.[5]

The most obvious indicator that what you've seen is a puma is its colour – ranging from light sandy shade to "tan" or "golden" all the way through to a reddish brown or dark chocolate hue and – as Suffolk Police data indicates – grey. The reported "dark chocolate" pumas could just as easily be misidentified black leopards – some black leopards still have their rosettes visible on parts of their bodies, they can have deep rusty brown fur in places as well as black. Black domestic cats often show the same phenomenon, developing a rich rusty brown coat with brown highlights during the summer months or as they age.

Pumas have been found living in the wild in Britain – Felicity the puma, as she came to be known, was captured near Inverness, Scotland in 1980. She was rather elderly and arthritic, and spent the rest of her life in the Highland Wildlife Park. On her death in 1985 she was stuffed. You can see her at the Inverness Museum.[6]

Officially there aren't supposed to be any black pumas. Very few black pumas have been photographed – always after being shot. One of the more convincing specimens was recorded in Costa Rica in 1959, it had light undersides and lighter fur on the insides of its legs, it wasn't black all over like a black leopard. European naturalists of the eighteenth century described the jaguarette, a particularly fierce, big puma-like cat of the Americas that was black with a white or light underside, so if they really are black pumas they may once have been less rare. A fair proportion of the sightings of pumas in some parts of the United States are of black individuals, but it's always possible that these are black leopards descended from released captive exotics, and that witnesses just assume (reasonably) that what they've seen is a variation on the big cat native to the Americas rather than an introduced exotic. Or these sightings could be just dark chocolate brown pumas seen in poor light.[7]

There have been recorded hybrids between American pumas and African or Asian leopards. These are known as pumapards – one with spots like a conventional yellow leopard's was born at a zoo in Hamburg in 1898. However, the pumapard is unlikely to account for any Suffolk big cats, as it was a dwarf, considerably smaller than either a puma or leopard. Contemporary photos show it with its terrier foster mother, the young pumapard wasn't much bigger than the terrier. You can see the pumapard at the Natural History Museum in Tring.[8]

Then there are the sightings where a witness had no idea whether they'd seen a puma or black leopard or lynx, or where there was just a report of a "big cat" and no more detail. Reports of the Haverhill Puma in particular talk about a "puma or lynx." Let's for a moment give these large felines the benefit of the doubt, and I've collected 43 of these non-specific large Suffolk felines (one of these a "multiple" sighting) plus another three nondescript Norfolk large cats of one sort or another, and one Essex border exotic whose exact species is unknown. I suspect, though, that nearly all of those indeterminate big cats will be pumas, and a few will be black leopards.

The 2011 big cat sighting by the driver on the 88A bus route from Blythburgh to Wenhaston, the earlier Haverhill Puma sightings, the big cat seen somewhere in Suffolk by a man testing his security light in 2008, and the "Shingle Street lynx" all fall into this vague category. We British are – unsurprisingly – not good at identifying big cats, although it's noticeable the less confidently identified Suffolk big cats tend to be in clusters – the Stour Valley, the Gipping Valley and bits of the Waveney Valley and North Suffolk. The North Suffolk cluster of big cats the witnesses couldn't identify was just west of another outbreak of encounters with big cats that can be more confidently identified as pumas.

Leaving out these indeterminate big cats whose witnesses weren't sure whether they were pumas or leopards or lynxes or whatever, that still means about a third of Suffolk big cats are pumas. My data seemed to show a statistically significant spike in Suffolk puma encounters around 2014, with a greater proportion of puma sightings at that time compared to other "county samples" across the UK, of the sort that Rick Minter described earlier. Over the seven years that I've been tracking big cats in Suffolk, though, puma reports have abruptly tailed off. It's been almost all black leopards that I've been hearing about since 2015, I've not heard a report of a Suffolk puma since 2018. I have, though, heard more reports of local lynxes and bobcats in recent years.[9] (See page 292 for my chart of Suffolk big cat sightings data.)

PART 3 – BIG CATS OF THE CURIOUS COUNTY

Lynxes and bobcats, servals and caracals

Let's not leave out the lynxes and the bobcats. When we factor in the 20 Suffolk lynxes and bobcats and the not easily identifiable big cats – the "puma or lynx" types and the odd long-bodied Norfolk "otter-cat" – out of a total of 178 Suffolk big cats that's 78 black leopards, 37 pumas and 43 indeterminate big cats. If only just over half the indeterminate cats turn out to be pumas, that's still 58 out of 178, which is about a third of our random big cat sample for Suffolk. That would produce a proportion of pumas higher than reported elsewhere.

The 20 "lynx or bobcat" types seen in Suffolk over the years include one which was the subject of multiple sightings in Wrentham, and one double sighting in Staverton Thicks at that unofficial campsite back in 1995 and – as we saw in Chapter 18 – a well-documented captive bobcat who was recently on a brief walkabout in West Suffolk. Of those 20, four were thought by informants to have been bobcats or in one case was known to be a bobcat.

Most of the Suffolk lynx sightings I've heard about were on or near the coast or in the land between the Orwell and the West bank of the Deben. (We'll return shortly to the solitary report of "lynx kittens" near Leiston.) This amount of lynxes is higher than the "handful" of lynxes usually found in patterns of big cat sightings in research by Rick Minter and others. "Lynx-like cats" sighted in West Suffolk were, with one exception, less confidently identified than those reported in East Suffolk, with the lynx-like cats seen on Suffolk's western edge more likely to fall into the tentative "puma or lynx" category.

As well as the Beccles lynx, there was Lara the Cricklewood lynx, found sitting on a wall of a garden in that neighbourhood of North London in 2000. She seemed quite tame, and was taken to London Zoo. (You can date her discovery by her name, it was in the early days of the *Tomb Raider* video game, featuring the then sensational computer game character Lara Croft.) Lara's capture came not long after a joint police and RSPCA operation confiscated two unlicensed lynxes from a ramshackle pen in Yorkshire.

In 2010, Max Blake, a volunteer at Bristol City Museum, stumbled upon specimen Ab4458. This is a small, ineptly stuffed Canadian lynx (and its bones), shot in Newton Abbot in 1903, that had come into the museum's stores and lain undisturbed for over a century. Judging by the lack of wear on of its teeth, it had probably been in captivity most of its life. According to the museum's records, the lynx had killed two dogs before it was shot.[10]

There's a big variation in lynxes, they are generally between 45-75cm at the shoulder. There are the Canadian lynxes (*Lynx canadensis*) and the slightly bigger Eurasian lynx (*Lynx lynx*), Iberian lynxes were probably always too rare to have ended up as pets in Britain. There's also much variation in how heavily spotted lynxes are (some have very faint spots) and on how stripey they are on their legs. They come in a big range of colours too, from rusty red to yellow to brown to grey.

Eurasian lynxes are particularly fond of "unbroken expanses of evergreen forest", of which there are plenty in Suffolk, lynx reports have come from Suffolk's Dunwich Forest and from Staverton Thicks on the edge of Rendlesham Forest. Lynxes are relatively tall compared to their length and have thick fur, making them seem bulkier than they really are.

Like leopards and pumas, lynxes are strong swimmers (note the clusters of sightings of big cats on both sides of the River Waveney, the River Gipping and the River Stour). The lynx's diet makes them even more adapted to Suffolk than pumas and leopards. While they will eat anything they can get their paws on, lynxes are foremost rabbit and hare specialists, and after that rodent specialists – going for rats, squirrels and mice. North American lynxes are usually very dependent on hares, but can "switch" their diet when there's a shortage of these, while the Iberian lynxes – now very rare and confined to Spain – seems to kill a lot of waterfowl as part of their diet. All these prey animals are plentiful in Suffolk. In Switzerland, where lynxes were introduced in 1970, their "importance for regulating the ungulate population" is now recognised, "ungulates" includes deer. The idea of re-introducing radio-tagged lynx to Suffolk, as we have noted, briefly appealed before those consulted realised that lambs and sheep were more likely to be on the lynx menu than deer. Both the Beccles lynx and the more recent West Suffolk escaped bobcat caused considerable destruction among livestock before being shot.

Unusual blue-grey coloured North American lynxes occasionally turn up, as do black bobcats. (The bobcats of North America are smaller than a lynx but very similar-looking and closely related.) At least one known black bobcat on closer inspection was more dark brown mahogany than pure black. Between them, melanistic or mahogany lynxes (or lynx-bobcat hybrids, known as blynxes or lynxcats) may explain the "black panther type… big animal… very long and quite stocky" with ears "tufted" seen at Ufford golf course in 2009. The animal had a long, thin tail, but there's much variation in size and tail length among lynxes.[11]

A more conventionally-coloured lynx could account for the sighting of the "feline creature twice the size of an ordinary cat… huge and spotty and not like an ordinary cat" seen on land behind Russet Drive, Red Lodge. If seen briefly, or in not very good light or from a long way off, the lynx's distinctive ear tufts often aren't that visible. This may explain the numerous "puma or lynx" descriptions from across Suffolk over the years – as we have seen, lynxes and pumas come in a similarly broad range of colours.[12]

Other possible explanations for some of the more extraordinary looking big cats that are reported are caracals and servals.

Caracals, native to Africa, Central Asia and southwest Asia as far as India, are usually twice the size of domestic cats (sometimes three times the size) and usually red-brown or golden in colour, although black caracals also exist. In their normal colouration, caracals look a little bit like a miniature puma with longer legs, except their ears end in black points with the most ludicrously elaborate tufts, hence their name, which is Turkish for "black ear". Caracals are in fact a species of lynx, *Lynx caracal*.

Similar to the caracal is the equally bizarre-looking serval (*Leptailurus serval*), which has a combination of spots and stripes, on a light orange-brown coloured background. The serval is about the same size as a caracal, with the same wiry shape and shortish tail. What particularly distinguishes the serval are its big, bat-like ears ending in tiny little black tufts – servals use these huge ears to listen for prey. While servals have been known to hunt down burrows, both servals and caracals usually hunt not by stalking like other cats, but by launching themselves at their prey – often rabbits or birds – with great leaps.

Caracals were said in the days of the British Raj in India to sometimes get together in packs in the wild and take down bigger animals, which was why captive caracals were trained to hunt birds and hares in India and Iran. They weren't actually very easy to tame, though.

Recent archaeological evidence in the form of what's thought to be a paw print of a caracal on a clay tile found at the site of a Roman villa in Aylsham, Norfolk points to Romans bringing caracals with them to East Anglia.

A recent Press Association investigation showed a surprisingly large number of lynxes, servals, caracals and other – smaller – species of exotic wildcats kept in captivity in Suffolk with Dangerous Wild Animals licences.[13]

Any serval on the loose in Suffolk would have its ancestry in a variety of the 13 known sub-species of the animal. Melanistic servals are quite common, particularly in the Abadare mountains of Kenya. These black servals look even weirder than the spotted and striped servals, so bizarre that an unfamiliar observer might think they're looking at jackal or a strange breed of dog. Perhaps some modern Black Shuck sightings are in fact black servals! There are also servicals and caravals – hybrids of servals and caracals, and one recorded lynx-serval hybrid in captivity.[14]

The leaping behaviour of caracals and servals may point to the identity of the animal seen by Ian Miller's wife around Blundeston some time before 2013 that "could jump six to eight feet." A melanistic serval or caracal could explain the "black panther" seen near Glemsford "hunting in the corn field", which "jumped up out of the corn with arched back and dived back in," according to the witness. A melanistic serval or caracal is probably also a closer match than a lynx to the "tufted" black cat seen at Ufford golf course, with its longer, thin tail.

As Rick Minter says, "We cannot just assume they [British big cats] are automatically strict leopards and pumas." We can't assume they're necessarily the other usual big cat suspects – lynxes, caracals and servals – either. [15]

It is possible that some are hybrids – hybrid puma-jaguars are known to exist, there are even leopard-lioness hybrids recorded in the Congo. There's a problem with hybridisation, though, and that's male sterility – the male hybrids are almost always sterile, only the females can reproduce, and then only if they breed with a pure-bred big cat. This could possibly help explain why big cat sightings come in local waves – big cats move into an area for a few years, look for a mate, but then the sterility of the hybrid males means they don't have any cubs, and the big cat extended family dies out.[16]

The leopards and pumas, and to a slightly lesser extent lynxes and bobcats, do like to wander. I've heard various figures for the distances covered by big cats in the wild on any given night – up to about 30 miles is one average night's wanderings for a male leopard, apparently. Pumas seem to be constantly on the move, going in and out of different habitats in search of different prey, and favouring different localities in different seasons. Jonathan McGowan estimates that a big cat released on the edge of London would show up in Cornwall (around 280 miles or 450 km due southwest of London by road) in about two weeks. As we saw back in Chapter 14, the British Big Cats Society claimed a decade ago to have assembled evidence of least 23 releases of big cats into the wild in the UK since 1976.[17]

Big cats will let themselves be known to each other by constant scent-marking of their territory, and by screams in the case of pumas. Could the Suffolk big cats have found a mate in Devon or Derbyshire? Or were they never really Suffolk resident big cats, but just passing through Suffolk on their way from Norfolk to Essex and onward to Cambridgeshire and even further afield? Or could they be part-time Suffolk big cats, with ranges that they've now established that cover the whole of the East of England?

Parts of the world that have known native big cats also have their own mystery cats that don't fit the description of the big cats known to live there. We've seen the unofficial "Eastern panthers" of the eastern USA, where pumas are supposed to be locally extinct. Big Cat Rescue say that when they get called out to deal with a reported "Eastern panther" seen stalking local Alsatians and in one case stalking a little old lady, it's more often than not a misidentified and not particularly big leopard cat or Bengal cat – a domestic cat-leopard cat cross. (We'll examine leopard cats shortly.) Texas, Arkansas, Oklahoma and Missouri are home to big cats, and they're also the alleged stomping ground of the Ozark Howler (*aka* Ozark Black Howler) a short-legged, shaggy furred mystery animal said by some to have horns and by others to be a misidentified big cat – possibly a gigantic dark-coloured lynx.

There are reports of the "onza", like a puma but more lightly-built, with longer ears, body and legs, said to live in the open grasslands of Mexico. The Indian state of Kerala, home to leopards and tigers, is said to also have a mystery big cat, the "pogeyan", a cloudy grey leopard without spots living in the hills around the tea plantations of Malabar, and so on.

Similarly, some of the Suffolk big cat reports by apparently reliable and sane witnesses, don't fit the standard descriptions of an exotic non-native big cat either. The Debenham Lion, was like a lion but smaller and with a long body, and with short ears ending in tufts. Then there was the black "tufted cat" of Ufford golf course. With its long tail, it doesn't quite match the melanistic versions of a lynx, bobcat, serval or caracal. The Peasenhall big cat, which Brenda Sore saw, sounds like a black leopard up to the bit where she describes its "pointed ears." Are these all Alien Big Cats introduced from faraway continents? Bizarrely, the answer to this mystery may lie closer to home.[18]

The "tufted-eared" black cat seen at Ufford Park Golf Course in 2009 doesn't fit the description of any known big cat, except possibly a black lynx or – as I've reconstructed it here – a black caracal. Both are rare, and melanistic caracals are more a ghostly grey in colour than pure black.

PART 3 – BIG CATS OF THE CURIOUS COUNTY

FOOTNOTES TO CHAPTER 21: What are the Alien Big Cats?

1. Big cats as "daimons" in *Mystery Big Cats*, Merrily Harpur, Heart of Albion 2006. Whatever you think of its conclusions, the book's gathering of evidence and first-hand accounts of British big cat encounters is perfectly sound. Black big cat transforming into a hare from "Shapeshifting big cats – Nick Redfern", website of Jim Harold, the paranormal podcast guy, 18 February 2016 http://jimharold.com/shape-shifting-black-cats-nick-redfern/ and Nick Redfern pers. comm. by email February 26 2016. Redfern notes that witches were traditionally supposed to transform into hares to make their getaways; "Rendlesham revealed: UFO investigator Brenda Butler", Richard Haugh, BBC Suffolk, 15 December 2010, http://news.bbc.co.uk/local/suffolk/hi/people_and_places_history/newsid_9291000/9291811.stm.

2. The muscular black leopard on the farm near Eye in 2013 was a different sighting to the more wiry black leopard seen in a meadow by the bridge at Lowgate Street, on the southern approach to the town five years earlier, although they could have been the same animal. British big cat investigator Jonathan McGowan has heard "more and more reports of a normal spotted leopard" from Kent, and says there is also at least one "chocolate brown leopard in the UK." Some of the leopard wool Jonathan and I pulled off barbed wire in Bournemouth was part yellow and part black, see "Large cat update", Weird Weekend, 2012 http://mattsalusbury.blogspot.co.uk/2012/10/jonathan-mcgowans-big-cat-large-cat.html There's also a jaguar-lioness hybrid – a jaglion – stuffed and mounted on display at the Natural History Museum, Tring, but it's a very unlikely candidate for any of Suffolk's big cats.

3. "That big cat is prowling again", *EADT*, 4 March 1996.

4. Texas Parks and Wildlife Department confirm that the Lone Star State is home to pumas, https://tpwd.texas.gov/huntwild/wild/species/mlion/.

5. Some describe these Eastern pumas (officially declared extinct in 2017) as a separate sub-species, *Puma concolor icoryi*.

6. http://scotcats.online.fr/abc/photoalbum/cannich.html

7. See "The Truth About Black Pumas", Karl Shuker, Shukernature blog http://karlshuker.blogspot.co.uk/2012/08/the-truth-about-black-pumas-separating.html)

8. Karl Shuker's blog, http://karlshuker.blogspot.co.uk/2014/07/pumapards-and-lepumas-unusual-feline.html.)

9. Rick Minter Pers. Comm. by email 14 November 2014. See page 17 for my most recent Suffolk puma report, from near Brampton Request Stop in May 2018. See page 262 for a puma at Isleham, Cambridgeshire, a mile from the Suffolk border, seen in late 2021.

10. "The Beast of Cricklewood is caged," *Daily Telegraph* 9 May 2001, http://www.telegraph.co.uk/news/uknews/1329632/The-Beast-of-Cricklewood-is-caged.html. Lara's capture was preceded by ten years of sightings of a puma-like animal on the fringes of North London and the adjoining county of Hertfordshire, dubbed The Beast of Barnet. Lara was transferred after three years to Parc Zoologique, Ammenville, France, where she found a mate and had many cubs. She died in 2009, following longstanding back complications probably brought on while she was living wild in London. http://britishbigcatresearch.weebly.com/latest-news/what-became-of-the-beast-of-barnet-times-series-investigation-reveals-cricklewood-lynx-laras-legacy-lives-on; Yorkshire lynx confiscation, http://scotcats.online.fr/abc/realcats/yorkshirelynx.html, quoting "Don't try this at home," BBC News, 30th January 2002 "A lynx, shot dead in England in c. 1903", Darren Naish, Tetzoo blog, http://blogs.scientificamerican.com/tetrapod-zoology/edwardian-lynx-from-england/.

11. "A melanistic bobcat from outside Florida," *Fla. Field Nat*. 23(1):13-14, 1995. http://fosbirds.org/sites/default/files/FFNs/FFNv23n1p13-14Tischendorf.pdf; There's also the desert lynx breed, alpine lynx and highland lynx, breeds of cat said to be domestic cat-bobcat hybrids.

12. The Press Association published in May 2016 the results of its Freedom of Information Act requests to all the local councils in England asking for data on animals kept in captivity in their areas with Dangerous Wild Animals Act licences, of which 179 councils responded. (The time and effort in bothering councils that didn't respond – and taking the matter up with the Information Commissioner's Office – is far greater than the initial FOIA requests.) Councils that responded included West Suffolk councils (St Edmundsbury Borough Council and Forest Heath District Council). West Suffolk reported two bobcats, seven lynxes, two caracals, four servals, two jaguaraundis (they're a long-bodied, small South American wildcat), one fishing cat. Mid Suffolk District Council recorded one serval. Waveney and Suffolk Coastal (now East Suffolk), Babergh and Borough of Ipswich had not responded at the time of publication. "West Suffolk home to lynxes, caracals, bobcats and more FOI into dangerous wild animals finds", *Haverhill Echo*, 23 May 2016, http://www.haverhillecho.co.uk/news/latest-news/west-suffolk-home-to-lynxes-carcals-bobcats-and-more-foi-into-dangerous-wild-animals-finds-1-7395800#ixzz49gPsRzL6. I was told by a former resident of the area around Santon Downham around 2011 that "everybody knew" about the Santon Downham Lynx Man, who kept lynxes as part of a captive breeding programme, and you could regularly hear the cries of lynxes locally.

13. "A Roman caracal in Norfolk," linked from http://bigcatsinsuffolk.com and see also *Fortean Times*, **FT 387**, http://mattsalusbury.blogspot.com/2019/10/a-roman-caracal-in-norfolk.html; by 1991, 21 years after their introduction into Switzerland, there were 100 individual lynxes in the country who had "huge" home ranges – 200-400 square km for males and 100 to 150 square km for females. When they were first introduced their territories were much smaller. See *Great Cats – Majestic Creatures of the Wild,* ed. Dr John Seidensticker and Dr Susan Lipman, Merehurst, London 1991; A successful reintroduction programme begun in 1973 has seen lynx return to the Slovenian alps and regions of Croatia.

14. Caracals live 10-12 years in the wild, according to Wingham Wildlife Park, Kent, who at the time of writing have one of them. There are currently servals in Suffolk's Africa Alive! wildlife park in Kessingland. No big cat escapes have ever been recorded from Africa Alive! to my knowledge; www.zootierliste.de/en/?klasse=1&ordnung=115&familie=11507&art=1120812 for captive caracals in Kent; for more on caracals used to hunt birds see Retrieverman blog, http://retrieverman.net/2012/10/04/the-hunting-caracal/; For caracal's reputation for livestock damage, see Predator Management Forum, South Africa, www.pmfsa.co.za/facts-2; for serval sub-species see www.servals.org/home.htm; serval-caracal hybrids from Messybeast, http://messybeast.com/genetics/hyb-serval-caracal.htm.

15. An ongoing study at the Royal Agricultural University in Cirencester is underway in which Dr Andrew Hemmings is examining the skeletal remains of mutilated livestock from the Cotswolds. He is studying the toothmarks left on the bones of 23 different carcasses, ranging from deer, sheep and wild boar. The results suggest these could have been killed by big cats. Rick Minter is acting as a consultant to Dr Hemmings, who uses dental putty to make casts of bones, and then digital callipers to make accurate measurements of imprints. New_study_could_help_prove_existence_of_big_cats/?ref=rss "Remains could prove that big cats exist in the UK", www.wiltsglosstandard.co.uk/news/cotswolds/10718835.

16. See Hybrid Big Cats in the British Countryside, Sarah Hartwell, MessyBeast, http://messybeast.com/big-cat2.html)

17. www.britishbigcats.org/news.php#oldnews6.

18. When compiling my very unscientific totals for Suffolk black leopards, pumas and lynxes, I've squeezed the anomalous big cats above into the nearest category that they seem to resemble. The Debenham Lion I've put with the pumas, for example, and I've lumped the ones that sound a bit like a serval or caracal but with too long a tail in with the lynxes. The black leopard lookalikes but with pointy ears I've included among the 78-odd black leopards. Really bizarre-sounding Suffolk big cats I've left out of the total altogether or included under the vague cop-out "puma or lynx" if they sound a bit puma-like or lynxy. Unscientific I know, but hey, it's a book on *mystery* animals. I invite an academic with a proper grasp of the statistics and of the zoology to get the funding to do it properly and peer-reviewed, an enterprise for which I am happy to share all my data.

Suffolk's wetlands like this one, in Eastbridge, are perfect big cat country. There's plenty of cover. Deer and other animals need to come there to drink.

Was the "huge spotted cat" seen in 2009 on this derelict land behind Russet Drive, Red Lodge, a Eurasian lynx?

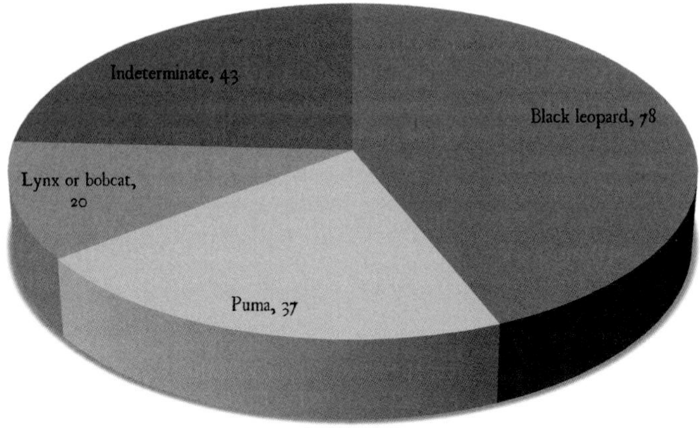

Pie chart of Suffolk big cat reports by type, from a sample of 178 sightings (including credible field signs and kill signs) for the period 1975 to 2021.

The village of Cattawade on the River Stour. The name is said to be Anglo-Saxon and to translate as "wildcat crossing".

PART 3 – BIG CATS OF THE CURIOUS COUNTY

22: East Anglian born and bred big cats?

If you enter Suffolk on the London to Ipswich train, your first sight of the county flashing past after crossing the muddy Stour estuary at Manningtree will be an industrial wasteland. There's a vast space on the Suffolk bank of the Stour where ghost factories gently decay, and where neat piles of rubble and hardcore from other recently demolished industrial units lie. A few factories in this Suffolk-Essex border industrial zone are still very much going concerns, tubes and chimney stacks, steam and all.

This is Brantham, which merges into the small settlement of Cattawade. (Different maps tend to disagree about where Brantham ends and Cattawade begins, what one map calls "Brantham Industrial Estate" appears as "Cattawade Industrial Estate" on another.) You can't really see Cattawade properly as it flashes past the train window, but were you to drive into this part of Suffolk from Essex, along the White Bridge that crosses the River Stour, you'd see an old stone bridge, a traditional old pub called The Crown and a surprisingly unspoilt village high street, given that it's on the edge of a half-ruined industrial estate. There's a slipway to take sailing boats by trailer down the edge of the Stour estuary here, on a mild day swans glide past on the water. A couple of signs to the slipway give the name of this place, Cattawade.

What interests us most about this surprisingly pretty backwater right next door to scene of industrial decay, offering such an unusual gateway to Suffolk, is the name "Cattawade". According to some scholars, Cattawade is Anglo-Saxon for "the crossing of the wildcat," a place where a wildcat could wade across a river.[1] Within Suffolk, there's also a Cat's Covert (*aka* Kendell's Wood) in Sibton, a Catt's Wood just north of Wickham Market, a Cat House and a Cat House Point on the bank of the Orwell River at Woolverstone. There's also a Cat's Lane in Sudbury, a Catkin Farm not far from Cratfield and a Tiger Hill near Assington.

The European wildcat had disappeared from southern England by the sixteenth century, and they're now very rare in Britain, confined to parts of Scotland. Lynxes – once native to Britain – are thought to have disappeared from England by the eighth century, at the time when the Wuffinga dynasty of the Anlgo-Saxon kingdom of East Anglia was gradually succumbing to the power of the kingdom of Mercia to the North.

But did the wildcats of England and Wales really die out? The Welsh poem the *Mabinogian* – generally accepted to have been written down between 1350 and 1410, is based on stories dating from sometime between 1060 and 1200. The *Mabinogian* mentions a larger than domestic cat-sized wildcat, Cath Palug, "the scratching cat," although it's not clear whether this is supposed to be actual Welsh fauna or a magical animal. There's much scholarly debate about whether the *Mabinogian* was seen by its narrators as mythology (it has relatively few obviously fantastic elements) and how much it was regarded as storytelling supposed to be about real people. The seventh century Welsh lullaby *Pais Dinogad* also apparently features a lynx – or at least a wildcat big enough that you'd hunt it with a spear.

There's a report in *A General History of Quadrupeds* from 1790 by Thomas Berwick stating "Some Wild Cats have been taken in this kingdom of a most enormous size. We recollect one having been killed in the northern English county of Cumberland, which measured, from its nose to the end of its tail, upwards of five feet (1.5m)." Berwick's report is likely to be second-hand at best, and probably an exaggeration. Then there was the "Gippsland giant cat" killed by Kurt Engel when he out shooting deer in the Australian outback in 2005. It was black, and charged at Kurt before he shot it. Kurt blew its head off with his high-calibre deer rifle.

Kurt claimed the cat he'd shot was 1.5 metres (nearly five feet) long. He photographed it, but as he was out on his motorbike in the middle of nowhere, he only had room to carry back the tail, which he cut off and took to Monash University. Their analysis revealed it had the DNA of a domestic cat. Sarah Hartwell in her MessyBeast website also mentions reports of Australian feral cats shot by farmers that reach "1.1 metres from nose to tail" (around 3 feet 7 inches). Domestic Maine Coon cats have been recorded of that length.[2]

If our information about the Gippsland Giant is correct, feral cats will have gone from the conventional-sized moggies known to have arrived in Australia in eighteenth century shipwrecks to puma-sized monsters in just two centuries. What could Britain's feral cats have evolved into during the two millennia since their arrival in Iron Age that preceded the Romans? And that's without introducing genes from some of the smaller exotic species of wildcats.

A BIIIG puddy-tat!

There was a tradition in Exmoor in the West Country going back to the early nineteenth century ("the early 1800s") of "fierce wildcats" bigger than domestic cats wandering the moors. A woman who lived on the Isle of Wight (on Yarmouth Marshes near the island's East Yarmouth – nothing to do with Great Yarmouth in Norfolk) recalled as a child being told to stay in at night as "double-sized" black wildcats with a distinct "woowee" call were out on the marshes at night, killing pets and livestock.

In the early 1960s, the Surrey Puma – one of the first well-known British "Alien Big Cat" panics – took hold, but everyone initially assumed at the time that if there was a Surrey Puma, it was a native feral cat that had somehow grown gigantic, before the idea of a "Puma", an introduced exotic, became suddenly fashionable.

Dr Maurice Burton, author of the 1968-vintage *Wild Animals of the British Isles* was among those who favoured giant wildcats or giant feral cats – domestic cats gone wild, and their descendants – as the explanation for British big cats. Belief that Britain's big cats were gigantic wildcats was widespread at the time of Surrey Puma, although Roger Tabor's study *The Wildlife of the Domestic Cat* in 1983 suggested there was little difference in size between domestic cats that stayed domesticated and the descendants of domestic cats gone feral.

After this, the "giantism" idea became unfashionable. When the "Puma" name attached itself to whatever it was out there in the Home Counties, the general public started to imagine all sorts of exotics from faraway continents. Most people who deal with urban feral cats today will tell you they are ever so slightly smaller in size than the domestic cat population.

However, Stanley, a former RSPCA inspector who contacted BBC Radio Suffolk's Jon Wright show, said that when he was stationed in Croydon in the 1960s, he had to trap and put to sleep a lot of "semi-feral cats" that were "slightly bigger than domestic cats." And a source at Framlingham and Saxmundham Cat Rescue told me in 2015 they'd noticed feral cats out in the countryside – usually black – that just keep getting bigger, although they also told me this is probably because there are proportionally more full adult males – or males neutered later in life than usual – out there than in the frequently early-neutered domestic cat population.[3]

I had the privilege to meet Chester, one of Fram and Sax Cat Rescue's guests, in his pen in 2012. He was almost two feet long. He was a long-haired male black cat with long legs, tufts on his ears and a long, sad face that looked just a little like the long sad face of a leopard. He gently nipped my arm with his massive, short, stud-like teeth. At the time, people were apparently dumping their unwanted cats in nearby Dunwich Forest (there was a spate of thefts of black Labradors from the Forest at the turn of this century too). So it wasn't clear if he was a domestic cat gone wild or whether he was born wild.

Another arrival at Fram and Sax Cats was George, who was rehomed in the summer of 2016. His web page, since taken down, said of him: "George is a large friendly black cat. If you like big cats then George is definitely the one for you! He is a big bruiser of a boy with a big personality to go with it. George looks older than his 4/5 years due to his hard and difficult time as a stray and he has obviously had to fend for himself for some time. That said, George loves attention, especially his tummy being rubbed."

Accompanying this text was a photo of an absolutely *enormous* domestic cat, said to be bigger even than Chester. His head is particularly large and broad compared to the rest of his body. One Fram and Sax Cat Rescue volunteer who got to know George said he was comfortably over two feet (60cm) long.

Dr Burton (he of *Wild Animals of the British Isles*) spoke to gamekeepers, who told him they "know how to keep a still tongue" about a phenomenon they revealed to him. They reported to him encountering wildcats or feral cats that were "enormous, big as a dog, twice as big as an ordinary cat." He said he'd even seen one of these himself in Devon. The gamekeepers told Dr Burton that if they ever shot one of these giant feral cats or wildcats, they would "bury the carcase as speedily as possible" and keep quiet about it.[4]

The Romans brought domestic cats with them to the province of Britannia – they would have looked more like the mottled tabby African wildcats from which they were descended. "Cat" is a word of Celtic origin, though, so the Romans may just have been adding to the gene pool of the cats the Iron Age Britons had around their settlements to keep down rodents in their grain stores. Archaeological evidence suggests that cats had become "familiar" in Britain sometime before the year 4 BC.

Even before selective breeding of different strains of exotic-looking domestic cats took off in the nineteenth century (we'll come to that), domestic cats had hundreds of years to get out there into wild Britain and breed with the wildcats, and around two thousand years for random mutations to take hold and turn them into "double-sized" versions of their cute little ancestors.[5] The Vikings also brought with them new varieties of domestic cat to England.

Then there is the lazy "escaped from a circus" (or zoo) explanation often given when a big cat is on the loose. As we've seen already, recorded escapes from zoos and circuses are few and far between, with the modern zoos of the East of England having a particularly good record. Recorded big cat escapes in East Anglia normally end with the cat being speedily recovered or shot.

I've heard a secondhand account of an elderly resident of somewhere in the Blythburgh area recalling as a child being in a dog and pony show that travelled the county living hand to mouth, that sometimes teamed up with bigger outfits that had more exotic animals. But no big cat escapes. We've already encountered Tornado Smith's wall-of-death performing lioness in the Suffolk village of Buxton, known to have spent her life in captivity without any escapes and dying without issue.

Lesser-known exotics

A lot of people posted overseas to Britain's colonial empire brought back with them exotic cats from Africa and India. Unlike (as far as we know) leopards and pumas, these intermediate-sized exotic cats can breed with domestic or feral cats.

There are the jungle cats, also known less commonly as swamp cats – *Felix chaus,* sandy coloured or sometimes glossy black, with the tiniest of tufts on their ears and a bizarre repertoire of sounds including chirps and something like a "bark". They have a considerable geographical range, through much of Asia and bits of the Middle East – they even go fishing for lungfish on the shores of the Sea of Galilee. Over their great geographical range (all the way from Egypt to Sri Lanka) they vary considerably in size – from about the size of a domestic cat to twice that size. In India and Pakistan, where they're generally at the smaller end of their size range, shiny melanistic jungle cats are common. They were brought over to the UK from India to Victorian England in the days of the British Raj because they were good "ratters". Then they were largely forgotten.[6]

We know jungle cats interbreed with domestic cats, as there's a fashionable exotic cat breed among cat fanciers in the US – the chaussie cat, which is a cross between a jungle cat and a domestic Abyssinian cat. Chaussie cats often end up in animal shelters, because – surprise, surprise – it turns out they're basically a wildcat after all and too much to handle for most pet owners. There's also the Euro-chauss, a man-made hybrid between the European wildcat *(F. silvestris)* and the jungle cat *(F. chaus)*, and there's a "jungle lynx", a hybrid between the jungle cat and bobcat, bred as an exotic pet.

Then there are the golden cats – the African golden cat *(Profelis aurata)*, and the Asian golden cat *(Pardofelis temminckii)*. We know some British empire civil servants brought back golden cats with them from their postings, African golden cats in particular. They started turning up being offered to Victorian zoos because they turned out not to make good pets after all. The African golden cat looks like a miniature puma, sometimes with spots, and apart from its size is quite hard to distinguish from a puma. And – yes – there are melanistic African golden cats and melanistic Asian golden cats too, as well as a grey version of the Asian golden cat.

We didn't hear much about these medium-sized cats, the jungle cats and golden cats – bigger than a domestic moggy, and probably much more common in captivity in the UK than the pumas, leopards, lions and tigers – after their arrival as spoils of the Victorian Empire. It's likely some of them got out, and bred with domestic cats. They would have had up to a hundred years to go through numerous generations, interbreeding both with domestics and with whatever else had got loose out there in the English woods by way of exotic cats.

Some of the descriptions of Suffolk big cats certainly sound closer to a "double-size domestic cat" than they do to an exotic leopard, puma or lynx. The "black, puma-like creature" seen by the Bloomfield brothers at Falcon Meadow, Bungay in 2004 had a head "like a house cat's but five times bigger." The animal seen late at night in the Haverhill Sainsbury's car park in 2008 was "tall and wiry with a white tipped tail, couldn't say how big it was," according to the witness, who "thought it was a fox at first…too big for a domestic cat."

Jonathan Mossman and Carl Scarfe on their walk to Claydon on that moonlight night in 2006 had a close encounter with a cat that was "all black, with the body shape of a feline," its shape was "pretty much (that of) a domestic cat." It had a long black tail whose form "matched that of a feline… long, slender", and Jonathan recalled then comparing what he'd seen to the tail of a domestic cat and noticing the similarity. David Barrington Barnes, the deerstalker at the end of Chapter 16 who gathered evidence of a puma on the Eve Estate somewhere in West Suffolk, couldn't say for certain whether the "big catlike" animal he'd seen in the headlights of his truck one night was a puma or just a domestic cat, "so fleeting was my view." He noted that if it was just a domestic cat he'd seen that night, then it was "a giant of the species."

PART 3 – BIG CATS OF THE CURIOUS COUNTY

Whether big cats in Suffolk's countryside are introduced exotics from other continents or indigenous British domestic cats gone wild might not be an "either/or" question.

Jonathan McGowan, the Bournemouth-based big cat investigator we met earlier, thinks some of the large cats sighted may be a hybrid between pumas and super-large feral domestic cats. Some of the black cats spotted do not have the "behaviour of leopards" says Jonathan. Some are "big black cats with small heads" while others are heard "yowling" – very un-leopard–like. But McGowan has also heard the leopard's distinctive "coughing" alarm call to its cubs in the British countryside.

"Complex hybridisation" between feral cats, Scottish wildcats and possibly some "exotics" is thought to explain the Kellas cat, shot by a gamekeeper near the village of Kellas in the Scottish county of Moray in 1984. It is slightly bigger than a domestic cat, with long legs and shiny black fur with random white wiry guard hairs scattered over its body. It is thought to be a hybrid between a Scottish wildcat and a domestic cat of some kind or an oriental strain – the shiny black fur, long legs and white wiry guard hairs recall a Bombay cat, a Burmese-black shorthaired cat cross, whose breeding was originally an attempt to produce at "miniature black panther." You can see the stuffed Kellas cat in the Elgin Museum in Moray.

A camera trap in Clashindarroch, Aberdeenshire filmed an "enormous" Scottish wildcat in March 2018. Four feet (1.2 metres) from nose to tail, it was "one of the largest wildcats recorded anywhere in the world" according to Kev Ball of conservation group Wildcat Haven.[7]

Then there are the Bengal cats, an affectionate breed of cat that's about domestic cat-sized (sometimes a little bigger) that likes to go for walks, you sometimes see them being taken for a stroll on a lead and a harness by their owner. They are yellow-brown in colour with leopard-like spots. Their name allegedly comes from an early encounter with one of them by early British settlers in India, seen from a boat swimming in the Bay of Bengal. They're a cross between a leopard cat (a small spotted wildcat with a coat reminiscent of a yellow spotted leopard's pattern, not to be confused with an actual spotted leopard) and domestic cats – most of them are at least fifth generation hybrids. Most Bengal cats seem to have some genes from the even more exotic fishing cat as well. The Dangerous Wild Animals Act of 1973 was partly in response to the surge in Bengal cats bred in the US, as well as "wolf dogs" (wolf-dog crossbreeds), both so new to the UK at the time that there was alarm at how they might turn out.

The Dangerous Wild Animals Act specifically banned pure leopard cats, that weren't yet being hybridized with domestic cats in the UK. In America, breeders keep breeding the fifth-generation Bengal cats back with pure leopard cats to get the markings – unfortunately it also gives their offspring a more wild leopard cat personality. Bengal cat hybrids are also being bred clandestinely in the US for their fur, some of which even ends up in quite reputable outlets there. Unscrupulous breeders pretend the bred-for-fur Bengal cats and leopard cats are non-existent "Lipi cats" from China, but the markings on the fur give them away as Bengal or leopard cats. Big Cat Rescue claim they get a lot of calls of "Florida Panthers" stalking local dogs, but when the animal rescue people show up, it turns out to be just a Bengal hybrid. Their wild personalities make them quite a handful, causing some desperate owners to turn them loose.

The Ultimate Guide to Cat Breeds notes that "selective breeding" of domestic cats took off in the 1870s, with Britain's first cat show at London's Crystal Palace in that year. Most "new breed characteristics arose through haphazard mutations – resulting in such traits as stub tails, abnormally short legs, bent or curled ears… human intervention is not responsible for some of the more distinctive mutations."

These "haphazard" characteristics have over the years resulted in the tailless Japanese Bobtail breed, which is supposed to look like a miniature bobcat, but it hasn't got any bobcat genes in it at all, it's just a spontaneous stumpy-tailed mutation. Then there's the Scottish curl cat, with its curled ears, the result of cross-breeding with some strange-eared feral cats found on a farm.

And then there's the new breed of "desert lynx." It isn't a lynx at all but a cross between various domestic cat breeds that coincidentally look a bit lynx-like and have – via spontaneous mutations in their ancestry – lost their tails or have stubby tails. In the US there are also "pixie-bob cats" – said to be hybrids between bobcats and domestic cats but these may not actually be a bobcat but just carrying genes from a tailless domestic cat mutant. The phrase "lynx hybrid cats for sale" is not uncommon in adverts in the US. But whether this really is lynx DNA in them or just sales talk about a domestic cats with something of the *look* of a lynx or bobcat about them is debatable.

Starting in the 1950s, cat breeding has been a "trend away from highly exaggerated looks back towards more natural, wilder-*looking* cats." (My emphasis added), including "semi-foreign" breeds with genes from domestic cats from Africa, or from breeds that look like they might have come from Africa. Often these breeds didn't actually have any African genes in them, they were just inspired by the *look* of African not-quite-wild cats, whose look breeders were trying to replicate by cross-breeding different varieties of domestic cat. Breeders who selectively bred such "semi-foreign" African-looking cats are looking to produce animals with " slender, muscular, wedge-shaped heads, oval paws, long, gently tapering tails, slender, muscular legs" on which they "stand taller".

Other examples of breeders' "effort to create wild-looking breeds" include the quite new breed of Ocicat, which "resembles an ocelot" but has no "wild" DNA. Could the Cambridgeshire "ocelot-like cat" encountered earlier have some connection to these Ocicats?[8]

The brown Burmese cats aren't from Burma at all, it turns out. They were a spontaneous mutation that arose in Thailand, where they ended up as temple cats. A lot of the exotic oriental names given to breeds of cat aren't anything to do with their origin, but just a distinctive, exotic-sounding name to make them sound cool. Bombay cats – a shiny black cat breed originating in a cross between a Burmese cat and a shorthaired black cat – weren't from India at all, but from Kentucky in the 1950s, their look inspired by the black panthers of a distant, imagined Bombay, India. (I know of at least one possible "black panther" misidentification in Dunwich Forest caused by a dogwalker seeing our own rehomed stray American Bombay cat taking himself for a walk in the woods, briefly glimpsed from a distance.) The Abyssinian cat was long thought to have been the result of British soldiers stationed in Abyssinia (now Ethiopia) in the nineteenth century bringing home local-bought kittens. But recent research points to the origins of the Abyssinian cat being actually somewhere in Egypt.

Yet another fancy pedigree breed is the Singaporean cat. These have distinctive round heads and big eyes, and originate from a feral cat colony found in a drain in the then British territory of Singapore. They're the result of yet another spontaneous mutation. The latest exotic cat breed to become popular in the last couple of years is the lykoi cat, bred to have a passing resemblance to wolves (in its coat and grey colouration mostly) and said to have behaviour more like a dog than a cat.

These weird-looking domestic cats have a long history. *Rural Sports* of 1813 includes a cat owned by a Mrs Finch in Malden, Essex, described a "curious long-haired cat." This was a male "about the usual size", tawny, sandy in places streaked with black, its face resembled "a lion in miniature" with hair protruding from its ears like the corkscrew moustaches fashionable among Thames water pilots at the time. Its tail was unlike that of a cat, more like a fox's.[9]

So domestic cats (including feral domestic cats) throw up some deeply bizarre mutations without any help from us. That's without humans selectively breeding domestic cats that already look like African wildcats and miniature black panthers. A quick look at the "cats for sale or adoption" websites shows how many "surplus" animals some pedigree cat breeders are looking to get rid of. It's conceivable that some of these super-exotic wildcat lookalikes are just dumped by less scrupulous breeders, or escape or just get lost. While the idea of feral domestic cats somehow growing to giant size in wild Britain may still sound unlikely, we've seen the apparent tendency for domestic cats to spontaneously evolve curly ears, round heads, stubby tails and other bizarre traits.

A short video by *The Oregonian* newspaper showed up on YouTube in 2010 showing what was thought to be a "huge feral domestic cat" found stuck in a *dog* flap and taken to an animal shelter in Oregon, USA, where staff named him Goliath. Could the same thing be happening in Britain? [10]

And that's without human-orchestrated selective breeding injecting "alien" DNA into domestic and feral domestic cats. As Carole Baskin, founder of Big Cat Rescue in the USA, so eloquently put it, "allowing the private possession of exotic cat hybrids is like strapping a nuclear warhead to the feral cat problem." (The keeping of most exotic cat breeds that would require a licence in the UK is still largely unregulated in many states of the US.)

Domestic cats have somehow been crossed successfully with servals, despite servals being two or even three times the size of a domestic cat. The offspring, known as Savannah cats, are larger and leggier than the domestic cat parents. We've already encountered the Bengal cat, as well as some other weird and wonderful domestic cat breeds. Of these, some are the result of hybridising with different breeds of wildcat, and some just the outcome of the throw of the dice that is genetics and random mutation, and others the result of a bit of both. And there are some breeds of domestic cat that are rather big, like the Maine Coon cat. What would happen if one of these became a feral cat and turned up in a wild Britain, already populated with potential mates with all sorts of exotic bits of genetic material in them?

Other such exotics worth mentioning are the Safari cats, a cross between a domestic cat and a Geoffroy's cat. The Geoffroy's cat is a domestic-cat sized species of wildcat from South America. What's interesting to note about Safari cats is that the males of these hybrids are – unusually – said to be fertile. Also, "hybrid vigour" – producing hybrids that are bigger than either parent – has been reported in Geoffrey's cats. There is a melanistic version of the Geoffroy's Cat as well.[11]

Where non-native exotic big cats from distant continents end and where indigenous wildcats that have somehow reached gigantic proportions begin is possibly a little blurred. Jonathan McGowan's belief about giant-sized feral domestic moggies being big enough to breed with pumas suddenly starts to sound more plausible, given the variety of spontaneously mutating moggies and the often reckless addition of exotic genes by pedigree cat breeders, genes that will inevitably get out into the feral cat gene pool .

The big cats of Suffolk (and of Britain) could indeed be a population of introduced black leopards, lynxes, servals, caracals and pumas – now in their third or fourth British-born generation. Or they could be domestic cats gone feral and somehow gone gigantic, and given an added spin by the acquisition of some exotic cat genes. Or they could be a bit of both.

Lynx kittens! Corsican cat-foxes!

Among the oddest Suffolk mystery cat reports, from "Simon from Ipswich", was that of two "lynx kittens" spotted one evening in October 2015, on the Eastbridge to Leiston road.

Given that not-yet-fully-grown lynx kittens and very unusual fully grown adult domestic cats would be about the same size, I'm tempted to think that what Simon and his daughter saw might not have been lynx kittens after all, but some really bizarre-looking feral mutant moggies, possibly helped along the path towards their strange appearance by the injection of fragments of DNA from some hybridised or foreign exotic species of wildcat.

From the French island *department* of Corsica in the summer of 2019 came news that a longstanding population of what were thought to be ordinary domestic cats gone feral and living in the woods may be a new species after all. These cats are known locally as Ghjattu Volpe – "the cat-fox" in the Corsican language because of their size (about 90cm or 35 inches from head to tail), their distinctive tail and the "very wide ears". Genetic analysis of 12 specimens caught in traps and later released show it's more closely related to the African wildcat *Felis silvestris lybica* than to the European wildcat. There is speculation that farmers arriving from the Middle East 6,500 years ago may have introduced the "cat-fox" before it went feral.

Living in a "very inconspicuous" colony of 16 known individuals, the cat-foxes are tawny coloured and striped with dark back legs and usually four rings and a black tip on thier bushy tails. They have "highly developed" canine teeth and a russet-coloured stomachs, and a reputation in local folklore for attacking the udders of sheep and goats. They are "very nocturnal" and hide out in areas with water and lots of cover where they can shelter from their natural predator, the golden eagle. The cat-fox's long, silky coat is a natural defence against ticks and lice. The island's National Hunting and Wildlife Service hope to have the newly-discovered animal "recognised and protected" soon.[12]

If a probable new species of wildcat can have hidden from us in a small woodland colony all this time, what else could be concealing itself out there in the countryside, in Suffolk or elsewhere in Britain?

Mrs Finch's cat from Malden, from 1813, shows that random mutations have produced bizarre-looking, big domestic cats for well over two centuries.
From *Our Cats and All About Them*, Harrison Weir, R. Clements, Tunbridge Wells, 1889, out of copyright.

FOOTNOTES TO CHAPTER 22: East Anglian born and bred big cats?

1. There's a story that the former Prime Minister Margaret Thatcher, when she was a chemist in the early 1960s, had her first job in a laboratory in the Brantham-Cattawade industrial estate with John Lyons, later ice cream giant Lyons Maid. The story goes that her brief was to put more air and more sugar and less ice cream into ice cream to create the Mr Whippy soft ice cream sold in cornets from ice cream vans. Investigation has shown this story is too good to be true – she was a chemist with John Lyons, but the story about forcing more air and sugar into Mr Whippy was an urban legend and she worked with the company in West London.

There's analysis of the Thatcher at Cattawade Industrial Estate/Mr Whippy legend at www.theguardian.com/politics/reality-check/2013/apr/17/margaret-thatcher-team-mr-whippy. Some of the piles of rubble on the Brantham industrial estate have recently been cleared, with planning permission granted for a housing development on one end of the site. Derelict industrial units are being demolished to make way for a proposed new train depot there as well.

2. Messy Beast http://messybeast.com/big-cat2.htm. We don't really know where the extra-large Maine Coon cats, the largest known domestic cat breed, came from. One of the most likely-sounding stories of its origins involves the – also large – Norwegian Forest Cats said to have been brought by Viking settlers to Newfoundland, and cats brought by early English seafarers have also been suggested. *A General History of Quadrupeds*, p. 228, Thomas Bewick, Hodgson, Beilby, Bewick, Newcastle, 1800, https://archive.org/details/generalhistoryof00bewi/page/228/mode/2up

3. Stanley was a caller to the Jon Wright show BBC Radio Suffolk 1 January 2015; a source in East of England animal rescue also told me they were "pretty sure some people out there are still keeping big cats.".

4. George's now defunct web page on Fram and Sax Cats was at http://framandsax.cats.org.uk/framandsax/adopt-a-cat/?cid=144295; *Wild Animals of the British Isles*, Dr Maurice Burton, Frederick Warne 1968. A resident of Dunwich in the early 1970s told me there were so many feral cats in Dunwich Forest in those days that the locals used to go on "cat shoots" in the forest with air rifles.

5. Iron Age British domestic cats in *The Ultimate Guide to Cat Breeds*, Louisa Somerville, Regency House Publishing 2004. See :"A Roman caracal in Norfolk, *Fortean Times*, **FT 382:57** and http://mattsalusbury.blogspot.com/2109/10/a-roman-caracal-in-norfok.html for recent archaeological evidence of a caracal in Norfolk during Roman times, as well as evidence (or the lack of it) for other big cats in Roman Britain.

6. Like jungle cats, the Sevenoaks Jackal was another animal presumed to have been brought back to England by an "old India hand", a British expatriate returned from a posting in India. In 1904, something killed two dozen sheep and did about £2000 of damage to livestock in the area around Sevenoaks, Kent, before it was shot and killed by a local gamekeeper. It turned out to be an Indian jackal. It was stuffed and displayed in a local pub. The Sevenoaks Jackal features on now rare and sought-after local postcards See www.scribd.com/article/51986732/Peculiar-Postcards.

7. Possible puma/giant domestic feral cat hybrids: **"**Jonathan McGowan big cats/large cats", August 2012, http://mattsalusbury.blogspot.com/2012/10/jonathan-mcgowans-big-cat-large-cat.html; Largest ever Scottish wildcat: www.independent.co.uk/news/uk/scotland-wildcat-video-aberdeenshire-forest-haven-clashindarroch-a8278196.html

8. *The Ultimate Guide to Cat Breeds*, Louisa Somerville, Regency House Publishing 2004. Among the breeds the book lists is the "Suffolk chocolate", also called the Suffolk brown, whose kittens change hands for around £400 online.

9. *Rural Sports*, Daniel, 1813, quoted in *Our Cats and All About Them*, Harrison Weir, R. Clements, Tunbridge Wells, 1889. Weir organised Britain's first cat show at Crystal Palace.

10. "Fat stray cat rescued, stuck in doggy door, *The Oregonian*, undated, 2007, 2010, www.youtube.com/watch?v=fN7eXTz35dI&feature=related.

11. Ligers – a hybrid between a tiger and a lion, also exhibit hybrid vigour and are enormous. As lions are animals of the open savannah and not suited to the British countryside, I haven't gone into lions as possible British big cats in detail. Sightings of "lionesses" in Britain are probably pumas. All the recorded modern escapes of lions form zoos or safari parks in Britain that I've come across ended with the lion being captured or shot within 48 hours.

12. "Corsica's cat-foxes, on the trail of what might be a new species", Maureen Coffland, *Phys Org*, 19 June 2019, https://phys.org/news/2019-06-corsica-cat-fox-trail-species.html.

Witch's cat on a weathervane at Blythburgh

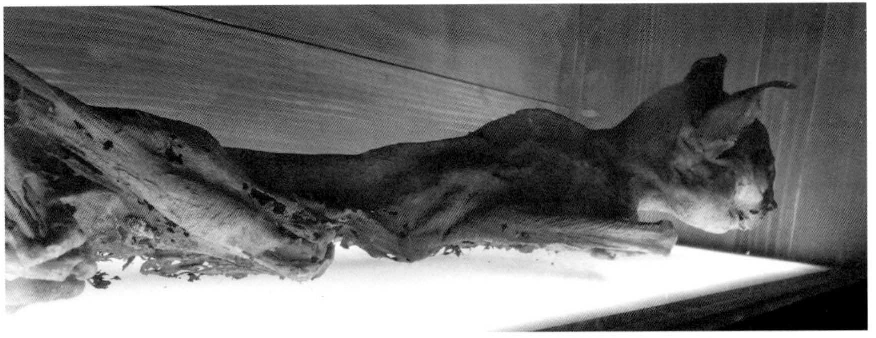

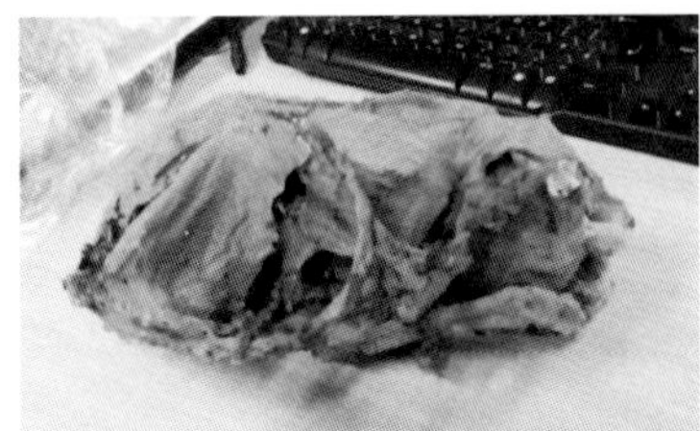

Mummified cats of West Suffolk: Rammeses at the Guildhall, Lavenham (top), at The Nutshell pub, Bury (left), a specimen now on display at the city's Moyse's Hall Museum (above, photo courtesy Alex McWhirter of Moyses's Hall Museum) and under the floor at The Mill Hotel, Sudbury (bottom.)

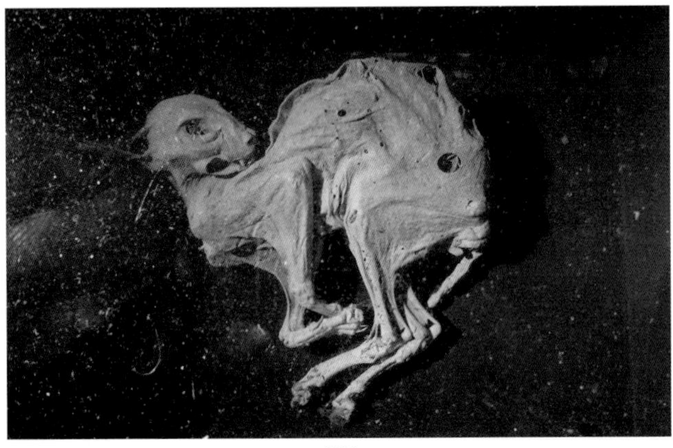

24: Conventionally-sized cat curiosities

And finally…

Whether or not Suffolk's alleged big cats actually exist, the county's domestic cats have at times been unusual and striking enough, even in death.

And you can actually get to see some of then, if you have a moderately strong stomach. One of Suffolk's more gruesome specialities is its mummified cats – found walled up inside old houses during restoration. Entombing cats or kittens (sometimes alive) in the walls of a house was supposed to bring good luck, and protect the house from both fire and witchcraft.

Bury St Edmunds is the epicentre of Suffolk mummified cats, there are several preserved mummified cats on display at its Moyse's Hall Museum, while Bury's The Nutshell pub – Britain's smallest pub – has a fine specimen of a mummified cat hanging from the ceiling, along with all the foreign banknotes that have ended up there over the years. Should you find yourself in the pedestrianised centre of Bury, The Nutshell is well worth a visit. Two pieces of advice, though.

One, The Nutshell is absolutely not for shrinking violets or wallflowers. It's so tiny that it's almost impossible not to get pulled into one of the conversations that's going on there, often among Bury's tiny bohemian "alternative" community. If you can't fight banter with even better banter, it's not for you.

And two, ask nicely for permission to photograph their magnificent mummified cat, and whatever you do, DON'T touch it. Like a lot of Suffolk mummified cats, there's said to be a curse attached to it. I heard an apocryphal story about The Nutshell's mummified cat being stolen, as a result of a prank by "other ranks" in a locally-based military unit, only for it to be returned not long after by a grim-faced off-duty soldier (out of uniform but still identifiable by his haircut) who turned up at the pub and handed it back with scarcely a word.

In Sudbury, The Mill Hotel has a mummified cat on display in a glass-topped casket. It was found in 1975 and reburied in its casket by the then Mayor of Sudbury, after Canon Peter Schneider of the Church of England reportedly declined to perform a religious ceremony for a dead cat. It's back on display under thick glass in a recess in the corner of the floor in the lobby, back in the building where it was found.

The restored Guildhall in Lavenham, now a National Trust property and local museum, also boasts a mummified cat on show, who goes by the name of Rammeses. He was found hidden in a roof in one of the nearby houses. Rammeses alone is worth the price of admission to the Guildhall. So magnificently well preserved is he that he still has the tips of his ears and most of his whiskers. None of the staff could tell me why he's called Rammeses (with two "m"s), although I suspect it's something to do with Egyptians and mummification – Egyptologist Robert Gayer Anderson and his twin brother Thomas settled in Lavenham in the 1920s and raised money to save the Guildhall.

Six mummified cats were discovered by builders doing work on a house in Fakenham Magna near Bury in August 1972. The builders reported being scared by unexplained tapping noises and footsteps.[1]

FOOTNOTES TO CHAPTER 24: Conventionally-sized cat curiosities

1. Sudbury mummified cat from *Lantern,* no, 12, Hidden East Anglia website, which quotes the *Eastern Daily Press* 15 November 1975, a dramatised account in *Suffolk Ghost Tales*, Kirsty Hartsiotis & Cherry Wilkinson, The History Press, Stroud 2017 says the Vicar of St Gregory's was "brought in" for the Mill Hotel cat's rebuial; Fakenham Magna discovery from *Bury Free Press*, 8 August 1972, Fakenham Magna is also said to be the haunt of a mysterious entity that goes by the name of "old yellow eyes". Many thousands of mummified cats buried in cemeteries at sacred sites in ancient Egypt were harvested and sent as ballast on British ships to England to be used as fertilizer, so it is possible that other mummified cats may turn up in some Suffolk field one day. I've heard unconfirmed reports of Suffolk detectorists turning up pre-Roman Egyptian jewellery in fields. If it's true, these would have been grave goods wrapped into the bandages of mummified Egyptian animals. The nitrates used in the mummification process meant mummies made good fertilizer.

This wooden carving in Aldeburgh's church remembers a local cat who used to regularly wander into the building and sit and listen to organ recitals.

Is this a domestic cat, or a heraldic panther, appearing as a gargoyle and water spout on the tower of St Peter's Church, Yoxford?

A sign seen in Blythburgh.

A cat on the statue of local boy Cardinal Thomas Wolsey, at the junction of St Peter's Street and Silent Street (above). A lion-like creature carved on the font made from dark Tournai marble imported from Belgium at the Church of St Peter's on the Waterfront (below), both in Ipswich.

Glossary

5th century (AD) the century from 400 to 499, during which the Anglo-Saxons arrived and established themselves in England and began to form what became its seven Anglo-Saxon kingdoms, including East Anglia.

15th century ("the 1400s") the century from 1400-1499 when Suffolk was at the heart of medieval England's wool industry and many of its churches were built.

8th Air Force US miltary unit with a big presence in Suffolk during World War Two."

95th Bomber Group (Bombardment Group, The 95th) the USAAF bomber squadrons based at RAF Horham in North Suffolk, which airlifted a few donkeys from Algeria to Suffolk.

ABC Alien Big Cat(s) – believed to be exotic big cats, not native to Britain, introduced to the UK by an escape or release of a big cat species from Africa, Asia or the Americas.

AD Anno Domini, the "Year of Our Lord" in Latin. In this dating system that has the presumed year of Christ's birth as zero, I write in 2022 (AD), the Roman Emperor Claudius's legions invaded Britain in 43AD, while Queen Boudicca of the Iceni's East Anglian rebellion was in 79 AD. I considered using a more secular system, but AD seemed appropriate as most AD dates used in this book are in the context of the struggle between Christians and pagans in East Anglia.

A roads in a county without motorways, the most important main roads are those designated 'A roads'. Some of Suffolk's A roads are even dual carriageways for some of their length.

The major A roads in Suffolk are the A12 (entering Suffolk at Stratford St Mary in the south and passing all the way through the county parallel with the coast and onward to Great Yarmouth in Norfolk), the A14 (entering Suffolk just north of Newmarket, passing through Bury and Stowmarket, bypassing Ipswich and ending at Felixstowe), the A134 (from Sudbury and north through Thetford Forest), the A143 (from Bury going northeast, crossing the Waveney and leaving Suffolk at Stutson), the A140 (from Stutson down to Needham Market), the A11 (Newmarket to Elveden) and the A1120 "scenic route" from Yoxford to Stowmarket.

The lower an A road's number is, the more important it is considered in terms of national infrastructure. Suffolk has numerous less important four-figure A roads. Properties "the wrong side of the A12", to the west of it and away from the coast, are less sought after than those nearer the coast.

Abellio Greater Anglia privately-owned subsidiary of Nederlandse Spoorwegen (Dutch Railways) that operates most of the railways in and into Suffolk and the rest of East Anglia. It was formerly Greater Anglia and before that Anglia Railways.

African golden cat see golden cat

Asian golden cat see golden cat

AONB Area of Outstanding Natural Beauty, an area designated for conservation, protected and subject to planning controls. The two AONBs in Suffolk are Suffolk Coasts and Heaths AONB (covering much of the Suffolk coast and the heaths inland) and Dedham Vale AONB along the banks of the River Stour and extending into Essex.

Anglia Railways see "Abellio Greater Anglia".

Angles one of the Germanic peoples from the areas that's now the northernmost provinces of Germany and its border with Denmark, who settled in Britain along with the Saxons and Jutes (from Germany and Denmark) in the period from 400AD onwards. By 600AD they had formed into the Anglo-Saxon kingdom of East Anglia.

They gave their name to what became the English people and language.

Anglo-Saxon (language) the Germanic language of the Angles and other Saxon peoples that settled in the East of England from 400AD onwards. The Undley bracteate, a gold pendant from Undley Common near Mildenhall, from the fifth century AD, bears the first known writing in a recognisably "English" variant of the Saxon (Germanic) language, distinct from the languages spoken in Germany. Many Suffolk place names are Anglo-Saxon in origin, such as Saxmundham ("Seizmond's Home"), Harkstead ("Herca's Place") and Cattawade ("Wildcat Crossing" according to some scholars.) Anglo-Saxon evolved into modern English.

assizes county courts sitting at regular intervals, their jurisdiction was transferred to the High Court and Crown Court in 1972. In Suffolk they were in Bury St Edmunds and later Ipswich, and at Thetford – part of Suffolk until 1832. Many Suffolk witchcraft trials were at the Bury or Ipswich Assizes.

B road important roads with lower traffic density than an A road, although in Suffolk they're comparatively busy. In Suffolk they're often former A roads that have been bypassed. They have a four-figure number starting with a "1". For example, the B1125 starts at Westleton and joins the B1122 near Theberton, and then goes all the way to Leiston, from where the B1119 goes all the way west to Framlingham.

B-17 Boeing "Flying Fortress", a heavy bomber aircraft in use with the US Army Air Force in World War Two, with many flying from bases in Suffolk.

Babergh (pronounced "Bay-burr") a District of Suffolk governed by Babergh District Council, based in Hadleigh. It's also officially known as South Suffolk. Roughly Gainsborough Country and Constable Country (see below). Its green logo features the sun shining over rolling hills. Babergh collaborates with Mid-Suffolk District Council in delivering many services.

barley a cereal grain crop with distinctive long "spikelets" protruding from the grains when it's still on the stalk. The poor, sandy, well-drained soil of much of coastal Suffolk is ideal for growing barley for malt (see below) used in beer.

BBCS British Big Cats Society, a big cat investigation group, active in the late 1990s and early 2000s. Its investigations included the Beccles Lynx.

BCIB Big Cats in Britain. A now less active group investigating British big cats. In the early 2000s they published annually a BCIB Yearbook detailing the reports of big cat sightings they had received, county by county.

big cat a non-scientific definition that strictly speaking includes tigers, lions, jaguars, leopards and snow leopards but most people generally include pumas, clouded leopards and cheetahs, or even lynxes, servals and caracals as well.

Big Cats in Britain see BCIB above.

Bigfoot (plural: Bigfoots) – a large, hairy apelike creature said to resemble a yeti, said to live in North America. It features in the traditions of many Native American nations. Also known as "sasquatch."

Black Shuck the phantom hellhound Black Shuck, usually (but not always) a large, male, often shaggy, black dog with shining red eyes.

black panther a melanistic leopard. Some are completely black, some are a very dark brown colour (almost black). In many cases, the spots can still be seen in a slightly darker colour.

bobcat a North American wildcat similar to a lynx, but smaller and generally with a very short tail (a "bobtail").

Bomber Group (Bombardment Group, Bomb Group) – a unit of the USAAF stationed in East Anglia in World War Two, this would consist of three or four bomber squadrons of twelve bombers each. The 95th Bomber Group, for example, was stationed at RAF Horham near Eye.

Borough of Ipswich the predominantly urban district of Suffolk administered by Ipswich Borough Council

The Brecks (Breckland) the area of northwest Suffolk and South Norfolk taken up by gorse -covered sandy heath with some woodlands (usually pines). It is the habitat for many rare species, some of which are seldom found elsewhere in England. Breckland is also the official name for a district of Norfolk. leopards

British Big Cat Research a low profile big cat research group investigating reports of big cats and possible big cat kills in the British Isles.

British Big Cats Society – see BBCS, above.

The Broads Officially the Norfolk and Suffolk Broads National Park, this is a conservation area of navigable lakes and rivers, managed by the Broads Authority. They are flooded medieval peat excavations. The Broads begins with the River Waveney at Lowestoft, and then goes inland to Oulton Broad, Barnby Broad, Beccles and Bungay before leaving Suffolk. Most of the Broads are in Norfolk.

Bury in Suffolk, Bury St Edmunds. Always pronounced "berry" (rhymes with "very", never pronounced to rhyme with "hurry"), and always leaving out the suffix "St Edmunds". Nothing to do with Bury in Greater Manchester.

Cambs. short form of Cambridgeshire.

caracal a species of cat about twice the size of a domestic cat, sandy or red in colour with long pointed black ears ended in extravagant tufts. (The name means "black ear" in Turkish.) It has a big range in the wild, from Africa to Asia. Some are kept in captivity. Some of Suffolk's big cats may be caracals.

carnassial – large teeth in carnivores, adapted for shearing flesh. Evidence of big cat kills includes bones neatly cut by carnassials, rather than crushed – as dog's carniassial teeth would.

catamount alternative name for a puma from

"cat of the mountain."

Centre for Fortean Zoology a group that investigates mystery animals internationally, based in Devon. It's "Fortean" in the belief that some of the animals reported couldn't possibly exist in the UK, and would have to be phantoms, or have some other explanation rather than being mortal, physical, living animals.

CFZ see Centre for Fortean Zoology

Chinese Water Deer (CWD) – a primitive species of deer native to China that lacks antlers and has downward pointing tusks or canine teeth. They escaped from English deer parks and are now breeding in the wild in the UK, spreading across Suffolk. Smaller than red deer or fallow deer, they are believed to be the preferred diet of British big cats.

Coast Path the Suffolk Coast Path is a 50-mile (80km) public footpath near the coast – sometimes on the dunes, sometimes further inland – along most of the length of Suffolk's coastline from Felixstowe to Lowestoft via Bawdsey and Aldeburgh. Part of it has been washed away by recent erosion at Eastern Bavants.

Cold War the period from 1945 to 1989 when the West, organised through NATO and led by the United States, was locked in a state of hostility with the Soviet Union and its allies in the Warsaw Pact countries. Although there was the constant threat of nuclear war, there was little by way of actual fighting, usually through conflicts supported by the West or the Soviets in the Third World. At the time, there was an enormous presence of the US military – mostly airbases for fighter planes and tactical bombers, some nuclear armed – in Suffolk. The Bentwaters Cold War Museum now occupies a former air base near Woodbridge.

Constable Country the area around East Bergholt and Dedham Vale in southeastern Suffolk and North Essex and around the banks of the River Stour, immortalised in the landscapes of the painter John Constable.

Constable, John (1776-1837) an English Romantic painter born in East Bergholt, Suffolk his most famous paintings were of local landscapes – *The Hay Wain* (showing Flatford Mill in Suffolk), *Dedham Vale*, also *East Bergholt House, River Stour Looking towards Manningtree* and *Stratford Mill* (near Stratford St Mary, Suffolk.) He painted rural scenes at a time of the great upheaval of the Industrial Revolution. He was elected to the Royal Academy and was influential in France, where he inspired the Impressionists.

county a province of the United Kingdom, run by an elected County Council.

county town the seat of the County Council of an English county. Ipswich is the county town of Suffolk.

coypu – see illustration below – the large aquatic South American rodent *Myopotamus coypus,* also known as the nutria or river rat, introduced to Suffolk in the 1940s originally for fur farming. Coypu escaped into the East of England countryside and became an invasive species notorious for eating sugar beet crops and damaging river flood defences. Following a series of eradication programmes they were declared extinct in the UK by the end of the 1980s.

Coypu Control the Ministry of Agriculture's successful East of England coypu eradication programme, which employed coypu men to patrol rivers and shoot them.

coypu men armed Coypu Control officers patrolling East Anglia's rivers in motorboats seeking and destroying coypu.

crepuscular most active around dusk and dawn.

crest in heraldry, the decorative figure on top of a helm (helmet) that rest on top of the arms

(shield). The crest on the arms of the county of Suffolk, for example, features a dragon-prowed Viking ship.

Cromwell Oliver Cromwell, born 1599, was MP for Huntingdon in Cambridgeshire. In the English Civil War (1642-1648) between the forces of King Charles I and Parliament, he was commander of the Eastern Association – a Parliamentary army – and later its successor the New Model Army. In 1650 he was made Lord Protector of the Commonwealth of England, its Head of State, until his death in 1658. During Cromwell's period of political influence, William Dowsing was given a commission to visit East Anglian churches to destroy or deface "idolatrous" church fixtures such as stained glass and sculptures that celebrated Catholic doctrine. Matthew Hopkins, self-styled Witchfinder General, was also active in East Anglia at this time. The period became known as the Cromwellian period.

Curious County, The short-lived and much-maligned slogan adopted by Visit Suffolk, the county's tourist board, in 2012. Now regrettably out of use, it lives on only in an under-used hashtag, #proudtobecurious.

cryptid a hidden animal, an animal not yet formally described by science Examples include Bigfoot and British big cats.

cryptozoology the study of animals up to now unknown to science.

CWD see Chinese water deer.

Defra the UK government's Department for Environment, Food and Rural Affairs agency for England. Within Suffolk, many of its statutory functions such as licensing of dangerous animals kept in captivity and of zoos and the reporting of escaped "exotics" (animals alien to the UK) have passed to Natural England (see below.)

detectorist a person (usually male) who looks for metal objects on farmland with a metal detector. They're a common sight in Suffolk's fields, especially after harvest time, as coins and other metal finds particularly from the Bronze Age, Iron Age, Saxon and medieval periods are abundant in the county. The three series of the BBC comedy drama *Detectorists* were filmed in and around Framlingham, Suffolk. Many recent finds of treasure in Suffolk such as the Bronze Age Wissett Horde and the woodwose gold spoon handle from near Woodbridge (see Chapter 1) were uncovered by detectorists.

District Suffolk has District Councils to which many of the functions of Suffolk County Council are devolved. These are the Borough of Ipswich, Babergh (South Suffolk), St Edmundsbury, Mid-Suffolk, Forest Heath, Suffolk Coastal (SCDC) and Waveney – the last two have formally merged to become East Suffolk. St Edmundsbury and Forest Heath have merged into West Suffolk.

Domesday Book King William I's survey of all of England following the Norman Conquest, it was completed in 1086 and it lists Suffolk villages still in existence today. It was expected to stand as the definitive record of the England's settlements until Doomsday, the day of the Last Judgement and the end of the world, hence the name.

Doom Doomsday, the end of the world in medieval Christian theology. There are several "Dooms" – scenes of the Last Judgement painted in Suffolk churches, most feature the resurrection of the dead and Christ and the angels dispensing justice on the souls of the departed. There are Dooms painted at Bacton, Chelsworth, Stoke by Clare, Yaxley and Stanningfield. But none are as spectacular as the one at Wenhaston, which features the Devil, imps and the gaping mouth of hell.

dormouse the hazel dormouse is an agile mouse-like rodent with a hairy tail and big ears, living in hedgerows and now very rare in the UK but recovering its numbers. Its name comes from its long hibernation, during which it is dormant.

DWA Dangerous Wild Animals Act. The legislation under which licences are granted (or not) to own and keep dangerous wild animals including big cats and wildcats under strict conditions.

DWAL Dangerous Wild Animals Act Licence, see DWA above.

Edmund the Martyr the last King of East Anglia, the Christian Saxon monarch was murdered by pagan Danish invaders in 869 somewhere round Hoxne. The Danes tied him up and shot arrows into him, then beheaded him. A mysterious wolf was said to have appeared to guard Edmund's severed head until it could be buried. His body was reburied at what became the abbey at Bury St Edmunds (named after him, the abbey is now a ruin). A cult of St Edmund the Martyr quickly followed, he was England's first patron saint until St George was adopted by crusaders.

EADT *East Anglian Daily Times*. The regional paid-for daily newspaper covering North Essex and Suffolk, based in Ipswich.

East Anglia – today, the counties of Essex, Suffolk and Norfolk. (But see footnote 1 on page 17!) The Anglo-Saxon Kingdom of East Anglia was roughly Suffolk, Norfolk and large swathes of Cambridgeshire. Founded in the sixth century AD, it was eventually conquered by the Kingdom of Mercia (now the Midlands) in 654, enjoyed brief independence after rebelling against the Mercians in 825 and ended with conquest by the Danes in 983. King Edmund the Martyr (buried at Bury) was the last King of East Anglia, and the Sutton Hoo ship burial near Melton, its grave items now in the British Museum, is believed to be a monument to the East Anglian King Rædwald, who reigned around 599-624.

Eastern puma a controversial population of pumas said to live in the eastern USA, despite pumas being regarded as hunted to extinction in that region and officially extinct there since 2021. Some claim that reports of eastern pumas (or eastern cougars or "Florida panthers") are misidentifications, or occasional specimens of the known puma population in the western USA that have wandered east. Others claim the eastern puma is a subspecies with distinctive behaviour.

East of England the counties of Suffolk, Norfolk, Essex, Hertfordshire, Buckinghamshire and Cambridgeshire. It became an "official region" in 1984 and there is an East of England Local Government Association based in Bury.

East Suffolk (county) from 1888 to 1974 the current county of Suffolk was divided into two counties – East Suffolk (its seat of government was at Ipswich) and West Suffolk (its county town was Bury). In 2017, Waveney and Suffolk Coastal district councils merged into a unified district council called "East Suffolk.".

East Suffolk Lines the two Abellio Greater Anglia railway lines, single track for most of their routes – from Ipswich to Lowestoft and from Ipswich to Felixstowe.

EDP *Eastern Daily Press*. The regional paid-for daily newspaper covering the northern end of Suffolk from around Southwold northwards and Norfolk. It's based in Norwich.

egret the little egret is a small white heron with black legs, now a common sight in Suffolk's wetlands It was hunted to extinction for its feathers used to decorate Victorian ladies' hats. In 1899 the *EADT* was already complaining that they had vanished from East Anglia. They re-colonised Suffolk from Africa starting in the late 1980s. Less common is the heron-sized great white egret, which is also now breeding in the UK again but more often seen as a summer visitor.

ergot a black-coloured fungal growth on rye and other cereals, it causes hallucinations if eaten, leading some to suggest it as a possible explanation for people seeing ghosts and fairies.

Eurasian lynx see lynx. Lynxes seen in the wild in Suffolk are probably Eurasian lynxes rather than the smaller Canadian lynx.

Evening Star the daily newspaper for Ipswich, which seems to take more of an interest in big cats than other newspapers in the county. Its online and weekly freesheet edition is the *Ipswich Star* and the titles are used interchangeably.

Fall, The in medieval Christian theology, the moment at which Adam and Eve – made in the "image of God" – were turned out of the Garden of Eden and punished for their Original Sin. According to this doctrine, mankind at that moment fell from a naïve State of Grace to the current degraded, sinful state we endure today. Therefore, Suffolk's wildmen would have to be humans that had become feral since The Fall.

field signs evidence of an animal having been in a particular place, such as scat (faeces), scent-marking with urine, scratches, paw prints, etc. as well as signs of them having eaten their prey (see kill-signs).

familiar (noun) a demon obeying and attending a witch, often in the form of an animal or a creature superficially resembling an animal.

farsee Suffolk dialect word for "fairy" in the eighteenth and nineteenth century. Some speculate that it originates from "far-sidhe", men of the hill in Irish Gaelic, either a very, very old Celtic word or brought by eighteenth century immigrants to West Norfolk from Ireland.

feline relating to a cat or a member of the cat family, or cat-like.

fen (also fenland) a type of fertile, mineral-rich wetland with grasses and mosses, often fens are drained marshland. They are now mostly used for pasture or horseculture (keeping horses for recreational use in paddocks) or nature reserves. Much of the edges of North Suffolk and West Suffolk are fen.

Fen Tiger the fiercely independent human inhabitants of the isolated fens in north Suffolk, Norfolk and Cambridgeshire, so-called by engineers whose drainage projects they tenaciously resisted. The name was applied to a mystery cat (not supposed to be a tiger but a thin black panther, puma or lynx or several different types of feline) sighted along the Cambridgeshire-Suffolk border from the 1980s.

feral animals born in the wild but descended from domestic stock that escaped or turned wild. Examples are feral cats (descendants of domestic cats) and feral ferrets, now hybridised into "pole-cat-ferrets". Feral cats are distinct from – for example – Scottish wildcats, a distinct species that was always wild. Some believe British big cats to be feral cats somehow evolved to giant size.

ferisher yet another Suffolk dialect word for

"fairy". Possibly connected to "fresher", a dialect word for a frog, as fairies were small, jumping creatures dressed in green.

Flying Fortress B-17 bomber made by Boeing, in service with the US Army Air Force in World War Two, flying from bases in Suffolk. There is a commonly held belief that US airmen used them to transport puma mascots to East Anglia from North America.

FOIA (pronounced "foyer") the Freedom of Information Act, under which public bodies have to respond to requests from members of the public for information. FOIA disclosures used in this book include Suffolk, Norfolk and Essex Police constabularies' published logs of calls from the public reporting big cats, and Natural England data on escaped exotics in Suffolk, including wild boar shot at Ixworth.

Forest Heath the district of Suffolk on the western edge of the county that includes Lakenheath, Mildenhall and Newmarket, now merged into West Suffolk.

Forestry Commission (Forestry Commission England) the government agency responsible for the management of forests, the exploitation of its timber resources, forest wildlife habitats and research into forests. which has its East of England HQ in Santon Downham, Suffolk. Forestry Commission-managed estates in Suffolk (some exploited by its commercial offshoot, Forest Enterprise) include Rendlesham Forest, Tunstall Forest, Dunwich Forest, Thetford Forest and the King's Forest near Bury.

Fort, Charles Author and philosopher who obsessively catalogued and commented on – often humorously – thousands of newspaper reports on unusual phenomena such as rains of frogs and fishes, luminous owls, mystery airships and so on. Fort was also interested in how orthodox science sought to explain away – or ignore – strange phenomena according to the intellectual fashions of the day. His four books *The Book of the Damned, Lo!, Wild Talents* and *New Lands* include accounts of plagues of aphids over Bury, gnat plagues over Beccles, a 1905 wildman on Martlesham Heath (probably an eccentric tramp, or a vagrant with learning difficulties), luminous owls over Norfolk and so on.

fortean (adjective) – relating to strange phenomena or inspired by the work of author and philosopher Charles Fort (see above). Current examples of fortean endeavours include the magazine *Fortean Times* and the Centre for Fortean Zoology.

Fram the town of Framlingham, short form used by those who live locally.

frairy (pronounced "fray-ree") Suffolk dialect word for "fairy" in the eighteenth and nineteenth centuries.

furze (also written "furzey") an old English word for gorse, still in use in East Anglia to describe now rare rough scrubland, not exclusively gorse.

Gainsborough Country the area around Sudbury and southwest Suffolk associated with the landscapes and portrait subjects of the artist Thomas Gainsborough. His childhood home in Sudbury is now the Gainsborough House museum in Gainsborough Street.

Gainsborough, Thomas (1727-1788) a landscape artist and portrait painter, he was one of the founding members of the Royal Academy. He was born in Sudbury in South Suffolk and had his studio first in Sudbury and then Ipswich in his early career, painting portraits for the local merchants and gentry. He worked at speed and combined portraits with landscapes. *Mr and Mrs Robert Andrews* is his most famous portrait, showing the couple at their estate near Sudbury. His landscapes included *Landscape in Suffolk* and *Cornard Wood, near Sudbury, Suffolk*. He inspired John Constable (see above).

galleytrot either a skeletal entity that frightens travellers on dark nights by removing its head, or a name for phantom dogs such as Black Shuck.

gelding a castrated male horse.

genus a grouping of organisms having common characteristics distinct from those of other such groupings. A genus is part of a "family" and is sub-divided into species (see below). A genus is indicated by a Latin name with a capital letter. For example, the genus *Panthera* includes tigers *(Panthera tigris)*, lions *(Panthera leo)*, jaguars *(Panthera onca)* and leopards *(Panthera pardus)*.

giantism a tendency towards abnormally large size, often caused by a genetic mutation.

gnat *Simuliidae* (black flies) and *Ceratopogonidae*, small two-winged mosquito-like flies, with biting and non-biting varieties.

golden cat the Asian golden cat *Catopuma temminckii* or *Pardofelis temminckii* is a heavily-built, golden brown or dark brown cat about two or three times as big as a domestic cat, native to South East Asia. The African golden cat *Caracal aurata* (not closely related to the Asian golden cat) is about twice the size of a domestic cat, with a small rounded head and long legs. Its colour varies from chestnut or reddish brown to grey, some individuals have black spots. Both African and Asian golden cats are kept in captivity and could account for some of Suffolk's big cats – they could be mistaken for pumas.

Heart of Suffolk Babergh District and Mid-Suffolk District together, cooperating on tourism and other services. The Brett Valley covers roughly the Heart of Suffolk area.

hellhound a hound from hell, a phantom or demonic dog such as Black Shuck (see above.)

helm the full-face helmet worn by knights in medieval warfare, which has a decorative crest on top identifying its owner.

heraldry the system by which coats-of-arms were devised and regulated in medieval times, still in use today.

Heritage Coast see Suffolk Heritage Coast

High Suffolk the part of Suffolk roughly west of Stowmarket (starting at Stowupland, the clue's in the name) where the sandy clay soil changes to chalky soil, and hills become more common.

hobby lantern (also hobby light) a mystery light, often seen in marshes or fields, that appears to move and in some cases react as if alive or under intelligent control. Some are believed to be self-igniting plumes of marsh gas.

hobby (bird of prey) *Falco subbuteo* – a bird of prey with swept-back wings that hunts swifts, swallow and dragonflies on the wing and lives in abandoned crows' nests. From North Africa, hobbys spend the summer in England, almost exclusively in Suffolk.

hops climbing plants whose female flowers are dried and used to make beer. They were previously grown a lot in Suffolk, especially around Stowmarket.

Hundred a now defunct administrative district of a county.

hypnogogic (also spelled hypnagogic,) the state of mind immediately before falling asleep. It's thought that many vivid encounters with ghosts and fairies occur in this state and are mistaken for real events.

Ipswich, Borough of see Borough of Ipswich

Ipswichian Interglacial a brief warm period between Ice Ages, named after the deposits and fossils found around Ipswich. It started around 135,000 years ago and finished with the last Ice Age 110,000 years ago.

Ipswich Star aka Evening Star the weekly freesheet version of the daily *Evening Star* newspaper, serving the area around Ipswich, and its website.

imp a small mischievous devil, a witch's familiar

jungle cat *Felis chaus,* a species of Asian wildcat slightly larger than a domestic cat. It's usually sandy in colour, although there are melanistic jungle cats too. Their natural range is from Egypt to southern China, although some are known to have been introduced into the wild in the UK. Hybrids of jungle cats and domestic cats are known as chaussie cats.

kill signs evidence of a kill by a big cat or other predator – the remains of an animal killed or partly eaten in a particular way, or flattened grass or a trail where a predator has dragged the body of its prey.

large cat some big cat investigators believe the UK's big cats aren't exclusively "big cats" such as leopards or pumas, but a variety of different animals such as hybrids of smaller wildcat species, or feral cats gone gigantic, and prefer to describe these as "large cats."

leopard A big cat species from Asia and Africa, usually yellow in colour with distinctive hollow black spots or "rosettes." Black (melanistic) leopards are rarer. For some reason, nearly all the leopards reported in the UK are black.

leopard cat *Prionailurus bengalensis,* a slender Asian wildcat the size a of domestic cat with a spotted coat like a leopard's. It was in response to concerns about leopard cats escaping from captivity that the Dangerous Wild Animals Act was introduced in 1976. Leopard cat-domestic cat hybrids, known as Bengal cats, are popular pets.

London overspill (also "London overflow", Expansion Towns) communities created as a result of a government policy of moving residents out of London to other areas from the 1930s to the 1970s, with new social housing estates built in those towns. The growth of Haverhill and Thetford in particular was as a result of London overspill, with Bury, Sudbury, Mildenhall, Long Melford and Great Cornard also part of this policy.

Lothing Land a former island in a giant lagoon north of Lowestoft, now drained. Most of it is in Norfolk, some of its villages are in Suffolk.

lynx a type of wildcat the size of a large dog, with yellowish fur (sometimes spotted), a short tail and tufted ears. It's believed to be the identity of some of Suffolk's big cats. Lynxes in England have been officially extinct since the eighth century AD.

malt cereal grains that have been soaked to make them sprout to allow the seeds to germinate and then dry off, with the aim of stimulating the production enzymes in them – starch, soluble sugars or the precursors to yeast. This process is known as malting. Malt from (in Suffolk mostly) barley and wheat is used in beer.

manimal a "man-animal", a creature with both human and animal characteristics. Bigfoot, woodwoses, dog-headed men and merfolk (mermen and mermaids) all fall into this category. Their existence is not accepted by science. Many would be an evolutionary impossibility and none of them could remain hidden from view in the UK and undiscovered for long. Nonetheless, people report encounters with them.

melanistic in animals, having a black colour, from the natural pigment melanin that is expressed in black-pigmented animals. Nearly all reports of leopard sightings in the UK are of melanistic leopards (these also occur naturally in Asia and Africa, but they're rarer than spotted leopards.) Melanistic lynxes and "black pumas" are also reported in the UK. Melanistic squirrels (an introduced melanistic variant of the grey squirrel) are currently found in Cambridgeshire, and are extending their range towards Suffolk.

Mid-Suffolk the district of Suffolk that covers Laxfield, Eye, Hoxne, Stowmarket, most of the Gipping Valley, Debenham, Stonham Aspal and Needham Market, where it has its headquarters. A small section of the "Midi" or Mid-Suffolk Light Railway survives as a museum near Wetheringsett. Mid-Suffolk includes much of the Norfolk-Suffolk border and Ipswich's northern suburbs.

mink (plural: mink) a dark-brown aquatic carnivorous mammal related to ferrets, weasels and stoats, but bigger, its diet includes fish and voles. The American mink *Neovison vison* was introduced to East Anglia after escaping from fur farms and is now considered vermin.

Motocross Cross-country racing on motorcycles. The area around Blaxhall hosts Suffolk's biggest annual Motocross event. The Westleton Scramble Races were a big Motocross event on Westleton Heath up to the 1960s, when the area became a nature reserve.

mountain lion alternative name for a puma in North America.

muntjac "barking deer", small, dog-sized Asian deer, the males have short antlers and tusks. They escaped from English deer parks and are now on their way to being Britain's most common deer species, the wild mammal you're most likely to *see* in Suffolk. They're ideal big cat food.

murmuration a huge flock of starlings flying together in close formation for protection against birds of prey as they catch insects on the wing in the hours leading up to them roosting in the evening. Murmurations in the hundreds or even thousands are common, particularly in autumn around Suffolk's coastal marshes and heaths.

mustelid a member of the family of carnivores that includes ferrets, weasels, polecats, stoats, mink and badgers.

Natural England (formerly English Nature) a UK government body for England whose responsibilities include a "green infrastructure", ensuring a sustainable "healthy natural environment", issuing licences for animal culls and enforcing licences to keep captive animals as required by the Dangerous Wild Animals Act. It took over many of these functions from Defra (see above) in 2006, Defra remains its "parent body." Natural England wardens can be seen at work on Suffolk's nature reserves.

nighthawker a clandestine metal detectorist (see above), detecting without the landowner's permission and trespassing on their property, sometimes at night.

North Sea the sea dividing England (including all of coastal Suffolk) from the Netherlands, Belgium, Germany, Scandinavia and Northern France.

North Suffolk generally considered to be the region that includes Lowestoft and environs, Beccles, Bungay, The Saints, Halesworth (depending on who you ask), the Suffolk coast from about Covehithe northwards, and inland the area around Eye and around the south bank of the Waveney

A murmuration of starlings over marshes near Walberswick

River and the Little Ouse River along the Norfolk border including Brandon. It's not an official district.

NT (the NT) the National Trust for England, the charity whose mission is to preserve England's cultural heritage. As well as various stately homes and historic buildings, its properties in Suffolk include the nature reserves Dunwich Heath and Orford Ness.

ocelot *Leopardus pardalis*, a South American wildcat resembling a dwarf leopard, some of which appear to have escaped from captivity in the UK. "Ocelot-like cats" have been reported in Cambridgeshire, but not yet in Suffolk.

omertà A code on silence regarding criminal activities and a refusal to talk to the authorities, originating in the Sicilian mafia.

Panthera the genus of big cats that includes lions, tigers, jaguars and leopards.

panther informal name for a leopard (in Asia and Africa) and a puma (in Florida in the eastern USA). Melanistic leopards are known as "black panthers."

Paranormal Database online database of strange phenomena in the UK and Ireland, without which this book wouldn't have been possible. It's particularly strong on hauntings. Started at the dawn of the internet age, its webmaster is based in Suffolk. www.paranormaldatabase.com.

peddler old word for an itinerant salesman.

Pharisee a member of a Jewish sect and social movement contemporary with Jesus, who in the New Testament denounced as hypocritical the Pharisees' strict religious observance. They somehow became conflated with fairies ("farsees" in Suffolk dialect, see above.) Fairy bread (in fact fossil sea urchins, resembling miniature loaves of bread) became "Pharisee loaves."

puma *Puma concolor,* a big cat from the Americas, usually sandy in colour. Many big cats reported in Suffolk fit the description of pumas. Strictly speaking, pumas aren't big cats as they're not in the *Panthera* family (pumas are in the *Felidae* family), they have a different arrangement of bones in their throats and can't roar.

RAF Royal Air Force – Suffolk military airbases are designated RAF, although nearly all of them are in fact US Air Force bases with a nominal RAF presence. Current RAF bases in Suffolk (actually in use by the RAF not the USAF) include the depot at RAF Honington and the air sea rescue helicopter base at RAF Wattisham.

Rendlesham Forest UFO Incident (also Rendlesham UFO Incident, Rendlesham Forest Incident, RFI) – mystery lights seen around Rendlesham Forest and the nearby airbases RAF Bentwaters and RAF Woodbridge on the night of Boxing Day 1980, believed by some to have been an alien craft that was the subject of a cover-up. Probably Britain's most well-known alleged UFO incident.

RFI Rendlesham Forest Incident, see above.

rhea large, fast-running white or grey South American flightless bird, related to the emu.

RSPB The Royal Society for the Protection of Birds, who own and manage the RSPB Minsmere nature reserve and some other smaller ones in Suffolk. Their staff are referred to disparagingly as "the raspberries" by some SWT workers.

scat animal faeces, especially from carnivorous mammals.

SNT area Safer Neighbourhood Team area, Suffolk Police's local districts.

St Edmundsbury The district of Suffolk covering Bury and Honington, Clare and Haverhill, now merged into West Suffolk.

samphire a salt-tolerant wild plant that grows near the water's edge in saltwater marshes, prized for its distinctive crisp, salty flavour when cooked for a few minutes. It's protected by wildlife legislation.

Saints, The a group of villages in North Suffolk between the Waveney and the Blyth, which all have the name of the saint followed by South Elmham or Ilketshall. (for example, St Peter, South Elmham, St Andrew, Ilketshall).

sasquatch see Bigfoot.

Sax short name for the town of Saxmundham.

sea urchin small spiny invertebrate sea creatures with a round shell, they are echinoderms – a group that includes starfish. In life they resembled hedgehogs (once also known as "urchins"). Their spines rarely survive fossilisation and their soft bodies resemble small loaves of bread, so their fossils were thought to be "fairy loaves."

serval a large African wildcat with long legs and a small head with big ears. Servals usually have black spots and stripes on a tawny background, although melanistic specimens are quite common. Some British big cats may be servals, or serval hybrids.

shilling in old money in circulation before 1971, a large coin worth 12 pence or one twentieth of a pound. It was made of silver until 1947.

shingle pebbles.

Shuck the East Anglian demon hellhound or phantom dog, often black in colour. Also an old Suffolk dialect name for a vagrant or tramp. See also Black Shuck.

shug another name for Shuck, believed to come from the Anglo-Saxon word *succa*, a demon.

shug monkey a bizarre creature said to resemble a huge black dog or lion with the face of an ape or baboon, with shining eyes. It reportedly lives around the villages of West Wratting and Balsham on the Cambridgeshire-Suffolk border and in Rendlesham Forest.

sika deer a species of introduced deer from Japan and Vietnam that escaped from deer parks and now breeds in the wild in England. A wild population is now establishing itself in Suffolk.

Sizewell the nuclear power station at the seaside village of the same name, on the Suffolk coast near Leiston. The white dome of Sizewell B is a local landmark

South Norfolk the southern half of the county of Norfolk, ending at the Waveney River that forms the border with Suffolk. It includes Harleston, Thetford, Attleborough, Great Yarmouth and Diss. There's an administrative district of Norfolk known as South Norfolk, but the term is also used to cover all of the southern part of the county.

South Suffolk see Babergh.

species a group of animals with similar characteristics that can generally exchange genes by interbreeding. The second word in the Latin name for an animal denotes its species. Big cat species include *Puma concolor,* the puma.

speedway a motorcycle sport that involves teams racing on a dirt track circuit, sliding on the surface on the bends, on motorcycles without brakes. Suffolk speedway teams include the Ipswich Witches and the Mildenhall Fen Tigers.

Stow the town of Stowmarket, to those who live there.

strigiform owl-shaped

Suffolk Coast Path see Coast Path above.

Suffolk Coastal Suffolk Coastal District Council (SCDC) administers the district covering the coasts and estuaries from the eastern edge of Ipswich all the way up to the Blyth River. It includes many of the county's seaside resorts – Felixstowe, Aldeburgh, Walberswick and Dunwich and has its headquarters in Melton. It's now merged into East Suffolk.

Suffolk Constabulary see Suffolk Police. A Constabulary is a police force.

Suffolk Heights a range of chalk hills from Bury west to Haverhill, Newmarket and beyond. Hills in the Suffolk Heights are usually steep with flat tops.

Suffolk Heritage Coast a conservation area on the Suffolk coast from the Essex border to Kessingland, and a surprisingly long way inland, all the way to Eye and Debenham(avoiding Ipswich). Its full title is the Suffolk and North Essex Heritage Coast.

Suffolk Wildlife Trust (SWT) the body that owns or manages many of the nature reserves in Suffolk as well as having a role in managing the RSPB's, the Forestry Commission's and other estates. It employs wardens and also relies on volunteers.

Sunrise Coast, The The stretch of coast from Southwold up to the northern end of the Suffolk coast above Lowestoft. It's so-called because it has the earliest sunrise in the mainland UK, as it's at its furthest point to the east. Not be confused with the Sunshine Coast in North Essex.

SWT See Suffolk Wildlife Trust

Tudor from the period when the Tudor dynasty ruled England, from 1485 to 1603. Tudor monarchs included Henry VIII and Elizabeth I.

USAAF The US Army Air Force during World War Two, when it was still part of the US Army. It became the autonomous USAF in the Cold War. There was said to be a USAAF base about every five miles in wartime East Anglia.

USAF the US Air Force today, with Suffolk airbases at RAF Mildenhall and RAF Lakenheath, with RAF Mildenhall scheduled to close down sometime in the 2020s.

Walk (in Suffolk place names) – an area for grazing sheep, for example, East Sheep Walk, heathland pasture near Walberswick and Toby's Walk near Blythburgh.

Waveney District the district of coastal North Suffolk from the north bank of the Blyth Valley at Southwold to Corton in the north. It includes the south side or the Waveney River, as well as Lowestoft, Southwold, Beccles, Bungay and Halesworth. It has its headquarters in Lowestoft. It's now merged into East Suffolk.

West Suffolk The district councils of St Edmundsbury and Forest Heath have combined most of their services anyway. Type in "St Edmundsbury" or "Forest Heath" in a search engine and you'll be taken to a page welcoming you to "West Suffolk."

A woodwose and its accompanying lions defaced by iconoclasts at Redlingfield church.

wildman a mythical feral human covered in hair in the traditions of Medieveal and Renaissance Europe, especially the Netherlands, Flanders and Germany. See also woodwose.

Witchfinder General the unofficial title Matthew Hopkins gave himself after receiving a commission from Parliamentary authorities to investigate allegations of witchcraft in the East of England in 1649.

woodwose The name given to wildmen in England, probably by Victorian antiquarians. The word is believed to be from the Anglo-Saxon word *wudewusa*, "wild being", so it has nothing to do with the woods. Nor are they Anglo-Saxon, most representations of woodwoses in Suffolk date from around 1490. Woodwoses are particularly common in carvings on Suffolk churches, especially on stone fonts but also carved on porches and on the tops of Suffolk church towers. There are also clusters of woodwoses in Norfolk churches, particularly around Norwich. Their origin is a mystery – it is thought they could be a cultural import from Flanders, the Netherlands or Germany. See also wildman.

Wool Towns, The Bildeston, East Bergholt, Lavenham, Lindsey, Kersey, Long Melford, Kentwell, Stoke-by-Clare, Hadleigh, Clare and Sudbury. These were South Suffolk medieval towns that grew wealthy as a result of the wool and cloth trade. Most of them are now villages, but their huge churches and historic timber-framed buildings still remain.

village sign a large, painted decorative sign made from metal or wood in a Suffolk village, bearing its name. The village sign usually depicts a well-known feature of the village. The Boxford village sign, for example, depicts Briton the Lioness in her sidecar, driven by Tornado Smith (see Chapter 12) while the Wissett village sign features a horse-drawn plough on one side and a tractor on the other.

Visit Suffolk tourist office for Suffolk that in 2013 briefly adopted the slogan "the Curious County" which is regrettably no longer in official use.

yard (measurement) three feet or 36 inches, 0.91 metres, used for distances.

zooform (noun and adjective) a creature or entity that has the appearance of an animal, or at least resembles an animal, but seems to be impossible, supernatural or a phantom rather than a living, flesh-and-blood animal.

zoology the study of the biology of the animal kingdom.

There's a guide to pronouncing Suffolk place names at www.foxearth.org.uk/blog/2005/07/suffolk-placenames-and-how-they-should.html

Select Bibliography

BBC News online:

BBC News website: 2 August 2004, "Anglers report Big Cat sighting" (BBC News England), http://news.bbc.co.uk/1/hi/england/suffolk/352954.stm; "Police report solves lynx mystery", BBC News, 21 March 2006, http://news.bbc.co.uk/1/hi/england/norfolk/4830320.stm; 1 August 2008, "National award for remarkable cat", http://news.bbc.co.uk/1/hi/england/suffolk/7537657.stm; 24 February 2014, "Dumped kittens with extra toes looking for new homes", www.bbc.co.uk/news/uk-england-suffolk-26321258; 4 September 2014, "Suffolk piglet rescued from sea by RSPCA" www.bbc.co.uk/news/uk-england-suffolk-30326967; 6 May 2015 (Essex section) www.bbc.co.uk/news/uk-england-essex-32609103; 12 December 2015, (Suffolk section), "Rare treasure found in Suffolk depicts medieval 'Wild Man'", www.bbc.co.uk/news/uk-england-suffolk-35050026

BBC Cambridgeshire, 4 March 2008, "Big cat history feature" www.bbc.co.uk/cambridgeshire/content/articles/2008/04/02/big_cat_history_feature.shtml

BBC Points East, 2010, Hintlesham ghost hunt by "paranormal investigators" www.youtube.com/watch?v=yoF4f0QDWJg

Books

Albion – A Guide to Legendary Britain, Jennifer Westwood, Paladin, 1985

Alien Animals, Janet & Colin Bord, Granada, London 1980

Annual Register, 1825-1826 (swimming a "witch" in Wickham Skeith) https://books.google.co.uk/books?id=FnNIAAAAYAAJ&q=wickham#v=twopage&q=wickham&f=true

The A-Z of British Ghosts, Peter Underwood, Chancellor Press 1993

Big Cats in Britain Yearbook 2006, ed. Mark Fraser CFZ Press, Wolfardishworthy 2007

Big Cats in Big Cats in Britain Yearbook 2007

Big Cats in Big Cats in Britain Yearbook 2008

The British Big Cat Phenomenon – Differing theories, eye witness reports, and the predator's diet, Jonathan McGowan, Hangar 1 Publishing, North Haven CT, 2022

The Book of Days , R. Chambers, W & R Chambers, 1863-4

Blything Hundred, P. M. Warner, University of Leicester PhD thesis, 1982, p.45***Cave Canem***, (ebook) Chris Huff, ASSAP www.assap.ac.uk/newsite/Docs/Black%20dogs.pdf

CFZ 2011 Yearbook, Centre for Fortean Zoology, Woolsery N. Devon, CFZ Publications, ed. Jonathan and Corinna Downes

Chronicon Anglicanum, Ralph of Coggeshall, www.bl.uk/collection-items/chronicon-anglicanum

The Complete Books of Charles Fort, Dover, New York, 1974

County Folklore Printed Extracts – 2: Suffolk, ed. Lady Evelina Camilla Gurdon, The Folklore Society, London 1893

The East Anglian; or, Notes and queries on subjects connected with the counties of Suffolk, Cambridge, Essex and Norfolk, 1640, https://archive.org/stream/eastanglianorno05whitgoog/eastanglianorno05whitgoog_djvu.txt

East Anglia – Walking the Lay Lines and Ancient Tracks, Shirley Toulson, Fontana 1976

The East Anglian Miscellany 1907-8, Note 2344

Encyclopedia Britannica Dictionary of Arts, Sciences, Volume XIX, 1823

Encyclopaedia of Witchcraft and Demonology, R. Hope Robbins, Hamyln, London, 1959

Encyclopedia of Haunted Places, Jeff Belanger, Career Press Inc, 2009
The First Fossil Hunters – Dinosaurs, Mammoths and Myth in Greek and Roman Times, Adrienne Mayor, Princeton University Press, 2011
The Folklore of East Anglia, Enid Porter, BT Batsford, London 1974
Flying Saucerers – a social history of UFOlogy, David Clarke and Andy Roberts, Alternative Albion, Loughborough 2007
Forgotten Ports of England, George Goldsmith Carter, Evans Bros, London 1951
Wild Animals of the British Isles, Dr Maurice Burton, Frederick Warne 1968
The Ghost Book, Alasdair Alpin MacGregor, Robert Hale 1956
A Ghost Hunter's Game Book, James Wentworth Day, 1958
The Ghost World, T F Thiselton-Dyer, Ward & Downey, London 1893, Project Gutenberg www.gutenberg.org/files/45362/45362-h/45362-h.htm
Ghosts of Blythburgh, Southwold & Walberswick, Allan Scott-Davies, Artspace, Suffolk, 2010
Ghosts of the Broads, Charles Sampson, Yatchsman, London 1931
Ghosts of East Anglia, Mills H. West, Countryside Books, Newbury, 2003
Ghosts of Suffolk, Betty Puttick, Countryside Books, Stroud, 1995.
Great Cats – Majestic Creatures of the Wild, ed. Dr John Seidensticker and Dr Susan Lipman, Merehurst, London 1991
Haunted East Anglia, Joan Forman 1974, 1985 reprint Jarrold & Co, Norwich
Haunted Lowestoft Revisited, Ivan A.W. Bunn and Henry Baker, published by the authors, Lowestoft 2010
Haunted Suffolk, Peter Jennings, Tempus Pubs, Stroud, 2006
The Helmingham Hall Bestiary, Yale Collections, http://collections.britishart.yale.edu/vufind/Record/2038220
Here Be Dragons, Ralph Whitlock, George Allen & Unwin, 1983
Historia Rerum Anglicarum, William of Newburgh, c. 1198
The History of Stowmarket, Rev. A.G.H. Hollingsworth, F. Pawsey 1844, 2003 edition by Mike Durrant
The Horse in the Furrow, George Ewart Evans, Faber and Faber, 1960
Here are Ghosts and Witches, James Wentworth Day, Batsford, London 1954
Holy Trinity Blythburgh: Cathedral of the Marshes, Hugh Roberts, Mary Montague, Barry Naylor, Jarrold, Norwich 1999
I Read it in the Local Rag, Pip Wright, Poppyland Publishing, Cromer 2006 www.pipwright.
In the Wake of the Sea-Serpents, Bernard Heuvelmans, translated by Rupert Hart-Davies, Hill and Wang, New York, 1969
LightQuest – Your Guide to Seeing and Interacting with UFOs, Mystery Lights and Plasma Intelligences, Andrew Collins, Alibris, andrewcollins.com
Lo! Charles Fort 1931, online at www.resologist.net/loei.htm.
The Lore of the Land – A Guide to England's Legends from Spring-Heeled Jack to the Witches of Warboys, Jennifer Westwood and Jacqueline Simpson, Penguin, 2005
The Mammals of Suffolk, Simone Bullion, Suffolk Wildlife Trust/Suffolk Naturalists' Society, Ipswich, 2009
Most Secret – the hidden history of Orford Ness, Paddy Heazell, History Press/National Trust, Stroud 2010
Mysteries of Britain, Janet and Colin Bord, Grafton/Collins, London 1987
Mysterious Creatures: A Guide to Cryptozoology – Volume 1, George Eberhart,

BIBLIOGRAPHY

CFZ Publications, Wolfardisworthy 2014 (Norfolk Gnasher)

Mystery Animals of Britain and Ireland, Graham J. McEwan, Richard Hale, London 1986

Mystery Animals of the British Isles: The Western Isles, Glen Vaudrey, CFZ Publications, Wolfardisworthy 2011

Mystery Big Cats, Merrily Harpur, Heart of Albion 2006

On The Deer Path, David Barrington Barnes, 2012, http://onthedeerpath.co.uk/books.html

Our Cats and All About Them, Harrison Weir, R. Clements, Tunbridge Wells, 1889

Paranormal Suffolk: True Ghost Stories, Christopher Reeve, Amberley, Stroud 2009

The Priory Church of St Mary Letheringham, WD Akester, 1979, updated 2007

Phenomena – a book of wonders, John Michell & Robert Rickard, Thames & Hudson, 1977

Pygmy Elephants, Matt Salusbury, CFZ Publications, Wolfardisworthy, 2013

The Register of John Morton, Archbishop of Canterbury 1486-1500: vol. III, Canterbury & York Society, 2000

Railway Ghosts and Phantoms, W B Herbert, David & Charles, London 1989 p16

The Seven Crystal Balls (The Adventures of Tintin) Herge, Casterman, 1948

Slow Travel – Suffolk, Laurence Mitchell, Bradt Travel Guides Ltd, Chalfont St Peter 2014

Dr Shuker's Casebook, CFZ Publications, Woolfardisworthy 2008

Shock! The Black Dog of Bungay, Dr David Waldron and Christopher Reeve, Hidden Publishing 2010

The Star-Crossed Stone: The Secret Life, Myths, and History of a Fascinating Fossil, Kenneth J. McNamara, University of Chicago Press, 2010

A Strange & Terrible Wonder: the Story of the Black Dog of Bungay, Christopher Reeve, Peter Morrow & Co, 1988

Suffolk Dialect, Louise Maskill, Bradwell Books, Sheffield, 2014

Suffolk Dragonflies, Nick Mason, Adrian Parr, Suffolk Naturalists Society, Ipswich 2016

Suffolk Ghosts and Legends , Pamela Brooks, Halsgrove, Wellington, Somerset 2009

Suffolk Ghost Tales, Kirsty Hartsiotis & Cherry Wilkinson, The History Press, Stroud 2017

Suffolk Tales of Murder & Mystery, Mark Mower, Countryside Books, Newbury 2006

A Summerie of Englysh Chronicles, John Stow, late 16th century

The Sutton Companion to British Folklore, Myths & Legends, Marc Alexander, Sutton Publishing, London, 2005, paperback edition p272

Tales of Old Cambridgeshire, Polly Howat, Countryside Books, 1990

This Haunted Isle, Peter Underwood, St Michael's Abbey Press, 1983

Three Men Seeking Monsters: Six Weeks in Pursuit of Werewolves, Lake Monsters, Giant Cats, Ghostly Devil Dogs... Nick Redfern, Paraview Pocket Books, New York 2004

Ultimate Guide to Cat Breeds, The, Louisa Somerville Regency House Publishing 2004

A Visit to Southwold, A. Barrett Jenkins, Southwold, 1985 (bears in East Anglian towns)

Westleton – Customs and Sayings recorded by the Women's Institute in 1922, Westleton WI, Leiston Press, Leiston 2008

William Dowsing's Journal www.williamdowsing.org/journalnoindex.htm

Witchfinder General – the Biography of Matthew Hopkins, Craig Cabell, Sutton, London 2006

Feature films:

Rendlesham UFO Incident, The, Altitude Films 2014 (*Hanger 10* in the US), www.youtube.com/watch?v=G4GijLIkmHM

Freedom of Information Act (FOIA) disclosures

Natural England, *Reported Sightings or Signs of Exotic Species Compiled by Natural England's Wildlife Management & Licensing*, September 2011

Natural England; *Reports received by Defra of escapes of non-native cats in the U.K 1975 to present day*

Norfolk Constabulary (Norfolk Police) – Freedom of Information Request Reference No: FOI 424/11/12, dated December 2011

Suffolk Constabulary (Suffolk Police) FOIA disclosure, Request Number: F–2013–03389, 23 November 2013; Suffolk Police FOIA disclosure Request no: F–2014–00782, 14 March 2014; Freedom of Information Request No: F–2014–02424 September 2014, request by Bethany Whymark of *Bury Free Press*

UK Defence Intelligence, *Unidentified Aerial Phenomena in the UK Air Defence Region: Executive Summary (2000, also known as Project Condign) Defence Region: Executive Summary* (2000, also known as Project Condign), www.disclosureproject.org/docs/pdf/uap_exec_summary_dec00.pdf

West Suffolk Council, Investigation into escape of bobcat in West Suffolk and records of animal escapes under the Dangerous Wild Animals Act (FOI 385), 17 February 2021, http://mattsalusbury.blogspot.com/2021/07/west-suffolk-bobcat-escaped-while-being.html.

Newspapers

Beccles and Bungay Journal: 14 April 2011, "Rare feathered visitor drops into Suffolk nature reserve," 3 June 2011, "Visitors reassured following Norfolk alligator sighting"

***Bury Free Press*:** 8 August 1972, Fakenham Magna mummified cat discovery; 14 March, 12 July 1996 big cat sightings; 5 September 2014, "Vigilance warning after copper is stolen from church roof in Great Barton"; 15 September 2014, "Suffolk woodland or foreign jungle?"; 15 September 2014; "Hunting for signs of the Beast of Balsham"

Bury Mercury, 23 October 2014, "Humpback whale off Minsmere?", 27 October 2014

***Bury Post*,** October 1789, 8 August 1855

Cambridge News, "Mysterious fen tiger seen…", 20 April 2014, "Shepreth Wildlife Park visitors fear they're on the menu rather than Easter eggs as tiger escape alarm set off", November 25, 2014 "Puma cubs' spotted in Red Lodge during search for lost dog"; " 'Large wildcat with big claws' spotted in central Cambridge", Ella Pengally, *Cambridge News*, 11 April 2020

Coastal Advertiser, 18 December 2009, "Farmers concerned about return of rare bird"; 6 August 2010, "X-files shed light on UFOs", 12 March 2010, "Claws back on the prowl"

Coastal Scene, 29 October 2014, "Could blue whales one day visit Suffolk's coast?"

Daily Express, 21 July 2013, "Curious tale of the Wall of Death rider who buried his lion…"; July 14 2015, "Listen: To US commander investigate 'UFO attack' at Rendlesham in 35-year-old recording"

Daily Mail* see *Mail

Daily Star, 29 January 2009, "Copper is attacked by big cat", (Wivenhoe big cat hunt)

Daily Telegraph see *Telegraph*

Darlington and Stockton Times, 17 October 2008, "Hooked on the tale of a flamboyant travelling showman" (Katterfelto)

***Diss Express*:** 6 May 1870 (death of Suffolk Giant); 23, 30 August 1996 (big cat sightings) 2006 big cat sightings – 2 April, 3 April (Hoxne grey panther), 12 May, 14 May 24 May, 25 May, 7 June, 10 June (Hoxne big cat), 16 June, 1 September 2006 (Bressingham sighting);

BIBLIOGRAPHY

"Dog walker sees 'Big Cat'" 27 October 2007; "Big cat spotted again" 16 May 2008.

East Anglian Daily Times (EADT):

12 January 1905, "A queer character at Woodbridge" (Martlesham Heath wildman in court), 13 May 1907; 4 March 1996, "That big cat is prowling again"; 6 March 1996, "Big cat sightings may be linked to ferocious attack"; 16 July 2003, "Black cat spotted in North Suffolk,"; October 15 2003 (Tommy the cat brings home a sturgeon); 20 March 2008; 29 March 2008, "More sightings of big cats come to light"; 29 March 2008, "Big cat sighting revealed in Suffolk"; 3 April 2008, "What lurks within the Suffolk countryside?", 19 November 2009, "Puzzled by big cat sighting", letter from Starston; 11 November 2010, "River Stour: Dragons, aliens and a princess,"; 19 July 2012, "Grundisburgh couple's unwelcome visit from ferocious turtle"; 18 October 2012, "Suffolk: Curious County slogan row may reach House of Commons"; 16 January 2013, (faun among sheep); 7 June 2014, 7 July 2014, "Heath ready for stardom after supporting role in Springwatch," 15 July 2014, "Black Shuck the Hell-hound legend that won't lie down," Martin Newell, 22 November 2014, 9March 2015, "Bewitched in the 'valley of the elves'"; "The lynx effect – wild cats could be released into Thetford Forest"; 19 March 2015, "Missing moggy moonlight's flit is finally over", 14 April 2015, "St Osyth Big Cat sighting"; 16 April 2015; "Exotic venomous snake found in delivery at Ransomes Europark"; 5 August 2015, "Is there a panther or big cat loose in Suffolk?", 12 August 2015, "Is a white wolf prowling Suffolk?", 19 August 2015, "My own big cat sightings", letter from David Willis; 20 October 2015, 20 October 2015, "Dogs struck down by mystery illness", 31 October 2015, "Are these the scariest places in Suffolk?" 20 March 2015, "Rare white stork spotted in Southwold day after white-tailed eagle sighting", 25 August 2015, "Clergymen and parishioners left devastated by theft of roof lead," 15 January 2016, "Jogger reports 'big cat sighting' in Suffolk field," 5 August 2016, "Suffolk emu which gave owner and police the runaround found in Glemsford garden"; "Suffolk police find Highland cow on A12 in 'fairly routine' call", Angus Williams, January 14 2021.

East Anglian Magazine Vol. 41, No. 9, July 1982, Patricia Willis: The Wraiths of Wissett

Eastern Daily Press (EDP):

July 1912, 15 November 1975, 20 June 1997, 18 March 2006, "Controversy over wild catalogue", Lorna Marsh; 29 February 2008, "More mink attacks in Felixstowe"; February 28 2013, "Police appeal after 'panther' sighting in Norwich"; 28 August 2013, "Norfolk puma spotted in Gorleston"; 5 January 2014, "Lost cocker spaniels, ET, ghosts, zombies" 10 August 2014, "Thieves steal three-foot tall lion statue from Norfolk church", 2 October 2014, 20 June 2016, "Scheme to reintroduce lynx to Thetford Forest is dropped", 27 August 2016, "Is this the infamous Norfolk panther prowling near Saxlingham Nethergate?"

***Evening Star* (also known as *Ipswich Star,* especially after 2012):**

21 September 1965, "Felixstowe Glowing Object Mystery"; 1 July 1996, "Huge cat seen near cemetery"; 16 March 2006; 16 October 2003, "Big cat seen in Suffolk," 23 October 2004; "Black cat sightings on the up"; 23 July 2006, (big cat sighting); 25 August 2006; 17 June 2008, Kirton big cat sighting; 25 November 2010, "Suffolk: New sightings of big cat 'Claws'"; 25 November 2010, "Wallabies on the loose in Suffolk"; 18 February 2012, "Akenham: Police receive reports deer attacked by big cat"; 16 August 2012, "Herbal medicines seized at Felixstowe"; 27 April 2013, "Trimley: Big cat spotted in Trimley St Martin!"

Gentleman's Magazine, The, December 1750 (Kessingland sea monster)

Halesworth Times and Southwold General Advertiser, September 1857, 3 December 1907

Harwich and Manningtree Standard, 21 September 2009 (Kirby Cross sighting); 21 June 2005, (Harwich and Jaywick puma-like animal sightings)

Haverhill Echo, 11 May 2006, "Hunting for the signs of the Beast of Balsham"; 11 November 2009, "Cat's lucky escape from mystery bird"; 5 July 2012, "I saw the Haverhill puma"; 10 July 2012, "Another sighting of Haverhill puma"; 7 August 2015, "Public reassured after big cat sighting", Josh Thomas; 23 May 2016, "West Suffolk home to lynxes, caracals, bobcats"
The <i> paper, "Call for wild boar cull after animals wreak havoc", 10 January 2015.
Ipswich Journal, 27 May 1721; 1877, "Brother Mike" Suffolk Notes & Queries reprint, original from 1751
Guardian, 17 April 2013, (Thatcher/Mr Whippy legend); 31 July 2016, "Escaped lynx recaptured in Devon"; 25 September 2015, "North Sea cod off Red List"
Ipswich Star* see *Evening Star
Independent, The (newspaper), 3 December 1997, "Politics: Questions about the Norfolk Gnasher bring out the beasts in Westminster"; 30 October 2008, "Mummy, there's a cheetah in the garden and it's eating my bike"; "Beast from the north... Enormous wildcat spotted in Scotland", Chris Green 29 March 2018, https://www.independent.co.uk/news/uk/scotland-wildcat-video-aberdeenshire-forest-haven-clashindarroch-a8278196.html.
Lowestoft Journal:
16 January 1976 letter by Southwold resident Mr A. Barrett Jenkins; 27 April 1997, "Big Cat Spotted", Terry Reeve; 10 April 2009; "Unsolved mystery of the Waveney monster"; 9 July 2012, "Emu spotted on Lowestoft to Ipswich train line"; 18 October 2012, Curious Suffolk tourism campaign leads to MP demanding action"; 19 November 2014, "Were whales spotted off Lowestoft coast same group as those seen near Essex?"; 23 October 2014, "Have you seen the humpback whale reported off RSPB Minsmere?"
***Mail, (Daily Mail,* Mail Online),** 31 March 2009, "Bear sighting in Suffolk woods was 'promotional' hoax staged by theatre group"; 23 June 2010, "On the run: The 4FT9ins rhea tearing through rural Suffolk"; 1 July 2010, "Giant runaway bird dies of panic attack after RSPCA tries to 'rescue' it," 25 May 2012 "Train driver's shock as giant South American bird appears on railway tracks," Suzannah Hills; 15 May 2014, "Is this the skeleton of legendary devil dog Black Shuck who terrorised 16th century East Anglia?"
Medical Daily 2 April 2015, "The real Ghostbusters investigate mold, not moans, within haunted houses", www.medicaldaily.com real-ghostbusters-investigate-mold-not-moans-within-haunted-houses-327950#
Mirror (Daily Mirror) "Is this new evidence of a big cat in Britain? Dog walker finds remains of terrifying creature near Scottish beauty spot", 18 May 2012; "Schoolboy comes face-to-face with huge black PANTHER when out running", *Mirror, (Daily Mirror)*
Newmarket Journal, 8 September 2008, "I tawt I taw a puddy cat, I did," (Haverhill Puma); 24 September 2008, "Second wild cat sighting in space of month"
New York Gazette 13 May 1751
New York Times 21 August 2014, "Neanderthals in Europe"
Newspapers in Suffolk website, Pip Wright, www.pipwright.com/newspapers.htm
Suffolk Wildlife Park press cuttings file, Suffolk Record Office Reference 1176/2/2/11/81
Saxmundham News, December 2014 (local record for carp fishing)
Suffolk Free Press (Sudbury), 12 June 2008, "Sudbury sighting of alien black squirrel"; 28 February 2012, "Look what we found lion in town gardens"
Sun, The, "Big Cat Rampage: Bobcat goes berserk and savages farmer's chickens after escaping owner before being shot and captured", 24 March 2020
Telegraph (Daily Telegraph), 9 May 2001, "The Beast of Cricklewood is caged"; 30 March 2009, "Mystery bear in Suffolk forest Shakespeare hoax; 7 October 2015, "Timeline: Pan

Through the Ages", 21 July 2016, "Beast of Dartmoor mystery solved after famous circus owner Mary Chipperfield 'set three Pumas free in 1970s'"

Thetford and Brandon Times, 4 February 2015, "Driver spots 'big cat' on late night A11 journey"

Wilts and Gloucestershire Standard, 4 October 2013, Royal Agricultural University study on remains could prove that big cats exist in the UK, www.wiltsglosstandard.co.uk/news/10718835.New_study_could_help_prove_existence_of_big_cats/

Pamphlets, broadsheets:

Arraignment of 18 Witches – see *A True Relation of the Arraignment of 18 Witches*

The Black Dog of Bungay, Christopher Reeve, pamphlet on sale in St Mary's Church Bungay, undated

A True Relation of the Arraignment of 18 Witches, London 1645

The Wonder of Our Times: Being a True and Exact Relation of the Body of a Mighty Giant dig'd up at Brockford Bridge near Ipswich in Suffolk... pamphlet, I. G , R. Austin, for W. Ley, London, 1651, Thomason Collection (British Library) list: E 646 (3)

Periodicals, magazines, journals:

FATE magazine, March 2006, "The Werewolves of Britain" Nick Redfern, http://cryptomundo.com bigfoot-report werewolves-uk

Florida Field Naturalist. (journal) "A melanistic bobcat from outside Florida," 23(1):13-14, 1995. http://fosbirds.org/sites/default/files/FFNs/FFNv23n1p13-14Tischendorf.pdf

Flying Snake vol 2 issue 1 www.flyingsnakepress.co.uk; www.facebook.com/Flying-SnakeMagazine

Folklore (journal), December 1892, "Folklore from S.E. Suffolk", Lady E. C. Gurdon, September 1959; Vol. 69, no. 3, "The Black Dog", Theodora Brown; December 2007, Vol. 118, no. 3, "The Wildman Inside and Outside Europe", Gregory Forth

Fortean Studies (journal), "The luminous owls of Norfolk," Dr David W Clarke, vol. 1, John Brown Publishing, London 1994; "Shug Monkeys and Werewolves – The Search for the Dog-Headed Men", Jon Downes and Richard Freeman, vol. 5

***Fortean Times* (magazine):**

FT101, 1996, ABC round-up; "Troublesome Things: A History of Fairies and Fairy Stories", (book reviews), December 2005, "Magic Lanterns," December 2006 (mystery lights). Elves in Anglo-Saxon England (book review), Jeremy Harte; FT220, Alan Murdie; FT278;16, August 2011, "Ghostwatch – Are Black Dogs wolves?" , FT278, August 2011, *The Star Crossed Stone* (review), http://mattsalusbury.blogspot.co.uk 2011 07 star-crossed-stone.html; FT280;31, October 2011, "UFO Casebook – my dog saw a UFO", FT297;33-37, "Spurious Spirits"; FT315;18, June 2014, Ghostwatch; FT318, September 2014, "The woodwoses of Suffolk," http://mattsalusbury.blogspot.co.uk/2014/10/the-woodwoses-of-suffolk.html; FT320; November 2014, Fairies Folklore and Forteana; FT321; 46-49, "The Music of Fairyland"; FT321;54-55, December 2014, "Cattle in the living room"; FT325;18, March 2015, Ghostwatch; FT321, December 2014, letter, "Woodwoses"; February 2015; FT323;75, letter from Gail Nina Anderson (on a ghost cat); FT329;15, July 2015, "Mouldy Old Ghosts", Ghostwatch; FT329;79 July 2015, "Phenomenomix - Dion Fortune 3"; FT340;18-19, May 2016 "The Hellhounds of East Anglia", Ghostwatch; FT343;33, August 2016, "The Enchanted Isle";; FT344;20, September 2016, "Big cats still stalk Britain," Paul Sieveking; "Letters", FT 391;72-73, April 2020 (enormous eels).

Hansard, 21 December 1966, Statement by the Minister of Agriculture on Coypu Control
The Historical Journal, 57(4), p1157-75, 2014 "The Making of the Early Modern British Fairy Tradition", Ronald Hutton, http://research-information.bristol.ac.uk files 38162235 Fairies4_1_.pdf
Journal of Natural History, Volume 16, Issue 3, 1982, "The taxonomic status of feral muntjac deer (*Muntiacus sp.*) in Britain," D.I. Chapmana & Norma G. Chapmana www.tandfonline.com/doi/abs/10.1080/00222938200770311
Lantern (Ivan A. W. Bunn and Mike Burgess, see also Hidden East Anglia website), 8, 1974-75, www.hiddenea.com/Lantern8.pdf; 9, spring 1975, www.hiddenea.com/Lantern9.pdf; 12; 13, "Timberrr.... it's a sea serpent!"; 17, p7 www.hiddenea.com/Lantern17.pdf; 18 ("Analysing the Hell Out of the Beast"), http://www.hiddenea.com/Lantern18.pdf; 25, Spring 1979, Water horses and The Monster in the Green, "The Needham Market Woodwose", www.hiddenea.com/Lantern25.pdf; 38; Wissett Shucks; www.hiddenea.com/shuckland/wissett.htm; 1973 Woodbridge Shuck www.hiddenea.com/shuckland/woodbridge.htm.
Oryx vol. 3, August 1956
Proceedings of the 15th International Congress for Analytical Psychology, "The Wolf of Gubbio and the Cambridge Tiger", British Association of Pyschotherapy (Jungian)
Quarterly Journal, Royal Meteorological Society, 32, p.170
Suffolk magazine (Archant): August 2015, "Suffolk's got animal talent",
Suffolk and Norfolk Life magazine, August 2010 "Recording Suffolk"
Suffolk Wildlife magazine (SWT), May 2015, "The Secretive Emperor", Liz Goodyear; May 2016, "A new mammal for Suffolk"
Tudor Studies, (journal) "Cardinal Morton's Register", Claude Jenkins, pp. 72-4, London, 1924 ***Wunderlust*** magazine, "Where to Spot UFOs in Britain", www.wanderlust.co.uk/magazine/blogs/weird@wanderlust/where-to-spot-ufos-in-britain

TV and radio broadcasts:

Ask The Fellows That Cut the Hay, recordings of George Ewart-Evans reading from his book, BBC, www.bbc.co.uk/programmes/b00rv8yk
BBC Suffolk, 30 October 2008, Roos Hall; www.bbc.co.uk/suffolk/content/articles/2008/10/30/roos_hall_gc_feature.shtml; 1 January 2015, audio clip of author on big cats on Jon Wright's Radio Suffolk show, (with permission) https://soundcloud.com/mattelgazette/big-cats-in-suffolk-clip-from-jon-wrights-bbc-radio-suffolk-show
The Film Programme, BBC Radio 4, 11 March 2012 (on *Drowning By Numbers*, filmed around Lowestoft)
Pathé newsreel –Briton, Sparky, Tornado and his wife "Marjorie Death" at Southend in 1936 www.youtube.com/watch?v=fFfGKljkkBo
Teletext, 25 May 1998 (big cat sighting)
The Today Programme, BBC Radio 4, 9 March 2011 – cranes returning to Suffolk

Websites, blogs

American Monsters website, "Felixstowe Fire Demon: (England)", Rob Morphy, 16 October 2011, http://www.americanmonsters.com/site/2011/10/felixstowe-fire-demon-england/
Apparitions of Black Dogs website, Dr Simon Sherwood, www.blackshuck.info/
Big Cats of Suffolk, http://bigcatsofsuffolk.com
Bigfoot Research UK http://www.bigfootresearchuk.com– page "Not found" as of 21 June 2015

BIBLIOGRAPHY

Bird Care website, www.birdcare.com/bin/shownews/219

Birdwatch News Archive, 19 July 2015, "Cranes fledge three young at Lakenheath", www.birdwatch.co.uk/channel/newsitem.asp?cate=__16010.

Brandon Forums, post by "Beaver Bob – Top Brandonian", 5 June 2014, post by "R2D2," 8 September 2014 and subsequently http://forum.brandonsuffolk.com/default.asp

British Big Cat Research (BBCR) website (site down as of December 2016):
sightings map 2013 http://britishbigcatresearch.weebly.com/sightings-map.html
"What become of the beast of Barnet?" http://britishbigcatresearch.weebly.com/latest-news/what-became-of-the-beast-of-barnet-times-series-investigation-reveals-cricklewood-lynx-laras-legacy-lives-on

British Big Cats, Hybrid Big Cats in the British Countryside, Sarah Hartwell www.britishbigcats.org/news.php#oldnews6

Bures village website www.bures-online.co.uk/dragon/history_files/WormDragon.pdf

Butterfly Conservation Suffolk website, www.suffolkbutterflies.org.uk/recording.html#Purple_Emperor

Cryptozoology News, August 23 2015, "'Bigfoot' Sighting in England, Claims Local Man", http://cryptozoologynews.com/bigfoot-sighting-in-england-says-local

Dash, Mike (Mike Dash website) – The Devil's Hoof Prints www.mikedash.com/assets/files/Devil's%20Hoofmarks.pdf

Dig Ventures website (skeleton of large dog unearthed at Leiston Priory) http://digventures.com/2014/10/28/digventures-and-the-bbc-one-show-devil-dog-black-shuck-returns/

Diocese of St Edmundsbury and Ipswich – woodwose bike rides www.cofesuffolk.org/index.cfm?page=yourchurch.content&cmid=464

Fairy Investigation Society website www.fairyist.com fairy-places east-anglian-fairies mermaid-s-pond-rendlesham-suffolk

Fortean Zoology blog, CFZ, Fortean Zoology blog, March 2009, "Return of the Shug Monkey", Still on The Track, http://forteanzoology.blogspot.co.uk/2009/03/return-of-shug-monkey.html; "The Gurt Dog Returns", Max Blake, comment by "Woody", 6 July 2009, http://forteanzoology.blogspot.co.uk/2009/07/max-blake-gurt-dog-returns.html)

Foxearth and District Historical Society, January 2005, www.foxearth.org.uk/blog/2005/01/rat-run.html (rats); www.foxearth.org.uk/blog/2005/01/brockford-giant.html (Brockford giant); www.foxearth.org.uk/blog/2005/04/weighed-down-by-bible.html (witch swimming in Stonham Aspal) Debenham FC match report with Debenham Lion reference, www.debenhamlc.co.uk/nmr.html

Gef! The Strange Tale of an Extra-special Mongoose, https://gefmongoose.co.uk/

Gun Dog Training Forum, 6 May 2012, Reach, Cambs. sighting www.gundogtrainingforum.co.uk/phpbb/viewtopic.php?t=11942#p142533

Hidden East Anglia website, Shuck encounter locations list www.hiddenea.com/shuckland/locationlist.htm; Thornington's missing Fairies Hill www.hiddenea.com/suffolk.htm#thorington

Historic Witches and Witchcraft Trials for England, Marc Carlson, 2004 www.personal.utulsa.edu%7Emarc-carlsonwitchtrialeis.html.

History Extra website (Katterfelto) www.historyextra.com/book-review/katterfelto-prince-puff

Iceni Post blog http://icenipost.com/the-kessingland-sea-serpent-or-may-be-an-oarfish/

Irish Wolfhounds website (Felixstowe Kennels) www.irishwolfhounds.org/felixstowe.htm

Know your cats – Jaguarundi, otter cat, https://www.knowyourcat.info/lib/jaguarundi.htm.

Lowestoft Witches website www.lowestoftwitches.com/the_trial_report.htm.

Made From History website, "20 of the Most Bizarre Creatures From Medieval Folklore", Alexander Collin, http://madefrom.com/history/medieval/weirdest-creatures-medieval/ com/localrag.htm

Matt Salusbury – see Salusbury, Matt

Melford Green Alpacas website www.melfordgreenalpacas.co.uk

Messybeast – serval hybrids http://messybeast.com/genetics/hyb-serval-; http://messybeast.com/big-cat2.html; lynx-serval hybrid; http://messybeast.com/genetics/hyb-serval-caracal.htm; "Domestic x roy's cat, jaguarundi, fishing cat hybrids", Sarah Hartwell, http://messybeast.com/small-hybrids/geoffroy-jaguarundi-hybrids.htm.

Mike Dash, see Dash, Mike

Monster USA blog, "Weirdness in the Woods: Strange Creatures of Rendlesham Forest," Nick Redfern, undated; http://monsterusa.blogspot.co.uk/2009/03/weirdness–in–woods.html

A Most Curious Murder (Katterfelto) www.amostcuriousmurder.com/BellGeordie.htm

Natural England – statement on lynx re-introduction www.gov.uk/government/news/natural-england-statement-on-the-possible-reintroduction-of-lynx

Norfolk Coast website, JM Barrie Thorpeness connection www.norfolkcoast.co.uk location_ suffolk vp_thorpeness.htm

Norfolk Wildlife Centre and Country Park www.norfolkwildlife.co.uk

Phys Org, "Corsica's cat-foxes, on the trail of what might be a new species", Maureen Coffland, 19 June 2019, https://phys.org/news/2019-06-corsica-cat-fox-trail-species.html

Redfern, Nick (Nick Redfern websites): "Shapeshifting big cats – Nick Redfern", website of Jim Harold, the paranormal podcast guy, 18 February 2016, http://jimharold.com/shape-shifting-black-cats-nick-redfern/; "Seeking the sinister shug monkey," Nick Redfern, Mysterious Universe blog, http://mysteriousuniverse.org/2012/09/seeking-the-sinister-shug-monkey/; "Out of Place Animals", Nick Redfern May 26, 2012, mania.com, "Weirdness in the Woods: Strange Creatures of Rendlesham Forest," Nick Redfern, undated; http://monsterusa.blogspot.co.uk/2009/03/weirdness–in–woods.html, see also *FATE, Three Men Seeking Monsters*

Retrieverman blog (caracals used to hunt birds), http://retrieverman.net/2012/10/04/the-hunting-caracal/

The Scottish Big Cats Trust website, Felicity the Cannich puma, http://scotcats.online.fr/abc/photoalbum/cannich.html; 2002 Yorkshire lynx confiscation, http://scotcats.online.fr/abc/realcats/yorkshirelynx.html; escapes of big cats in the UK listing http://scotcats.online.fr/abc/realcats/index.html

Saint Botolph Without Bishopsgate, London, www.botolph.org.uk/who-was-st-botolph/

Shuker (Dr Karl PN) – Dr Karl PN Shuker's Shukernature blog, Dr Karl PN Shuker, Clifden nonpariel butterfly, http://karlshuker.blogspot.co.uk/2014/07/the-clifden-nonpareil-bewitched-by.html; "The Truth About Black Pumas", http://karlshuker.blogspot.co.uk/2012/08/the-truth-about-black-pumas-separating.html; "Pumapards and lepumas", http://karlshuker.blogspot.co.uk/2014/07/pumapards-and-lepumas-unusual-feline.html

The Shark Trust website, www.sharktrust.org/en/british_sharks.

Salusbury, Matt (Matt Salusbury blog) , "Big cats in Dorset" http://mattsalusbury.blogspot.co.uk/2013/06/big–cats–in–dorset–london.html; Paul Crowther on soft toy black panthers; http://mattsalusbury.blogspot.co.uk/2008/06/weird-weekend-2006.html; "Large cat update", 2012; http://mattsalusbury.blogspot.co.uk/2012/10/jonathan-mcgowans-big-cat-large-cat.

html; Nick Warren's talk at Weird Weekend 2006, http://mattsalusbury.blogspot.co.uk/2008/06/weird-weekend-2006.html
Servals.org www.servals.org/home.htm
Simon Young – see **Young, Simon**
Suffolk Biological Records Centre via www.suffolkbrc.org.uk
Suffolk, County of, heritage website (Hulk's Grave) https://heritage.suffolk.gov.uk/hbsmr-web/record.aspx?UID=MSF686-Hulk's-Grave&pageid=16&mid=9
Suffolk Tourist Guide, "Thorpeness and Peter Pan," www.suffolktouristguide.com Thorpe-ness-and-Peter-Pan.asp
Suffolk Wildlife Trust, "Have you seen a pine marten in Suffolk?", 10 June 2020 www.suf-folkwildlifetrust.org/news/have-you-seen-pine-marten-suffolk.
Tetzoo blog (Darren Naish), "A lynx, shot dead in England in c. 1903, http://blogs.scientificamerican.com/tetrapod-zoology/edwardian-lynx-from-england/
Texas Parks and Wildlife Department (pumas), https://tpwd.texas.gov/huntwild/wild/species/mlion/.
UK Big Cats website (Bishop's Stortford big cat field trips) www.ukbigcats.co.uk/ourdiaryentry.asp?fieldtripvalue=13and
UK Butterflies website www.ukbutterflies.co.uk/species.php?species=boeticus
The Why Files, alleged stone falls in Rendlesham, www.thewhyfiles.net/rendlesham2.htm.
Wikipedia:
Great Thunderstorm of Widecombe, https://en.wikipedia.org/wiki/The_Great_Thunder-storm; Great Wratting http://en.wikipedia.org/wiki/Great_Wratting; Little Cornard https://en.wikipedia.org/wiki/Little_Cornard; Matthew Hopkins interrogated by Norfolk Assizes https://en.wikipedia.org/wiki/Matthew_Hopkins; Pharisees https:en.wikipedia.org_wiki_Pharisees; Tom Hickathrift http://en.wikipedia.org/wiki/Tom_Hickathrift
Ufo.se website, 1909 East Anglian airship wave, http://ufo.se/english/articles/wave.html.
Visit Suffolk: #TheOtherSide, www.youtube.com/watch?v=Lfs5lPr4cdE#theotherside; Mark Mower on the Waverney Monster at www.youtube.com/watch?v=Lfs5lPr4cdE #theotherside, Visit Suffolk video.
Weather Doctor website, "The Fire of St Elmo" www.islandnet.com/~see/weather/elements/stelmo.htm;
Week In Weird blog, "Do Animals Have Near-death Experiences?", Chris Savia, 28 April 2014, http://weekinweird.com/2014/04/28/animals-near-death-experiences/s
Young, Simon (Simon Young blog) "The Mysterious Rolling Wool Bogey," www.academia.edu/24973729/Young_The_Mysterious_Rolling_Wool_Bogey
Zootierliste (captive caracal in Kent) www.zootierliste.de/en/?klasse=1&ordnung=115&familie=11507&art=1120812 –

Index

INDEX

INDEX

INDEX

INDEX

INDEX

INDEX

A woodwose on the font at Harkstead church (above). It shows signs of once having been female.
A male wildman (woodwose) on the font at Stradbroke church (right).

About the author

Photo: © Hazel Dunlop

Matt Salusbury was born in Swinging Sixties London and raised in the capital, frequently visiting Suffolk from an early age to stay with his grandparents in Snape. He studied history at the University of Bristol in the 1980s, then worked as a London cycle courier before training to teach English as a Foreign Language.

Teaching took Matt to Turkey and then to the Netherlands, where he was head of department at a language school. He still has Dutch as well as British citizenship. Back in the UK in the late 1990s, Matt was a teacher then coordinator at a Kurdish community centre and also taught at Tottenham's College of North East London. More recently he has taught English on summer schools for overseas students of the London School of Economics and at Brunel University London and currently as an academic mentor on higher education courses for The Language Gallery London.

He studied journalism at the University of the Arts London in 2000 and has freelanced for titles including *BBC History*, *History Today, Times Higher Education* (on the revival of higher education in northern Iraq, following a visit in 2004) and the *Guardian*, for which he wrote a guide to getting personal data from the police using the Data Protection Act.

For over a decade he was news editor of English Language Teaching industry trade paper *EL Gazette* and he also co-editdc the *Freelance* newsletter for freelance journalists. He is a regular contributor to *Fortean Times* (tagline, "the world of strange phenomena") and a Core Participant in Sir John Mitting's ongoing Undercover Policing Inquiry.

This is Matt's third book. *Thatcherism Goes to College* (Canary Press, 1989) looked at the marketisation of higher education and got a mention in *Hansard*. His *Pygmy Elephants* (CFZ Press, 2011) took him to India to investigate reports of elephants just five feet (1.5m) tall.

Matt moved to Dunwich Forest in 2014 and has also lived in Chediston, while working at a café on the A12 at Darsham and at The Anchor pub, Walberswick. He's a volunteer at Dunwich Museum and Chair of the Dunwich Museum trustees. He is also BBC Radio Suffolk's "big cat expert", as well as woodwose consultant for Aldeburgh-based theatre company Wonderful Beast.

Matt is currently based mostly in Richmond Upon Thames with his partner Jane. He is a freelance journalist and a recent chair of the National Union of Journalists (NUJ) London Freelance Branch. He has also served on the NUJ's National Executive Council.

His hobbies include beachcombing for Dutch-language packaging that's washed onto the beaches of Sufolk after floating over the North Sea and also gathering reports of big cat sightings, especially in Suffolk.

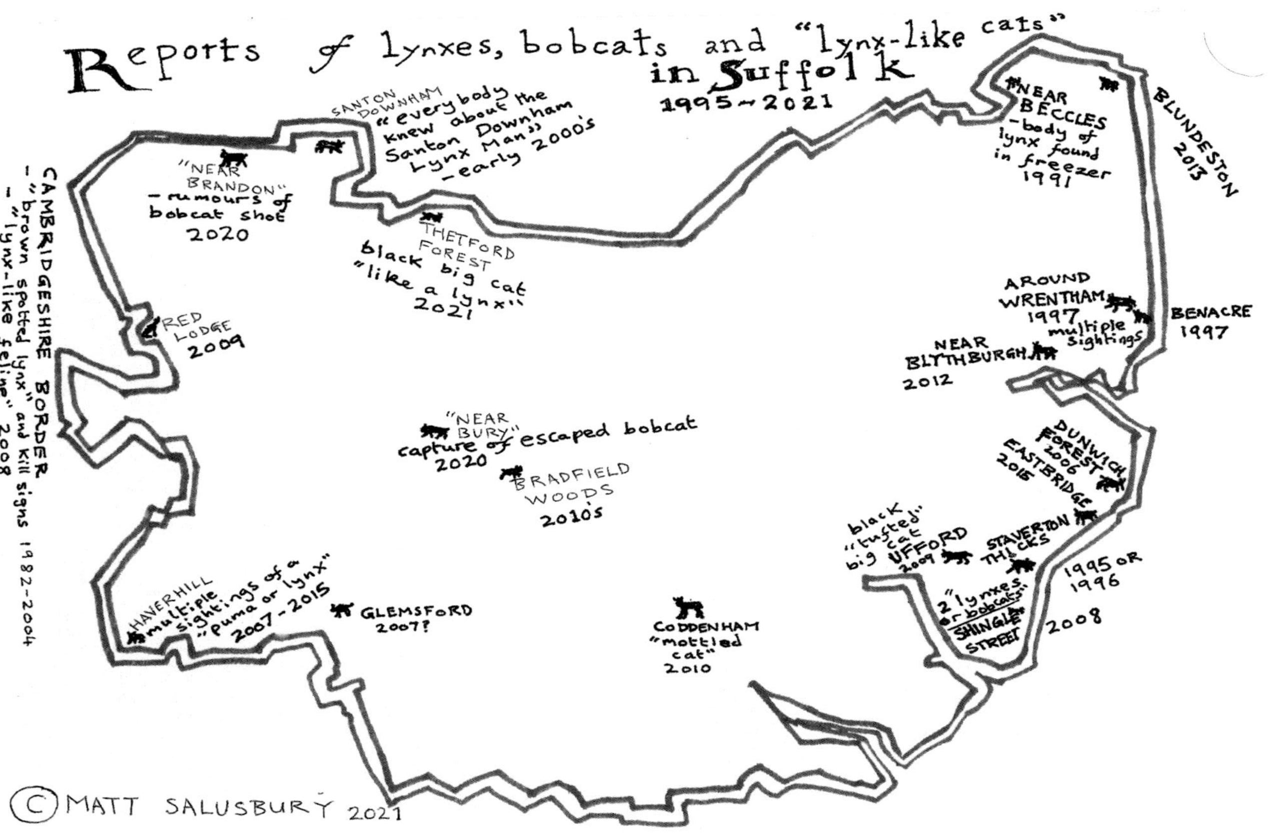
Reports of lynxes, bobcats and "lynx-like cats" in Suffolk 1995–2021
SANTON DOWNHAM "everybody knew about the Santon Downham Lynx Man" – early 2000's
"NEAR BRANDON" – rumours of bobcat shot 2020
THETFORD FOREST black big cat "like a lynx" 2021
RED LODGE 2009
"NEAR BURY" capture of escaped bobcat 2020
BRADFIELD WOODS 2010s
HAVERHILL multiple sightings of a "puma or lynx" 2007–2015
GLEMSFORD 2007?
CODDENHAM "mottled cat" 2010
NEAR BECCLES – body of lynx found in freezer 1991
BLUNDESTON 2013
AROUND WRENTHAM 1997 multiple sightings
BENACRE 1997
NEAR BLYTHBURGH 2012
DUNWICH FOREST 2006
EASTBRIDGE 2015
black "tufted" big cat UFFORD 2009
STAVERTON THICKS 1995 OR 1996
2 "lynxes or bobcats" SHINGLE STREET 2008
CAMBRIDGESHIRE BORDER
– "brown spotted lynx" and kill signs 1982–2004
– "lynx-like feline" 2008
© MATT SALUSBURY 2021

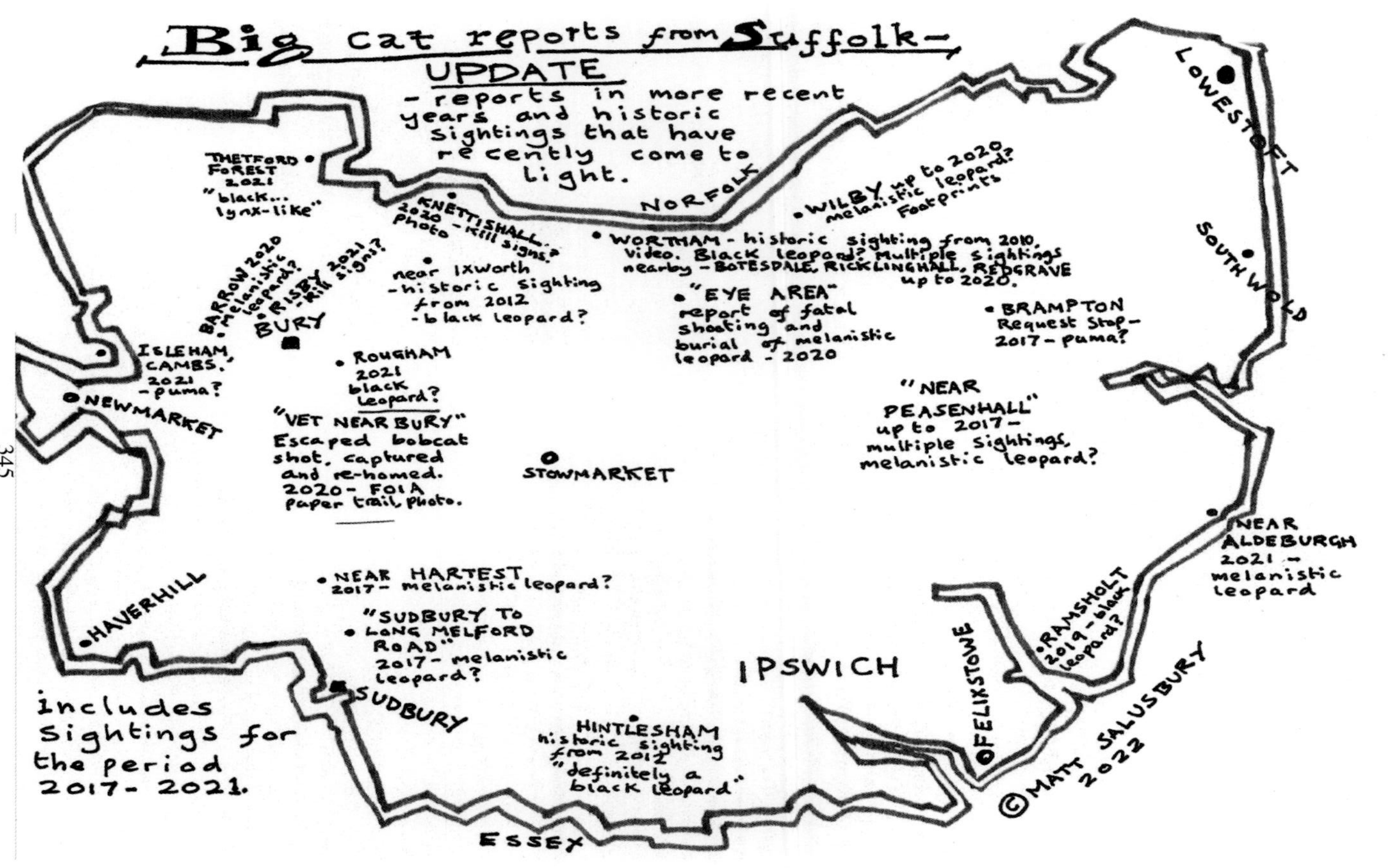
Big cat reports from Suffolk –
UPDATE
– reports in more recent years and historic sightings that have recently come to light.
THETFORD FOREST 2021 "black... lynx-like"
KNETTISHALL 2020 – kill signs, Photo
NORFOLK
WILBY up to 2020 melanistic leopard? Footprints
LOWESTOFT
SOUTHWOLD
BARROW 2020 melanistic leopard?
RISBY 2021 – kill signs?
BURY
near IXWORTH – historic sighting from 2012 – black leopard?
WORTHAM – historic sighting from 2010, Video. Black leopard? Multiple sightings nearby – BOTESDALE, RICKLINGHALL, REDGRAVE up to 2020.
"EYE AREA" report of fatal shooting and burial of melanistic leopard – 2020
BRAMPTON Request Stop – 2017 – puma?
ISLEHAM, CAMBS, 2021 – puma?
NEWMARKET
ROUGHAM 2021 black leopard?
"VET NEAR BURY" Escaped bobcat shot, captured and re-homed. 2020 – FOIA paper trail, photo.
STOWMARKET
"NEAR PEASENHALL" up to 2017 – multiple sightings, melanistic leopard?
NEAR ALDEBURGH 2021 – melanistic leopard
HAVERHILL
NEAR HARTEST 2017 – melanistic leopard?
"SUDBURY TO LONG MELFORD ROAD" 2017 – melanistic leopard?
SUDBURY
IPSWICH
FELIXSTOWE
RAMSHOLT 2019 – black leopard?
HINTLESHAM historic sighting from 2012 "definitely a black leopard"
ESSEX
includes sightings for the period 2017–2021.
© MATT SALUSBURY 2022

http://bigcatsofsuffolk.com

Still under construction at the time of publication, Matt Salusbury's **bigcatsofsuffolk.com** website will feature:

• video footage and still photos of big cats and their kill signs and field signs in the county.

• news, analysis and updates on big cat sightings in East Anglia and beyond.

• Freedom of Information Act disclosures on big cat sightings and escapes from around the UK.

• maps and much more.

Bigcatsofuffolk.com will serve as a reporting centre for sightings of big cat sightings in East Anglia, and also link to other organisations and individuals who are on the case regarding big cats locally, internationally and internationally.

The site will also have material on other mystery animals in the traditions of the county – especially East Anglian mystery lights, Black Shuck, wildmen, woodwoses, headless phantom coach horses and all their associated folklore.

Readers will also have the opportunity to support future endeavours in the East of England big cats investigation department through crowdfunding via Patreon, Kofi and Paypal.

http://bigcatsofsuffolk.com

Big Cat Conversations – a fortnighty podcast on UK big cat encounters **bigcatconversations.com**.

In each episode Rick Minter discusses big cat encounters with different witnesses, finding out what they experienced, how they felt about it and how these cases fit the bigger picture.

WEIRD WEEKEND NORTH.
27th April and 28th April 2024, Rixton and Glazebrook Community Hall, Warrington, Cheshire an annually around that time of year.

The Weird Weekend North is a must for anyone interested in ghosts, forteana, fairies, UFOs, folklore, cryptozoology and other fascinating stuff.
https://www.weirdweekendnorth.com

***Mystery Animals of Suffolk* is on Twitter at @MysteryAnimals**

Sign up for the mailing list for updates and details of *Mystery Animals of Suffolk* related events and develop- ments at:

mysteryanimalsofsuffolk @gn.apc.org

Pygmy Elephants

by Matt Salusbury, CFZ Press 2013

An investigation into reports of living dwarf elephants – said to be as little as five feet (1.5 m) tall at the shoulder – in remote regions of Africa since the early 20th century and in modern times in India.

This book looks in detail at the various known extinct pygmy elephants and pygmy mammoths of the fossil record and examines claims that there are pygmy elephants alive today.

The author travelled to Kerala, South India, to interview a key witness who described multiple sightings of the pygmy elephant knows as *kalaana* and also talked to some of India's foremost experts in elephant ecology. It includes photos of alleged pygmy elephants never before published.

Available from the CFZ Bookshop – https://cfz.org.uk/book/pygmy-elephants.

Join the mailing list – mysteryanimalsofsuffolk@gn.apc,org – for news of a planned forthcoming updated e-book edition of *Pygmy Elephants*.

Back cover images:
(From top) woodwose on the porch of St Michael's Church, Peasenhall; the River Lark at West Stow, location of some of Suffolk's many big cat sightings; flag of the County of Suffolk at Sizewell.
All photos: © **Matt Salusbury**